THE INSTITUTE FOR POLISH–JEWISH STUDIES

The Institute for Polish–Jewish Studies in Oxford and its sister organization, the American Association for Polish–Jewish Studies, which publish *Polin*, are learned societies that were established in 1984, following the International Conference on Polish–Jewish Studies, held in Oxford. The Institute is an associate institute of the Oxford Centre for Hebrew and Jewish Studies, and the American Association is linked with the Department of Near Eastern and Judaic Studies at Brandeis University.

Both the Institute and the American Association aim to promote understanding of the Polish Jewish past. They have no building or library of their own and no paid staff; they achieve their aims by encouraging scholarly research and facilitating its publication, and by creating forums for people with a scholarly interest in Polish Jewish topics, both past and present.

To this end the Institute and the American Association help organize lectures and international conferences. Venues for these activities have included Brandeis University in Waltham, Massachusetts, the Hebrew University in Jerusalem, the Institute for the Study of Human Sciences in Vienna, King's College in London, the Jagiellonian University in Kraków, the Oxford Centre for Hebrew and Jewish Studies, the University of Łódź, University College London, and the Polish Cultural Institute and the Polish embassy in London. They have encouraged academic exchanges between Israel, Poland, the United States, and western Europe. In particular they seek to help train a new generation of scholars, in Poland and elsewhere, to study the culture and history of the Jews in Poland.

Each year since 1986 the Institute has published a volume of scholarly papers in the series *Polin: Studies in Polish Jewry* under the general editorship of Professor Antony Polonsky of Brandeis University. Since 1994 the series has been published on its behalf by the Littman Library of Jewish Civilization, and since 1998 the publication has been linked with the American Association as well. In March 2000 the entire series was honoured with a National Jewish Book Award from the Jewish Book Council in the United States. More than twenty other works on Polish Jewish topics have also been published with the Institute's assistance.

Further information on the Institute for Polish–Jewish Studies can be found on its website, <www.polishjewishstudies.co.uk>. For the website of the American Association for Polish–Jewish Studies, see <www.aapjstudies.org>.

THE LITTMAN LIBRARY OF
JEWISH CIVILIZATION

Dedicated to the memory of
Louis Thomas Sidney Littman
*who founded the Littman Library for the love of God
and as an act of charity in memory of his father*
Joseph Aaron Littman
and to the memory of
Robert Joseph Littman
who continued what his father Louis had begun
יהא זכרם ברוך

'*Get wisdom, get understanding:
Forsake her not and she shall preserve thee*'

PROV. 4: 5

*The Littman Library of Jewish Civilization is a registered UK charity
Registered charity no. 1000784*

POLIN
STUDIES IN POLISH JEWRY

VOLUME TWO
Jews and the Emerging Polish State
Edited by
ANTONY POLONSKY

Published for
The Institute for Polish–Jewish Studies

The Littman Library of Jewish Civilization
in association with Liverpool University Press

*The Littman Library of Jewish Civilization
in association with Liverpool University Press
4 Cambridge Street, Liverpool* L69 7ZU, UK

www.liverpooluniversitypress.co.uk/littman

Managing Editor: Connie Webber

*Distributed in North America by
Oxford University Press Inc., 198 Madison Avenue,
New York,* NY 10016, USA

*First published in hardback 1987 by Basil Blackwell Ltd
First published in paperback 2008*

© *Institute for Polish–Jewish Studies 1987*

*All rights reserved.
No part of this publication may be reproduced,
stored in a retrieval system, or transmitted, in any form or by
any means, without the prior permission in writing of
The Littman Library of Jewish Civilization*

*The paperback edition of this book is sold subject to the condition
that it shall not, by way of trade or otherwise, be lent, re-sold,
hired out or otherwise circulated without the publisher's prior consent
in any form of binding or cover other than that in which it is published
and without a similar condition including this condition
being imposed on the subsequent purchaser*

*Catalogue records for this book are available from the
British Library and the Library of Congress*

*ISSN 0268 1056
ISBN 978–1–904113–78–2*

*Publishing coordinator: Janet Moth
Cover design: Pete Russell, Faringdon, Oxon.*

*Printed in Great Britain by
CPI Group (UK) Ltd., Croydon, CR0 4YY*

This volume is dedicated to the memory of
ERIC SOSNOW
*journalist, businessman, and philanthropist
born Kolno, Poland, 1910
died London, 20 February 1987*

*His advice and support were crucial to the establishment of both the
Institute of Polish–Jewish Studies and this yearbook*

———

The Institute for Polish–Jewish Studies, which sponsors *Polin*, has
benefited from the support of the following:

Mrs Sylvia Sosnow, Mr and Mrs Ronnie Fattal,
Mr Felix Posen, the M. B. Grabowski Fund,
the Lanckoroński Foundation, the American Jewish Committee,
the Polish American Congress, the Anti-Defamation League of B'nai B'rith,
Commentary magazine, the Oxford Centre for Postgraduate Hebrew Studies,
Gadsby & Hannah; Paisner & Co., Miller, Brener & Co.,
and the American Foundation for Polish–Jewish Studies

Editors and Advisers

EDITORS

Monika Adamczyk-Garbowska, *Lublin*
Israel Bartal, *Jerusalem*
Antony Polonsky (Chair), *Waltham, Mass.*
Michael Steinlauf, *Philadelphia*
Jerzy Tomaszewski, *Warsaw*

EDITORIAL BOARD

Chimen Abramsky, *London*
David Assaf, *Tel Aviv*
Władysław T. Bartoszewski, *Warsaw*
Glenn Dynner, *Bronxville, NY*
David Engel, *New York*
David Fishman, *New York*
ChaeRan Freeze, *Waltham, Mass.*
Józef Gierowski, *Kraków*
Jacob Goldberg, *Jerusalem*
Yisrael Gutman, *Jerusalem*
Jerzy Kłoczowski, *Lublin*
Ezra Mendelsohn, *Jerusalem*
Joanna Michlic, *Stockton, NY*

Elchanan Reiner, *Tel Aviv*
Jehuda Reinharz, *Waltham, Mass.*
Moshe Rosman, *Tel Aviv*
Szymon Rudnicki, *Warsaw*
Henryk Samsonowicz, *Warsaw*
Robert Shapiro, *New York*
Adam Teller, *Haifa*
Daniel Tollet, *Paris*
Piotr S. Wandycz, *New Haven, Conn.*
Jonathan Webber, *Birmingham, UK*
Joshua Zimmerman, *New York*
Steven Zipperstein, *Stanford, Calif.*

ADVISORY BOARD

Władysław Bartoszewski, *Warsaw*
Jan Błoński, *Kraków*
Abraham Brumberg, *Washington*
Andrzej Chojnowski, *Warsaw*
Tadeusz Chrzanowski, *Kraków*
Andrzej Ciechanowiecki, *London*
Norman Davies, *London*
Victor Erlich, *New Haven, Conn.*
Frank Golczewski, *Hamburg*
Olga Goldberg, *Jerusalem*
Feliks Gross, *New York*
Czesław Hernas, *Wrocław*
Jerzy Jedlicki, *Warsaw*
Andrzej Kamiński, *London*

Hillel Levine, *Boston*
Lucjan Lewitter, *Cambridge, Mass.*
Stanisław Litak, *Lublin*
Heinz-Dietrich Löwe, *Heidelberg*
Emanuel Meltzer, *Tel Aviv*
Shlomo Netzer, *Tel Aviv*
Zbigniew Pełczyński, *Oxford*
Alexander Schenker, *New Haven, Conn.*
David Sorkin, *Madison, Wis.*
Edward Stankiewicz, *New Haven, Conn.*
Norman Stone, *Ankara*
Shmuel Werses, *Jerusalem*
Jacek Woźniakowski, *Lublin*
Piotr Wróbel, *Toronto*

CONTENTS

STATEMENT FROM THE EDITORS 1

SYMPOSIUM: JEWS AND THE EMERGENCE OF AN
INDEPENDENT POLISH STATE 3

Eugene C. Black   Lucien Wolf and the Making of Poland:
Paris 1919 5
Paul Latawski   The Dmowski–Namier Feud, 1915–1918 37
Józef Lewandowski   History and Myth: Pińsk, April 1919 50
Daniel Stone   Polish Diplomacy and the American–Jewish
Community between the Wars 73
George J. Lerski   Dmowski, Paderewski and American Jews
(A Documentary Compilation) 95

ARTICLES
Sh. A. Cygielman   The Basic Privileges of the Jews of Great
Poland as Reflected in Polish Historiography 117
Eli Lederhendler   The Decline of the Polish-Lithuanian *Kahal* 150
Anna Żuk   A Mobile Class. The Subjective Element in
the Social Perception of Jews: The Example of
Eighteenth Century Poland 163
Maria and Kazimierz Piechotka   Polish Synagogues in the
Nineteenth Century 179
Mieczysław Inglot   The image of the Jew in Polish Narrative
Prose of the Romantic Period 199
Michael G. Steinlauf   The Polish-Jewish Daily Press 219
Szymon Rudnicki   From 'Numerus Clausus' to
'Numerus Nullus' 246

DOCUMENTS
David Engel   The Polish Government-in-Exile
and the Holocaust: Stanisław Kot's Confrontation with
Palestinian Jewry, November 1942–January 1943 –
Selected Documents 269
Bernadeta Tendyra   The Stanisław Kot Collection, Warsaw 310

COMMENTARY

Jan Błonski   The Poor Poles Look at the Ghetto   321
Polish-Jewish Relations During the Second World War:
  A Discussion   337

REVIEW ESSAYS

Edward Rogerson   Images of Jewish Poland in the Post-war
  Polish Cinema   359
Andrzej Bryk   The Holocaust – Jews and Gentiles.
  In Memory of the Jews of Pacanów   372
Władysław T. Bartoszewski   Jews as a Polish Problem   391

BOOK REVIEWS

Nahum Gross (ed.) *Yehudim ba-Kalkalah* by Jacob Litman   404
Jonathan I. Israel *European Jewry in the Age of Mercantilism:
  1550–1750* by Gershon David Hundert   407
Lucy S. Dawidowicz *The Golden Tradition. Jewish Life and
  Thought in Eastern Europe* by Jerzy Tomaszewski   412
Joseph Weiss *Studies in Eastern European Jewish Mysticism*
  (edited by David Goldstein) by Joseph Dan   414
Mathias Bersohn *Kilka słów o dawniejszych bóżnicach drewnianych
  w Polsce* by David Dawidowicz   417
Magdalena Opalski *The Jewish Tavern-Keeper and his Tavern
  in Nineteenth Century Polish Literature* by R. F. Leslie   418
Steven J. Zipperstein *The Jews of Odessa: A Cultural History*
  by Joseph Salmon   420
Stephen M. Berk *Year of Crisis, Year of Hope. Russian Jewry and
  The Pogroms of 1881–1882* by Alexander Orbach   424
Hans Rogger *Jewish Policies and Right-Wing Politics in
  Imperial Russia* by Dominic Lieven   425
Hans Rogger *Jewish Policies and Right-Wing Politics in
  Imperial Russia* by Daniel Grinberg   428
Heide W. Whelan *Alexander III and the State Council:
  Bureaucracy and Counter-Reform in Late Imperial Russia*
  by John D. Klier   430
Mary Antin *The Promised Land* by Moses Rischin   433
John Bodnar *The Transplanted: A History of Immigrants in
  Urban America* by Eli Lederhendler   434
Michael R. Weisser *A Brotherhood of Memory: Jewish
  Landsmanshaftn in the New World* by Jonathan Webber   437
Henryk Piasecki *Secja Żydowska PPSD i Żydowska Partia
  Socjal-Demokratyczna 1892–1919/20* by R. F. Leslie   440
Ber Borochov *Class Struggle and the Jewish Nation. Selected
  Essays in Marxist Zionism* by Robert S. Wistrich   442
Ehud Luz *Makbilim Nifgashim* by Joseph Goldstein   444

CONTENTS

Shmuel Nitzan (ed.) *Tnu'at Dror be'Galicia* by Israel Oppenheim	447
Ritchie Robertson *Kafka: Judaism, Politics and Literature* by Arnold J. Band	450
Sander L. Gilman *Jewish Self-Hatred: Anti-Semitism and the Hidden Language of the Jews* by Ritchie Robertson	453
Edward D. Wynot *Warsaw Between the World Wars: Profile of the Capital City in a Developing Land* by Joanna K. M. Hanson	456
Aleksander Biberstein *Zagłada Żydów w Krakowie* by Rafael F. Scharf	458
Shmuel Krakowski *The War of the Doomed: Jewish Armed Resistance in Poland, 1942–1944* by M. R. D. Foot	460
Nechama Tec *When Light Pierced the Darkness: Christian Rescue of Jews in Nazi-Occupied Poland* by John P. Fox	462
W Czerdziestą Rocznicę: Agonia, walka i śmierć warszawskiego getta; **Janina Jaworska** *Henryka Becka* by Joanna K. M. Hanson	464
Hanna Krall *Sublokatorka* by Michael C. Steinlauf	466
Randolph L. Braham and **Bélo Vágó** (eds) *The Holocaust in Hungary: Forty Years Later* by Maria Schmidt	471
Les Livres du Souvenir: Mémoriaux juifs de Pologne (présenté par Annette Wieviorka et Yitzhok Niborski) by Jonathan Boyrin	472
LETTER TO THE EDITORS	475
CONTRIBUTORS	477
OBITUARIES	480
Eric Sosnow	480
Arthur Sackler	483

POLIN
Studies in Polish Jewry

VOLUME 1 *Poles and Jews: Renewing the Dialogue* (1986)

VOLUME 2 *Jews and the Emerging Polish State* (1987)

VOLUME 3 *The Jews of Warsaw* (1988)

VOLUME 4 *Poles and Jews: Perceptions and Misperceptions* (1989)

VOLUME 5 *New Research, New Views* (1990)

VOLUME 6 *Jews in Łódź, 1820–1939* (1991)

VOLUME 7 *Jewish Life in Nazi-Occupied Warsaw* (1992)

From Shtetl to Socialism (1993): selected articles from volumes 1–7

VOLUME 8 *Jews in Independent Poland, 1918–1939* (1994)

VOLUME 9 *Jews, Poles, Socialists: The Failure of an Ideal* (1996)

VOLUME 10 *Jews in Early Modern Poland* (1997)

VOLUME 11 *Aspects and Experiences of Religion* (1998)

VOLUME 12 *Galicia: Jews, Poles, and Ukrainians, 1772–1918* (1999)

Index to Volumes 1–12 (2000)

VOLUME 13 *The Holocaust and its Aftermath* (2000)

VOLUME 14 *Jews in the Polish Borderlands* (2001)

VOLUME 15 *Jewish Religious Life, 1500–1900* (2002)

VOLUME 16 *Jewish Popular Culture and its Afterlife* (2003)

VOLUME 17 *The Shtetl: Myth and Reality* (2004)

VOLUME 18 *Jewish Women in Eastern Europe* (2005)

VOLUME 19 *Polish–Jewish Relations in North America* (2006)

VOLUME 20 *Making Holocaust Memory* (2008)

VOLUME 21 *1968: Forty Years After* (2009)

VOLUME 22 *Early Modern Poland: Borders and Boundaries* (2010)

VOLUME 23 *Jews in Kraków* (2011)

POLIN

We did not know, but our fathers told us how the exiles of Israel came to the land of Polin (Poland).

When Israel saw how its sufferings were constantly renewed, oppressions increased, persecutions multiplied, and how the evil authorities piled decree on decree and followed expulsion with expulsion, so that there was no way to escape the enemies of Israel, they went out on the road and sought an answer from the paths of the wide world: which is the correct road to traverse to find rest for the soul? Then a piece of paper fell from heaven, and on it the words:

Go to Polaniya (Poland).

So they came to the land of Polin and they gave a mountain of gold to the king, and he received them with great honour. And God had mercy on them, so that they found favour from the king and the nobles. And the king gave them permission to reside in all the lands of his kingdom, to trade over its length and breadth, and to serve God according to the precepts of their religion. And the king protected them against every foe and enemy.

And Israel lived in Polin in tranquillity for a long time. They devoted themselves to trade and handicrafts. And God sent a blessing on them so that they were blessed in the land, and their name was exalted among the peoples. And they traded with the surrounding countries and they also struck coins with inscriptions in the holy language and the language of the country. These are the coins which have on them a lion rampant towards the right. And on the coins are the words 'Mieszko, King of Poland' or 'Mieszko, Król of Poland'. The Poles call their king 'Król'.

And those who seek for names say: 'This is why it is called Polin. For thus spoke Israel when they came to the land, "Here rest for the night [Po lin]." And this means that we shall rest here until we are all gathered into the Land of Israel.'

Since this is the tradition, we accept it as such.

S. Y. AGNON, 1916

STATEMENT FROM THE EDITORS

In our statement introducing the first issue of our journal we gave our reasons for choosing the title *POLIN*. As we explained then, it is the Hebrew word for Poland and suggests to those knowledgeable in Jewish culture that mixture of affectionate and yet wary feelings that characterizes the long and complex relationship of the Jews to Poland and the Polish people. We commented then on the growing desire of both Poles and Jews to investigate their common past. To Poles this was the product, above all, of a desire to know more of the history of a people who for nearly a millenium lived in close proximity to them and whose evolution constituted an integral part of the development of the Polish lands. To Jews, the investigation of their Polish roots fulfilled a widely-felt desire to preserve the memory of a world from which so large a part of them are descended and from which Jewish civilization derives so many of the vital springs of its being. Our aim was thus to investigate both the relationship of Poles and Jews as well as the internal evolution of Jewish life. We are convinced that the response to the journal and the large amount of material for future issues which it has elicited have confirmed our belief in the vital significance of the tasks we have set ourselves.

In our introductory statement, we also wrote that 'our aim is to preserve and enlarge our collective memory, to investigate all aspects of our common past. We believe that there should be no taboo subjects and no topics which are too sensitive to be discussed. Our columns are open to all those of goodwill.' We hope that we have lived up to this bold ambition both in our first volume and in this issue. In Volume 1 we printed an article by Rafael Sharf, 'In Anger and In Sorrow.' in which he reflected on the complex nature of the Polish-Jewish relationship. This article was one of the spurs which impelled Jan Błoński to write in *Tygodnik Powszechny* 'The Poor Poles look at the Ghetto' which we reprint in this issue. We believe that the dialogue which has developed between Jews and Poles and between Poles and Poles on this topic has been both fruitful and necessary and we will do all we can to ensure that it continues.

This issue of *POLIN* follows the pattern of Volume 1 in all respects but one. This is the inclusion in it of a set of articles dealing with a specific topic, in this case the problems created for the Jewish population by the emergence in 1918 of an independent Polish state. We intend to have a similar core of articles in future issues. Thus, Volume 3 will deal with the history of Jews in Warsaw and its appearance will coincide with the publication of the Emanuel Ringelblum archive in Hebrew. In Volume 4 we will examine the way Poles perceived Jews and Jews perceived Poles and in Volume 5 we will investigate Jewish autonomy in pre-partition Poland. We should welcome suggestions from our readers for other suitable themes.

In conclusion, the editors would like to express their thanks to Professor Steven Zipperstein who is relinquishing his post of Associate Editor because of his move to U.C.L.A. He will be sorely missed but we are happy that we will still be able to seek his judicious counsel in his capacity as a member of the editorial board. His place as Associate Editor will be taken by Władysław T. Bartoszewski.

SYMPOSIUM

JEWS AND THE EMERGENCE OF AN INDEPENDENT POLISH STATE

LUCIEN WOLF AND THE MAKING OF POLAND: PARIS, 1919

Eugene C. Black

Organized Jewry brought competing formulations to the Paris Peace Conference of 1919. The Balfour Declaration of November 1917, the disintegration of the old multi-national empires, and the emergence of competing East European and Middle Eastern ethnic nationalism inspired Zionists to make particularly extensive claims. Confident of their friends in high places, especially in the American and British delegations, they pressed their cases with enthusiasm, vigour, and tactlessness. Western Jewish assimilationists, particularly British and French, worked tirelessly and patiently to defuse the Jewish Nationalism, to contain it, and, insofar as possible, to substitute the assumptions upon which Franco- and Anglo-Jewish elites had framed their diplomatic programs for almost half a century as the 'Jewish *desiderata*' for the Peace Conference. For Zionists and Jewish Nationalists such an agenda was worthless; anti-Semitism was ingrained in Western culture and Christian habit, and inescapable in European politics. Jews could never assimilate and remain Jews.

Western acculturated Jews – the self-styled 'moderates' – accepted the assumptions of liberal civilization. While the process might be uneven, moving in fits and starts with occasional regressions, Jews were part of Western culture. The diaspora was a fact of life. 'Next year in Jerusalem' was a spiritual aspiration, not a social reality. Education and economic progress would ultimately produce harmonious societies in which Jews could realize themselves within enlightened national cultures while preserving their Jewish identity and religion. Harmonious, well-defined Jewish subcultures had evolved and could thrive in the liberal west. Since all mankind would ultimately see that its best interests lay in the creation of socially harmonious and peaceful national cultures modelled upon that of Western Europe, history was on the side of assimilation and acculturation.

Enlightenment, liberalism, economic development, and social opportunity had not yet, 'moderates' conceded, come to all of the European world. But come they would, and once Eastern Europe provided the same economic, social, and political scope that the West already did, Jews would be contented, effective participants in their various national states. Western Jews even sought to expedite the process. Baron de Hirsch spent millions and offered more in an attempt to create opportunities, not merely for Jewish immigrants in new worlds, but for Jews remaining in Russia. Anglo-French Jewry, proud of the world it had shaped for itself, saw that carefully honed and cultivated image threatened by the intrusion of poor aliens. British and French Jewish leaders adopted two strategies to deal with the problem. On the one hand, they processed as many migrants as possible onwards to new worlds as far removed from their own as possible. They worked assiduously at the same time to educate and socialize those who remained on their hands, teaching them western languages, assumptions, and values. On the other hand, Western Jewish establishments also worked in tandem with each other through diplomatic channels in an effort to bring pressure through their own governments, particularly on Russia and Romania, to secure political and social conditions in Eastern Europe which would help to stem the immigrant tide.

Leading western Jews actively promoted such views and policies within the Jewish community and in the nations of which they were a part by the middle of the nineteenth century. Adolphe Crémieux (1796–1880), by virtue of his ministerial service in French governments and his leading role in the *Alliance Israélite Universelle*, established intimate connections between and *Alliance* and the Quai d'Orsay that continued into the twentieth century. The relationship proved mutually beneficial. Jewish interests received a hearing, if not accommodation, in French foreign affairs. The *Alliance*, by virtue of its school system scattered through the Ottoman Empire and North Africa, could serve as a potential stalking-horse for French cultural imperialism.[1]

For Anglo-Jewry, a small group handled diplomatic initiatives with the Foreign Office. The Conjoint Foreign Committee consisted of equal representation from the Board of Deputies of British Jews, the recognized representative body of British Jewry, and the Anglo-Jewish Association, which originated as a part of the *Alliance Israélite Universelle*. The AJA, ironically, achieved its august status by being the body through which Reform Jewish leaders could participate in communal leadership, since Chief Rabbi Dr. Adler stood foursquare for Orthodoxy as he understood and defined it. Montefiores and Goldsmids, however, could scarcely be excluded from the great panoply of Jewish leadership: thus the special importance of the AJA.[2] The Conjoint Foreign Committee preserved a delicate and decorous balance. The presidents of the Board of Deputies and AJA chaired alternate meetings. The Conjoint Foreign Committee reported back to and took 'instructions' from the two parent bodies. The Committee, however, by virtue of existing and being the medium through which most transactions went to the Foreign Office, achieved an importance and independence recognized by permanent officials, even by ministers themselves.

The Damascus Affair of 1840 and the Mortara case in 1858 had brought home to Western Jewry the need to create institutions to speak for their international interests, and the formation of the *Alliance* in 1860 established matters on a formal institutionalized basis. From their early days, the *Alliance* and AJA worked directly with foreign governments and through British and French diplomatic channels to secure full civic and religious freedom for Jews everywhere in East European and the evolving new Balkan states.[3] Adolphe Crémieux, president of the Alliance from 1863 to 1880, established that organization's forward position in foreign affairs. Never would the AIU play a more activist role in foreign affairs than it did during the Congress of Berlin in 1878.

Regular, organized Jewish activism in foreign affairs dates from that Congress. Having exerted themselves, particularly with Quai d'Orsay support, to secure civil and religious rights for Jews in Romania, Anglo-French Jews witnessed the systematic violation of those guarantees. They discovered, to their horror, that neither Britain, France, Germany, nor Austro-Hungary had any intention of enforcing such clauses so long as Russia remained hostile. Worse soon proved to be in store. Beyond the obvious diplomatic quandaries of the Bismarckian world, Anglo-French Jewry confronted an Eastern Europe appearing to go mad on the subject of Jews. The uncomfortably large number of Russo-Jewish immigrants moving westward in search of economic opportunity and cultural freedom exploded in the early 1880s as official and unofficial pogroms spawned panic flight. Both British and French Jewish leaders laboured assiduously, if unsuccessfully, to convince the Foreign Office and *Ministère des Affaires Étrangères* to intervene on behalf of persecuted Russian Jews.[4] Most organized Jewish international activity revolved around processing unprecedented numbers of human beings on the move, preferably to any country but their own. The British government, given its ostensible influence in Constantinople, suffered a Conjoint Foreign Committee barrage of Jewish Memorials and petitions from as far afield as Morocco and Persia, as well as a flood of grievances concerning Jewish refugees and settlers in Palestine.[5] After the death of Crémieux in 1880 and the problems of the Dreyfus case, the *Alliance* increasingly concentrated on educational, relief, civil rights, and anti-defamation work. The Conjoint Foreign Committee, although it often worked through the French, came increasingly to take the lead in matters of foreign policy.[6]

The Conjoint Foreign Committee saw Russian anti-Semitic policies at the heart of Jewish international problems. Romania's cynical violation of Jewish treaty rights infuriated Anglo-Jewry, but success in Romania still depended upon solving 'the Russian problem'.[7] No efforts were spared, but *Realpolitik* stood in the way. The French government, for which national security was wrapped up in its Russian alliance, was understandably cool to Jewish grievances. King Edward VII of England, who numbered Jews among his personal friends, attempted a personal intervention and actually chided his cousin, Tsar Nicholas II, for his anti-Semitic policies. Nothing changed, save possibly for the worse. And so the problem festered.

Before the outbreak of the first world war, Lucien Wolf (1857–1930) had become the secretary of the Conjoint Foreign Committee. Wolf, a journalist of consequence well connected with the Reuters News Agency, a scholar and distinguished historian, had his battle-scars of diplomatic experience. He edited *Darkest Russia*, a periodical that pilloried Imperial Russian abuse of Jews before the British public. The network of informants this nearly-blind diplomat developed, the clipping, translating services he arranged, his superb contacts in the Foreign Office, and the skill that he had already demonstrated, made him a central figure in the diplomacy of Anglo-Jewry. Although of relatively modest origins, he had moulded himself to and become a representative of the Jewish 'establishment'. An Anglo-Jew from hat to bootlaces, he shared the assumptions and values of the Jewish establishment. He enjoyed the confidence of those who mattered, particularly Claude J. Montefiore, president of the Anglo-Jewish Association, and David L. Alexander, president of the Board of Deputies. Through the intimate relations he developed through the war, particularly by early 1915, with Jacques Bigart, secretary of the *Alliance* Israélite, he also came to play a crucial role in Franco-Jewish diplomacy.

Both the *Alliance* and Conjoint Committee spent the first months of the war dealing with issues the war brought to the fore. Organized Jewry divided, flocking to their particular colours, demonstrating above all whether in London or Berlin, in Paris or Vienna, that they were English or German patriots, French or Austro-Hungarian. The cooperative network that had processed East European Jewish immigrants and refugees suddenly collapsed. Suddenly Jewish internees and prisoners of war demanded attention. Philanthropy and relief demanded reconstruction in the light of totally new circumstances.

Anglo-Jewry, perhaps because its international operating network had been less disrupted, also began to contemplate the ways in which the war might be turned to diplomatic good account for East European Jews. Poland brought the Alliance and Conjoint Committee to act together in concerted policies. While Anglo-Jewry contemplated ways in which pressure might be placed upon Russia to ease its anti-Semitic policies and give Jews at least the same rights and privileges accorded other 'subject' peoples within the Empire, Yehiel Tschlenow and Nahum Sokolow appeared with news of Russian outrages against Jews in wartime Poland. Anglo-Jewry took these matters in stride (or, because of its alliance with

Russia, felt compelled to downplay the news) and paid little heed to the Zionist appeal that accompanied the tidings. Zionism, while enjoying popularity among some Jewish professionals and intellectuals, had not yet gained the broad support it would soon develop in the East End. Zionism remained anathema to most Anglo-Jewish leaders, as they saw it as antithetical to all that had been achieved during the previous century. Herbert Samuel had just been rebuffed in his first attempt to fly that flag before the British Cabinet, and Chaim Weizmann had not yet seized effective leadership of the extra-parliamentary Zionist campaign.[8]

When Tschlenow and Sokolow flew their atrocities and Zionism flags in Paris in February 1915, however, Jacques Bigart, the long-time secretary and chief administrative officer of the *Alliance Israélite Universelle*, sprang into action. While Bigart understood that the *Alliance* could never take an overtly anti-Zionist policy for a variety of prudential reasons, he believed that Zionist principles, if ever ascendant, would wreak havoc for Jews in Western Europe. Bigart pleaded for Anglo-Jewry, with its avowed anti-Zionist stance, to assume the leadership in developing and executing policies that would secure true Jewish interests as Anglo-French Jewish leaders understood them and resist this Zionist threat. From February 1915 to the Paris Peace Conference and beyond, the *Alliance Israélite* and Conjoint Foreign Committee (reconstituted in 1918 as the Joint Foreign Committee) worked hand-in-hand on all matters of foreign policy.[9]

That policy, however, contained little that was new. Locked as they were into the liberal assumptions of the past half century, Anglo-French Jewry had few options. They hoped that the circumstances of war would enable them, particularly as the Western Allies became increasingly dependent upon American aid, to persuade their governments to press the Russian government to end Jewish disabilities. Anglo-French Jewry appealed to Russian self-interest as best they could with a mixture of inducements and implied threats.[10] Jewish 'demands' were modest enough. While the details varied from one proposal to another, Western Jewry asked the Russians to end restrictions upon Jewish settlement and education, and to abolish invidious religious discrimination in matters of passports and visas. Efforts to move either the British or French governments proved unavailing. Neither government was prepared to risk the Russian ill will that such pressure would engender. Private negotiations with Russian officials were no more successful. Russian behaviour, in fact, aggravated rather than eased the problem. The war in Eastern Europe, while stalemated as was that in the West, had a fluid battlefront which flowed back and forth through Galicia and the traditional Jewish Pale of Settlement. Russian generals regarded Jews as security risks, charged some with spying for the Germans or Austrians, and even developed a plan for substantial deportations to the Don basin.[11] While Grand Duke Nicholas sought to scapegoat Jews for his own military incompetence, Germans 'liberated' Polish Jews, just as they were later to do in Romania, by granting enough concessions to win Jewish favour while retaining Jewish dependency. Germans never, for instance, granted liberties to Jews that compromised their ability later to play to Polish nationalist sentiment.

Lucien Wolf found that, first, Sir Edward Grey, then Arthur Balfour, as Foreign Ministers resisted pressure to remonstrate about Russian abuses on the grounds that they could not interfere in the domestic affairs of an ally. The more Wolf and the 'moderates' pushed their case, the more irritated the British government became. They could do nothing, and Anglo-Jewry should understand that. Their good offices, while they might help after the war, had availed nothing before 1914. Lord Robert Cecil, the British Coalition Government Undersecretary for Foreign Affairs, charged, among other things, with Eastern European affairs, contended that the Jews in Britain and the United States were constructing their political position on 'the Russian difficulty'.[12] Cecil's observation reflected British and French fears about American politics. Both governments depended upon continued American support to prosecute their war effort. Both recognized the delicate balance in American politics. Both overreacted to anything that might appear to threaten the stream of financial and material aid. American Jews were overwhelmingly anti-Russian, and the German background of much of the American Jewish élite could be and was represented as dangerous. Both the British and French governments attempted to recruit Jewish support at home to play a missionary role for the allied cause in the United States. Since neither government was in a position to make the Russians 'behave', other options, particularly Zionism, became attractive cards to play. The French, who thought that Allied agreements meant the ultimate creation of a French-dominated greater Syria, dispatched a Zionist on a Quai d'Orsay sponsored lecture tour in 1915, while simultaneously bringing assimilationist Jews into a special propaganda bureau under Foreign Ministry and Chamber of Deputies sponsorship.[13] Lucien Wolf and Lord Robert Cecil had private discussions to the same purpose, but Wolf took a much stronger line than his French colleagues about limiting Palestinian commitments. Wolf understood that American Jewish leadership was more divided than Anglo-Jewry on the subject of Zionism. Something must be offered American Zionist as well as anti-Zionist opinion were a propaganda campaign to succeed. Wolf suggested a declaration for unrestricted settlement, equal rights, and a degree of Jewish communal autonomy. Knowing that the Zionists had established contacts with the British and French governments, he also hoped such a program would meet the political needs of the moment and preempt the Zionist position.[14]

What Wolf did not appreciate was that his government would see in Zionism the least difficult concession it could make to Jewish opinion. A half century of Anglo-Jewish pressure backfired. Equal rights for Jews in

Russia were clearly unattainable. Even if some half measures were secured, they would not satisfy the 'moderates' and would be meaningless to the growing and vociferous number of Zionists. Anglo-Jewish support was scarcely at risk for the British government. A Zionist policy might annoy the assimilated, but they had no place else to go. A Zionist statement would counter any German gains in East European, American, or neutral Jewish opinion. Both the British and French had private ambitions in the Middle East with which Zionism did not appear, at that time, to be incompatible. Zionism could be, as it was, an indirect way of pushing British claims in a region where British imperial interests collided with French. Some British statesmen believed in the cause. Herbert Samuel certainly did. Arthur Balfour possibly did. David Lloyd George assumed most positions at least once in his life. Sir Mark Sykes definitely came to believe in Zionism as well as other more grandiose and less achievable Middle Eastern goals. The Quai d'Orsay, not suprisingly, did much the same analysis with hopes that an early commitment to Zionism might benefit French Middle Eastern ambitions. Endorsing Zionism was the grand gesture the Western Allies could make to Jews without apparent cost, and, ultimately, in the British case, some benefit to themselves.

The French and British governments moved further into the Zionist orbit, pressing on even after Wilson's reelection. The February Revolution of 1917 with its dramatic promulgation of full Jewish equality did nothing to stem the Zionist momentum. Now the Allies sought any means to keep Russia in the war, at least until American forces could be mobilized and trained. Once committed to Zionism, moreover, they also feared conceding any 'Jewish' advantage back to the Germans. The united front of Anglo-Jewry, moreover, had broken. The uncompromising anti-Zionists at the Jewish Board of Deputies were overthrown in the summer of 1917. The mass of Jewish aliens, activated by the threat of being conscripted into either the British or Russian army, increasingly turned to Zionism. Both domestic and international considerations offered the British an opportunity to serve principle and self-interest. The French, having publicly committed themselves even before the Balfour Declaration was issued, were in no position to retreat. Woodrow Wilson, weighing matters judiciously, brought America into line at a more leisurely pace.

The Allied commitment to Zionism also encouraged East European Jewish Nationalists. They, too, rejected the 'moderate' formula of treaty guarantees for equal rights, and demanded, instead, the right to be different – to manage their own affairs in a quasi-corporative mode within their new national states. The Romanian experience seemed to them to demonstrate that only constitutional recognition and guarantee of Jewish autonomy within national states could guarantee Jewish freedom. But the right to their own schools, their own language and control of their lives flew in the face of the West European liberal conception of the national state, and that conception appeared to Western eyes to triumph in November 1918. Since the East European multinational empires had all been defeated – Russian, German, Austro-Hungarian, and Ottoman – liberal western-style nations were to be created, whether appropriate or not, through the Succession States.

This ostensible triumph of liberalism ultimately outweighed the momentary ascendancy of Jewish Nationalists. Zionism had previously offered the simplest concession to Jews. Now as the peacemakers confronted the unnerving ethnic map of Eastern Europe in 1919, Lucien Wolf and Anglo-Jewish 'moderates' offered a carefully calculated appeal. For Western anxieties about the bacillus of Bolshevism, the ethnically homogenized state appeared to form the best *cordon sanitaire*. What Wolf and the 'moderates' proposed implied 'stronger' states, western-dependent and western-oriented nations. Wolf demanded guarantees in each instance for Jewish civil rights, but was as anxious to contain Jewish Nationalist ambitions in Eastern Europe and at the same time to limit commitments to Zionists in Palestine. From Finland through the Baltic states to Poland, Czechoslovakia, the Ukraine, Austria, Hungary, and Romania, Wolf had a minimal and an optimal agenda.

Wolf laboured under no illusions about the depth of East European anti-Semitism. Untutored and uncontrolled masses were dangerous. He understood that folk prejudices, unrestrained by authority, meant endemic pogroms. Hostility towards Jews would only wane, as it had done in Western Europe, when Jew and gentile fused in a common culture respecting one another's individuality but speaking the vernacular, sharing patriotism, identifying one another as fellow citizens first. Reflecting back in September 1919 on the treaties he had done so much to help frame, Wolf observed:

> We cannot pretend to have solved the Jewish Question in Eastern Europe, but at any rate we have got on paper the best solution that has ever been dreamt of. We have still before us the task of working out this solution in practice. It will be difficult and delicate because we shall be confronted by two kinds of mischief-makers – on the one hand the violent anti-Semites, and on the other the extreme Jewish Nationalists. We have, however, in the Minorities Treaties so solid a basis to work upon that I think we can look forward to the future with a great deal of confidence.[15]

While Wolf was not above playing the disruptive implications of Jewish Nationalism, what he sought to convey to the peacemakers was the viability of the 'moderate' formula. Wolf simultaneously sought out and cultivated 'reasonable' East European statesmen and leaders who understood the difficulties of state-making, who favoured 'constructive' solutions, who would 'protect' Jewish minorities through that necessarily long and difficult process of moulding a new national culture. Thus Wolf sought and found East European national leaders who shared his vision and values – Beneš and Masaryk in Czechoslovakia, Ionescu in Romania, ultimately Paderewski in Poland – with whom to negotiate the best 'practical' arrangements.

At one particularly tense moment at the beginning of June 1919, while negotiating the Polish minority rights clauses, Wolf reminded his distinguished American colleague, Louis Marshall:

> The question to my mind is a political, and not a legal one. In everything I have done here since the Peace Congress has been sitting I have endeavoured to bear steadily in mind the permanent interests of our brethren in Eastern Europe and not to allow myself to be deflected from that duty by the conflicts and bitternesses of the moment. I look beyond the pogrom-stricken fields and the passions and recriminations to which ephemeral political conditions have given rise, to a time when on the basis of Equal Rights the Jews of Poland will be full partners in a State to which they will be patriotically attached, and of which they may be legitimately proud. But if this prospect is to be realised we must see that we do not poison the new relations of Poles and Jews at their source. And this we shall assuredly do if, for the benefit of Jews alone, we abridge in any way the sovereign rights of Poland and humiliate her before the whole world.[16]

The stakes were considerable. Jewish rights must be effectively secured. Jewish lives must not be at risk. But all of this had to be accomplished in a real world.

Covert as well as overt agendas had to be respected. The United States, in spite of lip-service to advanced principles, could not tolerate the suggestion of general League of Nations intervention on behalf of abused minorities. That might mean outside intervention on behalf of abused Japanese in California or, even worse, of Blacks in the American South. Minority rights could not, therefore, be obtained through the League of Nations charter. Each case would have to be managed in the individual treaty defining the new state. That meant tortuous negotiations in each instance. Poland, for its part, was unwilling to grant full rights to all national minorities. In the instances of Ukrainians or White Russians, the minorities had clearly defined territorial bases. Jews, on the other hand, were scattered throughout Poland. Poles, moreover, had no intention of granting minority rights to Germans within the Polish state. To aggravate difficult enough problems, the United States, France, and Britain feared Bolshevism and social revolution. The alleged extensive Jewish involvement in Bolshevism rekindled embers of western anti-Semitism and was even used to justify the brutal slaughter of Jews in Pińsk. And, finally, Jews, sharply divided between Nationalists and Assimilationists, also divided on matters of personality. Many rough edges had to be made smooth were any viable settlement to be produced.

Any Jewish agenda also had, in the first instance, to accommodate itself to great power wants and needs. The defeat of both Germany and Russia, not to mention the disintegration of the Austro-Hungarian Empire, made possible the reconstruction of Poland. While Poland could be resurrected given this power vacuum, Polish survival depended upon Poland either coming to terms with its more powerful neighbours or somehow developing the capacity to maintain its independence. Polish nationalists sought the frontiers of 1772. So vast an appetite – reaching well into overwhelmingly German provinces in the north and west, White Russian and Lithuanian areas around Wilno, and White Russian and Ukrainian lands to the east and south-east – invited discontent, if not war, and squared ill with grand pronouncements about rights of national self-determination.[17] Even in modified form, Poland would have to concede substantial minority guarantees before the nation could be reconstituted.

Beyond the immediate problem of securing concessions for Jews that neither Poles nor the allied powers wished to concede to Germany, lay the ebb and flow of the Bolshevik crisis. British, French, and American aid flowed, in ill-considered driblets, to White factions seeking to overthrow Lenin's government. American troops occupied Vladivostok, British troops Archangel. By late March 1919, the Jewish task became even more complicated. Béla Kun's spectacular rise to power in Hungary jarred peacemakers' priorities. Bolshevists in Hungary, like Spartacists in Germany, threatened to bring revolution from Russia to the west. The Allied military commander, Marshal Foch, considered Poland and Romania the necessary military bastions for resisting revolution in Europe. Clemenceau concurred, but both Lloyd George and Woodrow Wilson were less certain, Lloyd George, in particular, seeking pacification for disorder and unrest both at home and abroad.[18]

Wolf's first 'Polish' work during the war had been anti-defamatory, countering various charges about Jews spying for Germany. He first directly confronted Polish nationalism in 1915 when the Papacy made overtures to the *Alliance*, the Conjoint Foreign Committee, and the American Jewish Committee. François Deloncle, a French journalist, sometime diplomat, and politician, acted for the Vatican Secretary of State. Deloncle suggested that Jewish organizations and the Papacy should make common cause and develop joint agendas for the peace and conference that would follow the war. The Alliance and the Americans considered these overtures seriously, but Wolf asked the French to restrain themselves. Appointing himself to speak for both nations' Jewish organizations, Wolf suggested that the Pope could demonstrate his good offices best by improving Roman Catholic attitudes and relations with Jews in Poland. The Alliance concurred, and the Deloncle affair appeared to be over. Deloncle, however, returned in 1916 with a more elaborate program, one with strong Zionist implications. Wolf warned against allowing Jews to become spokesmen for Papal representation at the Peace Conference or allowing Jewish interests to become entangled on matters of Papal territoriality. He cautioned the French that supporting any Papal territorial claims, even in Vatican City, by extension might imply an endorsement of Zionist claims for Palestine. The Papacy offered a pronouncement against anti-Semitism conditional upon Jewish endorsement of various Roman Catholic proposals. On Polish national independence, for instance, Jewish opinion was divided, and Jewish organizations should never actively endorse policies as Jews that did not affect Jewish interests.[19]

Jewish interests were, however, directly involved in matters of new Russian anti-Semitic regulations in 1915 and 1916, removed only after extensive Jewish pressure had been placed on the British and French governments. Such successes could scarcely be represented as great 'improvements'. Zionism promised action, emancipation from European persecution, something new and dramatic that could capture the imagination.[20]

When Russia granted 'autonomous' status to Poland, some 80 per cent of Russian Jewry, according to contemporary estimates, confronted ethnic Polish nationalism. Matters were bad enough under Russian overlordship, but Roman Dmowski's Polish National Democratic Party, stridently anti-Semitic, asked the British and French governments to recognize it as the 'government in exile' of the Polish nation. Only those of the 'Polish race', contended the National Democrats, qualified for citizenship, and a 'Pole' had to prove that he had not been Jewish for three generations. Such a definition embarrassed the Foreign Office, now busily attempting to paint British policy in enlightened liberal terms. The National Democrats gave way and agreed to allow token 'Jewish' representation on the National Committee.[21] That changed nothing. The National Democratic Party continued to pursue its publicly-avowed policy of 'the forcible elimination or reduction of the Jewish population', harassing Polish Jews and particularly preventing Jewish refugees and victims of the wartime 'barbarous deportations' from returning to Poland.[22] Wolf's Foreign Affairs Committee of the Anglo-Jewish Association, rebuffed on its resistance to Zionism, made Poland its principal European preoccupation by the summer of 1917. The Committee consulted 'representative' Polish Jews and began negotiations in London with representatives of the Polish Progressive Party and Polish State Council. Besides equal civil and political rights for Jews, the Anglo-Jewish Association sought guarantees for Jews as 'a substantial nationality minority' with cultural autonomy and proportionate political representation.[23] Left politicians of liberal views on the Jewish question were a small minority. Dmowski's Polish Nationalists, however, were another matter. Dmowski and Paderewski had failed to secure British support in 1915, at least in part thanks to Wolf's well-orchestrated Conjoint Committee campaign in the London press,[24] and the British government was moving closer to formal recognition. Lord Weardale discussed the problem with Balfour, at the request of the AJA, on 23 November 1917, and found the matter was still 'under consideration'. That encouraged Lucien Wolf to have a long interview the following day with Lord Robert Cecil. The *Alliance Israélite* took the same approach with the Quai d'Orsay. Keeping both the Petrograd Committee, composed principally of 'moderate' Jews seeking accommodation with the Russian government after the February Revolution, and the American Jewish Committee, created in 1905 to safeguard Jewish international interests, apprised, Wolf's committee attempted to ward off British government recognition of Dmowski while securing government approval for a conference in some neutral country of representatives of Western Jewish communities and delegates from the progressive and Socialist parties in Poland.[25]

In Poland, however, the program of economic boycott of Polish Jews begun under Russian administration and applied intensely after 1912 'to nationalize Polish trade and industry in a narrow racial sense' continued. Worse still in 'moderate' eyes, the boycott was working, squeezing more and more Jews into poverty and forced emigration. Poland was replaying Russia in the 1880s, raising for Western Jewry the spectre of Eastern pauper hordes descending on their countries, draining resources and rekindling anti-Semitism. Wolf and 'moderates' sought to modify Polish behaviour, end boycotts and pogroms, and develop within Poland those institutions and conditions that would sustain the peace and allow for economic and social development. Such Zionist partisans as Balfour and Brandeis agreed with Wolf, Bigart and the majority of 'establishment' Jews on the matter of Jewish migration. They did not want 'those people' in their countries. The 'moderates' hoped to liberalize Poland, rendering emigration unnecessary. 'Establishment' Zionists saw Palestine as an option, another place to deflect immigration, whether Poland 'liberalized' or not.

Poland, by 1919, became a testing ground for Wolf's ideas, diplomatic skills, and political sagacity. Poland was the opportunity to win the long, unavailing struggle with Russia and Romania for decades past. If Wolf could find a way to fuse Polish national ambitions with properly framed Minority Treaties and safeguards for Jews, then it just might be possible to begin to quest for economic viability and social stability in this potentially most volatile and troublesome Succession State.[26] Wolf, anxious to minimize the Jewish Nationalist and Zionist impact upon the Peace Conference, saw Poland as an issue upon which the Allied delegations would be inclined towards what they perceived to be the least disruptive settlement. Extreme proposals for Jewish autonomy could be both exploited and discredited to reach 'our moderate formula of cultural autonomy'.[27]

Wolf always relied on the well-documented case to prevail. His careful research and tightly argued conclusions almost invariably gave him an advantage in discussion. To establish his assumptions as the basis of discussion and negotiation, he furnished the peace conference staff with his *Notes on the Diplomatic History of the Jewish Question*, a careful compilation of British State Papers to which he had been given access in 1915.[28] The Green Book, as it was usually called, proved one of Wolf's most useful weapons. He distributed copies to all national delegations and the more important members of the conference staff. Wolf's next step was to open direct negotiations with the Polish Nationalists. He began by calling upon Count Ostroróg, one of the Polish diplomats, the morning of 20 February. Ostroróg seems to have reacted well to Wolf, and Wolf found the Count 'very charming', as well as precisely the person who could facilitate negotiations with the Poles. The discussions encouraged Wolf to move without consulting the Zionists, a step that created gratuitous tension within the Jewish delegations, but unquestionably simplified Wolf's task.

Wolf's parallel problem was to carry the key members of the British delegation. With unerring instinct, he singled out J. W. Headlam-Morley, who was to be the principal treaty draftsman. Headlam-Morley, an educator, an intellectual, and historian as well as a diplomat, was precisely the sort of person with whom Wolf worked best. They shared the same values and unspoken assumptions. They saw one another as sensible individuals pursuing reasonable and just causes. Headlam-Morley was not initially encouraging. He doubted on 1 March that Wolf's formula for Jewish rights could be put into the treaty. The League of Nations, in his opinion, would regulate matters between states but would not intervene in internal issues. Woodrow Wilson and the Americans, he reminded Wolf, had removed the statement about civil and religious liberty from Article XIX of the Covenant. Wolf's French colleagues were also pessimistic. Bigart of the *Alliance* feared that, since Britain had already recognized the independence of Poland without insisting upon safeguards, the 'moderates' were already too late. Baron Edmond de Rothschild thought that the great powers, having made their declarations on Palestine, no longer wished to be annoyed with Jewish questions.[29]

Wolf hoped to be able to take Oscar Straus, as a leading American Jewish delegate, with him when he opened formal negotiations with the Polish Nationalists. Influenza, however, took its toll, and Wolf found himself engaged in a three-hour 'unofficial' discussion alone. The two principal Polish spokesmen were not regarded as being particularly well-disposed to the Jews. Piłsudski and Kozicki, the Secretary General of the Polish Delegation to the Peace Conference, joined Count Ostroróg, who had generally assumed a conciliatory role, in pressing the Polish case. Wolf reminded them that the Conjoint Foreign Committee had no interests of its own in this matter, that British and French Jews saw matters very differently from Polish Jews, but that the long history of Polish Jewish appeals for assistance led Anglo-French Jewry to offer its good offices in the search for peace and amity. Wolf conceded that Polish Jews asked for much that British Jews would not, but the Jewish problem in Poland was different and demanded settlement on its own terms. Wolf conceded that, when the Joint Foreign Committee undertook to confer with Count Sobański, it was prepared to encourage Polish Jews to accept a program that 'would make for a happy and contented Poland', and Wolf suspected that an appropriate settlement 'would be supported by moderate men in all great Jewish communities in the world'.

Wolf then proposed the five points of the Joint Foreign Committee resolutions of 3 October 1918 on minority rights as a basis for discussion. Issues of citizenship, the first two resolutions, presented no problem, but Jewish claims for educational, political, and linguistic rights seemed to the Poles merely a disguised form of national autonomy, making the Jews a nation within the nation. Lithuanians and White Russians might make such claims, for they were concentrated in specific lands, but Jews were scattered throughout Poland. Piłsudski conceded that serious difficulties existed between Poles and Jews that presented a problem 'of extreme gravity' to the Polish state. Wolf seized upon the statement as a satisfactory basis for discussion. A 'serious problem' cannot be resolved on ordinary lines. It demands special treatment, and the Joint Foreign Committee proposal is extremely moderate, aimed solely at 'cultural autonomy'. That remained a sore point for the Poles, who found the continued use of Yiddish as a medium of instruction in state-supported schools the symbolic as well as practical sticking point. Wolf responded that Yiddish had been the Jewish vernacular for 700 years, that 'Jews had been forced by historical circumstances' to make the language their own. Yiddish 'had become endeared to them by such use and by a considerable literature'. Poles and Jews must realize that Jews existed in Poland as a separate body through no fault of their own and could not become assimilated by statutory enactment.

> To refuse to recognise their separateness would be to martyrise this very separateness and thus to prolong the Jewish question indefinitely. It would be better to make reasonable concession to them on the facts. This, at any rate, would make for friendly relations

between the two races, and time and economic constraint might be trusted to do the rest in the way of bringing them still closer together.

The Poles took up Wolf's challenge to offer any reasonable amendment to this formula and agreed to consult the Warsaw government. At the same time, they asked Wolf about the Jewish problem in England. Wolf denied that such a thing existed. British Jews needed and had obtained certain legal concessions on matters relating to education and laws concerning Sunday trading. Wolf promised to furnish the Poles summaries of the English statutes on these points. English and Polish Jewish issues, he reminded the Poles, were not analogous. Yiddish was nowhere the permanent vernacular of any significant section of English Jews. Jews were less than 3/4 of one per cent of the English population, not the 14 per cent they were in Poland. Jews had not been in England for 700 years with their own language and institutions.[30]

Wolf, pleased that the Polish discussion had been more conciliatory in tone than he expected moved directly to the crucial issues and sought out E. H. Carr, the Foreign Office East European expert. He told Carr that Anglo-Jewry 'and practical politicians generally' considered the Polish question far more important than Palestine, for they understand that 'an amicable solution is essential to the stability of the new Polish State'. Wolf explained that the Zionists would themselves be organizing a bureau to deal with non-Zionist questions, and they would soon begin supporting the extreme Polish Jewish Nationalists. When Carr asked if Wolf would object to Carr alluding to Wolf's negotiations when talking to Polish delegates, Wolf suggested that it would be helpful and promised to furnish a copy of his report.

Wolf also continued privately to press Count Ostroróg to keep the negotiations moving. Yiddish remained the sticking-point, so Wolf reminded Ostroróg that Paderewski, speaking for the Poles, had suggested that Poland could make any concession that the United States did. Wolf believed that the Poles might ultimately accept Jewish 'control' rather than 'autonomy', a formulation that he realized would bother the Zionists, 'but they will have no real reason to complain, inasmuch as they will have the oysters while the Poles will only have the shells.'

Over the next several days, Wolf organized his campaign. On 18 March he laid out the Joint Foreign Committee case to H. J. Paton, the Foreign Office expert who was assigned particular responsibility for Poland, repeating his observation to Carr that 'moderate' success on Poland depended upon the degree of support that Allied Government would provide against the extreme demands of the Zionists. Paton promised his support. Wolf then approached Professor Sylvain Lévi, the French-Jewish orientalist of the Collège de France, whose Quai d'Orsay, *Alliance*, and Zionist connections made him an invaluable ally. Lévi, who had already broken the united Zionist front before the peace conference plenipotentiaries on 27 February, promised to secure Quai d'Orsay backing. Baron Edmond de Rothschild's representative thought that the baron might help. Wolf also went to the Ukrainians, who were anxious for any help they could gain in forwarding their own national claims, to secure their support for the Joint Foreign Committee formula. The Poles, Wolf felt, could scarcely afford to be behind the Ukrainians.[31]

The groundwork laid, Wolf then returned to his running struggle with the Zionists. The Americans were determined to make yet another effort to have all Jewry speak with one voice on issues of international policy. Louis Marshall, Cyrus Adler, Julian Mack, and Oscar Straus had their own differences of opinion, but they still hoped to be able to reconstruct a united Jewish front. Even the Zionists had internal quarrels. Weizmann, after all, quarrelled with Sokolow. On the nights of 5 and 6 April, the issue was fought out in the grand hall of the French *Consistoire*. Sokolow began by insisting that Jewish Nationalism was not revolutionary. Poland was hopelessly anti-Semitic, and Jews must have their ethnic and social rights preserved. This meant religious, cultural, and social autonomy, 'Jewish control of Jewish schools, with State aid, and a Jewish electoral curia which would elect Members of the Polish Parliament or any other Parliament in proportion to their numbers.' Subsequent Jewish Nationalist spokesmen swept away Sokolow's modest proposal. Menahem Ussishkin, in particular, announced that the privileges of a separate Jewish nationality within the succession states was but the first step. Jewish Nationalism would ultimately federate all Jewish communities everywhere in the world in one Jewish nation, argued the 'uncrowned King of Odessa', with a claim to be admitted to the League of Nations on an equal footing with all other nations. He warned assimilating Jews that this Jewish Nationality 'would set out to conquer them'. There were no French Jews, English Jews, or American Jews, 'but only Jews in France, England or America, who eventually would have to join the universal Jewish Nationality.' The Americans, with Judge Julian Mack in the lead, argued that the Nationalists must be allowed their way regardless of how Western Jewry felt about their ideas, 'even though we know they were mad and headed for self-destruction'. Louis Marshall attempted to secure a compromise by referring the matter to a small committee. Wolf, knowing the Alliance leadership was immovable, disingenuously stood aside, professing only his desire for 'unity', and allowed the French to veto the proposed accommodation.[32]

While allowing American tempers to cool, Wolf took the entire Anglo-Jewish delegation to the Czechoslovak Mission on the morning of 10 April. Beneš and Masaryk enthusiastically identified themselves 'with the best liberal traditions of Western Europe' and guaranteed Czech Jewish subjects with 'as happy and secure a position as their British and French co-religionists [enjoy] in their respective countries'. Sir Stuart Samuel invited the Czech government to seek loans from his bank and told Beneš that the British Government had entrusted Samuel Montagu & Co 'with several lines of the Credits opened for the Allies'. Such a happy resolution was a foregone conclusion, but Wolf realized that nothing could give the 'moderate' cause greater morale than such a clear triumph.[33] He could once again pick up the more difficult Polish issue, confident of support behind him. Wolf returned to lobby Headlam-Morley and Carr about Poland, warning them that the East European Jewish Nationalist delegations were readying memorials for a separate Jewish Nationality. All agreed on how 'very dangerous' it would be were such memorials to get into Polish hands. Headlam-Morley asked Wolf what they could offer Sokolow as an inducement to hold back the Nationalists. Wolf felt that a Polish government assurance that they would not gerrymander constituencies to the prejudice of Jews, and some liberal scheme of municipal self-government for all of Poland, not merely in White Russian and Lithuanian lands, would remove the justification for a Jewish Electoral Curia. At the same time, Wolf reminded them, the League of Nations must be made the special custodian for civil and religious liberty in Eastern Europe. Quite impossible as a general principle, contended Headlam-Morley with American reservations clearly in mind, but something might be managed on the specific treaty. All parted determined 'to promote a moderate compromise'.

Keeping both sides of his negotiations in tandem, Wolf lunched with Skrzyński, Prince Kazimierz Lubomirski, Count Ostroróg, and Jan Perłowski (the Parliamentary Secretary to Skrzyński) on 17 April. Skrzyński set the tone by denying the existence of Polish anti-Semitism and contending that special concessions to Jews depended upon Jews doing something special for Poland. Perhaps they might make a statement in favour of Poland acquiring Danzig and Teschen. Jews might also help to secure 'a conservative treatment of the Agrarian Question'. Wolf reminded himself that this was the Dmowski approach in slightly 'less aggressive' form. He responded coolly that Danzig and Teschen were international questions upon which Jews of different countries had different views. The Czechs had already asked Wolf for and been refused his support on Teschen, the Ukrainians on Lemberg. As to the agrarian question, surely that was one for Polish Jews themselves. When Skrzyński then trotted out the canards about Jews acting in harmony and controlling the press, Wolf firmly called him down. That myth lacked any foundation and was the source of much mischief. Turning the tables, Wolf added that 'kindness and generosity' would make Jewish Poles good citizens, ardent citizens, as conservative as they are in Western Europe. Radical anti-Semitism alone made them discontented and difficult.

Wolf declined to go further in discussions at that point, agreeing to see

Paderewski only after he had the opportunity to see the American Jewish delegation and demand its support. Oscar Straus and Cyrus Adler agreed. Straus specifically endorsed Wolf's 'equal rights' formula in preference to 'national rights'.[34] The Paderewski interview of 23 April went particularly well. The pianist-statesman acknowledged that Jews were very excited and discontented 'and that the problem was how to calm them and conciliate them'. The same was true of Poles 'who were also in an excited state and were disposed to look upon the Jews with anger'. The situation required patience. Wolf must understand, Paderewski continued, that his own desires 'to make great sacrifices in order to transform the Jews into good Polish citizens' were politically impossible in the present state of Polish public opinion. Of course they would be assured of equal rights. But what more could be done?

Wolf, as always, had a memorandum on hand. He was asking for no more than Jews enjoyed in Britain and France. The Diet must pass a Conspiracy Act 'which would be a tacit disavowal of the boycott', must secure religious and cultural minority rights, must pass an Electoral Law 'guaranteeing fair representation for the Jews', and deal with the issues of Sunday labour and trading for Jews. Paderewski was receptive. That brought Wolf to the Pińsk massacre. Paderewski did not deny the murder of Jews. He gave Wolf the official Polish reports 'which seem to show that the Poles had a measure of right on their side', while still conceding that 'the incident was deplorable'. Paderewski's welcome candour attracted Wolf. While pogroms and murder were intolerable, Wolf believed that Western Jewry confronted a difficult choice. Dmowski, the avowed anti-Semitic nationalist leader with whom Paderewski was at the moment on bad terms would clearly, if in power, make matters considerably worse. Paderewski surrounded himself with responsive, liberally-minded Poles, particularly Zaleski, whom Wolf felt to be the most warmly inclined towards accommodation with the Jews.[35] Impossible Jewish claims that might drive Paderewski from power would bring more dangerous leaders into authority and extend the already overlong nightmare of persecution and destruction. Leadership mattered. Were either the weak or ruthless, let alone both, to rule Poland, native savagery and political expediency would translate into endemic Jewish persecution.

Carr applauded Wolf's negotiations with Paderewski. He also reported that Sokolow and Mack, although they had considerably modified their terms, still were pressing for National rights, particularly separate Jewish Electoral Curiae. Carr felt, however, that some grounds for negotiation might be there. Wolf felt this was a testimony to the effectiveness of 'moderate' opposition to extreme Jewish Nationalism. Wolf's pleasure was even greater when he dined with Zaleski on the evening of 15 April. Paderewski was very satisfied with the Wolf interview and hoped to see him again soon. Zaleski was, in the meanwhile, to draw up a full report on the

Jewish question. Would Wolf supply him with documents relating to the various negotiations? Of course Wolf would. Zaleski also suggested that Wolf see Patek, leader of the Polish Parties of the Left, with whom Sokolow was already in negotiations. Wolf promised to do so as soon as he returned from London where he was going to 'be instructed' to stand firmly on the 1918 resolutions rather than 'National Rights'.[36]

Back in Paris on 3 May, Wolf found matters where he had left them. He gladly agreed to join Bigart and the *Alliance* delegation for a formal visit to Paderewski to present the French proposals when assured that they were essentially the same as his. He also found that Headlam-Morley had been appointed the head of a Committee of three to deal with the Jewish Question and Minority issues. David Hunter Miller sat for the United States, Philippe Berthelot for France, and E. H. Carr served as Secretary. Carr begged Wolf to furnish him useful documentation and reference material. Nothing could have pleased Wolf more.

> The appointment of this Committee is a great coup for us. It will probably postpone a settlement of the Jewish Question beyond the signature of the Peace Treaty, but it will be all the safer and solid for that. Instead of more or less banal Clauses in the Peace Treaty, we shall now have a detailed Statute of Minorities which will probably be the subject of special Treaties with the States concerned.[37]

Wolf believed that matters, once removed from the public glare of memorials, meetings, and presentations, would move into the hands of a handful of sensible people working to achieve reasonable, viable settlements. Behind-the-scenes negotiations, discreet diplomacy, were what he did best, and he had been at great pains in Paris and London to cultivate close personal relations and trust with those who mattered. From May to July, Wolf actually managed to shift the burden of negotiating with Zionists and Jewish Nationalists over to Carr, Headlam-Morley, Leeper, and the senior British peace conference staff. Keeping press contacts alive, to be used when needed, he cultivated Sir George Riddell, owner of *The News of the World*, one of Lloyd George's intimates, and information director for the British delegation.[38] Wolf was cordial enough when responding to individuals or groups who sought him out, but he had evolved a clear sense of priorities. Wolf covered his own rear by ascertaining that the Joint Foreign Committee and its parent bodies were kept appropriately informed, that Sir Stuart Samuel and Claude Montefiore were kept completely up-to-date, and that he was 'instructed' to do what he felt he should be doing. So successful was he in this tactic that Herbert Bentwich, his outspoken Zionist opponent and member of the Board of Deputies, unable to rein Wolf in from London through the parent committees, came to Paris on his own to disrupt Wolf's arrangements.

Bentwich arrived too late. Wolf had moved negotiations to circles Bentwich could not reach.

Wolf next ascertained that his allies were working in harmony with him. Jacques Bigart, Sylvain Lévi, and the Reinachs were in full accord with Wolf's views, so the *Alliance Israélite* was never a problem. The Americans, however, were another matter. Judge Julian Mack was an uncompromising Zionist and prepared to support any Jewish Nationalist position on the grounds that they were the best judge of their own problems. The unrepresentative nature of the East European Jewish Nationalist delegations bothered Mack not at all, for the cause he espoused was a minority position, and his commitment to it was total. Cyrus Adler, founder of the American Jewish Committee, while sympathetic to Zionist aspirations in Palestine, shared the 'moderate' view on European settlements. Henry Morgenthau, the financier and diplomat whose hostility to Zionism and Jewish Nationalism had led him to split with Stephen Wise, concurred completely with the Wolf position, but he had come to Europe to deal with issues of relief, not diplomacy. Louis Marshall, closest to President Wilson and the American delegation, stood somewhat between Mack and Adler. Never 'manageable', Marshall tended to think ill of solutions that did not appear to be his own. He had strong views on most people and things and an explosive temper that rendered him something less than an effective negotiator. Ultimately ground down, to some degree, between Wolf's unflappable persistence and the effective manoeuvres of the British peace conference delegation, Marshall tended, over time, to give way. While the American flank had an element of unpredictability and, at times, clear differences of opinion, Wolf attempted to see Marshall and other Americans almost daily, always conveying the same message of common purpose and cooperation.

Wolf simultaneously attempted to keep negotiations with the Poles on track. His candour, his openness, and his obvious sensitivity gave him a better reception and hearing than even he initially expected. He saw little hope in Dmowski and the extreme Polish Nationalists with their avowed anti-Semitic program and supported the Joint Foreign Committee policy of attempting to hold that faction in check through the Foreign Office. While warm to the Left, he was cautious to deal with it only after he had come to terms with President Paderewski and a spectrum of centre groups. Wolf's personal political preference, as a self-styled 'Manchester Liberal', were the Paderewski-Zaleski moderates. He also did well with Stanisław Patek, a Judge of the Court of Cassation in Warsaw, who was identified with the non-Bolshevik left and Piłsudski. Wolf and Patek had already taken the measure of one another in London in 1915, and they found it easy to work together. Patek had already encountered the Zionist-Nationalists at Paris. Sokolow attempted to persuade Patek to support Jewish National Autonomy. Patek knew that such a program would be political suicide and was delighted when Wolf indicated 'that I believed National Autonomy no longer had any practical importance ...'.[39] Wolf began his Polish negotiations with Count Ostroróg and Foreign Minister Skrzyński's people, tripped lightly past the French Clerical-Polish Clerical political connections, and worked his way to the only people he trusted to be able to carry an acceptable treaty and give it effect. So Wolf returned repeatedly to Paderewski and Zaleski, conveying the importance of taking a firm public stand on those pressing political issues which validated extreme safeguards in Western eyes. Something must be done about pogroms, and the issue of boycott must be met head-on. Wolf effectively conveyed Western Jewry's hopes – and they were very real – that Polish Jews could find security and fulfilment as Polish citizens. Wolf could speak from conviction. Neither Americans, nor French, nor English wanted Polish Jews in 'their' countries.

Wolf's Fabian strategy worked. By late May, even the more unruly Americans were anxious to re-establish their 'moderate' ties. Louis Marshall, irritated with Zionist leaders and anxious for some accommodation, sought Wolf out to test the waters on 'ethnic rights' rather than 'national rights'.[40] A more representative Polish Jewish delegation, highly Orthodox, finally reached Paris in mid-May. The Zionists denounced them as 'impostors' for good reason. They rejected the secular state of the Zionists in which they claimed religion would be subordinated to 'Nationality and Politics' and sought rather a true *Eretz Israel*. Their first concerns, however, were Sabbath Questions and the fear that a rigid ban of Sunday Trading was about to be introduced in Poland in order to re-enforce the widespread Polish boycott of Jewish businesses. Observant Jews would be severely penalized by losing both Saturday and Sunday trade. Wolf snapped up that point, asked for a memorandum of facts, and agreed to place the issue before the Council of Four.[41] Meanwhile, however, the Pińsk murders required management. Paderewski agreed to write a general letter deploring them, promising investigation and punishment. Pressed by Wolf, he agreed to remove an exculpatory paragraph that sought to mitigate the blame by suggesting that the dead Jews were Bolsheviks. Pogroms, unfortunately, were spreading. Tales from Wilno multiplied their horrors in telling. Facts helped. The 2,200 initially reported killed shrank to 200, and a Jewish leader reported arrested showed up quite unscathed in Paris a few days later.[42] Matters were not improved when the American Minister in Warsaw, Gibson, sent ill-informed reports claiming no such attacks had taken place. Gibson repeated every libel Dmowski had used through the years, 'all the legends of Jewish pro-Germanism, treachery, espionage, profiteering and bolshevism. He describes the whole Jewish proletariat – indeed all the Jews who are not Assimilants or Chassidim – as 'criminals'. His later denials and feeble argument that his reports were garbled in transmission made

Gibson appear doubly foolish and cast doubts on American diplomatic intelligence.[43]

Would-be friends and allies occasionally provided unexpected problems. Baron Alexandre de Gunzburg sallied into Paris from Switzerland, having heard that Jewish delegations were in a state of disarray. The Baron shared the fears that Maxim Vinaver, one of the founders of the Russian Cadet party, also voiced to Wolf that dividing Jews among succession states with their unconstrained racial hatreds was a greater danger than having them under the rule of a greater Russia. Wolf demurred and reminded them in turn that should Kolchak and Denikin actually defeat the Bolsheviks, pogroms would be the order of the day.[44] While Marshall shared Wolf's views on this, he still baulked, as did Wilson, at specifically committing to the League the role of policeman for minority rights preferring, ultimately, to fall back on great power guarantees.

Lord Robert Cecil waded into the fray in May. An uncompromising champion of the League, Lord Robert and his aide, Baker, proved highly receptive to Wolf's formulations of the right of appeal. Cecil and Baker accepted articles granting the League the right to act on its own initiative in emergencies and defining minority rights of appeal to the League. Cecil was 'determined to do his best to make the Treaties a real living Charter of Liberties for the Jews'. Lord Robert, however, required some reassurance 'about the relations of Jews with Bolshevism and revolutionary movements generally'. Wolf, who had often had to deal with that canard, calmly settled Cecil's anxieties.[45] No sooner had Wolf begun moving matters forward with Cecil, however, than Louis Marshall exploded again. He categorically refused to allow Polish Jews to become enmeshed in Polish courts on issues relating to their treaty-guaranteed rights. Wolf responded:

> The question to my mind is a political, and not a legal, one. In everything I have done here since the Peace Congress has been sitting I have endeavoured to bear steadily in mind the permanent interests of our brethren in Eastern Europe and not to allow myself to be deflected from that duty by the conflicts and bitterness of the moment. I look beyond the pogrom-stricken fields and the passions and recriminations to which ephemeral political conditions have given rise, to a time when on the basis of Equal Rights the Jews of Poland will be full partners in a State to which they will be patriotically attached and of which they may be legitimately proud. But if this prospect is to be realised we must see that we do not poison the new relations of Poles and Jews at their source. And this we shall assuredly do if, for the benefit of Jews alone, we abridge in any way the sovereign rights of Poland and humiliate her before the whole world.[46]

Marshall finally agreed to support the British proposal were the American formula not to carry. By 17 June, the Council of Five opted for the British formula on Minority appeals. Lacking American or French support, the more extensive Sunday Trading clauses upon which Wolf and Marshall had agreed, were lost. The next day, however, the Poles rejected the minority treaty 'on the ground that it is an intolerable interference with the sovereign rights of Poland'. Without being overly specific, the Poles pointed at the education clauses, with Yiddish language rights, and Sabbath Observance clauses, as inimical to military discipline. To recover the treaty, all influence had to be brought to bear on the Council to stand firm. Headlam-Morley told Wolf that he and Marshall must rally all their friends to bring pressure upon Lloyd George and President Wilson. Japan and Italy, for their own reasons, would stand firm with the British. Headlam-Morley warned that clerical interests at the Quai d'Orsay, unknown to Clemenceau, were actually encouraging the Polish resistance.

Wolf immediately spurred Sir Stuart Samuel to bring all possible pressure to bear on Lloyd George. He also explained matters to Herbert Samuel, then in Brussels, asking him to appeal to Lloyd George. Morgenthau was pressed into service to write a strong personal letter to Wilson. Since Wilson had just asked Morgenthau to investigate the Polish pogroms, he could scarcely resist such a request.[47] Baron Edmond de Rothschild and Israél Lévi cornered Cambon at the Quai d'Orsay to beg his support in this crisis and hint about the clerical intrigues. Marshall stood firm against any compromises to soothe Polish *amour propre*, and the crisis passed. The Council stood firm, although the Poles had brought their own delegation of Jews headed by Stanislas Natanson to plead the Polish nationalist case. The delegation was not heard, as it happened, until after the Council had reached its decision. The Council responded firmly to the Polish protest, ending 'with what is virtually an ultimatum to Poland to sign it next Saturday when the main German Treaty will be signed'. Wolf relished the fact that the Council drew its historical argument from his *Diplomatic History of the Jewish Question*.[48]

So it was that, on 28 June, the Polish treaty was signed. The Poles made no objection, Dmowski signing immediately after Paderewski. Signatures to the Polish Treaty marked only the symbolic beginning of the process of attempting to fuse Jew and Pole into one national state. Even as a symbol, that agreement remained vital. Each subsequent treaty – with Czechoslovakia, Austria, Finland, the Baltic States, Hungary, Yugoslavia, Romania, and Greece – used the Polish precedent. Some negotiations proved relatively easy; others, predictably but not exclusively Romania, proved extraordinarily difficult. On none could there be retreat. If there were, the Poles could rightly demand renegotiation of their terms. Writing the Polish treaty was one thing. Making it work was another. As far as Wolf was concerned, that was what mattered most. Jewish blood was being shed on Polish soil even as ink was being placed on paper. Pogroms continued.[49] The boycott, still applied with unremitting severity, must somehow be broken. Until that happened no constructive bridges could be built within Poland.

Jews at Paris were still speaking with discordant and disruptive voices. Once a Polish treaty existed, all claimed credit for it, Wolf in his diary and reports, others in more public forums. In one sense, Wolf was fortunate quite as much as he was skilful. Polish territorial ambitions were so far-reaching that Lloyd George was ultimately able to tilt Woodrow Wilson to his side. Great power determination to avoid being dragged into the perpetual quarrels between Poles and subject ethnic groups meant Jewish rights would receive more careful attention and support than they otherwise would probably have done. Lucien Wolf, however, understood how to exploit Jewish Nationalist ambitions, Polish pride, and peacemaker anxiety for a reasonable settlement in quiet diplomacy. The *Alliance Israélite*, particularly Jacques Bigart, applauded Wolf. Wolf remained a tactful diplomat to the end. We owe the victories of 1919 to 'the complete loyalty with which we all worked together'.[50] That was true. Sylvain Lévi's close connection with the Quai d'Orsay provided essential access to Cambon and Berthelot at crucial moments. Clemenceau's general sympathies were important.[51] The timorous *Alliance Israélite* executive committee occasionally summoned up unexpected political courage and tipped the balance towards moderation. Even Louis Marshall, who so often worked at cross purposes to Wolf and the 'moderates', helped to carry the day. In spite of his overbearing ego and explosive temper, Marshall found himself bridging the gap between the strongly pro-Nationalist Judge Julian Mack and 'moderate' Cyrus Adler. Marshall also personally sustained the link between East European Nationalist delegations and their Western opponents. Marshall's ties to and influence upon Woodrow Wilson and key members of the American delegation were, at crucial moments, helpful and served the great common cause. His visit to Paderewski, a man he personally disliked and distrusted, just before leaving France, helped to contribute to that sense of cooperation that Wolf argued was the only basis upon which a viable future could be built. The *Alliance* executive, in its effort to part as friends, told Marshall that he was the principal architect of treaty success and invited him to a celebratory dinner. Marshall, temperamental to the last, declined to dine and flounced off to Le Havre only to find his ship back to the United States idled by a strike. Leopold Greenberg, powerful editor of the *Jewish Chronicle*, knew what Wolf had done and praised him for it in a private letter. But Greenberg was also a committed Zionist, so England's leading Jewish newspaper attributed treaty success entirely to the Zionist-Jewish Nationalist alliance and spoke of the Polish Treaty as a triumph for Jewish nationalism. Zionists, stalled although not rebuffed on their Palestine ambitions, had to mark time until a proposed peace conference commission investigated the situation in the Middle East and reported back. Financially pressed, Zionists needed to claim some major victory to launch a new fund-raising drive. They needed to claim the Polish treaty as their victory.

The Zionist assertion, however, created a serious political problem. Since the Zionists represented the treaty as a triumph of Jewish Nationalism, Zionist self-congratulation and publicity continued to threaten the tidy Wolf settlement. From the outset Wolf realized that the Polish treaty could only give scope for a settlement, not resolve the Polish-Jewish problem. Throughout his negotiations he sought safeguards tolerable to Polish nationalists. He worried about words or issues that might poison the subsequent relations of Jew and Pole. Poland in 1919 was a land lacking facts but strong on rumours, prejudices, and fears. Retreating Germans had warned Polish Jews that their only hope lay with the Russian Bolsheviks, even leaving arms with those who appeared convinced. Subsequent murders and pogroms, particularly those in Pińsk, were laid to the door of 'Jewish Bolsheviks', who allegedly started the violence. Tales of pogroms lost nothing in the telling, but the worst were not inflicted by Poles. The hopelessly unsettled Ukraine saw the massacre of thousands and the devastation of dozens of Jewish communities. Milling refugees attempting to avoid Red-White conflict in the Russian civil war found themselves victimized on all sides, whether Jew or gentile.[52]

Eastern Europe could not be made better by treaty. The settlement could do no more than create the necessary conditions through which time and mutual self-interest could bring Jew and gentile together in interwar Poland. Designing such an agreement required suspension of disbelief and mutual forbearance.

> The magnitude of the Jewish population makes it necessary that patience should be strained to the utmost in order to secure a stable social peace in that country. Moreover the alleged infractions while undoubtedly causing a widespread insecurity do not afford material for a reliable case before the League. Finally, the political situation was one which rendered great circumspection imperative.[53]

Lucien Wolf could never have accomplished that task alone. Jews, even speaking in complete agreement, could not do so. The leaders of the Western Alliance – Georges Clemenceau, David Lloyd-George, and Woodrow Wilson – saw their Jews as national patriots and believed Polish Jews could be the same. Wolf never strayed from his belief that they and every East European Jew must slowly merge into their individual national cultures. Even after the 'moderates' had returned to England from Paris, Wolf, rather than Leo Motzkin and the Jewish Nationalist Committee remained the person to whom diplomatists and Jewish lobbyists still turned. Wolf amused himself by reminding Greenberg of the *Jewish Chronicle*,

> It is rather amusing that although our Delegation is no longer in Paris, all the Jewish work there is still being done by us. Yesterday's post brought me frantic appeals both from the *Alliance* and the Roumanian contingent in the Committee of Jewish Delegations. I managed to tranquillise them before the day was out.[54]

Years later, in 1925, when Count Skrzyński, the Polish Foreign Minister, sought an impartial representative to come to Poland to discuss the serious Jewish problems, he turned to Lucien Wolf.[55]

NOTES

1 Aaron Rodrigues of the University of Indiana has been studying the Alliance school system in the Ottoman Empire and, in a forthcoming work, will argue that the schools did not, in fact, serve this purpose. The Quai d'Orsay, however, did not ignore their potential exploitation.

2 The AJA also served a vital function for the AIU. Under French law, the *Alliance* could not 'own' properties such as the shares in the Jewish Colonization Association and the Baron de Hirsch fund. The AJA, however, laboured under no such disadvantage.

3 The Goldsmid-Crémieux correspondence from 1863 illustrates the range of AIU-AJA concerns. [Archives de] A[lliance] I[sraélite] U[niverselle]. Angl[eterre] I/J/3. The Serbian files starting with Goldsmid à Crémieux, 15 mars 1863, and continuing through the 1870s are particularly interesting. The AJA petition to the King of Serbia, 29 Oct 1872 is in II/D/5/3892.

4 The leading Jews even tried personal diplomacy. See, e.g., Mocatta à Loeb, 10 jan 1882. AIU Angl II/D/34/631. Jews also attempted to make common cause with Christian groups. When an Anglo-American Protestant delegation visited the Kaiser in an effort to have him petition on behalf of Protestants in the Russian Baltic provinces, the AJA attached an address on behalf of Jews. July 1871. Angl II/D/2/1984.

5 See, Board of Deputies of British Jews Papers (hereafter cited as BDBJ) C 11/2/1 and particularly Pauncefot to the AJA, 19 June 1889. See also, B/2/9/8, C 11/12/54 and C/14 *passim*.

6 Issues of procedure, often crucial in diplomatic history, suggest that the British ascendancy began very early in the twentieth century. See, e.g., Montefiore's criticism of AIU protocol. Duparc to Bigart, 11 Apr 1902. AIU Angl I/D/18. Cf. Adler to Bigart, 28 Jan; Loeb à Adler 31 jan 1892. AIU Angl I/B/54 bis/7769.

7 BDBJ C 11/2/2 has the CFC record on Romania, 1901–1910. See particularly the Foreign Office responses and negotiations of 1902 and 1907 and the 'Private and Confidential Memorandum on the Treaty Rights of the Jews of Romania', November 1908.

8 For the communal politics, see S. A. Cohen, *English Zionists and British Jews* (Princeton, 1982) Samuel's 'The Future of Palestine', Jan 1915 was printed but probably not fully circulated. His second try, 'Palestine', March 1915 came before

the Cabinet on the 19th. See, M. Gilbert (ed), *Winston Churchill: Companion Volume, 1914-1916* (London, 1979), 713-716.
9 Bigart à Simonsen, 29 déc; Bigart à Montefiore, 30 déc 1914, 9 fév 1915; Bigart à Wolf, 4 mars 1915. AIU Cdc S238/136-137, 139, 186, 214. See also, ibid., 36-37, 86, 90-92. Bigart expressed his outrage with Zionism to Winz in Berlin in October 1913. Cdc S 236/10. The Conjoint Committee Confidential File, 11 Jan 1915. [Mocatta Library, AJA Papers] AJ/204/4 explains why Anglo-Jewry was less disturbed by the Zionist visitors. See also, Wolf to Bigart, 22 Feb 1915. When the aged Narcisse Leven, President of the AIU, died in January 1915, Bigart effectively ran the AIU. Sylvain Lévi, the eminent Orientalist, eventually assumed the presidency, but it made no fundamental difference. Bigart continued, well into the 1920s, to dominate the organization.
10 American Jews had persuaded the Wilson administration not to renew its Russian commercial treaty before the war. Jewish bankers, both English and German, had boycotted Russian government loans in the past in futile attempts to win concessions for Russian Jews. See, e.g., Grey to Revelstoke, 6 Apr; Asquith to Campbell-Bannerman, 7 Apr 1906. Grey Papers. [United Kingdom. Public Record Office.] F[oreign] O[ffice] 800/100/26-30. The AIU reminded the Quai d'Orsay that the French foreign ministry had promised in 1906 to remonstrate with the Russian government about restrictions placed upon Jewish visitors and businessmen travelling to Russia. Sée à MAE, 13 juin 1916. [France] M[inistère des] A[ffaires] É[trangères]. Archives diplomatiques. Guerre.] A/1198/13-17; Wolf to Grey, 6 June 1916. AIU Angl II/D/26/5598.
11 Russian Foreign Minister Sazonov found the matter so embarrassing that he issued an elaborate explanation. Enclosed in Paléologue à Decassé, 15 Sept 1915. MAE A/1197/99-101.
12 Cecil to Spring-Rice, 29 Mar 1916. Cecil Papers. FO 800/196/141-144. Britain's Ambassador to the United States argued, 'If we make this demand from Russia we shall meet with a positive refusal and we shall not do the Jews any good. Some other means therefore must be taken of pleading their case and winning their sympathies'. Spring-Rice to Cecil, 17 March 1916. Spring-Rice Papers. FO 800/242/77-80.
13 On the Slousch lecture tour, see Jusserand à Briand, 17 déc 1915. MAE A/1197/115, encl 116-118. See also, *Appeal of the Consistory of the Jews of France to Jews of Neutral Countries* (Paris, 1915); Bigart à Wolf, 30 juil, 28 sept, 6 oct, 7, 10, déc; Wolf to Bigart, 28 July, 5, 12, Oct 1915; Bigart à Durkheim, 14 avr; Bigart à Sereni, 24 oct 1916. AIU Angl I/J/8/5311, I/G/4/5286; AIU Cdc S 239/35. 39, 233; S 240/15-16. MAE A/1198/100.
14 Wolf, Suggestions for a Pro-Allies Propaganda among the Jews of the United States, 16 Dec 1915. BDBJ C 11/3/1/3. See also, Wolf, 'Confidential Memorandum', 6 June 1917. BDBJ C 11/2/11; Wolf, Address to the American Jewish Congress, 1916. BDBJ C 11/2/8; de Bunsen to Wolf, 23 June; Wolf to de Bunsen, 29 June 1916. AIU Angl I/J/8/5649.
15 P[eace] C[onference] D[iary], 16 Sept.
16 Wolf to Marshall, 1 June 1919. [University College Library, London] Lucien Wolf, PCD, 1 June 1919.
17 Woodrow Wilson, although conscious of the considerable Polish-American vote and sympathetic to Polish nationalism, had quite enough of Polish pretensions before the negotiations began. 1 Apr 1919. P. Mantoux (ed), *Les Délibérations du Conseil des Quatre (24 mars-28 juin 1919)*, (Geneva, 1964), I, 112.
18 Paul Mantoux, *Les Délibérations du Conseil des Quatre*, I, 13 seq. Edwin Montagu, Secretary of State for India and, at the time, close to Lloyd George laid out so

restrained and perceptive a view of the Bolshevik problem that Lloyd George had it printed for secret Cabinet and peace conference circulation. Montagu to Lloyd George, 14 Feb 1919. GT 6861. CAB 24/75/275. A. J. Mayer, *Politics and Diplomacy of Peacemaking: Containment and Counterrevolution of Versailles, 1918–1919* (New York, 1967) advances the strongest case for anti-Bolshevism as a prime motive for the peacemakers.

19 Wolf to Deloncle, 17 July; Bigart à Wolf, 18 juil; Wolf to Montefiore, 16 July 1915. BDBJ C 1/2/6. Bigart à Wolf, 18, 22 juil, 22 août, 1 sept; Wolf to Bigart 20, 25 Aug 1915. AIU Angl I/J/8/5271; AIU Cdc S 238/375–376, 404–405. Successive lead stories in *Archives Israélites* on 27 avril and 4 mai 1916 reiterated the Wolf line. For an extensive file of both AIU and American Jewish Committee material, see MAE A/1197/121 seq. on the Deloncle mission and Benedict XV's statement for American Jews, see MAE A/1197/39, 44, and *passim*. See also, Le Sionisme et le Saint Siège, 19 juil 1917. MAE A/1199/98–101; CFC Conf, 16 July 1916. AJ/204/4. For 1916 discussions, see also Alexander and Montefiore to Marshall, 28 Apr 1916. AIU Angl I/D/13/5559; Bigart à Wolf, 15 mai, 5 juin, 5 juil; Wolf to Bigart 18 May, 18 Oct; Bigart à Duparc, 12 juin 1916. AIU Angl I/J/8/5559, 5738; I/G/4/5271; AIU Cdc S 239/298–299. 304, 320, 392; *Jewish Chronicle*, 9 June 1916; CFC Conf, 27 June, 16, 27 July 1916. AJ/204/4. See also Spring-Rice to Drummond, 30 Jan; Spring-Rice to Percy. 16 June 1916, Spring-Rice Papers. FO 800/242/28–29, 168–169.

20 Sée (AIU) à MAE, 13 juin 1916. MAE A/1198/13–17; Wolf to Grey, 6 June 1916. AIU Angl II/D/26/5598; Alexander to Bigart 28 Apr 1916. AIU Angl I/G/4/5529; LW to de Rothschild, 29 July; LW to Montefiore, 30 July 1915. BDBJ C 11/2/6.

21 Bigart à Wolf, 7 juin, 7, 13 nov; Wolf to Bigart 15 Mar, 21 May, 13 June, 16 Nov 1918. AIU Angl III/D/52/6181, 1403, 6344, 6424, 6830; Wolf to Bigart 5 Nov encl Sub-Committee on Negotiations, 28 Oct; Wolf to FO, 31 Oct 1917; Bigart à Wolf, 8 nov 1917. AIU Angl I/J/8/6/6183, 6193; Wolf, 'The Jewish Question', 14 June 1916. AIU Angl II/D/41/5731: CFC Conf, 27 July 1915, 17 May 1916, 3, 23 Oct, 11 Dec 1917; 31 Jan 1918. AJ/204/4.

22 L. B. N[amier], 'Poland', GT-2192. 4 Oct 1917. [United Kingdom. Public Record Office.] CAB[inet] 24/27/379 seq; GT-3912, 12 Mar 1918. CAB 24/45/34–41. See also, Sée à MAE, 18 juin 1916. MAE A/1198/18–19. For Wolf's files and cuttings, see [Mocatta Library] Wolf Papers ER-4(3).

23 The Russian February Revolution raised hopes overly high for settling the Polish-Jewish conflict. Jewish aspirations were 'sympathetically received', and further discussions planned. AJA/FAC Minutes, 22 Mar, 25 Apr, 3 Oct 1917. [Anglo-Jewish Association Archives. Mocatta Library.] AJ/204/4.

24 Stanislaw Patek and August Zaleski saw Lord Rothschild, Claude Montefiore, and Wolf to urge a 'liberal settlement'. They contended that Dmowski really only wished to drive 'Russian' Jews out of Poland. Wolf Confidential Memo, 30 June 1915; AJA/CC 27 July 1915. AJ/204/4. When Dmowski planned a 1916 lecture tour in Paris and London, the Alliance and Conjoint Committee brought government pressure to bear in view of his avowed anti-Semitism. Dmowski was not permitted to lecture in Paris, and his presentation at King's College in London, after a Foreign Office warning, proved innocuous. AJA/CC. 17 May 1916. AJ/204/4.

25 Polish political parties opposed to Dmowski meeting in Petrograd accepted national and cultural autonomy for minorities in principle. Jewish Nationalists, however, began to press for full 'national autonomy'. AJA/FAC 23 Oct, 11 Dec 1917, 31 Jan 1918. AJ/204/4; *The Times*, 20 Oct 1917; Wolf to Bigart, 31 Oct, 28 Nov 1917. AIU Angl I/J/8/6183, 6221. See also, Report of the Subcommittee on

Negotiations with Poland, 28 Oct 1917; Wolf to Balfour, 31 Oct; Wolf to Graham, 5 Nov 1917, ibid. 6193.
26 Joint Foreign Committee, *The Peace Conference, Paris, 1919* (London, 1920), 74; Blank to Wolf, 29 Nov 1918. BDBJ C 11/2/13; Wolf-Blank-Oliphant interview at FO, 2 July 1915. AIU Angl II/D/26/5271; Wolf's reflective report on the second meeting of the Assembly of the League of Nations, [16 Nov 1921]. AIU Angl III/D/52/9143; Wolf, Report to the JFC, 15 Dec 1920. AIU Angl III/D/52/8253. See also, FAC Confidential Minutes, 3, 23 Oct, 11 Dec 1917; 31 Jan 1918. AJ 204/4/54, 66, 71–72, unn. For the anxiety about emigration, see particularly Wolf to Bigart, 9 Feb; Bigart à Wolf, 9[!] fév 1920. AIU Angl III/D/52/8253.
27 Wolf, PCD, 19 Mar. Wolf returned to Paris from London on 9 February, having ascertained from the Joint Foreign Committee how much range he had for manoeuvre. While doing nothing to obstruct Zionist claims for Palestine, Wolf was determined to achieve his program in the European succession states. The Zionists, who however, having already stolen a march on the 'moderates' contended that their East European Jewish Nationalist delegations were fully representative of Jewish opinion. They were not, and a regular Polish Jewish delegation reached Paris in late April, but meanwhile Wolf had to fend off the Zionist-Nationalist claims of a delegation in being. See, e.g., PCD. 10 Feb.
28 Wolf to Oliphant, 15 June, de Bunsen to Wolf, 23 June, Wolf to de Bunsen, 29 June 1916. AIU Angl I/J/8/5649; Bigart à Wolf, 26 nov 1916. AIU Cdc S 240/68/6312.
29 PCD, 1, 3 Mar. the AIU and JFC had coordinated letters on the Polish question with their respective foreign ministries and conference delegations on 21 Jan. PCD, 21 Jan.
30 PCD, 5 Mar, 27 Feb; Henriques' summaries of the British statutes that Wolf furnished the Poles and British officials is in BDBJ C 11/2/14. See also the Minutes of the Joint Foreign Committee, 6 Mar, 14 Nov, 11 Dec 1918; Wolf to Marshall, 28 Nov 1918. BDBJ C 11/2/13.
31 PCD, 20 Apr, 19, 20 Mar; Sée & Bigart à MAE, 22 mai 1919. AIU Cdc S 243/3–5. The Ukrainians continued to seek Jewish support for their claims. See the circular letter to each Jewish organization asking for their participation in an investigation of reported pogroms from the President of the Ukrainian delegation, 11 Oct 1919. BDBJ C 11/3/1/3.
32 Wolf, Comité des Délégations, Report on the Visit of the Delegation to Paris [April, 1919]. BDBJ C 11/3/1/4; PCD, 24 Mar–16 Apr. The Joint Foreign Committee, including Lord Rothschild and Sir Stuart Samuel (both of whom favoured the Zionist formula in Palestine), approved of the refusal to accommodate Jewish Nationalism and instructed Wolf and the Paris delegation 'that they are not to agree to, or support the demands for Jewish National Rights'. 1 May 1919. BDBJ C 11/3/1/4. Sir Stuart Samuel, President of the Board of Deputies, initially toyed with accommodation, but by 11 April had shifted and 'deprecated' 'any Jewish political separatism in Poland'. PCD, 11 Apr. At the same time, the Joint Foreign Committee acted favourably on the Board of Deputies concern 'that Great Britain's intention to accept the mandate for Palestine will not be abandoned', since, as Claude G. Montefiore, the leading anti-Jewish Nationalist, added, 'any other arrangement would greatly hinder the immigration into that Country of those Jews who desire a new National Home'. BDBJ C 11/3/1/5. Woodrow Wilson, who felt that persecution of Jews was one of the problems most troubling world peace, when the Council of Four came to consider the issue of protection for national and religious minorities, took strong exception to any formulation granting autonomy to national minorities. 1 May 1919. Mantoux, *Délibérations*, I, 440.
33 PCD, 10 Apr. Sir Stuart Samuel had learned wisdom. At the *Consistoire* conference,

he had not opposed the Jewish Nationalists, but by this point he had shifted 'to deprecate any Jewish political separatism in Poland'. Ibid, 11 Apr. So had Headlam-Morley who, in utter frustration, asked Wolf what Polish Jewish Nationalists actually wanted. When Wolf told him that Jewish extremists were as mad as Polish extremists and that there was nothing to choose between Dmowski and Ussishkin, Headlam-Morley said, 'Well, they will all be murdered.' ibid, 14 Apr.

34 PCD, 17–22 Apr; Bigart à AIU, 25 avr; Bigart à Paderewski, 17 avr 1919. AIU Cdc S242/449; *Archives Israélites* LXXX/27, 29. 3, 17 juillet 1919.

35 Wolf's favourable impression of Paderewski outraged Louis Marshall. Morgenthau, however, although officially only working with the Red Cross, supported Wolf's position. PCD, 23–24 Apr.

36 PCD, 25 Apr.

37 PCD, 4–6 May; Mantoux, *Délibérations*, I, 440–442 (1 May) and 474–475 (3 May report from Berthelot, Headlam-Morley, and Miller and the Wilson-Clemenceau, Lloyd-George decisions).

38 Israel Cohen wrote a long article on behalf of the Eastern European Jewish delegates for *The Times* of 22 May 1919 in a desperate attempt to bring public opinion to bear and substitute the Jewish Nationalist for the 'moderate' formula in the Treaties. *The Times* editorially saved Wolf the problem of writing a response by coming out four-square for the 'moderate' position.

39 PCD, 17 May. By May 19th, the Big Three were attempting to restrain Poles from attacking the Ukrainians, who were rumoured to be slaughtering Poles wholesale in Galicia, not to mention their concern with stabilizing the situation in Hungary. Mantoux, *Délibérations*, II, 108–110.

40 Wolf, who had endemic quarrels with Marshall during the months of treaty negotiation, finally realized that Marshall was 'at heart a strong Tory', who allowed 'his views on general politics to affect his attitude on Jewish questions'. Marshall's personal, political detestation of the League as a danger to American interests, for instance, repeatedly led him to place the Jewish guarantees in the signatories to the Treaties rather than, as Wolf insisted, the League. Marshall's ego and temper, moreover, combined with his strong personal likes and dislikes to make him a most difficult and unpredictable colleague. PCD, 6, 27 June.

41 Montefiore agreed to ask Milner to present a letter to Lloyd George on the Sabbath Question. Marshall successfully convinced President Wilson on the point. PCD, 18–22 May. H. S. Q. Henriques, barrister and chairman of the Board of Deputies Law & Parliamentary Committee, prepared a summary memorandum for Wolf to give Paderewski on Jews and Education in England. BDBJ C 11/2/14. See also the report on the Warsaw Jewish Congress in *Archives Israélites*, LXXX/22, 29 mai 1919.

42 PCD, 14, 16 June. Part of the problem, as Wolf repeatedly reminded the Poles, was prompt action, control, and investigation. The Zionists' Copenhagen Bureau needed such horror tales to promote the Jewish Nationalist cause and forwarded exaggerated statistics that inflamed opinion. The Jewish Information Bureau in Copenhagen continued generally to be reliable.

43 Gibson's incompetence served as the justification for the elaborate Morgenthau mission to investigate the Polish situation. Esmé Howard, the British Minister to Warsaw, happened to be in Paris at the time, and Percy Wyndham, the chargé, did not handle matters well. Wolf later prepared a story on the Morgenthau report and 'Jews and Bolshevism' for the *Daily Telegraph* of 6 Nov 1919. Copy enclosed with Wolf to Montefiore, 6 Nov 1919. BDBJ C 11/2/14.

44 PCD, 26 May, 6, 8 June.

45 PCD, 28 May. Weizmann, as one of his gambits, played the 'Bolshevik' card, arguing that without Zionism, Jews might become the shock troops of world revolution. Hogarth to Clayton, 30 Mar 1919. [St. Anthony's College, Oxford] Hogarth Papers 14 (iv). Sir Mark Sykes, for one, was absolutely convinced. Sykes to Balfour, 27 Feb 1918. FO 800/210/129. When Weizmann told Oscar Straus 'that a failure of Zionism would mean a great immigration of Russian-Jewish Bolshevists in America', Straus acidly replied, 'Well we shall hang them.' PCD, 25 Mar. Balfour also believed that Jews were 'to a large degree, leaders in such [revolutionary] movements'. He continued by passing on the preposterous rumour, popular in British genteel circles, that Lenin 'on his mother's side was a Jew'. Brandeis, to whom he was talking on that occasion, told him that was nonsense, that Lenin 'on both sides is an upper class Russian'. Paris, 24 June 1919. FO 800/217/187. Bolshevism as a Jewish conspiracy was promulgated in print, apparently on the initiative of Colonel Townshend, General Ironside's Intelligence Officer of the British Archangel expedition. PCD, 2 Aug. See also, Wolf, Memorandum on the Jews and Bolshevism, 2 Oct 1919. BDBJ C 11/2/14.
46 Wolf to Marshall, 1 June 1919. Copy in PCD, 1 June.
47 Wolf, however, found this request entangled him in American Jewish politics. Even Cyrus Adler criticized Wolf for involving Morganthau, likening him, for Wolf's benefit, to Bentwich as a chronic 'mischief-maker' PCD, 20 June.
48 PCD, 28 May–28 June; Mantoux, *Délibérations*, II, 92–94, 331–332, 340–341, 451–453, 470–471, 486–490, 544–547.
49 Wolf continually sorted out real and exaggerated claims. See, e.g., his discussions with Stuart Samuel and Cyrus Adler on the Częstochowa incident. PCD, 29–30 June.
50 Wolf to Bigart, 7 July 1920. AIU Angl III/D/52/7896. Wolf's consistent support from Claude G. Montefiore and Sir Stuart Samuel as well as most traditional Anglo-Jewish leaders gave him indirectly access to Lloyd George and his circle of advisers. Montefiore, for instance, had ready access through Lord Milner.
51 When Margolin was lobbying for his Ukrainian cause, he called Clemenceau's attention to the 'rabid anti-Semitism of the Polish Government. "Yes, I know", said Clemenceau, "they are all reactionaries and anti-Semites, but they are going to get an ultimatum from us."' PCD, 26 May.
52 See, particularly, R. Ullman, *Britain and the Russian Civil War*, II–III (Princeton, 1967–1973). See also, Wolf, 'Memorandum on the Danger of Anti-Jewish Excesses from the Army of Denikin', 30 July 1919. BDBJ C 11/2/14; Bigart à Simonson, 6 Nov; Wolf to Bigart, 31 Oct, 10, 11, 12, 13, 19 Nov; Bigart à Wolf, 3, 12, 21 Nov; Bigart à Wolfsohn, 20 Nov 1919. AIU Cdc S 243/7175, 7178, 7210, 7219, 7241, 7145, 7255, 7607, 7619, 7643, 7675, 7685.
53 Wolf, Report to the JFC, 15 Dec 1920. AIU Angl III/D/52/8253. See also Wolf's Report on the Second Meeting of the Assembly of the League of Nations [16 Nov 1921]. ibid/9143; Wolf to Bigart, 6 July 1920. AIU Angl III/D/53/7887; Samuel to Wolf, 1 Sept 1920. BDBJ C 11/3/2/3. See also, Wolf's reports on the mission of Professor Szymon Ashkennzy to undo the Minority clauses in Poland. Wolf to Bigart, 12 June, 18 Aug, 8, 28 Oct, 5 Nov 1920. AIU Anglo III/D/52/7917, 8135, 8156 and W. S. Churchill, Report on the Situation at Vilna, 10 Oct 1920. CAB 1/29/222–223. See also, FO Political Intelligence: Poland 008, 20 Mar 1920. CP 937. CAB 24/101/161–162. Wolf believed the boycott was the most difficult issue to resolve in any ultimate settlement of the Polish-Jewish problem. Morgenthau, after the enquiry the summer of 1919, found eight principal outbreaks against Jews in Poland. While whitewashing nothing, Morgenthau was 'anxious to hold the balance fairly evenly between Poles and Jews', while Homer-Johnson preferred to

dwell on Jewish 'defects' and exculpate the Poles. The Report ultimately cited 282 deaths. 'Strictly speaking there were no pogroms, but only military excesses within the zone of military operations.' PCD, 2, 5–7 Oct. Wolf, while putting these tragedies in a balanced light, hoped that ultimately the resolution of the Russian civil war and restoration of peace there would create an opportunity for eastward Jewish migration and reduce the Jewish presence and problem in the small succession states. PCD, 9–11, 6 Aug, 5, 8 Sept.
54 Wolf to Greenberg, 9 Dec 1919. BDBJ C 11/2/14. Wolf did not always deal in 'tranquillity'. He regularly added to Sir Basil Thompson's dossiers about subversive or potentially subversive individuals who always seemed to be Zionists or Jewish Nationalists. See, e.g., Wolf to Thompson, 15 Apr 1921. BDBJ C 11/2/16.
55 Wolf to Bigart, 26 May, 26 July 1925. AIU Angl IV/D/54/6910, 7031.

THE DMOWSKI–NAMIER FEUD, 1915–1918
Paul Latawski

Roman Dmowski was the antithesis of Lewis Namier; by conviction, Dmowski was the archetypical anti-semite while Namier was a fervent disciple of Zionism. It was therefore no accident that these two men shared a vigorous dislike for each other. Namier, with characteristic hyperbole wrote that 'I am not actuated ... by any personal resentment against Dmowski and his whole Polish Black Hundred crew.'[1] In a less subtle manner, Dmowski contemptuously referred to Namier as that 'little Galician Jew'.[2] During the First World War these two men crossed paths in London where they both became involved with the Polish question and entered into an acrimonious feud centring on their respective visions of a future Poland. From 1916 onwards, they waged a very bitter and very personal struggle to discredit each other's views on the Polish question in the eyes of the British foreign policy establishment. In their duel for influence, each man revealed a startling dichotomy of character reflecting his undoubted qualities of genuine brilliance as well as his unsavoury attributes.

Roman Dmowski was the most important Polish right-wing ideologist of his generation. He began his political career in *fin de siècle* Warsaw and quickly established himself as the leader of the radical right National Democratic Party (*Narodowa Demokracja* – popularly *endecja*). His reputation as the voice of the Polish right wing grew after he became editor of the influential journal *Przegląd Wszechpolski* (All-Polish Review) in January 1895 and through the publication a number of important political tracts: *Myśli nowoczesnego Polaka* (Thoughts of the Modern Pole, 1903) and *La Question Polonaise* (1906). Dmowski's ideology transcended party political lines with his ideas on the nation forming the intellectual foundation of modern Polish nationalism.[3]

Dmowski could display considerable political acumen, but his efforts were frequently undermined by his prejudices and a proclivity to engage in the politics of the *boudoir*. Eduard Beneš, the future Czech leader, was 'immediately captivated by his shrewdness and the trenchant character of his political plans'. Beneš also observed that Dmowski 'often exhibited rather ostentatiously his anti-semitism'.[4] Dmowski's record of antipathy towards Polish Jewry included the notorious boycott of Jewish enterprises in Warsaw in 1912.

Like virtually all Polish politicians his ultimate goal was an independent Poland. In working towards this goal, however, Dmowski opposed revolutionary means of regaining Polish independence. Instead, he believed that the reconstruction of Poland could be forwarded only through a *rapprochement* with one of the partitioning powers. For Dmowski, this could only mean Polish autonomy within the Russian Empire. He dismissed the possibility of reaching an accommodation with Germany, arguing that 'the principal danger that menaces the national existence of Poland resides in the disproportionate growth of German power under the direction of Prussia.'[5]

With the outbreak of a general European war in August 1914, Dmowski, consistent with his political design, threw his support behind the Entente and remained staunchly loyal to the Russian cause, seeking autonomy for the Polish lands under the sceptre of the Tsar. His demonstrations of loyalty, however, yielded little in the way of Russian political concessions. Increasingly frustrated, Dmowski began to re-evaluate his approach during the spring and summer of 1915. With the German occupation of Warsaw in August, Dmowski had to shift his activities to Petrograd. His time in the Russian capital convinced him that a change of venue was in order; in October 1915 Dmowski left Petrograd, transferring his political activities to the West, remaining there for the rest of the war.[6]

Lewis Namier, in contrast to Dmowski, was a man of multifarious occupations. He is best remembered for his contributions to historical scholarship and his political activities in the Zionist movement. But among the least known and understood of his many callings was his stint in government service between March 1915 and April 1920. It was during this period that Namier became one of the leading British authorities on the Polish problem.

At the outbreak of the war, Namier volunteered for the army and entered the rolls of the Royal Fusiliers. His term in the army, however, was short. In March 1915 he was discharged and transferred to propaganda work at Wellington House. He obtained his position thanks to the patronage of his friend in the Foreign Office, Eustace Percy.[7] After entry into the civil service, Namier's career developed in three distinct phases: 1) Wellington House, 1915–1917; 2) The Intelligence Bureau, Department of Information, 1917–1918; and, 3) The Political Intelligence Department (PID), Foreign Office, 1918–1920. His early duties at Wellington House included a regular review of the Polish press and occasional papers related to British propaganda efforts among Poles in America. Later, at the

Intelligence Bureau and the Political Intelligence Department, Namier's task changed to studying and advising on more substantive Polish matters. With each change in Namier's official venue, he obtained greater responsibility and influence over British thinking on the Polish question.

On the surface, Namier's credentials to disseminate information on Poland appeared impressive. He was born in June 1888 at Wola Okrzyjska near Warsaw into a gentry family of Polonised Jews. Ludwik Niemirowski, as he was then known, grew up in the congenial atmosphere of the Polish manor house. His early life and education centered on his family's estate in Eastern Galicia. Namier's formidable intellect was firmly cultivated at an impressive array of institutions of higher learning: briefly at Lwów and Lausanne and then more extensively at the London School of Economics and Balliol College, Oxford. He took a first in modern history in Oxford in 1911. Finding Britain highly agreeable, Namier decided to settle there permanently; he changed his name and adopted British citizenship in 1913.[8]

Despite seemingly impeccable credentials, Namier was remarkably unsuitable for the task of supplying political information on Poland. According to his friends and colleagues, Namier held a strong antipathy towards Poland during his official tenure as expert on Polish affairs. Arnold Toynbee observed in his *Acquaintances* that 'there can be no doubt that, when Poland regained her independence, Lewis became a Polonophobe and a Zionist.'[9] Sir Eric Drummond, the private secretary to successive British Foreign Secretaries, wrote in 1917 that 'I profoundly distrust Namier's conclusions and statements.'[10] As if to confirm his earlier fears, Drummond commented two years later that 'Namier . . . is . . . bitterly opposed to a strong and independent Poland.'[11] In evaluating Namier, John Duncan Gregory, one of the few Foreign Office officials to take an interest in Polish affairs, believed that 'on the whole it has been a great pity that Mr. Namier was ever introduced into the F.O.' 'If only his prejudices didn't give him all the time an anti-Polish bias.'[12] James Headlam-Morley, Namier's immediate superior at the PID informed Namier: 'I know that nothing interferes so much with the value of your work as the feeling which you allow to appear that you have no sympathy with Poland at all.'[13] It is significant that both friends, such as Toynbee and Headlam-Morley, as well as long-time opponents, such as Drummond and Gregory, could reach a consensus of opinion about Namier. These British officials, who either worked intimately with Namier or regularly read his minutes and memoranda, found common cause in questioning his balance and objectivity.

The hostilities between Dmowski and Namier were formally initiated in the winter of 1915. When Dmowski arrived in London in November, the principal aim of the National Democratic leader was to garner British support for Polish aspirations. His opening approach to the British authorities was cautious. On 16 December 1915, Dmowski wrote to Lord Robert Cecil in the Foreign Office asking if existing obstacles could be removed to allow Polish relief to proceed. By picking what undoubtedly was a non-controversial subject, Dmowski hoped to use humanitarian relief as a useful entrance into the corridors of power. Namier, however, attempted to discredit Dmowski from the beginning. Eustace Percy, the man who brought Namier into government service, commented on Dmowski's request. No doubt repeating what Namier told him, Percy wrote: 'I sincerely hope that we shall keep M. Dmowski and every other Polish politician out of it.'[14] But Namier's first effort, albeit an indirect one, failed. Dmowski had his supporters in the Foreign Office who willingly defended him. Arthur Nicolson, who had known Dmowski since his time as Ambassador to Russia, wrote: 'Dmowski is a great influence among the Poles and stands apart from most Poles.'[15]

Unaware of Namier's machinations behind the scenes, Dmowski again approached the Foreign Office in the spring of 1916. On 11 March he submitted a memorandum arguing the case for the internationalization of the Polish question. In it he was careful not to overstep the bounds of British interests and he did not advocate Polish independence. The memorandum received a wide readership in the Foreign Office.[16]

The same month that Dmowski presented his memorandum to the Foreign Office, Namier again criticized the National Democratic leader, this time questioning the former's loyalty to the Entente cause. In the second week of February, Dmowski had attended a political conference of the Polish right held at Lausanne, Switzerland. Namier, in one of his press summaries, accused Dmowski of altering his political line and adopting a pro-Austrian position at the Lausanne conference.[17] This was a serious charge to place against a Polish politician from Russia who laid claim to the fact that he was staunchly pro-Entente. It was also well beyond the scope of Namier's duties to treat his press summaries as a platform for discussing the merits of the British government's association with Dmowski. But one thing was clear; it was an open attempt to sabotage Dmowski's bid for influence in Britain.

How true was Namier's charge that Dmowski was disloyal to the Entente at Lausanne in February? By Namier's own account, he based his accusation on information 'mostly from Zaleski'. Later Masaryk passed on to him an Austrian report from 'secret channels' which confirmed Namier's charge.[18] August Zaleski was the most prominent Polish socialist politician in London and, as a source, he certainly had partisan motives in handing Namier damaging information about Dmowski. Whether or not Tomaš Masaryk, the influential Czech leader, bore a grudge against Dmowski is unclear and it is impossible to assess Masaryk's information received from 'secret channels'. But what is certain, based on contemporary historiography, is that Namier's charge against Dmowski was absolutely unfounded. The Lausanne conference reaffirmed the pro-Entente and pro-Russia line that Dmowski followed.[19]

Namier's March attack on Dmowski did not pass unanswered. Rothay Reynolds, a friend of Dmowski employed in the Press Department of Military Intelligence at Watergate House, leaked the damaging press summary to him.[20] Once alerted to Namier's attack, Dmowski swiftly retaliated. On 6 May, Dmowski registered his complaint to Sir Arthur Nicolson at the Foreign Office. According to Nicolson's account of their conversation:

> M. Dmowski called on me this morning. He said that he had come to complain. He had been informed that this Office was deriving their information as to the recent Polish conference at Lausanne and on Polish affairs from M. Namier, a Polish Austrian Jew. . . . He stated that M. Namier had reported that he (M. Dmowski) had gone over to the Austrians and had deserted his former principles. . . . In regard to the charges against himself, he could only characterize them as a malicious falsehood.[21]

Dmowski's meeting with Nicolson resulted in a reprimand for Namier. Ernest Gowers, Namier's boss at Wellington House, informed Namier that he must confine himself to the requirements of the press summaries. More ambitious commentaries would require, henceforward, the approval of the Foreign Office.[22]

Dmowski, however, decided that he must thoroughly discredit Namier as well as other political opponents in Britain. In order to achieve his aims, Dmowski decided on an indirect approach with the willing collaboration of Count Jan Marie de Horodyski in June 1916. Horodyski was a freelance missionary of the Polish cause who had right wing political sympathies along with important contacts in the Foreign Office. On 12 June Horodyski met Sir Eric Drummond, the private secretary of the Foreign Secretary, Arthur James Balfour. Drummond recorded the following account of his conversation with Horodyski:

> Count Horodyski spoke to me yesterday with regard to M. M. Nemir, Zaleski, and Retinger. He said that he thought that these three gentlemen were, perhaps unwittingly, being used for pro-Austrian purposes and he urged that their correspondence should be closely watched and that it was desirable that they should not be allowed to travel about but should be confined to this country.[23]

The accusations of Dmowski's collaborator, Horodyski, placed Namier, Zaleski, and Retinger under a cloud of suspicion in the Foreign Office. Although an investigation failed to turn up any evidence of the three men's disloyalty, the Foreign Office continued to harbour doubts about Namier. But the inconclusiveness of the investigation also cast doubt on Dmowski's degree of innocence in inspiring these serious charges. These doubts divided opinion in the Foreign Office. Drummond vented his disenchantment with Namier on 15 June: 'I do not like the way M. Namier is always trying to have a hit at M. Dmowski, who I believe to be entirely reliable and a strong pro-ally.'[24] Lord Robert Cecil, however, had his doubts about the Polish National Democratic leader: 'All the same Dmowski is rather too clever for my taste.'[25] Despite mixed views in the Foreign Office, the episode worked against Namier and spelled a temporary decline in his influence. In late June, when Eustace Percy suggested that Namier be consulted on a Military Intelligence report on the Poles in Switzerland, he got a sharp rebuke. Clerk wrote: 'I do not think we need bother re: Namier.'[26]

The Dmowski-Namier exchange continued to occupy Foreign Office discussion in July and August 1916. When Cambridge University contacted the Foreign Office as to the advisability of awarding an honorary degree to Dmowski, the mandarins of British foreign policy engaged in some soul-searching on the merits and demerits of Roman Dmowski. Drummond wrote on 5 July: 'There are two opinions about Dmowski – one that with him and the pro-Russion party lies all hope for Poland – the other that he is a self-seeking politician surrounded by all that is least efficient, least trustworthy and most effete in Poland.'[27] Notwithstanding Drummond's mixed review, it did not result in a Foreign Office objection to an honorary degree from Cambridge University, which Dmowski received on 11 August 1916.[28]

The Foreign Office also tempered its criticism of Namier. In a letter to Sir George Buchanan dated 23 August 1916, Drummond outlined the Dmowski-Namier feud as it had progressed since early 1916. He was strictly even-handed towards both Dmowski and Namier: 'We naturally do not want to identify ourselves with anything hostile to Dmowski ... but as Namier wrote what he did write with the sanction of his immediate official superior it seems fair that he should be protected as far as possible.'[29] The Foreign Office was keen to drop the matter of the Dmowski-Namier feud although it would continue to crop up with monotonous regularity. In 1916, their intrigues were at a particularly ugly stage as each man, through his respective proxies, accused the other of treasonable activities. The opening clash between Dmowski and Namier ended in stalemate with neither man removed from a position of influence regarding Polish affairs in London.

In 1917, the Dmowski-Namier contest shifted from direct confrontation to a more behind the scenes struggle to win greater acceptance for their respective viewpoints among members of the British foreign policy establishment. The outbreak of revolution in Russia aided Dmowski's efforts to broaden the scope of discussion in official circles concerning the future of Poland. Likewise, Namier's transfer to the Intelligence Bureau of the Department of Information expanded his responsibilities, allowing him to comment directly on Polish political developments.

The collapse of Russian power in 1917 emboldened Dmowski into altering his political aims regarding the future of Poland. In a significant departure from his previous policy, Dmowski openly called for the creation of an independent Poland and articulated his territorial claims for the reconstruction of the state. Dmowski supplied an outline of his ideas in two memoranda to the Foreign Office in March 1917. He compiled the main points of these two short memoranda in his better known and more wide-ranging publication, *Problems of Central and Eastern Europe* (London, 1917).[30] Dmowski pressed a copy of this document into the hand of Balfour as he boarded a ship at Southhampton for America in July 1917.[31]

Dmowski's territorial programme for the reconstruction of Poland claimed from Russia the Congress Kingdom as well important segments of the western provinces including Lithuania and parts of the districts of Minsk and Volhynia. The claim from Germany included Poznań district, West Prussia, and Upper Silesia with the Baltic port of Danzig linked to Poland by a broad corridor. From the Austro-Hungarian Empire, Dmowski claimed Austrian Silesia (Teschen) and the entire province of Galicia. Reflecting his qualified definition of the principle of national self-determination, Dmowski believed that Poland could not be reconstructed on a 'purely linguistic basis'.[32] His territorial design for the reconstruction of Poland embraced territories that held large non-Polish speaking populations.

In the Foreign Office, Dmowski's memoranda and more extensive treatise aroused considerable interest in the spring of 1917. His documents received extensive scrutiny as the Foreign Office opened what may very well have been its first file on Polish frontiers. The Foreign Office debate on Dmowski's territorial programme revealed considerable doubts about the wisdom of some of his claims particularly from the western regions of Russia.[33] The interest Dmowski generated among British officials regarding his ideas on Polish frontiers nevertheless represented a milestone in his efforts to extend his influence on a major Entente government.

In the meantime, Namier used his new found freedom to write on Polish affairs to launch a 'memorandum-schlacht' to discredit Dmowski. Representative of Namier's efforts was the lengthy document he produced to debunk Dmowski's vision of the future Poland in September 1917. The memorandum appeared under the title of 'Remarks on "The Problems of Central and Eastern Europe"' and made its way into the Foreign Office file on Polish frontiers.[34]

What is remarkable about Namier's September memorandum is that in sixteen pages of text he only managed to devote two sentences to favourable remarks on Dmowski's programme. Virtually all of the memorandum criticized Dmowski's territorial claims against Russia deriding them as a violation of self-determination. Namier's memorandum was replete with language that was openly sarcastic and full of value judgements. When describing the basis of Dmowski's territorial schemes, Namier wrote: 'For his reflections on Austria, he is mainly indebted to memory, and for his facts about the Russian borderlands, to the toil of his imagination.'[35] Dmowski's territorial programme in the east was referred to as 'Polish imperialist claims' that were designed to support 'Polish landlords'.[36]

The Foreign Office found itself at odds with both the tone and the content of Namier's critique of Dmowski's *Problems of Central and Eastern Europe*. In a cover letter he attached to the document, Drummond commented that Namier 'is a violent opponent of Dmowski and much of what he writes and says is coloured by this dislike'.[37] Professor Charles Oman, a distinguished don from Oxford who was employed by the Foreign Office as a consultant on the Polish frontier question also criticized Namier's memorandum. According to Professor Oman: 'Mr. Namier's criticism of "The Problems of Central Europe" is written in a spirit of exaggerated hostility, making the worst of the Polish case whenever it is possible to do so.'[38]

Although the Foreign Office remained a bastion of support for Dmowski, Namier remained undeterred and assiduously cultivated important contacts within the British government. Phillip Kerr, the Private Secretary to the Prime Minister, was his most influential corrrespondent in high places. On four occasions during the course of 1917, Namier wrote to Kerr concerning the Polish question.[39] In each of his letters, Namier stressed the dangers of continuing relations with Dmowski.

Kerr instigated the first of these communications after meeting Namier at a social function in April 1917. From Namier, Kerr requested a *précis* of what policy His Majesty's Government should adopt regarding the Polish question. Namier willingly obliged and supplied Kerr with a six page letter devoted less to the Polish question than to the dangers of association with Dmowski.[40] The measure of Namier's concern over Dmowski's influence among British officials was made plain enough in his first letter to Kerr:

> There is one thing which I want to put before you and which I think ought to be rubbed into all the innumerable Government departments. You know me well enough to believe me that I am not actuated here by personal resentment against Dmowski and his whole Polish Black Hundred crew. After all from the very beginning it was not a personal question. I have never known any of their leaders personally and merely distrusted them as one disliked and distrusted their Russian reactionary confreres. But as all Poles have the appearance of having been 'persecuted' Englishmen have often

gone wrong and may yet easily go wrong with regard to the Polish reactionaries.[41]

The attack on Dmowski contained some implicit criticism of the Foreign Office. Namier's reference to the 'innumerable Government departments' could mean nothing else. What Namier did not know was that Kerr forwarded his letter to Sir Eric Drummond in the Foreign Office. In his reply to Kerr, Drummond reserved some harsh words for Namier: 'His attack on Dmowski and other Poles is, in spite of what he says, purely personal and quite unjust.'[42] Moreover, Drummond offered Kerr some firm advice concerning Namier's views on Poland: 'I think it would be very regrettable if you allowed yourself to be influenced by their plausibility.'[43]

Despite Drummond's admonition Kerr remained open to Namier's influence. In September Namier supplied Kerr with a copy of his memorandum criticizing Dmowski's *The Problems of Central and Eastern Europe*.[44] Two months later, Namier sent Kerr a translation of a *Przegląd Polityczny* article 'The Polish Question in International Politics.' The Polish journal was an organ of the National Democratic Party. Namier in his cover letter to Kerr argued that the article illustrated Dmowski's unwarranted pretentions: 'You will also mark that he reasons on the line "*l'État c'est moi*", or perhaps "*La Pologne, c'est moi*".'[45] Given the fact that Kerr was so close to the Prime Minister, Namier clearly reckoned that he could undermine Dmowski precisely in the centre of power in the British government.

What boded ill for Dmowski was that in 1917, Namier's acerbic prose and relentless persistence was winning converts to the anti-Dmowski camp. Bernard Pares, the noted scholar of Russian history at the outbreak of the Great War thought highly of the National Democratic leader: 'Dmowski has more remarkable gifts than I have met in any Russian and in my opinion must have a place somewhere between Parnell and Cavour.'[46] By 1917, Namier informed Pares of Dmowski's territorial claims, which led to Pares breaking off his 'very close' relations with Dmowski.[47]

The tide was inexorably turning against Dmowski in his contest with Namier for influence in British official circles in 1917. On the surface, however, the year had been marked with notable success for Dmowski and his political *confrères*. On 15 August 1917 Dmowski inaugurated the 'Polish National Committee' (*Komitet Narodowy Polski – KNP*), making himself president and opening offices in London, Paris and Rome. Two months later the *KNP* received recognition from the British government as an official agency, representing Polish political interests.[48] But Dmowski had hoped that Britain would recognize the *KNP* as the provisional government of Poland. The British hesitancy to offer such recognition was in part due to Namier's obstinate attacks against Dmowski throughout 1917.

Fortune continued to smile on Namier in his feud with Dmowski in the last year of the Great War. In February 1918, the Intelligence Bureau of the Department of Information became the Political Intelligence Department in the Foreign Office. This considerably strengthened Namier's official position by moving him into the Foreign Office. From his new post in the wheelhouse of British foreign policy, Namier was well placed to scupper Dmowski and his politics.

Namier's change of venue did not pass unnoticed by Dmowski. No doubt Namier's reappearance came as something of a shock to Dmowski who thought he had dealt the latter's influence a fatal blow two years earlier. Nevertheless, after learning of Namier's acquisition of the Polish desk at PID, Dmowski moved with characteristic ruthlessness. Relying on his tested method of denouncing his opponents to the British authorities, Dmowski handed a dossier on Namier to a contact in the Directorate of Military Intelligence (DMI) at the War Office in April.[49] When the DMI approached Sir William Tyrrell, Namier's boss at the Foreign Office, concerning the accusations, it got an angry response. Tyrrell defended Namier, calling the whole affair 'perfect rubbish'.[50]

Shortly after Dmowski delivered his dossier on Namier, an article 'Potash and Perlmutter' appeared in the 26 April edition of the *The New Witness*. It was a thinly veiled attack on Namier. About the source of inspiration for the article there can be little doubt that it was Dmowski. Its author, Robert Ussler, was a journalist who did press work for the Polish National Committee bureau in London. Ussler was a rabid supporter of Dmowski, writing of him that 'I do not believe that there is anyone living with a better knowledge of European politics, or a deeper insight into the real forces of the world.'[51] Moreover, in a letter to Alma Tadema, daughter of the famous landscape painter, Ussler wrote on 6 May: 'If this article can help to remove for ever from the scene an enemy of Poland, I should be very content.'[52] A fortnight later Ussler again wrote to Tadema and confidently predicted in reference to Namier: 'I believe he has received his *coup de grâce*.' Ussler, however, could not have been more mistaken.

Dmowski and his willing accomplice underestimated the strength of official displeasure with the entire episode of the dossier and *The New Witness* article. The incident earned Dmowski a rebuke from Drummond and Tyrrell in the Foreign Office.[54] Despite having received an official warning, Dmowski persisted in his attack on Namier. On 5 May another article openly attacking Namier appeared in the *KNP*-controlled London weekly *Tygodnik Polski*. It accused Namier of supplying anti-Polish articles to such publications as *The New Europe*. Namier brought the article to the attention of Tyrrell and the Foreign Office reacted swiftly.[55] Drummond wrote to Dmowski on 17 May and told him in no uncertain terms that the attacks on Namier must cease forthwith: 'You will I feel understand that what I want to convey is that it is a mistake for members of the Polish National Committee to inspire and authorize attacks on people who are actually working in the Foreign Office.'[56] In addition to the letter to Dmowski, Count Władysław Sobański, the *KNP* representative in London, received an official warning stating that any further articles assailing Namier would lead to the end of the British subsidy for the *KNP*.[57]

Faced with a curtailment of vitally needed funds, Dmowski beat a hasty retreat and, in replying to Drummond's letter, apologized for the misunderstanding and offered some unconvincing explanations in which he tried to distance himself from the authors of the press attacks on Namier.[58] But at the same time Dmowski believed that Drummond had assured him that Namier would be stopped from contributing to the press. Dmowski indicated this, both in his memoirs and in his letter to Drummond of 23 May.[59] Namier, when he read Dmowski's memoirs some time after the war, thought Dmowski was lying since he received no such instructions to cease writing for the press.[60] The truth probably rests somewhere between the two extremes of Namier's and Dmowski's account of events. It was no secret that Drummond was a Foreign Office supporter of the *KNP*. When he recounted the nature of his action to Lord Hardinge, he also emphasized that it was not the business of the Foreign Office to defend journals like *The New Europe* – an oblique reference to Namier.[61] In all probability, when Drummond first warned Dmowski, prior to their exchange of letters, he told him, in an attempt to placate him, that he would see that Namier kept out of mischief. Dmowski simply exaggerated a quiet verbal reassurance out of proportion.[62]

Dmowski's attempt to silence Namier's voice on Polish affairs utterly failed. His use of unsavoury political tactics damaged his reputation even among his supporters in the Foreign Office. Although both men would continue to play a major role in the international arena, Dmowski as head of the Polish delegation at the Paris Peace Conference in 1919 and Namier as the principal British expert on Poland until April 1920, their struggle for influence in London essentially ended with Dmowski's apology to Drummond in May 1918.

The outcome of the Dmowski-Namier feud seemingly vindicated everything Namier wrote about Dmowski's disreputable intrigues during the war. But Namier's tactics in undermining Dmowski differed so little from the National Democratic leader's methods that their mutual proclivity to engage in gutter politics made each man indistinguishable from the other. Moreover, Namier's triumph over Dmowski gave credibility to the former's views on Polish affairs that did lasting damage to Anglo-Polish relations. Namier, however, was destined to have the last word against Dmowski. Writing an obituary on his National Democratic rival in the *Manchester Guardian* in January 1939, Namier, no doubt recalling his wartime confrontation with his bitter foe, offered the following summary of Dmowski's political career: 'He was a child of the Warsaw riverside and reproduced its type in the arena of international politics.'[63]

NOTES

1 Letter Namier to Kerr, 2 April 1917, in: FO800/384 POL 17/4.
2 Roman Dmowski, *Polityka Polska i odbudowanie państwa*, (Częstochowa, 1937), pp. 279–81.
3 *Polski Słownik Biograficzny*, vol. 5, (Kraków, 1939–1946), pp. 213–55.
4 Eduard Beneš, *My War Memoirs*, (London, 1928), p. 313.
5 Roman Dmowski, *La Question Polonaise*, (Paris, 1909), p. 330.
6 Andrzej Micewski, *Roman Dmowski*, (Warsaw, 1971), pp. 220–5.
7 Julia Namier, *Lewis Namier A Biography*, (London, 1971), pp. 120–3.
8 Biographical data taken from: Namier, *Lewis Namier* and *Dictionary of National Biography 1951–1960*, pp. 763–6.
9 Arnold J. Toynbee, *Acquaintances*, (London, 1967), pp. 67–8.
10 Letter Drummond to Kerr, 6 April 1917, in: FO800/384 POL 17/4.
11 Letter Drummond to Kerr, 18 January 1919, in: FO800/215.
12 Gregory minute, 6 December 1919, in: FO800/149.
13 Letter Headlam-Morley to Namier, 3 February 1919, in: Sir James Headlam-Morley, *A Memoir of the Paris Peace Conference 1919*, (London, 1972), pp. 20–1.
14 Memorandum by Dmowski, 16 December 1915 and Percy minute in: FO371/2449–193104.
15 Nicolson minute, 18 December 1915, in: FO371/2449–193104.
16 Memorandum by Dmowski, 11 March 1916, in: FO371/2747–53414.
17 Letter Nicolson to Grey, 6 May 1916 and note Foreign Office to Gowers, 18 May 1916, in: FO395/25–95630.
18 Namier memorandum on his dispute with Dmowski c. 1925, in: private papers of Namier in the possession of Mr. John Brooke. Hereafter *Namier MSS – Brooke*.
19 M. Leczyk, *Komitet Narodowy Polski a Ententa i Stany Zjednoczone 1917–1919*, (Warsaw, 1966), pp. 50–1.
20 *Namier MSS – Brooke*.
21 Letter Nicolson to Grey, 6 May 1916, in: FO396/25–95630 and Dmowski, *Polityka Polska*, pp. 280–1.
22 *Namier MSS – Brooke* and note Foreign Office to Gowers, in: FO395/25–95630.
23 Letter Drummond to Grey, 12 June 1916, in: FO800/96.
24 Letter Drummond to Cecil, 15 June 1916, in: FO800/96.
25 Cecil minute, 15 June 1916, in: FO800/96.
26 Percy and Cecil minutes, 29 June 1916, in: FO371/2750–123998.
27 Drummond minute, 5 July 1916, in: FO395/26-131839.
28 J. D. Duff ed., *Russian Realities and Problems*, (Cambridge, 1917), pp. v–vi.
29 Letter Drummond to Buchanan, 23 August 1916, in: FO800/75.
30 Dmowski memoranda, March 1917, in: FO371/3000–63741 and FO371/3016–194676 and Roman Dmowski, *Problems of Central and Eastern Europe*, (London, 1917).
31 Dmowski, *Polityka Polska*, p. 263.
32 'Memorandum on the Territories of the Polish state' by Dmowski, 26 March 1917, in: FO371/3000–63741.
33 'Memorandum on the Boundaries of Poland' by Oman, 3 April 1917, in: FO371/3016–194676.
34 'Remarks in "The Problems of Central and Eastern Europe"' by Namier, 14 September 1917, in: FO371/3016–194676.
35 Ibid.
36 Ibid.

37 Letter Drummond to Balfour, 19 September 1917, in: FO371/3016–194676.
38 Letter Oman to Foreign Office, 26 September 1917, in: FO371/3016-194676.
39 The Namier-Kerr correspondence can be found in: Lothian MSS GD40/17 873/1 Scottish Record Office, Edinburgh. Hereafter *Lothian MSS*.
40 Letter Namier to Kerr, 2 April 1917, in: FO800/384 POL 17/4.
41 Ibid.
42 Letter Drummond to Kerr, 6 April 1917, in: FO800/384 POL 17/4.
43 Ibid.
44 'Remarks on "The Problems of Central and Eastern Europe"', by Namier, 14 September 1917 in: *Lothian MSS* GD 40/17 875/1.
45 Letter Namier to Kerr, 22 November 1917, in: *Lothian* MSS GD 40/17 875/1.
46 'The Polish Question' by Pares, 8 October 1914, in: FO800/74.
47 Bernard Pares, *My Russian Memoirs*, (London, 1931), pp. 481–2.
48 Letter Graham to Sobański, 15 October 1917, in: Archiwum Polskiego Komitetu Narodowego, mikrofilm 20754 teczka 28, *Archiwum Akt Nowych*, Warsaw. Hereafter *KNP Papers*.
49 *Namier MSS – Brooke*.
50 Ibid.
51 Letter Ussler to Alma Tadema, 29 March 1921, in: *Tadema MSS* 528, *Bodleian Library*, Oxford. Hereafter *Tadema MSS*.
52 Letter Ussler to Tadema, 6 May 1918, in: *Tadema MSS* 528.
53 Letter Ussler to Tadema, 21 May 1918, in: *Tadema MSS* 528.
54 *Namier MSS – Brooke* and Letter Drummond to Dmowski, 17 May 1918, in: *KNP Papers*, mikrofilm 20755 teczka 29.
55 Namier minute, 15 May 1918, in: FO371/4363-137.
56 Letter Drummond to Dmowski, 17 May 1918, in: *KNP Papers*, mikrofilm 20755 teczka 29.
57 *Namier MSS – Brooke*.
58 Letter Dmowski to Drummond, 23 May 1918, in: *KNP Papers*, mikrofilm 20755 teczka 29.
59 Ibid. and Dmowski, *Polityka Polska*, pp. 281–2.
60 *Namier MSS – Brooke*.
61 Drummond minute, 17 May 1918, in: FO371/4363-137.
62 Dmowski, *Polityka Polska*, pp. 281–2.
63 Dmowski obituary by Namier, 3 January 1939, *The Manchester Guardian*.

HISTORY AND MYTH: PIŃSK, APRIL 1919
Józef Lewandowski

Dedicated to Henry Rollet

Scientists know that the laws which govern the macrocosm are encoded in a single drop of water. Humanists are reluctant to employ such all-embracing concepts, but even their disciplines deal with a range of matters, great and small, important and prosaic. Every great event leaves an imprint on the fate of ordinary people and, vice versa, great 'historical' events are the result of actions of people who are usually unaware that they are shaping history. For this reason, researchers often take particular interest in what seems to be a banal phenomenon and by studying it hope to penetrate the actual structure in which the phenomenon was able to come into being and take form. I write this in order to assure the reader that the subject of this article is in actual fact closely bound to the most essential problems involved in the establishment of Polish independence after the First World War, and also to the difficult and sensitive issues of Polish historiography as a whole.

I will begin by referring to some correspondence of 1971 between myself and Professor Marian Kukiel. My original letter to him was prompted by a book he had recently published on General Sikorski.[1] I had never written about the book's hero but in working on contemporary history I had referred to other work by Kukiel. I had never had any personal contact with the author, but had felt grateful towards him for some time. I considered that making my own material available to him would be the best way of expressing my gratitude to a venerable scholar who was, for my generation, practically a living legend from the recent past. I had a particular detail in mind, concerning Sikorski's appointment in August 1919 as 'commander of the Polesie division on the Lithuanian-Byelorussian front' which, Kukiel suggested, was due to the particular significance of the Polesie region in the war then in progress. This statement seemed to me to be unjustified.

Of course, Polesie was of considerable strategic significance, as it became clear during spring 1920, when its marshy terrain forced the division into two groups of both the Soviet and Polish armies. Sikorski was certainly aware of the area's importance. A friend of his, Stanisław M. Kossakowski, the High Command's deputy civilian Commissar of the Eastern territories, noted the following conversation with Sikorski on 25 October 1919, 'I then looked at the first plan of strategic, antisoviet manoeuvres [indicated on the map by Sikorski]. The Bolsheviks had taken Kiev, that unhappy city – passed from hand to hand, but their 12th army is almost completely cut off, with no route by which to retreat. It would be enough for Col. S. to take control of the road from Mozyrz and the 12th Bolshevik army would be cut off. Denikin is pushing forward, his divisions are already at Briansk (the Malcowskie factories), Orel and Tuła.'[2]

Disregarding for the moment the debatable question of whether a single division could have succeeded in carrying out such a plan, the fact remains that on taking command in Polesie, Sikorski received no strategic or even general battle orders. This was a critical moment in the Russian civil war. At this point the 'Whites', led by General Denikin, had achieved one of their greatest successes which prompted the flowering of an intransigent nationalism and the refusal to recognize the independence and borders of the young states which had formed on the Empire's ruins. Poland and the other emergent states were theoretically allies in the battle against communism, but the unity of the empire was a greater priority for the leaders of the Russian counter-revolution than the defeat of the enemy. Poland observed the successes of the 'Whites' anxiously; their eventual victory would not bode well for her.

Sikorski's orders on taking command of the division hardly reflected the importance of the moment. He was instructed to maintain the peace, to straighten the line of demarcation and not to get involved in the war in Russia. He had only small active experience of battle, or indeed of leading a large unit. He was an engineer by profession, his military knowledge had been acquired at an Austrian Officer Reserve Army School and his position throughout the war had been primarily political, if not actually behind the lines – he had been head of the *NKN* (Main National Committee) army department. He did play an active role during the war with the West-Ukrainian Peoples' Republic, but his contribution was not widely praised. His predecessor in Polesie, General Antoni Listowski, was a professional officer who had served in the Tsarist army. He had had wide experience on the front and possessed the temperament of an ardent fighter, particularly valuable when directing the kind of manoeuvres necessary in a war conducted on the country's borders. If it was a question of the operational problem of the 9th Division, then replacing Listowski with Sikorski was a very rash move.

This was not, however, the case. Sikorski's appointment was a carefully considered, even a necessary step. The new leader had qualities his predecessor had lacked. Sikorski was an experienced organiser, a cultured man, free of the barrack-room psychology which prevailed to a greater or lesser degree in an army which had been through five years of war. He was – as Kukiel put it in his letter – a European. He was also one of the few superior officers on whom the Commander-in-Chief, Józef Piłsudski, could rely completely.

Many readers will be surprised by my last sentence. Collective awareness continues to retain the stereotyped image of an army unquestioningly devoted to Piłsudski and dominated by the legionaries, particularly those from the 1st Brigade. This stereotype has its roots in reality, but does not apply in the first years of independence. It is true the army had certain centrally-positioned interest groups at the time of regaining independence in the form of the *PSZ* and *POW* (Polish Military Organization) which were linked with Piłsudski. However, all available forces had been taken advantage of in the hectic organization necessary during a very dangerous and precarious time. As a result, the officers of the partitioning powers dominated the scene. Since Poles had not attained high rank within the German army (an exception being Colonel, later General, Raszewski), and only rarely in the Austrian, but had made careers on a large scale in the Russian army, it was officers of this last who were available and more willing to serve the Republic, especially as the Bolshevik revolution had robbed them of their positions and often of all their possessions. Although they had often been in the service of the Tsar out of practical necessity, it was, nevertheless, a service voluntarily undertaken and impeccably carried out, as the orders and ranks they received testify. Renegades were not accepted for service in Poland, and there was no lack of these, beginning with the fictional Major Plut and ending with real characters such as Warsaw's Governor-General Hutko Romeyko or Captain Siekierzyński. Those who had attained the peak of their careers in Russia, such as the Klebowskis – Napoleon Cezariewicz and Cezary Napoleonowicz – did not return. Not all those who returned were as culturally russified as General Dowbór-Muśnicki, whose period of service provoked Wańkowicz into writing a vehement pamphlet. Some officers had managed to balance their Tsarist service with their Polishness and a few had actively assisted the Polish liberation movement.

The sort of life led by the majority of officers from Russia was at odds with the ethos of the young state as expressed by Piłsudski. It also clashed with the convictions of the Legion's officers, young men with great ambitions, fewer stars on their shoulders and often accused of being revolutionary. Officers of the Russian army, with the exception of a few individuals, supported Piłsudski's opposition – the *Endecja*.[3] If we add the Officer *corps* of General Haller's army, which also supported the National

Democrats, to their number, then it turns out that Piłsudski 'could not rely on many of the commanding officers. Dowbór-Muśnicki, (Gen.) Haller and Michaelis are openly unsympathetic; Col. Haller is uncertain, Gen. Listowski had been won over by the opposition and Szeptycki, whom they are also diligently pursuing (. . .) has already betrayed his anti-belvederean hand. We are left with Rydz-Śmigły, Zieliński, Sikorski – in short, too few to balance out the opposition.'[4]

Sikorski did not belong to the Piłsudski camp in 1919 – by which time it was already a closed clan – but the situation in general did not allow Piłsudski to spurn allies from outside his own ranks. This division of strength in the army, which reflected 'civilian' political divisions, had repercussions on Piłsudski's political strategy; isolation forced him to compromise but also created an atmosphere of distrust, of division into 'us' and 'them'. It obliged him also to overlook sometimes grave shortcomings and faults if committed by 'one of us'.[5]

To go back to my original point – if Piłsudski could not count on many of the superior officers, if Sikorski was one of the few exceptions on whom he could rely, and if the division Sikorski took over had received no strategic directives, then we are faced with the question why Piłsudski should have buried a valuable colleague and authoritative figure in the Polesie backwoods when he was probably more necessary in Warsaw? There is also a related question. Why did Sikorski, who was more politician than soldier and an activist of considerable influence, decide to leave the capital in order to lead a single unit in an area with a tiny Polish population and of no political significance?

I will in due course set out my own theory. I explained it to Kukiel in a concise form – I was writing to a person, who was not only an outstanding historian, but a well-known political activist. What is more, Kukiel was a General, an exceptional military organiser who was familiar with the facts not only from the usual historical sources, but, more important, from his own experience. In my letter, I tried to show Kukiel maximum respect, but I was conscious of taking a radical step – I knew I was touching on a taboo subject. I was ready for a vigorous contradiction. His reply took me by surprise. It was brief and to the point. Kukiel wrote 'I am completely convinced by your hypothesis.' What is more, he clarified my own arguments with further interesting points where he could not give documentary evidence. Kukiel suggested that the proposal to entrust the command of the 9th Division to Sikorski came from Szymon Ashkenazy who '. . . was well in at the Belvedere, and well in with Sikorski; who knows, perhaps he drew attention to him as a progressive European.'

Here my correspondence with Kukiel ended. I ought to have been content that the author of Sikorski's biography had conceded my argument. But I was not. On the contrary, I was led to reflect on the difference between the history made accessible to the public and that discussed within the confines of small, confidential circles. In other words, on the taboos passed over in silence in the name of higher aims.

It is time to explain why Sikorski took charge of the 9th Division. The reason lies on the 'organizational' level. During the first months of independence, in a state of continuing war, the army's authority extended beyond the barracks. It was particularly in evidence where the Polish population was in a minority and unable to organise an authentic, civilian administration quickly. Polesie was in a particularly poor situation. It was an area which had been administered by the Russians. The towns were basically Jewish, the manors and intelligentsia mainly Polish, and the peasants who described themselves as 'local' spoke either a Russian or Ukrainian dialect. The capital of Polesie, Pińsk, was also rather singular in character. It was impossible to describe the towns of Eastern Poland according to European or even native Polish standards, but even Pińsk was particularly backward. When Sikorski took command 'the whole town looked like a neglected greenhouse garden. Such even, narrow, straight little roads, small, identical houses of moulded wood (...), a flat and monotonous landscape, triangular marketplace with a kosher butcher's shop revealing arches within, a church steeple, the cupola of an Orthodox Church – and that was all. The whole town.'[6]

Surrounded by the still waters of the Pripet river, cut off from the world by almost impenetrable marshes, the town had long vegetated. Though something of a cultural desert, it nevertheless played a large part in Jewish life; and emigration meant that the Jews of Polesie had many contacts abroad.[7]

The Germans had occupied it during the last years of the war. After their defeat army detachments began to move in from both sides, the Soviets from the East, the Poles from the West. In January the Soviets took Pińsk, in March the 34th Polish infantry regiment took over. Their commander wrote in his memoirs that 'the operation was not particularly complicated' and that 'the Bolsheviks did not put up much of fight and managed to escape beyond the river, leaving the armed Jewish population to cover their retreat, shooting at us from their windows.' Soviet sources indicate that the capture of the town was easier still – the regiment stationed in Pińsk simply went over to the Polish side. The town was taken with no shooting, there was no retreat, the survivors simply fled, and there were no armed Jews.

A dramatic event occured a month after Pińsk had been taken, on 5 April 1919. News of it reached the world three days later when the envoy and President of the Jewish Circle, Itzhak Grünbaum entered the tribune of the Legislative *Sejm* in Warsaw. The most important fragment of his speech went as follows:

The Government tells us that Poland's policies with regard to the borderlands are intended to win the sympathy and confidence of all people without exception from the Eastern territories. Unfortunately, I am unable to confirm on behalf of the Jewish people that this is so. On the contrary, all the news we receive seems to confirm that absolutely everything possible is being done to convince the Jewish people that they will never find happiness as members of the Polish state. This very day we have submitted a question to the *Sejm* concerning the shooting of forty innocent Jews in Pińsk . . .[8]

Grünbaum's revelation came as no surprise as the following section of the protocol reveals:

... (Voices: Because they had machine guns) Yes, of course, machine guns and Bolsheviks, we've heard that one already. We have a list of those shot, they are all Zionists and not Bolsheviks, (Voices: you are always innocent) no arms were found on these people (Voices: Step down and don't demoralize).[9]

The minutes quoted above contain two contradictory statements; one is Grünbaum's, the other is that of those who interjected. Two days later at the *Sejm's* next sitting the Jewish deputies revealed a list drawn up by a member of the American Provisions Committee, B. Cukierman, which confirmed Grünbaum's statement. In this version, on the afternoon of Saturday, 5 April, the local Jews of Pińsk gathered in order to discuss the distribution of flour sent from America to make bread for Passover. The meeting took place in the 'House of the People', a Zionist club. The meeting house was surrounded by the army which went on to shoot those who had attended in the town's main square. According to Cukierman, there were between fifty and one hundred dead. Cukierman had visited Pińsk that same day, but had left a few hours before the incident. He wrote the letter in the nearby town of Brześć where news of the events reached him.

The Minister of Military Affairs, Gen. Leśniewski, also took part in the discussion that day. On the one hand he made it clear that he could not possibly provide 'the House with a quick and exhaustive answer [to Grünbaum's question] today', but he repeated the news he had received via official channels. It amounted to the following. The Government had done everything to help the people of Pińsk, but a section of the Jewish community reacted in a hostile fashion even to aid in the form of food and this upset the black market. The area had not been completely cleared of Bolsheviks and soldiers had been shot at from windows.

This organized response was aimed at provoking an armed uprising in Pińsk, as the Jewish inhabitants of the town admitted to the delegate of the American Sanitary Commission's E. Frączak (...) On the morning of Saturday, 5 April a secret meeting of the Bolshevik organization took place, despite notices put up on street corners 'forbidding all gatherings' and announcing a state of martial law (...). A small red ribbon under the lapel was the agreed sign for admission to the meeting (...). The commandant in Pińsk, Major Łuczyński, was warned by a soldier of the Polish army, a Jew, that the meeting would discuss in detail the subject of arms and the murder of the Pińsk garrison on the night of 5 April; he sent out a small detachment of soldiers (...) Around 80 people were arrested and taken to the town command's headquarters (...) Of the 80 participants of the Bolshevik meeting, 33 were shot on the spot.[10]

One can assume that Gen. Leśniewski himself had doubts with regard to this explanation. A mere handful of soldiers had managed to arrest eighty conspirators preparing to murder the whole garrison directly after the meeting planning that murder. So he added that he had sent a commission to Pińsk and initiated a legal investigation. The minister's explanation was not discussed since it was immediately followed by the decision to establish, as well, a special parliamentary commission which would investigate in Pińsk the causes and background of the execution.

Thirty deputies signed the motion calling for the setting up of this commission. Some represented Jewish parties, but the majority were well-known Polish figures: Barlicki, Czapiński, Żuławski, Daszyński, Moraczewska, Błażej Stolarski, Niedziałkowski, Pużak, *PPS* and 'Liberation' Peasants Party activists. These signatures were significant for many reasons. Both these parties had a long tradition of speaking out against chauvinism and discrimination against minorities; this was central to their programme. It is sufficient to mention that during the first elections to the *Sejm*, the *PPS* put Feliks Perl forward as one of their most important candidates, fully aware that this would provoke both the *Endecja* and the clergy and would lose them the support of some floating voters. (Perl was one of the signatories of the urgent motion.)

The socialists had also anxiously observed the disquieting phenomena which accompanied the formation of the army. On 4 April, the day before the Pińsk tragedy, the unquestioned leader of the Polish socialists, Ignacy Daszyński, warned the *Sejm* about the 'hooligan in uniform' and demanded an end to the army's excesses. His speech met with 'energetic protests' from Gen. Leśniewski.[11] The army's behaviour in the eastern borderlands provided particular cause for anxiety. *Robotnik* had already published a particularly strong article on the subject in March when the army had only just entered the area.[12] Another fact which had particular implications was that the *PPS* and 'Liberation' were members of the so-called 'Belvedere camp', and constituted an important part of Józef

Piłsudski's parliamentary support. Formally speaking, Daszyński's statement, like the *Robotnik* article, was aimed at the Commander-in-Chief, but in actual fact it emerged as an act of support for him and this was how it was perceived by the public.[13]

Despite the unusually mild form of the motion – it contained no words of condemnation – its presentation to the *Sejm* evoked the opposition of the Right, articulated by Korfanty and Witos. As a result, it was passed in two stages and without a unanimous vote. But if one takes into account that the parliamentary majority had previously decisively rejected the urgency of any motions presented by the Left or by Jewish deputies, then it is obvious that something had stirred its benches. Was it the desire to remove the affair from the daily agenda by establishing a commission, or an admission that what had happened in Pińsk overstepped acceptable boundaries? Or perhaps it was the fear of Western reaction? All these factors probably came into play.

Creating the commission was an act of compromise – it did not condemn what had happened, but somehow raised hopes that justice would be done. Although it was the least radical form of action that the Jews and the parliamentary Left could allow themselves to adopt, it was simultaneously the most radical step that the Right, including the *Piast* Peasant Party and the Christian Democrats could agree to. There have been suggestions – and Kukiel supports them – that Szymon Askenazy made great efforts behind the scenes to bring about this compromise. He endeavoured to convince the world that acts of violence like that which had taken place in Pińsk and which had been repeated in other towns (the worst cases being in Lwów [14] and Wilno) were, nevertheless, sporadic and insignficant compared to those which were being perpetrated elsewhere. He wanted to persuade Jews in Poland to pursue the path of co-existence. This was particularly difficult when the army was involved, as Warsaw's authority over individuals and activists in the provinces continued to be illusory and relied a great deal on individual army commanders' sense of duty.

There were particularly disturbing signs in the area where the 9th Division was stationed. A lieutenant, stationed there at the time, future premier, Marian Zyndram-Kościałkowski, reported a systematic decline in pro-Polish sympathies, brought about mainly by '... excesses perpetrated by the Polish army, the police, administration and private individuals, particularly the landowners.[15] Similar reports came in from other sources. 'There was a group of us like-minded people,' wrote Wiktor Tomir Drymmer years later, then a young second lieutenant and information officer at the Division's headquarters. 'Officer cadets Włodzimierz Czajkowski, Henryk Kintopf and Jan Urbaniec were its leaders.' This group of friends began to produce an illegal paper. They objected to the character of the 9th Division and as a result 'our writing was very aggressive, revolutionary. We sent the paper through our own channels and by post to various deputies in the Sejm and to the press, beginning with *Robotnik* (...). Our paper, like all illegal literature, was read and commented on.'[17]

There was certainly something to write about. In Polesie, which had been occupied with the support of the local population, an opposition movement quickly began to grow, soon acquiring the character of a peasants' partisan force. The army treated this movement as if it was part of the Bolsheviks; they knew no other way of dealing with it. Unlike the Jews, the local peasants had no contacts beyond the borders of Polesie, no representation abroad and no access to the media, so the documentary traces of these events are practically non-existent. But their political significance was great.

There were two conflicting visions of the state in Polish politics at this time, two visions of Poland's position squeezed between two empires, the Russian and the German. The key to Poland's future position and her security was to be found in concepts determining the Poles' attitude towards those nations which had once formed part of the Polish-Lithuanian Commonwealth. Let us describe the concepts involved here. The first, the federal idea, aimed at an understanding with the minorities and the construction of a common organism, uniting Poland, Lithuania and Byelorussia. Only a federation of this kind could guarantee Poland any security in the face of Russian aggression, white or red. A necessary condition in realising this concept was persuading the minorities to accept it. The second concept, that of incorporation, aimed at a territorially smaller state, but one still containing minorities and ruled in the Prussian fashion, or one similar to the Russians in Poland with the goal of forcibly assimilating the non-Polish element. The federal concept was supported by the whole Belvedere camp including Piłsudski, but the army, fast developing into a national army, had little sympathy for it. It spontaneously and consistently followed a policy upholding the incorporation concept. The hostility expressed by the majority of superior officers, which I referred to above with reference to Kossakowski, was largely, if not exclusively, hostility towards the Left, towards equality of rights for all the nations involved and towards the federalist idea. Federalism also demanded certain concessions in the area of landownership in favour of the Lithuanian and Byelorussian peasants. The army, however, had little understanding for peasant movements and sympathized more readily with the landowners' demands for the maintenance of their lands.

It was not long before the 9th Division became a political problem yet again. This time the issue was the People's Militia. This was a force formed during the German occupation of the Congress Kingdom as the fighting wing of the *PPS* and included many young people from the *POW* (Polish Military Organisation) in its ranks. After liberation it was adopted by the state and became one of several political formations of the time. Artur Leinwand in his account of this question,[18] carefully gathered together all manner of fragments and rumours testifying to communist influences in the People's Militia, but with no convincing results. At the time a similar position was taken by the right-wing press. In fact, communist influence was minimal. This does not alter the fact that in striving to create a uniform administration and to liquidate paramilitary party forces, the authorities could not avoid liquidating the People's Militia.

In April 1919, the Ministry of Internal Affairs, in agreement with the High Command of the Polish Army, decided to send a division of the Militia to serve on a permanent full-time basis in the Eastern territories. This division would report directly to its own superiors. It would serve as a garrison, so its role was largely that of a police force. The arrival of this new division also provided an opportunity to restrict the wilful actions of those who exercised authority over the population, cutting down on looting and illegal requisitioning. It also meant restricting the authority of the gendarmerie.

As part of the re-ordering of the military structure in Polesie, a battalion of the People's militia from Kielce was also to be stationed there. The Commander of the 9th Division saw this as a measure taken to restrict his authority, and determined to oppose it. When the first units of the battalion arrived in Pińsk early in May, they were surrounded by the army and disarmed at gun-point, arrested and robbed of their meagre possessions. They were also not spared a lesson in patriotism, delivered by a professional Russian officer. This was particularly resented since the units were composed of members of the *PPS* and the Piłsudski *POW*.

The incident became a political issue. The *PPS* took the side of the Militia, the *Endecja* and the parties allied with it opened a protective umbrella over Gen. Listowski. The Belvedere remained silent. The situation became even more acute a few days later when deputy Niedziałkowski revealed in the *Sejm* that Gen. Listowski had formed a 'Unit of Russian Officers', handing them a standard on 22 June.[19] This group was simultaneously part of the 9th Division and of the 'White' Russian forces, who did not recognise Polish independence. This was not only an act of insubordination on Listowski's part, but an encroachment into the sphere of international politics.

In Warsaw, judging both by ambiguous and unambiguous allusions, there was some anxiety that Listowski might at some point place his Russian loyalties above his more recent allegiances to Poland and that, in the event of a decisive break-through by Denikin's army, he might cross over and join it. These fears proved to be exaggerated, but seemed justified in the circumstances. In August the leader of the gendarmerie who had failed to respond to these events, Capt. Wehr, a former Russian cavalry Officer, was arrested and accused of committing a series of crimes deserving the death sentence.[20] According to Kossakowski, the arrest provoked a violent reaction. The staff at the Division's headquarters resigned, together with the entire gendarmerie serving in the Eastern territories. Gen. Listowski also handed in his resignation. It was accepted. The nomination of the new commander, Col. Sikorski, had probably been decided earlier.

Sikorski found the division in a state of disintegration. The newly-appointed commander's evaluation of the situation has been preserved in a conversation with Kossakowski:

> Col. Sikorski says that he also comes into conflict with the civil authorities, but these clashes are different in character to those experienced by other leaders. He accuses the civil authorities of taking on too few duties. He is at present improving the terrible relations which Gen. Listowski allowed to develop. The stories one hears are enough to make one's hair stand on end. If a lad was indeed shot because he supposedly smiled sarcastically during an inspection in the presence of Listowski, if Wehr shot people in their dozens[21] because they looked like Bolsheviks in their poor clothes, if a dozen fugitives who had come from beyond the front in answer to an appeal issued by Listowski and had then been murdered so that peasants placed copies of the appeal under their heads in protest, if these people were robbed, flogged with barbed wire, burnt with red hot irons to elicit false confessions, then how can one express any surprise at the present campaign the population conducts against individual army units...[22]

Sikorski turned thirty-six officers over to the courts. I searched unsuccessfully for the results of the trials and for the names of the accused, finding only Wehr's. Incidentally, thirty-six officers represented a considerable proportion of the division's officer corps. Kossakowski has the following to say about all this, although it is unclear to what extent the sentiment is his own or Sikorski's: 'In Gen. Listowski's time the most despicable scum in our resurgent army ran wild.'[23]

Apart from legal action, Sikorski noted that several officers, despite the crimes and offences they had committed, would, if removed from undesirable influences and placed in a disciplined atmosphere, serve well and not come into conflict with the law.[24] His final conclusion reads as follows: 'A punitive expedition will bear no fruit here; methods of approaching the people must be changed. The guilty must be punished and the poorly-dressed allowed to live – this should be our new course of action.'[25] Both Kossakowski and his superior, the Civilian Commisar for the Eastern Territories, Jerzy Osmołowski, shared this conclusion.

Major Łuczyński did not face trial, nor was he made responsible for these events – we do not know why he was dealt with so leniently. Perhaps his regimental-legionary record carried more weight in the annals of history than the lives of thirty-three anonymous Jews. In other words, membership of the group with whose help Marshal Piłsudski had built Poland 'out of mud and reeds' was decisive. Łuczyński himself hints – I do not know on what basis – that he was held in particular regard by Sikorski and for this reason he fell into disfavour with Piłsudski's supporters. I do not doubt that many of these supporters did not approve the act that assured Łuczyński a place in history. But their disfavour was rather muted. 'The crime,' states Osmołowski, 'was hushed up and excused on the grounds of the officer's nervous derangement ... he continued to work and his career advanced swiftly.'[26] Łuczyński, who displayed no particularly outstanding qualities, quickly became a General and the Commander of the Army Corps No 5 in Kraków. Listowski also came to no harm. The storm which had broken around him quickly subsided and he was appointed head of another tactical unit.[27] He did not leave active service until after the war had ended, at the beginning of 1921. We can thus draw the tentative conclusion, that on the threshold of independence, the sway of Themis, the goddess of righteousness, was not very wide, certainly not wide enough for a law-abiding country.

In any case, Sikorski quickly brought the division to order. When in October of that year confidential negotiations began between the Polish and Russian Red Cross and, under this pretext, political talks between the Polish Captain Boerner and the Soviet Marchlewski, there was nothing to prevent them from being held at the small, peripheral station of Mikaszewicze, which was within the 9th Division's territory and under its protection. There were no excesses committed during the talks, no partisan activities and no information leaks. In the army, the character of the individual leader has an enormous influence on his subordinates.

At this point we shall pass from the events of over sixty years ago to another question, that of how these events are reflected in historical literature. Many years ago, while researching Polish policies in the Eastern territories in 1919, I tried to find material on the parliamentary commission I have mentioned, but without success. The archives had been cleared out, and what was left was falling to pieces. I have recently learnt that there was some material among Grünbaum's papers which have been preserved in Israel. However, I did find various incidental papers worth noting in Warsaw. Among the Polish National Committee's papers in Paris there is a copy of Franciszek F. Fronczak's statement made on the day of the incident. A Pole born in the States, he was a lieutenant-colonel in the American army at the time and a medical counsel in the Polish commission of the American Red Cross. He had connections with the National Democrats and by virtue of this was a member of the Polish National Committee in Paris, established during the First World War by Roman

Dmowski. His role in the committee was a humble one and seems to have been nominal only.

Fronczak arrived in Pińsk on 5 April, that is the day of the incidents, in order to visit hospitals and to inspect sanitary standards. His statement is 8 pages long.[28] The introduction contains the most important facts: on the evening of Saturday, 5 April 1919, in the town of Pińsk in the Mińsk province, on the orders of Major Jerzy Łuczyński, the commander of the Pińsk district, thirty three Bolsheviks or communists were shot for conspiring to obtain arms and to murder the small garrison stationed at this last outpost on Poland's Eastern borders.

The authorities were alerted to the existence of the conspiracy by an anonymous soldier, a Jew, '... who was forced into joining this communist organization' and who informed 'the district commander of the imminent threat of a massacre and of the night on which it would take place.'

Steps were taken and the house where the 200 conspirators were meeting was surrounded. Two soldiers were wounded during the operation, one of whom died. Fronczak does not name them. About 150 people escaped, but the rest, escorted by ten soldiers, were marched to the centre of the town. The author does not ask himself how such a slight force was able to overpower so many conspirators without the use of arms and without opposition, or why in a crowd of conspirators 200-strong there was not a single Russian, Pole or Byelorussian to be found, even for the sake of appearance. Shortly afterwards, Fronczak heard shots and found that thirty-three of the arrested had been shot. He went out and found bodies lying in the town square. Some people were still dying.

One of the dying had apparently said: 'Officer, how stupid we have been, I am still alive – put a bullet through my head.' The request was granted; he was shot in Fronczak's presence. It is strange that on hearing such a declaration, Fronczak did not trouble to ascertain any personal details about the man. Łuczyński had been humanitarian in sparing the women and old people. (Were the old also supposed to be participating in the attack of the garrison?) A search of the meeting place confirmed 'a store of ammunition and arms', but Fronczak did not see these arms for himself, nor did he explain why they were not used.

Let us go on to the other testimonies. Jerzy Osmołowski was the Civil Commissar for the Eastern Territories. A landowner and native of Wilno, educated and, in Kukiel's phrase, a European, he had connections with democratic circles in the capital. His function was rather vague. He appears to have worked mainly by influencing superior officers and through his good relations with Piłsudski. He did not get on so well with the landowners, who very soon lost confidence in him. Osmołowski's appraisal is short and to the point. I have quoted it already above (p. 61).

Osmołowski's deputy was Count Stanisław Michał Kossakowski who has also been quoted here several times. The possessor of a large fortune in Lithuania, he was not a member of any particular political party, but enjoyed some authority in right wing and conservative circles. He worked amicably with Osmołowski without rivalry or animosity. He left a diary, an irreplaceable source of information on the Second Republic. Unfortunately the volume covering the first half of 1919 has not survived. We do not know, therefore, what Kossakowski knew in April 1919 and how he assessed the situation at the time. While feeling no great sympathy towards Jews and revealing some indulgence towards the perpetrators of the murder, he had far less understanding for Listowski who, in his opinion, was at the source of all that was bad within the Division's territory.

The attentive reader will perhaps have noticed that the Major, later General, Łuczyński also published his memoirs.[7] They were written towards the end of his life, when the memory and capacity for enquiry tend to falter. The author even managed to confuse his own date of birth! A student who did not complete his education, a legionary, he advanced quickly, though it is difficult to see why. The most interesting point is that the act which assured him his place in history, the shooting of thirty-three Jews in Pińsk, does not appear anywhere in his memoirs! Of course, one can interpret silence in a variety of ways. The most likely explanation is that the author wished to avoid a burdensome memory in his old age. A natural and understandable reaction; memoirs are written primarily, if not exclusively, to shape the memory of oneself that is left behind – there are no exceptions to this rule. Also Łuczyński did not contribute to the stormy exchange that broke out at the beginning of the seventies in London's emigré press on the theme of the Pińsk incidents to which I shall return later.

I have already referred to the memoirs of Wiktor Tomir Drymmer. Their author was a high-school student when the First World War broke out, an activist involved in various splinter groups and *PPS*, later a legionary. In 1919 he became a reconnaissance information officer at the headquarters of the 9th Division. He lived in poverty for a few years after the war, but later made a very successful career as the Director of the Personnel Office in the Ministry of Foreign Affairs and in the inner circles of government. Brusque and peremptory, he is often held responsible, to an unfair degree, for the policies of the thirties. In 1919, however, he was a member of the Left. The diaries, written over many years, are the curious product of a man holding a variety of contradictory views. On the one hand, he was critical of the state of affairs within the division and denounced it in Warsaw, providing Niedziałkowski with material for very radical pronouncements. Towards the end of his life he was to write bitterly: 'Such was Polish reality during the first months of independence;' but these phrases can be understood only by the initiated, those already familiar with the historical details. For example, one has to have background knowledge to realise that Łuczyński has been conspicuously omitted in the register of the Legion's comrades-in-arms within the division. Drymmer was known to be candid, excessively so. But he was silent on the subject of Pińsk. He gave way to the general taboo on this topic.[29]

That which appears natural in a diary does not necessarily sit comfortably in historical records. Let us examine, therefore, how the incidents which resulted in Władysław Sikorski's nomination as commander of the 9th Division are represented in historiography. Let us start with Kukiel. I am sure he wrote as his memory dictated and that it dictated nothing on the subject of the themes that I have taken up. It must be strongly emphasized that he agreed with me in his letter, although he wrote and published something quite different. I would prefer that this agreement be stated publicly and not just in a private letter, but then I myself, armed with Kukiel's letter, should have published my notes without delay . . .

What of other historians? Over the years I have grown used when coming across problems new to me to referring in the first instance to Władysław Pobóg-Malinowski. I did so now. I looked at the geographical index, the index of names, but I found nothing. No shots in the Pińsk town square, no corruption within the division, no note of any resonance in either internal or international relations. Nor of the consequences in relations with minorities. His silence creates a particular atmosphere, a certain view of the past in which there exist wicked minorities and a state victimized by them. It can be said in Pobóg's defence that he was no model of objectivity, that his great work is written largely as a polemic in defence of his own position and that as a result we have a selectivity of facts, a limited field of vision. He was not an anti-semite; he simply had a narrow conception of the interests of the nation and state, closing his eyes to matters he found distasteful.

How do these problems appear in the written history which bears, to a greater or lesser degree, the official stamp of the Polish People's Republic? Let us refer to an official work, *Historia Polski* (The History of Poland) in several volumes issued by the Historical Institute of the Polish Academy of Sciences. Volume 4 is given over to the Second Republic, though the term volume is inappropriate as in the first, so-called 'model' version, what is involved is six large format books made up of a few thousand pages. In the introductory version, written in 1966, the events in Pińsk were dealt with by Henryk Zieliński. His account was brief but sensibly written and based on my research conducted earlier.[30] This version was later amended several times. Between 1966 and 1969 there was a 'change of paradigm' and the version which followed omitted the Pińsk incidents. The 1984 version also fails to mention them and a whole series of questions are dealt with in a single sentence which states that 'there were several incidents at the time involving soldiers raiding Jewish shops and beating up Jews, or at least remaining neutral in the face of such behaviour'.³¹ *Quelle délicatesse des sentiments!*

An abundance of biographies of Władysław Sikorski have appeared over the last few years. The author of one of these, Roman Wapiński, is a qualified historian and the author of several monographical studies and textbooks. His *Władysław Sikorski* appeared in 1978. The sections dealing with the inter-war period are written with some knowledge of the subject and there is much here that enriches our knowledge. But in writing about the 9th Division the author hesitates and his pen begins to grind a little. He knows his subject, he knows what was going on, and anyone who knows how to read will see that he has consulted all the necessary documents, but the knowledge therein is for the initiated. All the information is reduced to a single sentence: 'Sikorski's first tasks involved dealing with looting, an activity regarded as normal by some Polish officers in Polesie and which they saw merely as claiming the spoils of war.'³² Perhaps it is not a simple question of prudery? Of course, individual motives may vary, but collective motives, which are what concern us here, have some common denominator. Professor Norman Davies, in the conclusion to his history of Poland, states that one of the important instruments which serves to keep Poland in a state of dependence is the manipulation of the past, not only by means of censorship, but by 'appealing to Polish vanity'. This, he argues, is the modern equivalent of St Petersburg's one-time policy of praising the 'Golden Freedom' of the *szlachta*. History is made sterile not only by omitting the war of 1920 or Katyń, but by details which aim at a past image of the Polish character which is convenient for Moscow.

It is uncertain which works the author of the next biography, Olgierd Terlecki, has consulted. He rightfully draws attention to the fact that when Sikorski took over the division it was more of a motley band than a tactical unit. He also writes that Sikorski began by disbanding the Byelorussian Officers' Legion '. . . which displayed a complete lack of discipline'. There is not a word about the sins of the non-Russian cadre – though the author must have known something about it.³³ He prudently omits any notes on his references, and for this reason we are unable to ascertain the extent of his knowledge or his lack of it. The third biographer, Walentyna Korpalska, deals with the facts quite bluntly. She had come across Kossakowski's diary and makes selective use of it. The event in Pińsk she refers to as the invention of an 'oppressed minority' (her words) or as 'the so-called Pińsk pogrom'.³⁴ I do not doubt that the authors were anxious to display Sikorski's merits. But in this case, by avoiding unpleasant details they have belittled his qualities. Sikorski's role had to be diminshed in the interests of the nation. The result – a double deception in the representation of Sikorski as well as of Polish affairs.

At this point it is necessary to consider a series of related questions. We know that thirty-three Jews were shot in Pińsk. If one admits that a crime was committed, is it a phenomenon so banal that every historian researching the events of this year could without qualms of conscience avoid it or gloss over it? Can one argue that incidents of this type are common to the history of wars and armies all over the world and not specifically Polish? Should one consider the victims of a certain young officer to be merely an insignificant addition to the millions of human beings who have been victims of world war, revolution, counter-revolution, nationalist movements, lawlessness, anarchy, cruelty and the devaluation of human life? One may also ask: is this not too great a fuss to make about a single incident? Whatever one might think, Poland was a law-abiding country and murders such as the one in Pińsk, if not unique, were certainly not a daily occurence. Why open old wounds? After all, History – with a capital letter – has always been rather casual in her treatment of the nation lying between the German and Russian states. Would it be such a great misfortune if this nation were in turn rather casual with history – that with a small letter. Perhaps one should stifle unpleasant truths about facts which cannot be undone? These are not rhetorical questions, I put them to myself because of the way the problem of the 9th Division has been treated in Polish historiography.

Some years ago, a journalist claimed in *Wiadomości* that '... in 1919 in Pińsk, at the army's rear, a communist uprising broke out and was crushed with all the ruthlessness common in wartime. The uprising was organised by local Jewish communists and they were severely repressed. Anti-Polish propaganda in the West created a pogrom out of the incident. But had these been Poles and not Jews would the army have asked them in for vodka instead of shooting them?'[35]

When reason sleeps, phantoms begin to wake. No longer simple red ribbons under hasidic lapels, but an uprising which had to be crushed. When there is a lack of honest information, rumour steps in to take its place and acquires an autonomous life, taking whatever form might be most convenient. Łobodowski's article provoked an almost farcical discussion in which intelligent people who before the war had been accused by the Nazi-influenced press of currying Jewish favour (accusations then levelled at Łobodowski also) now felt obliged to defend the actions of the Pińsk Commandant, though they were perfectly aware he had committed criminal acts. Only Łuczyński said nothing.

The questions have been asked. It is time to attempt answers. We must first deal with the argument that side by side with the massacres which took place at that time the Pińsk incident is a mere 'drop in the ocean'. Without even counting the Russian, Polish and Ukrainian victims, but looking at the murder of Jews alone, Łuczyński's victims can be seen as an insignificant proportion. According to data from the 'Universal Jewish Encyclopedia', 31,000 Jews died during the pogroms and as a result of the confusion of revolution; of these, 17,000 lie on the conscience of the

Ukrainians, 5,000 on that of the White Russians, and 1,000 were victims of the Red Brigades. This was a time, after all, of widespread violence and brutality, of broad and fundamental demoralization.

The Polish point of view should be rather different. It is irrelevant that we have also lost many throughout our history. Poland's policy concerning its national minorities was bad and does not deserve to be defended from either a moral or pragmatic point of view. The behaviour of the officers in Pińsk conflicted clearly with all the state's articulated policies. But it cannot be ignored or wished away. The Pińsk affair must be seen as a symptom of what was happening in the state and society at the time. These excesses had an obvious influence on the situation within the country as a whole. Federalism could only work if all the nationalities involved recognized their common interest in linking their future with that of the Poles. Spectacular acts of violence against the minorities made federalism impossible, with implications which were felt long after. Feelings of patriotism came late to Polesie but it was precisely here during the 2nd World War that Ukrainian partisans operated and were the most persistent and irreconcilable in their hatred of everything Polish. In remembering them, let us not forget Capt. Wehr. Perhaps this hatred contained an element of reckoning for the events of not so many years ago?

When I read works on the relations between the Polish state and its national minorities which limit their research to the years 1921–1939 and studiously omit the time preceding the Riga Treaty, then it is difficult not to conclude that one is dealing with something that verges on historical deformation. A similar phenomenon can be observed in Pobóg-Malinowski, who omits to mention Lwów and Pińsk, and who writes about Łuczyński and Listowski only in a military operational context, and who then concludes that the Jews were negatively disposed towards the establishment of the Polish state.[36]

There is also another issue to consider, the effect on Poland's international position. The nationalities question, Poland's potential weapon in the face of the Soviet threat, became her weak point; anyone who felt like it could use the issue against her. At the very threshold of independence foreign attitudes to Poland became more relevant. They had undergone some changes. After the partitions, until the January Uprising, Poland was the inspiration of all the nations and was universally felt to be an Eastern bastion of Western culture, which was a part of the West, standing, poised against Asia as embodied by Russia. There was some romantic and naïve exaggeration in all this but Poland had its own élite to represent her in Europe and which was certainly European in every sense. There followed several decades when Polish affairs lost their immediate significance and knowledge about the Polish lands became quite rare in Western Europe. In this situation the news of what had happened in Lwów, Pińsk, Wilno and elsewhere did incalculable harm to the Polish cause. So too did the failure to recognize the need to deal fairly and justly with the new state's national minorities, above all the Jews, with their important informational connections. The murder of Jankiel was in fact the murder of Pan Tadeusz and the consequences were seen at the Paris Peace Conference.

Many Polish publicists have claimed that various states, interest groups and secret societies acted in this period against Polish interests. Yet one can safely say that it was undoubtedly the Poles who did themselves the most harm, beginning with Łuczyński and ending with Dmowski. Poland paid for Pińsk, Lwów, Wilno and Capt. Wehr and the 'antics' of Haller's men with the mines and steelworks of Upper and Austrian Silesia, East Prussia and the Minorities treaties. Arguments were already being formulated in 1919 which were to be used against Poland whenever it was necessary to find a stick – for example, when the Allies agreed to betray her at the end of the Second World War.

The 'Pińsk affair' allows one to comment on more than just past history. Through the prism of the affair and its discussion in Polish historiography one learns much about the present state of historical awareness. Many works have been written on the regaining of independence and the construction of the new state after 1918. Almost all suffer the same deficiency – they do not reflect the real, tragic problems of that time. Difficulties? The result of internal ambitions. Poles? Only the exceptional ones. A strange situation arises. In 1914 the riflemen and legionaries fought in isolation, and the words of the song 'First Brigade' expressing this isolation were more than just literary affectation. When the first cadre entered Kielce, the doors of Polish houses were literally and metaphorically slammed in their faces. Confronted with a pastoral letter from the local Bishop, the Legions' spokesman, Leon Wasilewski, had to prove that the riflemen were not a venereally diseased band of individuals. Four years later everyone was full of patriotic fervour, noble, reasonable and generous, only the national minorities seemed to put a spoke in the wheel.

To omit the unpleasant and the uncomfortable is to concoct history. It is worth considering what the consequences of such actions are. To say we obtain a false picture is a truism, because this very picture is the aim of falsification. Does one achieve anything positive? Lecturing on the history of Poland abroad, I discern differences between the way Poles and foreigners approach the past. Foreigners are not subject to either social censorship or indoctrination. I will take the German scholar Frank Golczewski as an example. He recently published an extensive treatise formally on Polish-Jewish relations from 1881–1922.[37] Golczewski's analysis is not above criticism. There is little in his book about the extent of the problem of the national minorities within the Polish territories. One finds nothing about the disputes surrounding these problems with Polish society and there is no awareness that one's relationship with the Jews formed a very strict dividing line affecting all other opinions. The author is also wrong to label as anti-semitic assimilatory and emancipatory strains of thought. But that is only one side of the coin. Golczewski has also gathered a wealth of material and provides an extensive account of events in Pińsk, based on Grünbaum's papers taken to Palestine just before World War II.

Some Polish authors who maintain the taboo on unpleasant subjects believe that they are acting in the national interest. They want to construct a blameless historical past for their native land, free of any stain. It is doubtful whether they will achieve their aim. If, instead of dealing with unpleasant facts by placing them squarely in their historical context, we omit to mention them at all, then we will encourage in others an image of ourselves which will increasingly contrast with our own.

There is another danger. In conditions as in Poland where the free expression of political opinions and the exercise of democratic rights are limited, the discussion of the events of the past assumes greater importance.[38] In these circumstances, history becomes entwined with tradition, knowledge with myth. Historical study becomes burdened with a task which provides it with no nourishment in the long run. History is always in danger of abandoning the scientific ideal, it surrenders easily to distortion. Historians (and others who write about the past) become the high priests of the nation's memory and memory itself acquires the characteristics of a cult; it becomes something one believes in. One cannot yearn for something that the memory finds embarrassing. We preserve our sufferings at the hands of others in our memory, the partitions, invasions, expulsions. There is no masochism in this, as foreigners often seem to think. We reflect on our suffering because, like great cultural flowerings, national uprisings, displays of athletic prowess and the achievements of emigrés, it testifies to our inexhaustible capacity to survive. If analogies with the fate of the Jews and Jewish historiography occur at all in the study of Polish affairs, then it is here that they are particularly striking, which should offer us no sense of relief.

There is, therefore, a place for painful episodes in this sort of history, but not for unpleasant ones. Yet history understood in this manner soon becomes sterile. The educative role of the historical discipline cannot survive without the discussion of unpleasant facts. This was demonstrated recently by Jan Józef Lipski in his work 'Two fatherlands – two patriotisms', which provoked a violent response in Polish circles, in love with their own past.[39] The philologist Professor Mestan has claimed that we do not know and probably never will know the first, early slavonic word for 'bear'. This beast was so feared that although his name was known, it was preferred not to 'call him out of the forest' and a paraphrase was used – 'he who eats honey', hence the word *medved* and its derivatives. The process by which history is converted into myth cannot by fully understood without recourse to theories of myth which applied, it seems, not only to primitive man.

Myth can exist just as effectively in a negative form, as silence or taboo. The bear was taboo, Pińsk and a few other places are taboo. A characteristic of myth-taboo thinking is the transfer of a particular phenomenon to the level of the general. A concrete, dangerous forest creature becomes a generalization. A murder, execution or pogrom in Pińsk was the act of a concrete individual, whether a frightened, drunken man or a confused officer. The events which followed later, the parliamentary discussion, the defence of the accused, the shielding of the division, transferred the act to the level of the general. This transformation of an event into a timeless taboo or superstition cannot be justified. If history belongs to the nation, then so does the historical taboo. The act of an individual rooted in time becomes timeless and common property. The rational step is to settle the account. For why should the son's teeth be set on edge because the father ate sour grapes?

NOTES

1 M. Kukiel, *General Władysław Sikorski*, (London, 1970), p. 280.
2 PAN Archive, 'Dyariusz S. M. Kossakowskiego', vol. 4/2, pp. 175, 255, henceforth appears as 'Diary'.
3 Cf. a brochure which in its time represented a programme for the Piłsudski camp: T. Hołówko, *Oficer polski*, (n.d. probably from 1922).
4 'Diary', op.cit., pp. 160–79.
5 The Civilian Commissar for the Eastern Territories, Jerzy Osmołowski informed Piłsudski, that one of the officers had attempted to claim and send out a few dozen wagons of war booty. Piłsudski's first reaction was a sharp one: 'Give me his name, I'll have the scoundrel shot!' but he changed his tone on finding out who it was. 'No, I cannot give you that officer! We need him ...' There followed the tragic statement which provides a key to many problems of the IInd Republic, 'I build Poland out of all the material available to me ... out of reeds and mud!' 'Pamiętniki Osmołowskiego' BN Rps. akc. 6797c, k. 80.
6 A. Stojowski, *Kanonierka*, (Warsaw, 1978), p. 37.
7 A. J. Narbut-Łuczyński, *U Kresu wędrowki. Wspomnienia*, (London, 1966), p. 269.
8 *Sprawozdania Stenograficzne Sejmu Ustawodawczego* (Parliamentary record of legislative *Sejm*, henceforth referred to as SSSU) 8 April 1919, p. XXXVIII/34. For some of the documentation on Pińsk, see J. Tomaszewski, 'Pińsk, 5 April 1919', *POLIN*, vol. 1.
9 SSSU, 8 April 1919.
10 Ibid. Sitting of 10 April 1919, p. XXIX/62.
11 Ibid. 4 April 1919, also 5 April 1919.
12 *Robotnik* no. 144, 12 March 1919, Mieczysław Łodzia: 'On the behaviour of soldiers in the borderlands'. Probably the pseudonym of Mieczysław Niedziałkowski, who came from Wilno and who was actively concerned with the politics of the Eastern territories.
13 Fr. Walerian Meysztowicz, writing in rather elevated tones about his days as a youth in the army in the cavalry regiment led by the legendary Major Dombrowski states, after years of denigrating *Robotnik*: 'We, who fought against Moscow were not at all an ideal detachment of knights. Beside the blameless – and there were few

of them – there was the common vulgar herd, there were moral troughs', *Gawędy o czasach i ludziach*, 2nd ed. (London, 1983) p. 173 passim.
14 The following is the only piece with any integrity to appear for decades: J. Tomaszewski, 'Lwów, 22 November 1918'. *Przegląd Historyczny* (1984), no. 2.
15 Almost a year later Kossakowski writes: 'As always in the army, the superior officers and army dignitaries understand the situation but even they cannot control their own apparatus,' Diary, vol. 5/1, pp. 23–1, entry for 13 January 1920.
16 Report from Leon Wasilewski's papers, National Library Rps. akc 4758.
17 W. T. Drymmer, *Zeszyty Historyczne*, vol. 28 (1974), p. 187.
18 A. Leinwand, *Pogotowie Bojowe i Milicja Ludowa w Polsce 1917–1919*, (Warsaw, 1972).
19 Deputy M. Niedziałkowski's question to the *Sejm* and the urgent resolution to dissolve the Russian troops in Gen. Lisowski's division (SSSU, 19th April, 1919). The urgency of the motion was overruled by the majority of the *Sejm*.
20 Drymmer wrote years later: 'Completing the set was the Chief of the field gendarmerie, also an old Russian cavalry officer, Lt Wehr. He was famous for his hatred of Bolsheviks, for whom he had one word *razstreliat* (shoot them). It is a good thing he wasn't at the front and had no opportunity to satisfy his instincts' (Drymmer, op.cit., p. 181). Drymmer says nothing about Wehr's arrest, although he was its instigator, see above.

I tried over many years to find out what happened to Wehr. The military annuals list no officer of that name, which leads one to suppose that he had been expelled from the officer corps. I found no personal details in the military Central Archive but there could be a number of reasons for this. Some incidental information about him: he ran his own farm near Łęczyca and continued to do so after the occupation. After the Second World War he was a starosta in Kalisz on behalf of the *PPR* and later the director of a large institution there.
21 According to Kossakowski, it was proved that Wehr had shot twenty-five people without trial. 'Diary', vol. 4/2, pp. 156–75..
22 'Diary' as above, pp. 140, 221, entry for 9 October.
23 As above, pp. 149, 230.
24 Sikorski's subordinate at the time, Col. Grobicki, described years later how Sikorski, letting him in late one night was visibly shaken for some reason and kept a pistol under a blanket. (*Zeszyty Literackie* 1963, 3; 1961, 9). And Grobicki in Sikorski's words: 'Captain Grobicki, a former superior on Listowski's staff is now kept on a tight rein and is perfectly all right. One can't give him free rein as a tyrant sleeps within him.' There follows such an extreme description of Grobicki's boasting that I feel obliged to cut my quotation short. I refer the interested reader to the 'Diary' op. cit., pp. 140, 221.
25 As above.
26 Osmołowski, k 60.
27 Listowski was made commander of a division stationed in Volhynia. Problems continued to arise. On 19 December, Niedziałkowski once again reported before the *Sejm* that abuses of power and armed uprisings seemed to follow in Listowski's wake. They had embraced the districts of Brześć, Kobryń and Prużany and Wołyń. It is possible that the *PPS*, nicknaming Listowski 'the *Endecja's* most reliable general' were guilty of tossing a metaphorical cuckoo's egg into the nest here, but if so, the *Endecja* accepted it. (*Robotnik* 18.8.1919 j.Cz. *Jeszcze jedna kompromitacja endectwa* – the *Endecja* discredited yet again.)
28 For Fronczak's report, see Tomaszewski, *Pińsk 5 April 1919*.
29 Drymmer, p. 187, The memoirs are to be found in *Zeszyty Historyczne*, (1974), no. 28.

30 *Historia Polski*, vol. 4, (1918–1939), part 1, (vol.) 1 Ed. Leon Grosfeld and Henryk Zieliński, (Warsaw, 1966). Cf J. Lewandowski *Federalizm*, (Warsaw 1962).
31 *Historia Polski*, vol. 4 (1918–1939), part 1. Ed. Tadeusz Jędruszczak, (Warsaw, 1978), p. 97.
32 R. Wapiński, *Władyslaw Sikorski*, (Warsaw, 1978), p. 97.
33 O. Terlecki, *Generał Sikorski*, vol. 1, (Kraków, 1981). The author writes very confusedly of these problems in an earlier version (*Generał ostatniej legendy*, Chicago, 1941), where the initiator and inspirer of the Officer's legion was . . . Piłsudski!
34 W. Korpalska, *Władysław Eugeniusz Sikorski. Biografia polityczna* (Wrocław, 1981), p. 90.
35 *Wiadomości*, (1970), 1/11 Józef Łobodowski.
36 Cf. Tomaszewski's convergent opinion, opus. cit.
37 F. Golczewski, *Polnisch-Judische Beziehungen 1881–1922 Eine Studie zur Geschichte des Antisemitismus in Osteuropa*, (Wiesbaden, 1981), pp. 218–29, 360.
38 I wrote further on this in the following article 'Funkcje szczególne historycyzmu w krajach systemu sowieckiego', *Zeszyty Historyczne*, (1973).
39 *Kultura*, (1981), no. 10.

POLISH DIPLOMACY AND THE AMERICAN JEWISH COMMUNITY BETWEEN THE WARS

Daniel Stone

American withdrawal from active political participation in European affairs in the interwar period reduced the importance of her relations to Poland and other European countries to the second rank for Polish diplomacy. Since the United States took no direct role in the pressing matters of concern such as Poland's boundaries, Polish diplomats concentrated their efforts in London, Paris, and Berlin. Nevertheless, it was obvious that the United States had become the economic centre of the world and could be the political centre, if she chose, so that she could not be ignored.

Economic questions played an important role in Polish-American relations. During much of the 1920s and 1930s the Polish diplomats tried to borrow large sums from American bankers to develop and industrialize Poland. They also encouraged direct American investment, but insisted that the Polish government supervise it closely. Despite these efforts, Poland never achieved the degree of support that it required or that the Poles felt they deserved. Negotiation of a $35 million loan from Dillon, Read and Co. in 1925 and a currency stabilization loan of $50 million from a banking consortium in 1927 represented the principal achievements of the interwar regime in this area. In addition, Poles floated some municipal bond issues in America. Harriman and Co. dominated direct American investment in Poland through its zinc mines in Silesia, but Harriman bid unsuccessfully to electrify more than one quarter of Poland in exchange for concessions which the government finally judged excessive. In addition, major American oil holdings in the Galician fields placed the United States in third place among foreign countries investing in Poland, after France and Germany. Although significant for the Polish economy, American investment in Poland consisted of only a small portion of American holdings abroad and paled in comparison with American investment in Germany, Poland's chief political rival at the time.

Political questions also played a role in Polish-American relations. Polish diplomats aimed at maintaining the good will of the American government and the American public. Lacking specific political issues, Poland's diplomats established personal ties with American political, social and intellectual élites. Unfortunately, the war-time enthusiasm embodied in Ignacy Paderewski's American triumph faded and governmental circles came to see Poles as 'politically immature, charming but naughty children [who] lacked realism and conducted business in a chaotic and shoddy fashion', while the press portrayed Poland even more harshly.[1] By the late 1930s, the United States judged Poland as only marginally important and was largely indifferent to her fate. Nevertheless, considerable reservoirs of sympathy remained, so that Poland might still compete for support. YMCA circles were extremely friendly and some intellectuals sympathized, notably Alfred A. Knopf, who published Polish novels in translation, and Professors Arthur P. Coleman at Columbia and William Rose at Dartmouth (later University of London). Several American foundations sponsored scholarly exchanges.[2]

The Polish-American community bridged the gap between the United States and Poland only to a small extent. During the First World War and the Polish-Soviet War, American Poles contributed handsomely to the Polish cause with money and military volunteers. The community was insufficiently developed to have much effect on the general public and the American government, however, having barely started its ascent from the immigrant working class to the middle class and the American power élite. Polish-American influence on inter-governmental relations failed to grow between the wars due to the Americanization of the community, which became increasingly preoccupied with improving its position within the political, clerical, and other influential élites at home which had previously been closed to it. Polish-American groups sympathized with, but showed little active support for, the state of Poland.[3]

America's Jews stood out as a principal interpreter of Polish affairs, based, not surprisingly, on their peculiar vantage, point so that Polish diplomats sought to establish a relationship with the American Jewish community based on their mutual interests. The existence of the large Jewish minority in Poland is too well-known to require much description. At about three million it comprised some ten per cent of the population of Poland. Other than a small but significant business and intellectual élite, Polish Jewry consisted largely of poor petty tradesmen and artisans. Relations between ethnic Poles and Jews had been generally fairly good by European standards over the centuries, but anti-semitic nationalist ideology developed in the early twentieth century which strained them seriously. Delegations of Jews from the United States and leading Western European countries went to Paris at the end of the First World War to speak to the Conference on behalf of their eastern brethren. Shrill claims and counter-claims by ethnic Poles and Jews resounded through the international press about anti-Jewish riots by Poles, on the one hand, and anti-Polish, pro-Bolshevik acts by Jews on the other. The numerous and widely reported incidents of anti-Jewish acts by ethnic Poles, Ukrainians, and Russians in the course of the Polish-Soviet War of 1920 particularly damaged Poles in American eyes and 'adversely affected the American image of reborn Poland'.[4] Against this background, strong Jewish lobbying convinced the Allies to require newly created states, including Poland, to enact Minorities Treaties with guarantees on ethnic freedoms applicable to non-Jewish as well as Jewish groups. The whole subject still arouses considerable heat today, even at scholarly meetings, and urgently requires investigation to determine the dimensions and significance of the incidents.

Relations between Polish diplomats and the American Jewish community between the wars break down into several periods, linked to the general shape of politics in Poland. Between the founding of the Polish state and Piłsudski's coup in 1926, the Polish parliament and government were run by centrist and rightist parties which regarded the Jews in Poland with some hostility but took few direct steps against them. After 1926, Jews hoped to achieve equal status with ethnic Poles, since Piłsudski himself was thought to be friendly to the Jews and since he came to power with strong leftist support; Polish socialists and communists generally regarded Jews as equals. After Piłsudski's death in 1935, the 'colonels' who succeeded him took an anti-semitic tack, more to gain political support at home than out of conviction. However, domestic concerns did not translate directly into foreign policy. The embassy in Washington naturally conducted most of Poland's business with the United States although the consulate in New York took on particular importance because of that city's financial and intellectual significance. Poland also established consulates in cities with substantial Polish immigrant communities such as Chicago, Detroit, Pittsburgh and Buffalo. On the whole, Poland did not send its top diplomats to America. The first envoy, Prince Kazimierz Lubomirski, owed his appointment to a reputation for business competence but accomplished little. His successor Jan Ciechanowski did better, thanks to his success in establishing political and financial contacts. The level of Polish representation declined in the 1930s with Ambassadors Tytus Filipowicz and Stanisław Patek who, while technically competent, owed their careers to their personal friendship with Piłsudski. Count Jerzy Potocki, the last inter-war ambassador, was a socialite whose skills were somewhat deficient.[5] Secondary personnel were better qualified. Hipolit Gliwic, an early commercial attaché, became a substantial figure in Polish business and political circles. Mieczysław Marchlewski came from the commercial stream of the foreign service, and Sylwester Gruszka specialized in the affairs of the Polish-American community.[6]

After 1921, the young Polish state sought contact with American Jewish organizations, particularly with the American Jewish Committee, the best established and most influential of the numerous American Jewish groups. Leaders of the Committee, together with Rabbi Stephen Wise, had appeared in Paris as lobbyists for the Minorities Treaties and continued to watch the allegations of pogroms during the Polish-Soviet War. The Poles saw the American Jewish Committee as a counter-weight to the Zionists in both Poland and America who they believed viewed Poland as fundamentally hostile to Jews, following the lead of Itzhak Grünbaum, Zionist organizer of the Minorities Bloc in the Polish parliament.[7] The American Jewish Committee generally accepted US government assurances from Ambassador Hugh Gibson and Special Envoy Henry Morgenthau, Sr. that the attacks stemmed from war-time confusion rather than deeply rooted anti-semitic policies. The relative friendliness of the Committee towards Poland was underlined by its close ties with the American-Jewish Joint Distribution Committee, an officially recognized social agency in Poland which spent two to three million dollars on emergency relief in 1919–21, much of it assisting ethnic Poles.[8] The American Jewish Committee expressed pleasure at the replacement of the openly anti-semitic tsarist empire by a Polish state that professed a democratic attitude towards all its citizens. Louis Marshall, president of the American Jewish Committee, assured the Polish minister in Washington, Kazimierz Lubomirski, that Polish Jews would be faithful to their new homeland and predicted that if Poland would 'give the Jew half a chance . . . he will make their present industrial desert bloom as the rose', adding that American Jews would help.[9]

Polish diplomats hastened to cash in on Marshall's words. Hipolit Gliwic, the commercial attache, approached Herbert Lehman, investment banker and chair of the Joint Distribution Committee's Economic Reconstruction Committee, in the hope of securing a development loan, while Polish Jews approached Cyrus Adler, Marshall's successor as president of the American Jewish Committee.[10] There was some hope of success since the Reconstruction Committee held a mandate to build up the economic structure of East European Jewry (rather than provide short-term charity) through a network of co-operative loan societies capped by the purchase and refinancing of the moribund Polish-Russian Bank of Warsaw.[11] Throughout the interwar period, these societies (*kassas*) underwrote several million loans, averaging less than twenty dollars, with little or no interest, to help Jewish artisans buy tools and help shopkeepers stay in business.[12] The Polish government hoped to take advantage of this mood to pay off the war-time debts that the United States government insisted on collecting as well as to secure loans for domestic purposes. Earlier efforts to float a bond issue through Polish-American sources failed to collect much money and the loan floated by a non-establishment Jewish source, the People's Trading Corporation of Chicago, had aroused controversy.[13]

Established German-American Jews did not intend to underwrite the new Polish state in defiance of market principles in order to assist their Polish co-religionists. Adler explained that providing a loan was 'an economic impossibility at the present time', while Lehman responded that he 'personally would be glad to see any sound financing done for Poland or its industrials in this country [but] I doubt very much, however, whether at this time the matter is practical on account of conditions here and abroad.' Lehman argued that Polish national prosperity would benefit Polish Jews and attempted to correct 'any impression that the Jews of this country are unfriendly to the efforts made by the Polish government or its nationals to finance here or elsewhere'.[14] Fragmentary evidence suggests that Lehman took the matter up with other Wall Street firms and may have been responsible for the major loan underwritten in 1925 by Clarence Dillon, an ambitious risk-taker and the son of a Warsaw Jew, Samuel Lapowski, who had settled in Texas after the January Insurrection. Despite his origins, Dillon had converted to Episcopalianism and did not identify himself with the Jewish banking community at all.[15] Unfortunately, Dillon's experience shows Lehman's assessment to have been correct, since neither Dillon nor the Polish government was pleased with the results of the loan issue, which sold too little for Dillon to realize acceptable profits; hence, he exercised his option to withhold a second bond issue. There is no evidence, as contemporary commentators, and some modern historians have alleged that Dillon was acting for German interests to sabotage Polish economic development.[16]

Nevertheless, Prime Minister Aleksander Skrzyński attempted to approach American Jewish bankers directly during his well-publicized trip to America in 1925. Skrzyński prefaced his trip with overtures to the Polish parliament's Jewish circle, which was dominated by Galician Zionists. The government and the Jewish circle signed an agreement (*ugoda*) amidst a fanfare of publicity by which the Jews repudiated the policy of minority bloc activities in favour of co-operation with the government. In exchange, the Jews were promised greater authority for the *kehillot* (Jewish Councils), greater language rights for Jewish schools, easier credit for Jewish merchants, the establishment of a Jewish department in the ministry of education, easier citizenship for Jews resident in Poland since 1910, and limited Sunday shop hours for Jewish tradesmen. The agreement was favourably reported in the American press.[17] Skrzyński came to America that summer and gave numerous lectures across the country which were widely reported, although only on the inside pages of newspapers. An important part of his trip was a meeting with members of the American Jewish Congress which passed in a friendly manner although without concrete result. The provisions of the agreement failed to lead to more widespread agreements.[18]

The Piłsudski coup of May 1926 ushered in a new period of Polish history which affected the Jewish question as well. Exaggerated hopes for major improvements in the status of non-Polish minorities were quickly dispelled, but the new government of Prime Minister Kazimierz Bartel, dominated by Jozef Piłsudski, adopted a policy of 'small steps' to win Jewish support, without fundamentally changing the Polish nature of state and society. After about two years of discussion and consultation with Jews, the government finally recognized Jewish communal organizations in eastern Poland and, after three more years, abolished tsarist restrictions on Jewish settlement and occupational patterns which the Polish state had inherited.[19]

Polish diplomacy in the United States hoped to exploit the somewhat improved position of the Jews in Poland by making fresh overtures to American Jews for support. The new Polish consul in New York, Mieczysław Marchlewski, was a foreign ministry economics expert who had negotiated a Polish-German trade agreement. Not surprisingly, he approached the problem of Polish-American relations from a financial angle, planning 'special attention to the enlargement of the economic section of the Polish consular office in New York'.[20] On arrival in New York in 1929, Marchlewski made subtle approaches to American Jews by initiating a good-will policy.

Concretely, Marchlewski turned from the American Jewish Committee to the Federation of Polish Jews in America, an organization founded in 1908 to unite a large number of *landsmanshaft* groupings from different Polish regions. These organizations had sprung up because the East European Jews felt that German-Jewish organizations, such as the American Jewish Committee, reflected different interests from those of the poor and more extreme (either politically or religiously) recent immigrants from Eastern Europe. Nonetheless, the Federation performed mostly social functions until the 1920s when its President Benjamin Winter, the Polish-born real-estate developer who converted Fifth Avenue from a fashionable residential street into a fashionable shopping area, and Zelig Tygel, a Zionist journalist in Poland until his immigration to the United States after World War I, sought a more active role in representing Polish-American Jews; Winter appears to have taken little interest in the day-to-day activities of the organization, leaving that to Tygel.[21]

Studying the American scene, Marchlewski observed that 'Jews play an enormous role in the life of the States, incomparably greater than the strictly Polish emigration' and that a quarter or a third of the American Jews were conscious of their Polish origins, 'maintain lively relations with [Poland], and are tied to Polish culture'. Hence Marchlewski looked to American Jews of Polish origin to invest in Poland and to travel there as tourists. He cultivated the Federation of Polish Jews, attributing its past protests over anti-Jewish discrimination in Poland to the influence of outside elements, particularly the Zionist leader in Poland, Yitzhak Grünbaum.[22] The Polish consul in Buffalo considered the Federation's leadership 'more capable, cleverer, richer, and more influential than our Polish emigration – but politically and socially unrefined, even primitive'. He too urged that quarrels be overlooked in order to maintain contact.[23]

Marchlewski demonstrated statesmanlike vision, noting that ties with Winter and Hungarian-born Rabbi Stephen Wise, head of the American Jewish Congress, an association of Jewish organizations, were particularly worth cultivating, but that the relationship could not bear fruit without significant moves in Warsaw to assist Polish Jews. The Polish consul in Chicago, Antoni Zbyszewski, another ally, lent support to Marchlewski's efforts in a joint memorandum urging Polish Ambassador Tytus Filipowicz to get Warsaw to open talks with American Jews of Polish origin concerning the formation of producer and distributor co-operatives for Jewish artisans, the improvement of credit facilities for Jewish businesses, the increase of exports of Polish-Jewish manufactures to the United States, and the establishment of a Jewish-American bank with sufficient capital to finance Polish-Jewish ventures. He also understood that long-range improvements in Polish-Jewish relations in Poland and America depended on hiring Jews in appropriate numbers in low-level state posts in such organizations as the railroads and post-office as well as in filling a few top positions with Jews. In the short run, Marchlewski established Polish-Jewish 'Committees of Good Will' to work on American public opinion, which needed to be cultivated at this time in view of Germany's worldwide diplomatic offensive to revise the Versailles Treaty, through abolishing the 'Polish Corridor'. In addition, he hoped to show Polish-Americans that Jews were not anti-Polish, so they would seek Jewish support for Polish-American electoral candidates. In the medium term, he hoped to convert Jewish philanthropic aid into constructive economic assistance and woo American Jews from public demonstrations against Poland. Marchlewski also urged the creation of good-will committees in Poland which would lead both ethnic groups into friendlier paths.[24]

Marchlewski had grounds to hope for strong support in Warsaw. He was in touch with a leading Piłsudski-ite politician, Tadeusz Hołówko, who had gained appointment as president of the Jewish section of the Institute for Research on Nationality Affairs (*Instytut Badań Spraw Narodowościowych*), in hopes of changing the overall approach of Poland to the Jews. Thanks to his view of Jews as loyal Polish citizens who should maintain their identity in Poland much as Jews maintain their identity in the United States, Hołówko established and maintained friendly relations with Polish Zionists until his assassination by Ukrainian terrorists in 1931. Hołówko's ideas on the Jewish question were a small part of his ambitious federal view of nationalities within the Polish state.²⁵ Marchlewski also exchanged some correspondence with Stanisław Paprocki, head of the Institute.

Polish Ambassador Filipowicz had reservations about Marchlewski's approach to Polish-Jewish relations, but did not stop him. Filipowicz feared that the Federation of Polish Jews in America would consider Marchlewski's friendliness a sign of weakness and would demonstrate greater hostility towards Poland.²⁶ Similarly, Władysław Sokołowski, the Polish embassy's first secretary, expressed concern that Marchlewski's effort to build bridges to the Jewish 'masses' through the Federation would have negative effects through the machinations of Zelig Tygel, the executive secretary, whom he termed 'the worst type of Jewish half-intellectual' who launched endless protests to prove his activity. Sokołowski had some regard for several members of the Federation's executive, however, and advised maintaining a modest relationship in the hope that Warsaw's hand would be strengthened in dealing with Itzhak Grünbaum and the Zionists in Poland.²⁷

The Committee of Good Will was launched at a festive dinner at the Hotel Del Monico in New York, where Ambassador Filipowicz delivered the keynote speech. Dr. Joseph Tennenbaum, a prominent member of the Federation of Polish Jews and of the American Jewish Congress, became chairman, and Paul Supiński, a Polish-American, became vice-chairman of the committee, which consisted of seven Polish-Jewish Americans and six Polish-Americans plus Consul Marchlewski.²⁸ Marchlewski started another Good Will Committee in Boston and planned others, with the help of other Polish consuls, for Buffalo, Chicago, Detroit and Montreal.

The policy brought quick rewards. Joseph Tennenbaum reported on behalf of the Federation of Polish Jews to the 1930 annual meeting of the American Jewish Congress that the Good Will Committee, which he chaired, was functioning well, that a Polish-Jewish conference seemed imminent in Warsaw, and that 'progressive Poles, who are not lacking among the representatives of the present government' would participate. Jewish members of the Good Will Committee and other prominent Jews, including one congressman, breakfasted at the Polish embassy.²⁹ A few months later, Tygel told the Federation of Polish Jews that 'one of our greatest accomplishments in the past year was the establishment of very close and cordial relations with the Polish authorities based on the firm foundation of mutual trust, understanding, and sympathy'. Tygel praised Marchlewski particularly highly for initiating the relationship and claimed, with obvious exaggeration, that 'generally speaking, our office slowly, slowly, assumed the function of an embassy of the Polish Jews in this country with virtual recognition by and consent of the Polish authorities'. He claimed with similar exaggeration that the Federation had played an important role in the final abolition of the irksome Tsarist Restrictions.[30]

Jewish members of the Good Will Committees spoke out at public meetings to support Poland. For example, Tennenbaum addressed a major rally of 3,000 Polish-American delegates in December 1930 in support of Poland's ownership to the 'Corridor'. Needless to say his statement that Polish Jews and non-Jews alike stood behind Poland evoked great applause and the conference sent a resolution to President Hoover and Senator William Borah, chairman of the Foreign Affairs Committee and proponent of revision. In addition American Jews offered no support to Ukrainians in their vehement protests over the brutal 'pacifications' occurring in Galicia and were moderate in their complaints against the economic problems of Jews in Poland, although some Embassy officials resented any complaints deeply.[31]

This manifestation of good will between Poles and Jews did not last long. Good relations broke down against a backdrop of anti-Jewish student rioting in November 1931 which closed schools and universities in Warsaw, Wilno and smaller cities and which the National Democrats exploited in their dual campaign against Jews and the Piłsudski government. While Polish accounts of the 1931 riots, including statements by some Jewish deputies in Parliament, indicated that the police acted energetically to quell the disturbances, their duration and widespread character excited reasonable suspicions among American Jews that the Polish government tolerated or even encouraged anti-Jewish activities. The incident also embittered Polish Jews, whose hopes for assistance from the Polish government fell flat.[32]

Relations broke down between the Polish consulate in New York and the Federation of Polish Jews under the pressure of daily reports of anti-semitic rioting Poland. Joseph Tennenbaum angrily resigned from the Good Will Committee in protest over what he considered inadequate government protection of Polish Jews, while Benjamin Winter, President of the Federation, denounced Ambassador Filipowicz for his efforts to defend Warsaw.[33] Even Marchlewski commented in a letter to the head of the Institute for Studies of Nationality Issues, Stanisław Paprocki, that the 'local Jewish masses were justified [in] their essential concerns' even if the Jewish press had exaggerated the seriousness of the incidents. He predicted that it would require extensive work 'to win again the beginnings of the trust and sympathy towards the government of Marshal Piłsudski ... which the initiators of the disturbances have destroyed.' Marchlewski continued to urge gestures favourable to Jews such as the declaration of a Berek Joselewicz Day in Warsaw honouring the Jewish hero of the Kościuszko Uprising and the Napoleonic Wars, and he inspired Aleksander Hafftka, a prominent Jewish politician, to accuse Zelig Tygel of having, 'with one stroke, destroyed the hopes which I placed on the aims of

... the Good Will Committee' as well as having committed a 'moral wrong' against Marchlewski, who, Hafftka said, had genuinely devoted himself to Polish-Jewish reconciliation. Marchlewski himself appealed to Benjamin Winter, assuring him that 'he understood the attitude of my Jewish friends' even if he found it 'painful ... to realize that our good will movement had to break down at a moment when there was the greatest need for it.'[34]

Ambassador Filipowicz saw to it that the breakdown in relations was not repaired. He inspired the vice-chairman of the Good Will Committee, Paul Supinski, to protest against Tennenbaum's 'uncalled-for and injurious [attacks on] the good name of the Polish people and Poland'. Filipowicz determined to await an approach from the Federation of Polish Jews before restoring relations – a gesture that never occurred. He soon told Warsaw that the whole good-will policy to Warsaw was finished, adding that the Committee had once been useful since the Christians had been under Marchlewski's control and the Jews had behaved themselves until their 'megalomania', their desire to influence Polish internal policies, had been frustrated, after which they turned hostile. Nevertheless, Filipowicz urged maintaining some contact with American Jews since they were influential in the press and on Wall Street, but he intended to re-establish relations with influential Jews in general, rather than Jews of Polish origin. The American Jewish Committee seemed to him the most promising group because it was concerned with Hitler's attacks on German Jews and might be sympathetic to Poland.[35] Remnants of the good-will campaign lingered in the visit of Dr. Henryk Szoszkies to the United States late in 1932 when the Zionist journalist and social activist reassured Polish-American Jewish groups about the situation of Jews in Poland and urged the formation of new Polish-Jewish committees in America to improve relations.[36] The good-will policy also had a European echo in mid-1932 with the formation of a good-will committee in Paris sponsored by the artist Artur Szyk and the editor of *Le Juif Polonais*, S. Londynski.[37]

Thereafter, Polish diplomatic contacts with the Federation of Polish Jews in America were primarily 'defensive', aiming at keeping informed of Federation activities and at preventing anti-Polish statements whenever possible.[38] Sylwester Gruszka, who replaced Marchlewski as consul, took particular pleasure at reporting the Federation's declining income during the Depression, passing on to Warsaw reports that an excessive proportion of funds collected by the Federation for charitable work among Polish Jews remained in New York to finance administrative costs and that the American Jewish Congress was taking over the political leadership of Polish-American Jewry.[39] Claiming that Winter and Tygel were making a vain show of activity to save the Federation from collapse, Gruszka requested that the Polish Foreign Ministry prevent Polish citizens from sending testimonials that might help the Federation raise funds.[40] Consul Gruszka and Ambassador Potocki ceased even answering letters after the Federation officially turned over political leadership to the American Jewish Congress, reserving only fund-raising activities for itself.[41]

In 1932, Ambassador Filipowicz's plan of establishing friendly relations with the influential American Jewish Committee had little chance of success, since that organization, like the Federation of Polish Jews, was fundamentally concerned with the fate of Polish Jewry at a time when its condition was deteriorating. Although the socially conservative members of the Committee sympathized with the difficulties encountered by the Polish government, which it considered well-meaning, in trying to alter ethnic prejudices at home, it nonetheless required positive action before it would offer any support.

Faith in Marshal Piłsudski's government had eroded. Morris Waldman, Executive Secretary of the American Jewish Committee had already identified the fundamental problems in the economy of Polish Jews in 1927 but had hoped for some improvement. He told a fund-raising meeting that Polish Jews were economically poorer in independent Poland than they had been in Tsarist Russia even though their political condition had improved. He felt that Poland's efforts to modernize its economy were 'working a vast and subtle revolution in the life of the Jewish people [so that] the industrialization of Poland [was] likely to prove – for some years to come, at least – a further misfortune for the Jews'. Waldman held these ill effects to be unintentional and called on the Jews to adapt to modernization.[42] Waldman continued to express faith that Poland's Jews would prosper only when Poland as a whole overcame its 'comparatively primitive condition of agriculture and industry' with the help of 'large financial credits badly needed by the government and municipalities of Poland and its financial and industrial institutions', but became increasingly suspicious that the Polish government was 'trying to obtain Jewish friendship and good-will without making any real effort to ease the Jewish situation'.[43] As a result, the American Jewish Committee made no public statements that might arouse Polish hostility and strengthen the National Democrats, but felt it 'equally undesirable' to support the Polish government as the Federation of Polish Jews was doing in the late 1920s. President Cyrus Adler maintained a cordial private correspondence with Ambassador Filipowicz and Consul Marchlewski in which he expressed his concern for the condition of Polish Jews.[44]

In 1931, the American Jewish Committee still took a moderate stand on Polish issues. Moris Waldman declined to join the Good Will Committee until the government remedied economic discrimination against Jews in taxation, licensing, and bank credits as well as by easing Sunday closing laws and ending the political monopoly enjoyed by the Orthodox Party, *Agudat Yisrael*, in communal affairs. But he hoped to demonstrate by meetings with Foreign Minister August Zaleski and other high officials that 'our group is greatly concerned, that we are keeping ourselves closely informed of developments, and that we look to the government as the agency with whom we very largely rest the opportunity and the responsibility for improving the situation'.[45] The American Jewish Committee responded to the student riots of 1931 more calmly than did the Federation of Polish Jews. The Committee exchanged notes with Ambassador Filipowicz and Consul Marchlewski expressing concern but refused to join public demonstrations since the Piłsudski government enjoyed 'an excellent record ... in preventing the spread of anti-Jewish manifestations'. Waldman believed that the government 'feels keenly embarrassed by what has been transpiring [and would] make sincere efforts to restore order and punish the guilty'.[46]

The following year, however, the Committee's restraint gave way when the continued decline of Poland's Jewry brought it to the conclusion that the government's attitude had changed or, at least, that the government could no longer keep local authorities in line. Renewed violence in Lwów and Warsaw brought a rare public statement from the Committee in conjunction with the American Jewish Congress, the B'nai Brith and the Federation of Polish Jews, condemning the police for failing to intervene and challenging Ambassador Filipowicz's statements on the incident which, the four groups claimed, minimized the seriousness of the matter.[47]

With the joint statement of 1932, relations between Polish diplomats and American-Jewish organizations reached a dead end. Polish diplomacy had created a modicum of good will in the American Jewish community as well as the Polish Jewish community, with a modest effort, but could not maintain the gains without more extensive reforms than the government would, or could, offer to Polish Jews. By the mid-1930s, there was little to talk about on either side, although this did not interfere with the distribution of charitable assistance from the Joint Distribution Committee and other agencies. Polish assurances that the renunciation of the Minorities Treaty of 1919, which Jewish-American groups had worked so hard to achieve, and the signing of a non-Aggression Pact with Hitler, both in 1934, would not affect Polish treatment of the Jews, were accepted quietly.[48] The American Jewish Committee continued to judge that 'since the situation is most complicated and difficult, it can ... only be aggravated by the barrage of criticism and abuse of the government, especially on the part of Jews outside of Poland'.[49]

The death of Marshal Józef Piłsudski fundamentally altered the political constellation of Poland, putting Polish Jews under greater nationalist pressure. As the American Jewish Committee reported with considerable exaggeration and misconstruction, 'the same [factors] are now at work in Poland as have been operating in Germany'. Although the Committee did not conclude that those forces had yet triumphed, the

Committee saw organized labour weakened and the government weakened, both of which had protected Jews against the forces of Polish anti-semitism. An early sign of the new situation was the removal of Jewish office holders from government posts and the inability or unwillingness of the government to stop anti-Jewish rioting, which lasted for several weeks in 1935.[50] Lacking Piłsudski's authority and charisma, his successors drifted towards extreme nationalism to rally the electorate and keep their rivals, the National Democrats, out of office. The Polish premier, Felicjan Sławoj-Składkowski, hoped to capture anti-semitic support by endorsing non-violent economic warfare against Jews. The government sponsored the creation of a mass organization called the Camp of National Unity, headed by Colonel Adam Koc, to support it. The Camp also endorsed non-violent economic warfare and barred Jews from membership, even if they should be Polish-speaking war heroes. Despite all of this, National Democrats and other extreme anti-semites found the Camp's policies deficient because it still guaranteed constitutional rights to all Polish citizens, including Jews.[51]

The principal measure which the government took to demonstrate its commitment to nationalism, a campaign for large-scale Jewish emigration from Poland, had little practical effect on Jewish life although its implications were ominous. Foreign Minister Józef Beck surprised the Economic Council of the League of Nations in the Fall of 1936 with a request for international assistance in relocating Polish Jews to Palestine, Africa, and Latin America. His arguments were continued by Adam Rose, Vice-Minister of Industry and Trade, and the permanent delegate to the League, Tytus Komarnicki. In Warsaw, the Ministry of Foreign Affairs entrusted emigration policy to its Consular Department, which viewed this unusually prominent assignment as an opportunity to display its skills and pursued it energetically.[52] The Polish government persisted in its emigration policy until the outbreak of World War II despite insignificant results and a corresponding distortion of priorities.[53]

Polish diplomats vainly hoped to garner American Jewish support for the scheme. American Zionists, like their Polish counterparts, opposed it as an expression of governmental anti-semitism, although they naturally hoped that Polish efforts to re-open Palestine to Jewish settlement would be successful. Rabbi Stephen Wise, a prominent Democrat, spoke for most American Zionists when he denounced Beck's speech to President Franklin D. Roosevelt as a 'a catastrophic declaration that of the three and a half million Jews in Poland, three million were superfluous and must emigrate'. The President quickly responded with a sentence in his inaugural address promising that 'the American Democracy would never hold any faithful and law-abiding group within its borders to be superfluous'.[54] Wise followed this with a vehement attack on Polish governmental anti-semitism in a fourteen-page open letter to Secretary of State

Cordell Hull on behalf of the American Jewish Congress, in which he called on the United States to intervene diplomatically with Poland as the United States had intervened on behalf of the Jews with Romania and Russia before World War I.[55]

A few minor victories helped Polish diplomats maintain the illusion that their policy might eventually bring results. Hull refused to intervene in what he considered a Polish internal question.[56] Roosevelt's friendship with Rabbi Wise did not stop him from directing the State Department to make inquiries in Latin America leading to the acceptance of several thousand Jewish immigrants, an insignificant number.[57] By 1938, the Polish embassy claimed that a new generation of American Zionist leaders, who were assuming greater day-to-day responsibilities within Congress, were taking a more 'practical' (i.e. favourable) look at emigration and that the torrent of protest was ebbing.[58] In reality, only the Revisionist Zionists whole-heartedly supported Jewish emigration. The leader of this rapidly growing segment of Polish Zionism quickly called for the evacuation of 750,000 Polish Jews to Palestine over ten years. An American revisionist paper, *The Palestine Flame*, publicized these ideas with the help of subventions from the Polish consulate, but Jabotinsky's American following remained insignificant. Both Revisionists and other Polish Zionists took advantage of special military camps on the eve of their departure for Palestine.[59]

Paradoxically, the American Jewish Committee, which rejected the Zionist principle of a single Jewish homeland in Palestine, proved marginally more sympathetic to the Polish initiative than the Zionists. The Committee forcefully insisted that 'the responsibility for finding opportunities for its Jewish population within its borders is exclusively' Poland's, but the Committee was willing to assist the government in winning free emigration of Jews to Palestine and elsewhere.[60] Recognizing that the National Democrats were far more anti-semitic, the Committee wished to maintain reasonably good relations with the government. The Committee may have gone too far in convincing the Polish undersecretary, Władysław Sokołowski, that the American Jewish Committee understood the Polish position, since he concluded that the American Jewish Committee would contribute substantial financial support to aid emigration.[61]

The Committee proposed an alternative plan to emigration, offering assistance to Polish Jews 'for revitalizing industry, draining and cultivating the Pinsk marshes, regulating rivers, etc'.[62] An important part of the plan was to be handled by Joseph Rosen, the Joint Distribution Committee's agriculture expert, who had recently settled 60,000 Soviet Jews in the Crimea, and who received a visa to travel to Poland at this time.[63] Ambassador Potocki, who heard the plan from the Director of the Joint Distribution Committee, Felix Waldman, in London, had some reservations about a lack of detail, but took it to Warsaw only to have Chief

Consular Officer, Wiktor Drymmer, reject it out of hand because it would have benefited only Jews and because it did nothing for emigration.[64]

Discussions continued on Potocki's return to New York, based on the premise of a general investment in Polish industry (rather than in specifically Jewish areas) by Jewish-American bankers and industrialists. It is hard to imagine that the Jewish proposals could have involved large sums of money since Joint was straining every resource to assist victims of Nazism in Germany and casualities of the Depression throughout Eastern Europe. Furthermore, Poland scarcely offered a more attractive location for profit-seeking investment capital in the Depression-ridden 1930s than it had in the more prosperous 1920s when few American bankers of any religion chose to invest in Poland. Nonetheless, a group of Jewish bankers called on Ambassador Potocki to offer funds for 'general improvement in the economic situation, especially in Polish industry' with some concentration on the Central Industrial Region which had just been created by the government. In exchange, the Jewish delegation wanted a clear programme to improve the Jewish situation and to fight anti-semitism. Potocki rejected the approach as unacceptable interference in Polish internal affairs.[65]

Meetings between Joint and New York Consul Sylwester Gruszka brought no greater results. Gruszka attempted to win the confidence of Alexander Kahn, George Backer, and Joseph Hyman with attacks on the Federation of Polish Jews and with appeals to them to support the forces of Polish moderation within the government by favouring Polish initiatives. He called emigration the only solution to the Jewish problem, hypothesizing that even $500,000,000 would not solve all of Poland's economic problems and he recommended a triple policy of industrialization, rural reform, and emigration. Jewish representatives agreed to give some assistance but refused to consider emigration 'desirable and necessary' on the grounds that Jews were entitled to remain where they already lived or to restrain 'protests, demonstrations, and talk of boycotts'.[66] Nonetheless, the Joint Distribution Committee expenditure climbed sharply in Poland in the later 1930s from $123,700 in 1933 to $464,529 in 1936 and $1,245,300 in 1936, reflecting both the greater sense of urgency in dealing with Jewish poverty in Poland (the money represented an increase from 18.5 per cent of total expenditures in 1933 to 32.7 per cent in 1938) and the improving revenue situation. As in the 1920s Joint devoted more of its attention to construction or industrialization and less to philanthropy. The Reconstruction Foundation restructured the free loan societies which it had established in the early 1920s, and appropriated $200,000 in 1937 to underwrite the loans, requiring strict business practices which Polish Jewish directors resented. The loan societies increased their lending to Jewish businesses from almost 11,000,000 zl. in 1933 (a little over $2,000,000) to 20,000,000 zl. in 1938 ($4,000,000) mostly in petty sums as before. Joint's activities in Poland also included vocational training and philanthropy.[67]

To counteract the Polish government's continued insistence on emigrations American Jewish groups, particularly the American Jewish Committee, proposed more specific investment and trade alternatives on a small scale which the Polish government accepted without attaching great importance to them. Much effort went into planning a somewhat hazy mission by M. S. Szymczak, a Polish-American member of the Federal Reserve Bank of Chicago, to Poland. Important Jewish businessmen approached him to go to Warsaw to get an agreement in principle for measures to improve Polish exports to the United States and to establish an import-export bank in London. They envisaged a private deal between American Jews and Poland without any direct US government involvement, although Szymczak insisted that the US government give its quiet approval. The plan failed, however, because Ambassador Potocki required assurances that certain Jewish organizations 'were willing to make a financial contribution toward either the properly financed emigration of Jews from Poland or towards the development of certain projects within Poland for the benefit of the Polish people, including the Jews.' The assurances were not forthcoming.[68]

Efforts continued, with some help from the Polish consulate. Samuel Lamport, a Jewish industrialist associated with both the Joint Distribution Committee and the American Jewish Committee, founded an American-Jewish Institute for the Advancement of Polish Commerce and industry, to collect information about American markets for Polish-Jewish products; he may have established a Warsaw counterpart, too.[69] Consul Gruszka expressed a willingness to contribute several thousand dollars towards improving existing import-export facilities and Joint contacted Jewish-American stores to find buyers for glass and leather products, samples of which were shipped from Warsaw.[70] Dr. Edwin Goldwasser, treasurer of the Joint Distribution Committee, proposed to Gruszka, that Poland take advantage of Anschluss to invite Austrian-Jewish industrialists, designers, and stylists to settle in Poland and reestablish their profitable textile industry. Goldwasser suggested that Polish capital be raised from private and governmental sources, and that the government guarantee the necessary export licences. Joint's role would lie in assisting the import of the goods into the United States. Goldwasser concluded that 'there are real possibilities for developing in carefully selected fields and in accordance with a well-formulated plan, a program which should result in a considerable increase of the export to the United States and other countries'. Goldwasser thought that private American, English and French Jewish money could also be raised for the project.[71] Joint executive secretary Joseph Hyman had some reservations about the business side of the project, but was willing to budget $50,000 for handicrafts and $50,000 for industrialization; he pledged more if the problems of the Zbąszyn refugees were solved.[72] US government sources indicated a Jewish company for the Exportation of Handicraft Articles had been formed in Warsaw in 1938 and had already secured large orders for gloves and linen suits in New York with the help of Joint, which was reported to be advancing $1,000,000 in credits and sending two representatives to Poland to help arrange sales estimated at $6,000,000 the following year.[73] While the details do not find confirmation in Joint sources, the optimistic report reflected current trends.

The improving economic climate, along with the growing German threat, helped restore relations between American Jewry and Poland in the last year before the outbreak of World War II. Jacob Landau, head of the Jewish Telegraph Agency, detected a certain nervousness in Ambassador Jerzy Potocki after the Munich crisis and noted that he was 'more accessible and reasonable than a year or two ago with regard to Jewish negotiation'.[74] Under advice from its Polish-born expert, M. Moskowitz, whom the American Jewish Committee had lured away from the American Jewish Congress in 1937, the American Jewish Committee remained sceptical of real change until the December 1938 municipal elections showed that 'a large majority of the Polish people voted for a democratic régime making the consolidation of all forces in Poland on a purely nationalistic and therefore anti-semitic basis ... impossible.'[75]

American Jews took an unambiguously pro-Polish stance as war with Germany approached. The Federation of Polish Jews pledged full support for Poland 'joining hands across the seas with our fellow Jews in Poland who for a thousand years have given their undivided loyalty and devotion'.[76] Similarly, the annual conference of the Federation in June 1939 'took place in an atmosphere of complete friendliness to Poland' and the congress 'expressed readiness to offer moral and material support to Poland in her present struggle to maintain independence against the wave of Nazi imperialism'.[77] The day before the German invasion, the Federation of Polish Jews offered Poland its full support and received official thanks from Ambassador Potocki.[78] Rabbi Stephen Wise, head of the American Jewish Congress, wrote to Potocki while the fighting continued, to express 'how deep is our sympathy with your country and how devoutly we pray that despite temporary reverses and defeats, the Polish Republic may move forward to victory and the renewal of its territorial integrity and its political sovereignty'.[79] With its traditional avoidance of publicity, the American Jewish Committee said nothing at the time, but later revealed its sympathies with its praise for the 'gallant ... resistance offered by Poland against vastly superior forces' and bemoaned Poland's 'cruel fate of being deprived of its independence and being shared as booty'. The Committee took pride in 'the Jews of Poland [who] immediately rallied to the defence of the country' and to the 'bravery and heroism of Polish Jewish soldiers'.[80]

American support for Poland in her moment of crisis showed that Polish diplomacy had done its work sufficiently to maintain some reservoirs of sympathy, even if American support for Poland had waned from its initial enthusiasm during World War I. The support that America's Jews offered Poland in 1939 testified to a positive relationship that had survived the strains of the interwar period. Of course, invasion by Nazi Germany put Poland in the best possible light, comparatively.

The relations between Polish diplomacy and the American Jewish community were important primarily as part of the broader question of Polish-American relations, which were carried on within the framework of America's withdrawal from political and military involvement on the European continent. Within these limits, Polish diplomats tried, with some slight success, to cultivate public opinion, in general, and gain support from the political, economic and intellectual power élites, in particular. Jewish support was primarily useful in winning over these groups and Jewish antagonism was important insofar as it might influence more important sectors of American society.

Polish diplomacy achieved many of its aims in its relations with the American Jewish community, which, in contrast with the 'revisionism' of Ukrainian and German groups, continued to support the existence of a Polish state in its current borders. Polish diplomats maintained correct relations with the German-Jewish establishment, which ran the American Jewish Committee and the Joint Distribution Committee, thereby helping Poland remain respectable in the eyes of the broader American establishment. Correct relations also aided the flow of American-Jewish philanthropic assistance and Polish-American trade, but did little to promote major investment, which market considerations made unlikely. Nevertheless, Polish diplomats could neither win the friendship of the German-American Jews nor their support of Poland's international claims because the condition of the Jews in Poland generally deteriorated throughout the inter-war period. Polish relations with American Jews of Polish origin (and with American Jews of Eastern European origin, in general) were more tempestuous. The American Jewish Congress and the Federation of Polish Jews publicly demonstrated substantial hostility to the Polish government, based, initially, on their understanding of the disorders, or pogroms, of 1918–1920, although Consul Mieczysław Marchlewski cleverly demonstrated that Poland could win active Jewish support under certain circumstances. Lacking deep connections within the American power élite, East European Jews had to rely on noisy demonstration to make their points. They also lacked the financial strength to supply much philanthropic, let alone investment, capital to Poland.

As one might expect, the American Jewish community, as a non-governmental pressure group might expect, for its part encountered less success in its dealing with the Polish government. Since the Polish government set its priorities according to its domestic needs, the American Jews failed to help their co-religionists very much against increasingly vociferous anti-semitism or to gain concessions from the government. Nevertheless, the 'carrot' of American German-Jewish economic aid and the 'stick' of East European Jewish demonstrations served to remind the Polish government that it had to work to maintain its reputation in American eyes.

The Jewish Question, which American Jewish groups kept before the American public, played a role in the general scepticism with which Americans viewed Poland between the wars. Like the economic difficulties and political instabilities that plagued inter-war Poland, its failure to solve the Jewish question detracted from the image of Poland as a democratic country. Had the Polish government initiated programmes to treat the Jews better, it would undoubtedly have received more favourable notice in American eyes. Had the government succumbed wholeheartedly to the extreme anti-semitism of the nationalist movement, the publicity would have been far worse and the United States might have reacted with complete indifference to Germany's invasion of Poland. To point to Polish-Jewish relations as a capstone of Polish-American relations with the West would be to exaggerate their importance out of all proportion; to overlook their significance as an index of broader, and more important, questions in international relations would also be a mistake.

NOTES

1 Piotr S. Wandycz, *The United States and Poland*, (Cambridge, Mass., 1980), p. 177.
2 Ibid., p. 229–33.
3 Ibid., p. 230; see also William John Rose, *The Polish Memoirs of William John Rose*, (Toronto, 1976) and Paul Super, *Twenty-five Years with the Poles*, (n.p., n.d. [Trenton, New Jersey, 1947]).
4 Wandycz, p. 168; see Arthur L. Goodhart, *Poland and the Minority Races* (New York, 1971 reprint [1920]) and Martin Weil, *A Pretty Good Club: The Founding Fathers of the U.S. Foreign Service*, (New York, 1978), pp. 24–45; Zosa Szajkowski, 'Western Jewish aid and intercession for Polish Jewry, 1919–1939', in *Studies on Polish Jewry*, (New York, 1974), pp. 150–241. Szajkowski skips through the 1920s but covers the 1930s extensively, based on similar American archival sources to those used in this article, from a Jewish nationalist perspective.
5 Wandycz, p. 232; 'Stanisław Patek', *Polski Słownik Biograficzny* (hereafter *PSB*) vol. 25, pp. 321–4; 'Jerzy Potocki', *PSB*, vol. 28, pp. 47–8.
6 'Sylwester Gruszka', *PSB*, vol. 9, p. 63.
7 Ezra Mendelsohn, *The Jews of East Central Europe Between the World Wars*, (Bloomington, Indiana, 1983), pp. 53–4; Antony Polonsky, *Politics in Independent Poland 1921–1939*, (Oxford, 1972), p. 92.
8 Yehuda Bauer, *My Brother's Keeper*, (Philadelphia, 1974), pp. 9–10.
9 Archives of the American Jewish Committee (hereafter AJCm), New York City, 'Poland, 1917–1924', 'Correspondence of Louis Marshall, President of the

American Jewish Committee with Prince Kazimierz Lubomirski, Minister of Poland and Leon Berenson, Secretary of the Polish Legation, October 1924'.
10 AJCm, 'Poland, 1917–1924', Frostig to Adler, 13 August 1924; Archives of the Joint Distribution Committee (hereafter JDC), file 324, 'Poland. General, 1921–32', Lehman to Warburg, 27 October 1924; Lehman had discussed banking with Hipolit Gliwic, the Polish commercial attaché, in 1922 and perhaps at this time as well, 'Reconstruction', file 392, Lehman to Gliwic, 20 January 1922.
11 Bauer, pp. 17, 23; JDC, 'Poland. Reconstruction', file 392; see also Zosa Szajkowski, '"Reconstruction" vs. "Palliative Relief" in American Jewish Overseas Work 1919–1939', *Jewish Social Studies*, vol. 32 (1970), no. 1, pp. 14–41, 11–47.
12 Bauer, p. 199.
13 Teresa Malecka, *Kredyty i pożyczki Stanów Zjednoczonych Ameryki dla Rządu Polskiego w latach 1919–1939*, (Warsaw, 1982), pp. 68–70; Wandycz, p. 182.
14 AJCm, 'Poland, 1917–1924', Adler to Frostig, 24 October 1924; JDC, 'Poland. General', file 324, Lehman to Warburg, 27 October 1924.
15 American Jewish Archives, Cincinnati (hereafter AJA), 'Lapowski Family'. Lehman wrote to Warburg that, approached 12–18 months before about placing a Polish loan, 'I put the people in touch with a very reputable and strong banking house here with the idea of interesting them in the matter.' Warburg, 27 October 1924.
16 Malecka, pp. 87–91; Wandycz, p. 190; see also Neal H. Pease, 'Poland, the United States and the Stabilization of Europe, 1924–1937', unpublished PhD dissertation, Yale University, 1982, pp. 367–8.
17 Harry M. Rabinowicz, *The Legacy of Polish Jewry, 1919–1939*, (New York, 1965), pp. 43–5; Herman Bernstein, 'The Polish-Jewish pact to end anti-semitism', *Current History* (October, 1925), pp. 78–81; Ezra Mendelsohn, 'Reflections on the Ugoda' in *Studies in Jewish History Presented to Professor Raphael Mahler on his Seventy-Fifth Birthday*, (Merhavia, 1974), pp. 87–102.
18 Mendelsohn, *The Jews of East Central Europe*, p. 56; Mendelsohn, 'Reflections', pp. 87–102; *New York Times*, 23 July 1 (8:2); see also 4 July (6:2), 6 July (5:2), 12 July II, 16:1, 13 July (4:3), 19 July VII, 3:1.
19 Andrzej Chojnowski, *Koncepcje polityki narodowościowej rządów polskich w latach 1921–1939*, (Wrocław, 1979), pp. 69–73ff., 135–7.
20 National Archives [hereafter cited as NA] 702.60c. II/163.
21 *Who's Who in American Jewry*, vol. III (1938–9), p. 1144; Z. Tygel, *Let's Talk It Over*, (New York, 1939), pp. 13–15.
22 Archiwum Akt Nowych (Warsaw), Konsulat Generalny Nowego Yorku [hereafter cited as AAN.KGNY] 408, Marchlewski to Filipowicz, 21 January 1930.
23 AAN.KGNY 408, Zbyszewski to Marchlewski, n.d. [June 1930].
24 AAN.KGNY 408, Marchlewski to Filipowicz, 21 January 1930.
25 Iwo Werschler, *Tadeusz Hołówko*, (Warsaw, 1984), pp. 205–7; Chojnowski, pp. 80–4 ff. The Piłsudski-ite party, the BBWR, invited Grünbaum to run for parliament in 1928 on its list; he declined. Andrzej Garlicki, *Od Maja do Brześcia* (Warsaw, 1981), p. 200.
26 AAN.KGNY 408, Weissbaum to Marchlewski, 17 March 1930; Filipowicz to Marchlewski, 16 May 1930.
27 Archwum Akt Nowych (Warsaw), Ministerstwo Spraw Zagranicznych [hereafter cited as AAN.MSZ] 2277, Sokołowski to MSZ, 29 June 1931.
28 AJCm 'Poland/1929–30/MDW'.
29 AAN.KGNY 408, Łepkowski to MSZ, 20 October 1930.
30 AAN.KGNY 408, n.d. [May 1931].

31 AJCm, 'Poland/1931-2/MDW', Waldman to Adler 2 December 1931; AAN.KGNY 408, Marchlewski to Hołówko, 10 December 1930; n.d. [May 1931].
32 Chojnowski, pp. 171–3. *New York Times*, November 3 (25:3), 5 (18:2), 7 (19:3), 8 (13:2), 10 (12:3), 11 (10:3), 13 (10:2), 15 (32:4) and others.
33 *New York Times*, November 20 (26:4), December 12 (12:8).
34 AAN.KGNY 492, Marchlewski to Paprocki 8 December 1931; Marchlewski to Winter, 12 December 1931; AAN, Archiwum Rzeczypospolitej Polskiej w Waszyngtonie [hereafter cited as AAN.ARPwW] 2620, Hafftka to Tygel, 8 March 1932; Marchlewski to Adam Koc, 2 November 1932.
35 AAN.ARPwW 2620, Filipowicz to MSZ, 1 July 1931.
36 AAN.KGNY 410, Zbyszewski to MSZ, 8 August 1932; MSZ-MSW, 1 October 1932.
37 AAN.ARPwW 2620, clipping from *Nowy Świat* (New York) 7 June 1932.
38 AAN.ARPwW 2623, Gruszka to Sokołowski, 27 January 1936.
39 AAN.MSZ 2297, Gruszka to Embassy, 5 January 1937.
40 AAN.MSZ 2301, Gruszka to MSZ, 8 November 1937.
41 AAN.MSZ 2311, Potocki to MSZ, 11 June 1938; Gruszka to MSZ, 16 May 1938.
42 Morris D. Waldman, 'Conditions up-to-date in Poland', Constructive Relief Conference of the JDC and the United Jewish Campaign, Chicago, October 22–3, 1927.
43 AJCm, 'Poland, 1927–1930', Memorandum, n.d.
44 AJCm, 'Poland, 1927–1930', Memorandum; Adler to Filipowicz, 22 December 1930; Adler to Marchlewski, 22 December 1930.
45 AJCm, 'Poland, 1931'. Memorandum to Poland; see also *American Jewish Yearbook 5693* (Philadelphia, 1932), volume 34, p. 316.
46 AJCm, 'Poland, 1931–1932', Interview with Dr. Marchlewski, 20 November 1931; Waldman to I.M. Rubinow, 17 November 1931.
47 AJCm, 'Poland, 1932–1940', Joint Statement: memorandum 'Recent anti-Jewish outbreaks in Poland', *American Jewish Yearbook 5695*, (Philadelphia, 1934), volume 36, pp. 452–3; *New York Times* 7 December 1932 (8:3) and 8 December 1932 (5:2). Rioting closed schools in Lwow and Warsaw as well as touching Kraków and Poznań, *New York Times* 14 November (6:5), 28 November (7:8), 29 November (7:5), 30 November (5:3), 2 December (7:5), 3 December (7:5), 4 December (32:7), 6 December (9:4).
48 'Poland, General. 1933–35. May.', Memorandum of meeting with Polish Ambassador Stanislaw Patek, 8 February 1934.
49 *American Jewish Yearbook 5695*, (Philadelphia, 1934), volume 36, pp. 414–5.
50 *American Jewish Yearbook 5697*, (Philadelphia, 1936), volume 38, pp. 614–7.
51 Edward D. Wynot Jr., 'A necessary cruelty: the emergence of official anti-semitism in Poland, 1919–1939', *American Historical Review*, vol. 76 (Oxtober 1971), no. 4, pp. 1037–44.
52 Wiktor Tomir Drymmer, 'Zagadnienie żydowskie w Polsce w latach 1936–1939; Wspomnienie z pracy w Ministerstwie Spraw Zagranicznych', *Zeszyty Historyczne* (Paris), 1968, volume 13, pp. 65–6.
53 See, for example, PAUS 66–7, 21 June 1937; 66–4, notatka dla Pana Amb. Potockiego, 29 July 1938; PAUS 66–7, 17 January 1939.
54 Franklin D. Roosevelt Library at Hyde Park, New York [hereafter cited as FDRL] PPF 3292, Wise to FDR, 15 January 1937; FDR to Wise, 23 January 1937.
55 *The Situation of Polish Jewry: Text of a Memorandum Submitted to the Secretary of State of the United States on July 12, 1937 by the American Jewish Congress*, (New York, 1937).
56 NA 860c.016/489, Wise to Hull, Hull to Wise, 12 July 1937; *Foreign Relations of the United States Foreign for 1937* vol. 3, (New York, 1937), p. 553.

57 NA 860c.56/236, conversation of Secretary of State Hull with Ambassador Potocki, 26 November 1937; Drymmer, 'Zagadnienie żydowskie', p. 66.
58 AAN.MSZ 2311, Potocki to MSZ, 8 February 1938; Potocki to MSZ 1 April 1938, Bruszka to MSZ, 13 June 1938.
59 Drymmer, 'Zagadnienie żydowskie', pp. 70–3; Mendelsohn, *The Jews of East Central Europe*, p. 80; AAN.MSZ 2301, Potocki to MSZ, 22 November 1937; MSZ 2311, Gruszka to MSZ, 20 December 1937, Wańkowicz to MSZ, 23 December 1937.
60 *American Jewish Yearbook 5697*, (Philadelphia, 1936), volume 38, p. 597; AJA, AJCm/b/Box 353, 5 November 1936.
61 Hoover Institution on Peace, War, and Revolution (Palo Alto, Ca.) Poland. Ambasada (US) [hereafter cited as PAUS] 66–4, 24 September 1936.
62 PAUS, 63–9, conversation of Waldman and Wańkowicz, 17 September 1937.
63 PAUS, 63–9, Szygowski to MSZ, 16 September 1939, Bauer, p. 103.
64 PAUS, 66–4, Notatka z konferencji z p. Amb. Potockim odbytej u pana D.D.K., dnia 18 maja 1937.
65 PAUS 66–4, 21 June 1937.
66 JDC. 'Poland.General', File 44–3, 17 November 1937.
67 NA 860c.4016/526, Memorandum of conversation between Ambassador Potocki and Undersecretary of State Sumner Welles; FDRL, Morgenthau Diaries, 20 December 1937, Book 103, pp. 129–33.
68 Bauer, pp. 194–209.
69 AAN.MSZ 2299, Gruszka to MSZ, report, 15 July 1937.
70 JDC, 'Poland.General.1938', File 44–3/44–21, Memorandum from Hyman to B. Kahn, 14 June 1938.
71 JDC, 'Poland.General.1938', File 44–3/44–21, Memorandum by Dr. Goldwasser for Consul Gruszka, 13 July 1938.
72 JDC. 'Poland.General.1938', File 44–3/44–21, Telephone Message from Mr. Goldwasser to Mr. Hyman, 23 December 1938.
73 NA 860c.4016/587, Biddle to Hull, 28 February 1939.
74 AJCm. 'Poland/1938–1939/MDW' Memorandum from Jacob Landau, 14 October 1938.
75 AJCm. 'Poland/1938–1939/MDW', A. Smolar to Waldman, 22 December 1938; personnel file, M. Moskowitz.
76 PAUS 66–7, 13 April 1939.
77 PAUS 66–7, Gruszka to Potocki, 23 June 1939.
78 *New York Times*, 30 August 1939 (3:4) and 31 August 1939 (3:3).
79 AJA. Wise Papers, Box 83, Wise to Potocki, 12 September 1939.
80 *American Jewish Yearbook 5701*, (Philadelphia, 1941) volume 42, p. 643.

DMOWSKI, PADEREWSKI AND AMERICAN JEWS
(A Documentary Compilation)
George J. Lerski

Jewish-Polish relations in the United States deteriorated substantially during and after the First World War, and as the author of an article on 'Jewish-Polish Amity in Lincoln's America'[1] I was determined to find the roots of this animosity which has not yet abated. Thanks to the kindness of Professor Piotr Wandycz of Yale University I was able to acquire revealing documents in this crucial matter in the form of Louis Marshall's bitter correspondence in 1918 with President Wilson and Ignacy Paderewski. At that time, Marshall was serving as the first President of the newly created but already powerful American Jewish Committee.[2] In both Dr. Wandycz's *The United States and Poland* and the late Professor Sukiennicki's *East-Central Europe During World War One* I came across descriptions of the Dmowski-Marshall encounter and Paderewski's uneasy reaction to his compatriot's foolishly provocative behaviour in New York.[3] This in turn drew my attention to Paderewski's correspondence published in 1973 in Poland and to Dmowski's own account of his second visit to the United States.[4] From all this, a clear picture emerges of the disastrous confrontation of these two strong-willed men, an encounter which had fateful consequences for the relations between Poles and Jews in the United States.

While his main antagonist Józef Piłsudski was interned by the Germans in the Magdeburg fortress, Roman Dmowski – the foremost Polish nationalist politician – was instrumental in organizing, first in Lausanne and then in Paris, the Polish National Committee, which was politically dominated by his National-Democratic colleagues ('Endeks') and other personalities involved before the war in the National League (*Liga Narodowa*). Their representative in America was the virtuoso pianist and composer Ignacy Jan Paderewski, who had established excellent relations during his long sojourn in the United States not only with his admiring Polish compatriots but also with influential Jews.[5] It was a wise choice on the part of Dmowski because the great performer, endowed with unusual charisma, was able to befriend such important public figures as Herbert Hoover [6] and Colonel Edward M. House, establishing through the latter close contacts with President Wilson himself.

Informed about Dmowski's pending visit to the United States, Paderewski asked the President in a letter full of compliments to grant him an opportunity to introduce the Polish leader. Referring to Wilson's famous Thirteenth Point concerning Poland's Independence, he wrote, early in September 1918:

> For a long time I have not been guilty of any attempt to rob you of your time, so precious to humanity. On this occasion however I could not deny myself the supreme honour and happiness of seeing you in order to introduce the head of our P[olish] N[ational] C[ommittee], the leading statesman of Poland, Mr Dmowski.
>
> The Polish problem is very important. With your incomparable power of vision you have been the first, Mr P[resident], to realize that importance and you have expressed it in such a way, that every Polish heart is blessing your name. I shall not exaggerate by saying that there has never been in our past a man, who during his lifetime, enjoyed such an uncontested, unanimous, absolute affection, reverence and gratitude as you do enjoy Mr President. You are the only man from whom we may ask and expect favours. As to the others, governments or individuals, we only expect and ask from them for a thorough understanding. While seeing the difficulties of the problem they generally overlook its importance.
>
> The difficulties are very great indeed. They are not only due to the unscrupulous greed and rapacity of the partitioning powers, which have been continuously endeavouring to oppress, to suppress our national life, encouraging, on the other side, separatistic, nationalistic aspirations of every small nation, of every tribe connected with the Polish people. Our own excessive liberalism in the past has been to a great extent responsible for the present state of things.
>
> Happily for our Christian conscience, unfortunately for our political unity and safety, we have never oppressed any race or creed within the borders of the Pol[ish] Republic . . .[7]

Paderewski also asked the proper channels in the State Department to facilitate the arrangement of an interview at the White House and received the following letter from Breckinridge Long on 10 September 1918:

> My dear Mr Paderewski,
>
> Referring to your recent request that the Department use its good offices in arranging an interview with the President for you and Mr

Roman Dmowski, I am pleased to inform you that I am in receipt of a letter from Mr Tumulty in which he states that the President will be very glad to receive you and Mr Dmowski at half after four o'clock, Friday afternoon, September 13th.[8]

At the same time as he undertook official contacts with the US government concerning the status of non-Polish nationals in the future Polish state, Paderewski also established working relations with the American Jewish Committee in preparation for Dmowski's visit. On 23 September, from the Gotham Hotel in New York on the official stationery of the Polish National Committee's representative in America he wrote to Louis Marshall, enclosing a statement of the Polish National Committee forwarded to him by Dmowski from Paris on 12 August, 1918:

> The enclosed statement of the Polish National Committee has been in my possession for about a month. It was originally my intention to give the publishing of its contents a solemn character. As however circumstances prevent my withholding it any longer, it gives me great pleasure to forward you this declaration in the hope that its spirit and sentiment will prove entirely satisfactory to you.[9]

The text of the Paris unanimous statement of the Polish National Committee reads as follows:

> Our aim is to create an independent Polish State, composed of all Polish territories inclusive of those which give Polish access to the sea; a strong State which would be able to keep in check its western neighbors, the Teutonic Empires, and would constitute a bulwark against their expansion in Central Europe and the Orient.
> We fully realize the fact that it is only with the assistance of the great free nations, in war against the Central Powers, that we shall be in a position to achieve the unification as well as to obtain the independence of Poland, and firmly trusting in their ultimate victory, which will be at the same time the triumph of liberty and justice, we consider ourselves as their Ally, not only for the duration of this war, but also after the conclusion of peace.
> We feel ourselves bound to those nations by unity of thought and struggle against the common enemy for the purpose of safeguarding the solemn rights of nations which are the basis of humanity's peaceful development.
> The Polish State must have a democratic constitution. It must govern along principles of liberty and justice, coordinated with principles of order. Without such principles, no effort towards civilization, no progress are realizable. No privileged classes should exist in

new Poland: *Polish citizens without distinctions as to origin, race or creed must all stand equal before the law*.[10]

The Polish National Committee's statement was discussed at a meeting of the Executive of the American Jewish Committee, and Louis Marshall as its President was authorized to respond to Paderewski's letter, raising some serious complaints and suggesting a conference between him and his associates on one side, and Dmowski on the other:

I have just received yours of the 23rd instant, with enclosed statement of the Polish National Committee bearing date August 12, 1918, and which you state has been in your possession for about a month.

I regret that you have withheld it until this time, especially in view of the fact that, since its receipt by you, the Convention of Polish organizations was held at Detroit, Michigan, at which Mr Dmowski, the president of the National Polish Committee, was present, and my friends and I were therefore prevented from having an interview with you and him before the Convention was held for the purpose of presenting our views with respect to what might be regarded as a satisfactory statement so far as the Jews of Poland were concerned.

I am informed that while the Convention was in progress Mr Rosenwald's secretary telegraphed to you for the purpose of ascertaining whether you had any communication to make to Mr Rosenwald, and that he had received no answer.

I have submitted your letter to a number of my associates who happened to be at my office today, and it is their belief that the statement made is inadequate, in view not only of occurrences in Poland during the past four or five years, but also of what has recently transpired in Poland indicative of the most unfortunate hostility by Poles toward the Jewish inhabitants of Poland. The sentiments expressed in the statement are admirable. Theoretically they are sound and welcome. But the difficulty is that a practical condition confronts the Jews of Poland. Their status has been made exceptional and they have been subjected to discrimination and hardships of the most poignant character. Mr Dmowski is credited with views which are in direct conflict, so far as practical operation is concerned, with the declaration that 'Polish citizens without distinction as to orgin, race or creed must all be equal before the law.'

In as much as the Jews of Poland are probably the only people within the boundaries of that New Poland which it is your ambition to create, a mere general declaration such as that which I have quoted will not suffice. Such a declaration was contained in the Treaty of Berlin, by which the Kingdom of Roumania was created, and yet Roumania for forty years disregarded the mandate of the treaty and defined Roumanian citizenship in such terms as to exclude the Jews from the benefits of the declaration made, which was intended to accord to them the right of equality before the law, which was withheld.

I understand that Mr Dmowski is still in this country. It might perhaps be advantageous to all concerned if it were possible to arrange for a conference at which my associates and I might present our views, in the hope that the outcome might be a more acceptable formulation of your declaration of principles so far as they affect the Jews of Poland.[11]

A meeting between Marshall and Dmowski was arranged by Paderewski at the Plaza Hotel in New York City on Sunday, 6 October, to be followed on 14 October by a larger dinner-meeting with Jewish-American leaders, devoted solely to Jewish-Polish relations in the past and future. Despite Paderewski's efforts, both meetings went badly, causing an even deeper rift and lasting disappointment on the part of the angry Louis Marshall, as is clear from two hitherto unpublished documents, his letter to President Wilson and the report he enclosed of his conversations with Dmowski which are mentioned by Piotr Wandycz in his study of American-Polish relations.[12] The crux of the matter seemed to be the 1912 boycott of Jewish business in Poland announced by Dmowski's National Democratic Party as reprisal for Jewish support of one Władysław Jagiełło, an obscure socialist candidate for the *Duma* elections in 1912 against the *Endeks'* candidate in Warsaw. Apparently Dmowski was also reluctant to accept Marshall's suggestion for the inclusion of a Jewish representative on his Polish National Committee. The fact that he declined such requests was termed by Marshall as 'simply monstrous'.[13]

On 7 November Marshall wrote to the President of the United States commenting in his letter on Jewish-Polish relations in recent years and suggesting specific provisions for the constitution of a future Polish state. After expressing general Jewish support for the re-emergence of an independent Poland as an act of international justice, he made such support conditional on a list of specific guarantees to be given to the four million Jews he claimed would fall under Polish rule. (Actually in 1918 there were less than three million Jews within the anticipated borders of what is nowadays often referred to as the Second Polish Republic.) Both documents are of great importance for understanding the roots of Jewish-American animosity towards Polish aspirations. Let us start with the full text of Marshall's letter of 7 November 1918 to President Wilson which includes not only the grievances but also the concrete proposals of the American Jewish Committee:

The President
The White House
Washington DC

It is generally recognized that one of the most important subjects to come before the Conference of Nations to be held at the close of the war, is the restoration of Poland. It necessarily affects the future of all of the inhabitants within the area of the re-created Polish State. Assuming it to be coextensive with the boundaries proposed by the Polish National Committee, of which Mr Roman Dmowski is the Chairman, approximately four [sic] million Jews who now dwell within that territory, will be directly concerned. Hence, whatever the geographical extent of the new State or its form of government, the civil, political and religious rights of these Jews must be safeguarded.

The American Jewish Committee has long sympathized with the aspirations of the Polish people for independence and the right of self-government. It heartily approves of the establishment of a State which shall, as far as practicable, be re-possessed of those lands which composed Poland during the Seventeenth century [sic] and which are essential to its industrial and economic rehabilitation.

Unfortunately, however, in 1912, there was inaugurated by the leaders of the Polish National Committee, and has ever since been carried on in that country, a policy looking to the practical destruction of the Jews of Poland through the medium of a most virulent economic boycott, which is still in full operation and has grown in intensity from year to year. In substantiation of this statement attention is called to the annexed report of a conversation between Mr Dmowski and the President of the American Jewish Committee, which took place on October 6th, 1918, and which explains the existing status of the Jews of Poland and the attitude maintained toward them by Mr Dmowski and his party.

The mere statement of the facts discloses an intolerable condition and bodes unspeakable evil unless immediate remedial action is taken by those who are seeking the recognition of an independent Polish State, to end this policy of extermination for which many of them are avowedly responsible, and unless the Constitution of the new Poland shall contain guarantees adequate for the protection of the Jewish inhabitants of Poland.

The Polish National Committee has recently intimated that the proposed Constitution of the Polish State would provide that 'Polish citizens, without distinction as to origin, race or creed, must all stand equal before the law.' Admonished by the unhappy experience of the Jews of Roumania, who were promised similar rights by the Treaty of Berlin of 1878, pursuant to which Roumania was created a kingdom and which for forty years has wantonly disregarded the terms of that treaty by withholding from the Jews of that country the rights which were sought to be secured to them, and warned by the frank avowal of Mr Dmowski as to his past and present attitude toward the Jews, the American Jewish Committee regards the proposed pronouncement as wholly inadequate.

When it speaks of 'Polish citizens' it affords the same loophole for evasion as that by which Roumania has hitherto successfully nullified the conditions of the instrument which called it into being – the lack of a definition of the term 'citizen'.

It also fails to forbid discrimination or restrictions or the imposition of disabilities.

Nor does it confer the right to employ any language other than Polish, commercially, socially or educationally.

The necessity of such a right is shown by the attitude of Mr Dmowski and the terms of a law enacted during the Polish revolution of 1862 [sic], which while purporting to grant to the Jews of Poland equal rights with all other citizens of the state, did so under the following condition:

> In consideration for their admission to the enjoyment of equal rights the Jews shall renounce the use of a language of their own in speech as well as in writing. After the promulgation of this act, no legal act, no will, no contract or guaranty, no obligation of any sort, no accounts or bills, no books or commercial correspondence shall be written or signed in Hebrew or Yiddish. All such documents shall in that case be held to be invalid.

The significance of this enactment lies in the fact that upwards of ninety per cent of the Jews of Poland speak and write and are deeply attached to their Yiddish tongue. As is well known, their religious services are conducted exclusively in Hebrew, as they have been for centuries. This legislation, though superseded by the Russian law, is still regarded by the Polish National Committee as being in full force.

This proposed declaration also disregards the fact that the new Poland is to include Austrian Jews, German Jews and Russian Jews who in all likelihood will not desire to retain the status of Austrians, Germans or Russians and who will expect to be recognized as Polish citizens.

Hence, the American Jewish Committee most earnestly prays that it be made a condition of the organization of the new Poland, that its Constitution shall contain specific provisions to the following effect:

(1) All inhabitants of the territory of the Polish State, who are not subjects of other states, shall for all purposes be recognized as of Polish nationality, provided, however, that those who have heretofore been subjects of other states and who are now domiciled in Poland who desire to continue their allegiance to such states may do so by a formal declaration to be made within a specified period.

(2) All Polish subjects, without distinction as to origin, race or creed, shall enjoy equal civil, political and religious rights, and no law shall be made or enforced which shall abridge the privileges or immunities of any of them, or impose upon any of them any discrimination, disability or restriction on account of race or religion, or deny to any person the equal protection of the laws.

(3) Polish shall be the official language, but no law shall be passed restricting the use of any other language, and all existing laws declaring such prohibitions are repealed.

(4) The Jews shall be accorded autonomous management of their own religious, educational, charitable and other cultural institutions.

(5) Those who observe the Jewish Sabbath shall not be prohibited from pursuing their secular affairs on any other day of the week so long as they shall not disturb the religious worship of others.

> Respectfully submitted
> American Jewish Committee
> By Louis Marshall
> President[14]

Marshall included with the letter his own minutes of his two-hour meeting with Dmowski, which started in a polite manner but developed into a heated confrontation on the subject of the 1912 boycott of Jewish commerce of which he had just been informed by the venerable Polish-born President of the World Zionist Congress, Dr Nahum Sokolow.[15] Dmowski, for his part, in his account of his meeting with Marshall argued that the latter not only committed many inaccuracies in his memorandum, but also published a pamphlet entitled 'My Discussion with Mr Dmowski' whose contents he did not show the Polish Leader prior to publication and which was used against him during the Paris Conference.[16] In his own brief summary of the discussion, Dmowski does confirm the main points of disagreement, concluding that the meeting did not produce any specific results.[17] Marshall's Memorandum reads as follows:

Pursuant to previous arrangement I called on Mr Dmowski at his apartments at the Plaza Hotel at three o'clock this afternoon. While all the incidents are fresh in my mind I have reduced the narrative to writing.

Mr Dmowski greeted me quite cordially and indicated that he had seen my letter to Mr Paderewski, of which I append a copy together with his communication. He proceeded to say that he regarded it as important for the Jews to cooperate with the Poles in their aspirations for a restoration of their national existence, and in substance spoke as follows:

'I wish to be entirely frank and to explain my attitude and that of the Poles toward the Jews of Poland. My father conducted fisheries and had close business relations with the Jews of our country. At his funeral there were probably more Jews present than non-Jews, and I looked upon them as friends. I am a biologist by profession and never expected to be engaged in politics. For centuries there was no anti-Jewish prejudice in Poland; there probably never would have been any had it not been for Russia.'

I interrupted him to say that the Polish nobility had evinced continued hostility and brutality toward the Jews of Poland, that the Church had from time to time evinced enmity, and I have him to understand that I was familiar with Jewish history in Poland. He replied that it was true that the nobility was brutal, but the brutality toward the Jews was of the same type as that which it practised upon the Polish peasants and proletariat generally. He continued:

'There never was a pogrom in Poland.' I again interrupted him by saying that there had been Polish pogroms since 1914, and that Georg Brandes had charged him, Dmowski, as the leader of the National Democratic Party, with having openly advocated pogroms in the newspaper called Zwa Groszi [sic]. He remarked that Mr Brandes was in error, had been misinformed, and had subsequently retracted that statement, which could be proven by Mr Luzzatti. I replied that this was new to me, but that I was fully acquainted with the economic boycott that had been in progress for six years and which was worse than a pogrom. He then said:

'I must confess that personally I have been hostile to the Jews and have as a leader of a political party deliberately engaged in a struggle against them, and am responsible for the economic boycott to which they have been subjected. I know your feelings in the subject, but I will give you the reasons which prompted my action. About 1908 a large number of Lithuanian Jews, who could no longer endure the treatment accorded to them by Russia, came to Poland. Strange enough they persisted, after they came to Poland, in speaking the Russian language obtrusively. They also began a movement whereby the Jews were induced to employ Jewish doctors and Jewish lawyers instead of Polish physicians and lawyers as theretofore. Consequently they began what I call a boycott. Although the Jews of Warsaw represented only thirty-eight per cent of the population, they took it upon themselves to advocate the election of a Jew to the Duma instead of a Pole, there being but one representative in the Duma from Warsaw. This culminated in the election for the Fourth Duma in 1912, in a serious conflict. On account of the peculiarity of the election laws and the attitude of the Polish electorate, it was found that the Jews who had availed themselves of the right of registration represented 24,000 voters and the Poles only 22,000 and as a result of this situation the candidate of our party was defeated. The Jews brought about the election of the Socialist candidate. This led to great bitterness, and from that time on we conducted the boycott of which you are complaining. There were other reasons which led to a clash between the Poles and the Jews. Poland is a poor country. Until recently the Poles were engaged in agriculture and as laborers exclusively. The Jews devoted themselves to commerce and industry. It became apparent to the Poles that it was desirable that they should also engage in commerce to enable them to gain a livelihood. That resulted in competition with the Jews, who resented the intrusion of the Poles in their economic field. Unfortunately it was a struggle for existence between two portions of the population, both of which were exceedingly poor. There were not crumbs enough to go around. It was therefore a question as to who should have the crumbs. Although the Poles are poor, the Jews were even more wretched. They have been exploited, their workshops are of necessity in their homes, are most unsanitary, and even with the assistance of their children they have found it difficult to earn enough to keep them from starvation. On the other hand, the Russians who exploited them were growing rich on the proceeds of the labor of these wretched people. Another reason for the growing hostility of the Poles against the Jews lay in the fact that the Jews persisted in speaking Yiddish, and that even their men of education, who had in and before 1862 been patriotic Poles, began to take the attitude that the Polish cause was a lost cause, that Poland was finished, and they therefore directed their activities into other channels. In Posen the Jews rapidly absorbed the German language and abandoned even Yiddish, and in towns in which they were in the majority they changed Polish names which had theretofore continued to be used [sic], into German names. All these things together contributed to the creation of a feeling of animosity, and it was for that reason that I and my party encouraged the boycott, which has been a very severe one and terrible in its operation, and which I am frank to say continues down to this moment and has been growing worse instead of better.'

Before he could resume his statement, I took up the thread of the conversation and said, in substance:

'Since it seems to be in order, I shall make an apologia pro mea vita of a different character from that which you have made. I was born in this State. My parents both came from Germany, my father in 1849, my mother in 1853. They came here practically as refugees. They could not endure the manifestations of hatred, bigotry and intolerance which prevailed in their native land. They prospered, thanks to the freedom and opportunities which our country accorded them, and they inspired in their children a feeling of love and devotion for the land which gave them equality of right and opportunity, and instilled in them the thought that the duties of citizenship were the correlative of the rights thus bestowed. From my earliest days I associated with Jews who had come to this country from Poland. They were men and women of sterling worth. I can point to many men of my acquaintance who were of Polish Jewish ancestry who attained a high rank in the professions and in business and have always been honored and respected by their fellow- citizens. One of my earliest enthusiasms, as well as one of my earliest sorrows, was Poland. As an American I felt a debt of gratitude to Kościuszko, who came to this country during our Revolutionary War to assist in the attainment of our liberty, and I grieved at the injustice which led to the division of Poland between Russia, Austria and Prussia. I also had the honor to become acquainted with Dr Marcus Jastrow of Philadelphia, one of the leading Rabbis of this country as well as one of its finest citizens, who fought in the Polish Revolution of 1862 and was imprisoned because of his participation in it, and who with other Rabbis of Warsaw, by way of protest against the tyranny of Russia, closed his synagogue. His sons are today professors in American universitied [sic]. I know, therefore, from direct contact with Polish Jews what their feelings toward Poles were. Although they had suffered and had come to this country to better their condition, they still felt a deep attachment for Poland. It came to me, therefore, as a shock when I first learned of the details of the boycott and of the explanation of its origin, which were communicated to me by no less a person that Mr Sokolov, and if you will permit me, Mr Dmowski, to use the expression, I regard the action of your party and of yourself as simply monstrous.'

Here he interrupted to say: 'I think that your characterization is not out of place. In fact I like the word monstrous.' I continued:

'I have followed your explanation with close attention. It is practically the same that was made to me and some of my friends some time ago, at a conference at which Mr Rosenwald presided, by Mr Paderewski. It is, however, neither an explanation nor a justification of what has taken place. To begin with, I cannot see the consistency of your arguments with regard to the effect of the presence of Jewish refugees from Russia as producing a pro-Russian propaganda. You concede that these people came to Poland because conditions in

Russia were intolerable. You have conceded in the course of your statement (which he had) that these men hated Russia, and yet you argue that they nevertheless were seeking to Russianize Poland. In the next place, you regard as a boycott on the part of the Jews the fact that Jews consulted lawyers and physicians of their faith. That comes far from establishing the claim of the creation of a boycott. The choice of a medical or legal adviser depends on many reasons other than the far-fetched theory of a boycott. The language question could certainly not have justified a boycott. You know how tenacious people are of their mother-tongue, and it is only a chauvinist who seeks to prevent people from speaking in the language familiar to them from childhood. I remember the indignation felt by the Poles, as well as by all reasonable and fair-minded men, when Germany sought by legislation to prevent the Poles who lived in Germany to speak, read or write in Polish. I have recently had a very interesting correspondence with the Governor of Iowa, who was of the opinon that nobody in this country should be permitted to use any language other than English. What would become of the Poles in the United States if such a course were adopted? Is it not a fact that they have clung to their language here in America, that they have their own schools in which they are taught in Polish, and their own churches and their own newpapers which are conducted in their native tongue? I may say that, in 1909, when I served as Chairman of the Immigration Commission of New York, this proposition, as applicable to the Poles of Buffalo, was brought to my attention. No objection whatever was made to the teaching of the Polish language or to its use in the Polish schools, the only qualification which we thought proper being that the language of the country should of necessity be taught in these schools as well as Polish.'

He then said: 'You are entirely right, but our opposition to Yiddish lies in the fact that its basis is German and that the natural tendency of continuing its use would be to make the Jews German instead of Polish in their sympathies in the event that differences should ever arise between the Poles and the Germans.'

I pointed out to him that this was entirely erroneous, that loyalty did not depend upon language, that that was demonstrated by the armies which we are now sending abroad, where there are tens of thousands of men who are of German birth or descent and who speak German and who nevertheless are loyal to America, as is shown by the casualty lists published daily in the newspapers. I then said that it was very clear to me, even from his statement, that the real basis of the boycott was political, and that it had apparently been decided in cold blood to destroy the Jews because of the exercise by them of their political rights and for voting contrary to the wishes of Mr

Dmowski and his party; that I understood that the Jewish opposition to his candidacy was due to his pronounced anti-Semitism and that he was unwilling to retire for a candidate who did not share his hostility to the Jews.

Thereupon he naively asked; 'But why should they not have voted for a Pole? Poland had only eleven seats in the Duma.' I replied that it was just as much for the interest of the Jews, who had a limited number of seats in the Duma, to be represented by one who understood their problems and difficulties and could advocate their rights, as it was for the Poles to be represented by one of their number. If the right of franchise meant anything and if the professed platform of Mr Dmowski was to be of any value, then every citizen of Poland should have the right to vote in accordance with his own belief as to what was desirable and according to his own conscience; that if a voter was to be punished because he did not vote as those of any other party wished him to vote, then it was apparent that there could be no liberty, and that even the grant of political rights would prove a source of danger. Referring to the Warsaw election, I said: 'The conditions which prevailed were in large measure due to the peculiar attitude taken by the Poles; if the Jews represented only thirty-eight per cent of the electorate, then the Poles, who represented the remaining sixty-two per cent, could have easily outvoted them, unless they were divided among themselves, and if they were divided among themselves, it was because they had the right to be. The fact, therefore, that the Jews were persecuted for the exercise of their political rights demonstrated the iniquity of the policy of the so-called Polish National Committee, initiated, as you, Mr Dmowski, have conceded, by you. You have protested against the suggestion that I have made, on the authority of Mr Brandes, that the Poles had conducted pogroms against the Jews. Let me say that, in my judgment, a pogrom is a thousand times less objectionable than the boycott which you have invented. A pogrom is an act of brutality, it is sporadic, it is an outburst of passion, which dies down almost as rapidly as it comes into being; there is bloodshed and loss of property. But such a boycott as you have created and which has now continued for six years, is a manifestation of hatred which grows by what it feeds upon. You have introduced poison into the system of the Polish people, who, you say, have previously been free from prejudice against the Jews. This poison works day and night. It becomes more virulent as the years go on. It is subtle and insidious in its operation. It passes beyond the control of him who first administered it, and in the end is destructive not only of the immediate victim, but of those in whom the venom has been engendered. If the Poles were free from religious or racial prejudice against the Jews before you carried your policy into operation, it is you who have lowered the moral fibre of the Polish people, and it is you alone who can and should persuade them of the error of their way and induce them to terminate this horrible boycott and to fraternize with the Jews of Poland. The Pope, a few years ago, recognized the injustice of this boycott and, as I understand it, through the leading clergymen of Poland, sought to put it down, but they did not succeed because of the opposition of your party.'

He walked up and down his room while I was making these remarks, and then said: 'Yes, I know what the Pope did, but you are perhaps unaware of the fact that I am not persona grata at the Vatican. While I fully appreciate all that you say, if I were now suddenly to change front and to deal with the boycott as you suggest, my party would immediately say that I was bought.'

I replied that I could not see how that would be possible if his party had confidence in him and if he was its leader as he conceded that he was. They knew as well as he the motive which had led them to unleash the bloodthirsty tiger and that it was in their power not only to make amends but to help the cause of Poland by destroying that tiger with their own hands. Moreover, the moral soundness of a policy which united the Polish people and which did away with the wickedness of the boycott could be made clear by the Polish press, on the forum and in the churches, and the same agencies that had created it could be directed toward its elimination.

He replied that after all the real cause of the boycott rested in the poverty of the country and in the fact that there were not enough crumbs to go around, and that, therefore, the Poles were obliged to save themselves from starvation by engaging in competition, however destructive, against the Jews who were engaged in commerce and industry. But he said: 'I am sure that if the New Poland is created, with all of the resources that it would have, we would occupy almost the same position as does the United States, because we could then take care of all of our people and there would be no such conflict of interest as that which now exists.' He then displayed to me a map of the New Poland, which covered not only Russian Poland as it has heretofore existed, but also Galicia, the Province of Posen, including Danzig, but excluding the region of Koenigsburg which he said was German, and a part of Silesia. That would give Poland tremendous coal fields containing sixty-four billion tons of coal, exceeding by more than twenty billions the tonnage of the Westphalian coal fields; salt mines, copper and iron mines, oil fields, an outlet upon the Baltic Sea, and the opportunity for finding markets; whereas if the New Poland would merely consist of Russian and Austrian Poland, it would be dependent on Russia, Austria and Germany for its markets and would be in precisely the same situation in which Serbia found herself of having an embargo placed upon her commerce at the boundaries. He therefore thought it important that the Jews of this and other countries should, in the interest of their own brethren, assist in the accomplishment of his plans, and, furthermore, that they should furnish capital with which to develop commerce and industries in Poland; that would provide for the Jews and would help the Poles, and, of course, create a feeling of friendship and unity.

I replied that, before the Jews could be asked to take any position on this subject, it was a sine qua non that the Poles should put an immediate end to the boycott, that they should show by their attitude toward the Jews that the era of hatred and conflict, or, as Mr Dmowski expressed it, 'of struggle,' was at an end, and that there should be a recognition of the injustice to which the Jews had been subjected. He said that that would all come in due time, but the only sure way of ending the struggle was to put an end to the real cause of it, which was the poverty of Poland.

I then said that I assumed that the [sic] cognizant of the publications of Professor Dewey and of others, who charged his party with being Czaristic and Royalist, and that the common people of Poland were not represented in it. He replied that he knew of these publications, but did not understand how such views could have originated because they had no basis. It was true that, at the beginning of the war, he felt that he would have to be either pro-German or pro-Russian. He saw no hope for Poland from Germany because the German ideas were to create a Poland which would be merely a new German province, whereas a better opportunity for independence could be achieved through the friendship of Russia. He also admitted that at that time it was his idea that Poland would have to be a monarchy, but his views on that subject had undergone a change, because he now saw that the days of monarchical governments were doomed throughout Europe, including Germany and Austria, and that, therefore, the only Poland that could now be possible would be a Republic of Poland instead of a kingdom.

I returned to the question of the membership of his party by calling attention to what I had read in the Evening Post, to the effect that at the Polish Convention held in Detroit the radical and labor elements were not represented, and that seemed to give some color to the charge of Professor Dewey that the party of Mr Dmowski was not a democratic but rather an aristocratic party. He replied that he had nothing to do with the calling of that convention, that it would have been out of place for him to have attempted to do so because the convention was one of Polish Americans, and that they would have resented any intrusion by him of his views; that the object of the convention was not political but related solely to the status of the Poles in America. I intimated that I had gained a different impression from the account of the proceedings of the convention, and especially since I knew that Mr Paderewski, who was Mr Dmowski's representative in this country, was extremely active in the convention.

This conversation lasted for over two hours. He finally said that he was very glad to have had this opportunity for an exchange of views, and that he was very anxious that there should be further conferences in the hope that a complete understanding could be reached; that it was his idea to take immediate action for the purpose of, by indirect methods, combatting the boycott. To which I replied, that I considered it the part of wisdom to take immediate and direct action to accomplish that end, because so long as the boycott prevailed, no Jew could look upon Poland as other than hostile.

In the course of the conversation I tried to impress upon him the importance of enabling the Jews of Poland to become for Poland what they have been for this country, a source of strength. In reply he stated that he recognized their usefulness, their industry, and commercial ability. He said that they are neither superior nor inferior to the Poles. He regarded their strength to consist in their wisdom as distinguished from their intelligence – thirty centuries of experience in all parts of the world, under every possible condition of prosperity and misery, had developed in them the quality of wisdom. Whereupon I retorted that, assuming that I was a true son of Israel, wisdom prompted me to impress upon him the importance of purging Poland of an evil which would certainly lead to destruction. I asked him to consider the effect that the exclusion of the Jews had upon Spain and Portugal, and other countries, even England, during the centuries when they were not permitted to dwell there. He replied that there are no Jews in Japan and Japan has prospered, but, he said, perhaps I am wrong there because I recognize the fact that but for Mr Schiff, Japan would not be what it is today. I fully acquiesced in his conclusion.

He escorted me to the elevator and then said that, in view of the political developments of the last few days, he felt that it was desirable for him to go to Washington and to remain in this country for some little time, and that he was very anxious to resume our discussion.[18]

There is no evidence that President Wilson ever answered Louis Marshall's letter on the growing crisis in Jewish-Polish relations, although it and the enclosed memorandum almost certainly contributed to the ultimate stand of the United States on the Minorities Treaties imposed on Poland and other countries of East-Central Europe at the Paris Peace Conference.

Dmowski's relations and through him those of the Polish National Committee with the American Jewish Committee deteriorated further as a result of his tactless speech at the dinner meeting of 14 October 1918. This we know from Paderewski's restrained but nevertheless firm public disagreement with Dmowski's views. Apparently the latter was officially asked to include a Jewish representative in the membership of the National Committee, and rejected this proposal. Remembering the warm receptions which he received as a performing artist from Jewish audiences, Paderewski favoured the inclusion of a Jewish representative but in his attempt at least partly to support the idea of the boycott, he introduced in a rather clumsy and inappropriate manner the painful issue of the 'Litwaks' – the partly russified Jews allegedly imposed upon Polish cities by the last Czar's government. Here is the text of his speech:

> You have heard Mr D[mowski]. Whether you like or dislike his way of talking, you must admit that he speaks with the utmost sincerity and courage. The other day Mr M[arshall] told me that Mr D[mowski] did not convince him. It will not cost me any effort to be just as courageous and sincere and I shall admit, here, in the presence of Mr D[mowski] himself, that he does not always convince me. As a member of the P[olish] N[ational] C[ommittee], a purely diplomatic body, the presence of which in the Allied countries was an imperative, absolute necessity, I submitted myself to his able, diplomatic direction, without necessarily sharing his political opinions, especially those concerning the internal affairs of our country.
>
> There are several matters on which I do not agree with Mr Dmowski, the principal of them having always been the Jewish question. We looked at it from two different angles. For him it was a question of statesmanship, for me that of humanity. He might have been right, I might have been wrong. Anyhow, and in spite of all that nice and graceful treatment which for several years I have been receiving at the hands of the Jews, I shall not change my stand, I shall not abandon my angle.
>
> I regard very highly indeed the splendid equipment of Mr D[mowski] as a statesman. I admire his vast knowledge, his brilliancy, the precision of his statements and above all I respect his absolute honesty, and yet I must confess that I am very often in the position of that French deputy who, when asked what was his opinion about a certain famous speaker of the day, answered: Oh, he is splendid, he is wonderful, he is the greatest orator I have ever heard. He will always have my applause; but not my vote.
>
> While enumerating the causes of that most unfortunate boycott in Poland, Mr D[mowski] did not, in my humble judgment, emphasize

strongly enough the principal one, which was of an exclusively sentimental nature, and which was the real foundation of the entire movement. Though not as passionate, impulsive and violent as your own race, the Poles are very emotional people and consequently very easily led by sentimental motives. The boycott was not only an economic symptom, a business proposition, it was before all a sentimental affair, a patriotic protest against a serious and, for an oppressed people, inpardonable offense [sic].

Some 25 years ago began the immigration of the Jews from Russia into Poland. Most cruelly oppressed by the Russian Government, most brutally expelled, these people came to us by thousands and brought with them the very seeds of discord and hatred. The newcomers entered our country like conquerors, because at once they became partisans, supporters and accomplices of our detestable oppressor, though their oppressor as well. Protected just as much in Poland as they were persecuted in Russia, ignorant of our language, they were not contented with offending our ears by speaking Russian everywhere as loud as they could, they organized societies for the promotion of the Russian language in Poland, they did more than that. Worthy descendants of ancient Khasars, aggressive in the extreme they soon got control of the less civilized but fanatical element among our Jewish population and started an active propaganda for the establishment of a Jewish state in historical Poland. Poland – Polsza in Russian, Pelsza in Yiddish was already Polish for them. Clever, energetic agents, among them a notorious Jewish journalist from Odessa, by the name of Jabotinsky, were touring our country, lecturing on the subject, exciting and demoralizing our Jews. The result could not have failed.

When, in November 1905, the so-called constitution was granted to Poland, when our people in Warsaw ventured to celebrate that event, the first sunshine in many years, by a solemn procession, numerous bands of young ruffians appeared on the streets, trying to interrupt the pageant, spitting at our flag, the symbol of our nation, the white eagle of Poland, shouting 'down with the goose', 'down with Poland'.

I have to your judgement, gentlemen, I have it to your conscience to decide, whether a nation oppressed, partitioned, tortured, fighting against 3 powerful empires could remain calm, at the appearance, most unexpected and unjustified appearance, of such an aggressive enemy in her own midst?

The Poles, incapable of cruelty, of brutality, did not respond by a pogrom, they answered by the boycott.

Mr D[mowski] flatters himself when saying that the boycott is his work. That boycott was born in the deeply hurt soul of the Polish people, who suddenly realized that not only the Russia, Prus[sia] and the Aus[tria] but also the Jews were greedy for their ancestral soil.

Mr D[mowski] is only responsible for having sanctioned that regrettable movement by the authority of this statesmanship. The task of a statesman is not strengthen animosity, to intensify passions, to increase suffering – his purpose and aim should be, on the contrary, to pacify, to establish harmony, to provide the maximum of prosperity and happiness. The days of 'divide et impera' are gone, let us hope, for ever. Mr D[mowski] it must be said, realizes it now and I am glad of it.

It may seem immaterial to you what are the causes of such an abnormal state of things. You only see a sort of social disease and you say 'it should be cured'. But let me say, that the methods you suggest are totally impossible. You are not, I presume, believers in Christian Science, consequently you know that such morbid cases could successfully be treated by prayer or persuasion. You are too liberal to believe, that nowadays there is any country, nation, tribe or community willing to accept orders from anyone.

There is but one way for making an end to these deplorable conditions. What has been established by sentiment must be removed by sentiment. Simila similibus. Our people are very emotional – I repeat it, I insist upon it – they are easily led by sentimental motives.[19]

That Paderewski was greatly annoyed by Dmowski's obnoxious behaviour towards the Jews in America is obvious from the cable he sent some time in October 1918 from Paso Robles, California, to Jan F. Smulski, President of the National Department of the First Convention of American Polonia (*Wydział Narodowy I Sejmu Wychodźctwa*) held in Detroit from 24 – 30 August 1918:

... President of our Committee being in this country I cannot independently negociate [sic] with Mr Marshall and associates. Such an action could be with some reason regarded as disloyal. Unfortunately Dmowski does not realize gravity of situation systematically underestimates strength and influence of opponents and believes that his arguing will win in spite of everything. I am sorry to say that his attitude however proud and truly patriotic has done immense harm to our cause. He wishes to talk with those people himself, intends to say that there are too many of them in our country which would mean absolute ruin of our work. Highly important recent events necessitate his presence in Paris or London and I am at a loss to understand why he prefers to stay here stimulating fresh animosity. If it continues I shall be obliged to resign ...[20]

Here is Dmowski's brief account of the same event:

> Later, together with Paderewski, we took part in a political dinner with Jewish leaders arranged by one of the New York activists. Present were Jewish Americans, who served in the past even in American diplomacy, also the Zionist leaders. There we were presented with some demands as a condition for their support of the Polish cause. One of these demands was that we introduce into our National Committee a Jew whom they could trust. But it appeared immediately that there is no such Jew, who would simultaneously possess their and our confidence. More important was the demand directed to me personally that I appeal to the Polish people calling for the cessation of the boycott of the Jews. I did not wish to give them a categorical answer, so as not to give them a chance to use this issue in a noisy campaign against Poland. So I said, well I will issue such an appeal, but under the condition that they first publish their appeal to Jews in Poland demanding that they loyally and faithfully serve Poland, that they work and struggle for the unification and independence of Poland. Their answer was the one that I was sure of beforehand – that this is impossible. In such a way the conference ended without any result.[21]

Dmowski ends his summary of the 1918 visit in America with the following bitter and self-righteous conclusions: 'When my sojourn in the United States came to an end, I knew what I already knew before I arrived – namely that during the Peace Conference we would have in the Jews the most vehement enemies of our cause.'[22] To a man of Dmowski's intelligence it never occurred that he himself by his aggressive behaviour had greatly contributed to that unfortunate animosity which soon took form in the Jewish lobby's insistence at the Paris Peace Conference on special guarantees for national minorities, especially in view of a number of anti-Semitic pogroms in eastern cities of the recent Polish state.[23]

On the other hand, American Jews should have realized that strong as Dmowski's political movement was in that period, it was not he but – partly as a result of semi-official American pressure – Paderewski who became the Prime Minister of reborn Poland early in 1919.[24] Moreover the first head of state was Dmowski's arch-opponent Józef Piłsudski. The *Endeks* were never able to gain a majority of votes and thus control interwar Poland, all of whose Presidents (Narutowicz, Wojciechowski, Mościcki, and Raczkiewicz) as former associates of Marshal Piłsudski were anti-Dmowski and anti-*Endek* in their political views. None of them could be categorized as anti-Semitic. The *Endeks* themselves, under their new name of the National Party (*Stronnictwo Narodowe*) ceased by 1935 to be the strongest political organization in Poland, a position which was acquired by the Peasant Party of Wincenty Witos and Maciej Rataj. Grave as Dmowski's political wrongdoings were, the Polish nation and its political leadership between the wars should not be forever held responsible for them. After all, the concept of 'collective guilt' is equally unjust in its application to the Poles as it was in the past to the Jews.

NOTES

1. George J. Lerski 'Jewish-Polish Amity in Lincoln's America', *The Polish Review*, vol. 18, (1973), pp. 34–51. Actually the term 'Amity' with reference to Polish-Jewish relations in the two years' period of 1861–3 was coined by Dr Abraham G. Duker in his thoroughly researched article 'Polish Political Émigrés in the United States and the Jews' published in December 1949 in *Publications of the American Jewish Historical Society*, vol. 39, part 2, pp. 143–67. I have been a philosemite since my student days in Lwów, as I have described in 'Lwowska Młodzież Społeczno-Demokratyczna, 1937–1939' in no. 47 of *Zeszyty Historyczne*, (1979), pp. 149–82. For that active involvement in the struggle against anti-semitism and efforts to rescue Jews in World War Two, I was awarded in 1986 the Diploma and Medal as one of the 'Righteous Among Nations' by the Yad Vashem Institute in Jerusalem which obliges me to work even harder with like-minded representatives of both nations which have suffered so much for much needed Jewish-Polish rapprochement.
2. While kindly forwarding those precious documents, Professor Wandycz indicated that he received them in turn from Dr Lucjan Dobroszycki of the New York YIVO Insitute for Jewish Research, being actually copies from Wilson's Archives. It is only just that I express my sincere gratitude to both scholars for giving me a unique opportunity to explain the hitherto unpublished sources of the painful Jewish-Polish conflict in America.
3. Piotr Wandycz, *The United States and Poland*, (Cambridge, Mass., 1980), pp. 465; and Wiktor Sukiennicki, *East-Central Europe During World War I; From Foreign Domination to National Independence*, vol. 2, (Boulder, Colorado, 1984), p. 1182.
4. Roman Dmowski, 'Ameryka' in his *Polityka polska i odbudowanie państwa*, (Warsaw, 1925), pp. 388–97.
5. See Charles Phillips, *Paderewski: The Story of a Modern Immortal*. (New York, n.d.), pp. 323–4, 431–3. Unjustly accused and even boycotted as being allegedly anti-semitic Paderewski once retorted in New York: 'I must tell you the truth – I am not a Polish Jew. But I have so many good Jewish friends that perhaps I might very well be called a Jewish Pole.' Ibid., p. 324.
6. See George J. Lerski, *Herbert Hoover and Poland: A Documentary History of A Friendship*, (Stanford, California, 1977), pp. 4–5.
7. 'Paderewski to Pres. Wilson'. In Witold Stankiewicz and Andrzej Piber (eds.), *Archiwum Polityczne Ignacego Paderewskiego*, vol. 1, 1890–1918 (Wrocław,), pp. 482–3. The rest of the communication deals with Ukrainian and Lithuanian matters.
8. Ibid., p. 483.
9. Ms of Paderewski's correspondence with Louis Marshall from the YIVO Archives. Similar letters were sent by Paderewski to other Jewish leaders, as evidenced by responses of a Zionist leader Justice Julius W.Mack and Jacob H.Schiff, Cf. *Archiwum Polityczne Ignacego Paderewskiego*, vol. 1, pp. 486–9, particularly 488.
10. MS 'Dmowski to Paderewski', (Paris) August 12, 1918.
11. *Archiwum Polityczne Ignacego Paderewskiego*, pp. 487–8.

12 Wandycz, 'Wilson and the Rebirth of Poland', *The United States and Poland*, pp. 104–69.
13 See Sukiennicki, op. cit., vol. 2, p. 1182 and vol. 1, p. 86. Also Zosa Szajkowski, 'Western Jewish Aid and Intercession for Polish Jewry, 1919–1939'. In Joshua A. Fishman (ed.) *Studies on Polish Jewry*, (New York, 1974), pp. 150–241. On the other hand Dmowski also complained that he was warned by some unnamed but allegedly reliable non-Polish informant that in New York there was an arranged Jewish plot within the 'Civil League' directed against his person by President Wilson's personal friend Rabbi Stephen Wise. See his *op. cit.*, pp. 395–396. After all there was no reason why he should have been loved by important leaders of American or any other Jewry.
14 MS 'Marshall to Wilson', 7 November 1918.
15 The author of this article established during the war friendly relations in London with Dr Sokolow's children. While Dr Celina, who liked to entertain the Poles such as Prime Minister Tomasz Arciszewski, followed her father as a ranking Zionist, her brother Florian distinguished himself as a Polish correspondent-journalist in pre-War and wartime London.
16 Dmowski, op. cit., p. 196. The author claims that in Paris he only had brief occasion to glance at Marshall's publication, and noticed various inaccuracies (*różne niedokładności*). Someone took the pamphlet from him and he admits never really reading it. I was unable to locate it either, even in the Union Catalogue unless Dmowski meant Marshall's pamphlet entitled *Jewish Rights in Eastern Europe* which was the text of the speech delivered before the American Jewish Congress at El-Hai Temple in Philadelphia on 15 December 1918 and published immediately in New York by the same Congress organization.
17 Dmowski, op. cit., p. 397.
18 MS 'Report of Conversation between Messrs. Roman Dmowski and Louis Marshall at the Plaza Hotel, New York City, on Sunday, 6 October 1918'.
19 *Archiwum Paderewskiego*, pp. 500–2.
20 Ibid., p. 492.
21 Dmowski, op. cit., p. 396. The text translated from Polish by this writer.
22 Ibid., p. 397.
23 Lerski, *Hoover and Poland*, pp. 7–8, 115–16.
24 See Wandycz, op. cit., pp. 158–67 and Titus Komarnicki, *Rebirth of the Polish Republic: A Study in the Diplomatic History of Europe, 1914–1920*, (London, 1957), pp. 291–7. The complicated problem of the 'Minorities' Treaties' is beyond the scope of this monograph and deserves separate coverage.

ARTICLES

THE BASIC PRIVILEGES OF THE JEWS OF GREAT POLAND AS REFLECTED IN POLISH HISTORIOGRAPHY*

Sh. A. Cygielman

The origin, formation and authenticity of the two basic Charters of Rights granted to the Jews of Great Poland up until the middle of the fifteenth century have frequently been examined by Polish historians. The first document was issued in Kalisz by Prince Bolesław the Pious in 1264, while the second – known also as the Extended Privilege – was granted to them later, when their position in the country improved substantially.[1] These two privileges together served as the source for determining the legal and social status of the Jewish community not only in Great Poland but also within the confines of the entire Polish Kingdom, from its emergence as a united kingdom, until its decline in the second half of the eighteenth century.

The attitudes of the Polish historians towards the privilege granted by Bolesław will assist us in clarifying how the different sections of society in Poland related to the Jewish population which, in the course of time, increased significantly, becoming a large and important community in world Jewry. However, our main concern here is the attitude of Polish historians to the later Extended Privilege – a document which, more than any other, contributed to the strengthening of the legal status of the Jewish community in Old Poland, and which for that reason, became a subject of controversy in Polish historical literature. Indeed, in the second half of the nineteenth century, some Polish historians pressed a charge of forgery, which reflected their negative image of the Jewish community and its leadership in Old Poland.[2]

The historical information available to researchers precludes any possibility of determining with certainty when this privilege was granted. The oldest documentation we have dates from the reign of Casimir IV (1453), although it is difficult to ascertain whether the Extended Charter was formulated in his time or already in that of Casimir III, the Great, in

* This is a substantially revised version of an article published in *Zion*, vol. 48, (1983), no. 3.

the fourteenth century, in a document that has not been preserved and was merely ratified again in the fifteenth century. It should be noted that in 1453 Casimir IV ratified several privileges which had originally been granted to the Jews of the whole of Great Poland, Little Poland and Red Russia by Casimir III, whose origin and authenticity have never been challenged.

Although claims that the Extended Privilege was a forgery emerged quite early,[3] until the mid-nineteenth century, Jewish leaders showed no interest in these accusations. This indifference may perhaps be explained by the fact that from the reign of Zygmunt I (1506–48) right up until the end of the second third of the eighteenth century, they were not faced with attempts to undermine the basic rights of the Jewish community or the authenticity of the Privilege, whose validity was not questioned by the Polish authorities. Only in the mid-nineteenth century, with the onset of Jewish Emancipation, were Jewish historians within Poland and elsewhere forced to confront the challenge posed by hostile critics of the charter in a dispute which still has echoes today and which we will examine later in this article.[4]

The status attained by the Jews of Great Poland with the granting of the Charter of Rights by Bolesław the Pious (1264) encouraged, during the second half of the thirteenth century and throughout the fourteenth, Jewish immigrants from Germany and Silesia, to settle within the borders of Great Poland. This was one of the most economically and socially developed regions in the kingdom and thus was well-suited for absorbing the Jewish immigration.[5] This movement gained momentum particularly following the crisis of the 'Black Death'. A considerable number of immigrants settled in the north-western districts of the kingdom which bordered their countries of origin. According to both Polish and Jewish sources, within a relatively short period, by the mid-fifteenth century, more than twelve Jewish communities had established themselves in the towns of Great Poland and attained a secure economic and social status.[7] Registrations in the District Court Books in Great Poland – in Poznań, Pyzdry, Kościan, Szamotuły, Gniezno and elsewhere – attest to the wide range of Jewish economic activity that at the end of the fourteenth century and in the first half of the fifteenth included providing credit to Christian merchants, landowners and members of the king's entourage as well as conducting various commercial transactions with Christian clients. However, at the beginning of the fifteenth century, with the strengthening position of the townsmen and their self-rule in accordance with the adoption of Magdeburg Law, competition between Jewish and Christian merchants and artisans increased and in its wake a struggle emerged to restrict Jewish economic activity. The townsmen secured the assistance of the Church and certain circles of the nobility and, as a result, rules limiting Jewish credit activites were formulated at the Warta Assembly (1423).

These new restrictions and the changes resulting from the numerical and economic growth of the Jewish community, boosted their desire to strengthen and safeguard their judicial, social and economic position, by legal means, thereby guaranteeing their continued existence under the new conditions. And indeed, in the first few years of Casimir IV's reign, favourable conditions were presented to the Jewish community representatives to seek royal approval for the Extended Privilege, and thus to improve the legal status of the Jews of Great Poland.[9]

Casimir IV was the younger son of Władysław Jagiełło, and ascended the throne in 1447. From the outset, he strove to destroy, or at least weaken the power of the aristocracy. He struggled against the strong opposition of magnates from Little Poland, who received support from the higher echelons of the Catholic Church led by Cardinal Zbigniew Oleśnicki.[10] To achieve his political objectives, Casimir IV attempted to take advantage of the financial and economic power of the Jews, and so paid little heed to the appeals of their opponents who wished to restrict their rights and freedom of activity.

Apparently, the Jews first approached the king during a visit to Poznań, shortly after he ascended the throne, and asked him again to ratify the Privilege – or perhaps to issue a new version of it – in order to strengthen the legal and economic status of their community.[11] They were refused. The Jews placed great importance on their appeal undoubtedly because their status had been undermined in Great Poland (and in other regions as well) as a result of the concessions made by King Władysław Jagiełło to the demands of the *szlachta* and by the publication of the Warta statutes;[12] The Jews claimed that they were also in need of a new charter since the original Charter of Rights given by Casimir III had been lost in a fire in Poznań.[13] On 13 August 1453, the King conceded to the request of the representatives and ratified an improved Privilege,[14] different in scope from that of Bolesław (1264) and other Charters of Rights given to the Jews of the whole of Poland. This was secured on 15 July 1364 with the help of the Jew Falko of Kalisz, and for the Jews of Little Russia and Red Russia on 25 April 1367. The charter also went beyond those granted to Jews outside the borders of Poland in other European countries.

The Extended Privilege contained several clauses (16,19,20,30) which granted the Jews rights that had been previously denied them by the Catholic Church; other clauses (32–7) guaranteed the possibility of expanding credit activities to large sums of money, and a series of additional clauses (10,11,25,27) defined and established more clearly the framework of Jewish self-rule in Poland.[15] The ratification of the improved Privilege provoked angry reactions in ecclesiastical circles and among townsmen who feared the growth of competition from Jewish artisans, merchants and financiers. The Franciscan monk Giovanni Capistrano, known for his sermons against the Jews of Italy, Germany and Eastern

Europe, arrived in Kraków at the end of August 1453, incited anti-Jewish activity and even threatened the king with harsh punishment for approving the Extended Privilege and other Charters of Rights to the Jews of Great Poland.[16] Capistrano, the loyal emissary of the Catholic Church, proceeded to despatch an irate report on this matter to Pope Nicholas V, appending to it a copy of all Jewish privileges approved by King Casimir IV.[17]

Cardinal Zbigniew Oleśnicki and the historian Jan Długosz, the leader of the Church in Kraków, joined Capistrano in his campaign of threats and vilification. Yet even when war broke out between Poland and the Teutonic Order in the spring of 1454, and led to increased pressure from Church circles to repeal the privileges granted to the Jews, King Casimir did not yield to their demands. Proof of this may be found in one of Jan Długosz's observations:

> The rights granted by the King and his *advisors* [my italics, Sh. A. C.] to the Jews were an insult to the Holy Faith [Christianity] and for this King Casimir was accused publicly and denounced by Zbigniew [Oleśnicki] the Cardinal, Bishop of Kraków and Johannes Capistrano, the God-fearing monk; but he did not wish to rescind them and thus the Lord poured forth his wrath on the King and the people.[18]

Yet following the defeat by the German forces of the army of Polish knights at a battle near the town of Chojnice (18 September 1454), the King was forced to consider the political and economic demands of the middle and lesser nobility. These circles formed, at the time, the social basis of the major part of the kingdom's cavalry. With the new Polish knightly corps assembled near the town of Nieszawa (November–December 1454) Casimir IV strove to ensure the support of the aristocracy in order to continue the war against the Teutonic Order, and so granted the *szlachta* additional and far-reaching privileges which bolstered their political standing substantially.[19] Among other things, it was agreed that the district assemblies of the *szlachta* (*Sejmiki*) would become the deciding bodies on all questions relating to the proposal of new laws and the conscription of the army.[20] Meanwhile, ecclesiastical circles, supported by the petty nobility, succeeded in repealing the Jewish privilege approved by Casimir IV since his ascension to the throne, under the pretext that it contradicted Divine Law and the law of the land.[21]

The abrogation of both the original and the Extended Privilege exposed the Jewish population to the arbitrariness of the municipal authorities and lent renewed validity to the Warta statutes.[22] Despite this, Casimir IV did not entirely abandon the Jews of Poland to the mercy of their persecutors. He continued to view favourably their various economic activities, tried to protect them wherever danger threatened and sometimes even meted harsh punishment and imposed heavy fines on towns in which disturbances against the Jewish community occurred, such as those of Kraków in 1463.[24] It is noteworthy that from the last third of the fifteenth century until King Zygmunt I's rise to power (1506), the Jewish population in Poland succeeded, without the support of valid or improved general Charters of Rights, in maintaining their economic and legal standing and even managed to establish an efficient community infrastructure and in many places to strengthen it significantly.[26] At the same time, it should also be remembered that Casimir IV never demanded from the Jewish leaders the return of the parchment scroll on which the official Charters of Rights were written.[27] They remained in the possession of Jewish institutions and in due course, when the right conditions arose, were submitted for re-ratification.

Close to a century after its repeal, the Extended Privilege won full and renewed re-affirmation by King Zygmunt August[28], and later by most of the kings of Poland, thus serving the Jews of Poland for many generations as the basic document protecting their rights.[29] Yet the Extended Privilege became a subject of controversy particularly from the nineteenth century in spite of its long established status as a respected state document which had served the Jews as a kind of basic law for hundreds of years.

The doubts of the Polish historians as to the genuineness of the Extended Privilege, were based mainly on formal flaws and on the existence of certain differences between its linguistic character and that of the official style that prevailed during the time of Casimir IV. According to their allegations the forgery had been carried out by Jewish dignitaries either at the time of Casimir III 'the Great', during the reign of his heirs, or possibly even shortly before the manuscript was submitted for ratification in 1453. This thesis was proposed by one of the most prominent legal historians in Poland, Romuald Hube (1803–90). Yet he also suggested that this accusation of forgery was a tool used by the Cardinal Oleśnicki and his associates, to instill doubt into the heart of King Casimir IV in order to persuade him to change his policy towards the Jews.[30] However, before we discuss this issue we must first examine earlier historical discussions of the genuineness of the Extended Privilege and other Charters granted to the Jews.

An important landmark for this discussion is the official compilation of Polish laws and royal privileges collected in 1505 by Jan Łaski, one of the senior Polish statesmen at the turn of the sixteenth century. The compilation included the Charter of Rights granted to the Jews by Bolesław the Pious in 1264[31] but omitted all other Jewish privileges approved since. This was justified by him in his introduction on the grounds that the inclusion of Bolesław's charter 'was not aimed at giving legal sanction to the privilege but rather only in order to provide protection [to the public] against the Jews'.[32] His anti-Jewish bias may be detected also in the version of the privilege granted by Bolesław he included in the compilation. This has flaws in several places: in one of them the distortion was left, possibly knowingly and perhaps even deliberately (the reference is to Clause 26 of the privilege which appears in the Łaski Codex as clause 25).[33] Although the original document of the Charter of Rights granted by Bolesław the Pious to the Jews has not reached us, with the aid of indirect evidence (which I adduce later) we may establish that, whereas the flawed clause in the Łaski Codex totally denied the right of the Jewish moneylenders to give loans against mortgages and promissory notes,[34] the original version of Clause 26 in the 1264 Charter of Rights – in copies dating from the reign of Casimir III and therefore in a version Łaski must have known – permitted Jewish loans against immovable property mortgages and promissory notes. The Jewish moneylender was also given the possibility to realize – if only partially – in the event of any violation of credit conditions, the mortgage and promissory note which were given as guarantees for repayment. The change which Łaski introduced into the original document evidently reflects his tendency to distort the picture of the basic rights that the Jews acquired since the early days of their arrival in Poland. On the basis of this distortion, the opinion that Bolesław the Pious' Charter of Rights prohibited Jews from lending money against bills and mortgages became established in Polish historiography. It also, no doubt, contributed to the consolidation of accusations concerning the forgery of the Extended Privilege.

By comparing the controversial Clause 26 in the 1264 privilege as it appears in the Łaski Codex with the original version, we may be able to clarify the approach taken by Polish historians in assessing the legal status of the Jews in Old Poland. This examination is based primarily on the most important source for the clarification of the authentic version of the privileges that served the Jews of Poland in formulating their legal status until the end of the days of Casimir III (1370) – namely, the Charter of Rights granted by Casimir III to the Jews of the whole of Poland, ratified in Kraków in July 1364. A copy of this privilege, dating from the fifteenth century, was preserved up until the Second World War, and was considered the oldest document that survived of all the General Privileges granted to the Jews of Poland up to the second half of the fifteenth century.[35] The study of this document has contributed significantly in clarifying controversial issues relating to the legal position of the Jews of Old Poland. Hube, who examined and published parts of it, determined correctly that its lack of mention of the Charter of Rights issued by Bolesław the Pious (1264) could not hide the fact that this document was an exact copy of the earlier charter.[36] In Clause 26 of the document which was first analysed by Hube, no sanction preventing Jews from lending money to magnates against promissory notes and immovable property mortgages is mentioned; moreover, in the document it was emphasized that the transfer of property to Jews as repayment for unpaid loans, would be protected by law.[37]

The content of Clause 26 in the Privilege that was discovered and studied by Hube, contradicts however the version of the corresponding clause (25) in Bolesław the Pious' Charter of Rights as it appears in its flawed and distorted form in the Łaski Codex. Hube never claimed that Clause 26 of the 1364 Privilege was forged or distorted; on the contrary, he asserted that the entire privilege was an exact copy of the Charter of Rights issued to the Jews of Great Poland in 1264. But he also contended that Bolesław the Pious' 1264 Charter of Rights forbade Jews from realizing promissory notes and immovable property mortgages pledged in exchange for loans.[38] Thus Hube joined the trend that led Jan Łaski and guided legal researchers and other Polish historians since the fifteenth century up to the present which culminated in the accusation that Jewish dignitaries attempted to extend by forgery the earlier privileges granted to the Jews of Poland.

Yet there is considerable evidence, appearing in legal documentary material of Little Poland and Great Poland since the end of the fourteenth and the beginning of the fifteenth century, that Jews did grant credit to landowners and others against mortgages and promissory notes. Documentary material clearly attesting to the scope and intensity of this 'forbidden' financial activity may be found in court ledgers and fortress registers of towns such as Kraków [39] Poznań,[40] and additional towns elsewhere in Great Poland,[41], as well as in Mazowsze, and particularly in the town of Płock.[42] From the documents it is evident that this activity was in accord with the legal and economic norms then common in Poland.[43]

Indeed had there not been an accepted legal principle in the Polish Kingdom that secured guarantees for Jewish moneylenders in the form of promissory notes and immovable property mortgages, there would have been no need to make new decisions on this matter at the szlachta meeting in Warka (1423). Yet Clause 19 in the *Sejm* Constitution, published after this assembly, prohibited Jews from granting loans in exchange for promissory notes and immovable property mortgages. This resolution was formulated with the support of the Church and under pressure by the nobility (mainly the lesser nobility) who were often in need of Jewish credit. Thus not infrequently they found it difficult to meet payments and as a result faced the danger of losing control over their assets.[44] And finally, it is hard to imagine that the representatives of the Jewish community – who undoubtedly took part in formulating the version of the Privilege submitted to Bolesław the Pious and his advisors – would have renounced an essential condition for the existence of so important a branch of Jewish economic activity in Poland of those days.⁴⁵ It is doubtful that without this clause, there would be any point to the whole document. Moreover, Bolesław the Pious was interested in winning the co-operation of the Jews in order to develop his country. Such an extreme measure against the Jews does not seem reasonable.

Accordingly, it seems logical to see Clause 25 in the Łaski Codex rather as a distortion of a clause in Bolesław the Pious' Charter of Rights. It is difficult to believe that this distortion resulted from a lack of reliable sources at the disposal of the editor considering the importance of his mission (King Alexander was about to present the Compiled Codex for ratification by the *Sejm* which was scheduled to convene in the city of Radom 1505). All the ledgers of the fortresses and branches of administration were open to him and the conclusion is unavoidable that this was a deliberate distortion on the part of Łaski.⁴⁶

Stanisław Kutrzeba, one of the most prominent modern Polish historians and a strong advocate of the claim regarding the Jewish forgery of the Extended Charter of Rights, wrote, in an apologetic tone:

> The *correction* [my italics] which Łaski made in the document may be explained thus – that at that time directives prevailed such as those based on the Warka Statutes of 1423 and on the Nieszawa Statutes [Rules of 1454]; and therefore Łaski *adjusted* [my italics] the directives of the Privilege to make them consistent with the directives of those of the Statutes.⁴⁷

It must be remembered that this adaptation of the Charter of Rights of the Jews of Poland made by Chancellor Łaski is still considered today by many Polish historians as the correct and authentic version of the document.⁴⁸ The attitude, then, of the Łaski Codex to the legal status of the Jewish community in Poland may be regarded as an important milestone in the history of the hostile perception, which is found among circles of Polish jurists and writers already at the close of the fifteenth century and which has led many modern Polish historians to allege that the Extended Privilege which was issued to the Jews of Great Poland is a forgery.

Let us now turn to the arguments of two prominent figures at the time of Casimir IV, Cardinal Zbigniew Oleśnicki and the historian and cleric Jan Długosz, who both laboured vigorously to rescind the Charter of Rights which the King granted to the Jews. Oleśnicki stood at the head of the opposition to the absolutist tendencies of Casimir IV; his attitude towards the Jews and towards the privileges they had received from the King was especially hostile, since he correctly saw that the enhancement of the status of the Jews was a deliberate measure in the policy of the King to augment his political strength. In his letter to Casimir IV in May 1454, he

THE BASIC PRIVILEGES OF THE JEWS OF GREAT POLAND   125

mentioned, among other things, the ratification of the Jewish privileges in 1453.

> At this time I shall not say everything, only the most important. Some time ago, you, your majesty the King, granted to the Jews, privileges and certain rights, several of which were awarded, so to speak, by King Casimir [the Great]. Your father [Władysław Jagiełło] may he rest in peace, despite the attempts of the Jews to win his heart with gifts, refused to ratify them. To this scene I was present and witness, and with my own eyes I read these distorted [49] privileges. And you, your Majesty the King, ratified them without having contacted me, even though I was present then in Kraków. Nor did you contact the lord advisors; moreover, you agreed [to include in them] several clauses[50] which contravene the principles of the Church and the Christian faith ... do not attempt, your Majesty the King, to make light of these matters and do not think that you are allowed to decide on matters pertaining to the church and the faith at your will. No person is so great and strong that it is impossible to oppose him when matters of faith are concerned.[51] Therefore, I ask and beg of you, your Majesty, please repeal these Charters of Rights and the privileges; prove, your Majesty that you are a Catholic monarch and remove those matters which cast disgrace on the name of the king and may yet bring about the greatest embarrassment.[52]

An analysis of this statement may help in reaching some conclusions relating to the Extended Privilege: Oleśnicki called all the Charters of Rights that King Casimir ratified at the time and which were re-submitted for ratification to Władysław Jagiełło *falcissima*; Stanisław Kutrzeba and other Polish scholars translated the word *falcissima* as meaning 'false' or 'forged' and thus apparently reinforced the thesis of forgery. Yet, this meaning of the word does not seem reasonable in the context of the passage. Oleśnicki, who served for many years as King Władysław Jagiełło's secretary, knew very well that the Charters of Rights – at least those granted to the Jews of the whole of Poland (1364) and the Jews of Little Poland (1367) – were authentic. Therefore, it is possible to assume that when calling them *falcissima* (neuter plural) Oleśnicki meant the other meaning of the word, such as 'faulty' or 'undesirable', or indeed both.[53] He was expressing his anger at the way the Jewish community of Poland had established legally certain rights. And if we assume that Oleśnicki wanted to employ the term 'forged' then his allegation appeared dubious, even to Hube and Kutrzeba, who never doubted the authenticity of the Charters of Rights (apart from the Extended Privilege) issued by Casimir III (the Great) and ratified by Casimir IV. From Oleśnicki's text, we may learn that Casimir IV's father – Władysław Jagiełło – also refused to ratify privileges granted by Casimir III that were submitted to him by emissaries of the Jewish community. It seems however that his refusal did not stem from any doubt as to the legitimacy of these Charters of Rights but rather resulted from the fact that, as a new Christian, he was greatly influenced by the heads of the Catholic Church who strove, as was customary, to drive out the Jews.

Oleśnicki's allegation that the King did not consult his advisors is also inaccurate. The King certainly did not summon Oleśnicki since the latter headed the opposition to the King's policy. Yet, from the comments of Długosz, who expressed great interest in the Jewish privileges in those same years, we know that the privileges and rights granted to the Jews were issued by Casimir IV, in collaboration with his advisors.[54] Indeed, Oleśnicki's accusations were not directed against the Jewish privileges as such, but against the King's domestic policy. There is no more in them than in the Church's usual and widespread anti-Jewish accusations. The Church opposed the King's policy without concerning itself too deeply with the character of the Jewish privileges. Oleśnicki's only open attack on the Extended Privilege is his condemnation of the clauses contradicting the principles of the Church (16,19,20,30).[55] His testimony only reinforces the view that King Casimir IV did take steps to establish the status of the Jewish community and liberate them somewhat from the restrictions laid down by Church directives and the Warka constitution.[56] It should be remembered, of course, that strengthening the economic status of the Jews would have benefited the state treasury, at a time when the King was preparing to implement his plans to extend the boundaries of Polish rule to the mouth of the Wisła river and the town of Gdańsk by attacking the fortifications of the Teutonic Order.

The second person who opposed the Jewish privileges that were ratified by Casimir IV was the canonist Jan Długosz, one of the leading members of the Catholic Church in Kraków. He was to become one of the most eminent historians and writers in Poland during the latter half of the fifteenth century. His personal involvement in the struggle against the ratification of the Jewish privileges and against the strengthening of the status of the Jews in Poland stemmed from his close association with Zbigniew Oleśnicki (Długosz was his ally and protégé) and from the close co-operation he maintained with the militant monk, Giovanni Capistrano during his stay in Poland and especially in Kraków.[57]

Długosz's position concerning the privileges is known to us mainly from his historical writings, composed about ten years or more after the events themselves.[58] The following passage below, extracted from his book *Historia Polonica*, is characteristic of Długosz's attitude, as a historian, towards the Jewish community.

At the request of the said Jewess, his mistress Esther, he [Casimir III] granted to several Jews, residing in the Kingdom of Poland, special priorities and liberties, although there are those who doubt the veracity of the documents and claim that they are an insult and offence to the honour of God, and still exude today a putrid odour.[59]

These words reflect Długosz's hostility to the Jews. Yet, in referring to the legality and legitimacy of the privileges, Długosz cautiously checked his language and confined himself to saying 'there are those who doubt'. In addition, there is an inaccuracy in his words for it seems that he confuses the granting of personal privileges to several Jews that were indeed granted by Casimir III, as in the case of the banker Lewko from Kraków and others, with the negotiations between the representatives of the Jewish community and the King.[60] Długosz's suspicious attitude – expressed in several places in his historical compositions – towards the authenticity and validity of the privileges that were awarded to the Jews of Poland by both Casimir III and IV, is clearly a consequence of his feelings about the Jews. He had been involved for many years in the activity of the legal instances of state and ecclesiastical rule and of its important offices and knew without a doubt that documents of this nature were written and edited with the care, precision and reliability expected of the King's secretariat. They were granted to the supplicants under the strict supervision of the Chancellor.[61,62]

Apart from the claims of the two figures mentioned above, we find no indication in Polish writings of this period of any accusations of fraud, forgery or illegal action concerning the Charters of Rights held by the Jews. In this context it is worthwhile examining the allegations made by the militant monk and persecutor of Jews, Giovanni Capistrano. Capistrano was summoned to Poland in August 1453 to wage war against the supporters of Jan Hus. He reached Kraków several days after the ratification of the Extended Privilege and many times urged the King to abandon his policy of supporting the Jews. In his letter to the King of 28 April 1454, he wrote that 'the privileges to the Jews that you have ratified without the presence of mind and unjustly, you have awarded to the enemies of the Cross – rescind and restore to them their *previous* form' [my italics].[63] This appeal to the King was written some eight months after the ratification of the privileges to the Jews of Poland, including the Extended Privilege, and shows that Capistrano did not doubt that the Charters of Rights were ratified legally. If he had harboured any suspicion as to the origin and authenticity of the documents, there is no doubt that he would have jumped at the opportunity to attack them. It is clear that Capistrano was familiar with the content of the privileges since he had taken great pains to send a copy of them to Pope Nicholas V. His demand must therefore relate to their content, particularly to the clauses contradicting the policy of the Catholic Church.

Indeed, in his letter to Pope Nicholas V of 13 September 1454, Capistrano wrote: 'The King of Poland did not heed my advice concerning the Jewish privileges. Your Excellency, Holy Father, I am sending you copies of the privileges, together with my other writings and books directed against heretics.'[64] In this document also there is no claim of forgery. Giovanni Capistrano was, of course, not involved like Długosz and Oleśnicki in the internal political struggles of Poland. He saw his main concern in strengthening the Catholic Church against the Hussites and in preaching against the Jews in general. The legal problems relating to the status of the Jews of Poland were not the focus of his interest.[65]

Many of the Polish writers who wrote in the second half of the fifteenth and throughout the sixteenth and seventeenth centuries on the legal and judicial affairs of the Kingdom, also dealt with Jewish rights. Many of them not only treated the Jews with open enmity, but also attacked the Charter of Rights which the Jews received from the rulers of Poland since the latter half of the 13th century. None, however, distinguished between one privilege and another: all were equally flawed in their eyes, and none of them showed any special interest in the Extended Privilege granted to the Jews of Great Poland and ratified by Casimir IV. In many of their works, the demand was made that all the privileges be rescinded, since they harmed Polish society. This claim was justified mostly by arguments derived from the Christian faith, Church policy, or it was based on views that stemmed from the economic and social preconceptions of feudal society. It is perhaps interesting to add that in the writings of that period, there prevailed a strong opposition to financial credit in general and to business loans by Jewish businessmen in particular. This opposition stemmed partly from the vast contrast between Polish feudal society seen as the possessor of a natural economy motivated mainly by non-economic incentives, and economic methods based on capital and monetary flow which already characterized the economic activity of the Jewish community (as revealed in the Polish and Lithuanian Metric Registrations).

The negative attitude to Jewish credit that was current among the Catholic clergy and the nobility – from which circles these authors generally came – obviously stemmed from church objections to usury and from the fundamental problem posed by business loans under static economic conditions. For example: several landowners who borrowed money from Jews became entangled in debts and were unable to meet their commitments. As a consequence they endangered their estates since their Jewish creditors sought to safeguard their own money by foreclosure or expropriating their income.[66] As is known, in many cases the borrowers did not use the money for productive purposes or for the improvement of their estates, but rather for the increase of their knightly prestige and the consumption of luxury goods. This use of monetary loans undoubtedly involved waste and frivolousness, and as expected, brought with it feelings of frustration among the debtors and their families. The fact that the money lenders were Jews, of course, contributed in kindling feelings of hatred and hostility. Under these circumstances, it is no wonder that Jewish money lenders or businessmen who demanded their money were presented in a negative light, as immoral figures with destructive qualities, such as skinners, robbers, tramplers, moneychasers, haters of good Christians and the like.

Jan Ostroróg (1436–1501), one of the leading Polish thinkers of his time devoted a chapter to Jewish rights in his tractate 'A memorandum on matters for the benefit of the Polish kingdom':[67]

> The Jews enjoy an unjust law enabling them to take interest, to retain and claim ownership over objects that are not theirs and not return them until repaid by the true owners the money they demand. This law should be rescinded. And when this right is taken away from them, many robberies will cease as a result.

Stanisław Zaborowski (died 1529), an expert on Polish law in the first third of the sixteenth century and a participant in the preparation of Łaski's Codex, composed a tractate on 'The nature of laws and the king's assets' (1507), and included a chapter on Jews.[68] In this chapter he denounced the right of the Jews to deal in usury and like Jan Ostroróg he saw in them a source of corruption in society. Similarly, Stanisław Orzechowski (1513–66), a thinker and writer on government and legal matters and a militant fighter against the Reformation, included in his tractate, which was submitted to the *Sejm* in Kraków in 1543,[69], comments condemning the right of Jews to engage in usury. He also opposed the Charter of Rights issued by Bolesław the Pious, which was in his words a disaster for Great Poland. He expressed sorrow that the validity of the document had been extended to the domain of the whole of Poland and complained that Jews and judges collaborated in oppressing Christians. Orzechowski also alleged that the law in Poland was powerless vis-a-vis the Jewish community and that because of the directives of the law whereby two Jewish witnesses determined the verdict of a Jew standing trial, Jews were guaranteed that they would never be punished.[70] From Orzechowski's allegations it appears that the Extended Privilege ratified by Casimir IV constituted a natural development of the Charter of Rights of Bolesław the Pious. Orzechowski, in his booklet, did not cast any doubt as to the legality of these privileges, nor did he hint at any act of fraud or any unusual measure on the part of the Jews.[71] He believed, rather, that the rulers of Poland should have refrained from granting Charters of Rights to Jews who wanted to settle within the confines of the Polish kingdom.

In conclusion, it can be said that both during and following the time of the ratification of the Extended Privilege by Casimir IV, expressions of hostility were indeed voiced against the Jews in Poland; yet no single voice was heard raising claims and objections similar to those asserted by the Polish historians who pursued this matter from the end of the eighteenth century onwards. No doubt had the charters been seen as forgeries, this would have been widely asserted.

From the end of the eighteenth century, a marked change emerged in the attitudes towards the judicial and constitutional position of the Jewish community in Poland-Lithuania. This change occurred against the background of a crisis which was to shake the foundations of the Polish state and eventually lead to its destruction, and was linked with the influence of the ideas of the Enlightenment – particularly those closest to the concept of political enlightened absolutism – the realization of which seemed to many thinkers to provide a means of extricating the state from its weaknesses. Thus the desire to enhance the status of the townsmen, both economically and politically, prevailed in Polish enlightened circles.[72] They hoped to achieve this by reducing and limiting the financial activities of the Jews in the cities of the Kingdom and by chipping away at the legal and social autonomy of the Jewish community.[73] The consolidation of the urban bourgeoisie and the decisions reached by the *Sejm* in the 1760s, led to the abolition of the right of Jews to conduct free economic activity in the cities of the Kingdom – a right which had been safeguarded for hundreds of years by the general privileges issued by the kings of Poland – causing far-reaching changes in the occupational composition and geographical location of the Jewish population.[74]

These trends also found expression in the compilation of the Polish laws collected by Stanisław Konarski (1700–73).[75] The first six volumes of this compilation were published in the 1730s and even today they are considered as the most authoritative collection on matters relating to the documentation of the legislative activity of Old Poland. Despite this, the compilation does not include the important General Privileges of the Jews of Poland, apart from the sole privilege that was also published in the Łaski Codex as mentioned above.[76] Yet, the compilation does contains in it extensive legislative material on the Jews of Poland-Lithuania[77] that serves to this day as an important source for the research of the history of the Jews in Old Poland.

Konarski's failure to include the basic laws that served the Jews of Poland for more than 400 years raises some questions, particularly in light of the fact that documents containing the privileges, among which the authorized text of the Extended Privilege is included, were available to him.[78] It seems that there is no explanation for this except that Konarski strove to conceal from the public eye the documents that served as the source of many Jewish rights and provided the foundation for the extended autonomy enjoyed by the Jewish community within the Polish kingdom. Konarski, deeply involved in the turbulent life of the kingdom and a staunch supportor of enlightened absolutism,[79] apparently supposed that in the not too distant future there would be a need to revoke the rights and social and legal autonomy of the Jews in order to integrate them into the social and legal framework of the absolutist state. This vision of the future of the Polish-Lithuanian kingdom, it seems, only reinforced his conviction not to digress from Łaski and not to give publicity to the Charter of Rights of the Jews of Poland. Moreover, as one of the leaders of the Catholic Church in Poland he no doubt shared its aspirations to halt Jewish attempts to strengthen and protect their rights.[80]

The claim of forgery of the Extended Privilege draws, then, its main inspiration from the historiographical picture described above. Formally, however, the claims are based only on flaws and defects supposedly existing in the document itself. Stanisław Kutrzeba, the main figure contesting the legitimacy of the privilege in the last fifty years, based his charge on one of the preambles of the privilege – that which was written in the name of Casimir III. His arguments may be summarized as follows: in the preamble there is a discordant title applied to Casimir III; there is a lengthy style alien to fourteenth century documents; and the names of administrative and registrative institutions cited are anachronistic.[81] In addition not only were the names of Casimir III's witnesses missing, but so was the exact date of the signature and ratification of the document.[82] Hence Kutrzeba's assumption that the document was forged. He alleged that the forgery was carried out in the fifteenth century some time during Władysław Jagiełło's reign or close to the time of its ratification by Casimir IV.[83] According to Kutrzeba 'This privilege [the Extended one] is undoubtedly a crude forgery. It raised suspicion from the beginning when it was submitted [for ratification to Casimir IV] as a copy with the explanation that the original had supposedly been consumed in a fire that struck Poznań.'[84] Kutrzeba concludes:

> The Polish privileges to the Jews ... were ... subject ... to distortion and defacement [uległy skorumpowaniu]. Moreover, in their flawed form, they actually served as a basis for their ratification and for granting new privileges, which transformed the flaws into legally binding norms. How is it possible to accept, under these circumstances, these privileges as binding resolutions.[85]

One of the more important documents to which we may turn for assistance in assessing the legitimacy of the Extended Privilege, is a record made in the Lwów Fortress books. This type of registration (referred to as *oblata*) was used in old Polish legal practice as an extremely reliable document.[86]

It was considered as a kind of declarative verdict, both in the legal and constitutional-political processes, for the purpose of re-ratifying Charters of Rights previously granted and for laying down rules and regulations founded on those Charters of Rights.[87] In the shortened record of the *oblata* known from the Lwów Fortress books[88] we learn that 'on 13 August, in the year 1453, in Kraków Casimir Jagiełło ratifies and extends the rights which Casimir the Great granted to the Jews'.[89] The abbreviated record summarizes authorized legal testimony that was registered in these books not too long after, it may be assumed, the ratifiction of the privilege by Casimir IV.[90] At this point, it should be stated that here the meaning of the term 'extend' is extremely hard to define clearly, and poses difficulties for us in learning whether the extension of the privilege was the result of Casimir IV's initiative. In any case, there is no reason to doubt the credibility and accuracy of the work of those researching the Lwów Fortress archive in the 19th century, who, after scrupulous enquiry, recorded the *Regest* (entry-calendar).[91] The primary importance of this document for us, lies in the illustration of the fact that during this period in Poland, legal documents were prepared carefully and painstakingly. It is inconceivable that an important royal document like the Extended Privilege could have been signed off-handedly without a thorough examination of all its particularities and details.[92]

Evidence of the credibility and accuracy of registration arrangements, and for our argument regarding the strict administrative arrangements made for all royal documents including the Charters of Rights concerning the Jews, is also found in other abbreviated registrars; the next chronological record in the Lwów Fortress books that deals with the Extended Privilege is the summary of King Zygmunt August's ratification issued towards the closing session of the *Sejm* in the town of Piotrków Trybunalski on 11 December 1548 in these very words: 'Zygmunt August, the King, ratifies a document of Casimir Jagiełło given to the *Jews* [my italics] in Kraków on 13 August in the year 1454.'[93] From this document it appears that the last king of the House of Jagiełło not only gave his approval to the Extended Privilege that was granted to the Jews of Great Poland by Casimir IV, but also extended – probably in accordance with a request made by the representatives of the Jewish community – the domain of the privilege's validity to include the Jews of the whole of Poland. This was done during the *Sejm* meeting openly and publicly and in the presence of nobles, representatives of the monarchy, senators and even Church heads. From then until the the second half of the eighteenth century, this document served the Jews of the whole of Poland as a general Charter of Rights. In the collection of the records of the Lwów Fortress additional summaries of ratifications of the General Privilege may be found. In one synopsis given by King Stefan Batory on 2 January 1580, in Warsaw, the King approved a Privilege granted to the Jews by King

Zygmunt August.[94] King Zygmunt III of the House of Vasa also ratified (on 12 April 1588) the privilege granted by his predecessor.[95] Towards the closing session of the *Sejm* at which he was crowned king of Poland, Michał Korybut Wiśniowiecki ratified the same privilege. In the summary of this ratification drawn from the Lwów Fortress register, it is written that King Michał approved and extended the document of Zygmunt III,[96] given in Warsaw on 12 April 1588.[97] This new document not only included the previous ratifications to the Extended Privilege, but also the additions that were added to it in agreement with the various kings of Poland since Zygmunt August. This copy of the Extended Privilege, which is also recorded in the notebooks of the Charters of Rights of the Kraków Jewish community, was divided into twenty-four original clauses and seventeen additional clauses that were added up until the reign of Michał Korybut Wiśniowiecki. Another copy of the same privilege, in a slightly flawed version, was found by Josef Perles, the Rabbi of Poznań, during the years 1862–71 in the community archives.[98] In this light, Kutrzeba's claims cannot be accepted: did the authorities in Poland treat for hundreds of years the general and local privileges granted to the Jews as they would a matter of minor importance, and would they have granted full power and legal authority to these documents without endeavouring to investigate into their authenticity?

Kutrzeba's claim that the Extended Privilege contains anachronistic terms and administrative institutions[99] is also not correct. In his textbook on the history of the state and law in Poland, Juliusz Bardach, a contemporary Polish researcher, notes that the first mention of trial books in Poland existed already in 1322 and that a Kraków district book dated 1374 (close to Casimir III's date of death) was found.[100] Kutrzeba's other allegations with regard to the legitimacy of the Extended Privilege are also unfounded. It is possible that the absence of a date and the names of Casimir III's witnesses is no more than negligence on the part of the transcribers or on the part of the officials preparing the ratification by Casimir IV.[101]

It is most likely that the leaders of the Jewish community of Great Poland, in negotiating with the King and his associates for the ratification of the Extended Privilege, brought with them a copy of an ancient Charter of Rights that was rescued from the fire and riots in Poznań in the years 1399, 1447 and 1450. Therefore, it is possible that the transcribers did in fact skip over several details that seemed of marginal importance and placed an emphasis on the formulation of the anticipated ratification by Casimir IV. Forgers would certainly not have had any difficulty in noting the names of the King's advisors (mainly in the copy), and perhaps would have made a special effort to include them in the document. One can also question Kutrzeba's remark on the lengthy style of the document. Its linguistic style and external form were undoubtedly clear to the courtiers of Casimir IV. It is difficult to imagine that they could have erred or that the forgery could be easily disguised.

In response to Kutrzeba's arguments regarding formal flaws in the document under discussion, it is worth while bearing in mind what was acceptable and customary in the writings of Charters of Rights at that time. Rulers not infrequently concealed the facts relating to the origin of documents (for the most part in order to give prominence to their own deeds and authority). Others saw fit to adorn the documents with unrelated preambles and symbols in order to lend greater weight to those documents in the existing network of political and social relations. For example, Casimir III, in granting a General Privilege to the Jews of the whole of Poland (1364), did not specify in the preamble that this document was an exact copy of the Charter of Rights given to the Jews of Great Poland by his grandfather on his mother's side, Bolesław the Pious.[102] Casimir IV, who granted more extensive rights to the Jews of Great Poland, operated differently and in the preamble of the privilege did not refrain from mentioning the name of his predecessor – Casimir III. If the privilege, in its final version, was really an innovation in the days of Casimir IV as a result of intensive Jewish mediation, it is possible to view the mention of his great predecessor as a means used by Casimir IV to give additional sanction to the new privilege. But even if we assume that Casimir IV ratified a Charter of Rights completely identical to that given by his predecessor, then it is reasonable to assume that the details of the preamble of Casimir III could have been distorted at a time when the document was being prepared anew. It is important to note that in the beginning of Casimir IV's reign the formulation of royal documents was not yet standardized. Yet, already at that time, the Royal Secretariat conducted orderly record books (the books of the Royal Metrics have been retained since the year 1447) and therefore it is difficult to believe that a document such as the Extended Privilege issued to the Jews of Great Poland would have been recorded without having received official authorization and without having been thoroughly examined.[103]

The declaratory verdict which ordered the registration of the Charters of Rights of the Jews of Great Poland in the Poznan Fortress books and which appeared in Bloch's publication at the head of the document, has not yet attracted sufficient attention from legal and political reserachers in Poland. Historians have not yet conducted a thorough investigation using accepted diplomatic and hermeneutic methods. In our discussion we shall concentrate only on the issue of Casimir's title which greatly preoccupied Kutrzeba. In the verdict of the *Starosta* the King's title appears as follows: *domini Kazimiri Dei gracia regis Polonie*.[104] This version of the title indicates that in the view of the *Starosta* of Poznań, while clarifying the registration of the Extended Privilege in the Fortress books, there was no doubt that it was indeed Casimir the Great who granted the leaders of the Jews of Great Poland the privilege under discussion. On the other hand, if they were referring to Casimir IV of the House of Jagiełło, the title of the king in the above-mentioned verdict would have also included the title 'the Grand Duke of Lithuania'.[105] The absence of both the name of the *Starosta* and the date of issue of the verdict, does point to a degree of negligence in transcribing Casimir III's preamble as well as in the decision of the court given at the time of the ratification of the privilege by Casimir IV or by one of his successors.[106]

As for ascertaining the date of the declaratory verdict, it could not have been given until after the death of Casimir III (5 November 1370),[107] or until the ratification of the Extended Charter of Rights by Casimir IV in the late summer of 1453.[108] Had the above clarifications at the court of the *Starosta* of Poznań in fact taken place after the ratification of the Extended Privilege, i.e. after 13 August 1453, there would certainly have been mention in the proclamatory verdict of Casimir IV. This was not the case.

Additional evidence for refuting the claim of forgery may be found in the legal-constitutional principle which was one of the foundations of existence of the Jewish people. The Jewish community and its leadership in Poland, as in other countries, accepted totally the principle *dina de-malkhuta dina* (the law of the land is the law). This principle was internalized and strictly upheld, since the acceptance of the authority of the kingdom was one of the fundamental rules of the existence of Jewish autonomy.[109] This would provide a strong reason for Jews to avoid falsifying royal documents.

The possibility that the dignitaries of the Jewish public in Great Poland digressed from this guideline is extremely remote. It is worth mentioning that Polish historians have never produced a single case in the history of Old Poland in which it was proved that an act of forgery had been perpetrated by leaders of the Jewish community (at least with regard to a royal privilege).

The General Privileges granted to the Jews, and, first and foremost, the Extended Privilege, merit a place in the compilations of legislative material accumulated in the Old Kingdom of Poland-Lithuania, both because of their great importance to the development of law and jurisprudence in Poland, and also because of their effect on economic and social life. The compilers of the legislative documentation that was included in the codices of Łaski and Konarski, identified, it seems, with the standpoint of those social and political elements who opposed the Jewish presence and activities in Poland; the contempt, scorn and selective approach to the basic Charter of Rights of the Jews struck roots in the outlook of the legal historians in Old Poland.[110] Polish historians studying the Extended Charter of Rights that was ratified by Casimir IV, linked the absence of this privilege from the Łaski Codex and that of Konarski with an alleged act of forgery, performed by the leaders of the Jewish community of Great Poland in an attempt to secure an approval.

The doubt cast on the legitimacy and authenticity of the Extended Privilege, despite the many ratifications by the kings of Poland, aided in cultivating an atmosphere of suspicion towards the Jews among Polish circles and nurtured the recurrent and repeated calls to reduce the legal basis for Jewish activity in Poland. It is also worth recalling that several Jewish researchers attempted to rebut the allegation of forgery of the Extended Privilege. Most prominent in this area were Philip Bloch (1892),[111], Moshe Schorr (1909),[112] and Yitzhak Schipper (1909).[113] A survey of the ways in which Jewish historians in Poland have tackled the complex challenge posed by the provocative claim of Polish historiography deserves a separate comprehensive discussion.

NOTES

1 The following are typical products of Polish historiography on our subject: *Jana Długosza Kanonika*; (Łaska Jan) *Commune incliti Poloniae*; *Statuty synodalne wieluńsko – kaliskie*, pp. 91–3; *Rocznik franciszkański krakowski*; *Księgi Ustaw Polskich i Mazowieckich*, index; Bandtkie, *Jus Polonicum*, pp. 20, 212–13, 289; Hube, 'Przywilej żydowski', pp. 426–42; idem., *Statuta Nieszawskie*, pp. 153–5, 165–70; Helcel, *StPPP*, par. 92, 110, pp. 25, 110–13, 150, 291, 320, 426–7; Kutrzeba, *HZDPP*, vol. 2, pp. 297–310; idem., 'Przywileje Kazimierza', pp. 4–5; idem., 'Stanowisko prawne Żydow', pp. 1008–12; Muller, *Żydzi w Krakowie*, pp. 5, 28–30, 48; Grodecki, *Polska piastowska*, p. 648, 652, 654; Sieradzki, 'Statut kaliski', pp. 132–42; Bardach, *HPiPP*, p. 422.
2 Authentic documents relating to the Extended Privilege, before its ratification by Casimir IV on Monday, 13 August 1453, are not known; several early official registers (*oblata*) of the Extended Privilege with minor changes of version were found in several Polish archives (Poznań, Lwów and elsewhere). In the compilation 'Inscriptiones Posnanienses AD 1539', pp. 59 ff. that was examined by researchers at the Poznań State Archives in the nineteenth century, was found the version of the Extended Privilege with the ratification of Casimir IV which was copied and published from its Latin source by Philip Bloch, *Die General-Privilegien*, pp. 102–20. Another registration of this same privilege together with the ratification of King Zygmunt August (11 December 1548) was in the same archive, in the compilation *Libri Civium AD 1535–1566*, pp. 450 ff. These versions have served historians as sources for the text (see Gumplowicz, *Prawodawstwo*, pp. 161–76; Perles, *Geschichte*, pp. 129 ff; Bandtkie, *Jus Polonicum*, p. 1, Cod B III). In the Archives of the Lwów Fortress (The Bernardines), vol. C 461, folios nos. 51–74, there is an official valid register of a copy of the Extended Privilege, ratified by Casimir IV. In this same file were added to the original Charter of Rights, between the sixteenth and eighteenth centuries, ratifications on behalf of the kings of Poland. (See *AGZL*, vol. 10, nos. 107, 2073, 2385.) Also in record books of older communities such as Kraków or Poznań were copies of the Extended Privilege – however these have not survived. The publication of the text of the Privilegium in

its original version is included by F. Piekosiński in the codex of documents of Great Poland (see *CDPM*, vol. 3, no. 1368).
3 Stanisław Kutrzeba wrote: 'The last [extended] privilege is undoubtedly a crude and vulgar forgery ...' (Kutrzeba, *HZDPP*, vol. 11, p. 301). Also see Juliusz Bardach, *HPiPP*, vol. 1, p. 422.
4 Among the Jewish historians who have treated this subject: Kraushar, *Historya*, vol. pp. 139–47; W-wa 1866, pp. 12, 62, 71, 75, 78, 80; Gumplowicz, *Prawodawstwo*, pp. 32–6, 107–8, 123–56; Perles, *Geschichte*, pp. 12–14; Graetz, *Geschichte*, vol. 7, pp. 200–1, 434; Bloch, *Die General-Privilegien*, pp. 74–8, 102–20; S. Dubnow, *Divrei Yemei Am Olam*, vol. 5, Paras (clauses paragraphs), 30, 62, 63, 64; Schorr, 'Krakovskyi svod', pp. 252–9; idem., 'Die Hauptprivilegien', pp. 524, 526, 530; Bałaban, 'Pravovoy stroy', pp. 162–5, 168.
5 Lament to Rab Israel Bar Yoel, p. 137; Schipper, *Studya nad stosunkami gosp.*, pp. 62–3.
6 Ibid., pp. 152–3.
7 Questions and Answers Israel of Bruna par. 264, p. 171; Questions and Answers Maram Mintz, Salonici Press, par. 109. Lemberg Press, 1851. Par. 114. Lekszycki, *Die altesten grosspolnischen*, index; *Księga ziemska Poznańska*, index; Łukaszewicz, *Obraz*, p. 72; Schipper, 'Rozwój ludności', pp. 28–31.
8 Bałaban, *HiLZ*, vol. 2, pp. 272–3; *StPPP*, vol. 1, p. 230.
9 Ibid., pp. 269, 276.
10 Kaczmarczyk, Leśnodorski, *HPiPP*, pp. 16–17; Topolski *Dzieje*, p. 26; Lewicki, *Zarys*, pp. 114, 116, 121–3; Bobrzyński, *Dzieje*, pp. 243–5.
11 This may be seen from a hint included in the words of the pretext for the annulment of the Privileges to the Jews, that was published by Casimir IV in the Nieszawa Regulations, 1454. See Łukasiewicz, *Obraz*, vol. 2, p. 192.
12 Mueller, *Żydzi w Krakowie*, p. 28; Bałaban, *HiLZ*, vol. 2, p. 278.
13 See para. 2 in the Extended Privilege: Bloch, *Die General-Privilegien*, p. 103, 'qui habuerunt a celebris memoria serenissimo principe domino Kazimiro ...'. It is possible that this was meant to decribe a fire in Poznań (and its Jewish Quarter) in 1447 at the time of the King's visit. A fire also broke out in 1450. See Walawender, *Kronika*, p. 263; Graetz, *Geschichte*, vol. 7, pp. 207, 441.
14 In this article the word ratified will be applied to the act of Casimir IV, though it is impossible to determine whether it was he or Casimir III who was responsible for the final version of the Extended Charter of Rights to the Jews of Great Poland.
15 Bloch, op. cit., pp. 107–15; Schorr, 'Krakovskyi svod', pp. 252–4.
16 See *Rocznik franciszkański krakowski*, pp. 46–52.
17 Hofer, *Capestrano*, pp. 525–37.
18 Joannis Dlugossi, *Opera*, ad a. 1454.
19 Roman, *Przywileje*, passim; *VL*, vol. 1, fols. 247, 254 (De judaeis et eorundem juribus praescriptionibus et obligationibus).
20 Bobrzyński, *O ustawodawstwie*, pp. 36–7; *pospolite ruszenie (expeditio generalis)*, Statuta nieszawskie.
21 Ptaśnik, *Miasta*, pp. 268–9.
22 Bałaban, *HiLZ*, vol. 2, pp. 276–8; idem, *HZK*, vol. 1, pp. 51–4.
23 Schipper, *Studya*, pp. 150, 152, 172, 185. After the signing of the peace treaty at Toruń (1466) with the Teutonic Order, the Jews began to enjoy renewed economic prosperity. See Lelewel, *Dzieje Polski*, p. 122.
24 Cromer, *De Origine*, p. 372; *StPPP*, vol. 2, no. 37776; Bałaban, *HZK*, vol. 1, pp. 55–6; many Polish researchers saw in King Casimir IV a guardian of Jewish economic activity; see, for example, Ptaśnik, *Miasta*, p. 352. Also see, *Codex epistol. saec.* vol. 16, no. 57.

25 The economic and legal status of the Jews of Kraków deteriorated as a result of the pressures of the townsmen, who succeeded in expelling them from the city in 1495. Yet, the Jewish exiles devoted themselves without delay to the expansion of Kazimierz. See Bałaban, *HZK*, vol. 1, pp. 59–65.

26 Elsewhere, in Lwów, Przemyśl, Poznań, and Łęczyca, the legal and economic conditions of the Jews improved. See *RYA*, vol. 3, nos. 7, 10, 14, 18, 19, 24, 26, 30, 32, 43, 45, 47, ; L. Charewiczowa, 'Ograniczenia gospodarcze nacyi schizmackich i żydów we Lwowie 15 1 16 wieków, *Kwartalnik Historyczny*, vol. 39, (1925), zeszyt 2; M. Horn, *Żydzi na Rusi Czerwonej*, (Warsaw, 1975), pp. 16–18.

27 See Kutrzeba, *HZDPP*, vol. 11, p. 303; Block, op. cit., p. 119. It is reasonable to assume that in the event of suspicion of forgery of the Extended Privilege, Casimir would not have left it in the hands of communal dignitaries with his signature and seal on it.

28 Jan Olbracht (1459–1501), Casimir's son, ratified the banishment of the Jews of Kraków (1494–5). His brother, Alexander, who replaced him 1461–1506, expelled the Jews of Lithuania and ordered the expropriation of most of their property in 1495. Their younger brother, Zygmunt I (1467–1548), signed one of the ratified copies of the Extended Privilege. See Papee, *Jan Olbracht*, (Kraków, 1936); idem., *Aleksander Jagiellończyk*, (Kraków, 1949); Bałaban, *HZK*, vol. 1, pp. 61–5; *PSB*, vol. 10.

29 This Charter of Rights was considered a General Privilege to the Jews of Poland, and served them as a legal basis from the beginning of the sixteenth century until the Partitions. Once the Council of Four Lands was established, the text of the Privilege was guarded in the Jewish community building in Kraków, along with other privileges. When these were burned in 1655, emissaries of the Council of Four Lands received from King Jan Kazimierz newly ratified copies, which won the ratification of later kings. On the fate of these documents (they served as substitutes for older documents), see Bałaban, *HZK*, vol. 1, pp. 561, 563, 565; vol. 2, pp. 744–6. On the ratifications of the Extended Privilege, see Schorr, 'Krakovsky svod', pp. 77, 100; Bałaban, 'Pravovoy stroy', pp. 165–6; Włodarski, *Chronologia*, pp. 435–6, 482–6. Philip Bloch found that one of the copies of the Extended Privilege was also signed by King Zygmunt I (1507), Bloch, *Die General-Privilegien*, p. 145.

30 *Commune incliti Poloniae regni*; Kaczmarczyk, *Jan Łaski*, (Warsaw, 1950), passim; Kutrzeba, *HZDPP*, vol. 2, p. 302. The uncertainty concerning the date of the forgery derives as far as these historians are concerned, only from the problems inherent in the date of the formulation of the Extended Privilege. See also Hube, *Przywilej żydowski*, who acknowledges that the argument of Cardinal Oleśnicki is not based on any evidence.

31 According to a version apparently written down in a copy of the year 1334. See Bandtkie, *Jus Pol.*, p. 289; Schorr, 'Die Hauptprivilegien', pp. 521–2.

32 These words appear in *Commune incliti Poloniae regni*, f. 163: 'Quod nos Alexander rex non confirmando speciale, sed ad cautelam defensionis contra Judaeos, privilegiis regni in istum condicem digestis adscribi mandavimus.' Compare with Kutrzeba, *HZDPP*, vol. 2, p. 302; Bałaban, *HiLZ*, vol. 2, p. 283; idem., *HZK*, vol. 1, p. 105, no. 43. It should be noted that Jarosław Leitgeber, a Polish researcher of the early twentieth century, saw the publication of this privilege by Łaski as aimed explicitly and solely at emphasizing that the guidelines restricting the Jewish activity remained intact. See Leitgeber, *Z dziejów handlu*, p. 70, no. 1.

33 In the version of the privilege from the days of Bolesław the Pious, published by Bershadsky (*RYA.*, vol. 1, pp. 1–25) the subject of the discussed clause (in the Latin text) bears the number 26 (ibid., p. 16). The difference in numbering was

caused by the absence of one of the clauses of the privilege in the Łaski Codex (paragraph 23 of the Latin version), see ibid., p. 14. The two other distortions in the Charter of Rights in the Łaski Codex almost certainly derive from a faulty understanding of the text. See Gumplowicz, *Prawodawstwo*, pp. 9, 10, 141; Kutrzeba, *HZDPP*, vol. 2, p. 302; Bałaban, *HiLZ*, p. 283.

34 In Łaski's Codex it is noted: *Si judaeus super possessiones aut literas bonorum immobilium pecuniam mutuaverit, id quoque ille cujus res est probaverit. Nos judaeo et pecunias et literatum pignu adjudicari statuimus*. *VL*, vol. 1, Alexander rex inseri mandat privilegium iudaeorum concessum a Boleslao duce, f. 314 (p. 143).

35 This document is included in a collection of the ancient manuscripts in the Library of Krasiński Institution in Warsaw (Biblioteka Ordynacji Krasińskich w Warszawie). This institution and its collection was destroyed by the Nazis during the 1944 Warsaw Rising; See T. Wierzbowski, *Vademecum* (Warsaw, 1926), pp. 242, 246; *Straty Bibliotek*, index. The document was published in full by Sergei Bershadski, *RYA*, vol. 3, no. 1, pp. 3–7. See also Hube, 'Przywilej żydowski', p. 424.

36 For different reasons Casimir III decided to attribute the General Privilege to the Jews of Poland of 1364 to his own initiative. See Kaczmarczyk, *Polska*, p. 138–9. This has led Hube to conclude erroneously that the privilegium of the year 1364 was given only to the Jews of Great Poland. See Hube, op. cit., pp. 436, 438–9.

37 Clause 26 of the manuscript according to Krasiński's collection. See *RYA*, no. 1, p. 6: *Item, si iudaeus super possessiones aut literas magnatum terre pecunias mutuavesit, et hoc per suas litteras et sigillum probaverit nos iudaeo iure aliorum pignorum possessiones assignabimus obligatas, et eas contra violentias defendemus*.

38 The flaws in Hube's argument were clearly exposed with the complete publication of the document by Bershadsky, see note 35.

39 Eugen Mueller, *Żydzi w Krakowie*, pp. 23, 30–1. Mueller, a researcher who dealt, among other things, with the economic activity of Jews at the end of the fourteenth century in the region of Kraków, made extensive use of legal material describing the credit deals of the Jews. Although the explicit content of the material attests to loans given by Jews to landowners in exchange of promissory notes and mortgages, Mueller, nonetheless, accepted the arguments of the Polish historians that such deals were prohibited. He based himself on the flawed version of Clause 26 in the Charter of Rights to the Jews of Great Poland, as it appears in the Łaski Codex. Mueller did not try to verify the version of the Codex.

40 At the end of the fourteenth and the beginning of the fifteenth centuries in Poznań and elsewhere in northwestern Poland, Jewish financiers lent large sums against promissory notes and the registration of mortgages in the Court House books. See Hube, *Prawo Polskie w 14w*, p. 205; *CDPM*, 111 (Poznań, 1879), no. 1904. In the District Court House book of Poznań for 1400–7 were included dozens, if not hundreds of such deals between Jewish moneylenders and noble estate-owners and the holders of senior offices in the regional and national administration. As guarantees to those loans were usually utilized promissory notes and mortgages. See *Księga Ziemska Poznańska*, nos. 382, 696, 816, 829, 830, 857, 901, 906, 946, 1594, 2206, 2826. Compare this with Eisenstein, *Die Stellung*, pp. 108–9.

41 In the Fortress books of the various towns of Great Poland were registered between 1380s and the second decade of the next century hundreds of Jewish loans to noble landowners as against mortgages of real estate, mainly against promissory notes and obligatories. See, for example, Lekszycki, *Die aeltesten grosspolnischen*, vol. 1, nos. 25, 40, 53, 95, 345, 382, 832, 888, 2376, 2787; vol. 2, nos. 1188, 1357, 1393, 1486, 1635, 2466.

42 The Register books of the court houses of Mazowsze (particularly in Płock and its

surrounding area) were examined by S. Trunk. Here are mentioned numerous credit negotiations of Jewish moneylenders with local noble landowners dating prior to 1437 – all of these are against notes and mortgages. In certain cases, when the debts were not met after several postponements of the date of payment, the Jewish creditors took over the holding or ownership of the debtor's land assets. It is also interesting to note that in mid-fourteenth century Mazowsze, there were deals also on urban property between Jewish moneylenders and their Christian clients as against promissory notes and mortgages. See Trunk, *Płock*, pp. 5, 14 and also Ringelblum, 'Ze Studyjów', pp. 322–4. Mazowsze became part of the Kingdom of Poland only after the end of the first quarter of the fifteen century. As a result, the Warka statutes (1423) were not in force here.

43 In 1390, Lewko, a well-known Kraków banker, lent the enormous sum of 500 marks to the King of Poland, against the King's own promissory note. In addition senior nobles of the court accepted the obligation of paying the capital in full with interest, if the King were unable to meet his obligations. See Bałaban, *HŻK*, vol. 1, p. 16, 18. A similar case occurred in 1405 when the sons of a nobleman of the Szczekociński family paid to the Jew, Canaan of Kraków, their father's debt to the sum of 3000 Hungarian florins, which was their father's share in a guarantee given at the time to the Jewish moneylender of a loan granted to Louis of Anjou, King of Hungary. See Helcel, *StPPP*, vol. 11, no. 1106. On Canaan see Bałaban, *HŻK*, vol. 1, pp. 16, 20–1.

44 The *Sejm* constitution was promulgated on 28 October 1423 in the city of Warta by King Władysław Jagełło. In abrogating Clause 19, the constitution relied on the regulations accepted at the Synod of the Church in Poland, held in Wieluń and Kalisz in 1420 under the leadership of the Archbishop Mikołaj Trąba, who had been head of the Polish delegation to the Council of Constance (Silnicki, *Mikołaj Trą*ba, pp. 170, 181, 185; *VL*, vol. 1, pp. 32, 111). According to Roman, this constitution was published in the year 1356–7. Roman St., *Geneza Statutów Kazimierza Wielkiego*, (Kraków, 1961), pp. 44, 153–4, note 161.

45 That this clause enabled Jewish financiers to grant credit to clients of the upper classes is evident from the version of the relevant clause in the Charter of Rights to the Jews of Austria, granted by the Duke Friedrich the Warrior on 1 July 1244. See Scherer, *Die Rechtsverhaeltnisse*, p. 183, no. 25. This same version was later incorporated into the Charters of Rights received by the Jews of Hungary (1251) and Bohemia (1254).

It is worth noting that in an article on the Privilege of Bolesław the Pious (J. Sieradzki, 'Statut Kaliski') the author does not discuss the controversial Clause 26 of the Charter of Rights of the Jews of Great Poland (1264) and stresses the alleged generosity of Bolesław the Pious toward the Jews. He also attempts to absolve the Jews of Poland of the thirteenth and fourteenth centuries of any blame for making the granting of credit their main source of livelihood (see ibid., p. 137).

46 Barycz, *Szlakami*, p. 23 stresses the 'propagandistic tendency' in the Łaski Codex.
47 Schipper, *Studya*, pp. 75, 88–91; Kutrzeba, *HŻDPP*, vol. 11, p. 203.
48 Roman Grodecki in his history of Jews in Poland up to the end of the fourteenth century adhered to Łaski's approach, and, like him, ignored other Charters of Rights granted to the Jews during the days of Casimir III (Grodecki, *Polska Piastowska*, pp. 646, 648, 652, 654).
49 In Latin: *privilegia falcissima* (in the plural). See note 52.
50 See *SJP* (D), vol. 7, p. 727, no. 6.
51 ' ... jeśli chodzi o wiarę ...'. Its being dealt with on matters concerning the Catholic faith.
52 '... Teraz wszelako nie wszystko, lecz co najbardziej dojmuje opowiem. Dawniej

WKM ... pewnych przywilejów i wolności Żydom udzieliłeś, jaky przez króla Kazimierza im nadane, które ś.p. Rodzic Twój w mojej obecności, gdym sam tego był świadkiem i samem te zmyślone przywileje czytał [in Latin it is written in the neuter plural: *privilegia falcissima] lubo ujmowany wiela darami przez Żydów, wzbraniał się potwierdzić, i te WKM zatwierdziłeś, nie zniósłszy się ani zemną*, który wówczas w Krakowie bawiłem, ani z Panami rad, a co większa na niektóre w nich punkta, wierze i religii chrześciańskiej przeciwne przyzwoliłeś ...' '... Nie chcieś WKM, lekce sobie tego ważyć, ani rozumiej, iż w rzeczach wiary i religii chrześciańskiej możesz stanowić coć się podoba. Nikt nie jest tak wielkim i tak potężnym, żeby nie można mu się oprzeć gdzie chodzi o wiarę! I dlatego proszę i błagam, abyś WKM te tam przywileje i wolności odwołać raczył. Pokaż WKM, że jesteś Królem katolickim i usuń wszelki powód do niesławy Twego imienia i do prawdopodobnych większych jeszcze zgorszeń.'

Wiszniewski, *Kronikarstwo polskie*, pp. 80–1; Codex epistolaris saeculi decimi quinti, vol. 3, 1392–1501. (Kraków, 1879), *Monum. Medii Aevi*, vol. 2, p. 146; Dzieduszycki, *Oleśnicki*, vol. 2, p. 481.

53 As for the word *falcissima*, see Lexicon IV (fasc. 29), p. 57, E 2, 3. Also see Schipper, *Przegląd*, nos. 6, 8, 12; Eisenberg, *Die Stellung*, pp. 115–6, 120.
54 See the excerpt from the *History of Poland* by Długosz, op. cit. p. 8, as well as note 18.
55 See Bloch, *Die General Privilegien*, pp. 109–10, 112.
56 A policy similar to that of Casimir IV was followed by Casimir III in the Charters of Rights to the Jews from 1364 and 1367. See Bałaban, *HiLŻ*, vol. 11, pp. 268–9.
57 See Bałaban, *HŻK*, vol. 1, pp. 44–8, 50–2; Hofer, *Capestrano*, index.
58 See *PSB*, vol. 5, pp. 176–80; Bobrzyński, *Długosz*, index.
59 *Joannis Dlugossi seu Longini Historia Polonica Libri XII*, (Frankfurt, 1711), liber 9, columna 1110, sub a. 1356.
60 Wyrozumski, who based himself on Długosz, nonetheless doubts Długosz's argument that the influence of the concubine Esther led to the ratification of the Privilege to the Jews. See J. Wyrozumski, *Kazimierz Wielki*, (Wrocław, 1982), p. 212.
61 Sułkowska-Kurasiowa, *Polska Kancelaria*, pp. 43–7, 59–68; idem., *Dokumenty Królewskie*, pp. 21–4, 79–81.
62 Note the clash, basically economic in character, between Długoszem and the Kraków Jewish community, in the 1460s. Długosz tried to acquire a considerable part of the Jewish quarter and did so after considerable pressure and threats. This confrontation weakened the position of the local community against the incessant attacks of the townsmen, leading to their eventual expulsion. See Chmiel, *Zbiór dokumentów*, no. 20, pp. 35–7; Bałaban, *HŻK*, vol. 1, pp. 56–65.
63 Compare Wadding, *Annales Minorum*, vol. 12, p. 195; Hofer, *Capestrano*, pp. 535–6; Kraushar, *Historja*, vol. 11, p. 80; 'Przywileje nierozważnie Żydom już przyznane i niesłusznie nieprzyjaciołom Krzyża udzielone, odwołaj i sprowadź do dotychczasowej formy.'
64 See Hofer, op. cit., pp. 525–8, 535–6; Wadding, op. cit., p. 197.
65 Ibid., ibid.
66 See note 39.
67 *Jana Ostroroga Pamiętnik, ku pożytkowi Rzeczypospolitej zebrany*, ed. T. Wierzbowski, (Warsaw 1891), p. 23; A. Pawiński, *Jana Ostroroga żywot i pismo o naprawie Rzeczypospolitej*, (Warsaw, 1884).
68 *Tractatus de natura iurium et bonorum regis ... Quem in lucem*, ed. Stanislaus Zaborowski, *StPPP*, vol. 5, pars. 1 (Kraków, 1878), p. 17.
69 *Respublica Polona proceribus Polonis in conventu generalis A.D. 1543*, Cracoviae

congregationis salutem, *Orichoviana*, Operat inedita 1543–66, *Biblioteka Pisarzów Polskich*, vol. 19, (Kraków, 1891), p. 22.

70 It is possible to connect the argument of Orzechowski to Clause No. 1 and also (partially, at least) to Clause 43 of the Extended Privilege. These clauses were designated to defend Jewish economic activity and it seems that they were vital to its existence. See Bloch, *Die General Privilegien*, pp. 104–5, 117–18.

71 See note 69.

72 For example, Lublin, Kraków, Wilno, Poznań, Gniezno, Toruń. Compare *Diarjusze sejmowe*, p. 60.

73 *Materiały do Dziejów Sejmu*, pp. 78–93.

74 Compare *Istorii Evreiskogo naroda*, vol. 11 (Moskva, 1915), pp. 273–7; Bałaban, *HiLŻ*, vol. 11, pp. 321–5, 347; Surowiecki, *O upadku*, pp. 116, 230–57. Surowiecki tries to refute the opinion that the Jews caused the decline of the towns in Poland (ibid., p. 230). He also notes the role played by Jews in helping to introduce more advanced economic methods into the Polish economy, see *Lustracja woj. łęczyckiego*, pp. 16–17.

75 See *VL*, volumes 1–7, Konarski, one of the leaders of the Polish enlightenment was among the heads of the Piarist Order and was active in the education of the sons of higher nobility. See *PSB*, vol. 13, pp. 471–7; Konopczyński, *Polscy pisarze*, pp. 59, 70, 75, 85, 88, 131, 156, 160, 185.

76 *VL*, vol. 1, fols. 309–16.

77 *Inwertarz Praw, Statutów, Konstytucyi Koronnych y WXL przedrukownych*, (Warsaw, 1789), pp. 36, 123–4, 258, 261–2, 266–7, 271, 273, 276–8, 281, 289, 324–30, 334, 337, 342–3, 390, 456, 620–4; *Inwentarz Nowy Praw*, (Warsaw, 1782), pp. 82–5, 91–2, 94–6, 166.

78 It is clear that Konarski and his assistants from the Piarist Order read with great scrutiny all the constitutional documents in the Register Books of the King's Secretariat and the Grand Duke of Lithuania. Among them may be found the registrations of the General Privileges granted to the Jews. According to Władysław Smoleński: 'The learned Konarski refused to publish at the opening of his Compilation of Laws the most ancient of all the documents of Polish legislation, since he believed that it was not proper to open such a codex with a document relating to a tribe with such wayward moral standards.' See Smoleński, *Stan i prawa*, p. 26; Gumplowicz, *Prawodawstwo*, pp. 121–2.

79 In 'Rozmowa Ziemianina ze swym sąsiadem o teraźniejszych okolicznościach', (Konarski, *Pisma Wybrane*, vol. 1) Konarski preaches the need to strengthen the King's rule and also the state bureaucracy and military.

80 Ibid., A, pp. 126, 128; St. Konarski, *O Skutecznym rad sposobie*.

81 See Bloch, *Die General-Privilegien*, pp. 102–4. The version of the titles of Casimir III that are registered in the Preamble of the Extended Privilege is slightly different from that which appears in the Charter of Rights to the Jews of Little Poland that received its approval on 25 April 1367 (see Bloch, op. cit., p. 12).

82 Kutrzeba, 'Stanowisko prawne Żydów', pp. 1008–11; idem, 'Przywileje Kazimierza', pp. 4–5.

83 Kutrzeba, *HŻDPP*, vol. 11, pp. 301–2.

84 Ibid., p. 301.

85 Kutrzeba, 'Stanowisko prawne Żydów', p. 1009.

86 See *SJP* (D), vol. 5, p. 469; *SJP* (L), vol. 3, p. 391. According to the opinion of K. Liske, who examined thousands of documents of the sort, only a few belong to the mid-eleventh century. *AGŻL*, vol. 10, pp. v, vi.

87 The Statutes of the Wojewoda Tęczyński from 1527: Bałaban, *HŻK*, vol. 1, p. 365; a judicial statute by King Zygmunt August from 1554; ibid., pp. 361–2; a statute

for the Jews of Lwów ratified by the King in 1569; Pazdro, *Organizacja i praktyka*, p. 163; the statutes of the Wojewoda Czarniecki from the year 1660; ibid., pp. 171–5. Many other examples could be cited.

88 See *AGZL*, p. 7, no. 107 in the Books of the Secretariat of Lwów Fortress, in vol. 461, pp. 55–68.

89 'W Krakowie, 13 sierpnia 1453 r. Kazimierz Jagiellończyk potwierdza i rozszerza prawa, które Kazimierz W. przyznał żydom.' A researcher into the history of Polish law, Oswald Balzer ascribes the ratification by Casimir IV of the Charter of Rights of Bolesław the Pious to 'the forgery of the Jewish Privilege of Casimir the Great'. See: Balzer, *Corpus iuris*, pp. 35, 46, (no. 21:5) p. 61, no. 154. He accepts as self-evident that the privilege of Casimir the Great is the privilege of Bolesław the Pious, which was forged by the Jews.

90 It is reasonable to assume that with the ratification of the Privilege the Jews hastened to provide for copies to it and to confirm validation by having them legally registered.

91 Confirmation of the view that Casimir IV extended the rights granted to the Jews by Casimir III may be found in the version of the privilege published by P. Bloch. The final section of the second preamble reads: '... idem jura innovare ratificare et confirmare dignaremur gracoise'. Bloch, *Die General Privilegien*, p. 103. (This version is also cited by Kutrzeba, Kutrzeba, *HZDPP*, vol. 11, p. 309.) The usual meaning of 'confirmare' in Poland in the fifteenth century is 'to grant', 'to strengthen' (*Lexicon, fasc.*, vol. 14, pp. 936, 939). The term in this case served as a formula which enabled Casimir to extend the rights of the Jews of Great Poland beyond those granted to them in the previous Charter of Rights.

92 For registrations of the Extended Privilege made in other Register Books, see Schorr, 'Krakovskyi svod', pp. 252–3, 259; 'Die Hauptprivilegien', p. 532.

93 *AGZL*, vol. 10, p. 52, no. 787, cf. 461, pp. 54–69; see also Bloch, op. cit., pp. 119–20.

94 *AGZL*, vol. 10, p. 137, no. 2073, cf. 461, pp. 53–70; This document is several pages longer than its predecessor because of the addition of the ratification of the privilege registered in the Books of the Lwów Fortress during the days of Zygmunt August's reign.

95 *AGZL*, vol. 10, p. 155, no. 2385, cf. 461, pp. 52–70.

96 In the text the phrase 'to the Jews', which is self explanatory is missing.

97 *AGZL*, vol. 10, p. 308, no. 5128, cf. 461, pp. 51–74.

98 See Perles, *Geschichte*, pp. 12, 22, n. 25. The version in Latin that Bloch published was divided into 46 main clauses: Bloch, op. cit., pp. 102–20. See also the version with the 24 clauses in Gumplowicz, *Prawodawstwo*, pp. 161–76. A. Tomczak holds that the ratification of the Extended Privilege of 13 August 1453 can also be found in the Fortress Register Books of Łęczyca (Great Poland); it was kept there in the Town Archive at least until 1820. This leads Tomczak to accept the view that Casimir IV ratified the rights granted to the Jews by one of his predecessors, above all Casimir III and extended them in the above privilege. Tomczak, *Lustracja woj. łęczyckiego*, p. 11. This privilege is also mentioned by the Mayor of Łęczyca, Jan Kuber (before 23 August 1820) who links it with the activities of Bolesław and Casimir. See Kaczmarek, *Źródła*, no. 37, pp. 139–40.

99 Libri castrenses, Libri terrestres, Tabulae iudicii.

100 Bardach, *HPiPP*, vol. 1, p. 379. According to his words (ibid.) in the second half of the fourteenth century it is possible to divide Law Books into two types: District Books and Fortress Books. It is not impossible, therefore, that in the mid-fourteenth century registrations were made in the District Books.

101 See Schorr, 'Krakovskyi svod', p. 255.

102 See above, p. 289 and also note 36.
103 Maleczyński, *Rozwój dokumentów*, pp. 244, 267, 270–2.
104 See *Zbiór*, vol. 8, nos. 2530, 2533, 2536; Bloch, op. cit., p. 102.
105 Compare *Zbiór*, vol. 3, no. 799, 800, 802, 834, 836, 839, 847; vol. 8, nos. 2506, 2512, 2521; *VL*, vol. 1, pp. 68, 72, 83, 88; Wuttke, *Posen*, pp. 59, 61, 64–5, 67, 69.
106 For examples of registrations in the Fortress Books of Great Poland from the end of the fourteenth century containing details of names of holders of offices who sat in judgement and the dates of verdicts, compare vols. 1 and 2 of the collection (compilation) of documents published by Lekszycki. The concluding paragraph of the Extended Charter of Rights to the Jews of Great Poland which includes the ratification of Casimir IV (see Bloch, pp. 119–20) is additional evidence of the authenticity of the whole document; the King and his close assistants who were present on the occasion of its signing and who included the most senior members of the ruling élite approved the Charter of Rights. This fact by itself proves that the Privilege was examined in all its details by those people usually responsible for the issuing of official documents. The text of the whole privilege was prepared for signature according to the command of the Chancellor Jan of Koniecpole and his Deputy, Peter of Szczekocin and was handed over in a ceremonial occasion to the Jewish dignitaries of Great Poland by the Chancellor himself. There is no reason therefore to doubt its legitimacy.
107 Written there is 'sacre regie majestatis'.
108 Gąsiorowski, *Starostowie wielkopolskich miast*, p. 59.
109 See, for example, Ben Sasson, *The History of the Jewish People* (Hebrew), vol. 2, pp. 110–13; Allon, *Ha-Mishpat ha-Ivri* (Hebrew), pp. 354–5, 639, 642, 661–2. The constitutional implications of the maxim 'the law of the land is the law' (*dina de-Malkhuta dina*)for Jewish life in Old Poland were not discussed exhaustively in the rabbinical literature, since at that period no fundamental dispute on this issue arose within the Jewish community. It has also not aroused much interest among the historians of Polish Jewry. Z. Falk, ('On the clarification of the constitutional perception', p. 86) reached the conclusion that the Jews obeyed the basic laws which governed them, including Charters of Rights and privileges of any kind, because of the general rule of *dina de-Malkhuta dina*. He also alludes to the standpoint of Rabbenu Tam. Urbach (*The Ba'alei Tosafot*, p. 323) held the opinion that the rule of *dina de-Malkhuta dina* held sway for the Jewish community in those cases where it was a question of obeying privileges and basic laws that were established by the early rulers. He bases himself on the judgement of the MaHaRaM Bar Baruch. One could also add the opinion of the Rashba who claims that 'every land of a Monarch is his property and he may tell you that if you do not obey his commands, he will expel you from the country' (Innovations of the Rashba, *Nedarim*, 28A in the name of Rabbi Elazar ben Shmuel of Metz). A similar opinion on the validity of the kings' laws was also expressed by Shlomo Luria, one of the greatest Jewish scholars in Poland in the mid-sixteenth century (MaHaRaShaL, *Baba-Kama*, chapter 6, par. 14). Shilo (*Dina de-Malkhuta Dina*, pp. 68, 79, 83, 143, 147–9) examines the constitutional aspect of the maxim and relies on the opinion of the RaMaA who claimed that constitutional legislation which was accepted at the time by the Jewish community has to be respected (*Shulhan Arukh, Hoshen Hamishpat*, 369, par. 11). Shilo also stresses (p. 146) that the Rabbis saw in official commands of rulers to act in accordance with the laws of the kingdom a confirmation of the validity of the principle. The scholars of *halakha* (Jewish law) did not often refer this principle explicitly, perhaps because they saw it as standing beyond any debate.
110 The arguments of the best Polish researchers (St.Staszic, J. W. Bandtke, A. Helcel,

R. Hube, W. Łozinski, Eug. Muller and others) were used by others for polemical purposes, for example: Marylski, *Dzieje Sprawy Żydowskiej*, pp. 35, 89–90; Jeske-Choinski, *Historia*, pp. 74–6, 91–2; Zawadzki, *Polska*, pp. 52–4.

111 Philip Bloch was the first researcher to examine thoroughly the Extended Privilege to the Jews of Great Poland. He made important efforts to refute misleading assumptions that were widespread on this question at the time. See Bloch, op. cit., pp. 62–79, 102, 120.

112 Professor M. Schorr, when examining the Note Book of the Charters of Rights of the Kraków community (Sumaryusz przywilejow) in preparation for publication, devoted some attention to refuting the claims of some historians, who saw in the above Extended Privilege a forged document. See Schorr, 'Krakovskyi svod', pp. 252–9; idem., 'Die Hauptprivilegien', pp. 524–9; idem., *Organizacya Żydów w Polsce*, p. 8.

113 Y. Schipper investigated the circumstances of the granting of the Extended Privilege during the last years of the reign of Casimir III. See Schipper, 'Przegląd', no. 12.

REFERENCES

AGZL – *Akta Grodzkie i Ziemskie z czasów Rzeczypospolitej z Archiwum tzw. bernardyńskiego we Lwowie*, I–XXV, Lwów 1868–1925.

AVAK – *Akty izdavayemye Vilenskoyu Archeograf. Kommissiyeyu (Vilenskoy Kommisyeyu dla razbora drevnich aktov)*. I–XXXVIII, Vilna 1865–1914.

AYZR – *Archiv yugo-zapadnoy Rossii izd. Kommissiyeyu dla razbora drevnih aktov*, parts 1–8 (v. XXVII), Kiev 1859–1911.

Bałaban, *Dzieje* – M. Bałaban, *Dzieje Żydów w Galicji i Rzeczypospolitej Krakowskiej*. Lwów 1914.

Bałaban, HiLZ – idem, *Historia i Literatura Żydowska*, v. II–III, Lwów 1920–1925.

Bałaban, HZK – idem, *Historia Żydów w Krakowie i na Kazimierzu, v. 1:1304–1655*. Kraków 1931.

Bałaban, 'Pravovoy Stroy' – idem, 'Pravovoy stroy yevreyev v Polshe', *Yevreyskaya Starina*, II (1910), p. 39–59, 161–191, 324–345.

Balzer, *Corpus Iuris* – O. Balzer, *Corpus Iuris Polonici medii aevi, Program wydania zbioru ustaw polskich sredniowicznych oraz regesta tychże ustaw*. Lwów 1891.

Bandtkie, *Jus Polonicum* – J. W. Bandtkie, *Jus Polonicum Codicibus veteribus manuscriptis et editionibus*, W-wa 1831.

Bardach, *HPiPP* – J. Bardach, *Historia Państwa i Prawa Polski do polowy XV wieku*, W-wa 1957.

Bartoszewicz, *Antysemityzm w Literaturze* – K. Bartoszewicz, *Antysemityzm w Literaturze Polskiej XV–XVII w.*, W-wa 1914.

Barycz, *Szlakami* – H. Barycz, *Szlakami Dziejopisarstwa Staropolskiego*, Wrodaw 1981.

Bersohn, *Dyplomaturyusz* – M. Bersohn, *Dyplomataryusz dotyczący Żydów w dawnej Polsce*, W-wa 1910.

Bloch, *Die General-Privilegien* – Ph. Bloch, *Die General-Privilegien der polnischen Judenschaft* Posen 1892.

Bobrzyński, *Długosz* – M. Bobrzyński St. Smolka, *Jan Długosz, jego życie i stanowisko w piśmiennictwie*, Kraków 1893.

Bobrzyński, *Dzieje* – M. Bobrzyński, *Dzieje Polski w zarysie. Szkice i studja historyczne*, I Kraków 1927.

Bobrzyński, *O ustawodawstwie* – idem, *O ustawodawstwie nieszawskiem Kazimierza Jagiellończyka*, Kraków (U.J.) 1873.

Brann, *Geschichte* – M. Brann, *Geschichte der Juden in Schlesien*, Breslau 1896.
Brückner, *Dzieje Kultury* – A. Brückner, *Dzieje Kultury polskiej*, I–IV, W-wa 1946–1958.
CDPM – *Codex Diplomaticus Poloniae Majoris*, ed. F. Piekosiński, I–V, Posnaniae 1877–1908
Chmiel, *Zbiór dokumentów* – A. Chmiel, *Zbiór dokumentów znajdujących się w Bibliotece hr. Przeździeckich w W-wie*, Kraków 1890.
Commune incliti Poloniae regni privilegium . . . – *(Laski Jan) Commune incliti Poloniae regni . . .*
Cromer, *De origine* – M. Cromer, *De origine et rebus gestis Polonorum*.
Diarjusze sejmowe – *Diarjusze sejmowe z wieku 18, III*, ed. Wł. Konopczyński, W-wa 1937.
Dzieduszycki, *Oleśnicki* – Dzieduszycki, *Zbigniew Oleśnicki*, Kraków 1854.
Encycl. Jud. – *Encyclopaedia Judaica*, Jerusalem 1971, I–XVI.
Glatman, *Szkice* – L. Glatman, *Szkice historyczne*, Kraków 1906.
Graetz, *Geschichte* – H. Graetz, *Geschichte der Juden*, Vierte Ausgabe.
Grodecki, *Polska piastowska* – R. Grodecki, 'Dzieje Żydów w Polsce do końca 14 wieku', *Polski piastowska*, W-wa 1969, pp. 595–702.
Gumplowicz, *Prawodawstwo* – L. Gumplowicz, *Prawodawstwo polskie względem Żydów*, Kraków 1867.
Helcel, *StPPP* – A. Helcel, *Starodawne Prawa Polskiego Pomnikie*, I, W-wa 1856.
Heppner, Herzberg, *Aus Vergangenheit* – A. Heppner-J. Herzberg, *Aus Vergangenheit und Gegenwart der Juden in Posen*, Koschmin 1914.
Historia Polski – *Historia Polski*, ed. H. Łowmiański, I, W-wa 1969.
Hofer, *Capestrano* – I. Hofer, *Johannes von Capestrano. Ein Leben in Kampf um die Reform der Kirche*, Wien 1936.
Hube, *Prawo polskie w 14 w.* – R. Hube, *Prawo polskie w 14 wieku. Sądy i ich praktyka*. W-wa 1886.
Hube, 'Przywilej żydowski' – idem, 'Przywilej żydowski Bolesława i jego potwierdzenia', *Bibliotece Warszawska*, CLXXV (1880), pp. 426–439.
Hube, *Statuta Nieszawskie* – idem, *Statuta Nieszawskie z 1454 roku*, W-wa 1875.
Jana Długosza Kanonika – *Jana Długosza Kanonika Krakowskiego Dziejów Polski Ksiąg dwanaście, przekład K. Mecherzyńskiego*, V, Kraków 1870, ad A.D. 1454.
Jeske-Choiński, *Historia* – T. Jeske-Choiński, *Historia Żydów w Polsce*, W-wa 1919.
Joannis Dlugosi, *Opera* – *Joannis Dlugosi, Senioris Canonici Cracoviensis Opera Omnia cura. Przeździecki*, V, Cracoviae 1867.
Kaczmarczyk, Leśnodorski, *HPiPP* – Z. Kaczmarczyk-B. Leśnodorski, *Historia Państwa i Prawa Polski*, II (do 1795r.), W-wa 1957.
Kaczmarczyk, *Polska* – Z. Kaczmarczyk, *Polska czasów Kazimierza Wielkiego*, Kraków 1964.
Kaczmarek, *Źródła* – R. Kaczmarek, *Źródła do historii miast łódzkiego okręgu przemysłowego*, W-wa 1958.
KDW – *Kodeks dyplomatyczny Wielkopolski*
Kitowicz, *Opis* – J. Kitowicz, *Opis obyczajów za panowania Augusta II*, Wrocław 1950.
Konarski, *Pisma wybrane* – St. Konarski, *Pisma wybrane*, I–II, W-wa 1955.
Konopczyński, *Polscy pisarze* – W. Konopczyński, *Polscy pisarze polityczni 18 wieku*. W-wa 1966.
Kraushar, *Historya* – A. Kraushar, *Historya Żydów w Polsce*, I–II, W-wa 1865–1866.
Księga ziemska poznańska – *Księga ziemska poznańska 1400–1407*, ed. K. Kaczmarczyk-K. Rzyski, Poznań 1960.
Księga Ustaw Polskich i Mazowieckich – *Księgi Ustaw Polskich i Mazowieckich staraniem Lelewela drukiem ogłoszone*. Wilno 1824.
Kutrzeba, *HZDPP* – St. Kutrzeba, *Historia Źródel Dawnego Prawa Polskiego*, I–II, Lwów 1925–1926.

Kutrzeba, 'Przywileje Kazimierza W.' – idem, 'Przywileje Kazimierza Wielkiego dla Żydów', *Sprawozdania z czynności i posiedzeń PAU*, XXVII, XII, 1922, N. 10, pp. 4–5.
Kutrzeba, 'Sądownictwo nad żydami'– idem, 'Sądownictwo nad żydami', *Przegląd Prawa i Administracyi*. XXVII (1902), pp. 925–945.
Kutrzeba, 'Stanowisko prawne Żydów' – idem, 'Stanowisko prawne Żydów w Polsce w 15 stuleciu', *Przewodnik Naukowy i Literacki*, XXIX (Lwów 1901), pp. 1007–1018, 1146–1155.
Kutrzeba, 'Studya' – idem, 'Studya do historii sądownictwa', *Przegląd prawa i administracyi*. XXVII (1902). pp. 828–849.
Kutrzeba, 'Życie społeczne' – idem, 'Życie społeczne, *Kultura Staropolska, Materiały do zjazdu im. Jana Kochanowskiego (8–10, VI, 1930)*. Kraków 1932, pp. 19–39.
(Łaski Jan), *Commune incliti Poloniae* – (Łaski Jan), *Commune incliti Poloniae regni privilegium et constitutionem indultuum publicitus decretorum aprobatorumque cum nonnullis iuribus tam divinis quem humanis per Allexandrum . . . Regum Poloniae*. [Kraków] 1506.
Leitgeber, *Z dziejów handlu* – I. Leitgeber, *Z dziejów handlu i kupiectwa poznańskiego w dawnej rzeczypospolitej*. Poznań 1929.
Lekszycki, *Die ältesten grosspolnischen* – I. von Lekszycki, *Die ältesten grosspolnischen Grodbücher*, I–II, Leipzig 1887–1889.
Lelewel, *Dzieje Polski* – J. Lelewel, *Dzieje Polski potocznym sposobem opowiedziane, Dzieła*, VII, W-wa 1961.
Lewicki, *Zarys* – A. Lewicki, *Zarys historii Polski (do r. 1795)*, London 1944.
Lexicon – *Lexicon Mediae et Infamae Latinitatis Polonorum*, I–V (fasc. 1–41), Wrocław 1955–1982.
Łukasiewicz, *Obraz* – J. Łukasiewiez, *Obraz historyczno-statystyczny miasta Poznania w dawnych czasach*, I–II, Poznań 1838.
Lustracja woj. łęczyckiego – Lustracja województwa i powiatu łęczyckiego roku 1789, ed. A. Tomczak, W-wa 1977.
Maleczyński, *Rozwój dokumentu* – K. Maleczyński, *Rozwój dokumentu polskiego od XI do XV w.*, Wrocław 1971.
Marylski, *Dzieje sprawy żydowskiej* – A. Marylski, *Dzieje sprawy żydowskiej w Polsce*. W-wa 1912.
Materiały do dziejów Sejmu – Materiały do dziejów Sejmu Czteroletniego, VI, ed. A. Eisenbach, E. Rostworowski, J. Woliński, Wrodaw 1969.
Moszczyński, *Pamiętnik* – A. Moszczyński, *Pamiętnik do historyi polskiej*, Poznań 1858.
Müller, *Żydzi w Krakowie* –Eug. Müller, *Żydzi w Krakowie w drugiej połowie 14 stulecia*. Kraków 1906.
Olszewski, *Sejm* – H. Olszewski, *Sejm rzeczypospolitej epoki oligarchii (1652–1763)*, Poznań 1966.
Otwinowski, *Pamiętniki*, – E. Otwinowski, *Pamiętniki do panowania Augusta II*, Poznań 1838.
PAU – Polska Akademia Umiejętności.
Pazdro, *Organizacja i praktyka* – Z. Pazdro, *Organizacja i praktyka żydowskich sądów podwojewodzińskich*. Lwów 1906.
Perles, *Geschichte* – I. Perles, *Geschichte der Juden in Posen*. Breslau 1865.
PSB – *Polski Słownik Biograficzny*, I–XXV, Kraków 1935–1982.
Ptaśnik, *Miasta* – J. Ptaśnik, *Miasta i mieszczaństwo w dawnej Polsce*. Kraków 1934.
Riabinin, *Materiały* – J. Riabinin, *Materiały do historii Lublina*, Lublin 1938.
Ringelblum, 'Ze studjów' – E. Ringelblum, 'Ze studjów nad dziejami Żydów na Mazowszu'. *Przegląd Historyczny*. XXVI (1926), pp. 299–339.
Rocznik franciszkański krakowski – Rocznik franciszkański krakowski, Monum. Poloniae Histor., III, W-wa 1961.
Roman, *Przywileje* – St. Roman, *Przywileje nieszawskie*, W-wa 1957.

RYA – *Russko-Yevreyski Archiv*, ed. S. A. Bershadskyi, I–III, SPb 1882–1903.
Scherer, *Die Rechtsverhaeltnisse* – I. E. Scherer, *Die Rechtsverhaeltnisse der Juden in der deutsch-oesterreichischen Laedem*, Leipzig 1901.
Schipper, 'Przegląd' – I. Schipper, 'Przegląd krytyczny literatury odnoszący się do historii Żydów', *Wschód*, 1909, No. 8–12.
Schipper, 'Rozwój ludności' – idem, 'Rozwój ludności żydowskiej na ziemiach dawnej Rzeczypospolitej', *Żydzi w Polsce Odrodzonej*. I, W-wa 1932, pp. 21–36.
Schipper, *Studya nad stosunkami gosp.* – idem, *Studya nad stosunkami gospodarczymi Żydów Polsce podczas średniowiecza*, Lwów 1911.
Schorr, 'Die Hauptprivilegien' – M. Schorr, 'Die Hauptprivilegien der polnischen Judenschaft.' *Festschrift Adolf Schwartz zum Siebzigsten Geburtstage*, Berlin 1917, pp. 519–538.
Schorr, 'Krakovskyi svod' – idem, 'Krakovskyi svod yevreyskih statutov i privilegyi', *Yevreyskayz Starina*, I (1909), pp. 247–264; II (1910), pp. 76–100, 223–245.
Schorr, *Organizacja Żydów w Polsce* – idem, *Organizacja Żydów w Polsce (az do r. 1792)*. Lwów 1899.
Silnicki, *Mikołaj Trąba* – T. Silnicki, *Arcybiskup Mikołaj Trąba*, W-wa 1954.
Skarga, *Żywot* – P. Skarga, *Żywot Szymona z Trydentu, Żywoty świętych*.
Smoleński, *Stan i prawa* – W. Smoleński, *Stan i prawa Żydów polskich w XVIII wieku*. W-wa 1876.
Smolka St. – St. Smolka, Bobrzyński, *Długosz*.
Sommersberg, *Silesicarum rerum* – F. M. Sommersberg, *Silesicarum rerum scriptores aliquce adhunc inediti, accedunt codicis Silesiae diplomatici*, I–III, Lipsiae-Vratislaviae 1729–1732; II, *Diplomatarii Bohemo-Silesiaci continuatio*, Lipsiae 1730; III, *Silesicarum rei historicae et genealogiae accessiones*, Vratislaviae 1732.
Statuta nieszawskie – *Statuta nieszawskie. Księgi Ustaw polskich i mazowieckich staraniem J. Lelewela drukiem ogloszonych*, W-wa 1824.
Statuty Kazimierza W. – *Statuty Kazimierza Wielkiego. cz. II, Statuty Wielkopolskie*, ed. L. Łysiak, W-wa 1982.
Statuty synodalne wieluńsko-kaliskie – *Statuty synodalne wieluńsko-kaliskie Mikołaja Trąby z r. 1420*. Kraków 1951.
StPPP – *Starodawne Prawa Polskiego Pomniki*, Kraków 1870.
Straty Bibliotek – *Straty Bibliotek i Archiwów warszawskieh w zakresie rękopiśmiennych źródeł historycznych*. I–II, W-wa 1956.
Sułkowska-Kurasiowa, *Dokumenty królewskie* – I. Sułkowska-Kurasiowa, *Dokumenty królewskie i ich funkcja w Państwie Polskim 1370–1444*. W-wa 1977.
Sułkowska-Kurasiowa. *Polska Kancelaria* – I. Sułkowska-Kurasiowa, *Polska Kancelaria Królewska w latach 1447–1506*, Wrodaw 1967.
Surowiecki, *O upadku* – W. Surowiecki, *O upadku Przemysłu y Miast w Polszce*, W-wa 1810.
SJP(D) – *Słownik Języka Polskiego*, red. W. Doroszewski, I–X, W-wa 1958–1968.
SJP(L) – *Słownik Jezyka Polskiego*, przez S. B. Linde, wydanie drugie, I–VI, Lwów 1854–1860.
Topoloski, *Dzieje* – I. Topolski, *Dzieje Polski*, W-wa 1976.
Tyloch, 'Die Judenschutzbrief' – W. Tyloch, 'Die Judenschutzbriefe von Boleslaw dem Frommen von Grosspolen und Kasimir dem Grossen, König, von Polen', *Kairos*, XXII (1980), pp. 114–121.
VL – *Volumina Legum*, ed. I. Ohryzko, SPb 1859–1860.
Wadding, *Annales Minorum* – Wadding, *Annales Minorum*, tertia editio, Romae 1933.
Walawender, *Kronika* – A. Walawender, *Kronika klęsk elementarnych*, II, Lwów 1935.
Wielkopolskie roty sądowe – *Wielkopolskie roty sądowe XIV–XV wieku*. I–IV, ed. H. Kowalewicz, Wrocław 1959–1974.

Wiszniewski, *Kronikarstwo polskie* – U. Wiszniewski, *Kronikarstwo polskie 15 wieku, Historia literatury polskiej*. IV, Kraków 1842.
Włodarski, *Chronologia* – B. Włodarski, *Chronologia Polska*, W-wa 1957.
Zawadzki, *Polska* – A. Zawadzki, *Polska przedrozbiorowa a Żydzi*, W-wa 1939.

cz   – *część*
r   – rok
SPb – St. Petersburg
UJ   – Uniwerstytet Jagielloński
w   – wiek
W-wa – Warszawa

THE DECLINE OF THE POLISH-LITHUANIAN *KAHAL*

Eli Lederhendler

Ever since Simon Dubnow, Israel Halperin and others established the central significance of Jewish autonomous institutions in the study of East European Jewish history, the *kahal* or *kehillah* (community as a corporate body) has been the object of continual attention. Some of the most recent works on Polish and Russian Jewry in the eighteenth and nineteenth centuries, while examining a wide range of issues, devote a good deal of discussion to the local Jewish community as a social phenomenon. Interestingly, the wider framework of Jewish corporate autonomy in Eastern Europe – the provincial and national *va'adim* (councils) – has not received the same kind of attention in recent years; nor has the question of the vitality and authority of the local *kahal* been linked to the question of joint or supra-communal activity.

Two main views have been expressed in the recent literature about the local *kahal*. Levitats and Shochat tend to regard state interference in and legal suppression of the *kahal*'s official status as secondary to the empirical sociology of Jewish life in Eastern Europe. They emphasize the continuity and longevity of the *kahal*, or at least the hegemony of rabbis and lay leaders and the array of social and religious institutions active in communal life, well into the second half of the nineteenth century.[1] Similarly, Stanislawski, while arguing that state pressure was a decisive factor in the way Jewish communal life evolved during the reign of Nicholas I, agrees that local communal rule – under another name – survived the official abolition of the *kahal* as such.[2] The other view, taken by Rosman and Cohen, is that the *kahal* had lost most of its autonomy to the powerful Polish magnates and their officials long before the end of the eighteenth century.[3]

At issue here is a larger question: that of continuity and change in the organizational aspects of East European Jewish society. Rosman and Cohen, for example, argue that the character of Jewish communal life underwent major changes in the period before the Polish partitions.

Stanislawski, along with Levitats and Shochat, stress the basic stability in the Jews' inner life prior to the third decade of the nineteenth century: a stability, they argue, which allowed the local community to shift gears when the shocks did come and was thus able to prolong its effective existence.

This essay attempts to attack this issue from another angle: that of the supra-communal or national context. It will re-examine, for the period between the demise of the Polish and Lithuanian *kahal* councils (1764) and the 1820s, the way in which the Jewish political system functioned. Particular attention will be given to the impact of the absence of a regulatory intercommunal apparatus, and to the issues of conflict and cooperation as they reveal the extent of the deterioration of the *kahal* system.

As a political institution, the Polish-Lithuanian *kahal* inherited most of its characteristic features from the medieval Jewish corporate community. What distinguished the medieval *kahal* from earlier models of Jewish self-government was the fact that it was designed for a dispersed people, living under different rulers and in different cultural environments, and was thus autonomous vis-a-vis other Jewish communities. What made the medieval *kahal* different from modern forms of Jewish community structures is that it performed governmental functions, with powers of enforcement which were granted by the ruler of the district, country or empire in which the *kahal* was situated. It was thus autonomous vis-a-vis the other, non-Jewish, corporate bodies in the same political jurisdiction.

Dispersed as they were, the individual communities were also bound together by basic similarities in purpose, in governance and in structure as well as by a web of interrelations and mutual responsibilities. The leagues of communities that existed in Poland-Lithuania at the provincial and national levels – the *va'adim* – were a particularly well-developed expression of the principle of mutual responsibility within Jewish society. The local *kahal* had a long-established mandate to provide for the welfare of its members and to maintain the rule of Torah law within its jurisdiction. This mandate implied more than purely local or administrative responsibility, however. The collective values of the larger Jewish community, when affirmed by the local Jewish administration, were the source of legitimacy and authority for the local *kahal*. The local *kahal* was therefore a basic unit in a more complex socio-political structure.

The *kahal* and the intercommunal bodies also played another role: that of intermediary between the ruling powers of the state and Jewish society. They functioned as the crown's fiscal and judicial agent within the Jewish sector of the population. Indeed, the powers of taxation and enforcement granted to the *kahal* by the state were crucial to Jewish communal governance. This was not because the *kahal* gained legitimacy or authority in this manner (the internal tradition of Jewish self-government provided these), but because it needed the *power* gained from its reciprocal relationship with the state. The traditional, normative values of Jewish self-rule applied to the *kahal* as an abstract idea, but in practice the authority of a particular set of men at a given place and time was never accepted absolutely. The fact is that the Jewish community in dispersion lacked political power of its own. The men at the head of the Jewish communities thus depended on an outside source of power to reinforce their authority.

Because power was derived from gentile sources, dissent and conflict within the community were also linked to gentile power: those who sought to undermine the established leaders or to evade their jurisdiction had recourse to such tactics as informing or appealing to gentile courts or to the protection of gentile patrons. By the same token, the *kahal* could also use these methods in combatting dissent and disobedience. The defining characteristic of medieval Jewish politics, then, was the inextricability of internal from external affairs. The compass-point toward which virtually all political activity was oriented was the seat of gentile power.

An examination of the available sources on the Polish-Lithuanian *kahal* shows that these features, inherent in the structure of medieval Jewish politics, were all similarly to be found in Poland.[4] It is precisely the intimate connection between the internal and the external politics of the Polish-Lithuanian *kahal* that renders all but irrelevant the question of whether Jewish autonomy as expressed in the system of provincial and national councils was a product of Jewish initiative or was imposed on the Jews by the state for reasons of fiscal policy. This is a question whose examination, more often than not, follows certain subtexts of an ideological rather than historical character: were the Jews the 'subjects' or the 'objects' of their own history (a common debate between Diaspora-affirmers and Diaspora-negators)? Did the Jews really constitute a state within a state (as charged in pre-war Polish nationalist writings and as denied by Jewish apologists)? Clearly the *va'adim* could not have come into existence without a context in which both the Jewish communities and their Polish-Lithuanian rulers had an interest in erecting such formal political structures.

Given the imbalance of relative power between the authorities (both crown and manorial) and the Jewish communities, however, it was sufficient for official support to be withdrawn from the provincial and national Jewish councils for these institutions to collapse. They were not self-sustaining parts of the Jewish social system, but a political mechanism intended to facilitate coordination in a variety of spheres. They bound together geographically dispersed communities with great disparities of demographic and economic strength, and which owed political allegiance to a variety of overlords. In Poland-Lithuania, which itself was far from being a centralized state, the fragility of such a structure is hardly surprising.

Yet although not always very successful in such matters as arbitrating the conflicting jurisdictional claims of the larger communities and in managing Jewish indebtedness, the councils were more effective in organizing joint political representation, providing the cash needed for political lobbying, keeping a vigilant watch over Jewish interests in judicial proceedings, and lending added weight to rabbinical court judgments. Despite their failings, the councils therefore represented a high point in Jewish political development. For all that the Polish-Lithuanian case was clearly exceptional, it nevertheless offered a standard against which communal life would be measured by future generations of East European Jews. Even more important in the present context is the fact that the supra-communal structures gave concrete form to the idea that the local *kahal*, independent though it may have been in its internal administrative affairs, was implicitly (and in this case also formally) part of a much larger Jewish polity.

According to both Rosman and Cohen, by the time the *va'adim* were abolished the autonomy of the local community had been considerably undermined through the intervention of landowners in *kahal* affairs, through the declining independence of the rabbinical judicial system, and through the high-handed behaviour of wealthy and eminent members of the communities no longer willing to accept communal discipline.[5] The contrary view – that Jewish communal life remained more or less intact – is based on the fact that the local *kahal* survived the abolition of the provincial and national councils: the legislation of June 1764 left the local community responsible for collecting Jewish taxes. One historian, Artur Cygielman, has even claimed that the demise of the *va'adim* went quite unnoticed by the Jewish community because of their minor role in Jewish life.[6]

Yet it would seem that the abolition of the councils was but the first step in a major assault against the entire structure of Jewish autonomy, including the already weakened local community. During the state reform debates of the Four Year *Sejm* (1788–91) Jewish autonomy became the focal point of public discussion of the Jewish question and both Polish and Jewish pamphleteers urged the necessity of doing away with the *kahal*.[7] The proposals of the Jewry-law committee of the *Sejm* were not finalized in time to be incorporated into the new constitution of May 1791, but were discussed in the *Sejm* and in official circles with a view toward implementing a major reform. It is at this stage that we can already point to the deleterious effects on Jewish political activity of the absence of a supra-communal structure. Although the Jewish communities were well aware of what was being proposed in the *Sejm* and in the public press, Jewish communal delegates did not meet to draw up a plan to counter these proposals until the summer and fall of 1791.[8] A combination of factors prevented the *Sejm* from enacting any Jewish reform laws during the next several months, and thus the *kahal* was spared for another thirty years in Poland (lasting in Russia until 1844). There can be no doubt, however, that Jewish political action had in this instance been much less effective than had been the case generally under the *va'adim* system.

One area in which the lack of a mechanism for intercommunal discipline was keenly felt was the struggle between *hasidim* and their opponents (*mitnagdim*) – a struggle that lasted some thirty years from the early 1770s to the turn of the nineteenth century. In 1772 – quite some time after Hasidism had become firmly entrenched in its original southern communities, but coinciding with its more recent introduction into White Russian and Lithuanian communities – a writ of excommunication (*herem*) against the sect was issued by the Jewish community of Wilno. The ban was circulated to other communities where similar documents were issued.[9]

The proclamation issued in Brody is particularly instructive as to the mitnagdic camp's feeling of weakness in the face of a concerted hasidic 'threat':

> Some years ago there arose just such evildoers.[10] Then we had eminent sages and the leaders of the [Polish] Council of the Four Lands who repressed them and made the public aware of their wickedness, until we were finally rid of them. Today, alas, the crown is removed from us and we are poor in men of true faith who would stand up to the wicked ones, and so they have sprouted again.[11]

The political efficacy of the national council and their leaders is contrasted here with the sense of disorder and disorganization that existed in intercommunal relations in the absence of such an institution. As a result, the proper enforcement of communal sanctions was difficult.

The fundamental weakness of the mitnagdic position in the absence of a state-sanctioned, nationally authoritative body was underscored when *hasidim* in Grodno burned copies of *Zamir aritsim*, an anti-hasidic collection printed in Olexeniec later that year. The bans had only limited effectiveness, and the *hasidim* flouted it openly where they had the strength of numbers to do so. The Wilno *kahal*, in a letter to its counterpart in Brody, noted further that little could be done to avenge what it termed 'the blasphemous act' in Grodno:

> They [the *hasidim*] are unscrupulous criminals, with wily tongues which they use in high places, before the courts of governors and rulers, so that we risk, God forbid, all of our communities being placed under restraint [...][12]

The struggle was renewed in 1780–1 in the wake of the appearance of the militantly partisan hasidic tract, *Toledot Ya'akov Yosef*. In response, the major Lithuanian and White Russian communities' representatives, following the lead of the Wilno *kahal*, proclaimed a new and more stringent *herem* against the non-conformists.[13]

Yet what is most striking about the successive attempts to cow the dissidents and purge the community is, of course, their ineffectiveness – despite the cooperation within the northern communal leadership. In the past, intramural jurisdictional disputes had been resolved in one of two ways: either the conflict was submitted for arbitration to courts of the supra-communal *va'adim*, or else one (or both) of the parties sought recourse to gentile courts or protective patronage. In the case of the confrontation between the hasidic movement and the communal authorities, only the latter option remained. When the simmering conflict erupted for the third time in 1798, it was only resolved after an appeal to the state by both sides. The tsarist Jewry Law of 1804 gave tacit recognition to hasidic rabbis and synagogues.[14]

At the same time that the Lithuanian and White Russian communities were plunged into this pitched battle over authority, they were also drawn into a more local dispute which, before it finished its rather squalid course (in 1791), involved several central Jewish communities, two rival Lithuanian magnate houses, the Lithuanian courts, the Polish king and the *Sejm*. This was the power struggle within the Wilno community between the *kahal* and the rabbi, Shmuel ben Avigdor, backed by their respective supporters.

In its barest outlines, the affair concerned the decision of the *kahal* to alter the terms of the rabbi's lifetime contract. This step was undertaken in the wake of the rabbi's independent behaviour, his penchant for currying favour with both the local authorities and the community's artisan and middle classes, and his attempts to pack the *kahal* administration with relatives and supporters. The dispute began in 1762, but by 1781 some of the issues had still not been resolved. The *kahal* at this stage decided to break its contract with the rabbi entirely, which it succeeded in doing in 1785 with the help of the Wilno *wojewoda*, Karol Radziwiłł. Rabbi Shmuel, for his part, won the support of the Bishop of Wilno.

The *kahal* of Wilno, in deposing Rabbi Shmuel, explicitly rejected the right of any other Jewish jurisdiction to interfere. It maintained that the regulations of the defunct Lithuanian Council were no longer operative, and when the communities of Słuck and Grodno (in concert with Pińsk and Brześć) summoned the Wilno *kahal* to appear before a court of arbitration, Wilno refused to recognize their authority to do so. Rabbi Shmuel, his recourse to other Jewish courts blocked, found that his only option lay with the bishop and with litigation in various Lithuanian and Polish courts. The case was further complicated by efforts by both parties to take over the Wilno *kahal* board, with the political and at times physical help of their gentile patrons and their troops. Thus, a dispute of seemingly little initial consequence rapidly assumed regional, even national, proportions.[15]

Together with the hasidic controversy and other, more localized conflicts over *kahal* powers (Mińsk, Witebsk and elsewhere), the Wilno rabbinate affair seems to demonstrate not only the level of civic demoralization in Jewish politics at the end of the eighteenth century, but also the structural inability of a Jewish community shorn of supra-communal restraints to maintain even that precarious balance between internal control and external interference which had been maintained during the previous two centuries.

The abolition of the national and provincial *va'adim* made all but impossible the kind of policy coordination and collective lobbying activity that had been the *forte* of the Jewish supra-communal system. We know of few instances in which chosen representatives of the communities met on a regional basis to determine a course of action on a range of issues. When they did occur, these meetings were usually motivated by the need to deal with a specific problem. Such was the case of the meeting of Jewish representatives held in 1791 to discuss ways to counter the proposals for a new Jewry law being promoted in the *Sejm*.

The piecemeal incorporation of the White Russian, Lithuanian, Ukrainian and Polish provinces into the Russian empire certainly militated against cross-provincial communal coordination, and this difficulty was only accentuated by the divisions between the hasidic-dominated south and the anti-hasidic bastions of the north.

One view of the general state of Jewish communal politics around 1804 was given by Rabbi Hillel ben Ze'ev-Wolf. The *va'adim* of the past, he stated, had had the power to discipline their communities, and they had taken the responsibility for 'directing the affairs of the province in accordance with the way of the world, by collecting funds with which to gain the favour of the rulers. Not so today,' he continued,

> woe to such a generation, that since the borders were divided and the frontiers closed[16] [. . .] there is no [central] council and the provincial council is no more. With no conferences of elders there is no one to plan ahead and to go before the officials or petition the king [. . .]. Nor is there proper law and judgment, seeing that authority and governance has been impoverished along with the leadership [. . .]. Each one is for himself, so that no common counsel is taken to find a remedy in the face of harsh new decrees.[17]

The absence of a regular intercommunal forum was partially offset by the growth of regional political 'nerve centers' like that of Yehoshua Zeitlin's court in Ustiye, near Shklov.[18] But here, the pattern of individual and local efforts at dealing with officials of the government tended to replace the vestiges of the previous era of planned communal activity. Zeitlin, who enjoyed the patronage of Potemkin, was a free agent who held no communal position or responsibility. It was his prestige and his influence alone, rather than the combined efforts of the Lithuanian and White Russian communal leadership, which enabled an unofficial network to function.

Zeitlin's informal methods came into conflict with a community-based collective representation in the years between 1802 and 1804, when the Jewry Law commission in St Petersburg invited the Jewish communities to send their own delegates to the preliminary discussions. Such delegates were sent from the provinces of Mohilew, Mińsk, Podolia and Kiev, while Wilno already had two spokesmen in St Petersburg at this time. They came with little if any previous influence in or knowledge of the capital, and their requests that key provisions of the proposed law be suspended for twenty years were rejected. In general, the role they played seems to have been negligible.[19]

In 1807, a year before the Jews were to be expelled (by provision of the Jewry Law of 1804, par. 34) from villages where they had long been established as innkeepers and distillers, Count Kochubei began campaigning for the postponement of the order. In putting his case, he urged the convening of a group of Jewish representatives, as a counterweight to the possible political impact of the Parisian Assembly of Jewish Notables (1806) and the 'Sanhedrin' (1807) convened under Napoleon's orders. A modified version of this proposal was put into effect: the Jewish communities of eight provinces were asked to elect representatives who would present their views on the 'best means of implementing' the 1804 statute. The delegates were to report to the provincial governors.[20] Here the initiative was clearly that of the state and the representatives' function was strictly defined. Once they had rendered their opinion, the delegations were disbanded.

A major effort to restore a system of intercommunal coordination was undertaken in the years between 1815 and 1818. During the war against Napoleon, two Jewish contractors to the Russian army, Zundl Sonnenberg and Eliezer Dillon, had transmitted Jewish petitions to the highest government circles and, at an audience with Alexander I in June of 1814, were referred to officially as the 'deputies of the Jewish people'. It remains unclear just who sent Sonnenberg and Dillon their instructions. It is, however, unlikely that Sonnenberg would have drafted on his own initiative the detailed memorandum which he submitted in 1813 asking for the abrogation of restrictions on Jewish trade in the Russian empire, the restoration of the Jewish community's right to employ the ban (prohibited by the 1804 statute), and other privileges.[21]

Both men, it should be noted, came from communities in Lithuania and White Russia, and it is likely that they maintained links chiefly with the communities of Wilno, Mińsk and Witebsk. It was, in fact, at a meeting of the main Lithuanian and White Russian communities at Zelva in 1815 that the delayed response came to the Tsar's proposal made in 1814 to Sonnenberg and Dillon, that a permanent Jewish deputation be sent to St Petersburg. Nothing, however, was done for an entire year, and the rabbinical and communal leaders of the northern provinces met again in Mińsk in 1816 to attempt to put the idea into practise. The resolutions adopted at this conference, which referred to itself as a *va'ad medina* – a term which had last been used officially in 1764 – show that the communities aspired to a more formalized political mechanism. The operative section of the Mińsk resolution not only called for the raising of a special fund throughout the Jewish communities, but also assigned officers in each province to supervise the collection and to serve as the communications link between local districts and the provincial and national leaders. At the district level, chosen officers were to forward to the provincial centre their list of grievances and instructions for the representatives to take to St Petersburg. The leaders at Mińsk clearly had in mind a hierarchical structure reminiscent of the Lithuanian Council and the Polish Lands Council.[22]

The resolution invoked the Tsar's instructions to Sonnenberg and Dillon, no doubt to lend weight to the authoritative character of the project; but in fact, the government had no intention of recognizing a permanent representative body on the *va'adim* model, and quickly stepped in to insure that the collection of funds be controlled by the administration. Moreover, while it was prepared on this basis to accept a Jewish fund-raising campaign, it stopped short of actually mandating the execution of the plan.[23]

The 1816 resolution clearly reflects the fact that the entire effort to win general cooperation was to be based solely on moral persuasion. The conference members, headed by Rabbi Haim of Volozhin, pleaded with the local communal leaders not to take their instructions lightly. 'We have,' they said, 'complete faith in our brothers of the people of Israel, who normally fulfill their communal obligations, that they will certainly rouse themselves to collect the necessary funds out of their own good will – for surely Israel must not be accused of lacking solidarity!'[24]

Dillon's and Sonnenberg's letters from St Petersburg in the latter part of 1816 and the first part of 1817 make it abundantly clear, however, that they were left to their own devices and reduced to pleading for funds and the assistance of other deputies.[25] Despite a new election of deputies that took place in Wilno in 1818, the deputies continued to operate with little financial or political backing, and there is no evidence that intercommunal consultation was maintained once the deputies were elected. By 1823 the deputation had all but ceased to function, and in 1825 it was formally abolished.

We continue to hear of local efforts to coordinate political action only in connection with ad hoc contingencies. Such an instance was the appeal by the Tykocin *kahal* in 1822, sent to Lublin and several other communities, to convene a conference of delegates and to send a committee to Warsaw in an effort to stave off an expulsion order. It is not known whether such a meeting took place.[26] In a memorandum of 1833 the *kahal* of Wilno proposed to Nicholas I that a Jewish representative body be reestablished – if only to consist of four men – to advise on projects concerning Jews and to serve as a means of communication between the government and the Jewish population.[27] This may or may not have been a regional initiative, but in any case it was not heeded.

The inability of the Russian Jewish communities to act together in defence of common interests, for both internal and external reasons, indicated that the *kahal* as a system and as a concept had been weakened at a very basic level. The fact that, despite the government's conditional approval, the communities themselves could not bring to fruition the plan for sustaining a collective, responsible deputation shows that the *kahal* had already lost a great deal of its political and moral stature by 1816.

Because the traditional system of Jewish autonomy had depended on the support of the state for its effective functioning, the withdrawal of state support from the system, which was first felt on the national level, was bound in consequence to affect the entire structure. Jewish voluntary support for communal institutions could not sustain a formal network for common defence or for the resolution of conflicts beyond the local level. The local community, now more than ever subjected to official pressure and interference, lacked a collective framework to shore up its own authority and legitimacy.[28]

The public character of traditional Judaism insured that the local community would retain its importance as the focus of Jewish social and religious life for at least several decades – as Shochat, Levitats and Stanislawski point out. But the signs of its *political* decay were quite clear by the time Nicholas I came to the throne. The Jewish communities lacked effective political representation on a collective level, while on the local level the legal status and prestige of the community and its officers were drastically eroded. The abolition of the *kahal* in Russia in 1844, though it left some of the old communal machinery in place, deprived the local community of the last shred of the reciprocity that had once governed its relations with the state. This was the final stage of a process begun in 1764 with the abolition of the provincial and national councils of Polish and Lithuanian Jewry.

Underestimating the importance to Jewish political life of the *va'adim* of pre-partition Poland, or focusing on the continuities of Jewish life at the local level without regard to the impact on Jewish politics of the breakdown of collective structures, probably derives from a Jewish historiographical tradition that has usually not considered Diaspora Jewish societies as political phenomena. The reasons for this lie partly in the way that modern Jewish historiography first developed, with its emphases on social, cultural, religious-intellectual or legal studies; and partly in the way that political studies first developed, with their basic orientation toward the state and its functions in a way that ruled out the examination of the political development of stateless societies or small social groups. By re-examining the developments in Jewish society from this angle of vision, however, it is possible to shed some light on the chain of events that led to later, unquestionably political, processes.

During the half-century between the late 1820s and the late 1870s the belief by prominent members of the acculturated Jewish intelligentsia (the *maskilim*) that the lack of a collective framework for the Jewish communities constituted a major obstacle to a modern reform of Jewish society became an increasingly important theme in Jewish public discussion. Thus Isaac Ber Levinsohn came to advocate the institution of a hierarchical provincial rabbinate. Others (including Max Lilienthal, Moisei Berlin, Alexander Tsederbaum, Osip Rabinovich and Menashe Margulis) either harked back to the positive qualities of the old *kahal* and supra-*kahal* system or pointed to the advantageous features of the more modern social and political structures of Western Jewish communities. Their awareness of the decline and fragmentation of the Jewish communal apparatus played a key role in preparing them to think in terms of reconstructing such an apparatus. This in turn had clear implications for the development, in the period that began in 1881, of Jewish political movements that had as their aim the political 'regeneration' of the Jews.[29]

NOTES

This essay is based on sections of my doctoral dissertation, 'From Autonomy to Auto-Emancipation: Historical Continuity, Political Development, and the Preconditions for the Emergence of National Jewish Politics in Nineteenth-Century Russia' (Jewish Theological Seminary of America, 1987). Research for the longer work was made possible by generous grants from the Revson Foundation, the National Foundation for Jewish Culture and the Memorial Foundation for Jewish Culture. A major part of the thesis was written while I was in residence as Junior Fellow at the Oxford Centre for Postgraduate Hebrew Studies. I would like to express my thanks to all of these institutions for their support.

1 Isaac Levitats, *The Jewish Community in Russia 1772–1844*, (New York, 1943), pp. 44, 121–2, 269; idem, *The Jewish Community in Russia 1844–1917*, (Jerusalem, 1981),

pp. 84, 201; Azriel Shochat, 'Ha-hanhagah be-kehillot rusia im bitul ha-kahal', *Zion*, vol. 42 (1977), pp. 143–233. A similar opinion was expressed on the Polish Jewish community after 1821 by Jacob Shatzky, *Geshikhte fun Yidn in Varshe*, vol. 1, (New York, 1947), pp. 274–8.
2 Michael Stanislawski, *Tsar Nicholas I and the Jews: The Transformation of Jewish Society in Russia 1825–1855*, (Philadelphia, 1983), pp. 124–7, 185–6.
3 Murray Jay Rosman, 'The Polish Magnates and the Jews: Jews in the Sieniawski-Czartoryski Territories 1686–1731', (doctoral dissertation, Jewish Theological Seminary, 1982), p. 440; Benjamin Cohen, 'Ha-reshut ha-voievodit ve-hakehillah ha-yehudit ba-meiot ha-16—18', *Gal-Ed*, vol. 3 (1976), pp. 9–32.
4 For a detailed discussion, see chapter 2 in Lederhendler, 'From Autonomy to Auto-Emancipation'.
5 Rosman, op. cit., pp. 108–9, 126, 378, 403–40; Cohen, op.cit., pp. 10–12, 30–2. Attempts to fight against such phenomena are amply reflected in the records of the communities. See, e.g. *Pinkas Va'ad Arb'a Aratsot*, ed. Israel Halperin (Jerusalem, 1945–6), no. 352 (1676); *Pinkas Medinat Lita*, ed. Simon Dubnow (Berlin, 1925), no. 908 (1700); *Dubna Rabbati*, ed. H.Z. Margaliot (Warsaw, 1910), p. 64b (1734).
6 Most recently (1986), at a lecture presented to the seminar in East European Jewish history that meets periodically in Jerusalem.
7 On this episode see Simon Dubnow, 'Evreiskaia pol'sha v epokhu poslednykh razdelov', *Evreiskaia starina*, vol. 4 (1911), pp. 441–63; idem, *History of the Jews in Russia and Poland*, 3 vols. (Philadelphia, 1916), vol. 1, pp. 270–91; Raphael Mahler, *Toledot ha-Yehudim be-Polin (ad ha-meah ha-19)* (Merhavya, 1946), pp. 440–56; N. M. Gelber, 'Die Juden und die Judenreform auf dem vierjahrigen Seim', *Festschrift Dubnow*, (Berlin, 1930), pp. 136–53; Valerian Kalinka, *Der vierjahrige Polnische Reichstag 1788 bis 1791*, (Berlin, 1898), Book 2, pp. 341–6 and Book 5, pp. 503–4; Israel Klausner, 'Hamaavak hapenimi be-kehillot rusia ve-lita ve-hatsa'at r. Shimon ben Volf le-tikunim', *He'avar*, vol. 19 (1972), pp. 64–73, with the appended translation of Shimon ben Volf's pamphlet, 'He'asir be-niesvizh' (originally published in 1789 as *Więzień w Nieświeżu do Stanów Sejmujących o potrzebie Reformy Żydów*).
8 Mahler, pp. 453–4; Dubnow, *History*, vol. 1, pp. 290–1.
9 A collection of these was printed in Olexieniec, near Brody, in Volhynia, under the title *Zamir'aritsim ve-harvot tsurim*, and republished by Dubnow: *Chasidiana*, (St Petersburg, supplement to *He-'avar*, vol. 2 [1918], repr. Jerusalem, 1969); also in Mordecai Wilensky, *Hasidim u-Mitnagdim: le-Toledot ha-Pulmus she-beineihem ba-shanim 5532–5575* [1772–1815], (Jerusalem, 1970).
10 For example, the messianic sect of the Frankists active in Poland and Bohemia-Moravia in the 1750s and 1760s.
11 Wilensky, vol. 1, p. 46; Dubnow, *Toledot ha-Hasidut*, (Tel-Aviv, 1974 [1930]), p. 120.
12 Wilensky, vol. 1, p. 72.
13 Dubnow, *Toledot ha-Hasidut*, p. 138; Wilensky, vol. 1, pp. 101–21; Iulii Gessen, 'K istorii religioznoi bor'by sredi evreev v kontse XVIII i v nachale XIX v.', *Voskhod*, no. 1, 1902, p. 120. The four communities joining the ban were Grodno, Breść, Słuck and Pińsk.
14 For the course of events between 1798 and the second arrest of the hasidic master, R. Shneur Zalman, see: Israel Klauser, *Vilna bi-Tekufat ha-Gaon*, (Jerusalem, 1942); Gessen, 'K istorii religioznoi bor'by'; the documents published by Dubnow in 'Vmeshatel'stvo russkago pravitel'stva v antikhasidskuiu bor'bu (1800–1801)', *Evreiskaia starina*, vol. 3 (1910), pp. 84–109, 253–82; and W. Z. Rabinowitsch, *Lithuanian Hasidism*, (New York, 1971). The 1804 statute is recorded in the *Polnoe*

sobranie zakonov rossiiskoi imperii, first series, vol. 28, no. 21,547. Paragraph 53 of the law referred to the 'sects' in the Jewish community.
15 The definitive account of the affair is that of Klausner in *Vilna be-tekufat ha-gaon*; cf. Israel Zinberg, 'Di makhloykes tsvishn di roshey hakohol un dem rov in vilne in der tsveyter helft 18tn yorhundert', YIVO *Historishe shriftn*, vol. 2 (1937), pp. 291–321. Lithuanian and Polish court decisions appear in *Akty izdavaemye vilenskoiu komissieiu dlia razbora drevnykh aktov*, vol. 29: *Akty o evreiakh*, docs. 231, 234–40.
16 A reference to the partitions of Poland.
17 *Hillel ben Shahar*, (Warsaw, 1804), p. 22b.
18 On Zeitlin, see Shmuel Zitron, *Shtadlonim*, (Warsaw, 1926), pp. 28–51; Shmuel Yosef Fuenn, *Kiryah Neemanah*, (Wilno, 2nd rev. ed., 1915), pp. 271–3; S. Y. Hurwitz, 'Sefer hayai (zikhronot)', *Ha-Shiloah*, vol. 40 (1923), pp. 3–7.
19 Gessen, 'Deputaty evreiskago naroda pri Aleksandra I', *Evreiskaia starina*, vol. 2 (1909), p. 18; idem, *Istoriia evreiskago naroda v rossii*, vol. 1 (Petrograd: 1916), p. 322; Levitats, *Jewish Community*, vol. 1, pp. 95–6.
20 Gessen, 'Deputaty', pp. 20–1; idem, *Istoriia*, vol. 1, pp. 318ff.; Dubnow, *History* vol. 1, pp. 347–9.
21 Gessen, 'Deputaty', pp. 22–4; cf. S. Ginsburg, *Otechestvennaia voina 1812 goda i russkie evreii*, (St Petersburg, 1912), p. 85.
22 See the text published by David Maggid, 'Iz moego arkhiva: k istorii evreiskikh deputatov v tsarstvovanie Aleksandra I', *Perezhitoe*, vol. 4 (1913), pp. 181–6 (doc. 1); cf. Levitats, *Jewish Community*, vol. 1, pp. 99–100.
23 Gessen, 'Deputaty', pp. 198–201.
24 'K istorii evreiskikh deputatov', p. 185.
25 Ibid., pp. 186–8 (Dillon's letter of December 1816, doc. 2); cf. Levitats, *Jewish Community*, vol. 1, pp. 100–1. On Sonnenberg's and Dillon's activities in St Petersburg, see Zitron, *Shtadlonim*, pp. 103–37; Gessen, 'Deputaty', pp. 203–6.
26 YIVO *Historishe shriftn*, vol. 2 (1937), documents section (doc. 2): 'A kol-koyrey fun Tiktiner kehille vegn der gzeyre fun geyrush un vegn a baratung fun yidishe kehilles', pp. 573–4.
27 'Zapiska vilenskago kagala o nuzhdakh evreiskago naroda (1833 g.)', published by Gessen in *Evreiskaia starina*, vol.4 (1911), pp. 107–8.
28 For a detailed discussion, see Lederhendler, 'From Autonomy to Auto-Emancipation', chapter 3.
29 Ibid., chapter 4.

A MOBILE CLASS.
THE SUBJECTIVE ELEMENT IN THE SOCIAL PERCEPTION OF JEWS: THE EXAMPLE OF EIGHTEENTH CENTURY POLAND

Anna Żuk

I apply the term 'mobile class' to a social grouping, which becomes the object of emotions usually directed towards several different classes. A characteristic feature of a mobile class is that its place in the subjectively-perceived social structure changes, depending upon who is making the assessment and the degree of his familiarity with the group. The aim of this paper is to show how Jews can be considered a 'mobile class', since they are the subject of emotions usually directed by more highly-placed social groups to the lower classes, and, conversely, by the lower social strata to groups of higher social ranking. To illustrate my argument I shall use examples from eighteenth century Poland.

For a mobile class to come into being, a pre-requisite is, in most cases, the decay and disappearance of those characteristics which indicate social ranking. What then occurs is identification of the group on the basis of attributes belonging to various social strata. However the kind of perception which results is brought about by subjective factors. It consists essentially of a number of generalizations that do not have a real basis in reality; or which are based on some specific features of the group, rather than all its characteristics.

The Jews in eighteenth century Poland belonged, together with the burghers and the peasants, to the lower classes. Some of them were engaged directly in servicing the magnate and gentry classes. The subjective categories in which Jews were included were two-fold: the upper classes regarded the Jews as belonging to the lower orders and bestowed upon them emotions reserved for these classes. To them this seemed justified by the position of Jews in the social order. In turn the lower classes tended – especially during periods of social conflict – to identify all Jews on the basis of functions which some of them performed for the upper classes.

Thus they looked on the Jews as a group with emotions normally reserved for these classes.

In both cases, subjective categorization becomes at the same time generalization; feelings which might have been justified if directed towards a section of the Jewish community were extended to the group as a whole. Before discussing this problem, I should like to point out that the phenomenon of the mobile class is not the only area of the sociology of affect, in which Jews were in the past, or are currently, the subject. It should also be stressed that this study contains a series of hypotheses, the validity of which should be tested in research which goes beyond the history of Polish Jews and the framework of a single historical era. Furthermore, while it is not only the Jews who can be characterized as a mobile class, they are a prime example – almost the embodiment – of this phenomenon.

JEWS AS SEEN BY THE UPPER CLASSES

The question of the functions performed by a section of the Jewish community in the service of the upper classes in old Poland requires further research. At this stage I would merely like to emphasize the political aspect of these functions. They were usually services of an economic nature, and explanations for this have been sought either in the cultural sphere (for example, the fact that the nobility [*szlachta*] were prevented from engaging in commerce), or else in the personal traits of the upper classes. Thus Graetz writes that Jews 'brought benefits to the frivolous and masterful Polish lords'.[1] In accordance with this view it is argued that the nobility and gentry entrusted their interests to Jews in order to devote themselves wholeheartedly to frivolity. Some individuals were certainly motivated by considerations of this nature. Yet on the whole, the practice has a certain logic and can be seen as contributing to the continuing domination of the noble class. If one wishes to maintain a monopoly of power and privilege, it is a considerable advantage if a serving group does not aspire to the prizes which social advancement offers, but is satisfied with merely financial rewards. To use a simple comparison, the Jews serving the nobility were in the position of a foreign work-force accepting half-pay. The full payment accorded to a serving group which provides services directly and possesses qualifications (particularly in the field of management) consists, as a rule, apart from financial remuneration, of rewards of a social and political character – in the shape of rights and privileges. This is one of the mechanisms by which members of the lower class advance to middle class status. The serving class becomes a pressure group, directing its aspirations towards areas of privilege and decision-making which are within the domain of the class being served.

Since the latter attach considerable importance to those they consider indispensable, the aspirations of the servicing group sometimes meet with a favourable response. As a rule, however, the situation as it unfolds is one of conflict. How, and by what means, this conflict is resolved may depend upon the particular circumstances. It lies in the interests of the upper classes, who wish to retain their dominance, to avoid not only the conflict itself, but also the possibility of its arising. One way of achieving such security would be to recruit a serving group which does not harbour any aspirations towards those rights and privileges which are the preserve of the upper classes.

In the case of the Jews of old Poland, their social aims were limited. They were restricted to the confines of their own community, which was isolated both culturally, and, because of the self-government granted to them, also politically. The Jews were not the only group which can be seen to have been optimally functional in a service role and, at the same time, to have been 'protective', i.e. unlikely to seek conflict itself, while insulating the nobility and gentry from other groups which had the potential for conflict. Another such group was the lower clergy. In this case too, the reference system of values and rewards – in the sense, for example, of social and political advance – lay outside that monopolized, at least at the parish level, by the nobility. The conflicts which did arise in the political arena related rather to the Church hierarchy and the ruling élite, two circles which it is not always easy to separate. At the parish level the clergy were able to provide the nobility and gentry with support. This went beyond simply legitimizing power and assumed more direct forms. A foreigner who travelled in Poland at the time of King Stanisław August Poniatowski noted:

> A very small part of his [the vicar's] affairs concerns matters of religion; most of the time which his church and household leave him, he spends with the squire or is engaged in the latter's affairs. Hence one often meets, whether at home or abroad, a Polish nobleman in the company of a clergyman. The other of his inseparable companions is the Jew. They, like two guiding spirits, protect at each step every Pole of importance. All matters which are thought to be too important or too sensitive for a Jew are entrusted to the clergyman and, therefore, the priests are often, and for long periods, absent from their parishes.[2]

The clergy and the Jews, groups that were socially distant and culturally opposed to each other, in practice, in everyday life in old Poland were bound by frequent social contact centred on the squire and his interests. These contacts may have been reflected in some customary practices. Thus a foreigner found in a Polish inn that 'the postmaster, an old drunken Jew, drank vodka with a stalwart and corpulent village priest.'[3]

Summarizing these reflections, it is clear that the political role of those Jews directly involved with serving the nobility contributed towards the stabilization and preservation of the upper class monopoly of power. In this role, apart from Jews, there were also some members of the lower clergy and also foreigners, such as Germans. Their usefulness and efficiency as a group serving the economic – and indirectly the political – interests of the upper class, resulted from their membership of social spheres which were culturally or institutionally isolated, a fact which excluded them from the political game.

To underline the importance of the problem, let us imagine a situation in which the squire administered his domain with the help and cooperation of its inhabitants. This would imply a degree of peasant emancipation which can not be reconciled with serfdom. It therefore endangered the class domination of the nobility. The Cossacks, by contrast, were an example of a group which provided services of a specific kind, but at the same time possessed considerable potential for conflict. This conflict potential, the effects of which were decidedly harmful for Polish statehood, stemmed largely from the fact that the Cossacks demanded social and political rights as payment for their military services.

The link which bound the squirearchy together with the Jews who serviced it may be defined as comparative exploitation. Its relative character becomes evident when comparison is drawn with other groups which, if they had fullfilled the same functions as the Jews, would have been rewarded differently.

The stereotype of the Jew held by the upper classes, and its subjective colouring, may reflect this relative exploitation. As a consequence, features which should have been evident because of the Jews' functions and their contacts with the nobility disappear from their actual status. The question of rewards in the area of social and political rights or prestige also disappears, since the stereotype does not include those cultural and personal attributes which could form the basis for the grant of such rights.

And so, at the time of the Four Year *Sejm*, in upper class journalism, the Jews were presented stereotypically as an undifferentiated mass: 'greedy, cunning, fanatical, marked by a low cultural, mental and moral level'.[4] We should note that upper classes frequently formulate their feelings towards lower classes in this kind of language. A 'low cultural, mental and moral level' is usually attributed to lower classes, irrespective of who they are. We can see this process at work, for example, when a peasant or a worker is defined as 'uncultured, dirty, ignorant,'. Only the term 'fanatical', as applied to religious practices and customs, is linked specifically to the stereotype of the Jew. The adjective 'greedy' is applied to the underprivileged classes to such a degree, since it serves to deny or restrict their rights to acquisition and ownership. In the minds of those who regard the privilege of ownership as belonging exclusively to themselves, an acquisitive drive on the part of the underprivileged classes is judged in terms that are morally negative; the man is 'greedy' if he wishes to acquire goods or services, and 'cunning' if he is able to realise that wish. In the culture of Polish stereotypes, such attributes are also ascribed to peasants.

This stereotype of the Jew contains an element of mystification originating from the principle of taking the part for the whole. It leaves out a large number of Jews who did not fit the stereotype of the lower classes, for the simple reason that they did not belong to them. The proximity referred to, which included contact on the social plane, excluded individuals of a 'low cultural and mental level'. Its frequency is hard to ascertain, but in eighteenth century memoirs, for example, the Jewish agent or manager is described as a member of the household,[5] and a foreigner visiting Poland wrote; 'It is certain that in any other country an infected Jew would not be admitted to a nobleman's house.'[6] Hence the conclusion that even a reasonable excuse, such as disease, was not used as a barrier to continued contacts with Jews in Poland.

And yet the day to day presence in upper class houses of Jews, fulfilling both functional and social roles, does not seem to have had any significant effect on the stereotype of the Jew, in which he is denied cultural and moral virtues. The general attitude of the nobility and the gentry towards the Jews is best described in the words of Adolf Pawiński:

> In relation to the lower strata, discriminated against politically and socially, there prevails in the main an indifference to their fate or even a tendency to oppress them. And so, for example, Jews who have long lived either in the villages or in towns, or even in the cities, are an object of aversion or contempt as well as being exploited in financial and fiscal terms. In the eyes of the ruling estate they do not deserve any kindness. On the contrary, in the instructions of the *sejmiki* (regional assemblies of the gentry) attention is repeatedly drawn to the Jews as a convenient and necessary source of financial pillage for the benefit of the Republic. Whenever the need arises in the Sejm to vote a tax for defence purposes, and the gentry and nobility are called upon to contribute, they point to the Jews as the first and most plentiful source (...) After each taxation measure or increase of the tax levels affecting Jews, there follows a new demand issued by the deputies of the *sejmiki*. It all reminds one of the digestive processes of an animal's body; satiation is followed by emptiness, and emptiness by renewed filling of the stomach.[7]

The nobility and gentry push the Jews aside, ascribe them without exception to the lower orders and, at the same time, establish them as an object of exploitation. This occurs despite the many benefits derived from Jews, either in the form of services of various kinds, or through direct material profit.

The political benefits which accrued to the upper classes were considerable, but they were disregarded or unappreciated by them. Nathan Hannover, for example, writes in his chronicle dating from the period of the Cossack wars in the seventeenth century: 'The Jews in Ruś were lords and rulers of Ruthenian towns; hence the misfortunes which befell the Jews.'[8] This sounds improbable, but Hannower is not guilty of misrepresentation; he merely uses language which is inadequate to describe the political system in the Ukraine, in which Jews did, to a certain extent, participate. Apart from the role of 'middleman' in economic life, Jews in Old Poland were very important in the circulation of information. In such a vast, underpopulated country they were often messengers, and because of their mobility and the nature of their occupations, which required meeting people regularly, they acquired a relatively large stock of information.

Adam Moszczeński, describing the period of the Humań massacre, recalls; 'As for the provincial governor (*wojewoda*) of Kiev, his door was always open to the Jews, and he believed their tales and complaints to such lengths that if any official or cashier had the Jews against him, he could not retain his post.'[9] This seems possible, as the Jews in the Ukraine were the only possible ally of the gentry classes. There was no other social group which could provide support for the ruling power; the burgher class was insignificant, while an immense social gulf, as well as economic and religious conflicts, separated the nobles and gentry from the peasantry. Relations with the Cossacks were similarly plagued with conflict. Nevertheless, irrespective of the benefits which the gentry classes received from the Jews, the latter were treated in the way an upper class treats a lower one, and were accorded the emotional response usually reserved for the lower classes.

This relationship is well captured by Marchlewski:

> Within the conservative, gentry camp ... there was an active tradition of treating Jews with contemptuous patronage, a tradition maintained since the times of serfdom. This relationship is expressed in one word which hides an infinity of contempt: *żydek*. ... Even among people of unquestionably high cultural level, who had, however, absorbed the ideas and assumptions appropriate to their class, there was the same tone and the same attitude towards Jews. So, for example, J.I. Kraszewski tries to be 'fair' to the Jews, but whenever he writes about them one senses the gulf which separates him from these pariahs. He treats them in almost the same way as a European ethnographer would describe an exotic African tribe. For him, a gentleman with his own coat of arms, it would be out of the question

to consider a Mosiek or a Lejbuś as his peer. Until now, for politicians of this camp, the 'Jewish question' existed only in the sense that decisions regarding the Jews' future need to be taken; equality of rights for Jews is a notion which eludes their grasp completely ... It is, however, this same gentry tradition which will not be reconciled to anti-semitism, to the struggle against the Jews. Between the nobles and their *żydki*, whatever we think about the policies of the gentry class, there was always that sense of lordliness which recoils from flattering the instincts of the masses and attempts to retain a semblance of culture ... Journalists of this camp too did not degrade themselves by exploiting zoological anti-semitism for political purposes. They had no need to dirty their hands.[10]

The nobility and gentry bestowed on the Jews emotions reserved for the lower classes, treating them with disrespect, patronisingly, fully confident of their own superiority. But this was not anti-semitism, which, according to this gentry scheme of values, was plebeian and therefore unworthy.

JEWS AS SEEN BY THE LOWER CLASSES

Here the paradoxes which lead to the creation of a mobile class are fully revealed; the inclusion of Jews in a subjective category with groups with which, in objective terms, they have little in common, and this categorization process carried out on the basis of very scanty evidence. Emotions are clearly the motive force behind generalization.

Our hypothesis as to how the Jews appeared to the lower classes is as follows: these classes exhibited a tendency to include Jews in the same subjective category as the privileged classes on the evidence of the service function performed by certain Jews for these classes and the type of social dependence (patronage) involved. The extensive mystification process involved here consisted of all Jews being subjected to the emotions which may have been justified in relation to a small number of them, so that Jews who occupied an equally low and underprivileged position in society as those who attacked them became the object of aggression directed against the upper classes. This allows us to explain the different interpretations of certain events which are sometimes treated as anti-Jewish or anti-semitic, but are also interpreted in terms of class conflict.

So, for example, according to Kitowicz, the expulsion of Jewish artisans from Warsaw in 1794 frightened contemporaries, who saw in it the beginnings of a social upheaval along the lines of the French Revolution.[11] Kitowicz, in his description of the Warsaw riots, gives the following sequence of events: 'The first outbreak' – Warsaw artisans demand the expulsion of Jews. 'The second outbreak' – appeared to be modelled on the intitial stages of the French Revolution. Three villains were seen at Krakowska Street with cockades fastened to their caps. They were immediately taken off to the guardhouse on Marszałkowska Street. Nothing else was heard of them and it was dangerous to ask lest the enquirer were counted as one of their companions.[12] 'The third outbreak' − anti-Jewish excesses break out in the wake of the attack by the tailor, Fox, on a Jewish tailor. The furrier, Mariański, who had said; 'Today the apprentices are rioting; tomorrow it will be their elders', was dragged from his bed by soldiers who forced their way into his house ... and led him down to the guardhouse.[13]

In the light of these events 'the *Sejm* considered banning the indulgence festival at Bielany on Whit Monday, which had always attracted Varsovians in their thousands to the forest of the Cameduli monks, − and also the public processions during Corpus Christi. A request was also made that detachments of soldiers disperse all crowd gatherings in which twelve or more people took part.'[14]

However the Bielany festival and the Corpus Christi procession 'passed off peacefully as usual'. Kitowicz, in his description of the Warsaw riots concludes that 'the Warsaw mob is not as frightening as, for example, the French'. Examining this question in more detail, he anticipates Tocqueville's later argument that the social basis of revolutions are not those who are underprivileged absolutely, but those whose underprivileged status is relative and who aim to improve their position:

> The Polish mob is not supported by the gentry, and it has no access to the army because officers and members of the cavalry are recruited exclusively from the noble class. Its voice carries no weight in public debates. All legislative, defence and financial functions of the state are in the hands of the noble estate. Hence the Polish mob could never be as dangerous to this country as the French mob became. It might become so when the burgher class is admitted to the legislature and to other public offices.[15]

These conclusions, which may be recognized as a valuable contribution to the sociological theory of revolution, were reached by Kitowicz on the basis of events which could be defined as an anti-Jewish riot. In this latter interpretation the facts alone are taken into account, while in the version given by Kitowicz, the thoughts and motives of those involved are considered, and here, in fact, the Jews appear as an intermediate element in the conflict between the mob and the upper classes. In the thoughts, and even more, in the emotions, of the common people these riots are not solely anti-Jewish, but have a further object in the shape of the privileged classes. The privileged group grasps this true context, and hence the severe measures taken against the artisan who spoke of a further stage of rebellion; hence also the discussion of such radical measures as the prohibition of meetings or the ban on public Catholic rites. And yet the fear which provoked the above sentiments proved unfounded, since 'the Polish mob is not as dangerous as, for example, the French mob'.

In the seventeenth and eighteenth centuries during the conflicts between the nobility on the one hand and the peasants and Ukrainian Cossacks on the other, the full force of what we have termed 'subjective generalization' is revealed. In the heat of the dispute the Jews, together with the Catholic clergy and the gentry, are lumped together in a single category of adversaries. In this case, and it is a rare occurrence in Jewish history, these attitudes had grounds for justification; their logic is borne out by consideration of the system of power relations and the position of Jews within it.

Some contemporary Jews were conscious of this. Nathan Hannover writes in his Chronicle:

> Some Cossacks were freed from taxation and enjoyed the same freedom as the nobility and the gentry. But the remainder of the Ruthenian people worked as serfs on the estates of the magnates and gentry who oppressed them. They dug clay and made bricks and laboured hard in the house and in the fields. The gentry class placed a heavy burden on their shoulders and some of the gentry used dreadful measures to force them to accept the faith of their rulers. They were degraded to such an extent that all nations, even that poorest of all [i.e. Jews] ruled over them.[16]

However such a measure of rationality in according Jews the emotions reserved for the ruling classes is a very rare occurrence. As a rule, the image of the Jew in the emotions of the lower classes is a highly mystified one, and the generalization is constructed on the basis of features that are unrepresentative of Jewish society as a whole. The social consciousness of the common people, touched to only a small degree by intellectualism, seems to suffer from the mis-application of empiricism. What is experienced directly is thought to hold good as a general rule. Hence, a part is identified with the whole and appearance with essence. In the feudal order, this arises when the peasantry direct their hopes and aggressions not against those who really dispose of power, but against those who are intermediaries.[17] All kinds of requests are addressed to leaseholders, estate stewards, and similar officials who also become the first victims of a desperate peasant rebellion. Jews are victims of emotions which should properly be addressed to members of the groups in power: the nobility, or else the clergy. Jews become victims because of this misuse of empirical knowledge; it is they whom the Ruthenian peasant encountered most frequently in the market place or in the inn, and the repression which the peasant experienced flowed directly from them, although its true source lay beyond them.

The mechanism of this kind of subjective construct can be illustrated by one of Spinoza's reflections: affect leads to a vision in which a part is identified with the whole; if this part is bad, then the whole may be treated with antipathy and aggression. 'But one must observe that in ordering our thoughts and images, we should always take into account what is good in each thing, so that we are always moved to action by feelings of joy.' The perception of the whole through what is bad and partial is:

> ... the common characteristic of all those whom luck does not favour and who are weak in spirit. Thus a miser, even a poor one, talks unceasingly of the financial abuses and failings of the wealthy, tormenting himself and showing others that he cannot tolerate with equanimity either his own poverty, or the riches of others. Those who are ill-received by their mistresses talk in the same vein, thinking only of the volatile nature of women, their deceitfulness and other commonplace faults of this kind; it is all forgotten when the mistress accepts them back again.[18]

Such emotions are seemingly a natural tendency of human kind and are present in force in popular thinking, which is little penetrated by reason and is, as a rule, associated with the lower and oppressed classes, those 'whom luck does not favour'. Yet where the treatment meted out to Jews by their Christian neighbours is concerned, the tendency to emotions of this kind is both more specific and intense. This may be explained by the general attitude of the Church towards the Jews, an attitude which does not, as is usually argued, originate in the assertion that the Jews 'killed Christ' or refused to recognise him (which would be a Freudian rationalisation), but in their failure to recognize the Church itself – a step which, of course, would be impossible without recognising Christ too. For centuries the Church had been an institution which tended towards totalitarianism, a system which in the very nature of things behaves with intolerance and aggression towards groups threatening its legitimacy.

A totalitarian institution – and this is proved in the twentieth century by the experience of peoples living under totalitarian systems – rejects groups which challenge its legitimacy. There is no threat or warning issued – 'We shall persecute you because you do not recognize us.' The non-conformist groups are simply branded as sick, evil and in conspiracy with a demonic force which is interpreted according to the particular social and historical context. The Christian-Jewish conflict, rooted in the question of legitimacy of Church power, provided an environment in which Christians were inclined to see in Jews all that is evil, and to equate the part that is evil with the whole. Where popular consciousness was concerned, this tendency is particularly strong and it increased in the case of those 'whom luck does not favour'.

The nature of the understanding appropriate to a Ruthenian peasant in the eighteenth century, has been characterized as a distorted empiricism. It had particularly unfortunate effects when it came into contact with popular Jewish consciousness, which in turn was marked by distorted *apriorism*. This *a priori* thought results from enclosure in a particular ethnic, cultural and religious environment, and it produces patterns of thought and behaviour determined in advance by what was regarded as compatible with Jewish tradition. *A posteriori* thought – the process of reconciling knowledge and assumptions with experience and reality – was comparatively weakly developed. If the values of individual and collective life are established by such *a priori* thinking, and are shaped to only a small degree in accordance with external reality, the result may be that grasp of that reality is lost and the group becomes unable to foresee the dangers that reality bears. The social consciousness of the Jews, largely determined by *a priori* thought, and the social consciousness of the lower classes within Christian society, interacted and produced a tangled knot of mutual incomprehension and antipathy.

For centuries the Jews depended upon a system of logic and reasoning which restricted their ability – already limited in the conditions of the Diaspora – to act or exercise influence in the political sphere. From the point of view of the sociology of knowledge it is interesting that this *a priori* style, in a purer intellectual form, was quite widely represented in Jewish historiography. Majer Bałaban writes:

> In science research is usually based on facts – most importantly derived from the observation of phenomena – and only subsequently followed by conclusions arrived at by deduction. The scholar does not look to left or right and his conclusions sometimes destroy what generations have sanctified and centuries accepted as dogma. And this is true science, free from the influences of the street, from the considerations of the moment and of factions or groups. In the historiography of Polish Jews it is usually the other way round. The author has a chosen thesis and looks for evidence with which to back it up – he has the conclusions and seeks merely the initial premise.[19]

It can even be argued that these characteristics can be observed to a significant degree in present-day Jewish historiography, perhaps because of the persistence even in scholarly work of sublimated traits of that common Jewish consciousness or, in other words, the misapplication of *a priori* thought.

In conclusion, we may advance the following hypotheses: First, the perception of Jews in the group consciousness of the lower classes was based on a false analogy, which seemed to have a logical base but was rooted in emotion. One part, usually the 'bad' part, would became the whole. An intermediary role in carrying out a decision would be conceived as the process of decision-making itself. A typical feature of the feudal order – peasants focussing their hopes and emotions towards those who mediate between them and the true wielders of power – can be seen as typical of a far more general phenomenon.

Second, the ability of Jews to influence or determine events remained severely limited while they maintained their separate national and cultural identity under the conditions of the Diaspora. Jewish group consciousness, which concentrated on preserving that separate identity, diminished this ability even further, testifying to the weakness of *a priori* thought. It meant that the perception of reality was formed to only a small degree by contact with it, so that the values of individual and collective life (religious, national or cultural) were determined by abstract principles.

The combination of these two factors: peasant cognitive thought directing aggression against what was immediately perceived, and Jewish group consciousness which shaped cognition by *a priori* thinking, and resulted in a weak perception of reality, seem to have created a situation which for the Jews was particularly unfortunate. It made possible the manipulation of the Jews, putting them in a mediating position as a highly visible link which became the focus for the aggression of the lower and oppressed classes. This state of affairs existed during the seventeenth and eighteenth centuries in the Ukraine, where the Polish nobility made the Jews the visible tool of their own exploitative policies.

LANGUAGE AND THE JEWS AS A MOBILE CLASS

In Polish memoirs of the eighteenth century the linguistic order in which basic social groups are described seems to reflect the order of their stratification. The sequence in which these groups are cited is as follows: nobility peasants, Jews. This order follows from the way in which the social order was perceived, yet it also has a subjective basis: a generalization of speaking habits – 'I and you' rather than 'you and I'. In other words the feeling towards oneself or one's own group is very warm and positive. When Poles say 'Poles and Jews', and Jews – 'Jews and Poles', Czechs – 'Czechs and Slovaks' and Slovaks – 'Slovaks and Czechs', that priority given to one's own group of origin is a linguistic habit rooted in well-defined emotions. This linguistic principle is particularly apparent when the utterance expresses emotion. Let us take, as an example, a sentence from an eighteenth century memoir: 'All the Starzeński family liked greyhounds extraordinarily, but they detested Germans.'[20] Greyhounds are mentioned first, since they were liked, whereas the Germans, since they are disliked, are relegated to second place.

If we have in the Polish language of the eighteenth century an established sequence 'nobility, peasants, Jews', which reflected the order of social stratification and also the order of emotions, we may ask whether this order is ever reversed. This does sometimes take place in particularly dramatic occurrences, such as when death disrupts the sequence of these terms. Because the expressions 'gentry, peasantry, Jews', and nowadays 'Poles and Jews', come to one's lips readily, as if they were single phrases whose sense in common speech is not reflected upon, we may assume that breaking the internal order of such expressions demands some mental effort. The first requirement is a degree of analytical sense, or the awareness that behind the formal structure of the expression lies content and meaning. The second requirement is motivation, the desire to express a new content on the level of syntax. These two prerequisites must be satisfied for a linguistic pattern of this kind to be broken up. So, a modern Pole, irrespective of his attitude towards Jews and of the subject being considered, would say 'Poles and Jews'. It is the pattern of language which determines the phrase, and the reversal of order, to the extent that it is consistent and goes beyond mere chance or accident, requires both analytical sense and motivation.

The Polish language of the eighteenth century was, in some respects, more precise than present-day Polish, seen in terms of the sociology of knowledge. This could be attributed to the influence exerted by the system of direct democracy, a system which produced an analytical sense as a matter of course, because a forum in which contradictory views are brought into agreement generates a definite linguistic culture in which concepts must be sharp and sentences clear. Similarly the fact that the Talmudic hermeneutics of Jews in old Poland were dominated by the analytical method of the *pilpul* can be explained by the influences exercised by their social organization, based also on the principle of the clash of opinions. Its functioning required skill in reconciling contradictory views, since the essence of *pilpul* lay in bringing opposed viewpoints into agreement. There is a close relationship between the type of social organization and the type of hermeneutics used.

The way in which language was used in eighteenth century memoirs seems to indicate a high degree of awareness, so that already at the level of syntax it produces meaningful pronouncements. When human groups or things are listed, the order as a rule is from the most to the least important and from the largest to the smallest. Apart from the analytical sense which is perhaps due to direct democracy, we also find reflected a vision of the social world in terms of an inflexible hierarchy, which is believed to be in harmony with the objective state of things. So Kitowicz writes that in 1794 'the Muscovites engaged in considerable pillage of noblemen's palaces, the gentry's mansions, churches and the Jews; and last, of the humble peasants.'[21] The order in which the listing is made reflects both the social hierarchy and the scale of the plunder.

Even in the sight of the executioner the gentry take precedence over Jews. Writing about criminal offenders threatened with death for the crimes they had committed, Kitowicz writes: 'when a member of an influential family committed a crime... or a Jew'.[22] In another passage, he observes that the rebellious Cossacks 'pillaged noblemen and gentry, Jews and peasants',[23] or: 'members of the Roman Catholic faith, Jews and various Ruthenians'.[24]

Although the ordering of social groups, expressed in the terms 'nobles and gentry, Jews, peasants' or, more rarely, 'nobles and gentry, peasants, Jews', is a linguistic convention well established in the social reality of eighteenth-century Poland, the convention could collapse when particularly dramatic events were being described. As stated earlier, death sometimes forces an interruption in the linguistic sequence. And so, we find in a memoir that: 'Cossacks ... committed terrible abuses and cruelties against the Jews under the pretext of avenging the death of the Saviour; at the same time they did not spare village vicars and landowners.'[25] The Jews, as the group suffering most, are mentioned before the clergy and gentry class.

Interesting material, relevant to our theme, can be found in the accounts of the Humań massacre of 1768. According to some Polish accounts, the Jews were the main defenders of Humań. The daughter of the governor of Humań, who survived the massacre, wrote: 'I remember seeing ... Jews with singed beards and sidelocks who were shooting and defending themselves with great spirit – only Jews, I might add.'[26]

In Tuczapski's manuscript of 1788 we read:

> Szafrański, having collected all the guns, armed Jews with them and was thus in active command of the armoury and the entire defence. When the rebels approached the gates, leading peasants armed with hatchets to cut down the palisade, they were struck by cannon fire from the soldiers, while the Jews, shooting through the palisades, forced them to retreat. The Jews contributed actively to the defence and executed all Szafrański's orders.[27]

Adam Moszczeński's account reveals that the Jews in Humań conducted themselves with greater dignity than the gentry. It is true that Moszczeński does not write about the role played by the Jews in defending the fortress, but from his description of events, it appears that the Jews were more far-sighted and less prone to panic than the gentry. He writes:

The Jews, seeing how the noblemen Ciesielski, Młladanowicz and Rogaszewski treated the Cossacks and their commander unjustly, naturally realised that it would bring repercussions when Żeleźniak approached at the head of the rebellious peasantry and the Cossacks. They went to the nobleman Ciesielski and suggested to him that Gonta was sure to have some agreeement with Żeleźniak.[28]

The Jews' warnings were disregarded. On the whole the image conveyed of their behaviour is more positive than that of the gentry. Moszczeński does not praise the Jews in so many words but, significantly, he breaks with linguistic convention and in his account, as a rule, gives the Jews precedence over the gentry:

Here Gonta joined forces with the hordes led by Żeleźniak, and they marched together on Humań; wherever, on their way, they found Jews, gentry and Poles, these were cut to pieces.[29] . . . And then they covered the whole town of Humań with corpses. The deep well in the market place was filled with the bodies of dead children. The peasants in the villages robbed and killed Jews and their children, while the gentry and landowners were bound up and taken by cart to Humań where drunken Cossacks were killing them.[30]

Although in her memoir cited earlier, Mrs Krebs, the daughter of the governor of Humań, refers to the Jews as the main defenders of the fortress, the linguistic convention does not change when she writes that in Humań 'there were many merchants, Turks, Greeks, Muscovites, and Jews.'[31] In Moszczeński's account, however, 'many Jews, Greeks, Armenians, Turks and Tartars had settled [in Humań].'[32]

Generally speaking, the sequence in which people and objects are listed can be regarded as an expression of emotion, or as a reflection of social hierarchy in social consciousness, or both; our interpretation would depend on the context. Let us consider, for example, the meaning contained in one sentence, written by the Prussian subject George Forster, during his travels in Poland: 'At seven I arrived at Kęty, a miserable little town, where, because of the fair, the place was packed with carts, horses, peasants, oxen and swine, and also Jews.'[33]

This kind of ordering is completely unknown in Polish literature, although its essence can be found in the sentence quoted earlier, written by a nobleman who, in accordance with family tradition, gave greyhounds precedence over the Germans.

In conclusion we can state that, generally speaking, language used at the level of common speech is subjected to strong schematization. Although in eighteenth century accounts the phrase 'nobles and gentry, Jews, peasants' is usually found – and more rarely, 'nobility and gentry, peasants, Jews' – when particularly dramatic events are being described, engaging deep emotions and moral judgments, this schema can break down. So, Jews could be mentioned first, before the gentry, when they are the victims suffering most or when, in a given situation, as in Adam Moszczeński's account of the Humań massacre, evaluation in moral and subjective categories places them ahead of the noble and gentry class. Thus in language too, although in a limited sense, the Jews appear to be a mobile class.

NOTES

1 H. Graetz, *Historia Żydów*, vol. 8, (Warsaw, 1929), p. 52.
2 *Polska Stanisławowska w oczach cudzoziemców*, vol. 2, (Warsaw, 1963), p. 321.
3 Ibid., p. 95.
4 See A. Eisenbach, *Z dziejów ludności żydowskiej w polsce w XVIII i XIX wieku. Studia i szkice*, (Warsaw, 1983), p. 34.
5 *Z dziejów Hajdamaczyzny*, vol. 2, (Warsaw, 1905), p. 48.
6 *Polska Stanisławowska w oczach cudzoziemców*, vol. 2, p. 299.
7 A. Pawiński, *Rządy Sejmikowe w Polsce 1572–1795*, (Warsaw, 1978), pp. 169–70.
8 Natan Hannower, 'Jawein Mecula, tj. Bagno głębokie. Kronika Zdarzeń z Lat 1648–1652', translated by M. Bałaban in: *Sprawy i Rzeczy Ukrainne*, (Lwów, 1914), p. 18.
9 Adam Moszczeński, *Pamiętniki do historii polskiej w ostatnich latach panowania Augusta III i pierwszych Stanisława Poniatowskiego*, (Poznań, 1858), p. 137.
10 J.B. Marchlewski, *Antysemitizm a Robotnicy*, (Kraków, 1913), p. 55.
11 See J. Kitowicz, *Pamiętniki czyli Historia Polska*, (Warsaw, 1971).
12 Ibid., p. 439.
13 Ibid., p. 441.
14 Ibid., p. 441.
15 Ibid., p. 443.
16 Ibid., p. 443.
17 See W. Kula, *Teoria ekonomiczna ustroju feudalnego*, (Warsaw, 1983).
18 B. Spinoza, *Etyka*, (Warsaw, 1954), pp. 348–9.
19 M. Bałaban, *Z historii Żydów w Polsce. Studia i szkice*, (Warsaw, 1920), p. 23.
20 M. Starzeński, *Na schyłku dni Rzeczypospolitej*, (Warsaw, 1914), p. 2.
21 J. Kitowicz, *Pamiętniki czyli Historia Polska*, (Warsaw, 1971), p. 595.
22 J. Kitowicz, *Opis obyczajów za panowania Augusta III*, (Wrocław, 1970), p. 263.
23 Ibid., p. 304.
24 Ibid., p. 329.
25 M. Starzeński, *Na schyłku dni Rzeczypospolitej*, p. 25.
26 *Opis autentyczny rzezi humańskiej przez córkę Gubernatora Humania z Młodanowiczów zamężną Krebsową*, (Poznań, 1840), p. 23.
27 *Z dziejów hajdamaczyzny*, p. 57.
28 A. Moszczeński, *Pamiętniki do historii polskiej* ..., pp. 139–40.
29 Ibid., p. 142.
30 Ibid., p. 144.
31 *Opis autentyczny rzezi humańskiej* ..., p. 10
32 A. Moszczeński, *Pamiętniki do historii polskiej* ... p. 145.
33 *Polska stanisławowska w oczach cudzoziemców*, vol. 2, p. 48.

POLISH SYNAGOGUES IN THE NINETEENTH CENTURY
Maria and Kazimierz Piechotka

The fall of the Commonwealth of Poland and Lithuania and the partition of the state weakened the institutions which had kept the Polish Jews communally united. These had existed until the end of the eighteenth century despite the abolition of the Council of the Four Lands in 1764.[1] New integrating factors emerged because of the changes in state dependence and the legal and economic position of the Jews, their relations with the Polish population and the administrations of the partitioning powers, as well as the emancipation processes and acquisition of real and formal equality, assumed different forms in the three areas of partitioned Poland. Of great relevance, as well, were the internal factors – Jewish attitudes toward inherited forms of communal organization and the distinctive features of this religious and cultural life. In the nineteenth century, processes developed which were already evident among the Polish Jews in the pre-partition period. Economic, social and cultural stratification accentuated. But it is chiefly religious divisions which are important to us here, since they affected how and why synagogues were built.

In the first half of the nineteenth century, *mitnagdim*, the followers of classical rabbinical Judaism, were largely recruited as members of the superintendence of synagogues.[2] (This institution was introduced in the 1820s in the Congress Kingdom of Poland and Galicia, to replace the *kehillah* organization.) It was *mitnagdim* who were typically put in charge of communal property, which included synagogues, *batei midrash* (study houses), ritual baths and the like, and who made decisions concerning their management.

Hasidism grew in opposition to rabbinical Judaism. Originating in the eighteenth century in Podolia, during the nineteenth century it spread across Galicia, the Congress Kingdom of Poland and the Russian partition zone, becoming increasingly dynamic and popular among the Jewish masses. The religious life of the Hasidic Jews was centred around the homes of their spiritual leaders or *tsaddiks*. The *hasidim* did not normally take part in religious services held in the synagogue, and they prayed in their usually small *shtibels*, frequently located in private houses. Occasionally a few *shtibels* were situated in the same town, each one attracting the followers of a different *tsaddik*. *Hasidim* also erected their own large synagogues (for instance, Glancer's synagogue in Lwów, the synagogues at Kowno, Sadagóra).

The Jewish Enlightenment movement (*Haskalah*) grew mainly in large towns.[3] Its followers, the *maskilim*, were supported by the new Jewish intelligentsia and bourgeoisie. Polish *maskilim* were inspired by the German Jews. The influence of German culture on them is *inter alia* reflected in the names of the first, so-called 'progressive' synagogues (*die dajcze szul*) built at the time and also by the fact that German prevailed for a long time as the language used in sermons preached in these synagogues.[4] There were relatively few East European *maskilim* and especially at the beginning of the nineteenth century their activities were resisted by the traditionalist Jewish masses; indeed, the *mitnagdim* and *hasidim*, who were traditional enemies, united in the hatred of the *maskilim*. Moreover, the 'enlightened' received little official support.[5]

After 1815 the bulk of the Jewish population found themselves in the territories acquired by Russia. They lived in two areas which were administratively distinct – the Russian zone, which included the former provinces of Byelorussia, Lithuania and the Ukraine and which were annexed directly by the Russian Empire, and the Congress Kingdom of Poland. Together with the Jewish population of Galicia they constituted the largest, and most expanding concentration of Jews in Europe.

In the territories that belonged to Russia and Austria the Jewish population not only increased in size but also as a proportion of the overall population. During the nineteenth century the number of Jews in Galicia increased more than fourfold – from 200,000 (5.5 per cent) in 1816 to 872,000 (11 per cent) in 1910, despite emigration to the Congress Kingdom, which had begun in the 1840s, and to the West and America in the 1870s.[6] In the Congress Kingdom the growth rate was even more dynamic – from 213,000 (7.8 per cent) in 1816 to 719,000 (13.5 per cent) in 1865, reaching 1,320,000 in 1897 (14.5 per cent of the overall population and 28.3 per cent of the urban population)[7] which practically meant a sevenfold population increase. There was a relatively small number of Jews in the provinces which belonged to Prussia; the majority of them inhabited the territories of the Grand Duchy of Poznań (around 50,000 in 1816). The Jewish population was much smaller in Silesia (around 16,000), and there was only a tiny number in Pomerania (2,800).

Attachment to traditional forms of worship, which prevailed in Russian and Austrian Poland, together with the poverty of Jewish communities in small towns, helped to preserve a considerable number of synagogues built in the pre-partition period. Though they had to be rebuilt frequently or

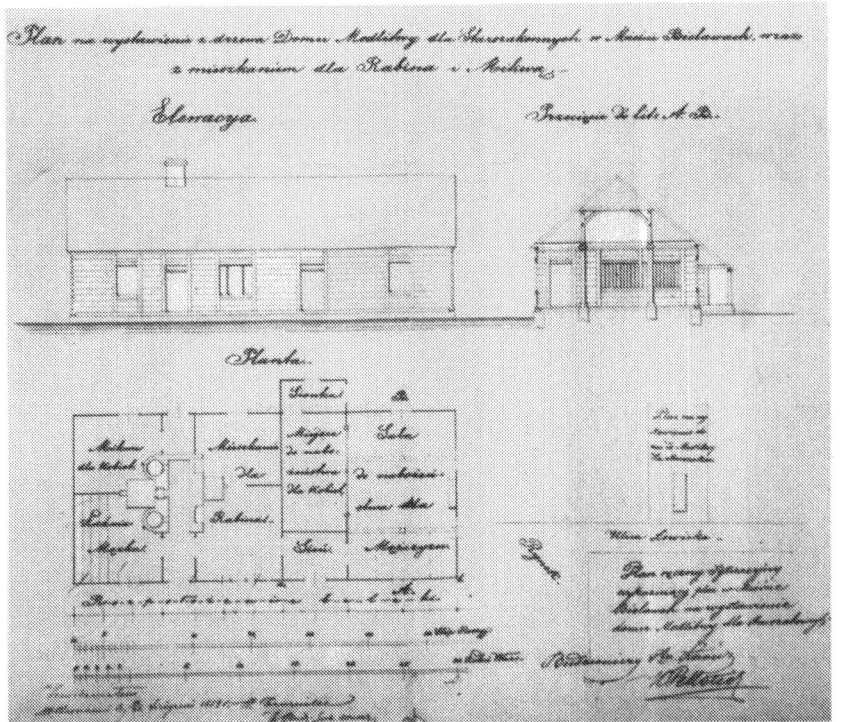

1 BIELAWA – Synagogue with rabbi's dwelling and *mikve*. Designed by T.K. Pelletier, 1856. AGAD – CWW.

2 KUZNICZKA – First half of the nineteenth century. Photo, Czubrykowski, before 1939. Photo archives of IS-PAN.

3 DZIAŁOSZYCE – Designed by F. Frankowski, 1852. Photo, Dobrowolski, 1950. Photo archives of IS-PAN.

4 KLIMONTOW – Built about 1851. Photo, T. Przypkowski, 1952.

5 MOGIELNICA – First half of the nineteenth century. Surveyed by ZAP before 1939.

6 CHOMSK – First half of the nineteenth century. Photo, T. Bochnig, 1929. Photo archives of IS-PAN.

7 WARSAW – PRAGA, Szeroka Street. Designed by J. Lessel, about 1830, pulled down in 1961. Photo, K. Beyer, about 1860. Photo archives of IS-PAN.

8 ŁOMZA – Version I, unexecuted. Designed by H. Marconi, 1832. AGAD – the Marconi collection.

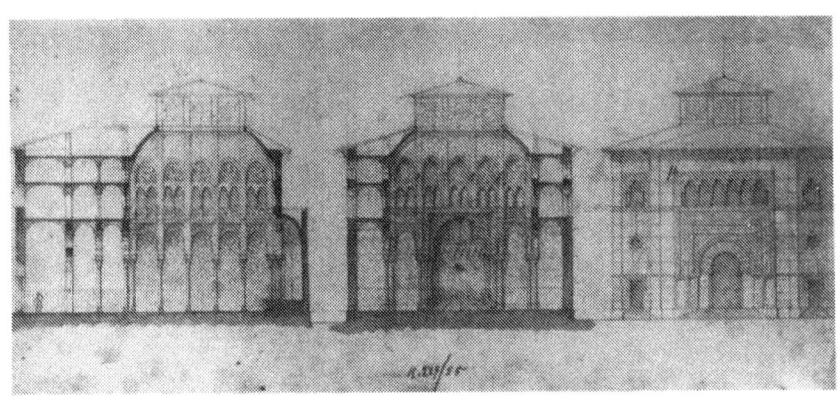
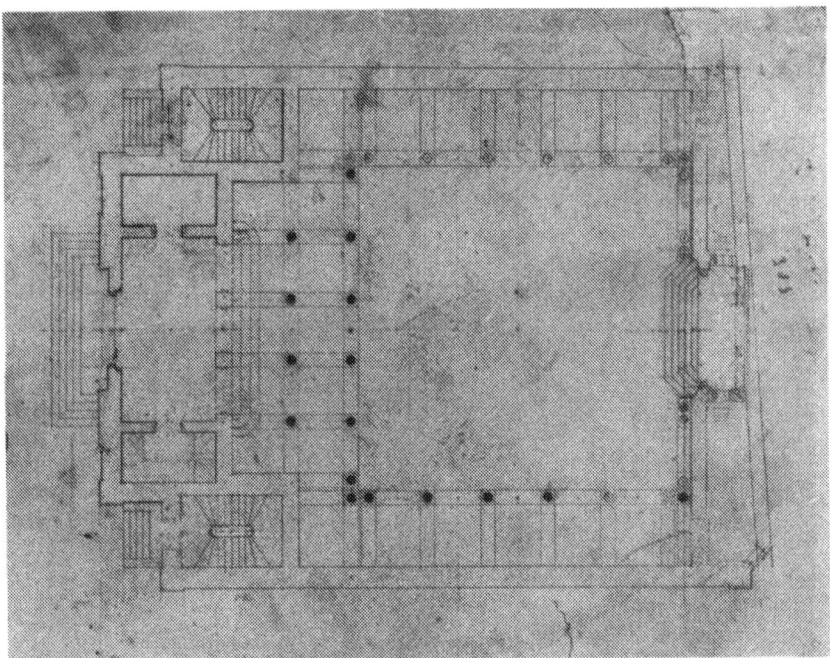

9 WARSAW – Franciszkańska Street. Version I, unexecuted. Designed by H. Marconi, 1850. AGAD – the Marconi collection.

10 LWOW – Progressive Synagogue, 1846. After M. Bałaban, *Historia Postępowej Synagogi we Lwowie*. Photo, J. Morek.

11 LWOW – Progressive Synagogue. As above.

12 KRAKOW – Tempel, 1862. Photo, M. Krajewska, 1985.

13 KRAKOW – Tempel. As above.

14 WARSAW – Great Synagogue at Tłómackie. Designed by H. Marconi, 1875. Photo, H. Poddębski. Photo archives of IS-PAN.

15 WARSAW – Great Synagogue at Tłómackie, 1875. *Kłosy* (1888), No. 1183, p. 139. Engraved by Witoszewicz.

16 BEDZIN – Second half of the nineteenth century. Photo archives of IS-PAN.

17 WŁOCŁAWEK – Designed by F. Tournelle, 1847. Engravd by A. Kozarski. *Tygodnik Ilustrowany*, 1872, pp. 254–5.

18 STANISŁAWOW – ca 1879. Photo archives of IS-PAN, before 1939.

19 ŁODZ – 'Italian' Synagogue. Designed by H. Majewski about 1880. After *Architektura Łodzi Przemysłowej*, reproduced by G. Russ.

20 PRZEMYSL – Szajnbach's Synagogue about 1910. Photo archives of ZIH.

21 RADYMNO – about 1910. Photo J. Zurowski, 1961. Photo archives of ZIH.

22 WILNO – Subocz Street. Designed by A. Dubowik, 1927. AAN.23

WIELKIE OCZY – Nineteenth century synagogue. Photo c. 1950. Photo archives of IS-PAN.

enlarged, they often still served communities. The Jewish demographic increase required that additional rooms be added to accommodate women or as prayer rooms for brotherhoods and guilds. Interiors were often modernized, galleries for women were built into the older structures. Occasionally the exterior was modernized. Most frequently sunken roofs, which were difficult to maintain, were removed and replaced with sloping ones. In such cases parapets were demolished and the more prosperous communities had elevations decorated. The finest synagogues of the sixteenth, and especially the seventeenth and eighteenth centuries survived in the eastern and central provinces of the Polish Commonwealth until the Second World War. Elsewhere, in the former Prussian territories, such buildings were not preserved by the turn of the century. Jewish mass emigration further discouraged the erection of new synagogues and was unfavourable for the preservation of the old ones. This was noted in 1939 by Sz. Zajczyk[8] when he wrote about the paucity of examples of synagogue architecture in the western provinces of Poland. It was only in the nineteenth century that huge synagogues, designed by German architects and modelled on German synagogue architecture, were erected in Silesia and the big cities of Great Poland and Pomerania (such as Gliwice, Racibórz, Bytom, Katowice, Gdańsk, Bydgoszcz, Poznań).

The rapid increase in the number of Jews, along with interval migration patterns, created a need for new synagogues, *batei midrash*, ritual baths and slaughterhouses. The authorities of the Congress Kingdom were aware of this. Correspondence between the presidents of the Kalisz and Mazovian provinces and the Government Board for Instruction and Public Worship has survived from 1818 on how to grant permission to erect new synagogues 'where they had never been built before' because of the 'growth of the resident population of the Judaic Faith in the Kingdom'.[9] Attempts were also made to regulate organisational dependence of those new communities. The increasing Jewish populations of small towns tried to escape from dependence on the *kehillot* elsewhere. Complaints were occasionally lodged of excessive taxation and of the accumulation of wealth by the synagogues of dominant *kehillot*. Such a complaint was made in 1822 by the Jews from Serock and Nowe Miasto Pułtuskie against the Nasielsk *kehilla*.[10] The Jews of Wyszków also struggled for independence from Maków Mazowiecki (correspondence about this dates from 1837 to 1859). They tried to create the conditions necessary for each community to act independently. It was decided that, until a new synagogue could be built, rooms would be rented for common prayer and the synagogue service accommodated in this way. Though these efforts failed to produce the expected results, the community did act independently and eventually built a synagogue without official permission.

The rise of new communities was generally encouraged by the owners of private towns, who would provide sites for synagogues, and often established them themselves (for instance, in Aleksota, Izbica Kujawska). Their ability to do so decreased over time.[11] First, *kehillot* and, from 1821, the superintendence of synagogues was subjected to the control of both provincial and central authorities. Under these conditions the cost of the normal maintenance of existing structures was ensured but not money to erect new buildings. Synagogues and other buildings necessary for the religious needs of the community therefore usually had to be built out of the funds collected especially for that purpose from Jews, and occasionally with the help of large donations. If a community wanted to undertake a building project, the authorities would examine how it was to be financed. They evidently feared in such cases that the 'elders' of the community, who usually figured among the more affluent members, would undertake excessive financial obligations which they would then impose on the Jewish poorer elements, who made up the bulk of the Jewish population. Such control was exerted in 'national' as well as private towns.[12]

The Prussian and Austrian authorities carefully supervised the construction of all sorts of buildings including religious ones, and comparable supervision was later adopted in the Duchy of Warsaw, and the Congress Kingdom. New laws forbade the erection of buildings, including synagogues, *batei midrash*, ritual baths or slaughterhouses, without the approval for the construction of these designs. These procedures were identical to those for other religions. District and provincial architects were responsible for drawing up plans and helping to execute them.[13] Final projects were then approved by the provincial authorities, checked by the architects from the Government Board for Internal Affairs, and accepted by the Government Board for Instruction and Public Worship and the bodies which replaced them. Therefore the comments and signatures of architects who worked in the Warsaw offices (including H. Marconi's) are often found on the plans beside the authorities' decisions.

There was inevitable conflict between the economic restraints imposed by the authorities responsible for the distribution of funds and the desire for appropriately 'magnificent' synagogue exteriors from the architects who commented on the plans.[14] To satisfy the architects, the Government Board for Instruction and Public Worship thought it necessary to lay down a suitable architectural formula for synagogues and other buildings, and it therefore promoted model plans.[15] Many complications arose, of course: communities might also have particularly pressing needs for a new building, such as after a fire, while in other cases the indolence of officials encouraged builders to erect synagogues without offical permission. When this was discovered, enquiries were held, the building site was visited, lengthy negotiations conducted and letters exchanged. Typically these led to an acceptance of the status quo, for despite the protests of local authorities to higher ones, it was impossible to pull down buildings. This state of affairs had a deleterious impact on building and frequently hampered rational planning and regulation of the urban environment.[16]

At the end of the eighteenth century both wooden and masonry synagogues ceased to be designed with a high main hall, covered by a multi-tiered roof, and surrounded by rooms with galleries and corner pavilions. This design disappeared, together with the Baroque way of arranging space. At the same time the widespread general impoverishment and decline of patronage created unfavourable conditions for building in the previous sometimes lavish way. The synagogues' interiors were now also poorer. The main hall, which was still very lavish, especially in wooden synagogues into the late-eighteenth century, was simplified. The multi-tiered, false vaultings, built into the roof framework, disappeared – the last known instance of such vaulting is the wooden synagogue at Warka, built in 1813. Vaulting gave way to flat ceilings or mirror vaults (flat ceilings with a high concave cove running around the hall). As well as halls without internal supports, nine-bay and three-nave arrangements were still employed, the piers, however, being used to support key beams. Similar ceilings also appeared in masonry synagogues. The introduction of roofing paper and sheet metal made it possible to reduce the roof pitch. The high-pitched, multi-tiered, gabled or half-gabled roofs with four slopes started to be replaced by ones with low, two or four slopes.

The nineteenth century brought a change of attitude towards timber as a building material. Its specific properties had allowed such shapes as false vaultings or hanging galleries, which were impossible to execute with other materials. But it was now no longer used. Because of the risk of fire and because it had a short life, timber was reserved for building more modest buildings intended for the poorer classes. Consequently it was primarily employed as a building material in villages and small towns, where its availability and the ease with which it could be worked encouraged its wide use. Timber was also now of poorer quality – sawmill timber appeared, cheaper and in short lengths. The building authorities moreover pressed for masonry synagogues to be built. They had practical and aesthetic advantages – masonry synagogues were considered more 'monumental'. But they required larger funds and the use of larger numbers of skilled workmen. Consequently masonry synagogues, often replacing wooden ones, were built in the big cities or towns where the communities were older, more prosperous and better established, or where the donors were particularly generous. On the other hand the poor communities in the small towns struggled to be allowed to build in timber, which was cheaper and readily available. Often it was possible to get hold of it free from the local landowner and have local carpenters erect simple and modest buildings.[17]

The nineteenth century synagogues on a traditional lines were usually erected on the 'longitudinal' plan. The main hall, intended for men, was square or squarish, with the holy ark up against the east wall and the *bimah* in the centre, and was entered from the west through the vestibule, with a prayer room above it for women. The latter was occasionally extended by galleries built into the hall. In both masonry and wooden synagogues the 'longitudinal' plan was normally employed in its basic form: the height of the walls of the main hall was equal to that of the vestibule and the women's section added together. All these made up a compact structure, under one roof, with eaves all around at the same level. A variation on the 'longitudinal' plan was occasionally used in small, poor synagogues and *batei midrash* (called *przyszkółki*). Here the walls of the main hall were lower than those of the vestibule and the women's section; the latter was above the vestibule, and was completely, or partially, built into the loft. One-storey synagogues and *batei midrash* were built as well, resembling the small single-storey town buildings, that surrounded them. They consisted of a porch, and the hall for men, joined by small openings in the wall to the smaller hall for women, which was accessible directly from the outside. All the rooms were low (240–250 cm), with a ceiling at the same level; the roof was shingled, tiled or even thatched. *Batei midrash* and occasionally even small synagogues were attached to the rabbi's or scholar's rooms, or the ritual bath and under the same roof. A plan from 1865 has survived from the House of Prayer at Bielawy and this shows that the same building was to house a small synagogue, the rabbi's home and a ritual bath. The project was drawn up by K. Pelletier, an architect from Łowicz district. Because of lack of money only a small synagogue was built.[18]

Houses of prayer were also set up in private dwellings, and were supported by groups of the faithful. In 1826 the Municipal Office of Warsaw informed the Government Board for Instruction and Public Worship that because of the lack of a synagogue in the capital 'the services are only held in private dwellings, where the neighbours gather for common prayers, sharing the cost of rent, fuel and light', and that 'it [the office] granted temporary permission for their further activity.' The letters enclosed listed 101 houses of prayer in Warsaw and ten in the Praga suburb, and also included the addresses and names of 'supporters'. Depending on their size the houses could take twelve to one hundred worshippers; the majority consisted of two rooms, but as many as twenty-nine had only one, and only two had three rooms.[19] Throughout the nineteenth century the number of such prayer houses was increasing, especially in the large cities. In Warsaw there were already 217 by 1891.[20] The situation was analogous in other towns.[21]

The basic version of the 'longitudinal' design, worked out at the turn of the sixteenth and seventeenth centuries, was employed until the inter-war period. Its simplicity allowed different architectural styles to be used in synagogue building while conforming to the traditional arrangement and shape of rooms, determined by the rules of worship. This was of special importance in the nineteenth century because of contemporary historical thinking, which led to stylistic pluralism.

The elevation at the entrance was the main one. It screened the fact that the western part of the building was divided into two storeys, which could, but need not be, reflected in the elevation: light could enter the women's section in the upper storey through windows in side walls too. Similarly the stairs could either be placed against the elevation (outside stairs) or remain hidden inside the building. The size and position of windows on side elevations depended on the arrangement of the interior. Usually they were different in the two-storey western part and in the high main hall. In synagogues with side galleries turning along the whole wall, there were usually two tiers of windows. Since the Holy Ark was placed inside the synagogue, against the eastern wall, this consequently determined how the eastern elevation would be built. The central part of the wall could not have windows up to the level of the ark. The shape of roofs in the nineteenth century, once the practice of building vaults into the lofts had been abandoned, depended on their framework and the material used to cover them.

In the first half of the nineteenth century architecture was dominated by classicism. In the constitutional period of the Congress Kingdom the authorities enforced the use of the classical style when edifices were built or rebuilt for them, and it also tended to be imposed on government architects, who designed sacred buildings among others. Classical forms continued to be employed throughout the nineteenth century until the end of the 1920s. They ensured that the plans employed would be generally approved: architectural rules were viewed as a reflection of eternal ones which contributed to the imperishable grandeur of the edifice.[22] In the case of sacred buildings, they expressed the timeless character of religious truths. The principles of 'ordered' architecture were taught in every architectural college. They made it easier to draw up projects. Rules were followed which almost automatically determined the proportions of a building, its architectural divisions, the position of openings and the choice of detail. In the first half of the nineteenth century architectural orders were associated with the social 'position' of its founder or of the class the building was designed to serve.[23] The use of columns, together with Ionic and Corinthian orders, was considered proper for upper classes, whereas the urban middle classes were entitled to either pilasters of Doric or Tuscan orders, or else to not using orders but architecture based on classical canons. When government edifices were erected, their architectural style had to correspond with the position of the city in the administrative hierarchy. Albums filled with designs, for churches as well, were used for this. Piotr Aigner, professor of architecture at the University of Warsaw, who was employed by the Government Board for Internal Affairs and Police and was one of the most outstanding architects of the first quarter of the nineteenth century, published a book in 1825 called, *Budowy kościołów część pierwsza zamykająca cztery Projekta Kościołów Parafialnych różnej wielkości w dziewięciu tablicach* (Church Building. Part I: Four Designs for Parish Churches of Different Size in Nine Plates).[24]

As far as synagogue architecture was concerned, it was considered proper to follow the designs ascribed to urban middle classes, though this rule was not strictly observed. Usually the 'grand order' was employed: the pilasters articulated all the elevations, or only the front one along the whole height of the wall. The front elevation could occasionally be emphasized by a columnar portico (most frequently three-axial, added, recessed or only blind), crowned with a triangular pediment, set against the background of a stepped gable, screening the high-pitched roof (Kuźniczka, Pabianice, Wieniawa near Lublin, Płońsk, and others). There is a striking resemblance between these elevations and the model churches designed by Aigner. They were a continuation of the Palladian tradition, which appeared in palace and church architecture in the last thirty years of the eighteenth century. Then the palace at Tulczyn, owned by the Potockis, was built, and the synagogue as well, whose front elevation imitated the Venetian church of San Giorgio Maggiore.[25] Porticoes with pediments were added to synagogues with roofs with four slopes (Kępno, 1815). At Klimontów (1851) a portico of this type screens the outside stairs. The synagogue at Działoszyce (designed by I. Frankowski in 1852) has a saddle roof, crowned with pediments, and pilasters articulate all the elevations; it is worth noting that the Tuscan style was correctly designed. The synagogue in Biała Podlaska, rebuilt after a fire in 1826, had a recessed portico hiding a gallery in the storey, and flanked by two square towers, reminiscent of former pavilions.

The revival of classical forms was seen in wooden synagogues too. The synagogue at Mogielnica had a columnar portico; at Raków the pillars of the outside gallery were crowned with small Tuscan capitals. Similar heads were put on the pillars of the gallery at Zabłudów which at that time was added above the vestibule of the seventeenth century synagogue. A columnar portico, set against a stepped, boarded gable appeared as well in the unexecuted plan of 1825 for the synagogue at Aleksota. Walls were decorated with the pilasters, rustications and cornices, characteristic of masonry architecture.

The use of 'Gothic' styles dated back to the third quarter of the eighteenth century. They were believed to show the ancient lineage or, as it was called, the 'antiquity' of the family, social group or institution for which the building was designed. It recalled the splendour of the monarchy of Casimir the Great, the royal law-maker, who was associated with 'bringing the Jews to Poland'. In the nineteenth century Gothic styles were used to rebuild castles, erect buildings intended to house the relics of the nation's past, and from the 1820s they were adopted widely in Christian sacred architecture.[26] Similarly there are a few instances known of synagogues built on the traditional, longitudinal plan, as well as *batei midrash* where neo-Gothic styles were employed. In the synagogue at Chomsk a high-pitched, stepped gable was added to the western elevation (narrower than the elevation itself), buttresses were built, and the windows acquired an ogival shape. Often, however, the builders confined themselves to the shape of the openings, which were occasionally combined with details borrowed from various styles (for example Szawle, the portico in Witebsk). Gothic styles were also imitated in wooden synagogues. When the synagogue at Wyłkowyszki was renovated in 1839 or 1852, an ogival door was introduced into the vestibule. Presumably at the same time ogival windows were constructed at Szawlany. Although the synagogues with neo-Gothic elements appeared across vast territories throughout the nineteenth century, there were few of them. This situation was because the neo-Gothic style was becoming widespread and typical in church architecture, with which Jews did not want to identify. In the cases described above the inventiveness of architects was reduced to adding to the traditional scheme; they were primarily classical, but Gothic as well, and later 'oriental' and neo-Romanesque ones also appeared. The faithful accepted them, provided the traditional arrangement of rooms and location of the holy ark and the *bimah* were preserved. Any attempts to alter this layout encountered opposition. The synagogue at Terespol was not built according to the plan accepted by the provincial authorities in 1856, but a traditional synagogue was erected instead on the longitudinal plan, with an outside gallery supported by pillars.

In the 1830s the first attempts were made to abandon the longitudinal layout. Such a synagogue was built about 1830 at Praga in Warsaw, and for many years this was the only community synagogue in the capital. The structure was designed by J.Lessel as a rotunda. That the synagogue was executed with so little respect for traditional solutions seems to have been possible because of the approval and support of its founder, Berek Szmulowicz (Bersohn). H. Marconi's synagogue plans have also been preserved.[27] In 1832 he drafted the first version of the project for the synagogue in Łomża. It was planned as a central building and was based on five squares with bevelled corners. The same layout was designed for the main hall and four corner pavilions adjoining it, connected by rectangular joins. The galleries above for women ran around the hall. Both the high hall and lower pavilions had flat octagonal cupolas over them. This version, however, must have been rejected, for a new plan was produced in 1835 which followed the traditional arrangement of rooms and masses but which were interpreted in an oriental fashion. The square hall with nine bays and two projecting corners on the west side, which were partly modelled on eighteenth century pavilions, had quadrilateral domed roofs, looking like a flattened 'donkey's back', and the windows were finished with horseshoe arches. The front elevation of the synagogue at Kolno, designed by Marconi in 1847, also had an arched horseshoe portal and similar windows. Marconi, who had already employed oriental forms in palace interiors, the 'Moorish' hall in the Pac palace in Warsaw, and the palace at Jabłonna,[28] presumably used them to emphasize that 'Jews are eastern people'. The synagogue at Łomża seems to be one of the first in which 'Moorish' forms appeared. They were further embellished and elaborated by Marconi in the two versions for the unexecuted vast synagogue in Franciszkańska Street in Warsaw in 1850. In the first version the square hall was surrounded on three sides by galleries in the first and second storey, and light was additionally provided by a 'lantern'. The second version provided for three naves with side galleries. In both versions the Moorish motifs were consistently used on the elevations and in the interiors. Marconi's plans were drawn up when the supporters of the 'Enlightenment' were increasing in number and beginning to play an important part in the economic life of the Congress Kingdom.

The supporters of the reforms believed that the basic aim of religion was to improve the morals of the faithful. This was to be achieved by teaching and sermons, which, together with prayers, became central elements of the services. The rabbi-preachers not only required religious knowledge but now had also to be talented speakers. The faithful were expected to participate in the service. To achieve this a few innovations were introduced into the Reform synagogues: the services were conducted in German and eventually in Polish; well-trained cantors were employed, choirs and, later, organs.[29] This led to changes in the layout of synagogues. A spot had to be found for the preacher so that he could face the faithful and so that they could focus their attention on him. Supervisors of the synagogue wished, moreover, to highlight their own importance by placing their seats in prominent locations. There was also a need for a spot for the choir, and possibly the organ. Unlike in the traditional interiors, where Jews could shift their pews to concentrate on the Holy Ark against the eastern wall or the *bimah* in the centre of the hall, in the Reform synagogue the fact that attention should be focussed in one particular direction was emphasized. The *bimah* was moved directly in front of the ark and lost its 'canopy'. A pulpit or rostrum for the speaker was put between the *bimah* and the ark, and benches were placed next to it for him and the synagogue supervisors. Consequently, a kind of a presbytery emerged – one raised above the floor of the hall and occasionally emphasized, as in Christian churches, by the apse. The interior, as in Protestant churches, was surrounded by galleries for women. These, unlike in former synagogues, could now watch the service and be seen from below. The isolation of galleries was becoming increasingly token and eventually entirely disappeared.[30] Undoubtedly reform of worship and the layout of progressive synagogues were influenced by the forms of services introduced by Protestantism.[31] This influence was already evident in the eighteenth and the first half of the nineteenth centuries in some traditional synagogues, where benches invariably were directed towards the ark, and especially with the introduction of galleries for women in the main hall along one or both side walls.

Such reform was initiated by German Jews.[32] Their assimilation and rising social status encouraged them to erect synagogues of a size and architectural style reflecting their social, economic and cultural position. But attempts were made to make Jewish sacred architecture look different from religious buildings of other faiths throughout the nineteenth century not only in Germany. The building of a new synagogue stimulated architectural competition and encouraged heated discussions, in which the most outstanding architects took part. These, however, did not lead to any unanimously accepted solutions.[33] The structures built at that time conformed to contemporary eclectic ideas and were usually a compilation of forms borrowed from different styles and cultures. The break in the tradition of synagogue building, which occurred in the majority of German countries (in some it had already begun in the Middle Ages), resulted in attempts to find the origins of synagogue architecture within Jewish history. Some were attracted to the architecture of countries where the Jews originated (Egypt or Arab lands); others to that of those countries in western Europe inhabited by Jews for long periods of time and where Jewish culture had flourished (Spain, Italy and Germany). Consequently inspiration frequently came from both Moorish and early-Christian architecture as well as from that of the Italian Renaissance and German Romanesque. The adherents of the latter declared, in the words of E. Oppler, who designed numerous synagogues himself, including those in Głogów and Wrocław, 'In Germany a German Jew must build in the German style ... The Romanesque style is completely German'.[34] Both this view and Bałaban's comment on the Germanization of Jews under Prussian rule are well illustrated by the Great Synagogue in Poznań, which was built in 1910 in the same style as an emperor's 'Romanesque' castle.

The *maskilim* in the Congress Kingdom and Galicia came from a similar *milieu* to German Jews: they were recruited from the Jewish intelligentsia as well as bourgeoisie and plutocracy, whose economic importance was gradually increasing. The first Reformed house of prayer in Poland was the *minyan*, founded in Warsaw in 1802 by Flattau, a banker from Germany, in his own home, and the orthodox Jews called it the 'German *shul*'. The *maskilim* attached to it in 1843 built the first progressive synagogue in Warsaw in Daniłowiczowska Street. It survived until the 1870s, and was then replaced by the great synagogue at Tłumackie.[35] From the 1830s, the *maskilim* in Lwów tried to build a progressive synagogue. They followed the example of the 'progressive' Viennese with their synagogue in the Seitenstettengasse, built in 1826. In 1846 the synagogue in the Rybi Square in Lwów was ceremoniously opened. It was initially called *Deutsch-Israelitisches Bethaus*, and the sermons were preached in German until 1903, when its name was changed to the Community Progressive Synagogue and Polish was introduced as well as German.[36] Its spatial aspects did not follow traditional arrangements: it was modelled on the central Protestant churches. The synagogue was based on the plan of a cross with arms of the same length and its octagonal hall had a high cupola above with a lantern. The central character of the interior was emphasized by at first two, and then three, tiers of galleries running along the hall. To meet the needs of the Reformed worship the *bimah* was placed near to the ark against the east wall. The arrangement of the exterior architectural shape was characteristic of the trend to not using orders but classical architecture which developed at the turn of the eighteenth and nineteenth centuries. In Kraków from 1845 the Progressive Synagogue was housed in a school building. It was only after opposition from the *mitnagdim*, who ran the community, had been overcome, that permission was granted to erect the *Templum*. The construction of the *Templum* was finished in 1862, and it has survived to the present day and continues to fulfil its purpose. As a result of successive rebuildings (1868, 1883, 1893, 1893–94, 1924) the main hall, originally on the square-shaped plan, has been extended to the east by two bays; the apse, aisles and staircases have been added, and the front elevation been transformed, retaining, however, its original neo-Romanesque character.[37]

The construction of synagogues in Lwów and Kraków was opposed by the communities' boards, which had controlled their own synagogues for centuries. In Warsaw the situation was rather different. The municipal authorities had, for many years, blocked the organization of the community.[38] It was only in 1830 that the synagogue at Praga, founded by Berek Szmulowicz (Bersohn), was built. In Warsaw itself prayers were conducted in numerous small synagogues. As late as 1900 the synagogues founded by the Nożyks (6 Twarda Street) and Sardiner (4 Twarda Street) were the property of the community.[39]

In 1859 the *maskilim* attached to the synagogue in Daniłowiczowska Street, realized that their building was too small and started plans to build a new and vast Progressive synagogue. However, it was not until the 1870s that it was possible to put this idea into practice. The members who built it were representatives of the growing number of assimilated Jewish plutocracy and intelligentsia. Their synagogue committee included Jews who played an important role in Polish culture. In order to obtain the best design a competition was announced in 1873 in which noted architects participated. The projects of Br. Żochowski, T. Lemke and J. Heurich, were awarded prizes in the competition, but not accepted by the synagogue committee. Eventually the synagogue was built to the plan of

Leander Marconi (Henryk's son).[40] It had a three-nave hall; the nave was enclosed by the apse, and galleries for women were located in the storey over the aisles. It housed around 1,500. The use of the 'grand order' in a portico, and the accumulation of structures, crowned by a cupola, produced a monumental building modelled on the classical and neo-Renaissance traditions of Warsaw architecture, begun by the neighbouring edifices in Bank Square (now the seat of Warsaw's People's Council). The combination of a cupola and a crown emphasized the character of the structure as a Jewish sacred building and must have fulfilled the intentions of the Synagogue Committee, whose members participated actively in both Jewish and Polish social life. This also accounts for the rejection of St. Adamczewski's design, as he borrowed ideas from other sources. His views are described in the literature as representing contemporary ways of thinking.[41] Adamczewski wrote: The edifice is designed in the monumental Egyptian style for historical reasons: the principles in Moses's laws for the Chosen People came from Egypt, and moreover, that way of building, emphasizing dignity and power, is a reminder of the dignity and power of ecclesiastical dogmas, that is of the law at that stage of struggle.' In fact the structural arrangement was classical and its 'Egyptianness' lay in the use of certain details, but, above all, in the symbolic meaning ascribed to particular elements of the building – for instance, in the twelve columns that represented the twelve tribes of Israel, two columns with stars for the past triumphs of the Israelites, the cupola for the power of the law over the nation.[42]

The general economic prosperity in the rapidly industrializing towns of the Congress Kingdom and the larger cities of Galicia in the 1870s and 1880s, resulted in the building of many substantial synagogues, both traditional and progressive. They were erected by communities and religious societies as well as by private persons. Ample funds were provided by the Jewish bourgeoisie and plutocracy with the equality of rights. Additional rooms were designed to serve the community's social life. The buildings were occasionally crowned with cupolas or tall, domed roofs (Częstochowa, Łódź, Płock, Tarnów, Słonim). Small cupolas and towers also appeared (Będzin) as well as turrets like minarets, which flanked the western elevation or emphasized the corners of the building (Stanisławów). These structures became part of the urban skyline, and occasionally even dominated it (Tarnów, Będzin).

Synagogue architecture ran the whole gamut of neo-styles, except perhaps neo-Gothic, and were frequently mixed. Large neo-Renaissance synagogues were erected in Łódź and Częstochowa – the so-called Italian Synagogue, designed by H.Majewski in 1880 in the former, and the New Synagogue in the latter. In the way the nineteenth century interpreted architectural styles, they were designed to demonstrate the links between Jewish and European culture, like the neo-Romanesque synagogues in

Warsaw, founded by Nożyk, Łowicz, Węgrów, Sosnowiec, Kałuszyn. The oriental trend, begun by Marconi's designs mentioned above, emphasized the Jews' connections to the East. This tendency persisted in the synagogue erected at Włocławek in 1854, designed by Marconi's disciple, F. Tournelle, and afterwards in numerous synagogues built in the Congress Kingdom and Galicia until the First World War, including the synagogues at Stanisławów (1870), Wołkowysk, Łódź, Kielce (1901–2), Białystok (1909–13), and elsewhere. Such elements as cupolas, horseshoe, trefoil and 'donkey's back' arches, borrowed from Islamic architecture and occasionally combined with neo-Romanesque, neo-Gothic, neo-Renaissance, and even neo-Baroque (Wołkowysk) styles, identified a synagogue in much the same way as the Star of David, the tablets of stone of Moses and the seven-branched candlestick placed on the front elevation.

Elements borrowed from various historical styles, such as towering gables, pinnacles, arcaded friezes, semi-circular and horseshoe arches, were eagerly employed in small synagogues as well, and here generally adopted traditional layouts. Many of them were erected at the same time in small urban centres in the Congress Kingdom and Galicia; around 1910 in Galicia *art nouveau* forms also appeared (such as in Radymno). The final effect produced by the building of course depended on the inventiveness and skill of an architect but also on the funds provided by those who commissioned them and the technical possibilities allowed them. Since these were frequently limited, many buildings appeared lacking style or with their stylistic provenance merely hinted at and often in simplified forms by the shape of openings, their frames, and the profiles of cornices. Similarly, throughout the nineteenth century, wooden synagogues continued to be built in small towns throughout central and eastern Poland. There were in 1910 at least 90 such buildings existing in Galicia only, 20 of them being classified as 'recently built'.[43]

Contrary to the eclecticism, which borrowed and combined elements from different styles and epochs, attempts were made to create a Polish national style.[44] While such aspirations were not limited to Poland, they were particularly understandable in a nation deprived of its own state, and living in a divided country. The desire to stress national identity and unity had its impact on all spheres, including architecture. Research into the Polish architectural past as a source of inspiration, began in the 1860s and then developed extensively in the 1880s, and was to affect small towns and villages as well. It was discovered that a number of elements which had been traditionally recognized as specific to Polish architecture had also been employed in synagogue building: these were, for example, the high-pitched, multi-tiered roofs, arcades and pavilions in wooden synagogues, and parapets in masonry ones. In 1903, at the same time as eclectic synagogues were being erected, and when *art nouveau* was beginning to appear, the synagogue was built at Oszmiana, whose huge, cuboid shape, with the traditional arrangement of interiors, was covered by a high-pitched, three-tiered, shingled roof with an octagonal wooden cupola built into it.[45] It almost precisely copied the traditional layout of Polish eighteenth century synagogues. In 1910 A. Szyszko-Bohusz published his own plan for the synagogue in Charków, modelled on styles characteristic of Polish provincial Baroque.[46]

The outbreak of the First World War ended the period of building vast synagogues. Architects began to rebuild the towns and villages destroyed by the war. An exhibition was organized in 1915, which resulted in the publication in 1916 of 'The Village and the Small Town'.[47] This included photographs of Catholic and Orthodox churches, manors, town and village houses, granaries and inns, as well as sixteen synagogues built in the territories of the Polish Commonwealth. They were not intended to serve as models, but as a source of inspiration. After independence, especially in the early years, architects found inspiration in this collection. Similarly continuity of tradition was emphasized with pre-partition Poland. Numerous plans have survived of wooden and masonry synagogues designed between 1921 and 1928.[48] Many of them repeated the traditional arrangement of interiors and structures. The halls were unispatial, nine-bay or three-nave. High-pitched, multi-tiered roofs reappeared, and even false vaults built into them (Lachwa), as well as reminders of corner pavilions, outside galleries (Bielsk Podlaski), lofts (Łuck, the so-called 'Purycówka'), gables modelled on Baroque ones (Pustelniki), and small cupolas (Wilno-Subocz). Moreover, the schemes not directly modelled on traditional forms (Otwock, Młądzka Street, designed by M. Weinfeld) were actually based on the well-established spatial arrangements. In the period between the wars, buildings were also constructed with no architectural style or pretence, occasionally naively imitating so-called 'modern architecture'.

Most Polish synagogues dating from the nineteenth and early twentieth centuries, like those dating back to earlier periods, have been destroyed. The structures destroyed first were those that attracted attention by virtue of their style and grandeur. Some were rebuilt and given new use. This entailed changing the arrangement of interiors, and occasionally altering their original architectural shape. Others were demolished. Undoubtedly, this architectural value (and this applied not only to synagogues), was not properly appreciated. They were considered of little value and were not given due care and attention. This is still partly the case. Interest in the architecture of this period did not develop until the late 1960s, while research on synagogues has hardly begun. In the historical or architectural literature they are typically mentioned only in passing.[49] We do not even possess a complete list of surviving monuments and their survey. Archival research is still at a very preliminary stage. The few publications devoted to particular buildings deal primarily with the history of communities and congregations connected with them; those that examine architectural problems specifically, are exceptional.[50] Consequently it is impossible to present a full range of problems connected with the Polish synagogue architecture of the nineteenth and twentieth centuries in their complicity. This will be possible only after completing the investigations initiated two years ago by the Institute of Art PAN. The authors of the present paper are fully aware of this state of affairs and the present paper is intended to draw attention to the value of those structures and urgent necessity to preserve the existing ones and to provoke discussion rather than serve as a comprehensive or conclusive investigation.

NOTES

1 The dissolution of the Council of the Four Lands in 1764 did not entirely destroy the internal organization of Polish Jews. The Jewish question continued to be discussed by Poles and Jews. Jewish plenipotentiaries were active during the Four-year Diet. Royal permission allowed representatives from over 100 communities to meet; memorials and projects were worked out, and there were negotiations between Jewish plenipotentiaries, members of the Polish Diet and royal deputies. See A. Eisenbach, *Z dziejów ludności żydowskiej w Polsce w XVII i XVIII w.* (Warsaw, 1983), particularly the chapter entitled 'Sprawa żydowska w Polsce w okresie stanisławowskim'.
2 'Supervision' was ordered by a letter of the Government Board for Internal and Religious Affairs in 1856 because of the unfortunate accident in Lublin. They were intended to control the safety of existing synagogues. During a 'supervision' the number of Jews who attended synagogues was specified as well. AGAD Acts CWW, vol. 1441.
3 S. Łastik, *Z dziejów oświecenia żydowskiego*, (Warsaw, 1961).
4 M. Bałaban, *Historia Synagogi Postępowej we Lwowie*, (Lwów, 1937); S. Silberstein, 'Postępowa Synagoga na Daniłowiczowskiej w Warszawie', *Bulletin of ŻIH*, no. 47; H. Kroszczor, 'Wielka synagoga na Tłumackiem', *Bulletin of ŻIH*, no. 95.
5 A. Eisenbach, op. cit., 'Problem praw obywatelskich Żydów w dobie porozbiorowej'.
6 M. Bałaban, *Dzieje Żydów w Galicji i Rzplitej Krakowskiej 1772–1868*, (Lwów); A. Eisenbach, op.cit., 'Rozwój i urbanizacja ludności żydowskiej'; J. Tomaszewski, *Rzeczpospolita wielu narodów*, (Warsaw, 1985), see particularly the chapter 'Żydzi polscy w Niemczech'.
7 R. Kołodziejczyk, 'Miasta Polskie w okresie porozbiorowym', *Miasta Polskie w 1000-leciu*, (Wrocław, 1965), vol. 1; A. Eisenbach, op. cit.
8 Sz. Zajczyk, 'Bożnica w Kępnie', *Bulletin of History of Art and Culture* [BHSiK], (June 1939), no. 2 – reprint *Bulletin of ŻIH*, no. 43–44.
9 Archiwum Główne Akt Dawnych, Warszawa – Akta Centralnych Władz Wyznaniowych [AGAD – Acts CWW], vol. 1441.
10 AGAD – Acts CWW, vol. 1679.
11 AGAD – Acts CWW, vols. 1821, 1715.
12 AGAD – Acts CWW, vols. 1441, 1715.
13 AGAD – Acts CWW, vol. 1441: The Committee of the Kraków province raised on

29 November 1827, the matter of costs for making the plans and *anszlagi* of 'neglected synagogue houses'. In response the Government Board for Internal Affairs and Police stated that making them was part of the professional duties of district builders, who were obliged to prepare plans and *anszlagi* and were to be repaid only for the costs of travelling and stationery. 'Synagogue houses, as they are public and devoted to the service of an officially tolerated faith, will remain under government protection, like churches and church houses' – the term 'church houses' in the letter applied to synagogues, baths and churches.

14 The plan for a small synagogue at Bielawy, when presented to the architectural authorities, was objected to on the grounds of its being too poor. It was declared that the synagogue, despite the modest means available, should be more impressive and 'different from the simple hut that had just been planned'. AGAD – CWW, vol. 1752.

15 The Board for Instruction and Public Worship rejected the plan for a synagogue presented by the owner of the estate of Aleksota, who intended to have it erected at his own expense. It recommended instead the use of the plan it had previously commissioned for Filipowo, 'which would probably be more suitable', since 'a synagogue constructed according to this plan would be decorative and truly beautiful'. AGAD – CWW, vol. 1821. Unfortunately we do not know the plan for Filipowo.

16 A fascinating exchange of letters on the building of a Jewish school at Działoszyce (Działoszyn) without official permission, in a place formerly designated for a new street, lasted from 9 February 1836 until September 1840. AGAD – CWW, vol. 2306.

17 The letters of the Jews from Działoszyce, who wanted to build a school out of timber, as it was available 'everywhere' and much cheaper. AGAD – CWW, vol. 2306. Z. Gloger in *Encyklopedia Staropolska*; the entry 'Synagogue' stated that 'elaborate building was much easier for them, as in the majority of cases they did not need to purchase timber: an ancient custom, preserved until our times, was that when a synagogue was to be built, the *kehillahs* would visit the neighbouring manors of nobles and landowners to collect timber; often they were given more than they actually needed'.

18 See note 14.

19 AGAD – CWW vol. 1441.

20 H. Kroszczor, op. cit.

21 L. Infeld, *Szkice z przeszłości*, (Warsaw, 1964); M. Bałaban, the introduction to *Historia Synagogi Postępowej we Lwowie*.

22 W. Krassowski, 'Problemy architektury polskiej między trzecią ćwiercią XVIII w. drugą XX w. dwudziestego wieku', *Architektura*, (1978), no. 11–12; A. Miłobędzki, *Zarys dziejów architektury w Polsce* (3rd ed. Warsaw, 1979).

23 W. Krassowski, op. cit., after S. Sierakowski.

24 P. Biegański, 'Teoretyczne projekty Kościołów Aignera', *BHSiK*, (1938), no. 4, file 6; A. Miłobedzki, op.cit., (1st edition, Warsaw, 1963), 213–214; T. S. Jaroszewski, *Christian Piotr Aigner – architect warszawskiego klasycyzmu*, (Warsaw, 1970). Aigner's work was not the only publication. It was preceded by standards and 'model plans' (*Musterpläne*) published in Galicia (*Einhundert und vierzig Kupfertafeln zum praktischem Baubeamten vom Jahre 1800*). See T. Mańkowski's review in *Dawna Sztuka* (1939), no. 3, file 2. In 1824 Hilary Szpilowski, a builder in the Mazovian voyevodship, published *Wzory Kościołów parafialnych*.

25 T. S. Jaroszewski, op. cit., contended that *Budowy kościołów* would only serve as a practical guide for the less independent provincial architects. To satisfy the need for recognized models, necessary for the government enterprise of building churches, Aigner used his own and other architects' experience. The plans in his

publication are a product of the eighteenth century spirit in architectural planning. T. S. Jaroszewski lists a number of churches, built before and after Aigner's work, which were inspired by the facade of St. Ann's Church in Warsaw, built in 1786–8 and designed by St. Kostka Potocki and Ch. P. Aigner on Palladian models. This list could be enlarged to include numerous synagogues. This is understandable, if one remembers that they were probably planned by the same architects who worked for the government. R. Wischnitzer, *The Architecture of the European Synagogues* (Philadelphia, 1964), includes T. Loukomsky's drawings. Although the author is right to draw attention to the links between the elevation of the synagogue at Tulczyn and the Palladian churches of St. Giorgio Maggiore and San Andrea della Vigna in Venice, she has misinterpreted them as being influenced by the Russian translation of *I quattro Libri dell Architettura*, published in 1798. For, as St. Lorentz has contended in *Efraim Szreger* (Warsaw, 1986), already at the end of the 1770s and the beginning of the 1780s a few palaces had been built in the south-eastern territories of the Commonwealth in the style of Palladian classicism, including the palace at Tulczyn (1775–82). In St. Lorentz's opinion it was E. Szreger who 'transferred great classical conceptions to the Ukraine'. See also T. S. Jaroszewski, 'Materiały do dziejów pałacu Potockich w Tulczynie', *The Annual of the National Museum in Warsaw*, (1982), no. 26.

26 W. Krassowski, op. cit.; P. Krakowski, 'Teoretyczne podstawy architektury XIXw', in *Zeszyty Naukowe Uniwersytetu Jagiellońskiego*, (Warsaw-Kraków, 1979).

27 AGAD – the Marconi collection.

28 T. S. Jaroszewski, 'Orient w architekturze polskiej XIXw', in *Orient i Orientalizm w Sztuce*, (Warsaw, 1986).

29 M. Bałaban, *Historia Synagogi Postępowej we Lwowie*, pp. 142–51. In 1887 a harmonium was purchased, in 1893 a mixed choir with professional female singers was introduced – it was located in the gallery. The organist, Prof. Wojnowski, was employed – according to the record book the organist should be non-Jewish. In 1897 organs were bought.

30 M. Bałaban, op. cit., pp. 44–5, quotes the description of the synagogue and its consecration from *Gazeta Lwowska*, 24 September, 1846, no. 11:

> ... basically it is a synagogue like many others, though with a few alterations which are now being adopted in Vienna and Germany. The interior looks magnificent enough, owing to the elevated, spherical dome, although the positioning of benches, as in an amphitheatre opposite the gallery erected for the elders, spoils slightly the impression usually produced by any holy place devoted to prayers. The sight of the whole congregation was both interesting and absorbing ... The most favourable impression, however, was produced by the upper galleries, surrounded with grilles, and filled with the beautiful faces of the daughters of Israel, whose dress, as we have noticed, has gradually come to resemble our own.

31 M. Bałaban, op. cit., 'Reforma czy oświata'. Dr Jezechiel Lewin, a rabbi, in his opening sermon on 8 September, 1928 compared styles and doctrines, reform and education. He contended: 'So the work and efforts of a century of Jewish history led to the ultimate overthrow of reform, which aimed at Protestantizing our religous life, our houses of worship. The sound instinct of the nation triumphed. Having to choose between reform and education, it decided to favour education. This has already started to breathe new life into Jewry and to penetrate all aspects of our culture, in all stages of its evolutionary development.'

32 M. Bałaban, op. cit.

33 H. Eschwege, *Die Synagoge in der deutschen Geschichte*, (Dresden, 1980); Brien de Breffny, *The Synagogue*, (Jerusalem-Tel Aviv-Haifa, 1978); P. Krakowski, op. cit.; H. Hammer-Schenk, 'Ästetische und Politische Funktionen historisierender Baustile in Synagogenbauten des ausgehenden 19 Jahrhunderts', *Kritische Berichte* (1975), no. 14.
34 H. Hammer-Schenk. op. cit., trans. by P. Krakowski, op. cit.
35 H. Kroszczor, op. cit.; S. Silberstein, op. cit.
36 M. Bałaban, op. cit.
37 M. Bałaban, *Historia Żydów w Krakowie i na Kazimierzu*, (Kraków, 1936), vol. 2; M. Bałaban, *Przewodnik po żydowskich zabytkach Krakowa*, (Kraków, 1935); H. Kozińska, 'Typy architektoniczne synagog w XIXw. w Polsce (ze szczególnym uwzględnieniem Galicji)' the typescript of an MA thesis of the Jagiellonian University.
38 A. Eisenbach, op. cit., particularly the chapter 'Ludność żydowska w Warszawie na przełomie XVIII i XIX w'.
39 M. Bałaban, *Zabytki historyczne Żydów w Polsce*, (Warsaw, after 1929).
40 H. Kroszczor, op. cit.
41 W. Krassowski, 'Aestetyczna ozdoba w architekturze drugiej połowy XIXw.' in *Sztuka II poł. XIXw.*, (Warsaw, 1983); *Inżynieria i budownictwo* (1880), no. 39, p. 158; P. Krakowski, 'Teoretyczne podstawy architektury XIXw.', op. cit.
42 An example of drawing inspiration from ancient traditions was J. Zachariewicz's project to rebuild a progressive synagogue in Lwów. M. Bałaban wrote in *Historia Synagogi Postępowej we Lwowie*, p. 142 ff:

> Zachariewicz, having started from the erroneous assumption that Jewish synagogues were the successors of the Lord's Temple on Moria (that of Solomon and Herod), began to study construction and preservation, and conceived the plan for the reconstruction of the *templum*: the vestibule and the apse were to be enlarged, and two massive towers in the eastern style, as high as the apex of the dome, were to be placed over the vestibule. New appendages were to house the council's assembly hall, or possibly a prayer room for winter, a rehearsal room for the choir, and the like... Fortunately, there were not enough funds for the major restoration, and the community was satisfied with minor rebuilding, which did not alter the outward appearance of the *templum*, which was so admired for half a century.

The plan was published in *Czasopismo Techniczne*, (Lwów, 1896).
43 Warsaw National Library, to Czołowski's Archives, MS 5635, 'Wykaz drewnianych synagog w Galicji', drafted by K. Notz in 1910.
44 Andrzej K. Olszewski, 'Przegląd koncepcji stylu narodowego w teorii architektury polskiej przełomu XIX i XX w.' in *Sztuka i Krytyka*, (1956), no. 54; A. Miłobędzki, op. cit. W. Krassowski 'Problemy architektury', op. cit.
45 The date for the building of the synagogue has been taken from *Encyclopaedia Judaica* (Jerusalem, 1972), vol. 12, p. 1496.
46 T. S. Jaroszewski, 'Architektura neobarokowa w Polsce' in *Sztuka I poł. XVIII w.*; materials from the meeting held by *SHS* (*Stowarzyszenie Historyków Sztuki ...*) in November 1978, in Rzeszów (Warsaw, 1981). A. Szyszko-Bohusz's plan was published in 1910 in the annual *Architekt*, (1910), no. 9, file 11, plates 33–4.
47 *The Materials for Polish Architecture*, vol. I, *Wieś i Miasteczko*, (Warsaw, 1916).
48 In AAN (Archives of New Acts) in Warsaw; in the Acts of the Ministry of Internal Affairs, there are twenty-four projects for synagogues accepted by the Ministry of Civil Engineering in 1921–8.
49 W. Krassowski, 'Aestetyczna ozdoba', op. cit.; P. Krakowski, op. cit.

50 M. Bałaban, *Historia Synagogi Postępowej we Lwowie*; S. Silberstein, op. cit.; H. Kroszczor, op. cit.; A. Penkalla, 'Synagoga w Klimontowie', *Bulletin of ŻIH*, (1980), no. 4, p. 116; A. Penkalla and J. Szczepański, 'Synagoga w Kielcach' *Bulletin of ŻIH*, (1981), No. 4, p. 120.

51 The history of the reconstruction and rebuilding of the synagogue at Piotrków Trybunalski is an exception. J. Baranowski and H. Jaworowski, 'Historia i rozwój przestrzenny synagogi w Piotrkowie Trybunalskim', *Bulletin of ŻIH*, (1966), no. 57.

ABBREVIATIONS

AAN – Archiwum Akt Nowych, Warszawa ... Archives of New Acts, Warsaw

AGAD – CWW – Archiwum Główne Akt Dawnych, Warszawa – Akta Centralnych Władz Wyznaniowych ... Main Archives of Old Acts – Acts of Central Denominational Authorities

IS – PAN – Instytut Sztuki Polskiej Akademii Nauk ... Institute of Art of Polish Academy of Sciences

WAPW – Wydział Architektury Politechniki Warszawskiej ... Department of Architecture of the Polytechnic of Warsaw

ŻIH – Żydowski Instytut Historyczny ... Jewish Historical Institute

ZAP – Zakład Architektury Polskiej ... Institute of Polish Architecture

THE IMAGE OF THE JEW IN POLISH NARRATIVE PROSE OF THE ROMANTIC PERIOD

Mieczysław Inglot

Anyone attempting to present an image of the Jew in Polish narrative prose of the period 1822–63 has to consider, at the outset, factors that conditioned this image.[1] First of all one must mention the social and psychological environment and the stereotype of the Jew which emerged from it.[2] As Alexander Hertz recalls:

> An image of one social group reflected in the consciousness of every member of another social group is one of the most interesting and important problems of sociology and cultural anthropology. The investigation of this image and how it evolved is of the utmost importance for understanding the relations of groups and individuals. In our relations with people belonging to different groups we use definitions derived from images drawn from our own collective experience about other groups and their members. These images and the definitions stemming from them are never the results of sober thought and do not correspond to reality. They are an inadequate representation of it. And it cannot be otherwise. They come from our everyday experiences which have nothing to do with the detailed and scrupulous search for truth of the scientist. These experiences are merely based on casual meetings and incidental judgements where emotion outweighs reflections. Consequently stereotypes are constructed which are a part of 'knowledge based on supposition' and ideas about others.[3]

Hertz's comments apply to the stereotype, in other words to several clear and characteristic traits of the model which have both an emotional and cognitive character.[4] Pierre Reboul introduced, in his work with the rather misleading title *Le Mythe Anglais dans la Littérature Francaise sous la Restauration* (Lille 1962), the similar concept of *images illusoires*. The title is misleading because in Reboul's work myth has nothing to do with the constructions of religious consciousness in primitive societies: like the stereotype, it is an idea for expressing 'false consciousness'. Reboul, however, emphasized the important role of literature in the formation of the myth. 'The leading and most important writers were always influenced by collective thoughts, although they sometimes escaped them and tried to shape them. The myth existed more vigorously among writers than among other people of other professions.'[5]

A second factor influencing and shaping the literary image of the Jew were tales in general circulation.[6] People who have investigated these stories distinguish those of folk creation (rural and urban folklore), of popular literature from those of 'highbrow literature'. We too draw a distinction between the image of the Jew created in literature intended for peasants and in literature written for the educated reader.

The final criterion is that of the specific literary *genre* involved. As Władysław Bełza has noted, 'In Polish poetry Jewish characters are almost always positive. Our poets expressed a particular and magnanimous sympathy for them which could even transform them into pleasant and normal everyday characters . . . .'[7]

Jan Winczakiewicz in his collection of verse on Jewish themes assessed Polish poetry the same way:

> The reader may be struck by the fact that the attitude of almost all poets to Jews is usually positive, and quite often they show great sympathy for them. Therefore, my choice is completely objective. In case I am accused of being too pro-Jewish, I have searched for anti-Jewish verses and I have found only two which I have quoted. On the other hand it must be admitted that Jews do not appear in Polish poetry until 1834 (Jankiel in *Pan Tadeusz*) and that previously their presence is only found in frivolous comments, epigrams and satire.[8]

It is worth adding that the Polish poetic tradition clearly influenced the image of the Jew in nineteenth century verse. Old Polish verse was greatly affected by the Psalms which show Jews as part of religious mythology. Similarly, in romantic verse and then in twentieth-century poetry, Jeremiah, Moses and Ezekiel were characters used to express Polish national problems and were even models for describing how one should view the world.[9]

The image of the Jew in drama was many-sided. As is to be expected in comedy, amusing, cunning and cowardly characters predominated, reflecting the folk stereotype of the little Jew (*Żydek*). Examples of these characters can be found in such comedies as *The Jewish Deserter; The Polish Jew or Everybody Has His Day; The Jew Who Was Changed Into Glass; Useless*

Jewish Matchmaking; The Jew in the Barrel or One Million Moneydealers or *The Jew as King*.

But several different characters can be found even in this literary type. For a start, in the Polish political comedy of Ludwik Dmuszewski (*Barracades in Prague, Farewell*) and Alojzy Żółkowski (*Foray in Lithuania*) there appear favourable representations of Jewish leaseholders and dealers who are looked upon as Poles of the Mosaic faith.[10] Similarly, Józef Korzeniowski (1843), in his drama *Jews*, introduced definitely positive characters.[11]

In the widely read, frequently edited and popular novels of the Romantic period, the image of the Jew is also a versatile one. In a dozen or so texts intended for the educated reader, one can find various ways of representing Jewish characters. These romances or sentimental and pre-Romantic works very early on introduced the theme of love between a Christian and Jewess (more often) or between a Jew and a Christian woman (more rarely) as a metaphor of the conflict between romantic and civil law. One can also find the character of the Jew as a patriot whether portrayed realistically or romantically, inspired not so much by the political comedies we have mentioned as by the archetypical image of Jankiel.[12]

Finally, Jewish characters were also created as in Balzac's *Human Comedy*. A whole gallery of human types appears in the realistic novels of national life, which were popular at this time. A common theme was that of the image of the Jewish plutocrat buying his way into the aristocracy. The image of the Jew also appeared in short stories and homilies intended for the peasants.

It should be said that the novels and short stories of the Romantic period about Jews in Polish were written only by Poles. It was not until 1863, and strongly influenced by Józef Ignacy Kraszewski, that works appeared by authors of Jewish extraction (J. Goldszmit, Z. Librowicz, Melwina Meyersohn).

In writing about the literary image of the Jew I have paid most attention to the stereotypes because they dominate both kinds of literary works, popular and 'high-brow'. Mythical characters appeared only rarely, mainly in the romantic stories about King Casimir the Great and the legendary Jewess, Esther.

Scholars of nineteenth century literature have identified two main themes in the treatment of the Jewish question. On the one hand, the complete strangeness, difference and even hostile attitude of Jewish society towards Poles is accentuated – the ethnic, linguistic, cultural, custom and religious differences, as well as the Jewish wish to remain separate from others, are stressed. It is possible only for some 'more civilized' individuals to integrate with the Polish nation. By contrast, more liberal attitudes depicted the complex mixture of guilt and injuries that had led to the separation, distrust and hostility. The supporters of this view thought it necessary to make Jews become more like Poles in their customs and civil duties. The entry of the adherents of the Mosaic faith into Polish society was treated by them not as something depending on the individual, but as something to be achieved by mass action.[13] Hertz also indicated a third Polish attitude towards Jews, which was not expressed in journalism but mainly in the literature of Adam Mickiewicz and Władysław Syrokomla. These writers did not look on Jews as a secretive community composed of enemies or of potential converts to Christianity and to Polish nationality. They introduced into literature the image of the Jew as a good family man similar to the Armenian or Byelorussian who was a part of the patchwork of the multinational Polish Republic. He was an individual retaining his overriding class and religious identity but at the same time working productively for the benefit of the whole nation. Thus, he fully deserved the name of Polish patriot.

These three attitudes form a framework for analysing the literary treatment of the image of the Jew. I will now examine this problem in more detail in romances, novels of national life, essays and stories for peasants. It is striking that although the first works in Polish literature mentioning Jews appeared at the same time as the beginning of romanticism, they were written as typical sentimental, pre-Romantic 'love stories'. The famous work by J. U. Niemcewicz *Lejbe and Siora or Letters of Two Lovers* (sometimes subtitled: *A Jewish Romance*) appeared in 1821. In the same year there also appeared the forgotten and almost unknown short story of Anna Nakwaska *Le Juif Abraham*.[14] Another sentimental work was the short story written by J. F. Królikowski (1830) (adapted from the novel of Ludwik Borne) called *Romance in Romance* dedicated to the unconsummated marriage between a Jew and a Polish aristocrat.

The elements of the Jewish love story are also to be found in *Tsarevich Constantine and Joanna Grudzińska or The Polish Jacobins* by J. Czyński (1833), in *The Jewess* or *Saxons in Kępa* by Paulina Krakowowa (1839) and in *Rachel* by I. Hołowiński (1847). In the years following even more works of this type were published, such as *Novel With No Name* by J. I. Kraszewski (1854), *Charming* by T. T. Jeż (1860) and *Noble Unknown* by A. Wilkoński (1862). I will comment on only the more interesting of them.

Three historical novels describe the legendary love story of Casimir the Great, the last Polish king of the Piast dynasty, and Esther. These are *Nałęcz* by F. Bernatowicz (1828), *Casimir the Great and Esther* by A. Bronikowski (1828) and *Esterka* by T. Bułharyn (1829). Kraszewski also returns to the theme in one of his best historical novels *The King of the Peasants* (1883).

Emotional attitudes in culture are often the chief mode of expression of societies threatened and humiliated.[15] Therefore, two typical models of love were expressed in the novels of this period. First of all they reflected the renaissance of Tristanism, the ideal of the equality of lovers facing a moral dilemma. Such an attitude clashed with the traditional view of the role of women. Social and economic reality ensured that the female partners of their Tristans were victims of Nazarene love, that is love where a sacrifice was made to their parents in accepting husbands chosen by them or in submitting to a higher ideal. It has to be pointed out that such conflicts were an expression of the movements for the emancipation of individuals from various repressed and derided classes.

The unconsummated love of a Jewish physician for an aristocrat in *Noble Unknown* was presented by Wilkoński in the same way as an affair between another aristocrat and an educated peasant in the novel *The Vengeance of Milk-Brother*.[16] Niemcewicz stressed the need for Jews to assimilate to Polish customs. He was influenced by Moses Mendelsohn, the creator of the *Haskalah* movement. In his novel, *Lejba Son of Abraham*, his eponymous hero supported this movement. He played the role of Tristan towards Sarah, the daughter of the merchant Moszka, an ardent talmudist. Their conflicts reflected arguments between conservative and progressive circles in the Jewish community. Moszka had promised that Sarah should become the fiancée of Jankiel, a fervent talmudist, as well as a cripple and villain. The author drew the melodramatic characters in contrasting black and white colours. He was evidently influenced by picaresque novels (*Moll Flanders, Manon Lescaut*) and depicted the talmudists as evil men who controlled the Jewish people by their ability to elucidate difficult problems of religious ritual. Count Edmunt Teczyński, a school-friend of Lejba, saved Sarah from a dark cellar where she had been thrown by the talmudists. He fell in love with her and made this plain to her, but because of his friendship with Lejba, he respected her rejection of him.

Friendship, which was rated as highly as love by the sentimentalists, was the main theme of the short story 'Abraham the Jew'. As we have seen, Polish writers quite often used the name of the biblical patriarch and the partner in the Covenant between God and the people of Israel for their positive characters. Abraham acted as a good Samaritan to Squire Kazimierz Milewski who was suffering temporary misfortune. He saved Kazimierz from being punished for his alleged desertion from the army and helped him return home and regain his property. His reward for this was to be given the privilege of living for ever near the palace and having the place of honour at the heir's table.

Niemcewicz's melodrama, despite its tragic conflicts, ends happily, as do the majority of novels written in this style. This was a reflection of the enlightenment's belief in the success of social and educational reforms. On the other hand, Jan Czyński found a different solution for the affair between the Jewish girl, Noa Hondelsman (sic) and Jakub Horowicz. Noa supported the Polish patriots fighting against the Tsarist regime and its Polish lackeys. 'The time will come when you Poles will treat us justly and will unite with us to overthrow the pharoahs who oppress us all terribly.'[17]

The oppressors were General Różniecki, who was the favourite of Tsarevich Constantine and was courting Noa, and Mr. Birnbaum, a Jewish spy, bandit and police agent, a character similar to Vidocquo, the archetype of Balzac's Vautrin.[18] As can be seen, Czyński made ample use of the tradition of picaresque novels. It is worth adding that Birnbaum, in trying to get Noa to submit, used the myth of Esther. To no avail, because his vile action was revealed by Jews who said: 'This is worthy of all Hamans who oppress our people.'[19]

In his novel, Czyński depicted the November uprising as a succession of lost opportunities.[20] The leaders of the insurrection were accused of collaborating with the enemy and of being afraid of a peasant rebellion. The insurgents failed to take the opportunity to win the Jewish people to their side. The progressive Jew, Jacob, dies after being falsely accused of spying. Old Handelsman curses the defeated insurgents: 'Let Poles ... learn what the disaster means, scattered among the nations like Israelites persecuted by those for whom they fought.'[21]

Hołowiński also wrote his novel in the style of a patriotic adventure tale, as well as a romantic love story. Rachel, the beautiful innkeeper's daughter with black hair and eyes, broke with her family with some help from the young heir Karol. Hołowiński thus described the drama of a person who had broken his ties with his own class.[22] The individual acted alone, or almost alone, against the crowd.

Niemcewicz had already described similar conflicts. The drama of Rachel was an even more profound one because she loved her parents who also loved their only daughter. Hołowiński confronts the intense love of a daughter for parents with even more intense feelings of an unusual type. Rachel was not in love with Karol. She left her home because of her love for the Christian God revealed to her through worshipping the Virgin. While playing with peasant children she had visited the Lady Chapel and decorated it with flowers on several holy days. Mystical ties were established between the Jewish girl and the Virgin. Rachel, the literary archetype of Saint Bernadette, took Karol's appearance as a sign from God. 'Oh, how I love you, beloved messengers from Our Lady Mary. In her goodness, to make an orphan happy, she inspired and sent your good selves to me. But ... my greatest fortune is to talk to Mary directly, without any messengers,'[23] she told Karol and Klara when they visited her in the cloister where she had taken refuge. Rachel was kidnapped by talmudists and suffered for her faith in a rabbinical dungeon, where she died united with Christ. Karol found comfort in Klara's arms.

Although Hołowiński made more use of the tradition of the adventure novel than his predecessors, he introduced elements of realism by creating the character of the rabbi and describing a tavern. This is also evident in his use of popular proverbs, such as 'when it thunders, the thief becomes honest,' 'when in need, go to the Yid: when in misery, go to the priest.'[24] However, his portrait of Rachel remains a totally romantic one. As in Norwid's *Assunta or Looking towards Heaven*, 'in the expressions in her face one could see higher feelings and sad thoughts. Apparently she did not pay any attention to her own physical characteristics.'[25] Rachel lived on two levels, the spiritual and mundane, and this duality influenced her appearance and actions.

In *Novel With No Name*, Kraszewski created a similarly soulful character, Sarah, the beautiful daughter of Białostocki, a merchant from German Street (which was the actual name of the street where Julian Kleczko, the convert and future eminent literary critic, was then being brought up). A student from Wilno, Stanisław, who lived with the Białostockis, became the teacher of the beautiful Sarah.

> Sarah entered majestically, quietly, without hesitating or blushing. She looked at the young boy with his large dark eyes, and he was deeply moved. The girl was dressed exquisitely, and nothing betrayed that she was a Jewess. Two huge tresses of dark hair sweeping down her back made her even more charming. She greeted the teacher and when he began to speak, she looked at him with such curiosity and intelligence that all the difficulty he expected disappeared. He found he had met a remarkable person, not a simple child of an exiled and pygmy nation but a flower chosen by fortune, one reflecting the colour and charm of a lost epoch and vanishing life.[26]

Thanks to romantic love at first sight our hero found himself in 'a paradise of delusion'. Sarah, or mainly her large thoughtful dark eyes, was a gate leading to metaphysical spiritual heights, a reflection of a vision of lost innocence. There was a symbolic unity between Sarah and the mythical Eve.[27]

Such wonderful love could not be consummated in this world. Sarah, rejected by her own society, knew that both she and Stanisław would also be ill-treated by Christians. When she realized that Stanisław's life would be in danger, she came to the decision to become an actress and mistress of a wealthy aristocrat. Thus, she became a modern Messalina who by disgusting her lover could neutralize their love.

These were the most important Jewish Isolde characters, partners of romantic Tristans. In the background can also be found a distinct group of characters related to Esther, the legendary mistress of Casimir the Great (1310–70). The novels describing the Polish King's love for the beautiful Jewess derived from a pre-Romantic interest in the personality of the

King[28] and they echo the biblical *Book of Esther*. The father or grandfather of Esther is called Mordechay (Bronikowski, Bułharyn). They were accused of using women to conquer Poland. 'She does what she wants, and Jews seize everything. The Jews have all the gold, it makes my blood boil to see them: you need a Haman, yes a Haman,'[29] cried one of the heroes of Bułharyn's novel. And Bronikowski described the diabolic plans of Mordechay in this way: 'He would change Polish land into Judaic, and the ancient tomb of Esther built in Łobzów would have the same significance for Polish Israelites as Mecca for followers of Mahomet.'[30]

The story of the Jewish conspiracy to conquer the world was thus introduced into Polish fiction. This view was later developed in the *Protocols of the Elders of Zion* and in twentieth-century racist writings such as *The Fall of Israel*.[31] The source of these ideas can already be found in the pamphlets of French counter-revolutionaries like A. Barruel, who connected the events of 1789 with a Jewish-masonic plot. It is also worth pointing out that the creators of the characters described (except Bronikowski) rejected the story, suggesting that it was concocted by magnates hostile toward the King.

Bernatowicz and Bułharyn described Esther as a beautiful girl who loved the lonely and unhappy King. This view is the opposite of Bronikowski's characterization of Esther as a tool in the hands of cynical Jewish conspirators. According to Bernatowicz, King Casimir was bewitched by the exotic Jewess, by her 'beautiful dark tresses falling loose to the ground like the long branches of a birch tree and showing her charming snow-white neck and marvellous waist between the tresses'.[32]

The novels were full of secret meetings, intrigues, chases and Jewish plots directed by the *Kahal* or inspired by Polish magnates. The characters of the Jewish plotters were painted in dark colours, and Bronikowski even associated the evil character, Mordechay, with magic and diabolic practices. At that time the evil characters were quite often redheads, following the way villains were presented in melodramas. The writers, in the fashion of Niemcewicz, condemned the conservatism of Jewish communities and their hostility and vindictiveness towards those who had deserted them. However, Bernatowicz violently opposed the deeply-held belief that Jews practised the ritual murder of Christian children.[33]

The most important trend in the Polish realistic novel after 1831 (the November uprising) was the attempt to fill its pages with everyday living characters. The writers fully realized that a distinct historical period was passing. This was the period of lost national independence which was worth preserving in literature. The faithful reproduction and preservation in popular memory of dying national customs was believed to be the essential purpose of patriotic literature.[34] In 1842, in the journal *Petersburg Weekly*, a prospectus was published for a joint work called *The*

Lithuanians. It was to be a series of literary portraits of such characters as the steward, provincial nobleman, tenant, tax collector and Jewish broker. The series never appeared in the press but the idea was realized by Józef Ignacy Kraszewski in his works (*Pictures from Life and Travel, The Magic Lamp* and *Types and Characters*).

Kraszewski became the main founder of the 'retrospective' movement which developed artistically from Stendhal's descriptive prose where the narrator acted as a mirror for what was happening about him. Thus, the relater was a landscape and portrait artist in the Flemish style, adopting techniques used in Dutch seventeenth-century painting. Kraszewski and other 'genre' writers used the method called 'the realism of presentation' by Ian Watt.[35]

However, the gallery of characters introduced into Polish prose by Kraszewski and others had been created earlier by Adam Mickiewicz in the pages of his great epic poem *Pan Tadeusz* (1834), 'the most brilliant and the most innovative Polish novel of that time'.[36] I will therefore begin my analysis of the image of the Jew in the Polish novel of this school by describing Jankiel, the innkeeper, one of the most interesting characters of *Pan Tadeusz*.[37] Jankiel appears for the first time in volume 4 of the poem, in the scene in the tavern, which was the usual place where people from various classes and nationalities met. It used to be the favourite observation point for narrators of the 'novels of the road'. The poet described in detail Jankiel's clothes and the characteristic configuration of his hands: he kept his left hand under his belt while he smoothed his long white beard with his right hand. He characterized Jankiel's personality further as well as his role as a political prophet and Jewish folk artist popularizing national and folk songs. Jankiel was known as a clever man and was therefore invited to settle quarrels. Jankiel's wisdom and talents were evident during the concert given for Polish troops entering Lithuania with Napoleon's army. The folk melodies, documenting various periods of Polish history from the Four-Year Diet until Napoleon's time formed the basis of the virtuoso dulcimer player's impromptu.

One can detect two main trends in realistic literature. Numerous writers, in reviewing the decaying past, tended to venerate characters from the past and show little sympathy for approaching changes. Others, on the contrary, liked to stress the richness and many-sided nature of reality and to create new characters.

The main representative of the first trend, Ignacy Chodźko, in introducing the character of Abraham Ilski, the innkeeper, called him 'the figure'. In his description he clearly showed his sympathy for the Jew as a representative of the chosen people and at the same time a citizen of beloved old Poland. He wrote: 'His name suited his appearance because his face was aged and noble, his beard was white and grave, his forehead was high and bald, his black eyes were lively and intelligent ... a painter would find him like a patriarch or even see him as a model.' There then followed a detailed description, in true Flemish style, of Abraham's clothing. The portrait finished with a characteristic tone of regret: 'Very rarely nowadays, and soon never, can one see such venerable characters among Israelites. They are disappearing from the present generation which is being changed into one common European people . . . .'[38]

Abraham Ilski was presented as a descendant of an old family with roots in a definite piece of land and having connections with the magnates. Chodźko, as well as Mickiewicz, emphasized the wisdom and unselfishness of his hero. His good advice helped solve the drama in the family described by him. Therefore, his sympathy for the Jew enabled him to describe accurately that ethos of knowledge and wisdom so highly prized by the Jewish community, traits rarely ascribed by Polish writers even to rabbis.[39]

Józef Korzeniowski was an author who emphasized the new characters. In the novel *Collocations* (1847) he introduced the character of Shlom, innkeeper and adviser to a nouveau-riche magnate. Shlom was a modern, fashionably-dressed Jew, a so-called *sheyne-moreyne*. He was a graduate of the famous Krzemieniec high school and he had wanted to study medicine. However, as Korzeniowski put it, 'his Jewish nature prevailed'[40] and he turned from books to business.

Kraszewski was the leading analyst and presenter of realism. In one of his earliest works, *The Magic Lamp* (1843–4), he introduced into the novel the fashion of presenting individualized and many-sided Jewish characters.

> I cannot understand why anyone writing about Jews is satisfied with always describing our Jews in the same way, as ragamuffins in skullcaps with dangling corkscrew curls and beards. There are Jews and Jews, ones as different from one another as heaven and earth.
>
> Look at this poor man, bent double, in grey gaberdine, his hat in holes and his cap threadbare, in shabby shoes, with his little box on his back, a Jew selling Berdycz calendars, lucifers, curry-combs, shoe-polish, etc. Does he really look like Moreyne with his perfumed beard, highly polished shoes, his cane with its silver ferrules, beaver hat and gloves, approaching the market hall? Between them are hundreds of intermediate characters from the officious factor to the wholesale merchant, learned rabbi and so on.[41]

Through the image of the Jew the writer introduced into literature a whole panorama of human types. One can find more mature and individualized images in the second series of his novels, for example in the fragment of *The History of Hershek*. The narrator used the same technique for presenting his characters as he applied in his novel *The History of Sawka*. Its theme was the ennoblement of Hershek, an average Jewish hawker and smuggler. This mirrored the presentation of the Ukrainian peasant, Sawka, who was also a man from the lower classes. However, Kraszewski was a realist and he presented Sawka's life as one narrated by the author, commenting that Sawka could not present his story himself. On the other hand Hershek's fate was shown in part as the product of his own character. However, in the second part of the Hershek story, the author explained the origin of Jewish wealth. He did not condemn it. On the contrary, he stressed the thriftiness, frugality and self-denial of Jews, including our Hershek. He claimed that able Jewish merchants were fulfilling those socially necessary functions neglected by Poles.[42] In this way realistic fiction was interwoven with the arguments of a reporter trying to describe real characters.

This stress on realism and contemporary accounts of the image of the Jew were typical traits of the novel of national life. Scholars of *Pan Tadeusz* have shown that almost all aspects of Jankiel's life were based on fact.[43] In creating the characters of rabbi, street bookseller, factor and innkeeper, the writers had in mind characters well known to them and to their noble readers, and ones demystified in a way which was unusual in the romantic novels.

Thus Jews were observed from the outside in the taverns known to all noblemen. 'The tavern and its keeper . . . formed an inseparable whole: it was impossible to imagine one without the other. Anyone remembering *The Organist* tavern had at the same time to think about Chaim the humpback . . . ,'[44] wrote Walery Łoziński. *The Organist* was described in detail by the author, who paid great attention to its keeper and how he treated his customers.

However, in the novel of national life, the image of the Jew did not always resemble a snap-shot from the family album. When events occurred which threatened the former social élite, elegiac tones were replaced by acute satire, although the realistic method of presenting events was retained. This method was seen particularly in the description of Jewish bankers and industrialists.

In the mid-nineteenth century, Józef Symeon Bogucki, a second-rate Warsaw writer, made nouveau-riche Poles the heroes of his novel *Capitalists* (1852). Somewhat later, Korzeniowski in his *Relatives* (1857) presented two Jews, the convert Olkuski and the Orthodox Geldson, in the role of capitalists. Korzeniowski reacted to a new phenomenon missing from Bogucki's writing, namely the development of Jewish counting houses and banks in Warsaw in 1840–50, that is, in the years when these novels were set. It is worth adding that the character of Olkuski, according to his creator, was based on the story of Sylwian Jakubowski, a poor messenger boy, who became one of the richest bankers of the capital city in 1836–52.[45]

In his rather negative characters of Olkuski and Geldson, Korzeniowski developed one of the most essential themes of social critics. This was the description of people from the lower classes who by pure chance (at that time the economic factors were underestimated) rather than by birth or hard labour, entered the ranks of the aristocracy. Although this time the story concerned Jews, it resembled Fredro's drama of Mr. Geldhab, a despised nouveau-riche banker of German origin.[46] It is also worth adding that this well-known character from Fredro's comedy was interpreted as being a Jew when performed in Warsaw theatres in the late nineteenth century.[47]

Kraszewski also created the rich magnates of *The Illnesses of Our Century* (1856) and *Metamorphoses* (1859). Similar characters can also be found in *Jewish People* by Zygmunt Kaczkowski (1860). It was a specifically Polish problem. These three novels were intended to criticise western materialism which, according to the writers, was menacing the Polish national, spiritual and aristocratic tradition. In *Metamorphoses* Kraszewski wrote, 'The predictions were fulfilled: the Kingdom of Israel appeared and the banker became King of the world' (vol. 3, pp. 28–9). The word 'Israel' had a symbolic meaning that expressed a materialistic viewpoint and financial speculation and it was also used when referring to Poles. In creating the Jewish character of Krzesław Żydowski who was a moneylender exploiting poor people, Kaczkowski was attacking not only Jews but also the 'Rothschild ethos' so popular in Jewish folklore.[48] The author wrote of his character in this way; 'Every Żydowski [adj. Jewish], like every Jew, knows the financial affairs of all his neighbours; he even understands the Jewish language because he uses it in taking to Jews. Such a man was Krzesław. This did not prevent his defrauding Jews as well as Christians.'[49]

Thus Jewish magnates were attacked as well as anyone who crossed the old barriers between classes and who climbed the feudal ladder. Jews, Germans, Francophile and Anglophile Poles were all criticized as propagators of western ways of making their fortunes through finance and trade. The term 'Jew' was, in effect, a slogan applied to wider social phenomena. It should be stressed however that an outright and unbridled attack on Jewish bankers did not occur until the end of the nineteenth century, when the Polish bourgeoisie became stronger and when such neglected values as frugality and saving material goods were being resurrected. This problem is however found in the romantic short story *The Stockbrokers* by Walery Wielogłowski. A Polish banker, who acted as an industrial spy and tried to take over from inside a Jewish business which threatened Polish concerns, was the hero of this story.[50]

In contrast to the romantic novels where the Jewish heroine (or more rarely hero) was either one of the leading figures or even the leading figure, with their name used as the title (eg. Esther or Rachel), in the realistic novels Jewish characters played secondary roles. This was not to change until 1863 when Kraszewski published his novel *The Jew* (1866) and Eliza Orzeszkowa published *Eli Makower* (1875) and *Meir Ezofowicz* (1879).

'Until now we have been used – with occasional exceptions – to find Polish works only providing caricatures of Jews, usually black characters despite the fact that even among us there are noble souls. You were the first person to do justice to us, showing Jews, their books and science in their true light,'[51] Nehemiasz Landes wrote to J. I. Kraszewski offering at the same time to translate his novel *The Jews* into German, as was in fact done.[52]

Similar views on how Jews were presented in Polish literature appeared more often after 1863. A popular contemporary reviewer, Waleria Marrené Moszkowska,[53] and another journalist from the newspaper *Izraelita*[54] discussed the problem of Jews being either depicted as evil characters or as comic figures. Both stressed that Kraszewski played the main role in destroying these stereotypes. As Moszkowska noticed, because of Kraszewski the 'whole school of novelists for whom the Jew was "a sort of punchinello or pierrot" disappeared and he just became a Jew'.[55]

However, this hasty generalization went too far and it is not coincidental that she went on to give examples from Wilkoński, the author of popular literary anecdotes. In these he described such comic characters as a cunning factor, Szymsia, and funny little Jews like Swarzec who dressed up as a Turk and organized a horse parade to greet and entertain Napoleon.

Whereas in the 'high-brow' novels of Kraszewski, Chodźko, Czyński, Korzeniowski and Jeż, the image of the Jew was a real and serious one, in the low-brow literature aimed at mass readers, the stereotype of the Jew as villain and/or comic figure prevailed. In the anonymous popular novel *The Mystery of Berlin* (1847), one of numerous imitations of *The Mystery of Paris* by Eugene Sue, Jewish criminals of villainous character were introduced. They kidnapped a prince's child and brought him up as a Jew with the name of Szmerles. One of the members of the gang explained their purpose:

> Our aim will only be fulfilled when this man whom we have turned into a knave and who has suffered and been beaten by many people, becomes a prince so that he can give our people special protection and benefits. Let our intentions be fulfilled, then we will see whether they dare to charge us that our crimes stem from our blood: we have shown them that their blood is no better than ours.[56]

The novel ends happily when the contrite criminals are punished and Szmerles's goodness triumphs. He is reborn as a decent man and he meets his brother Prince Jan Promiński. Thus, in this novel we can see a revival of the trend of presenting Jews as criminals and conspirators, as in the romantic works.

The picaresque image of the Jew was strengthened by an image of the tavern as a den of thieves which appeared in several novels of national life, such as in Kraszewski's *The Old Servant* and in the political novel *The Spring of Nations*. In such works as Łoziński's *Grey and Crimson Noblemen* (1858) or *Saint Jur* (1862) by Jan Zachariasiewicz, the tavern was the meeting place for insurrectionary peasants where the innkeepers fenced goods stolen from country houses.[57]

In short stories intended for a peasant audience, the Jew was characterized as a comic swindler. This image was presented together with his role as a merchant in the rural community which misjudged the purpose of a calling which was alien to them. According to Hertz:

> This Jewish stereotype was a man with a foreign faith, language and customs, as well as foreign morality. He was cunning and evasive. He thought only about his profits, always trying to cheat Christians. He had all the traits that the folklore of pre-capitalist economies is accustomed to bestow upon every merchant. In Poland, where the Jews were the only merchants, especially small merchants, these traits were attributed to the whole caste.[58]

In one of his short stories, Jan Kanty Gregorowicz introduced the character of the cunning Jew.[59] He was like another comic swindler, Mosiek in *The Kuba of the Market* written by Walery Wielogłowski.[60] It is worth adding that this way of presenting the Jew clearly recurs not only in folklore but also in the comic images. Comedy had an influence on the composition of the stories and on the construction of their characters. The stories quite often used a form of dramatic dialogue. Wielogłowski was the master of such forms but they can also be found in the journalist Władysław L. Anczyc's writings, such as *The Drinking, Loss and Misery of Peasants*. In the fourth volume of *Pictures* by Gregorowicz, a bridegroom enters during the wedding party dressed like a poor Jewish merchant 'with a bag full of shards from broken pots'. The attendant 'shook the bag for a joke, from time to time moving it round from back to front to make everybody merry'.[61] Such a character was probably derived from folk comedies, such as the Christmas plays which were very popular at that time among the peasants. Here the role of the malevolent Jew was of course played by Herod.

Anyone reading the literary works of the Romantic period about Jewish problems will appreciate the importance of various sources influencing the creation of the Jewish stereotype. Students of poetry noticed this before anyone else. At that time, the Jew as a hero of narrative prose was not yet a character in his own right. Almost invariably he was used to symbolize wider events. In romantic novels or 'love stories' he was the character in the foreground and sometimes the book was even given his name. However, love between Jew and Christian served as the apotheosis of a humiliated and wronged people. The feeling played a role in helping to improve the relationship between representatives of various social classes. Jewess and Jew expressed the idea of equality in love, in the same way as a young peasant girl in love with a fine gentleman either from the bourgeoisie as in Schiller's *Love and Intrigue*, or from the country as in Moniuszko's *Halka*, or finally as an educated peasant falling in love with an aristocrat as in Kraszewski's *Ostap Bondarczuk*. These characters were usually apotheosized. The narrators were in fact expressing their antipathy to social prejudices, whether Polish or Jewish. The traditions of the picaresque novels were used in presenting the conservative characters.

Although Jews usually played secondary roles in realistic novels, they were important elements in the colourful mosaic of the comedy of human life. But they were put in the shade by the leading characters from the noble class. Therefore, the traditional Jewish characters were invested with added stature, from a nostalgia for the splendours of the former great Poland, like the 'last of the Mohicans'. The nobleman's hostility towards social and cultural change, towards urbanization and industrialization as tendencies supposedly alien to the Polish agricultural nation because they were imported from the West, also meant, however, that all sorts of nouveaux riches were condemned, including Jewish 'money-grubbers'. In rare cases too, the conflict between Polish and Jewish upstarts was presented in fiction.

Adam Mickiewicz created the unique Jewish character, Jankiel, who combined love for tradition with deep knowledge and understanding of the new Polish social and national ideals, especially the struggle for freedom and independence.

In the literary works intended for peasants, the Jew stayed in the background while the main characters were Polish folk heroes. The Jew was the small merchant trader, innkeeper or peddler. He was credited with such traits as astuteness, cunning and hatred of gentiles. His language and manners were mocked. However, pre-capitalist peasant folklore gave all foreign merchants these traits. Only in rare cases and in such pedestrian novels as *The Mysteries of Berlin*, was the Jew given the demonic traits of a villain. One is tempted to suggest that Jews here took on the role of Gypsies who initially served as black characters in picaresque and romantic novels.

In conclusion, a few characteristic stereotypes were created. First of all there was the Jewess or Jew as idealized lover, who supported the democratic changes in society which aimed at breaking down social barriers. The only exception was Bronikowski's Esther who was shown as the deceitful romantic 'femme fatale'. Demonic traits were reserved for minor characters in the form of conservative Jews, knaves, malicious rabbis, smugglers and innkeepers sheltering the thieves.

The realistic stories created the characters of the good little Jew (*Żydek*), innkeeper and trader, friend of magnate families – a type of man disappearing with the epoch that created him. On the other hand, accounts in the realistic novels also described Jewish characters as parvenus and capitalists, harbingers of industrial ideas hostile to aristocratic society. Finally, tales meant for the peasantry made use of the stock comedy character of the little merchant, cunning and funny, treated with suspicion as the representative of a despised professon and of a foreign nationality.

Thanks to the great talent of Mickiewicz, the character of Jankiel, symbolizing tolerance and wisdom as well as sincere and progressive Polish patriotism, has retained a much greater appeal than other types. However, such traits were rarely seen in the portrayal of Jews in the Romantic period. The positive character of the Jew does not appear very often until after the 1863 uprising when the novels of Kraszewski, Orzeszkowa, Prus and Konopnicka were written.

NOTES

1 For the image in literature in general see M. Polanyi, 'Where is the image?', *Dialogue – USA* (American Embassy, Warsaw, 1975) no. 3.
2 For characterization see for example W. Steiner, 'The Semiotic of the Genre: Portraiture in Literature and Painting', *Semiotica*, vol. 21 (1977), pp. 1–2, 113 and H. Markiewicz, 'Postać literacka i jej badanie', *Pamiętnik Literacki* (1981), p. 2.
3 A. Hertz, *Żydzi w kulturze polskiej* (Paris, 1961), p. 224, chapter on Obraz Żyda.
4 A. Schaff, 'Pragmatyczna funkcja stereotypów', *Kultura i Społeczeństwo* (1979), no. 4, p. 55. According to Schaff the stereotype is the structure that represents something or an image of it, based on current experience, and because of its apriority, automatism and its repertory of 'black and white' traits, it may integrate the society faced by natives and foreigners.
5 P. Reboul, *Le Mythe Anglais dans la Littérature Française sous la Restauration* (Lille, 1962), p. 191.
6 The term 'stories in general circulation' was introduced into the theory of culture by S. Żołkiewski in the work: *Kultura, Socjologia, Semiotyka Literacka* (Warsaw, 1979). Hertz drew our attention to the role of the Jew in folklore which showed the Jewish stereotype in Polish peasant expressions. In these we find the Jew who is dishonest in business. These are also many expressions ridiculing traits ascribed to Jews such as cowardice or strange rituals (A. Hertz, op. cit., p. 232).
7 See Cz. Hernas, 'Potrzeby i metody bedania literatury brukowej', in *O współczesnej kulturze literackiej*, eds. S. Żołkiewski and M. Hopfinger (Wrocław, 1973), vol. 1; J. Maciejewski, 'Obszary trzecie literatury', *Teksty* (1975), vol. 4; M. Inglot, 'Nauczyciel polonista wsród obiegów kultury', *Polonistyka* (1983), no. 3.
8 W. Bełza, *Wstępne słowo do 'Żydzi w poezji polskiej'* (Lwów, 1906, 2nd ed.), p. 5.
9 J. Winczakiewicz's introductory comments to 'Izrael w poezji polskiej', *Antologia* (Paris, 1958), p. 15.
10 See W. Borowy, 'Z historii równouprawnienia Żydów w powieści polskiej', *Pamiętnik Literacki* (1925–6).
11 The main investigators of this problem are K. Dresdner, in 'Żydzi w powieściach J. Korzeniowskiego', *Przegląd Humanistyczny* (1933), vol. 3 and A. Żyga, 'Problem

żydowski w twórczości J. I. Kraszewskiego', *Rocznik Komisji Historyczno-Literackiej* (Kraków, 1964), vol. 2.
12 A. Żyga describes the voluminous literature about the character of Jankiel in Polish literature.
13 T. Łepkowski, 'Poglądy na jedno – i wielo-etniczność narodu w XIX w', in *Swojskość i cudzoziemszczyzna w dziejach kultury polskiej*, ed. Z. Stefanowska (Warsaw, 1978), pp. 242–3.
14 Only M. Borowy writes about him.
15 See the stimulating comments of J. Bachórz, 'Realism without "head in the clouds"', *Studies on the novels of Józef Korzeniowski* (Warsaw, 1979), p. 291.
16 See M. Inglot and M. Jakóbiec-Semkowa, 'Przodkowie i potomkowie Ostapa Bondarczuka. Problem chłopa-inteligenta w literaturze polskiej okresu romantyzmu', *Prace Literackie*, vol. 10.
17 J. Czyński, *Cesarzewicz Konstanty i Joanna Grudzińska czyli Jakobini polscy*, ed. K. Bartoszewski (Warsaw, 1956), p. 244.
18 'He entered dressed in black, in a decent civilian suit. His long bronzed face, small sharp eyes, raven locks and narrow eyebrows forming two coterminous arcs, had much the same effect as a traveller meeting an armed bandit in a forest. It was the German Jew, the secret-police agent whose skill made him the favourite of the Tsarevitch,' J. Czyński, op. cit., p. 88.
19 Ibid., p. 267. The word 'Haman' was used as a term of abuse by the Jewish characters in the realistic novels. It is possible that the name was, and perhaps still is, part of Jewish folklore.
20 See K. Bartoszewski's 'Introduction to J. Czyński, *Cesarzewicz Konstanty* ...' op. cit., p. 55. See also A. Eisenbach, *Wielka Emigracja wobec kwestii żydowskiej* (Warsaw, 1976).
21 See J. Czyński, op. cit., p. 382.
22 As Hertz writes: 'The caste is a closed group. Everybody who belongs to it, or is born in the caste, also dies in the caste. To leave the caste is very difficult, often quite impossible. Quite often the way out looks like escaping from the caste, and it is connected with attempts – not always successful – to cover over the tracks of the past', op. cit., p. 75.
23 I. Hołowiński, *Rachela* (Wilno, 1847), p. 180.
24 Ibid., p. 78.
25 Ibid., p. 128.
26 J. I. Kraszewski, *Powieść bez tytułu* (Kraków, 1974), vol. 2, p. 103.
27 See J. Bachórz, op. cit., p. 330.
28 They derived from the *organicznik* programme promulgated by Prince K. Lubecki, the minister of the Polish Kingdom, and can be found in numerous dramas dedicated to the King.
29 T. Bułharyn, *Esterka* (Warsaw, 1829), p. 20.
30 A. Bronikowski, *Kazimierz Wielki i Esterka* (Warsaw, 1828), vol. 2, p. 184.
31 This book was written by Henryk Rolicki (1933). 'The author proved that Jews were the cause of the fall of the great powers and of the creation of all heresies as well as revolutionary ideas', (A. Hertz, op. cit., p. 276).
32 F. Bernatowicz, *Nałęcz* (Warsaw, 1828), vol. 3, p. 15.
33 This time-honoured belief was based on the horror stories spread by nuns about children kidnapped by Jews and rolled in barrels with nails inside them. In the nineteenth century even Jews tried to combat these rumours, e.g. J. Tugendhold in the essay, which appeared in two editions, called *O czynionym ludowi starozakonnemu zarzucie potrzeby krwi chrześcijańskiej do jakiego obrzędu religijnego* (see A. Żyga, op. cit., p. 157).

34 Michał Grabowski, one of the leading contemporary literary critics and champion of the native historical novel, wrote, 'The spirit of nations answers our questions best from afar, like an echo. Therefore it speaks specifically from the past.' M. Grabowski, 'Literatura romansu w Polsce', part 1, in *Literatura: krytyka* (Wilno, 1840), vol. 2, pp. 39–40.

Similarly, Eustachy Tyszkiewicz wrote to Placyt Jankowski, 'Everyone who knows and loves his nationality, is deeply moved by the content and form of contemporary pieces of work. Instead of Korydons from the past, instead of descriptions of alien places, one can find everywhere the Judge and his wife, the Regent with Bernardine snuff, the innkeeper Abramek, the steward, bailiff . . .' (cit. according to W. Charkiewicz, *Placyt Jankowski, Życie i twórczość* [Wilno, 1928], pp. 43–4).

35 'The convention aimed at giving the impression that the story was a complete and authentic tale of the human experience in a definite time span and particular place.' See A. Brodzka, *O kryteriach realizmu w badaniach literackich* (Warsaw, 1966), pp. 79–81.

36 K. Wyka, *Pan Tadeusz. Studia o poemacie* (Warsaw, 1963), vol. 1, p. 184.

37 Jankiel is 'different by his faith, customs, profession, clothes'. However, at the same time his 'dissimilarity' is merged with his 'domestic character' as in something that is more general, wider and more essential. Mickiewicz is indifferent to the fact that there are different things and values inside this 'domestic character'. This is the diversity that enriches and develops (A. Hertz, op. cit., p. 41). Mickiewicz describes Jankiel in the following way:

The host stood in the midst in his long gown
With silver clasps, that to the floor reached down,
One hand within his black silk sash was pressed,
The other gravely his grey beard caressed,
With roving glance he walked around the hall
Commanding, serving none, but greeting all.
With some he would begin a conversation
Of other pacify an altercation.
The Jew was old, and through the years had gained
A name for honesty. None ever complained
Or gentleman or peasant, nor they should,
For everyone knew Jankiel's drinks were good.
He kept a strict account, nor cheated ever,
Permitted merriment but drunkards never,
Loved every entertainment and not least
A wedding party or a christening feast.
As a musician Jankiel was renowned
Once with his dulcimer he wandered round
The country houses and much praise had gained,
Both by his playing and his voice well-framed.
Though Jewish he had good pronunciation
and specially loved the ballads of the nation.
And brought back many from his travels west.

. . . .

So Jankiel, full of fame and wealth withal
Hung his sweet dulcimer upon the wall
And turning inn-keeper had settled down.
As under-rabbi in the neighbouring town
He was a welcome guest and counsel-giver

And knew the trade in grain along the river
Which in the country's useful information,
And was a loyal Pole by reputation.

Adam Mickiewicz, *Pan Tadeusz or the Last Foray in Lithuania*, translated into English verse with an introduction by Kenneth Mackenzie (London, 1964), vol. 4, pp. 82–3.
38 I. Chodźko, 'Pustelnik w Promiunach', *Podania litewskie*, 3rd series (Wilno, 1858), p. 196.
39 A. Hertz recalls: 'Wisdom and knowledge are valued most in the Jewish character. ... In the Jewish world an uneducated man – even a very rich one – was always treated as inferior to a learned man. It is striking that this main trait of the Jewish character has been completely ignored in the stereotypes created by the outside world, which insists that the Jews gave wealth the highest value', (op. cit., p. 96).
40 J. Korzeniowski, 'Kollokacje', *Biblioteka Narodowa*, ed. S. Kawyn, ser. 1 (Wrocław, 1959), no. 28, p. 32.
41 J. I. Kraszewski, 'Latarnia czarnoksięska', *Obrazy naszych czasów*, ser. 1 (Kraków, 1964), pp. 229–30.
42 Ibid., ser. 2, p. 62.
43 See S. Pignoń, 'Wstęp do Pana Tadeusza', *Biblioteka Narodowa*, ser. I (Warsaw, 1980), no. 83, pp. 210–11.
44 W. Łoziński, 'Zaklęty dwór', *Biblioteka Narodowa*, ed. J. Krzyżanowski, ser. 1 (Wrocław, 1959), no. 96, p. 5. This point of view profoundly influenced the description of a Jewish town in the humorous story of J. U. Niemcewicz, called *Moszkopolis, Year 3333 or the Unbelievable Dream* (1817). The building of this town looked like taverns surrounded by stables. The taverns lined by the dirty street where ducks, hens, geese and turkeys tracked through the mud.
45 See S. Kawyn 'Introduction to J. Korzeniowski, "Krewni"', *Biblioteka narodowa*, ser. I (Wrocław, 1955), no. 156, p. xli. For the development of wealthy Jewish society in the capital city also see J. Tomaszewski, 'Zarys dziejów Żydów Polskich w XIX i XX w.', in *Żydzi Polscy, Dzieje i Kultura*, ed. M. Horn (Warsaw, 1982), p. 34.
46 See K. Wyka, 'O Panu Geldhabie', *Pamiętnik Literacki* (1951), vol. 3/4.
47 Alojzy Żółkowski, the Younger, the leading contemporary comic actor interpreted the role of Geldhab in this way. He played Geldhab in 1865 giving him the traits of a well-known Warsaw banker, Epstein, who was delighted by the similarity and offered him a diamond pin (see S. Dabrowski, R. Górski, *Fredro na scenie* [Warsaw, 1973], pp. 212–13.)
48 For the ethnocentrism in *Choroby wieku*, see J. Jedlicki 'Polskie nurty ideowe lat 1790–1863', in *Swojskość i cudzoziemszczyzna w dziejach kultury polskiej*, ed. Z. Stefanowska (Warsaw, 1973).
49 See A. Hertz, op. cit., p. 175.
50 Z. Kaczkowski, *Żydowscy* (Lwów, 1872), vol. 1, p. 197.
51 As the Polish businessman Faustyn confesses,

> I dislike this nation but I feel its superiority – I don't like it, but I admire it. I don't trust it, but I would follow its advice and warnings. They are like old souls which have undergone enduring slavery and have experienced both trial and suffering.... They appear to serve the whole world, and they dream about possessing it. Everyone remembers their past greatness and all look secretly and hopefully to the future. They are masters of all branches of science, arts and handicrafts. They have climbed over everyone to the top of society and become respected. They can read all our thoughts, but who can read their private thoughts?

(W. Wielogłowski, 'Magnaci giełdowi', in *Społeczeństwo dzisiejsze w obrazach* [Kraków, 1859], pp. 100–1.)

A. Wilkoński, the satirist, in the essay 'O dorobkiewiczach' went against the general disapproval of parvenus. He distinguished those who had become rich by honest toil from those who had made money by wicked speculation (see *Ramoty i romotki* [Poznań, 1862], vol. 5, pp. 200–1).

It is necessary to point out that Niemcewicz in the humorous story mentioned before described Warsaw as well as the whole country as being dominated by Jews. He showed the former rulers of Poland transformed into serfs or urban labourers. The author meets the descendant of the Zamoyski family, a poor cabman who explains to him how this happened: 'They did not conquer the Poles by arms but by trickery, deceit, bribery. I do not know exactly how it came about, but when they became eligible for all offices and had the right to buy landed estates, nothing could block their tireless cunning and dodges. As time passe they squeezed out Christian Poles and they dominated everything, and because nobody wanted the dirty kingdom, they elected their king and called old Poland, Palestine.' (J. U. Niemcewicz, op. cit., *Przegląd Poznański* [1858], vol. 26, p. 346.) This story was not printed during the author's lifetime. It appeared for the first time in *Przegląd* (Review). It is worth adding that the editors of the journal declared its pro-Jewish attitude with the discreet statement that 'the satire goes further and beyond the Jews'. Thus, they suggested that the story was also relevant to Germans who were then oppressing Poznań. However, the editor of *Dziennik Poznański* (no. 203–5, 1912), while reprinting the humorous story, warned his readers that the victory of Jews in the elections to the Warsaw municipal council might be dangerous for Christians.

52 N. Landes to J. I. Kraszewski, b.d., cit. after A. Żyga, op. cit., p. 219.
53 W. Marrené, 'Kwestia żydowska w powieści współczesnej', *Tygodnik Ilustrowany* (1879), no. 200, p. 267.
54 'There was a time when the Jew was an indispensable character in every novel that claimed a wider public. He used to be the so-called "black character" or the comic part of the work', *Izraelita* (1879), no. 3, cit. after A. Zyga, op. cit., p. 214.
55 W. Marrené, op. cit.
56 *Tajemnice Berlina*, *Z pamiętników urzędnika sądu kryminalnego* (Warsaw, 1847), vol. 2, p. 13. I am obliged to Dr. B. Bednarek for drawing my attention to this little book.
57 More details about this problem can be found in my work *Polska proza fabularna o Wiośnie Ludów*, forthcoming.
58 A. Hertz, op. cit., p. 85.
59 'The Jewish factor, looking at money like a turtle at eggs, contrasted with the careless but good-natured features of our peasants. His whole person showed complete absorption and impatience when he came to look at money and a sluggish and slow account.' (J. K. Gregorowicz, *Obrazki wiejskie* [Warsaw, 1852], vol. 3, p. 64.)
60 See W. Wielogłowski, *Obrazki z obyczajów ludu wiejskiego*, 4th edition (Kraków, 1882), pp. 377–8.
61 J. K. Gregorowicz, op. cit., vol. 4, pp. 377–8.

THE POLISH-JEWISH DAILY PRESS
Michael C. Steinlauf

In the period between the two world wars, the Polish-Jewish daily press was undoubtedly the most successful example of Jewish cultural creativity in the Polish language. Unfortunately, precious little has been written about this major cultural institution of modern Polish Jewish life. Over and beyond the obstacles to historical research created by the vast destruction of Polish archival institutions in World War II, difficulties which apply, though in different measure, to the reconstruction of both Polish and Polish Jewish history, particularly in the period just prior to the war, there is here a further barrier: the aversion albeit increasingly anachronistic of many Poles and Jews to phenomena whose locus is neither purely 'Polish' nor purely 'Jewish', as a result of which, the memory of the Polish-Jewish press has slipped into the void between two mutually exclusive national self-conceptions. Therefore this article. What follows is a sketch based on the skimpy existing literature[1] and a preliminary reading of the Warsaw daily *Nasz Przegląd*; my object is to assemble basic historical data, characterize general tendencies, and suggest areas for further detailed investigation – in short, to trace the rough dimensions of a marvellously complex yet neglected domain of recent Polish Jewish history.

FROM *IZRAELITA* TO *NASZ PRZEGLĄD*

The existence of the Warsaw daily *Nasz Przegląd* [*Our Review*][2] (1923–39), along with its sister publications in other large Polish cities, *Nowy Dziennik* [*New Daily*] (1918–39) in Kraków and *Chwila* [*Moment*] (1919–39) in Lwów,[3] represents a unique phenomenon in modern Jewish history: a daily press in a non-Jewish language.[4] Ever since the beginnings of the *Haskalah* (Jewish Enlightenment) at the end of the eighteenth century, there had been periodical publications published by and for Jews, at first primarily in the languages of the co-territorial nations, later, towards the end of the nineteenth century and particularly in Eastern Europe, increasingly in the Jewish languages – Hebrew and Yiddish – as well. Periodicals in the non-Jewish languages were published at intervals of a week, a month or more – they were never daily publications since it was assumed that once a Jew could read the language of the country in which he lived, he would avail himself of daily newspapers in that language for general news, and then turn to the Jewish press for subjects of Jewish interest. The first mass-circulation Jewish dailies arose to meet the needs of a large Jewish readership little conversant with non-Jewish languages, but who demanded the kind of window on the modern world which only a daily newspaper could furnish. Such dailies, inevitably in Yiddish,[5] were also intimately linked to the rise of Jewish national consciousness in Eastern Europe. Thus, the Warsaw Yiddish dailies *Haynt* (1908–39) and *Der moment* (1910–39), for example, both founded in the years just prior to World War I, furnished their readers with a complete account of world, local and Jewish community events, championed Jewish political struggles for civil and national minority rights, and were instrumental in publishing and supporting the newly-emerging Yiddish literary culture. With many adaptations based on the new conditions of life in an independent Polish state, the Yiddish daily press – which for most of the interwar period consisted of a least five dailies in Warsaw alone[6] – retained this fundamental profile as both news-purveyor and instrument of national renewal and resistance.[7]

The Polish-Jewish daily press, in contrast, did not come into its own until the end of World War I, and by virtue of a radical break with its past. For many decades, the Polish-language Jewish press, the oldest Jewish press in Poland – beginning with the short-lived *Dostrzegacz Nadwiślański* (1823–24)[8] and ending with the well-established and increasingly staid weekly *Izraelita* (1866–1913)[9] – upheld an assimilationist ideology which preached the transformation of Jews into 'Poles of the Mosaic faith' ['*Polacy wyznania mojżeszowego*'], and with the rise of Jewish national movements, opposed as 'separatism' any expression of national consciousness, be it Zionism or yiddishism. *Izraelita*'s social base was the Warsaw banking and commercial plutocracy which, tacitly supported by the orthodoxy, controlled the Warsaw *kehillah* (Jewish community council).[10] It was supported as well by certain groups of progressive Polish intellectuals, particularly the 'positivists', who welcomed assimilated Jews as partners in the development of Polish productive forces and political freedom. As both Jewish and Polish national movements – the latter frequently with an anti-Jewish orientation – began to gather force, however, *Izraelita* and what it represented began to be challenged, and several attempts were made in Warsaw to develop a different sort of press: *Izraelita* itself under the editorship of Nahum Sokolow (1896–1902);[11] the Zionist anthology *Safrus* (1905) edited by Jan Kirszrot;[12] the short-lived Zionist weekly *Głos Żydowski* (which was banned and then reappeared as *Życie Żydowskie*) edited in 1906–07 by Yitshak Grünbaum;[13] and from 1913–14, a daily newspaper – *Przegląd Codzienny*.

Przegląd Codzienny was founded at a prophetic moment in modern Polish-Jewish relations: when, amidst the furore resulting from the Duma elections of 1912 in which Jewish votes helped elect a candidate not supported by the nationalist Polish coalition, these groups declared a boycott against Jewish participation in Polish economic and cultural life.[14] The campaign, whose chief instrument was the new mass-circulation nationalist press, enlisted the support of many Poles previously well-disposed toward Jews, including the leading exponent of Polish positivism, Aleksander Świętochowski.[15] The editor of *Przegląd Codzienny* was Stanisław Mendelson, who had been an activist in the Polish Socialist Party, but had begun to move toward a Jewish national perspective (he was Nahum Sokolow's son-in-law). The paper, as Mendelson envisioned it, was intended for Jews (it covered in great detail the notorious blood libel trial of Mendl Beylis in Kiev),[16] but also for Poles; it was to provide for Polish society, he declared – in an expression identical to those that would be used in the interwar period by Polish-Jewish journalists to characterize their own activity – 'a mirror of Jewish life'.[17] Among the journalists it employed were Jakób Appenszlak and Natan Szwalbe, later founders of *Nasz Przegląd*, but also – unlike the interwar Polish-Jewish press – a number of Polish journalists as well.[18] Upon Mendelson's death and the start of World War I, *Przegląd Codzienny* folded.

With the collapse amidst a wave of anti-Jewish violence after World War I of the belief by significant numbers of either Poles or Jews that Jews could or should be assimilated into Polish society, and the passing, as a rule, of Jewish communal control out of the hands of assimilationist and religious oligarchies and to more democratic nationally-minded representatives, the Polish-language Jewish press emerged completely transformed. Although a small number of assimilationist Jewish publications continued to appear in the interwar period, their influence was minimal.[19] Rather, a new group of well-educated, largely middle-class journalists, whose notions of Jewish nationality had been shaped by the Yiddish and Hebrew press, who were primarily Zionist and frequently partisans of the Hebrew cultural revival[20] – began to found Polish-language Jewish publications. Thus in Warsaw, Appenszlak and Szwalbe, joined by Samuel Hirszhorn, Saul Wagman and Samuel Wołkowicz,[21] who had continued throughout the war and in the years immediately following to found short-lived Polish-Jewish newspapers, in 1923 established *Nasz Przegląd*. But why did this new generation of Polish-Jewish journalists found *daily* newspapers, a situation so unlike that in Western European countries? Why the need for a daily newspaper, a staple of modern life more commonplace than a telephone, to be 'Jewish', and what, if not language, did such an identification entail?

A JEWISH DAILY PRESS IN A NON-JEWISH LANGUAGE

Of greatest importance in the rise of the Polish-Jewish press was the rapid spread of the use of Polish among Jews. With the sudden availability of free primary education in the new Polish state, and despite the growth of Yiddish and Hebrew school systems, the majority of Jewish students in the interwar period nevertheless attended state schools in which the language of instruction was of course Polish.[22] Bi-lingualism (Yiddish and Polish) became increasingly prevalent among Polish Jews. Moreover, especially but by no means exclusively among educated youth and in sections of the middle and professional classes, Polish – particularly as a written language – began to make inroads over Yiddish.[23] In such circles, a preference for Polish over Yiddish and even an ignorance of Yiddish led to an estrangement from Jewish culture – yet rarely however to a renunciation of Jewish national identity. The irony is that precisely when the pre-World War I assimilators' dream of mass Polish-language education for Jews was finally fulfilled, linguistic assimilation was accompanied by relatively little of the national assimilation which had been their ultimate goal. Indeed, just the opposite was the case: Jews on the whole increasingly regarded themselves nationally as Jews, whether their language was Yiddish, Polish or both.[24] And it is precisely a population that was increasingly at home in Polish *yet* increasingly Jewish-identified that could constitute the mass base required for a Polish-Jewish daily press.

The strengthening of Jewish consciousness was, of course, at least in part a reaction to the growth of anti-Jewish feeling and violence in the interwar period. In an interesting defence of the Polish-Jewish press made, significantly, by a Yiddish journalist in a Yiddish daily, Sh. V. Stupnitski describes the origins of the Polish-Jewish daily press as follows: 'At a time when Jewish life developed, when Jews became involved in general political life – it then turned out that a Jew desiring to find out what is going on in the external world, as well as a non-Jew wanting to know what is happening among Jews, had simply no opportunity to do this, since nearly the entire Polish press is reactionary, Catholic, anti-semitic.'[25] Characteristic of the Polish press, Stupnitski points out, was that perhaps alone in all of Europe, it was '*judenrein* [free of Jews]', and even if occasionally there was a Jewish contributor, he was forced to change his name or sign his article with initials, and, certainly, could never write sympathetically of Jewish affairs. These then, concludes Stupnitski, were the 'objective reasons' for establishing a Jewish daily in Polish. 'It was simply a necessity for us, it was an act of national self-defense'.[26] This analysis is supported by the case of Jakób Appenszlak, the editor-in-chief of *Nasz Przegląd*. From an assimilated home, educated in Polish schools, Appenszlak began his journalistic career prior to World War I as theatre critic for the major Warsaw daily *Kurier Warszawski*. His decision to found a Polish-Jewish daily was partly a 'protest' against the pressure to change his name while he worked for the Polish paper.[27] Even more instructive is the origin of the Kraków daily *Nowy Dziennik*, founded during the last months of World War I as a direct result of Jewish outrage at the murder of a Jew by Polish hooligans, and the subsequent cover-up of the crime by the liberal Polish newspaper most widely read by Jews.[28] Moreover, the first Polish-Jewish daily, the short-lived *Przegląd Codzienny*, was, as we have seen, founded amidst the poisonous atmosphere of the first modern anti-Jewish press campaign in Polish history. Even when it was not overtly hostile to Jews and Jewish interests (for example, *Robotnik*, organ of the Polish Socialist Party), the Polish press was simply ignorant of and indifferent to Jewish matters.

To the 'objective reasons' for a Polish-Jewish daily press, Stupnitski then appends 'subjective reasons which justify [its] existence':

> Our development does not move along the path of Western Jews, among whom there rules a dualism, a double-entry bookkeeping in the relations between Jew and human being. The German Jew during the course of the entire week would read the *Frankfurter Zeitung*, a progressive, modern daily, and on Saturday would receive the weekly *Der Israelit* in order to square himself with Jewishness.[29] We read a newspaper as human beings and at the same time as Jews. We want therefore to find in it everything that can possibly interest the human being in the Jew and the Jew in the human being. As a result, there can exist among us a Polish-Jewish paper, whereas in France and England it is unneeded. . . .[30]

Stupnitski's words point to a significant difference between the sense of Jewish identity of Western and Eastern European Jews. In the West, the encounter with secularization generally meant the progressive diminution of the realms in which one could express one's 'Jewishness', its delimitation to family, synagogue, 'Sunday school', charitable institution or weekly newspaper. In interwar Poland, for a variety of reasons beyond the scope of this article, the transformation from traditional to secular world-view was, in this respect, not as disruptive, and was accompanied by the rise of an immense network of national institutions and ideologies within which one's day-to-day identity as a Jew could generally be taken for granted. Precisely *because* it was such a commonplace of everyday life, for many Polish Jews a daily newspaper, regardless of language, had to be Jewish as well.

CIRCULATION

Responding to these needs, the Polish-Jewish daily press rapidly attained a wide readership.[31] Establishing circulation figures, however, for these newspapers, and indeed for all of the Jewish press and even for the Polish press of the interwar period, is no easy matter. As a result of the massive destruction of Warsaw in the Second World War, most of the records of publishers and printers disappeared. For most of the years since the war, the only source of circulation statistics has been the catalogues, published during the interwar period by two Polish advertising firms,[32] to which the various newspapers themselves sent in figures. These are the data consistently utilized by Marian Fuks in his monograph on the Jewish press in Warsaw.[33] More recently however, Andrzej Paczkowski has turned elsewhere: to the records of the Polish Ministry of the Interior (that is, police) for the interwar period. These records are fragmentary: they do not exist at all for the 1920's, and for the 1930's only for certain years. Moreover, the manner in which they were obtained is unknown. However, Paczkowski makes a good case for the supposition that these figures, consisting of samplings often as frequent as every two weeks, and compiled exclusively for internal ministry use, are much more reliable than the single figure contributed to the advertising catalogues by newspaper publishers, and reproduced without any independent verification. Paczkowski first published the raw data in his article, '*Nakłady dzienników warszawskich w latach 1931–1938*',[34] and then published a monograph on the interwar Warsaw daily press, *Prasa codzienna Warszawy w latach 1918–1939*,[35] basing his conclusions as to circulation on an analysis of the data in his article. Since the figures for the Jewish press cited in his monograph are general

TABLE 1: AVERAGE CIRCULATION OF WARSAW JEWISH DAILIES, 1932–38

	Fuks	*Police Data*	*Nr. of samplings*
Nasz Przegląd	40–50,000	21,520	57
Piąta Rano[38]	40–50,000	14,745	57
Haynt	45,000	26,615	39
Der moment	30–40,000	23,315	42
Unzer ekspres	40–60,000	15,183	42
Folkstsaytung	18,000	16,494	42
Yudishe togblat	15–30,000	13,515	35
Hayntige nayes	75,000	19,843	41
Varshever radio	—	25,090	43

estimates, however, it seemed advisable to return to his sources. Therefore, in Table 1, I have presented average circulation figures for the nine major interwar Warsaw Jewish dailies in the 1930's (two Polish-Jewish morning papers, five Yiddish morning papers, and two Yiddish afternoon papers) according to Fuks, and according to my own analysis of Paczkowski's data in '*Nakłady dzienników warszawskich* . . .' (along with the number of samplings on which the latter figures are based).[36]

As is to be expected, the circulation figures based on the police data are, as a rule, significantly lower than those of Fuks. This is however in keeping with Paczkowski's overall analysis of Polish press circulation. Thus, for 1938, the only year for which comparable data are available, Paczkowski computes total circulation of the Polish daily press to have been 1,210,000 according to the advertising catalogues, and 770,290 according to the police data.[37] Moreover, the only case in which the figures are similar, that of the Bundist *Folkstsaytung*, supports the reliability of the police data, since Paczkowski independently notices a similar phenomenon for the Polish Socialist Party daily *Robotnik* (for which the police figures are actually higher than those in the catalogues), and attributes it to the possibility that the catalogue publishers reduced circulation figures for the socialist press.[39] The lower police figures receive further confirmation from Nakhman Mayzil, who in 1931 wrote that none of the five Warsaw Yiddish dailies attained a week-day circulation equal to that of the Moscow *Emes* – 31,000.[40] Furthermore, actual circulation figures were probably even lower than those given above, since Paczkowski calculates that about one-third of all Polish-language dailies were returned unsold;[41] if we assume that a similar proportion held for Yiddish papers (no statistics are available), then all the circulation figures in Table 1 must be reduced accordingly.

Using the police data, it is possible to compute total average circulation for the various types of daily newspapers in Warsaw in the 1930's. This has been done in Table 2. Based on these figures, the Polish-Jewish proportion of the total Warsaw Jewish daily press was 20.6 per cent, that is, for roughly every four Warsaw Jewish newspapers printed daily in Yiddish, one was printed in Polish. This proportion becomes more significant when viewed in the light of the fact that more of the Warsaw Yiddish than Polish-Jewish

TABLE 2: AVERAGE CIRCULATION OF
WARSAW DAILY PRESS, 1932–38

Polish-Jewish[42]	42,014
Yiddish[43]	161,450
Jewish (Polish + Yiddish)[44]	203,463
Polish (non-Jewish)	632,058[45]
Total (Jewish + non-Jewish)	835,521

dailies were printed for readers outside Warsaw.[46] Furthermore, these figures may be compared to those for the period prior to World War I when, in 1906, for example, there were in Warsaw eight Yiddish and Hebrew dailies with a total circulation of 108,200, but no Polish-language Jewish dailies, and six Jewish weeklies with a combined circulation of 40,000, of which the two in Polish (*Izraelita* and *Głos Żydowski/Życie Żydowskie*) had a total circulation of 2,000.[47]

The police records also permit, to a limited extent, an analysis of the development of the daily press, at least in the 1930's. In Table 3 I have presented average circulation figures for two two-year periods: 1932–33 and 1937–38.[48]

TABLE 3: AVERAGE CIRCULATION OF WARSAW DAILY PRESS, 1932–33, 1937–38

	1932–33	1937–38
Polish-Jewish	48,057	35,970
Yiddish	170,249	152,650
Jewish (Polish + Yiddish)	218,306	188,620
Polish (non-Jewish)	546,499	717,617
Total (Jewish + non-Jewish)	764,805	906,237

The small decline of the Jewish press – 13.6 per cent – is made more significant by the simultaneous expansion of the non-Jewish Polish press – 31.3 per cent. Thus, in the course of a six-year period, the Jewish share of all the daily newspapers published in Warsaw declined from 28.5 per cent to 20.8 per cent.[49] Paczkowski suggests a number of possible reasons for this phenomenon: the relatively faster growth of the Polish population of Warsaw in the 1930's, the increase in the sale of Polish dailies outside Warsaw, but also, the increasing proportion of Jewish readers who turned to Polish papers.[50] He concludes: 'If the data on circulation on which I base my conclusions are true – and much indicates that they are – then it is possible to speak of an emerging crisis situation in the Warsaw Jewish press'.[51]

In order to specify the nature of the 'crisis' in the Jewish press, I have computed circulation figures for the major Warsaw Jewish dailies for the periods 1932–33 and 1937–38. These are presented in Table 4. The figures document a greater or lesser decline in the circulation of every major daily with the exception of *Nasz Przegląd*. Yet circulation of the other Polish-Jewish daily, the tabloid *Piąta Rano*, declined as well, so it would seem difficult to draw conclusions along linguistic lines. However, one of Paczkowski's major conclusions in his monograph is extremely helpful: 'If we

TABLE 4: AVERAGE CIRCULATION OF WARSAW JEWISH DAILIES, 1932-33, 1937-38

	1932–33	1937–38
Nasz Przegląd	20,391	22,649
Piąta Rano	16,167	13,322
Haynt	27,529	25,700
Der moment	25,130	21,500
Unzer ekspres	15,366	15,000
Folkstsaytung	18,737	14,250
Yudishe togblat	14,030	13,000
Hayntige nayes	21,951	17,734
Varshever radio	25,179	25,000

were to attempt to point to the most characteristic, the most important shift in the structure of the Warsaw press during the years of the Second Republic, then undoubtedly at the head, before all others, emerges the growing significance of the sensational press'.[52] The Jewish press was no stranger to this phenomenon: much was written about the 'pernicious' and apparently growing influence on Yiddish readers of the inexpensive afternoon tabloids such as *Hayntige nayes* and *Varshever radio*.[53] However, the above figures demonstrate, I would suggest, that if the Jewish reader was increasingly turning to tabloids in the late 1930's – as was his Polish counterpart – then it was not to Yiddish tabloids, nor even to a Polish-Jewish tabloid such as *Piąta Rano*, but to the non-Jewish sensational press in the Polish language.[54] On the other hand, among the readers of the more 'serious' (and more expensive) daily Jewish newspapers, Yiddish readers – as is to be expected by the spread of linguistic assimilation – declined, but Polish readers increased, an increase, however, which did not make up for the larger decrease in Yiddish readers.[55]

THE POLISH-JEWISH PRESS AND THE YIDDISH PRESS

In its overall democratic and Jewish national political orientation, in its function as guardian of Jewish civil and national rights in Poland and defender against anti-semitic attacks, in its consistent support for the development of Yiddish and Hebrew culture and struggle, as we shall see, against the 'danger of assimilation',[56] and in its ongoing concern for the building of a Jewish homeland in Palestine – the new Polish-Jewish press was very similar to the mass-circulation Zionist Yiddish press. Similar but not identical, however, the Yiddish press as a whole was more highly 'ideologized' than the Polish-Jewish. Thus during the interwar period, even *Haynt* and *Der moment*, which had been founded as politically independent newspapers, drew closer to and at various times formally affiliated with various Zionist factions.[57] *Nasz Przegląd*'s Zionism, in contrast, was 'non-party' and therefore independent, more of a 'tendency' than a firm 'ideology'. Only in *Nasz Przegląd*, for example, could one encounter – on the same page – articles by David Ben-Gurion and Vladimir Jabotinsky![58]

The philosophical similarity between the Polish-Jewish and the Zionist Yiddish press reflected many personal and organizational ties. Journalists and editors in one press often worked for the other as well; moreover, the same publisher was frequently responsible for publications in both Yiddish and Polish. Of the founders of *Nasz Przegląd*, for example, Natan Szwalbe, was diplomatic correspondent for *Haynt* in the 1920's, and both Samuel Hirszhorn and Samuel Wołkowicz were regular contributors to the Yiddish press as well as – most interestingly – founders of the Folkist Party, one of whose principles was the recognition of Yiddish as the national language of the Jewish people.[59] On the other hand, two of the figures whom Khaym Finkelshteyn, in his monograph on *Haynt*, calls 'the "big three" in the "*Haynt*-family"',[60] – Yehoshua [Osjasz] Thon and Nahum Sokolow – were closely involved with Polish-language publications[61] and were, indeed, skilled writers, editors and orators in Polish (as well as in Hebrew). This is also true of Yitshak Grünbaum, the charismatic Zionist politician who was probably the single most popular Jewish public figure of the 1920's. Grünbaum was instrumental in solidifying *Haynt*'s links to organized Zionism, and for a number of years was the paper's guiding spirit; he was simultaneously an editor and regular contributor to the Hebrew, Yiddish and Polish-Jewish press.[62] Moreover, the publishers of *Haynt* were directly involved in founding a number of Polish-language Jewish publications. Among them were the dailies *Kurier Nowy* (1919–20), *Nasz Przegląd*'s earliest post-World War I predecessor, whose editorial offices were the same as those of *Haynt*,[63] and *Nowe Słowo* (1931–32), and the weekly *Opinja* (1933–39).[64] The latter two, the most successful of these ventures, established partly in response to the supposed slackening of *Nasz Przegląd*'s oppositional politics, were edited by Mojżesz [Moyshe] Kleinbaum, a close associate of Yitshak Grünbaum.[65] '*Opinja*', states Finkelshteyn, 'said in Polish what *Haynt* propagated in the mother-tongue [*mame-loshn*, i.e., Yiddish]'.[66]

TWO KINDS OF 'BRIDGES'

And yet – despite this web of practical as well as ideological interconnection, the frequent identity of writers, publishers, political positions – language, in interwar Poland, was hardly an incidental matter, and a Jewish press in the non-Jewish language found itself before problems and opportunities which the Yiddish press did not face, and which, moreover, on occasion led it into conflict with it. First of all, employing the same language as the surrounding Polish nation meant that one was also speaking *to* it; a Polish-Jewish newspaper was therefore involved, as no Yiddish paper could or wanted to be, in the endeavour of 'reveal[ling] for Polish society, with whom we live on one land', as the first issue of *Opinja* puts it, 'a mirror in which it can see a faithful image of Jewish society',[67] or, in the words of Jakób Appenszlak in the founding issue of *Nasz Przegląd*: 'rendering accessible to Polish society an understanding of our national self, its laws and ideals'.[68] In relation to governing circles, the Polish-Jewish press attained the status of unofficial press organ of the Jewish community, in which reaction to policy could be gauged and political concerns noted. It also responded quickly and consistently to the Polish press, searching out rare expressions of goodwill, polemicizing with the proliferating anti-Jewish onslaughts, and thereby placing itself at the eye of the storm provoked by the 'Jewish question'. As a result of its 'visibility' in the Polish world, the tones of *Nasz Przegląd*'s political articles, for example, was generally less strident than that of its Yiddish counterparts. Moreover, *Nasz Przegląd* often stressed, more so than the Jewish-language press, Jewish patriotism to the Polish state.[69] The paper, in short, attempted to function as a bridge from 'darkest Nalewki'[70] to Polish society; but whether – aside from occasional Polish politicians and a multitude of journalists hungry for polemics – it reached any significant number of ordinary Polish readers is very doubtful.

In relation to its Jewish readers, *Nasz Przegląd*'s function as a bridge was more successful. First of all, it offered its Jewish readers a view of the Polish world they could not always find in the Jewish-language press: extensive national news, regular reviews of Polish theatre, accounts of behind-the-scenes parliamentary intrigues.[71] More important, however, was its role in returning 'Jewishness' to Jews. In the words of Appenszlak: 'For some may [the paper] be a gate of return, a stage in the approach to one's own nation [...] Among our own brothers we wish to intensify national feeling, expand the consciousness of the creative power and spiritual values of Jewry'.[72] In its founding issue, *Opinja* is even more explicit: 'our weekly undertook as a primary task to acquaint the Polish-reading Jewish intelligentsia with the breadth of Jewish knowledge, the history of the Jewish nation, the pearls of Hebrew and Yiddish literary creativity'.[73] Thus, the

Polish-Jewish press published articles by such eminent Jewish historians as Majer Bałaban, Ignacy Schiper and Mojżesz Schorr, who, although they also appeared in Yiddish and Hebrew publications, had chosen to write their major works in Polish, and were ultimately most at home writing for the readers of *Nasz Przegląd*. Even more important was the popularization of Yiddish and Hebrew culture. *Nasz Przegląd* published a great number of translations from Yiddish and Hebrew literature, both the 'classics' (Mendele Mokher Sforim, Sholem Aleichem, Y. L. Peretz, David Frishman) as well as contemporary authors (Sholem Asch, Z. Segalowicz, Y. Y. Trunk, Moyshe Nadir, Uri-Zvi Grinberg, A. Shlionski). New Yiddish and Hebrew books were extensively and seriously reviewed, as were Jewish music and theatre by writers thoroughly at home in several cultures.[74] One such writer, not untypical of this group, was the theatre and literary critic, feuilletonist and political commentator Mojżesz [Moyshe] Kanfer, who was based in *Nowy Dziennik* and published throughout the Polish-Jewish press. Kanfer, a childhood friend of the Hebrew writer Sh. Y. Agnon and a popular lecturer on Yiddish theatre and literature, was instrumental in founding the Kraków Yiddish Theatre, the first Yiddish theatre in Poland entirely financed by a Jewish community.[75] There were as well Yiddish and Hebrew writers, journalists and critics who wrote directly in Polish for the Polish-Jewish press.[76] As a result of these various efforts, in Warsaw for example, as Pola Appenszlak recalls: 'the fastidious crowd [of intelligentsia] which used to fill the Polish theatres and literary cabarets, began, thanks to [*Nasz Przegląd*], to attend the theatre of the Vilne Trupe, the Turkov-Kaminska theatre, Vaykhert's Yung Teater and the Azazel *kleynkunst* theatre',[77] and more generally: 'Yiddish culture, in *Nasz Przegląd*'s translation and under its patronage, acquired "civil rights"'[78] among Jews previously estranged from Jewish life. That is, through the mediation of *Nasz Przegląd* and its sister papers, Yiddish culture began to be associated with some of the prestige-value of high Polish culture.

UNIQUE FEATURES

Such dedication to Jewish literature and theatre was hardly unusual among Jewish newspapers. The Yiddish press had, after all, since its inception consistently written about Yiddish culture and published the work of Yiddish writers. Indeed, nearly all of the most prominent Yiddish prose writers first published their major works in the Yiddish dailies; the Yiddish press was their major source of readers and livelihood. What was unique in these endeavours of the Polish-Jewish press was entirely a function of language – the use of the Polish language to strengthen national consciousness and oppose 'assimilation' by transmitting an awareness of

Jewish culture to a group of readers who lacked the ability or inclination to find it in the Jewish-language press. The act of translation, moreover, permitted a symbolic reconciliation: Yiddish and Hebrew writers, frequently at odds ideologically, co-existed in the same newspapers, often on the same page, as nowhere else in the Jewish press. There were, however, in addition, several aspects of the Polish-Jewish press which were not a function of translation, which were not, that is, simply a Polish version of the Jewish-language press. These were features unique in themselves, and therefore also most relevant towards establishing a true picture of the extent and depth of a Polish-language Jewish culture in interwar Poland; here it is possible only to point toward areas which future research will fully document.

First of all, a pre-condition: the matter of style and aura. It was, after all, a very different thing to function amidst the middle-class world of Polish-speaking Jews and amidst the Jewish masses and their *mame-loshn*. Melekh Ravitsh, from a vantage point at the centre of interwar Warsaw Yiddish culture, recalls Jakób Appenszlak's 'Polish-aristocratic' manner,[79] and characterizes Paulina Appenszlak as the archetype of the young lady ['*panienke*'] whom young Yiddish poets dreamed of impressing: elegant, assimilated, and cosmopolitan.[80] And he marvels that a man such as Appenszlak, whose office was in the midst of Yiddish-speaking Warsaw, could remain so aloof in spirit and in practical knowledge of the Jewish masses around him.[81] The distance between these worlds was a matter of language, but also of class, a reproduction within the Jewish microcosm of the larger gulf between Polish and Jewish cultural circles.

The influence of class attitudes partly explains the commitment of the Polish-Jewish press to the popularization and support of Jewish fine arts. This is not to say that the Jewish-language press ignored Jewish painters and sculptors; yet, also doubtless because of remnants of the traditional Jewish preference for the written over the visual representation, Jewish visual artists, it seems, did not receive the same exposure in the Jewish-language press as their literary counterparts. In an article ironically entitled 'Is Jewish Art Needed?', a writer in *Nasz Przegląd*, for example, complains that 'publications such as *Haynt* and *Der moment* treat art with peculiar neglect'.[82] In the pages of *Nasz Przegląd*, on the other hand, a comparatively large amount of space was devoted to gallery reviews, criticism of past and contemporary Jewish art, Jewish art history, and, in the weekly illustrated supplement, reproductions of new works. Moreover, an organization founded by Jakób Appenszlak, the Society for the Propagation of Fine Arts [*Towarzystwo dla Krzewienia Sztuk Pięknych*], dedicated itself to raising money to enable young Jewish artists, to whom Polish galleries were frequently closed, to exhibit their works.[83] In an age when fine arts, even more than writing or music, constituted a link to a cosmopolitan

Western modernist culture, *Nasz Przegląd*'s efforts on behalf of Jewish art were encouragement for the 'europeanization' of Jewish culture.

Furthermore, the Polish-Jewish press also hosted the emergence of a new and as yet virtually undocumented literary phenomenon: a group of writers who chose to write fiction and poetry on Jewish themes in Polish. The most well-known of this group was Roman Brandstaetter, poet, translator and Zionist publicist;[84] the group included: Maurycy Szymel,[85] Anda Ekerówna, Horacy Safrin, H. A. Fenster, Daniel Ihr, Karol Dresdner, Stefan Pomer, Karol Rosenfeld, and Minka Silberman.[86] These were exceptions to the more well-known phenomenon of 'Polish writers of Jewish descent' such as Bolesław Leśmian, Julian Tuwim, Antoni Słonimski, Józef Wittlin and Mieczysław Jastrun – major Polish poets who, while widely attacked in the anti-semitic press for their supposed 'judaization' of the Polish language, in their interwar writings remained aloof from Jewish themes.[87] Yet there is also the case of Mieczysław Braun [Bronsztejn], whose modernist poetry rarely ventured into Jewish subject matter, but whose prose writings, frequently published in *Nasz Przegląd* and the Polish-Jewish weekly *Ster* (Warsaw, 1937–38), often did. And in an article entitled, 'Polish Writers or "Jewish Writers writing in Polish" or "Polish-Jewish [Writers]?"', Braun forcefully defends the first of these formulations and adds: 'The attachment of a Polish writer, a Jew, to the Jewish nation [...] is not incompatible with the natural tie which binds him to Polish culture and language in organic unity. There is no duality in this: belonging to the Jewish nation and to contemporary culture in its Polish form are reconcilable'.[88] Further research will doubtless reveal a broad and complex spectrum of approaches to the tangle of 'Polish-Jewish' literary identity.

In addition to its support of Jewish artists and Polish-language writers, *Nasz Przegląd* in particular also sponsored two special publications. One was *Mały Przegląd* [*Little Review*], which appeared as a regular supplement to *Nasz Przegląd* written exclusively by and for children. *Mały Przegląd*'s editor and guiding spirit was the legendary educator and writer of children's books Janusz Korczak, martyred, along with the children of his orphanage, at Treblinka in 1942.[89] The second of these publications was the weekly *Ewa* (1928–33), a journal for women edited by Paulina Appenszlak, the wife of the editor of *Nasz Przegląd*. *Ewa*, which announced in its founding issue that it would 'reflect the opinions, thoughts, problems and aspirations of the contemporary Jewish woman, struggling for complete liberation and active direct participation in the development of Jewish national life,'[90] was 'European' and broadly feminist in orientation;[91] it also, however, participated in another unique activity organized by *Nasz Przegląd*: the annual 'Miss Judaea' beauty contest.

'ASSIMILATION'

Despite the manifold ties between the Yiddish and the Polish-Jewish press, it was probably inevitable that the Yiddish press would come to regard a successful Polish-Jewish press with suspicion and often with outright hostility. First of all, since, as we have seen, a large proportion of Polish Jews in the interwar period were bi-lingual, Yiddish and Polish-Jewish papers were competing for many of the same readers. Thus, for example, in a bitter article in the Yiddish literary weekly *Literarishe Bleter* the young I. B. Singer accused the Lwów daily *Chwila* of manipulating the closing of its Yiddish rival *Lemberger togblat*, the last Yiddish daily in Galicia.[92] Moreover, the Yiddish press, indeed like all of Yiddish culture, consistently perceived itself as an embattled institution: one of the most commonly encountered words in the lexicon of contemporary Yiddish criticism was the word 'crisis', and one of the most commonly cited reasons for the 'crisis' was the increasing linguistic assimilation of Polish Jews, a perception which, of course, much in this article substantiates. Furthermore, there was in Polish Yiddish culture (as there was in Hebrew culture – and not only in Palestine) a tendency to perceive its mission as linguistically exclusive, that is, as the only 'authentic' Jewish culture. However much this tendency compromised with Hebrew culture (and when it did not, fanatical conflicts were the result), to the possibility of a Jewish culture in the Polish language it allowed no quarter. For all these reasons, it was also therefore inevitable, and this despite the commitment of the Polish-Jewish press to Jewish culture and national awareness, that the animosity directed toward it would take the form of accusations of 'assimilation' – that is, of seeking the disintegration of Jewish national consciousness in much the same way as its nineteenth century predecessor *Izraelita*. This was, after all, the occasion for Sh. Y. Stupnitski's previously cited 'justification' for the Polish-Jewish press.[93] And even in the pages of *Opinja*, a publication founded, as noted, by the publishers of *Haynt* and described as nothing else than its Polish version, space had to be devoted to refuting such charges. Replying to the reproach that the Polish-Jewish press was 'an instrument for the assimilation of Jewish society', and therefore had no right to participate in protests over the abrogation of the National Minorites Treaty,[94] an editorial in *Opinja* argues:

> If not malice, then amazing ignorance must have guided the author of this reproach. Isn't it known that every day the ranks increase of Jewish youth who emerge from Polish schools, denationalized and polonized, and therefore bereft of the opportunity of availing themselves of literature in Yiddish, and all the more so in Hebrew? Isn't is known that in assimilated Jewish circles hitherto

completely estranged from the life of the Jewish masses — there has recently arisen a movement for a return to Jewishness [...] And shouldn't we, precisely for all these Jewish circles, create a bridge which would link them to Jewishness, and which only the Jewish press in the Polish language can constitute?[95]

To the evidence already brought undercutting such charges of 'assimilation', a final example: when, during the 1931 census, which failed to include a question on national affiliation, the Jewish press mounted a campaign to encourage Jews to use the question on 'mother-tongue' as a declaration of national identity,[96] that is, to answer Yiddish or Hebrew even if their primary language was Polish — the Polish-Jewish press participated as well. 'Entire Jewish families who speak neither Yiddish nor Hebrew', complains a writer in the assimilationist monthly *Zjednoczenie*, listed Yiddish as their mother-tongue 'because they were instructed to do so by the Jewish press *printed in the Polish language*'.[97] That is, for the sake of Jewish national interests, the Polish-Jewish press opposed documentation of the fact that many of its own readers existed!

CONCLUSION

Far from being a 'tool of assimilation', the Polish-Jewish daily press — as well as, I would suspect, the larger system of Polish-language Jewish culture which is yet to be explored — was an integral part of the complex, tri-lingual web, what Chone Shmeruk terms the 'polysystem',[98] of interwar Polish Jewish culture. The Polish-Jewish press, linked in a multitude of practical and ideological relationships to Jewish culture in Yiddish, and secondarily in Hebrew as well, shared with them the 'mission' of developing a modern Jewish national culture. Because Polish, however, was not an 'a priori' Jewish language, the Polish-Jewish press and the cultural system it represented lacked the ideological vitality, but also the frequent intolerance of Yiddish and Hebrew cultures. In contrast to the Yiddish and Hebrew cultural systems, each of which was associated with specific political ideologies (Bundist, Folkist, left Zionist, or non-assimilating Communist in the former case, Zionist in the latter), the Polish-Jewish cultural system as a whole 'had no well-defined overall political-ideological character'.[99] Thus, *Nasz Przegląd*'s readers, broadly Zionist or a-political, were generally less intensely 'politicized' than their Yiddish or Hebrew-reading counterparts. This apparent weakness of the Polish-Jewish press, in terms of the highly political standards of the age, was, however, in our own post-ideological hindsight perhaps, also its strength: a humility based on a consciousness of the limitations of its own possible claims to 'authenticity', which allowed it, first, to mirror the real breadth of Jewish cultural creation in Poland, and second, to continue to adhere to the flickering hope of fraternal relations with the non-Jewish world.

NOTES

1 Chone Shmeruk's article, 'Hebrew-Yiddish-Polish: a Tri-Lingual Jewish Culture' (to be published in Israel Gutman, Ezra Mendelsohn, Jehude Reinharz and Chone Shmeruk (eds) *The Jews of Poland between two World Wars*), is both from a theoretical perspective and on the basis of the observations and references with which it is filled, a fundamental starting point for the study of the Polish-Jewish press, and indeed for the study of interwar Polish Jewish culture in general. The authoritative bibliography of the Polish-language Jewish press is Paul Glikson's *Preliminary Inventory of the Jewish Daily and Periodical Press Published in the Polish Language, 1823–1982* (Jerusalem, 1983), with additions (soon to be published) by Alina Cała. For the interwar Yiddish press, the corresponding bibliography is Yechiel Szeintuch's *Preliminary Inventory of Yiddish Dailies and Periodical Publications Published in Poland Between the Two World Wars* (Jerusalem, 1986). Marian Fuks' pioneering monograph on the Jewish press in Warsaw, *Prasa żydowska w Warszawie, 1823–1939* (Warsaw, 1979), is an important but occasionally flawed source. Fuks is most reliable on the Polish-language press, but must, however, be used cautiously even here (see, for example, nn. 47 and 76 below). Andrzej Paczkowski's recent monograph on the interwar Polish daily press, *Prasa codzienna Warszawy w latach 1918–1939* (Warsaw, 1983), as well as an earlier statistical article, 'Nakłady dzienników warszawskich w latach 1931–1938' (in *Rocznik Historii Czasopiśmiennictwa Polskiego* [Wrocław-Warsaw-Kraków-Gdańsk], v. 15, 1976, pp. 68–97), examine the Jewish press as well, and bring new data to bear particularly on the question of circulation. (See pp. 214–7 below.) The anthology *Di yidishe prese vos iz geven* (Tel Aviv, 1975), edited by Dovid Flinker, Mordkhe Tsanin, and Sholem Rosenfeld, is a collection of reminiscences by Jewish journalists and editors; the following articles are relevant: Pola Appenszlak, '*Nasz Przegląd*', pp. 223–31; Moshe Sneh, '*Nowe Słowo* – a kemferishe tsaytung in der poylisher shprakh', pp. 232–35; Sholem Yededia, '*Piąta Rano*', pp. 235–36; Dovid Lazer, '*Nowy Dziennik* – 1918–1939', pp. 301–15. (Pola [Paulina] Appenszlak was a journalist and wife of the editor of *Nasz Przegląd*; Dovid Lazer worked for *Nowy Dziennik* from 1921 and was editor-in-chief during the latter 1930's; on Moshe Sneh see n. 65 below.) Melekh Ravitsh's quirky and illuminating *Mayn leksikon* (v. 1, Montreal, 1945; v. 2, 1947) includes profiles of several Polish-language Jewish journalists. Khaym Finkelshteyn's partly memoiristic monograph, '*Haynt*' – *a tsaytung bay yidn, 1908–1939* (Tel Aviv, 1978), contains incidental material on the Polish-language Jewish press as well. In addition: Pola Appenszlak, 'Ha-itonut be-polanit', *Enziklopedyah shel galuyot*, v. 1, Tel Aviv-Jerusalem, 1953, cols. 505–14; and Avraham Levinson, *Toledot yehudei Varshah*, Tel Aviv, 1953, pp. 305–06. For the sake of completeness, two pre-war Polish anti-semitic works: Paweł Czajkowski, 'Prasa żydowska w Polsce', *Przegląd Judaistyczny* (a pseudo-scholarly periodical devoted to the Jewish 'menace'), v. 1, 1922, pp. 197–212; and Zygmunt Jamiński, *Prasa żydowska w Polsce*, Lwów, 1936.
2 As if to emphasize the use of Polish for Jewish purposes, the word 'our' [*nasz, nasze*] was extraordinarily prevalent (over 12 per cent of Glikson's entries) in the titles of interwar Polish-Jewish publications.
3 For the purposes of this article there is little reason to distinguish among the papers published in these various cities. It should however be borne in mind that the

linguistic make-up of the Jewish populations of the Galician cities of Lwów and Kraków was very diffierent from that of Warsaw in Central ('Congress') Poland. The 1931 Polish census lists the following percentages of Jews declaring Yiddish as their mother tongue in these three cities: Warsaw, 88.9; Lwów, 67.8; Kraków, 41.3. (Cited according to Yankev Leshtshinski, 'Di shprakhn bay yidn in umophengikn Poyln', *Yivo bleter*, v. 22, 1943, pp. 147–62; these figures are somewhat inflated – see n. 24 below.) Thus, Kraków did not have a single Yiddish daily; Warsaw usually had at least five. Yet Jewish cultural and political life developed with a force of its own in Kraków, and primarily in the Polish language. And *Nowy Dziennik* in Kraków could become something that *Nasz Przegląd* never could in Warsaw: *the* Jewish newspaper.

4 As Shmeruk has pointed out ('Hebrew-Yiddish-Polish . . .'), the existence of a small number of obscure and widely scattered Jewish dailies in non-Jewish languages (see for example the listing of Jewish publications in *Jüdisches Lexikon*, v. 4, Berlin, 1930, pp. I–XXXV [insert to cols. 1104–05]) are exceptions which only underline the significance of the interwar Polish phenomenon.

5 Although Hebrew dailies existed in the interwar period (*Ha-zefirah*, with interruptions, to 1931, and *Ha-yom* from 1925–26, both in Warsaw), and in many circles great prestige was associated with the reading of a Hebrew newspaper, there were, however, never enough Hebrew readers in Poland to make a Hebrew daily a viable competitor of a Yiddish or even a Polish-Jewish daily, and a Hebrew paper could only exist because it was subsidized by Zionist organizations, for whom its existence was an important political statement. In the interwar years, moreover, as Shmeruk has pointed out, Poland increasingly lost ground to Palestine as the centre of modern Hebrew publishing. The circulation of the Hebrew dailies during the interwar period was a negligible proportion of the total circulation of the Jewish press.

6 In addition to *Haynt* and *Der moment*: *Unzer ekspres* (1927–39), an independent tabloid; *Folkstsaytung* (1921–39), organ of the Jewish socialist Bund; and *Yudishe togblat* (1929–39), organ of the orthodox Agudas Yisroel. *Haynt* and *Der moment* also published inexpensive afternoon tabloids: *Hayntige nayes* (1929–39) and *Varshever radio* (1924–39), respectively. In addition, almost all of the many Jewish political parties and 'tendencies' maintained their own, frequently irregular, periodical publications. Szeintuch lists a total of 1708 Yiddish periodical publications throughout Poland in the interwar period; a good number of these, of course, were short-lived.

7 If we interpret the notion of 'nationality' broadly enough, this may be said to characterize even the orthodox *Yudishe togblat*.

8 The weekly *Dostrzegacz Nadwiślański/Der Beobachter an der Weichsel*, printed in Polish and in Hebrew-character German, antedated by some forty years both the first Yiddish and Hebrew newspapers: *Varshoyer yudisher tsaytung* (1867–68) and *Ha-zefirah* (1862–1931), respectively. *Dostrzegacz* was a symbolically important but anomalous historical phenomenon: financially supported by the Russian government, it could not attract enough readers to justify its existence. *Dostrzegacz* has a comparatively large literature: Mordkhe Spektor, 'Di ershte tsaytung bay yudn', *Yudishe folks-tsaytung* (Warsaw), February 25, 1903; Majer Bałaban, 'Tsum 100-yorikn yubiley fun der yidisher prese in Poyln', *Bikher-velt* (Warsaw), v. 2, 1923, cols. 427–38, and 'Nasi poprzednicy i nauczyciele; prasa polsko-żydowska w XIX wieku', *Nasz Przegląd*, September 18, 1938; Azriel Frenk, 'Der "yontev" un zayn historisher hintergrunt', *Tsukunft*, March 1924; Nakhmen Mayzil, 'Di ershte yidishe tsaytung in Rusland mit hundert yor tsurik', *Tsukunft*, March 1924, and '125 yor zint der ershter yidisher tsaytung in Poyln', *Yidishe Kultur*, December 1948;

Yisroel Tsinberg, *Di geshikhte fun der literatur bay yidn*, v. 88, New York, 1943, pp. 220–21; Gershom Bader, 'Dray momenten in der antviklung fun der yidisher prese in Poyln', *Der polyisher yid, 11-ter yorbukh*, New York, 1944, pp. 60–61; Yankev Shatski, *Geshikhte fun yidn in Varshe*, v. 1, New York, 1947, pp. 290–92; Pola Appenszlak, 'Ha-itonut be-polanit'; S. Łastik, *Z dziejów oświecenia żydowskiego*, Warsaw, 1961, pp. 176–79; and Fuks, pp. 21–40. In terms of actual influence, the first Polish-language Jewish publication was the weekly *Jutrzenka* (1861–63). Significantly, although by the 1850's in Warsaw a potential readership for a Polish-Jewish periodical already existed, such a publication was only established under the impetus of the first Polish attacks on Jewish assimilation, the so-called 'Jewish War' of 1859. On *Jutrzenka*, see: B. Vaynrib, 'Tsu der geshikhte fun der poylish-yidisher prese', *Yivo bleter*, v. 2, 1931, pp. 73–79; Yankev Shatski, 'Der kamf arum geplante tsaytshriftn far yidn in Kongres-Poyln (1840–1860)', *Yivo bleter*, v. 6, 1934, pp. 61–83, 'A tsushtayer tsu der biografie fun Daniel Neufeld [editor of *Jutrzenka*] (1814–1874)', *Yivo bleter*, v. 7, 1934, pp. 110–16, and *Geshikhte fun yidn in Varshe*, v. 2, New York, 1948, pp. 245–47, 253–55, and v. 3, 1953, pp. 298–300, 318–19; Majer Bałaban, 'Nasi poprzednicy ...'; Pola Appenszlak, 'Ha-itonut be-polanit'; and Fuks, pp. 41–61.

9 On *Izraelita*, see for example: Yankev Shatski, *Geshikhte fun yidn in Varshe*, v. 3, pp. 319–21; Fuks, pp. 85–102; and Alina Cała, *Kwestia asymilacji Żydów w Królestwie Polskim (1863–1897): Postawy, Konflikty, Stereotypy*, doctoral dissertation, Historical Institute, Polish Academy of Sciences (PAN), 1985.

10 See for example, Shatski, *Geshikhte fun yidn in Varshe*, v. 3, pp. 110–29.

11 The story was told that since by this time neither *Izraelita*'s subscribers nor its editorial board read the paper – they supported it as an institution, but in these circles actually reading a Jewish paper smacked of 'separatism' – it took years until someone noticed that this very 'separatism' had explicitly crept into the paper and Sokolow was fired. (See S. Hirszhorn, 'Początki żydowskiego ruchu narodowego w Polsce', *Nasz Przegląd*, September 18, 1938.) Nahum Sokolow (1859–1936), the most productive and influential of a number of tri-lingual nineteenth century Polish Jewish journalists, began working for *Izraelita* in the 1880's. For many years he also edited *Ha-zefirah*, founded numerous other Hebrew publications, and was closely involved in the birth of the earliest Warsaw Yiddish periodical, Y. L. Peretz's *Di yudishe biblyotek*. The Hebrew poet Haym Nahman Bialik said of Sokolow that if someone were to undertake the project of gathering all of his writings he would need three hundred camels to carry them. After World War I Sokolow served in the Zionist Executive, and in the 1930's as head of the World Zionist Organization. Although he lived in England for most of the interwar period (where he produced an English history of Zionism), Sokolow continued to publish in Poland in the tri-lingual Jewish press; among Polish Jews his authority as Zionist elder statesman was immense. For a bibliography of works about Sokolow and the Jewish press, see Robert Singerman, *Jewish Serials of the World: A Research Bibliography of Secondary Sources*, New York-Westport, Connecticut-London, 1986, pp. 109–112. On Sokolow and *Haynt*, see p. 218 below.

12 In the preface to *Safrus*, Kirszrot contrasts the old romantic promise of assimilation, 'a living idea, a creative and winged conception', with the contemporary result: 'a soul-less and mechanical process performed its work without a superfluous word, the work of disintegrating the nation, whose intelligentsia, tearing itself from the family trunk, in frenzied haste demolished all roads to the human soul'. ('Wstęp', p. 7.)

13 On *Głos Żydowski*, see the article by Hirszhorn in n. 11, and Fuks, pp. 153–55; on Grünbaum (1879–1970), see pp. 218–9 below. In the more democratic and

polonized situation in Galicia, Polish-language Zionist publications appeared with greater regularity: the fortnightly *Przyszłość* (Lwów, 1890–99?); and the weeklies *Wschód* (Lwów, 1900–12) and *Moriah* (Lwów, 1903–14); indeed, the Galician Zionist press as a whole was a Polish-language press.

14 The Duma was an elected representative body which met in St. Petersburg. Granted by the czar after the 1905 revolution, by 1912 the Duma's political importance was minimal. On the Duma elections of 1912 and the resulting anti-Jewish boycott, see for example *Żydzi w Polsce Odrodzonej*, Warsaw, [1932–33], pp. 482–85; the memoirs of the Polish-Jewish journalist Bernard Singer, *Moje Nalewki*, Warsaw, 1959, pp. 164–69; Finkelshleyn, p. 49–56; and Frank Bolizewski, *Polnishe-Jüdische Bezichungen 1881–1922* (Wiesbaden, 1981).

15 In 1913, in a major article entitled 'Jew-Poland' ['*Żydo-Polska*'], Świętochowski prophesied a 'war' between the Polish nation and the 'nation of Israel'. (*Tygodnik Illustrowany*, nr. 8.)

16 Fuks, p. 151.

17 Herman Czerwiński, 'Ze wspomnień dziennikarskich', *Nasz Przegląd*, September 18, 1938.

18 See Czerwiński.

19 In particular, the publications of the Union of Poles of the Mosaic Faith [*Zjednoczenie Polaków Wyznania Mojżeszowego*] such as: *Rozwaga* (1915–28) and *Zjednoczenie* (1931–33); for further sources, see Shmeruk.

20 The editors of the Kraków daily *Nowy Dziennik*, for example, were considered the most 'Hebraist' of any Jewish paper in Poland: most had received a Hebrew education and read and spoke Hebrew. On a visit to this Polish-language paper's offices, Haym Nahman Bialik is reported to have said: 'Here one can at least speak Hebrew!' (Lazer, p. 311.) The relationship between the small but prestigious Hebrew cultural circles and those Jewish circles among whom Polish was the language of choice was often particularly close. Polish-educated Jewish youth seeking a way back to 'Jewishness', for whom Yiddish was still – if sometimes only unconsciously – tainted with its lower-class origins and nineteenth century designation as 'jargon' (not to mention the new Zionist accusation that it was a product of Jewish exile [galut] and must be 'negated' along with it), often discovered in elitist Hebrew culture a bridge to a new Zionist identity. An example of this phenomenon is the case of the Polish Zionist youth group Hashomer Hatzair, whose members generally came from Polish secondary schools, had been influenced by Polish nationalism avoided Yiddish, and devoted their energy to cultivating a new and 'healthy' Jewish youth steeped in manual labour and Hebrew culture. (See Ezra Mendelsohn, *Zionism in Poland, the Formative Years, 1915–1926*, New Haven, Connecticut and London, 1981, pp. 81–87, 120–30, 290–96.) Another instructive example: in an article on the bitter Hebraist-yiddishist conflict, a writer in *Nasz Przegląd* (Jakób Zineman, 'O naszej kwestji językowej', September 6, 1928), while announcing an even-handed approach to the issue, in fact attributes most of the blame for the conflict to the 'barbarism' of the yiddishists, and accepts the correctness of most Hebraist arguments. For an enlightening discussion of the political aspect of this tie – the influence of Polish nationalism on Zionism, see Ezra Mendelsohn, 'A Note on Jewish Assimilation in the Polish Lands', in Bela Vago (ed.), *Jewish Assimilation in Modern Times*, Boulder, Colorado, 1981, pp. 141–49. The Hebrew-Polish nexus as a linguistic and literary phenomenon deserves further attention.

21 On the founders of *Nasz Przegląd*, see p. 15 below.

22 It should, however, be pointed out that many elementary school students attended public schools in the mornings, and religious or secular Jewish schools in the

afternoons. On the secondary level, more Jewish students attended private or community-supported Jewish schools than state schools, but in the majority of these schools Polish was the language of instruction. For an analysis of the trilingual Jewish educational system in Poland and for further sources see Shmeruk.

23 One example: in an article intended to reply to the widespread accusation that Yiddish culture was on the wane in Warsaw, Nakhmen Mayzil ('Vi halt es mit yidish in Varshe', *Literarishe bleter*, nrs. 18–19, May 3–10, 1935) nevertheless cites statistics that show that among the libraries of eight Warsaw Jewish secondary schools containing over twenty thousand volumes, there were only one hundred books in Yiddish! The phenomenon was most widespread but not limited to the middle classes. Thus, Zygmunt Turkov (*Di ibergerisene tkufe*, Buenos Aires, 1961, pp. 247–48) recounts how the organization Kultur-Lige, one of the bastions of Yiddish culture in the interwar period (among its activities was to manage one of the two Yiddish publishing houses in Poland), whose practice it had been to purchase blocks of seats to Yiddish theatre performances for its Warsaw working class membership, began in the late 1930's to patronize Polish theatre instead. Further research is required to establish whether such phenomena were more pronounced in Warsaw than elsewhere in Poland.

24 This is borne out by the results of two Polish censuses: in 1921, 74.2 per cent of those Jews declaring themselves Jewish by religion also identified themselves as Jews by nationality; in 1931, in the absence of a category for national affiliation, and in the face of a campaign mounted in the Jewish press to use the category of 'mother-tongue' (a particularly inappropriate notion in relation to the bi-and trilingual reality) as a political statement about national identity – 79.9 per cent of all Jews by religion declared Yiddish as their mother tongue and 7.8 per cent declared their mother tongue to be Hebrew. In Warsaw for example, there were more 'native' speakers of Hebrew (19,743) than of non-Jewish languages including Polish (19,305)! The percentage of 'native speakers of Jewish languages' in 1931 exceeded by 13.6 per cent the percentage of 'Jews by nationality' in 1921. Although these results are an unreliable source for Jewish linguistic affiliation, they are an excellent indicator of the growth of Jewish national consciousness – which appears to have been notably strengthened after ten years of independent Poland. (The figures are from Yankev Leshtshinski's analysis of the 1931 census cited in n. 3 above. On their actual significance, see Shmeruk, 'Hebrew-Yiddish-Polish ...', as well as Leshtshinski.) It should be kept in mind, however, that there was a big difference between what a Zionist or Bundist, on the one hand, and an orthodox Jew, on the other, would have *meant* by Jewish nationality.

25 Cited from a Polish paraphrase of Stupnitski's article: (h), 'W młynie opinji. Czy potrzebne jest pismo polsko-żydowskie?', *Nasz Przegląd*, June 14, 1928. The original appeared in *Lubliner togblat* apparently as a reply to a 'great Jewish literary figure' who had stated in the *Sanacja* (government) newspaper *Głos Prawdy* that a Jewish daily in Polish was unnecessary. I have been unable to locate the original.

26 'W młynie opinji. Czy potrzebne jest pismo polsko-żydowskie?'.

27 Pola Appenszlak,'*Nasz Przegląd*', p. 227.

28 The victim, an orthodox Jew, was dragged from a trolley and beaten to death by a gang of Piłsudski's Legionnaires; on the following day the liberal *Nowa Reforma* carried a brief notice about the death, attributing it to a heart attack; at demonstrations surrounding the victim's funeral, the demand was raised for 'a daily Jewish national newspaper in the Polish language, which would serve as a combative tribune' against the wave of anti-semitism following the dissolution of the Hapsburg monarchy and the rise of an independent Polish state. (See Lazer, pp. 301–02, 304.)

29 Similarly, a Boston Jew today might read the daily *Boston Globe* and the weekly *Jewish Advocate*.
30 'W młynie opinji. Czy potrzebne jest pismo polsko-żydowske?' These lines play on the well-known dictum of the nineteenth century Hebrew poet Yehudah Leyb Gordon: 'Be a Jew in the home, and a man on the street'.
31 During the 1930's there were between two and four Polish-Jewish dailies in Warsaw; for periodical publications throughout Poland in the interwar period, Glikson and Cała list some 700 titles, of which about 150 appeared only once.
32 The firms of Teofil Pietraszka and Franciszek Krajny, the latter later known as PAR (*Polska Agencja Reklamy* [Polish Advertising Agency]); the catalogues were published more or less every two years beginning in 1921.
33 See n. 1.
34 See n. 1.
35 See n. 1.
36 Because of an insufficient number of samplings, I omitted figures for 1931 and 1936; in addition, because of many apparent irregularities, I omitted figures for June 30, 1932. I then computed average circulation for each of the years 1932, 1933, 1937 and 1938, and took the average of these figures. Thus, for example, of the 57 samplings of the circulation of *Nasz Przegląd*, there were 19 for 1932, 24 for 1933, 7 for 1937, and 7 for 1938. Fuks' figures are on pp. 263, 275, 189, 197, 208, 215, 206, 189, respectively, of *Prasa żydowska* . . . .
37 'Nakłady dzienników . . .', p. 68.
38 *Piąta Rano*, a Polish-Jewish tabloid, was published from 1931–39; see further n. 54 below.
39 'Nakłady dzienników . . .', p. 69. Another possibility, suggested to me by Professor Joshua Rothenberg, is that they inflated circulation figures for the non-socialist press, but not for the socialist press which, in any case, was of small interest to the catalogue publishers since it carried very little advertising.
40 'Vu haltn mir mit unzer tog-prese in Poyln?', *Literarishe bleter*, nr. 22, May 29. This figure may not reflect the true circulation of *Der emes*; what is relevant here, however, is the figure itself and how it compares with Fuk's for the Warsaw press. Mayzil's statement that this is a week-day circulation figure suggests a further question, since it is well known that the circulation of the Yiddish dailies was much larger on Fridays – namely, was Friday circulation included in the police samplings in a statistically consistent manner? Checking the 45 cases of samplings for which specific dates are given permits an affirmative answer: 6 were on Fridays.
41 *Prasa codzienna* . . . , p. 260.
42 Based on the circulation of the following dailies: *Nasz Przegląd*, *Piąta Rano*, *Nowe Słowo* (Glikson nr. 308), *Pismo Codzienne* (nr. 348), and *Nasz Głos* [*Wieczorny*] (nr. 245) for the years 1932, 1933, 1937, 1938. For *Nasz Głos* in particular there is a degree of discrepancy between its dates of publication as given in Glikson and dates of samplings in the police data.
43 Based on the circulation of the following dailies: *Haynt*, *Der moment*, *Unzer ekspres*, *Folkstsaytung*, *Yudishe togblat*, *Hayntige nayes*, *Varshever radio*, *Tsvey baytog* (Szeintuch nr. 1523), *Dos vort* (nr. 685), *Dos naye vort* (nr. 1217), and *Yudisher kurier* (nr. 999) for the years 1932, 1933, 1937, 1938. For *Yudisher kurier* in particular there is a degree of discrepancy between its dates of publication as given in Szeintuch and dates of samplings in the police data. In addition, no distinction is made in the police records between *Dos vort* and *Dos naye vort*, and *Tsvey baytog* appears as '*Cwaj Bajtos*'.
44 From 1932–39 there were no Hebrew dailies in Warsaw.

45 Paczkowski's figures for the Polish-language daily press ('Nakłady dzienników...', p. 69) less my figures for the Polish-language Jewish daily press.
46 Paczkowski, *Prasa codzienna* ..., pp. 242–43. *Nasz Przegląd*, for example, encountered more competition in other major cities from *Nowy Dziennik* and *Chwila* than did *Haynt* from local Yiddish dailies; *Nasz Przegląd* was therefore more of a 'Warsaw paper' than *Haynt*. Probably only Wilno, with its well-established Yiddish press, was an exception to the high level of penetration of Warsaw Yiddish dailies into other cities. On the other hand, more of the Warsaw Jewish daily press as a whole was printed for 'export' than was the case with its Polish counterpart (Paczkowski, *Prasa codzienna* ..., pp. 259–60); in other words, the Jewish press in Poland was much more centralized in Warsaw than was the Polish press.
47 The statistics for 1906 from the offices of the Warsaw censor [*Warszawski Komitet Cenzury*], a rare and important find, are published in Fuks, p. 298. Fuks chooses to include the daily *Gazeta Nowa/Ludzkość* (with a circulation of 10,000) as a Jewish paper, but although its editor was Jewish, its politics were liberal and it was probably read primarily by Jews, it never explicitly addressed itself to a Jewish audience.
48 It should be noted that there are over three times as many samplings for the first period than for the second.
49 According to Paczkowski's calculations, the Jewish share of the Warsaw daily press declined from approximately 25 per cent for 1931–33 to 20 per cent for 1937–38; the first figure, however, is based on data which include the year 1931 which I omitted because samplings of Jewish press circulation for that year were extremely sparse. See *Prasa codzienna* ..., p. 263 and the table on p. 257; there are other minor differences in Paczkowski's figures.
50 *Prasa codzienna* ..., p. 263.
51 *Prasa codzienna* ..., p. 263.
52 *Prasa codzienna* ..., p. 275.
53 See for example, Nakhmen Mayzil's diatribe, 'Vu haltn mir mit unzer tog-prese in Poyln?', cited in n. 40.
54 Stanisław Świsłocki, the editor of *Piąta Rano*, expecting a large readership for a Polish-language Jewish tabloid, launched his paper in 1931 with a circulation of over 40,000, but was quickly forced to cut back to 'more realistic' numbers, and this at a time when the share of the sensational press as a whole in the Warsaw daily press went from 55 per cent in 1932–33 to 60–65 per cent in 1937–38. See Paczkowski, *Prasa codzienna* ..., pp. 248–49 and 264–65.
55 Professor Joshua Rothenberg has brought to my attention a relevant and apparently undocumented phenomenon concerning readership of the Yiddish press in the 1930's. With the increasing pauperization of the Jewish population, coupled with the increasing sense of urgency about world news, the practice developed of paying 5 groszy (*Haynt* and *Moment* cost 25) to read a Yiddish paper on the premises of the local newspaper or book dealer, and then returning the paper to be sold or 'loaned' again. Yiddish papers inveighed against this practice, and even began to staple together the pages of their newspapers, but this didn't help: with the newspaper-seller's permission, the staples were removed and then replaced after the paper was read. Readers of *Nasz Przegląd*, generally of a wealthier class, did not need to 'share' their paper in the same way. Professor Rothenberg's observations stem from Radom and the shtetl Sandomierz. More research, including interviews with those who remember the period, is required in order to establish the prevalence of this phenomenon in Poland and its effect on the figures above.
56 Pola Appenszlak, '*Nasz Przegląd*', p. 226; see pp. 223–4 below.
57 *Haynt* affiliated with Yitshak Grübaum's *Al Hamishmar* faction of the General

Zionists, *Der moment* (after a link to the non-Zionist Folkist Party) first with the competing *Et Livnot* group, and in 1938 with Vladimir Jabotinsky's Revisionists. On the split in the Polish Zionist Federation, see Ezra Mendelsohn, *Zionism in Poland...*, pp. 245–52.

58 See for example *Nasz Przegląd*'s fifteenth anniversary issue, September 18, 1938. Ben-Gurion and Jabotinsky were leaders of two of the most antagonistic Zionist parties: Labour Zionists and Revisionists, respectively.

59 Hirszhorn (1876–1942), whose early years were spent in Polish-speaking circles, came to Yiddish as an adult. He was the author of a popular sketch of Polish Jewish history (*Historja Żydów w Polsce, od Sejmu Czteroletniego do wojny europejskiej [1788–1914]*, Warsaw, 1921) which he translated into Yiddish, and editor and for the most part translator of a Polish anthology of Yiddish literature (*Antologia Poezji Żydowskiej*, Warsaw, 1921). He liked to say that he wrote with two pens, Yiddish with the right hand and Polish with the left (Ravitsh, v. 2, p. 114). Wołkowicz (b. 1891), who was also a Yiddish-Polish translator, founded the series 'Biblioteka Pisarzy Żydowskich' which published Polish translations of Yiddish literature; in addition he was one of the founders of the Yiddish school system Tsisho. On Hirszhorn and Wołkowicz see *Leksikon fun der nayer yidisher literatur*, v. 3, New York, 1960, cols. 159–60 and 287–88, respectively; on Hirszhorn see also *Polski Słownik Biograficzny*, v. 9, Wrocław-Warsaw-Kraków, 1960–61, pp. 535–36. Appenszlak (b. 1891), on the other hand, read Yiddish fluently, but spoke with difficulty and with the 'accent of a *ger* [convert]'; see Ravitsh, v. 2, p. 98.

60 p. 146. The third was Moyshe Yustman [B. Yeushzon] (1889–1942), an extremely popular Yiddish columnist.

61 Thon (1870–1936), who served in the Polish *Sejm* [parliament], worked with *Nowy Dziennik* and also published in *Nasz Przegląd*; on his involvement in *Haynt* see Finkelsheyn, pp. 152–54. On Sokolow, see n. 11 above; on Sokolow and *Haynt*, see Finkelshteyn, pp. 154–57.

62 Finkelshteyn, pp. 132–45. On Grünbaum, see also p. 211 above. It would be worthwhile to compare the writings of a figure such as Grünbaum in Yiddish, Hebrew and Polish, in order to see how a political message may have changed depending on the linguistic audience.

63 Fuks, p. 258.

64 *Opinja*, an important and heretofore unexamined source for Polish-Jewish cultural history of the 1930's, was moved in 1935 from Warsaw to Lwów, where it appeared until 1939 as *Nowa Opinja* (according to Glikson, nr. 342) or *Nasza Opinja* (according to the catalogue of the Polish National Library). The publication may not have been able to continue in Warsaw because of political reasons: Cardinal Kakowski's displeasure over a Polish translation of Yosef Klausner's Hebrew study of the life of Jesus (Finkelshteyn, p. 302).

Other Polish-language Jewish publications published by *Haynt* were the dailies *Nowiny Codzienne* (1922) and *Nowy Czas* (1929), and the weekly *Nowa Palestyna* (1935) (Paczkowski, p. 248; Finkelshteyn, pp. 301, 302, 424, respectively). In 1939, after negotiations with the editors of *Nasz Przegląd*, the publishing cooperative 'Alt-Nay' (the publishers of *Haynt*) made plans for an illustrated Polish-language Jewish weekly which would begin to appear in September of that year (Finkelshteyn, pp. 300–03). The publishers of *Der moment* also founded Polish-language Jewish papers, among them the daily *Nowy Głos* (1937–38) (Paczkowski, p. 250).

In September 1929, Sh. Y. Yatskan, the flamboyant founding editor of *Haynt*, established an inexpensive a-political Polish tabloid with the purpose of weaning a mass Polish audience away from the popular anti-semitism fostered by the existing large-circulation Polish dailies, and thereby implicitly advancing Polish-Jewish harmony. The paper was launched by scores of newsboys distributing a special issue which proclaimed: 'Greatest sensation of the day! Revolution in press history! Daily of the newest type ...!' *Ostatnie Wiadomości*, among the first successful attempts at yellow journalism in Poland, quickly attained a circulation of 100,000, making it the largest-selling Polish daily; throughout the 1930's, however, it gradually lost readers to other tabloids. Yatskan's involvement with the paper ended in 1934. (See Paczkowski, pp. 208–13, 264–65; Finkelshteyn, pp. 35–36.)

65 Kleinbaum (1909–1972), whose ties to Grünbaum inspired the nickname 'Kleingrünbaum', inherited Grünbaum's mantle when the latter emigrated to Palestine in 1933; under the name Moshe Sneh, he was the head of the Haganah (Jewish defense forces) in Palestine in the 1940's, and from 1951 the leader of the Israeli Communist Party (Maki). See Finkelshteyn, pp. 182–84, 301–02; and Sneh, pp. 232–34.

66 p. 301.

67 'Cele i zadania', nr. 1, February 5, 1933; as cited in Fuks, p. 279.

68 'Na posterunku', nr. 1, March 25, 1923; as cited in Jakób Appenszlak, 'Pietnastolecie "Naszego Przeglądu"', *Nasz Przegląd*, nr. 263, September 18, 1938.

69 Much was written, for example, about the Jewish part in Polish insurrections of the nineteenth century. This emphasis was generally balanced, however, by a realistic assessment of the actual state of Polish-Jewish relations, and demands for their improvement. Both these elements are implicit in the words with which Appenszlak continues the statement (written in the relatively hopeful early 1920's) cited above: 'As citizens of the Polish commonwealth, we desire a strong and enduring Poland, free and freedom-granting, drawing its power and prosperity from the concerted cooperation of all citizens without regard to creed, nationality, or point of view'. ('Na posterunku.')

70 A well-known street in the Warsaw Jewish quarter.

71 Bernard Singer (pseudonym 'Regnis', 1893–1966), *Nasz Przegląd*'s regular and extremely popular parliamentary correspondant, was on 'old-boy' terms with many Polish politicians. Characteristically, Singer wrote in Yiddish and Hebrew as well. See Finkelshteyn, pp. 197–99; and Ravitsh, v. 2, 121–23.

72 'Na posterunku.'

73 'Cele i zadania.'

74 The Polish-Jewish press was also highly receptive to Jewish writers in other non-Jewish languages. And therefore, for example, it was through the Polish-Jewish press that Franz Kafka was introduced to Polish readers. Of all the reviews, excerpts and mentions of Kafka's work in the Polish press in the interwar period, eighty per cent were in Jewish publications. See Eugenia Prokopówna, 'Kafka w Polsce Międzywojennej', *Pamiętnik Literacki*, v. 76, 1985, pp. 89–132, and especially the appended bibliography on pp. 131–32.

75 There is no entry for Kanfer in any of the Jewish or Polish encyclopedias or biographical dictionaries. The theatre he founded operated from 1926–28 with a permanent company of young amateur and professional, often Polish-trained actors; among the plays it produced were Yiddish versions of Stanisław Wyspiański's *Sędziowie* and *Daniel*, the latter staged for the first time in Poland, directed by the Polish director Antoni Piekarski. The theatre gained such artistic renown that, in a highly unusual gesture of recognition, the Kraków municipal council appropriated funds for its support. On this fascinating example of the complexities of interwar Polish Jewish culture, see: Sholem Fraynd, 'Dos ershte yidishe gezelshaftlekhe teater in Poyln (krokever yidish teater)', *Yidish teater*, v. 1, Warsaw-Vilna, 1927, pp. 214–30, and 'Krokever yidish teater', *Literarishe bleter*, May 27, 1927; Yonas Turkov, 'Ha-teatron ha-yehudi be-Krako', in *Sefer Krako, ir ve-*

em be-yisrael, Jerusalem, 1959, p. 352; and Rokhl Holtser, 'Yidish teater in Kroke', in *Yidisher teater in Eyrope tsvishn beyde velt-milkhomes, Poyln*, New York, 1968, pp. 276–85.

76 Among Yiddish writers: Leo Finkelshteyn and S. L. Schneiderman; among Hebrew writers, Yehudah Varshaviak, for example, published essays and reviews of Hebrew literature in *Nasz Przegląd*. Future research on the Polish-Jewish press will have to distinguish between writers who wrote directly in Polish and those whose works appeared in translation. Chone Shmeruk correctly criticizes the work of Marian Fuks for failing to make this important distinction. ('A Pioneering Study of the Warsaw Jewish Press', *Soviet Jewish Affairs*, v. 11, 1981, nr. 3, p. 38.)

77 '*Nasz Przegląd*', p. 228. These were the major Yiddish 'art' theatres in interwar Poland.

78 '*Nasz Przegląd*', pp. 228–29.

79 v. 2, p. 98; for many years Ravitsh was secretary of the Union of Jewish [i.e., Yiddish and Hebrew] Writers and Journalists, better known by its address, 'Tłomackie 13'.

80 pp. 100–01.

81 p. 101. For a comical comparison of the readers of five Warsaw dailies, including *Nasz Przegląd*, see: Der Tunkeler [Yoysef Tunkel], 'Der tsaytungs-farkoyfer', in *Dos amolike yidishe Varshe*, Montreal, 1966, pp. 318–22.

82 Norbert Rosse, 'Czy sztuk żydowska jest potrzebna?', May 19, 1925.

83 Pola Appenszlak, '*Nasz Przegląd*', p. 228.

84 After World War II Brandstaetter (b. 1906) converted to Catholicism, and is today a leading Polish Catholic writer and dramatist. He has published Polish translations of Psalms, Song of Songs, and Proverbs.

85 In the mid-1930's Szymel suddenly threw over a promising career as a Polish-language poet and, no longer as 'Maurycy' but as 'Moyshe', turned exclusively to Yiddish. See Ravitsh, v. 1, pp. 261–63.

86 Eugenia Prokopówna, a doctoral candidate at the Jagiellonian University in Kraków, is completing a dissertation on these writers. She has recently published an article on the depiction of the Jewish Sabbath in Polish literature which draws on some of this material: 'Sobota', *Fołks-sztyme* (Warsaw), nrs. 20–23, May 17–June 7, 1986; and see also her article in the forthcoming anthology *The Jews of Poland between Two World Wars* cited in note 1.

87 On such writers, see Artur Sandauer, *O sytuacji pisarza polskiego pochodzenia żydowskiego w XX wieku*, Warsaw, 1982.

88 'Pisarze polscy czy "pisarze żydowscy piszący po polsku" albo "polsko-żydowscy?"', *Ster*, 1937, nr. 16, as cited by Janusz Maciejewski in the introduction to his edition of Braun's *Wybór poezji*, Warsaw, 1979, p. 27. Braun (1902–42) is a relatively forgotten Polish poet; Maciejewski's small volume is the only edition of his poetry published since the war. Braun was also one of the rare Polish writers who attempted to direct the attention of Polish literary circles to Yiddish literature; see 'Literatura żydowska a polskie środowisko literackie', *Nowe życie*, v. 1, 1924.

89 Korczak wrote a book about Jewish children entitled *Mośki, Joski i Srule*, and a book about Polish children entitled *Józki, Jaśki i Franki* (See: c., 'Z piśmiennictwa', *Izraelita*, nr. 3, May 6, 1910). On *Mały Przegląd*, see: Janusz Korczak, *Ktavim pedagogiyim*, Tel-Aviv, 1954, pp. 135–58; Marian Fuks, '"Mały Przegląd" Janusza Korczaka', *Biuletyn Żydowskiego Instytutu Historycznego w Polsce* (Warsaw), nr. 105, 1978, pp. 3–28; and Leon Harari, '"Kleine Rundschau" – Korczaks Zeitung für die Kinder', in Werner Licharz (ed.), *Janusz Korczak in seiner und in unserer Zeit*, Frankfurt/Main, 1981, pp. 118–28.

90 'Od redakcji', February 19, 1928, as cited in Fuks, p. 282; on *Ewa*, see Fuks, pp. 282–85.

91 It should be noted that the orthodox Yiddish press often included a section in Polish for women, since many women in hasidic homes read Polish more fluently than Yiddish. Obviously, such women's publications were very different from *Ewa*.
92 B. Zinger, 'Der krizis fun der yidisher prese in provints', *Literarisher bleter*, nr. 129, October 22, 1926.
93 See pp. 212–3 above.
94 The treaty, guaranteeing Jewish political and cultural rights in independent Poland, was signed by Polish representatives as part of the Versailles Accords. Much Jewish political energy was expended during the interwar period attempting to realize its provisions.
95 'Pro domo sua', nr. 38, September 23, 1934, as cited in Fuks, p. 279. The article replies to an accusation made by 'one of our best journalists . . . at a certain Jewish journalists' conference'. Shmeruk ('Hebrew-Yiddish-Polish . . .') identifies the writer of the article as Moyshe Kleinbaum.
96 See n. 24 above.
97 'Statystyka a etyka', v. 1, 1932, pp. 10–12; as cited in Shmeruk, 'Hebrew-Yiddish-Polish . . .', emphasis in the original.
98 'Hebrew-Yiddish-Polish. . . .'
99 Shmeruk, 'Hebrew-Yiddish-Polish. . . .'

FROM 'NUMERUS CLAUSUS' TO 'NUMERUS NULLUS'

Szymon Rudnicki

Almost from the beginning of its activities the National Democratic movement used nationalist slogans in its propaganda campaigns, chiefly antisemitic ones. This propaganda eventually achieved the desired results. Clearly, though, the policy of the National Democrats was only one part of the so-called 'Jewish question', and the events described below were only a small part of the political programme of the National Democrats.

From the first days of the independent Polish state the National Democratic movement worked to curb the rights of the national minorities, particularly those of the Jews. Only a month after the assembly of the *Sejm Ustawodawczy* (Constituent Parliament) on 19 March 1919, the *Związek Ludowo-Narodowy* (Popular National Union) pointedly tabled a motion which resulted in a Commission for Jewish Affairs being set up. Its task was 'the comprehensive examination of the Jewish question, employing a questionnaire designed by those circles most familiar with the matter, and the presentation of conclusions so derived, with a view to resolving the problem'.[1] In the power struggle the *Endecja* (National Democrats) eagerly employed anti-semitic slogans, counting both on their universality and that they would be readily taken up by voters.[2] The slogans were matched by deeds. In the lands which had once belonged to Austria-Hungary, Jewish railway workers were dismissed. It began to be increasingly difficult for Jews to find work in state and municipal enterprises. As early as 1919, Itzhak Grünbaum complained about the introduction of a percentage quota system for students admitted to Poznań University.[3]

The universities became the testing ground for the National Democrats' propaganda and methods. The susceptibility and responsiveness of youth to patriotic appeals were exploited, and it proved simple to transform them into nationalist slogans. Advantage was taken too of the severe economic situation and poor employment prospects. Because of the lack of employment opportunities for intellectuals, it was easy to convince young people that posts occupied by others should belong to the host community – to the ethnic Poles. A fundamental rallying cry of nationalist youth, which it used to gain control at the universities, was the campaign against what it believed was the excessively high level of young Jews entering higher education. Although the Jews were the prime target for such attacks, in Lwów a campaign was also waged against the Ukrainians.

There were three stages in this campaign: (1) The 1920s and the efforts by young nationalists to gain power and influence in the universities. (2) The first half of the 1930s when the 'numerus clausus' slogan was replaced by the 'numerus nullus' one and the campaign over the 'ghetto bench' began. The campaign had also moved from the propaganda level to that of physical confrontation. (3) The second half of the 1930s, which was characterized by an intensification of campaign methods and notable successes for the young nationalists.

The young nationalists were initially concentrated in the *Narodowe Zjednoczenie Młodzieży Akademickiej* (*NZMA* – National Union of Student Youth) which they barely managed to control. They credited themselves with 'awakening resistance to Jewish influences'. And it is worth noting a sentence from the first issue of their journal *Głos Akademicki* of May 1920, that 'until recently our organization stood completely on its own in this struggle'. Since this reflected the contemporary situation, it was also an indication, as we shall see, of what an appropriate propaganda campaign, waged with persistence and ruthlessness, could lead to. Although a considerable number of students remained indifferent to this struggle at the universities and were concerned only with their studies, and the members of nationalist organizations were never in a majority, they nevertheless managed to gain control of the student organizations and impose their own views.

The battleground fought over by socialist and democratic organizations at the beginning of the 1920s was the *Bratnie Pomoce*, student self-help organizations. The first one to fall to the young nationalists was the *Bratnia Pomoc* of Poznań University. It was controlled by a Nationalist Bloc incorporating student associations and fraternities as well as the *NZMA*. After their success in elections held on 10 April 1921, they passed a resolution calling for Jews to be excluded from student organizations.[4] This pattern was to be repeated at other universities.

On the 25–26 March 1922, the first Congress of *Młodzież Wszechpolska* (All Polish Youth) took place. This was a nation-wide organization where adherents of the nationalist programme were concentrated. It immediately joined in the political campaigning before the 1922 parliamentary elections. From then onwards, the disparate activities at separate universities began to take on an organized shape.

From the beginning the nationalist students directed their activities towards limiting the number of Jews at universities to the same percentage they had in the nation as a whole; in other words, introducing the 'numerus clausus'. Why so many Jewish students should have been entering the universities is a question outside the scope of this paper. It should be pointed out, however, that they were chiefly concentrated in the Faculties of Medicine and Law – professions which could be pursued in private practice. In other faculties, and at other academic institutions, they were much less in evidence. For example, at Poznań University they never reached more than two per cent of the student total.

Młodzież Wszechpolska began a nationwide campaign aimed at forcing the government to introduce legislative measures for a Jewish quota. Their demands, however, did not end there. In a special issue of *Głos Akademicki*, of November 1922, devoted entirely to Polish-Jewish relations, they also called for a ban on the admission of Jews to student organizations and associations, and warned against maintaining social contact with Jews.

The 1922–3 academic year began with a series of rallies at different universities. As early as September a memorandum was addressed in Lwów to the senates of all universities demanding the introduction of a 'numerus clausus'.[5] At this time Jews were 42.5 per cent of the students at the Jan Kazimierz University, but at the Polytechnic they amounted to only 13.9 per cent, and only 13.7 per cent at the Academy of Veterinary Science. To back up their memorandum, a rally was called for 1 October, and the demand was renewed in February 1923. Among the resolutions passed at the rally was a call to restrict the number of Jewish students to 11 per cent of the total.[6] This was to be repeated at other universities with the exception of Poznań, where a limit of 1 per cent was demanded, the same percentage of Jews in the Wielkopolska region.[7] The fact was ignored that if this principle were applied to the other regions of Poland, then the percentage of Jews admitted would have come to considerably more than the stipulated 11 per cent.

In Kraków the Rector of the Jagiellonian University at first refused to agree to a rally of this kind. A number of student organizations also protested against attempts to hold one. After renewed requests, permission was granted and the rally took place on 23 October. Demands were made for a 'numerus clausus' for Jews in training colleges as well as in academic centres, and if necessary, in faculties of philosophy and law. These demands were renewed at a further rally on 19 March 1923, and on this occasion an appeal was also made for help in communicating these demands to the *Sejm*.[8]

The situation seemed much the same in Warsaw. A rally on 23 November 1923 passed a motion calling for the imposition of a 'numerus clausus'. This was handed to the Vice-Minister for Religious Affairs and Public Education. No Jews were admitted to this public meeting and no representative of the young socialists was allowed to address it. From then on this procedure became the norm. In addition, a students' association 'strong-arm squad' found its way into a meeting of the *Zjednoczenie -Organizacja Polskiej Młodzieży Akademickiej Pochodzenia Żydowskiego* (Organization of Young Students of Jewish Descent) – and broke down the doors of the hall where it was taking place.

These activities in Warsaw culminated in the all-student assembly called for 19 March in the Filharmonia. Here a resolution was passed, with a fourth point which stated that 'Jews should be excluded from membership of Polish ideological, training, scientific, self-help and other organizations, and [the assembly] expresses its approval and support for those organizations already observing these principles'.[9] The nationalists subsequently managed to introduce these principles into the *Bratnia Pomoc* organisations at the university and the polytechnic.

At the close of the assembly it was decided to hold a *Zjazd Ogolnoakademicki* (All-Student Rally) in Lwów at the end of May and the beginning of June. Delegates were chosen, in spite of the protests of young left-wingers, at local meetings on the majority vote system. Furthermore, at these meetings strong-arm squads, composed of members of *Młodzież Wszechpolska* and the student fraternities, admitted only their own followers and ejected those holding contrary views from the hall. In this way the desired composition of the national assembly was achieved. Young delegates of the Peasant parties, elected in Kraków, refused to participate. At first, the Catholic group *Odrodzenie* also wanted to withdraw from the convention. However, it eventually took part but abstained from voting on motions calling for a limitition on the number of Jews at Polish universities to the same proportion as in the overall population; and the waging of a struggle to support this measure using 'all necessary means to reach a successful outcome'. The assembly also approved the statute of the *Związek Narodowy Polskiej Młodzieży Akademickiej* (National Union of Polish Student Youth), which banned Jews from being members of the organization.[10] An unforeseen result of the assembly was a break in what had been, despite some violent differences of opinion, a solid, nation-wide student movement. After this convention, *Młodzież Wszechpolska* began to wield increasing influence at the universities.

Following resolutions passed at the assembly, a Main Committee and Local Academic Committees were set up to deal with the 'numerus clausus' issue. An action programme, extending far beyond the university sphere, was drawn up by the secretary of the Main Committee, Zbigniew Stypułkowski. He believed the ideal solution to the problem would be 'to employ those methods towards Jews, which would eradicate them and their influence from all Polish soil'. Because this was not possible for various reasons 'we must aim at a complete separation of Jews from Poles, and thus exclude them from all spheres of Polish life – government, national, economic, cultural, moral, family, social, etc. – leaving them complete freedom to organize their own ghetto.' As Dariusz Jarosz has shown, an identical demand was contained in the programme of *Młodzież Wszechpolska*, approved in 1925.[11]

The Parliamentary Club of the Popular National Union in the *Sejm* supported these demands. They did so after their defeat in the struggle for the presidency and at an unfavourable time for the National Democrats, following the assassination of Gabriel Narutowicz. On the one hand they wished to divert attention from recent events, while on the other the anti-Jewish campaign was treated as a part of a drive for support among young people. On 16 January 1923 a motion was proposed for changes in articles 85 and 86 of the Universities Act of 13 July 1920. These articles related to student admission procedures. In particular, attention was drawn to article 86, which gave faculty boards, with the approval of the Minister of Religious Affairs and Public Education, the right to limit the number of students accepted. The proposers of the motion wanted to add the following sentence to article 85, 'in Polish institutions of higher education, the number of students admitted to any given department who are of non-Polish nationality or of Jewish faith, must not exceed, as a percentage of the overall number of students of the same department, the percentage of the said national group, or Jewish faith within the overall population of the Polish State.'[12] As can be seen the motion was formally aimed at all minorities, in keeping with the doctrines of Polish nationalism. In practice, however it only applied to Jews, since only they exceeded the quota in the proposal.

The Education Committee of the *Sejm*, which considered this proposal, appointed as its spokesman the famous historian, Władysław Konopczyński. Besides being a professor at the Jagiellonian University, Konopczyński was also a deputy representing the *Związek Ludowo-Narodowy* and a member of the *Liga Narodowa* (National League). After he had spoken, Jewish and Socialist deputies rose to oppose the resolution. They demanded that the motion be sent to the Constitution Committee to test whether the proposed changes in the Constitution could be adopted legally.

The subject produced a bitter debate in the Constitution Committee. Ranged against the motion were Adam Pragier (PPS) and Ludwik Chomiński (*PSL-Wyzwolenie*) who argued that it was unconstitutional. I. Grünbaum asserted that it was the first step towards changing the Constitution. Władysław Kiernik (*PSL-Piast*) agreed that, as it stood, the proposal could not be reconciled with the Constitution. He redrafted it in consultation with *ZLN* members, linking the quota with the issue of a reduction in overall student numbers. Percentages were no longer mentioned, only a fair numerical relationship.[13]

The motion was returned to the Education Committee in its revised version and was then distributed to faculty boards with a query if its adoption would affect the running of higher education. Out of forty-two faculty boards, nine rejected the proposal, declaring themselves in favour of the *status quo*. Twenty-seven supported the proposal in its entirety. Seventy-five per cent of professors approved limiting student numbers and about half were in favour of a percentage quota.[14] In Kraków nine professors out of fifteen in the law faculty declared themselves in favour of limiting student numbers, and eight were in favour of percentage quotas. The medical faculty was unanimously in favour of such quotas. However, the professors in the philosophy faculty considered the proposal went against the dignity of the academic community. Thirty professors voted against the proposal, including the chairman of the Polish Academy of Learning, Kazimierz Morawski, and thirteen voted in favour of the quotas.[15] The Poznań members demanded a reduction of the quotas to one below the proportion of Jews in the population as a whole. The issue of percentage quotas also came up at the Conference of University Rectors (5–7 February 1923), but it did not generate any discussion.[16] In fact a number of faculties were already using percentage quotas, but the most extreme case, as mentioned above, was that of Poznań.

When the Education Commission received these figures and prepared to discuss the matter once more, the representative of *PSL-Piast* tabled a motion requesting its deferment until his party had formulated its own policy on the question. The motives behind this step are none too clear. Most probably, however, the move was connected with simultaneous discussion about the formation of a majority bloc in the *Sejm*, in which the *Piast* group would participate. As a result of these talks the so-called 'Polish majority' was set up in the *Sejm*, headed by the *ZLN* and *PSL-Piast*. One of the principles on which they cooperated was the tenet: 'Young Poles will be guaranteed the chance to be educated at secondary and tertiary level and at vocational institutes, according to the appropriate proportions of the national groups within the state.'[17] As can be seen the principle was also extended to secondary and vocational schools, and the issue was couched in terms which gave the impression that it was young Poles who needed defending, whereas in reality it was young Byelorussians and Ukrainians who were being the most unjustly treated.

The government of Wincenty Witos was formed on the basis of this agreement. Its Minister for Religious Affairs and Public Education was Stanisław Głąbiński, former chairman of the *ZLN*. At the same time, Kiernik's motion, in a slightly amended form, was returned to the Education Committee for further consideration and was approved on 19 June 1923 by sixteen votes to thirteen. Jewish representatives voiced their concern by tabling a counter motion, calling for the following passage to be added to article 86: 'the above restrictions [on admissions to universities] should not be applied on the grounds of nationality or faith.'[18]

With the resolution being passed by such a slender majority, the opposition demanded a third reading. The President of the *Sejm*, Maciej Rataj, sent the motion to the Legislative Committee. Here it came to a stop, since *PSL-Piast* considered it undesirable to introduce the 'numerus clausus' before reforming the Treasury. And this was the end of a first attempt to legislate for a percentage quota to be applied to students entering higher education. In the circumstances the only course open to Głąbiński was to transfer his authority to restrict the number of students admitted to the faculty boards. He did so by a letter circulated on 12 July 1923. The activities of the boards in this area were terminated by the May Coup in 1926.

The government formed after the Coup embarked on several initiatives aimed at reaching agreement with the national minorities. These moves culminated in the passage through the *Sejm* in January 1931 of a bill repealing emergency regulations relating to descent, nationality, language, race or religion. Jewish members had been pressing for such a bill since the first days of independence. If the Jewish minority were pleased with the bill, the mood of the Ukrainians following the pacification campaign of 1930 was one of hostility towards the government.

In the universities, this policy was expressed in the actions of the different ministers who assumed responsibility in turn for higher education. Before the start of the academic year, on 20 September 1926, Antoni Sujkowski cancelled the instructions circulated by Głąbiński. In July 1927 his successor, Gustaw Dobrucki, issued a reminder that the relevant law did not allow the introduction of limits based on nationality or religion. He received Jewish members of the *Sejm* at the beginning of the academic year and told them that 'the government of Marshal Piłsudski is absolutely opposed to the 'numerus clausus'.'[19] Continuing this policy, Sławomir Czerwiński advised university senates to be cautious in allowing assemblies which might result in anti-semitic brawls.[20]

These measures, however, were not matched by appropriate action in the universities. In fact, ceilings continued to be applied. The Rector of the Jagiellonian University, Leon Marchlewski, commented on this at a conference of university rectors, where consideration was given to which departments they should be introduced and in what form. Taking part in the discussion, the Minister, Dobrucki, declared that 'the recording of the actual number of Jews admitted by any one faculty is not desirable, since this cannot remain a secret.' In the end it was unanimously agreed that the Ministry should leave the 'numerus clausus' question untouched.[21] In fact it was not needed for, in practice, a Jewish percentage quota existed in places where the provision of laboratories had caused problems. The *Kurier Codzienny* of 2 October 1931, disclosed that this percentage was 12 per cent in medicine, 10 per cent in dentistry, and 8.5 per cent in pharmacy and veterinary science.

The medical faculties led the way during this early period of the campaign against the Jews. One pretext for the increasing number of

confrontations which occurred each year was the so-called 'affair of the Jewish corpses'. On 26 June 1926 the director of the anatomy department of Warsaw University sent out a circular stating that because of a shortage of cadavers, Jewish students wishing to attend lectures and demonstrations would only be admitted if the Jewish community provided corpses.[22] It was claimed that the reason for this dispute was not political, but the result of the objection to Jews 'profaning consecrated corpses'.[23] The Jewish community could not provide the requisite number of corpses since Orthodox Judaism forbade dissection.

Młodzież Wszechpolska had no intention of abandoning its propaganda campaign. In May 1927, the Fifth Congress of Polish Student Youth (which it organized) advised its newly elected leaders to petition the academic authorities and the government to limit the number of Jews at university institutions.[24] Continuing efforts were being made, with some success, to exclude Jews from certain student organizations.

The economic crisis added a new dimension to the problem since it was a convenient starting point for unleashing chauvinism and anti-government activities. The governing council of the *Stronnictwo Narodowe* (Nationalist Party) organized a boycott of Jewish businesses. Similar activities were adopted among young people by the *Ruch Młodych Obozu Wielkiej Polski* (Youth Movement of the Camp for a Great Poland), which had been set up in April 1927. *Młodzież Wszechpolska (MW)* became an integral part of the latter organization as its student section. A special 'Jewish department' was created, attached to the central bureau of *MW*. Its activities were not confined to propaganda. In Lwów *MW* organized a blockade of Jewish shops, refusing to allow 'Christians' to enter them. The move was then repeated in other towns. During this period nationalist students began to sport green ribbons as a sign of their anti-semitism.

The nationalist camp was aware that the economic crisis facilitated the spread of anti-semitic propaganda. Appealing to feelings of social injustice, anti-semitism identified its source in a very primitive way, but one which was close to the popular imagination, in the figure of the Jew as competitor, the Jew as exploiter. In particular, the lower-middle-class who were suffering increasingly could see the elimination of Jewish competition as a way of solving all their problems. In the difficult economic situation, therefore, there was considerable support for the call for an economic boycott of Jews. It also attracted increasing support in the countryside. Similarly, the same argument was used in propaganda aimed at young people, namely that they were the victims of 'injustice' in their own country.

An advantage enjoyed by the anti-Jewish programme was its concrete nature and its convenient topicality. It provided a ready explanation for all the complex and negative phenomena of social, political and economic life. Hatred for a common enemy acts as an integrating force, welding together people from different social strata, classes and groupings and from different cultural levels. In Poland it was the Jew who was the obvious candidate for the position of public enemy. Not real Jews, although it was they who suffered from these policies, but mythical Jews – a mythologized, irrational group, the cause of all evil past and present. Consistent with this theory was the belief that the presence of Jews and Judaism meant disruption and disintegration for the Christian community, which was the ideal one by its very definition, and especially for the Polish Catholic community.

The nationalist camp's press organs stirred up the atmosphere to an even greater pitch of excitement.[25] At the beginning of December 1931, the official journal of *Obóz Wielkiej Polski* (*OWP*), *Szczerbiec*, reported: 'The ambition of the younger generation of Poles, who are now beginning to play an active part in social and political life, is to settle the Jewish question.' This policy statement was published at a time when a wave of anti-semitic disturbances, organised by *MW*, was sweeping across university campuses. The intention of the organizers was to influence young people beginning their studies. They aimed at provoking clashes with the police, which would then facilitate anti-government agitation and demonstrate the extent of its power to the youngsters.

Incidents started at the Jagiellonian University, beginning with the affair of the corpses: Jews were not admitted to anatomy lectures or practical experiments. Because of these incidents, lectures were suspended for a week, beginning again on 28 October. At Warsaw University trouble broke out in the faculty of law, which was a bastion of *MW* and where the greatest number of Jews in relative terms were studying. The result of these incidents, as *MW*, admitted, was to leave several dozen Jews severely beaten.[26] On 6 November lectures at the University were suspended, and similar action was taken at other institutions in the capital during the next few days. This step, which rectors frequently employed after such incidents, was inconvenient to the majority of students who had taken no part in the troubles, because it extended their term of study. Another 'inconvenience' was the announcement of fresh registration at the university.

Incidents also took place in other towns, including Wilno. Here, during an anti-Jewish demonstration after Jews had been turned away from the main university building, events culminated in tragedy. A Polish student of the law faculty, Stanisław Wacławski, was struck on the head by a stone during a brawl and died later in hospital. A wave of strikes and rallies organized by *MW* hit academic centres all over the country. Here motions demanding the introduction of a 'numerus clausus' were passed and, probably for the first time, the call for a 'numerus nullus' was heard, a slogan which replaced the other over the coming years.

The Senate of Warsaw University deplored these incidents. A number of individual professors protested against them, as they had done in 1923.[27]

Members of left-wing organizations consistently opposed them, risking threats and persecution. However, only the *Związek Polskiej Młodzieży Demokratycznej* (Union of Polish Democratic Youth) of the *Sanacja* organizations took an unequivocal stance, condemning the excesses and defending those attacked.

Just as in 1923, a resolution of the Nationalist Party of 18 December 1931, to regulate student numbers in academic institutions, came to be seen as an expression of support, which strengthened nationalist youth in its conviction that it was fighting for a just cause. The number of students was to be set annually by the Faculty Councils. 'Care should be taken in admitting students,' warned the movers of the resolution, 'that the number of Christian students in relation to the overall level outlined in Clause 1 should not be lower than the overall number of Christians in the national population as recorded in the last census.'[28] Unlike in 1923, it was rejected and was restricted to the Jewish population.

The resolution was sent to the Commission but never appeared before the *Sejm*. Its reading apparently led to stormy exchanges during sittings of the Educational Committee, but we have no records to indicate the positions adopted by individual Committee members. We know, however, the views of Professor Wacław Komarnicki, who moved the resolution. He justified it first on pedagogic grounds – to remove anything which might disturb academic work. Next he used arguments based on economic grounds. According to Komarnicki, young Jews were better off than their peers. As a direct result of too many of them entering universities, Jews were forcing Poles out of the professions. He insisted the state could not remain indifferent to the composition of the intelligentsia, all the more so as the influx of Jews into the arts and sciences was harmful. The introduction of a 'numerus clausus' was therefore a measure of national defence. To overcome the scruples of members of the Committee he cited the examples of restrictions on Jews introduced in Hungary and Rumania.[29] This statement was the broadest and most comprehensive expression of the motives behind the demands of the nationalists. By this time, however, these were not enough to satisfy *Młodzież Wszechpolska*. In May 1932, at a meeting of this Steering Committee, the previous demands on the Jewish question were extended considerably. Now all Jews were to be deprived of 'political rights with all that entails, and prevented by changes in the existing law from participating in the individual and collective life – both cultural and economic – of the Polish nation'.[30]

A further development of this resolution was the formulation of the 'Basic Principles underlying policy towards the Jewish, German and Slavic minorities' published in November 1932. The statement was published by the student section of the Warsaw *OWP*. Most space in the 'Principles' was devoted to the Jewish question. They assumed a complete separation of the two communities, with no chance of crossing the divide.

Mixed marriages, for example, would have been forbidden. All the restrictions would have appled to Jewish Christians as well. In the area we are discussing, they assumed the introduction of the 'numerus nullus' principle in all schools, starting from elementary level. Jews would have been forced to attend only their own lower and middle schools, which would not have enjoyed state rights. It was clearly a racist programme. Indeed, in the 'Principles' the concept of 'race' was used, although the nationalist press on the whole had avoided it.

From the outset the universities were an enclave of considerable independence. Both lecturers and students were critical of the regime. As a consequence, it might have been expected that the government would have tried to gain some say in the running of the universities, as well as acquiring a greater degree of control over faculty members and students. This would have been consistent with the general line taken by the authorities in the legislative sphere. After their victory at the 1930 elections and the achievement of a decisive majority in the *Sejm*, they began to introduce laws which increased their control over the nation. Consequently this was a period of considerable government activity in framing and carrying through legislation. On 1 March 1932 a bill was passed regarding assemblies and gatherings, on 27 October one regarding associations, and, following this, a bill relating to local autonomy. The high point of this anti-democratic course adopted by the government was the new constitution, which came into effect in 1935.

Government policies over schooling moved in a similar direction. On 12 January 1932 the government submitted the draft bill of a resolution for the reorganization of the school system. In the section dealing with the universities, it was proposed that the Minister for Religious Affairs and Public Education should have the power, after consultation with the faculty councils, to set compulsory, supplementary examinations at some universities and university faculties.[31] This proposal roused the anger of representatives of the national minorities. Milena Rudnicka, a Ukrainian representative in the *Sejm*, recognized that it gave legal sanction to a 'numerus clausus' which had existed in practice for several years over Ukrainian students. Emil Sommerstein, pointing to the decline in the number of Jews at the universities, condemned the proposal strongly, declaring that 'we have here the "numerus clausus", not in its brutal, naked form, as presented in the resolution of the Nationalist Group, but in a covert form, which has to rely entirely on those who are to carry it out.'[32]

A real storm erupted over the resolution relating to the universities. Even before it was submitted, on 21 January 1933 the Minister for Public Education spoke at a sitting of the *Sejm* Budget Committee. He pointed out that the academic authorities had not managed to use the relevant act to nip anti-semitic brawls in the bud, and this showed the need for a change in the law.³³ The draft bill, however, left no doubts as to the true intentions of its authors – the complete subordination of the universities to government control.

In principle the whole academic community opposed the scheme, although for widely differing reasons. The nationalists were concerned with defending the ground they had won; left-wingers considered it meant the destruction of the last vestiges of democracy. Scholars perceived a threat to academic values in the new proposals.³⁴ The opposition in the *Sejm* waged an unequal struggle against the bill. Representatives of the *Stronnictwo Narodowe* were also concerned at its far-reaching effects. The speeches of Professors Wacław Komarnicki and Bohdan Winiarski were calm and objective – pointing out the harm such measures would cause to academic life at the universities. But a very different voice sounded from the benches of the Nationalist faction. Tadeusz Bielecki declared that the new proposal would help Jews and was an attempt to 'disrupt the struggle of the younger generation against the Judaisation of the Polish community'.³⁵

Immediately after the bill was passed the Minister for Public Education began to exploit the opportunities which it afforded him. Amongst other things the activities of student associations were only permitted on the site of specific universities. This resulted in the dissolution of all the nationwide student organizations which were controlled by the nationalist camp. Almost simultaneously the nationalists suffered an even more severe setback. The administration dissolved the *Obóz Wielkiej Polski* throughout the country. In practical terms this meant the end of a unified nationalist youth movement, since a split soon occurred, which led to the creation of the *Obóz Narodowo-Radykalny* (National-Radical Front).³⁶ All of these factions, however, adopted a uniform policy on the Jewish question.

The new law could not solve the very problem which had been one of the prime arguments for its introduction. Anti-semitic outbursts continued, increasing in force and brutality. On 24 October 1933 lectures were suspended at the University of Warsaw for one month because of clashes between a gang of toughs recruited by *MW* and members of the *Legion Młodych* (Youth Legion). A second reason was the introduction for the first time at Warsaw academic institutions of a 'ghetto bench'.

Anti-semitic activities grew in strength during 1935 after Piłsudski's death, when the National Democrats assumed for a while that they would gain power. 'The *Endecja* understood,' wrote Ludwik Krzywicki, 'that anti-semitic slogans were a useful means of controlling crowds and igniting passions. Indeed, students were to act in the vanguard in striking at the government with anti-Jewish slogans.'³⁷ The use of anti-semitic propaganda meant that the government could be attacked for its apparent philo-semitism, while the Left could also be attacked as an agent of 'international

Jewry'. This led to a series of street demonstrations throughout the country, symbolised by those at Przytyk, Mińsk Mazowiecki, and Myślenice. In 1936 a number of court cases occurred where members of the *Stronnictwo Narodowe* and the *Obóz Narodowo-Radykalny* were accused of placing bombs outside Jewish shops and similar activities.

Definite moves towards the introduction of a 'ghetto bench' began during the 1935–36 academic year, and gained in momentum during successive years. Disturbances began, as usual, at the beginning of the academic year, and because of this they were called 'autumn manoeuvres'. Often they were linked to events commemorating the anniversary of Wacławski's death.[38] They became wilder and more violent. Memoirs of students from the period are full of descriptions of those beaten and maimed, although the names of the organizers of these brawls are invariably missing. However, the attitudes of the latter are summed up in a leaflet, dated 26 January 1937:

> Progress, Learning, Democracy – they all sound wonderful. But what is hidden under this facade? The repulsive Jewish spirit. And this disgusting use of clubs which makes you recoil, is in fact a glorious struggle to free the nation from its Jewish fetters. Just think: you meet a Jew or a Communist in some dark place. And you set about him! You lay into him, driving the metal into his teeth! Just don't back away, you milksop![39]

Everyone came in for a beating, most of all Jews, but also those people who protested against the club-wielders – among them people who were not attached to any organization, but were motivated simply by common humanity.

Student organizations which protested against and actually opposed the activities of these gangs of thugs were the communist *Życie* (Life), *Związek Niezależnej Młodzieży Socjalistycznej* (Union of Independent Socialist Youth), *Legion Młodych-Fracja* (Youth Legion – Faction), the *Związek Polskiej Młodzieży Demokratycznej* (Union of Young Polish Democrats), and the academic grouping *Wici* (the youth movement of the Peasant Party). A number of these organizations formed the *Komitet Obrony Honoru Akademika* (Committee for the Defence of Students' Honour). They noticed that anti-semitism, besides its nationalist and racist face, was also an instrument which potentially threatened *all* liberal and democratic views.[40]

Individual professors frequently spoke out, dismayed by what was happening in the universities. Those who did so were not only people associated with the democratic camp. One of the most critical articles on the subject was written by Antoni Sobański, in the columns of the conservative periodical *Czas*.[41] Maria Dąbrowska also joined in the chorus of protest, throwing her personal popularity and moral authority on the scales. The voice of this author, sensitive to the human injustice being committed, and at the same time disturbed by the views of a section of the student body, was full of concern.[42] Her words, a reflection of the views and attitudes of the best section of the Polish intelligentsia, raised the spirits of the injured, but they did not affect the perpetrators of the violence, especially as many professors tolerated the thugs, or even supported them.

In February 1936 the Minister for Public Education, Wojciech Świętosławski, declared that he would not allow 'a handful of politically-motivated students to disrupt the normal work of the overwhelming majority'. A year later, in January 1937, he announced that he would not agree to the official introduction of student segregation: 'I regard the issuing of such an order as impossible.' Further statements along these lines were made.[43] They were composed in a tense atmosphere, when a number of the universities were closed because of attempts forcibly to introduce 'ghetto benches'. These attempts were being increasingly successful. Gradually more and more rectors were caving in.[44]

On 23 December 1936, a conference of university rectors approved a proclamation where the rectors attributed the nationalists' excesses to the influence of Hitlerism. They nevertheless acknowledged that the Jewish question was a difficult and serious one. While the proclamation denounced the violence, it was regarded, as Andrzej Pilch writes, as an encouragement to the troublemakers because in one section it admitted that students had the right to seek their own way of removing those ills that affected the life of the nation.[45]

Lack of decisive action encouraged the bully-boys. On 12 January 1937 the Rector of Wilno University, Władysław Jakowicki, having lost control of the situation, offered his resignation. However, support for the trouble-makers came from the former president of the *Sejm*, Julian Szymanowski. He accused the Jews of causing the disturbances by not accepting the Rector's proposal that Poles occupy separate seats. Attempts were made to impose segregated seating, amongst other places in the law faculty. All Jews were turned out of the university buildings and the library.[46] On their way out, ten Jews were set upon and beaten.

Although it was not a decisive factor, much depended on the attitudes of the faculty members. There was one case where a lecturer deliberately came late for class to allow time for Jews to be ejected from the lecture-theatre. Different attitudes can be seen clearly in the case of Wilno. Professor Tadeusz Czeżowski would not permit any disturbances at his lectures. When trouble threatened, Jews who did not want to occupy the seats intended for them and indicated by cards placed there were forced to remain standing during the lecture. Professor Pruffe recommended that the proctors remove the cards which divided the seating. The engineer Krasnopolski replaced his lecture with a talk on 'the systematics of culture'. Professor Panejko, however, requested all the Jews standing in the lecture-hall to leave before he would begin his lecture.[47] Professor Szymanowski's position has already been referred to. Similar events and similar attitudes could be encountered at other universities, among them Lwów, where the 'ghetto bench' had already been in force for a year.

In the circumstances the immediate action undertaken by the Minister proved ineffective. On 30 March 1937 he ordered the disbanding of the *Młodzież Wszechpolska* organization at Warsaw University, as well as the *Narodowy Związek Polskiej Młodzieży Radykalnej* (National Union of Radical Polish Youth) – the student wing of the *ONR*. It did not have a great deal of meaning or effect, since these organizations over a number of years had become used to acting on the edge of the law. This apart, the *Związek Młodej Polski* (Union of Young Poland) began to be active – a youth affiliate of the government *Obóz Zjednoczenia Narodowego* (Camp of National Unity). There was little to distinguish the *ZMP*'s views from *Młodzież Wszechpolska* or *ONR*, since the union was organized by members belonging to a wing of the latter body. This was all linked with the broader process by which the *Sanacja* began to appropriate for itself the slogans of the nationalist camp.

Partly because of this, the measures taken by the Minister could not put a brake on the action already set in motion. What is more, recourse to legal action was rendered impossible. In Lwów, during November and December 1936, eight students appeared in court accused of forcing Jews, by threats and by beatings, to occupy segregated seats. After a hearing at a Preliminary Court had found the defendants not guilty, the County Court confirmed this on appeal. *Wszechpolak* – the journal of *Młodzież Wszechpolska* – triumphantly informed its readers that, 'The ghetto cannot oppose the law.'

In July 1937 the Universities Act was amended. On the basis of this, at a rectors' conference of 24 September, the Minister made a further concession by allowing the rectors to issue public order instructions concerning segregated seating for Polish and Jewish youth in lecture theatres. This concession was received by the young nationalists as a great victory. A measure designed to calm the students had precisely the opposite effect. On 3 November 1937 *Młodzież Wszechpolska* proclaimed a 'day without Jews' at all institutions of higher education in Lwów. In following years a 'day without Jews and Ukrainians' was to appear. This initiative was seized on by other universities. The Executive Branch of *ONR* issued the following internal order: 'In bringing about the "numerus nullus", all *ONR* members are advised, when encountering a Jew at university, to beat him soundly and eject him from the campus. Should there appear to be too many Jews, or proctors who might come to the Jews' defence, then other colleagues should be called in to support you. The above order must be carried out ruthlessly. The "numerus nullus" must be forced through, as the "ghetto bench" was a year ago.'[48]

It was not only Jews who fell victim to the young 'nationalists'. On 18 July 1936, in the centre of Warsaw, distributors of the *ONR* journal *Falanga* repeatedly stabbed the young socialist leader, Stanisław Dubois. Cases of socialist and communist students being beaten up were not rare. In March 1939 members of strong-arm gangs broke into a talk organized by students affiliated to the Peasants' Party. The press reported that four victims of this attack lay in a critical condition in hospital.[49]

Various measures were employed against those faculty members who opposed the extravagant behaviour of the thugs. Explosive charges were laid at the doors of flats belonging to Konrad Górski in Wilno, and Kazimierz Bartel in Lwów. Mieczysław Wolffke was pelted with rotten eggs, and smoke canisters were thrown into the hall where he was to lecture. Cases of attacks on faculty members also occurred in 1933 during the dispute over the proposed Higher Education Bill. On this occasion a new device was introduced: lists of scholars, both Jewish and 'of Jewish descent', began to be published. On one of these was the name of Leopold Caro, vice-chairman of the Polish Primate's Social Affairs Council. This was linked to the demand, also being voiced at the time, for the imposition of a 'numerus nullus' for research staff as well. The so-called 'Aryan paragraph' – prohibiting Jews from belonging to certain organizations – was approved in 1937 by the Union of Non-Professorial Staff in Lwów Institutions of Higher Education. In the following year it was approved by the national Union of Associations of Non-Professorial Staff in State Institutions of Higher Education. Jews previously belonging to these organizations were immediately struck off the membership list.[50] This phenomenon extended far beyond university campuses. Similar resolutions were adopted by other associations and organizations, among other social and professional groupings composed of engineers, architects, doctors and so on. Exclusion from these organizations made continuing in one's profession difficult, if not impossible.

The issue spread to even more areas of public life. An attempt was made to divide city market-places into Polish and Jewish parts. Such a division was put into effect in Kalisz on 13 July 1937. The Association of Property Owners at Inowrocław passed a resolution calling for the eviction of Jews. But the most extreme step was taken by the local branch of the *Stronnictwo Narodowe* at Częstochowa, which proposed that Jews be banned from the town. A similar campaign was launched in Brześć nad Bugiem. The *Stronnictwo Narodowe* officially launched a campaign for residential ghettoes.[51] All this was done in accordance with the call to create a Catholic state of the Polish nation. Kazimierz Kowalski, chairman of the *SN* wrote that 'the one basic obstacle in achieving this goal is the Jews.'[52]

The number of street attacks on individuals, on Jewish shops and market-stalls, increased. When such incidents took place, the police generally arrived too late, or else ignored them. The economic crisis and the boycott action, often linked with the destruction of goods, caused a considerable decline in the part Jews played in trade and business.

The number of Jews at the universities fell rapidly. The Rector of Wilno University, Father Aleksander Wójcicki, wrote in his report for 1937 that, of those admitted to the first year of study, in the humanities eight out of eighty students were Jews, in law thirteen out of 150, in pharmacy four out of forty-five and in agriculture none. No Jews were admitted to Poznań University, to the medical faculty of the Jagiellonian University, nor to a number of other universities and faculties. Whereas, during the academic year 1928–9, 20.4 per cent of the overall student total were Jews, by 1936–7 this figure was 11.7 per cent and in 1937–8 only 7.5 per cent (1,183 out of 15,591 admitted); the figures in Warsaw were 4 per cent, in Lwów 7 per cent, in Kraków 10 per cent, in Wilno 7.3 per cent, and in Poznań none.[53] This reduction in the universities was achieved by means graphically described in *Wszechpolak* of 16 October 1939:

> Then the time arrived to apply for university places. The youth movement blocked the way of Jews so that it was difficult for them to complete all the formalities. There were cases at the medical faculty of UJK [the Jan Kazimierz University in Lwów] where a Jew, who had managed to get to the Dean's office and submit his application, had to be escorted out by ten proctors, and even then he could not leave by the main gate, but had to jump out of a window. Some could not manage to turn up for the entrance examination and even those who had already been admitted, turned up on registration day to find slogans scrawled up, saying 'Day without Jews', and then 'Second Day without Jews', and so on. Those who still wanted to make their way on to the university campus, faced being beaten up with knuckle-dusters and sticks decorated with razors.

This description of events at Lwów, which applied just as well to other towns and cities, preceded a confrontation with the Rector, Stanisław Kulczyński. He refused to allow a 'ghetto bench' to be introduced and, on 7 January 1937, offered his resignation. He defended his decision to resign in an open letter, where he maintained that he would not be a part in sullying the good name of the University. He would not give in to the terrorism of the young 'nationalists', who were trying to force the legal authorities to do the impossible. He asserted further that he was not against free choice over seating, but the introduction of a 'ghetto bench' took the issue of free choice 'on to the stage of emergency measures directed against a single national or religious group'. In this atmosphere academic life could not continue.[54]

Other rectors supported Kulczyński's views,[55] although the Rector of Poznań University did not. Although praiseworthy and honourable, Kulczyński's stand was of little avail. His successor, Rector Longchamps, issued an order on 12 January, the day that lectures were due to begin, that the segregated seating scheme should be imposed. The Pro-Rector Professor Ganszyniec refused to comply and wrote a letter of protest. He said, 'by submitting to the terror practised by *Młodzież Wszechpolska*, you have made the Rector's office both the expression and the executor of the absurd demands of these young people, and have sacrificed the victims of this campaign, without in return guaranteeing that peace or freedom to study, or the health and life of those condemned to the student ghetto, will be assured.' He commented, with regret, that he had failed to find in the Rector's order any words of condemnation of the organizers of the brawls.[56] Immediately afterwards, on the 6 February 1938, an article appeared in *Wszechpolak* claiming that Ganszyniec was in debt to the Jews, that he was an atheist and a socialist, and that his Jewish assistant was his lover. The late Rector, Kulczyński, on the other hand, was alleged to be a mason. In a similar way, twenty-six professors led by Bartel, protested against the introduction of an official ghetto at the Polytechnic, but the proposal was still approved by the senate.[57]

Voices were also raised in favour of the moves. After the above letter from the twenty-six professors had been made public, they were answered by Stanisław Głąbiński. He regarded it as improper to accuse the Rector of the Polytechnic, and other rectors, of acting contrary to the law by introducing segregation. They were only carrying out their duty. This argument was continually repeated. Głąbiński concluded his riposte with the demagogic assertion that in his student days seating had also been allocated.[58]

The Lwów professors were not the only ones to protest. Group petitions were drawn up and individuals spoke out, steps which demanded considerable moral courage in the circumstances. In December 1937 fifty-eight professors – the cream of Polish academic life – protested publicly against the introduction of restrictions based on creed, nationality or race. They came from various backgrounds and different political standpoints. They did so 'with a feeling of joint responsibility that the very thing which we have failed to prevent is now a dominant influence at the majority of universities'.[59] A number of them, in an expression of solidarity with Jewish students, delivered their lectures standing up. Henryk Lukerc wrote, '... although it may appear, judging from the words of some professors, that they criticize only the attack on academic freedom, forgetting other evils of totalitarianism outside the walls of the university, this movement is not exclusive, but is linked with the wider political movement of Polish democracy.'[60]

On 19 October 1937, Professor Mieczysław Michałowicz protested publicly in the auditorium of the Paediatrics Clinic of Warsaw University and explained his actions in this way, '... I want to follow my conscience, knowing I have remained faithful to Christian principles.'[61] This was not the first protest which appealed to religious principles. Immediately after Michałowicz's statement, however, two priests, Fathers Seweryn Popławski and Marceli Nowakowski, replied in an open letter, supporting the stand taken by the young nationalists.[62]

The propaganda of the nationalist movement followed closely on the heels of these representatives of the clergy. It did not take long for the effects of this activity to become apparent. On 16 January 1938, at an open meeting of the student Marian Sodality, it was agreed that individuals of Jewish origin could not become members.[63] A baptised Jew, Father Puder, was struck by an assailant in church. The Catholic press condemned this crime, but a few days after the incident, on 6 February 1938, Stanisław Mackiewicz wrote in *Słowo* that 'the one logical, clear criterion is, in fact, that adopted by Hitler. A Jew is a person who is of Jewish descent.' Ten days later he asserted that 'anti-semitism without racism is incomplete.' Voices were also raised demanding the enactment in Poland of anti-Jewish legislation along the lines of the Nuremberg Laws.[64]

Attitudes of this kind resulted in increasingly severe physical conflicts, involving ever wider sections of the community and inflicting new casualties. This is hardly surprising when one considers that, as a result of a search of three student hostels in Lwów in March 1939, the police found sixteen revolvers, two fowling-pieces, thirteen hand-grenades, thirty-four canisters filled with caustic gases and fluids, explosive materials, and so on.[65]

We do not know every incident that occurred. As Krzywicki writes, the censorship either did not allow articles on anti-Jewish excesses to appear, or else itself decided the guidelines on what should be written.[66] The searches described above took place following the murder in 1938 of three Jews, students of Lwów Polytechnic. A year later two university students were murdered, and in May that year, seven were severely beaten up, one a first-year student named Markus Landsberg, dying in hospital.[67]

Periodicals hostile to such deeds wrote of the incomprehensible tolerance, of the paralysis in acting against the wielders of clubs and cudgels, and they even wrote that there was silent admiration or support in some quarters. After the Landsberg killing, the Rector suspended lectures, and the senate condemned the crime. The Young Socialists' journal, *Młodzi Idą* commented bitterly on the steps taken by the university authorities: 'Here we go again. Events are following their usual course.' It called for resistance to such acts in deed as well as in word.[68]

The will to act was lacking. The administrative apparatus did not act, and when it did, it took inadequate steps and failed to achieve the desired results. This attitude should come as no surprise given the way the government bloc was evolving. Democratic, workers' and socialist organizations proved too weak to resist this wave of hate and barbarism. A regaining of collective sanity only occurred shortly before the outbreak of war, when the problems of national defence became the priority.

NOTES

1 Emergency motion of ŻLN representatives concerning the establishment of a Sejm Commission on the Jewish Question. *Druki Sejmu Ustawodawczego RP*, no. 119.
2 One of the young socialist leaders wrote, 'Does anyone have any illusions that if it were possible to arouse the passions of the Polish people using some other platform than anti-semitism, that the *Endecja* would be prepared to discard immediately its anti-semitic propaganda . . .?' S. Dubois: 'Ohydna dywersja' in *Wyższe uczelnie pod blokadą reakcji* (Warsaw, 1937), p. 19.
3 Speaking during the discussion on Prime Minister Skulski's admission, 19 December 1919. *Sprawozdania Stenograficzne Sejmu Ustawodawczego*, p. 19.
4 D. Jarosz, *Młodzież Wszechpolska, 1922–1926* (Warsaw, 1983), p. 146.
5 'Memoriał w sprawie zachowania polskości lwowskich akademickich uczelni', *Głos Akademicki*, November 1922.
6 'Środowisko lwowskie', *Akademik*, 20 March 1923.
7 'Wiec akademicki młodzieży poznańskiej', ibid., 25 January 1923.
8 'Młodzież akademicka w Krakowie w sprawie numerus clausus', *Goniec Krakowski*, 21 May 1923. Also D. Jarosz, op. cit., pp. 122–3.
9 'W sprawie numerus clausus', *Gazeta Warszawska*, 20 March 1923. Also Jarosz, op. cit., pp. 106–8.
10 'III-ci Ogólny Zjazd Polskiej Młodzieży Akademickiej we Lwowie', *Akademik*, 30 June 1923. See also *Prąd*, June–July 1923, and Jarosz, op. cit., pp. 48–51.
11 Z. Stypułkowski, 'My i Oni', *Wiadomości Akademickie*, 10 December 1924; also Jarosz, op. cit., p. 7?
12 *Druki sejmowe*, Okres I, Druk nr 94; for an account of the struggle to have this resolution accepted, see 'Walka o numerus clausus', *Przegląd Wszechpolski*, November–December 1923, pp. 848–72.
13 The text of the motion is in W. Komarnicki, *Numerus clausus w szkołach akademickich* (Warsaw, 1932), p. 28. The speech was delivered before a sitting of the Education Committee of the *Sejm*, on 3 March 1932.
14 Ibid.
15 The latter declared that 'the universities are being flooded with Jews', the introduction of the numerus clausus will calm the ferment at the universities, and is not incompatible with the moral and constitutional equality of rights. 'Declaration of a minority of professors of the Philosophy Faculty of the Jagiellonian University concerning the "numerus clausus", decided at a sitting of the Faculty Council on 9 March 1923', *APAN Kraków, Teki Zielińskiego*, file no. 7837.
16 *Konferencje rektorów szkół akademickich w Polsce w latach 1919–1931* (Warsaw, 1932), p. 55.
17 'Zasady współpracy stronnictw polskiej większości parlamentarnej w Sejmie w r. 1923', *Materiały źródłowe do historii polskiego ruchu ludowego*, vol. 3 (Warsaw, 1967), p. 81.
18 K. Czerwiński, *Szkoły wyższe w Polsce. Ustrój, organizacja studiów* (Warsaw, 2nd ed. 1930), p. 26.

19 'Numerus clausus', *Akademik Polski*, 18 October 1927.
20 A. Pilch, *Studencki ruch polityczny w Polsce w latach 1932–1939* (Kraków, 1972), p. 129.
21 'Twelfth Conference, 23–24 April 1927', *Konferencje rektorów* . . ., p. 118–20.
22 'Okólnik', *Akademik Polski*, 20 January 1927.
23 J. Zański, 'U progu nowego roku akademickiego na medycynie', ibid., October 1930.
24 'Uchwały Piątego Zjazdu Ogólnoakademickiego w Poznaniu', ibid., 20 June 1927.
25 The conservative *Dzień Polski* of 15 November 1931 commented on these attempts as follows, '*Gazeta Warszawska* writes in a language which incites its readership not only to spread violence and confusion, but at times even to pogroms. The National Democrats do not pause to consider what effects these Hitlerite policies may have when transferred to Polish territory.'
26 'Zajścia antyżydowskie', *Akademik Polski*, December 1931.
27 R. Ganszyniec, *Sprawa numerus clausus i zasadnicze jej znaczenie. Antysemityzm akademicki jako objaw antysemityzmu społecznego* (Warsaw, 1925), p. 23. Also T. Kotarbiński, 'Po burzy 22 XI 1931', *Racjonalista*, December 1931, pp. 177–84.
28 *Druki Sejmowe*, Okres III, Druk nr 434.
29 W. Komarnicki, op. cit., pp. 31–40.
30 'Zjazd Rady Naczelny M. W. (15–17 V)', *Akademik Polski*, 7 June 1932.
31 *Druki sejmowe*, Okres III, Druk nr 451.
32 Stenographer's report of the 61st session of the *Sejm* on 22 February 1932, pp. 38 and 51.
33 One of the supporters of the bill, Professor Wałek-Czarnecki wrote: 'In Poland the government of Marshal Piłsudski represents a solid tower of strength against which all the efforts of Hitler's imitators will fail. This government will not look on with indifference while the "nationalist" club-wielders and their protectors among the older generation indulge in their antics.' T. Wałek-Czarnecki, *Sprawa szkół akademickich* (Warsaw, 1933), p. 47.
34 These problems have been discussed in an article by S. Rudnicki, 'Ustawa o szkolach akademickich z dn. 15 III 1933', *Więź*, 1985 no. 4–6, pp. 166–80.
35 Stenographer's report from the 91st session of the *Sejm*, on 20 February 1933, p. 111.
36 A book devoted to these issues is that by S. Rudnicki, *Obóz Narodowy-Radykalny. Geneza i działalność* (Warsaw, 1985). See p. 392.
37 L. Krzywicki, 'Burdy studenckie', *Wspomnienia*, vol. 3 (Warsaw, 1959), p. 292.
38 'On the anniversary of Wacławski's death, Jewish blood must flow. On that day Jewish homes and businesses, acquired by wrongs done to Poles, and even by their deaths, must burn.' *ONR.AAN, Druki ulotne*, vol. 154.
39 B. Chrzanowski, *Wspomnienia. Rozdział o miłości i dobroci*, BN III 6480/2 (typescript). The following is an extract from an *ONR* leaflet quoted by *Czas* on 2 November 1936: 'You will shudder at the idea of so many setting on one person. The sight of blood will disturb you . . . . Don't be put off by the blood – keep hitting, beating everywhere, strike with whatever comes to hand, use whatever suits you best.'
40 The *OMTUR* journal wrote: 'Anti-Jewish demagogy is just a screen for these unruly knights. Behind it are hidden the reactionary, fascist endeavours of Dmowski-ism.' 'Nauka i kastet', *Młodzi Idą*, 15 November 1936. A representative of *Wici* wrote in a similar fashion: 'The *Endeks* are advocating a biological, animal kind of anti-semitism. "Beat the Jew" – just because he is a Jew. They are attempting to use this racial hatred to drown all the aspirations of the peasant masss towards real and necessary changes of attitude.' T. Rek, 'Endecki antysemityzm', *Młoda Myśl Ludowa*, June–July 1936.

41 A. Sobański, 'W odpowiedzi panu Dembińskiemu' *Czas*, 8 November 1936.
42 M. Dąbrowska, 'Doroczny wstyd' *Dziennik Popularny*, 24 November 1936.
43 Speech by the Minister for Religious Affairs and Public Education at a session of the *Sejm*, 21 February 1936, *Oświata i Wychowanie*, ii, 1936, p. 103. 'You must not assume that the behaviour of any of you will be tolerated, where that behaviour is incompatible with the law, and with a sense of honour and dignity.' J. Ujejski (Vice-Minister of Religious Affairs and Public Education), 'O lepsze warunki życia młodzieży akademickiej', Address delivered over the radio, 5 October 1936, ibid., p. 640.
44 'A number of rectors were unhappy about the disturbances and unhappy about the anti-semitic excesses and the creation of ghettoes within the precincts of the universities. But their desire for peace and quiet was even greater. Peace at any price.' L. Krzywicki, op. cit., p. 348.
45 A. Pilch, op. cit., p. 160.
46 'He was working in the university library on one of the upper floors. ONR supporters broke into it, dragging him out by his hands and feet and hurling him down onto the marble floor of the lobby.' H. Obiezierska, *Pamiętnik* (in private hands).
47 'Żydzi są sami winni zamknięcia uniwersytetu w Wilnie', Copy of an article by Professor J. Szymanowski, *Wszechpolak*, 21 January 1937. 'Zajście żydowskie na USB', ibid., 11 February 1937. 'Zajście żydowskie na Uniwersytecie Wileńskim', ibid., 18 February 1937. 'Prowokacje zydowskie na uniwersytecie wilenskim', ibid., 25 February 1937.
48 S. Rudnicki, op. cit., p. 306.
49 J. Swirski, 'Protestujemy', *Młoda Mysl Ludowa*, February, 1939.' Hitlerowska napaść', *Epoka*, 15 March 1939.
50 'Paragraf aryjski w Związku Asystentów', *Wszechpolak*, 4 February 1937. S. Ossowski, 'Nowa grupa etniczna w szkołach akademickich', *Epoka*, 25 February 1939.
51 'O ghetto terytorialne', *Wszechpolak*, 17 October 1937. 'Ghetto akademickie', ibid., 10 November 1937. 'Ghetto w Inowrocławiu', ibid., December 1937.
52 From the foreword to J. Giertych, *O wyjściu z kryzysu* (Warsaw, 1938), p 8.
53 'Odżydzenie USB', *Wszechpolak*, 17 October 1937. 'Z materiałów liczbowych WRiOP', *Oswiata i Wychowanie*, vol. 6 (1938) pp. 556-7. A. Pilch, op. cit., pp. 157-8.
54 S. Kulczyński, 'Nie chciałem złożyć podpisu. List otwarty', *Dokumenty chwili* (Kraków, 1938), pp. 17-19.
55 Letter to Rector Kulczyński, ibid., p. 14.
56 R. Ganszyniec, 'Zarządzenie sprzeczne z etyką i elementarną sprawiedliwością', ibid., p. 15.
57 'Open letter by Lwów professors', *Epoka*, 5 February 1938.
58 'Professor Głąbiński's reply', *Wszechpolak*, 6 February 1938.
59 'Lux in tenebris lucet', *Epoka*, 5 January 1938. The list of signatories is also in S. Rudnicki, op. cit., pp. 373-4.
60 H.L., 'Spisek przeciwko szermierzom światła', *Epoka*, 5 February 1938.
61 'Statement by Professor Michałowicz'. In *Dokumenty chwili* . . . , p. 10.
62 They wrote: 'Because those comments may cause some mental anguish among the young, we the undersigned, experienced teachers of young people, wish to assert that the positive attempts of the faithful in choosing to separate themselves from Jews, does not conflict with the aims, the teaching and the dictates of the Church.' Quoted from *Czas*, 24 October 1937.
63 Concerning the aryan paragraph in the *ASM*, *Wszechpolak*, 30 January 1938. The moderating priest of *ASM* annulled the resolution.

64 S. Rudnicki, op. cit., p. 375.
65 A. Pilch, op. cit., p. 156.
66 L. Krzywicki, op. cit., p. 377.
67 *Kurier Warszawski*, 28 May 1939; *Epoka*, 15 March 1939, 5 June 1939.
68 'Na innych szpaltach', *Młodzi Ida*, VI, 1939.

DOCUMENTS

THE POLISH GOVERNMENT-IN-EXILE AND THE HOLOCAUST: STANISŁAW KOT'S CONFRONTATION WITH PALESTINIAN JEWRY, NOVEMBER 1942– JANUARY 1943 – SELECTED DOCUMENTS
David Engel

The latter half of 1942 marked a turning point in the development of the free world's awareness of the nature of German designs upon the Jews of occupied Europe. During this time reliable information first reached the West about the existence and operation of a comprehensive Nazi programme to kill all Jews within the German Reich's reach.[1] Much of this information came from Polish sources and was addressed in the first instance to the Polish Government-in-Exile in London.[2] Other reports were sent by Jewish sources inside Poland, via channels operated by the Polish underground, to Jewish leaders in Great Britain and the United States.[3]

The leaders of the Jewish community in Palestine did not have such direct contact with occupied Poland as their counterparts in the West were able at times to maintain. Through most of 1942 their knowledge of what was happening to their fellow Jews in Europe was obtained second hand through sources in London, New York, Geneva, and posts in various neutral countries, as well as via the wire services of the major international news organisations. Their first substantial direct encounter with news of what has since come to be known as the Holocaust came only on 18–19 November 1942, when a group of Palestinian citizens who had been detained in Nazi-occupied Europe at the outbreak of war arrived in Palestine in exchange for a contingent of German nationals similarly held in the Allied countries. Many of these had spent the first three years of the war in Poland and were able to provide eyewitness corroboration for reports of the wholesale slaughter of Jews that had previously been widely discounted as unconfirmed rumours.[4] Their message finally brought home to Palestinian Jewish leaders the awful reality from which they had previously recoiled; from then on a major portion of their attention was to be directed to finding ways to rescue whatever Jews could still be saved.[5]

It happened that at this very moment a high-ranking official of the Polish Government-in-Exile was visiting Palestine. Stanisław Kot, former interior minister and ambassador to the Soviet Union and close confidant of Premier Władysław Sikorski, had come to the country, ostensibly for a rest, prior to assuming his new post as government delegate in the Middle East.[6] Since it had become clear that Poland had been designated by the Germans as the principle arena for carrying out the murder of Jews from all over Europe, it was obvious that Polish cooperation could be an important determinant of the success of rescue efforts. The leaders of Palestinian Jewry thus had a vital interest in meeting Kot and in laying before him their thoughts and plans about aid for their threatened fellow-Jews in the occupied Homeland.

In fact, Jewish leaders had expressed a desire to confer with the Polish official even before the testimony of the exchangees had placed rescue at the head of their agenda. They wished to raise with him a series of allegations of anti-Jewish discrimination in the Polish exile army in the Soviet Union under the command of General Władysław Anders and in the civilian relief apparatus maintained by the Polish Embassy in that country that had reached them during the previous months.[7] They were especially concerned with this issue, it seems, because to their minds the purportedly anti-Jewish attitudes of Polish officials in the Soviet Union had led to a disproportionately low number of Jews being included among those Polish citizens evacuated to Palestine from Russia together with the Polish army in 1942.[8] For them, bringing Jews out of the Soviet Union to Palestine was no less an act of rescue than was seeking aid and protection for the Jews of Nazi-occupied Europe, and they viewed the exertion of pressure upon Polish officials to increase Jewish representation in the ranks of the Polish evacuees as one of their most important missions at this crucial time in Jewish history.

Jewish spokesmen had been voicing their complaints about the alleged unfair treatment by Polish authorities of Polish Jewish refugees in the Soviet Union since the previous spring, when the first small group of Jewish evacuees had arrived in Palestine, and in subsequent months their remonstrances had grown ever more vocal. This had sharply stung the Polish Government-in-Exile, which maintained that the blame for the phenomena that so angered the Jews lay with the Soviets rather than with the Poles. Polish leaders feared that Jewish complaints could easily be exploited by the Russians for their own anti-Polish propaganda purposes, given what they assumed to be a high level of sensitivity and solicitousness towards Jewish concerns on the part of Western public opinion. Some Polish spokesmen even believed that in voicing their complaints, Jewish organisations were willingly cooperating with the Soviet Union against Poland in the struggle over the disputed territories on Poland's pre-war eastern frontier. Many Polish officials appear to have been convinced that

Jews could play a crucial role in influencing British and American policy on the eastern border issue, and they were vitally concerned with seeing the allegations of Polish anti-Jewish discrimination laid to rest. In this connection, several Polish leaders had visited Palestine during the second half of 1942 and had attempted, by means ranging from mild cajolery to unabashed extortion, to dissuade the Jewish leadership in that country from persisting in its complaints.[9] Kot's own visit to Palestine undoubtedly was intended, at least in part, also to contribute to this campaign.

Thus it appears that precisely at the moment that Jews needed the sympathy and support of the Polish Government the most, tension between the Government and world Jewry was at its height. As the following accounts of Kot's discussions with Palestinian Jewish leaders at the end of 1942 and the beginning of 1943 show, this tension could not be separated from the issue of rescuing Polish Jewry in the minds of either party, and it lent the meetings an atmosphere of confrontation. The records of these discussions thus comprise a crucial piece of evidence not only in the investigation of the responses to the Holocaust both of the Polish Government-in-Exile and of the Jewish community in Palestine, but even more in the attempt to understand the thinking and emotions that underlay them.

The following documents relate to eight of the over a dozen meetings held by Kot with various important figures in the Palestinian Jewish community in late 1942 and early 1943. Three of these were private meetings – one with David ben Gurion, chairman of the Executive of the Jewish Agency for Palestine (Palestinian Jewry's official political representative body), and two with Yitzhak Grünbaum, a former deputy of the Polish *Sejm* and the doyen of Polish Zionist politicians, who at the time chaired the special Rescue Committee that the Jewish Agency had only recently created. Two others were held with a delegation from the Representation of Polish Jewry (*Reprezentacja Żydostwa Polskiego*), a body consisting of former Polish Jewish leaders from all Zionist parties save the breakaway Revisionists, as well as from the non-Zionist religious party *Agudas Yisroel*[10]; speaking on behalf of the Representation were Moshe Kleinbaum (Sneh), a young (age 33) protégé of Grünbaum serving at the time as head of the National Command of the clandestine Jewish defence force Haganah, Anshel (Anzelm) Reiss, a labour Zionist activist from Galicia who had been among the founders of the World Jewish Congress, and Abraham Stupp, a former secretary general and vice-chairman of the Eastern Galician Zionist Federation. A delegation from Agudas Yisroel also met with Kot separately. In addition Kot held two general meetings, one for leaders of Palestinian Jewish communal institutions and another for representatives of the Palestinian Jewish press. The arrangements for these meetings were facilitated by Henryk Rosmarin, a former Polish

Zionist activist and *Sejm* deputy who in 1939 had been appointed Polish consul general in Tel Aviv.

The descriptions of the discussions with Grünbaum and of the first meeting with the Representation of Polish Jewry come from Jewish sources. For the second meeting with the Representation, both a Polish and a Jewish source are extant, and both are given here. The descriptions of the remainder of the meetings are from Polish sources. The documents come from various locations; these are given as part of the rubric for each.

NOTES TO INTRODUCTION

1 See, *inter alia*, Walter Laqueur, *The Terrible Secret: Suppression of the Truth about Hitler's 'Final Solution'*, (Boston, 1980), pp. 41–122; Martin Gilbert, *Auschwitz and the Allies*, (New York, 1981), pp. 39–105.

2 For a comprehensive discussion of the news received by the Polish Government-in-Exile during this period, as well as of the Government's response, see David Engel, *In the Shadow of Auschwitz: The Polish Government-in-Exile and the Jews, 1939–1942* (Chapel Hill and London, 1987), pp. 173–202.

3 The most important of these were the letter from the General Jewish Workers Federation (Bund) of May 1942 and the message from the underground Bund and Zionist organisations in Warsaw delivered by the Polish emissary Jan Karski in November of the same year. These are described in the various works listed in notes 1 and 2 above.

4 For the testimony of one of the members of this group, see Reprezentacja Żydostwa Polskiego, *Sprawozdanie z działalności w latach 1940–1945*, n. p., n. d., pp. 46–51 (henceforth cited as Reprezentacja, *Sprawozdanie*). For general descriptions of the group's arrival and message, see Laqueur, *Terrible Secret*, pp. 190–93; Gilbert, *Auschwitz*, pp. 88–9.

5 On the reception in Palestine of the news brought by the exchangees and its impact upon the leadership of Palestinian Jewry, see Dina Porat, *Hanhagah be-Milkod: Ha-Yishuv nochah ha-Sho'ah, 1942–1945* (Tel Aviv, 1986), pp. 59–67 and passim.

6 It is more likely that Kot's visit was motivated by concern over political developments in the upper ranks of the Polish army, which was at that time based in Palestine. See [Jan Drohojowski], *Jana Drohojowskiego wspomnienia dyplomatyczne*, Kraków 1969, pp. 214–20; cf. 'Rozmowa z Min. Prof. Kotem', 13 January 1943, Central Zionist Archives, J25/2.

7 See Reprezentacja, *Sprawozdanie*, pp. 51–2; Eliyahu Epstein to Moshe Shertok, 10 November 1942, Central Zionist Archives, Z4/14652. On these allegations, see Engel, *Shadow of Auschwitz*, pp. 125–47 passim.

8 Of 115,000 Polish citizens evacuated from the Soviet Union under official Polish auspices during 1942, at most 6,000 were Jews. On the other hand, Jews comprised over one fourth and perhaps as much as one third of the total number of Polish citizens who had found refuge in the USSR during the war. Engel, *Shadow of Auschwitz*, pp. 139–40.

9 For a detailed discussion of these visits and of Polish Government reactions to Jewish complaints, see David Engel, 'Ha-Sichsuch ha-Polani-ha-Sovieti ke-Gorem be-Hityahasutah shel Memshelet Polin ba-Golah la-Sho'ah', *Shvut*, vol. 12 (1987), or, alternatively, Engel, *Shadow of Auschwitz*, pp. 147–52.

10 Kot actually held four meetings with a delegation from the Repesentation; the minutes of the first two are given here.

Document No. 1
[Minutes of Kot's first meeting with the Representation of
Polish Jewry. Reprezentacja,
Sprawozdanie, pp. 52–56]

27.XI.1942.

Conference with Minister Kot

Present: Minister Professor Kot, Consul General Dr. Henryk Rosmarin, Dr. M. Kleinbaum, Dr. A. Stupp.

11:40 am.

Dr. Stupp: First of all we apologize for bothering you while you are on holiday, but in view of the situation that has arisen we could not postpone our conference.

Prof. Kot: I understand. There is no problem.

Dr. Stupp: I should like to report to you briefly what people who arrived from Poland several days ago tell us about the present situation there. We are told by them that a special commission that goes from town to town murdering nearly all Jews has been active in the occupied homeland for months. Generally all the Jews of a given locality are assembled in a square; then the greater part of them is separated out and marked for 'resettlement', while a smaller part, usually a very small part, remains behind. For the most part the ones remaining are those who work in war industry. All older persons, women, and children are sent off in special transports that never reach any destination. People say that somewhere in the vicinity of Treblinka and Małkinia, as well as in Bełżec, there are installations specially built for the purpose where Jews are being murdered on a mass scale. Some die during the journey, while the rest are killed by shooting or gassing. There has never been a sign of life from the deportees.

Minister Kot: Doctor, why are you telling me all this? Do you think that I do not know about it? These facts have been known to us for quite some time. The Government has frequently written and spoken about these matters. Yet thus far we have not seen any reaction from the Jewish side. I must say that during this war Jewry has not been active. I do not see any activity worthy of the name either here in Palestine or in America. There is no need to persuade us to do something. We began to put pressure on the Allies to put an end to these murders quite a while ago. I shall show you gentlemen the materials that have reached us from inside Poland.

Dr. Stupp: We have not heard of these things. We were not informed either by the Government in London or by its agencies here. As late as several weeks ago Dr. Schwarzbart[1] corresponded with us from London about addresses for parcels to be sent to Poland. We sent thousands of addresses which, it seems, are no longer of any use in view of the existing situation. Only recently we received a reply from Minister Raczyński[2] that this news has not been confirmed and that the Government is attempting to obtain reliable information.[3]

Minister Kot: But these matters are well known and have appeared in the press. They have been raised at various press conferences.

Dr. Kleinbaum: All of this information has reached us only now, and in this connection we have a number of requests that we wish to address through you to the Government. We request:

1: a declaration by the Government and the National Council concerning the responsibility of all those who participate in the murder and persecution of Polish Jews.
2: that the Government attempt to influence both the Allied countries to take suitable measures against the Germans and the neutral countries to put pressure on the Germans and to aid those Jews who are able to escape from German occupation. Perhaps the Government could also do something by intervening with the Vatican.
3: that broadcasts directed to Poland instruct the Polish population not to give in to anti-Jewish agitation and to oppose the barbaric deeds of the Germans. Reports reaching us from Poland prove that such educational work is necessary.
4: that the Polish clergy be persuaded that it must raise its voice and protest against what is happening, just as the French clergy did.

Minister Kot: Decisions have already been taken in these matters, and more will be taken.

Dr. Kleinbaum: It is important to synchronize this campaign. All over the world protests and demonstrations are taking place; thus we consider it essential for the Government to speak out once again at this moment.

Minister Kot: Very well, all this is possible; but the most important thing is to influence Britain and the United States. There is no need to put requests to us. For months now the Polish Government has been demanding repressive measures from the Allies, but neither America nor Britain wants to hear of it. Only the smaller countries support us; English-speaking countries, on the other hand, find such measures unethical, against the teachings of religion, and not permissible. It is important therefore to move public opinion; and you gentlemen must do something in that direction. The neutral countries are unable to do much. Just look at who they are; Turkey would not lift a finger for a Pole or a Jew; Switzerland is surrounded on all sides; Sweden is frightened. As to the Vatican, you know what grievances we bear towards the Apostolic See. It seems that what we can do before anything else is to demand the true facts from the Vatican so as to become aware ourselves of the true situation. Only then can we appeal to the Vatican to do something on its own. As to the clergy, I really do not know to whom to turn: Hlond[4] is not in London;

Radoński⁵ might be a possibility. In any case I shall be glad to do whatever I can in this matter. I believe that the Polish population is helping wherever it can. Naturally there may be isolated exceptions, but this does not change the whole picture. Such incidents can happen on the Jewish side as well. Take, for example, what happened in Oszmiana, where the Germans brought the Poles and Jews together and demanded that the Poles shoot the Jews. The Poles refused, whereupon the Germans made the same demand of the Jews. Some Jews, no doubt out of fear, picked up weapons, ready to shoot at the Poles. At this point the Germans began to incite the Poles against the Jews: 'Here, you have just seen, the Jews were ready to shoot you.' In the end the Germans killed both the Poles and the Jews. I repeat, the Polish Government will gladly do everything [that it can], but you too must not remain silent. You are collecting evidence; fine, let the Government have it. But let me point out that your materials must be thoroughly checked and confirmed; for should the British or the American catch us in even a single inaccuracy, they will say that everything is a lie. It is more convenient for them not to believe everything. Public opinion in these countries is under the influence of old maids and women who think it impermissible to resort to repression. So get to work.

Dr. Kleinbaum: It seems to me that the Government overestimates our capabilities. You may believe that Jews can do everything, but to us it seems that the Government can do much more than we can. The Jews are constrained by the policies of the governments of the various countries; nevertheless the Jews in America have organised a great protest demonstration to which both Roosevelt and Churchill sent their messages.

[...].⁶

NOTES TO DOCUMENT NO. 1

1 Ignacy Schwarzbart (1888–1961) – General Zionist leader from Kraków. From 1923–29 served as president of the Zionist Federation of Western Galicia. Elected to Sejm in 1938. Escaped from Poland to West via Romania in 1939; in December 1939 nominated to Polish National Council.
2 Count Edward Raczyński (b. 1891) – Polish diplomat. Served as ambassador to the Court of St. James from 1934–45. During the period between the signing of the Polish-Soviet Agreement (July 1941) and the death of Premier Sikorski (July 1943) acted as director (kierownik) of the exile Polish Foreign Ministry, in effect taking on the functions of foreign minister.
3 The reference is to a telegram despatched by Raczyński on 23 November 1942 and forwarded to the Representation of Polish Jewry by the Polish Consulate General in Tel Aviv on 25 November, in which the acting foreign minister, replying to an earlier request from the Representation for confirmation of Palestinian press reports that the population of the Warsaw ghetto had fallen from half a million to 100,000, indicated that such reports could not yet be confirmed. See Reprezentacja, *Sprawozdanie*, p. 44. In the event, this denial was disingenuous; see Engel, *Shadow of Auschwitz*, pp. 197–98.

4 Augustus Cardinal Hlond – archbishop of Gniezno-Poznań, primate of Poland. Fled Poland in 1939, first to Rome, then to France. Interned by the German authorities in France in February 1944 following his refusal to issue a summons to the Polish people to join Germany in the fight against Communism, thus frustrating his own plans to return to occupied Poland.
5 Bishop Karol Radoński – bishop of Włocławek. Fled Poland in 1939; in February 1942 appointed to Polish National Council.
6 References to minor details mentioned by Kot during course of conversation omitted.

Document No. 2
[Polish summary of Kot's discussion with David ben Gurion. Yad Vashem Archives, 055/2]

Summary of Minister Kot's discussion with Ben Gurion, Chairman of the Jewish [Agency] Executive, on 3 December 1942, at the Jewish Agency in Jerusalem, in the presence of Mr. Korsak, Consul General of Poland.

1. Ben Gurion inquires whether the Polish Government would be in a position and would agree to send a number of confidential agents nominated by the Jewish Agency through their facilities. [These agents] would make contact with the Government delegates and send exact news about the situation of Jews in Poland through the channels available to the Polish Government.

Minister Kot replies that the Polish Government could send such men, but they would have [first] to make their way to London and establish contact with our Interior Ministry. At the same time, Minister Kot explains that messages from people who have been sent to Poland reach the Government with great difficulty and delay, that these people have no possibility of return, and that most information travels through neutral countries like Sweden or the Vatican. Sometimes messengers manage to reach Italy, where they are able to despatch news. Minister Kot indicates that the Government is in possession of exact and fully reliable information from Poland dating from the end of October. This information is completely accurate as to facts; only the numbers might be inexact.[1]

2. Next Ben Gurion inquires about the situation of Polish Jews in Russia and the possibilities for their departure from the USSR. Because of lack of time this question is discussed only generally, leaving the discussion of the details to the next meeting, set for Monday, 7 December 1942, at 2:00 [pm].

Ben Gurion mentions that according to the explanation received from the Soviet Embassy in Washington, the departure of Polish Jews from

Russia depends solely on the good will of the Polish authorities, as the Soviet authorities do not oppose their departure.

He also refers to the reputed declaration of General Zhukov that the Soviets will not hinder the Jews' departure, but that this depends only on the Polish authorities.[2] He asks whether the Polish Government would be able to transport Jewish children who are at present in Iran to Palestine without obtaining clearance from Iraq.[3] This could be done, if need be, by dressing them in military uniforms as members of a youth labour brigade to be discharged later on in Palestine. He holds that such methods are permissible in time of war, and that the British authorities would certainly have nothing against it, as they have expressed their agreement in principle to the entrance of these children into Palestine. The difficulty lies only in the absence of clearance from the Iraqi authorities.

In his answer Minister Kot emphasizes that in all talks with the Soviets about evacuation the Polish authorities did not make any distinction between Poles and Jews; what was discussed was the question of evacuation of Polish *citizens*. He mentions that the Soviet authorities take the position that all Jews who lived in the territory of the USSR before 1 November 1939 are Soviet citizens.[4] No departure was made from this principle, with the sole exception of a particular woman who received permission to leave. Permission to leave was given to soldiers' families, but in this case as well the aforementioned principle was adhered to. The Minister speaks about the Soviets' heightened sense of prestige which to a great extent influences various moves on their part, such as, in this case, the decree annexing the Polish territories, in connection with which they consider the local population as Soviet citizens, excepting only genuine Poles from this rule.

As to the children, the Minister explains that efforts were made to evacuate 10,000 Jewish children, but the Soviet Government agreed to only 600 (taking this figure from the number of Polish and Jewish children found at the time near the border in Ashkhabad). However, General Anders succeeded, through his personal efforts and intervention, in removing some 1,000 children to Iran. Minister Kot considers the suggestion to transfer Jewish children from Iran to Palestine in military uniforms unacceptable, as uniforms should not be used for purposes of disguise. The children could be transported, if the British authorities agree, in a British convoy which would not need Iraqi visas. He advises seeking such agreement. He suggests trying to obtain permission from the British to transport these children from Iran to Palestine in ships carrying arms and ammunition from ports in the Middle East, some of which return here afterwards. However, he indicates that the British should not be told that the dates and schedules of the ships' departure are known to the Agency.

Minister Kot emphasis that of the 10,000 Polish children in Iran only

2,000 came in labour brigade uniforms, and these were already in military formations in Russia.

Further talks on this subject are postponed until Monday.

NOTES TO DOCUMENT NO. 2

1 The reference is presumably to the Karski report of November 1942.
2 A number of Jews who left the Soviet Union with evacuating Polish troops testified upon reaching Teheran that at a meeting of Jewish leaders with NKVD General of State Security Yurii Zhukov on 19 August 1942 the Soviet officer had stated, in the presence of Polish Chief-of-Staff General Zygmunt Bohusz-Szyszko, that, in contrast to the Polish claim, the Soviet Government had no objection to the inclusion of Jews among the evacuees. Bohusz-Szyszko and other Polish leaders consistently denied that such a statement had ever been made.
3 The reference is to some 1,000 Jewish children who were evacuated from the Soviet Union with the Polish army in 1942 and quartered in Teheran. The Jewish Agency wished to bring them to Palestine; but at first no means of transportation could be found, owing largely to the refusal of the Iraqi Government to allow the children to pass through Iraqi territory. Eventually a solution was found, and these so-called Teheran children were able to make their way to Palestine.
4 On the Soviet attitude towards the citizenship of Polish Jews under Soviet jurisdiction, see Yosef Litwak, 'Shèelat ha-Ezrahut shel Yehudim Yotsèei-Polin be-Vrit ha-Mòatsot (1941–1943)', *Behinot* VII (1977); Engel, *Shadow of Auschwitz*, pp. 271–72.

Document No. 3
[Minutes of Kot's second meeting with the Representation of Polish Jewry. Reprezentacja, *Sprawozdanie*, pp. 68–73]

Second Conference with Minister Kot

Saturday, 5 December 1942, 4:00 pm (Gat Rimon, Tel Aviv).

Present: [On behalf of the Polish Government] – Minister Kot, Consul General Dr. Rosmarin, Vice-Consul Jenicz; on behalf of the Representation [of Polish Jewry] – Mr. A. Reiss, Dr. Kleinbaum, Dr. Stupp.

Mr. Reiss: Begins by introducing the Representation, its origins and composition. He emphasizes the double task that the Representation has set for itself – to cooperate in rebuilding an independent Poland and to ensure full equality for the Jewish people in the Poland of the future. Unfortunately, though, circumstances have arisen that have made it difficult for us to speak today about the various matters that we had intended to lay before you. In view of the terrible news coming from Poland, we no longer know whom and how many Jews we represent. Simply in the most general terms we should like to tell you how our relations with the Government have taken shape during the time the Representation has been in existence. In our view, the Government's attitude towards us is unsatisfactory; in an entire series of issues things are happening that must leave us dissatisfied and that do not, in our opinion, serve Polish interests either.

The evacuation from Russia was carried out in a way that caused us a great deal of harm, though by now this has been overshadowed by the situation that has arisen in the Homeland. In this connection the question of the Government's influence on the Polish people in the Homeland, the question of aid for the Jews there, comes to the fore. We are not convinced that everything possible has been done in this respect. In any event, we have no knowledge that in its broadcasts to Poland the Government has undertaken a clear educational campaign aimed at [inculcating] a proper attitude among the Polish community. We have approached the Government several times about our possible participation in bodies whose task is to maintain liaison with the Homeland. Thus far, these matters have not been favourably resolved. We are absent from the Planning Commission where, in any event, the foundations of the future Poland are being laid, and we believe that we ought to have the opportunity to participate and to share responsibility in this area. Finally, I should like to raise again the question of the Jewish children who have come from Russia to Teheran. It happened that thanks to somebody 900 Jewish children got there, and you understand what each Jewish child means to us at this moment. There are difficulties in bringing these children to Palestine. We are very concerned about this; we do not know what is going to happen to these children, and we should like to ask the Government to help us bring them to Palestine.

Dr. Kleinbaum: The world has witnessed a change in Polish foreign policy; a change in internal policy is noticeable as well. However, the general impression remains that with regard to the Jews nothing has changed. Poland will be one of the decisive factors – I do not say *the* decisive factor, but one of them – in the settlement of the Jewish question on a world scale. But should this question remain unsolved after this war as well, should the world continue to regard the Jews as a people of lesser value than others, then indeed the blood shed will have been in vain. The solution of the Jewish question means the establishment of a Jewish Palestine, the concentration of the major part of the Jewish people here, and full equality of rights for Jews in the countries where they remain. To approach the Jewish question in this spirit a certain disposition is necessary, and this requires a measure of educational work on the part of the Government. Thus far we have not seen such work. If Poland is really to enter the path of democracy, then the Government, the army, the civil service, the political parties, [and] the Polish community [as a whole] must undergo a radical change in their attitude towards the Jews and the Jewish people.

Dr. Stupp: I should like to come back to purely Polish-Jewish matters. I suppose that even without having talked to us and without our complaints, you would certainly have realized that the Palestinian sector has not been treated fairly by the Government. Here is the Jewish centre; the leaders of Polish Jewry – the Representation – are located here; yet the Polish Government seems not to desire to make use of all this and has not sought [our] collaboration. In our first memorandum to the Government we proposed working together, but the Government has maintained hardly any contact with us. Here and there we have received a telegram with an evasive answer to our requests. For that reason the Representation is glad you have come; but fate has decreed that you should arrive at a time when it is difficult to discuss matters in concrete terms, as we do not know how current [these discussions] are. It is possible to speak only in general terms, and in general we can say that the Government's contact with us to this point has been insufficient and unsatisfactory and could not give us the conviction that the Government really intends to work together with us. We ask you to work for a change in these relations after you return to London.

Minister Kot: Polish Jews have not supported democracy; rather they went hand in hand with Sanacja.[1] The atmosphere in Russia was caused by the behaviour of the Jews under Soviet occupation. Many Poles suffered because of denunciations by Jews. In some places Jews joyfully welcomed entering Soviet troops, helped disarm Polish officers and police, tore off their insignia, and then collaborated with the Russian regime and brought about many arrests and deportations.[2]

Dr. Stupp: If I may interrupt you, Mr. Minister, you probably know that in many areas of the Homeland Polish people, convinced that the Soviet army had come to help, also welcomed the troops with flowers.

Minister Kot: Well, let us leave aside the welcome, but [what about] all the other things that happened later on? But I understand that this is not the time for recriminations and that a change is necessary in the mutual relations between Poles and Jews. I myself have worked a great deal in this direction, explaining to Poles that such a change is in the interest of the state. I recruited so many Jewish officials that Poles actually spoke about a numerus clausus for Poles in the Embassy.[3] I have not always been able to convince people everywhere; some have said right to my face that they would never forget the wrongs done to them by Jews and would speak of this openly, everywhere and at all times. Of course, I know that not all Jews supported the Bolshevik regime, but there was a sufficiently large number of those who did. At least such was the opinion of the people in Russia. Regarding the general Jewish problem, the government will be glad to support any effort concerning Palestine, but let the Jews state in clear terms what they want the Polish Government to do in this regard. At the moment the only thing Jews talk with us about is Poland; they don't speak about Palestine. You say, Gentlemen, that the Government has not invited you to work together [with it], but you did not have to wait for it to invite you. For it is the duty of all citizens to do all they can for their country; but at the moment the Jews are sitting quietly, doing nothing, not showing any great activity in any respect. They become active only when it comes to protesting against Poland. And here something interesting happens. The typical Jew who speaks with me tells about his attachment to Poland and claims that he cannot live without his Lwów or his Wilno; and I believe that this is so and that he would be glad to do everything for Poland. But we see no action on the part of the various agencies, representations, and the press. These institutions exhibit great idleness in these matters. Do we have to appeal to the Jewish people over the heads of these institutions? We shall do it if we have to, but we should rather not.

I return to Russian matters. Here and there there were shortcomings. But in general we have done all that we could. I have explained so many times that if the Jews are not let out of Russia, the fault does not lie on the Polish side. The Jewish children who are at present in Teheran got there not 'thanks to someone', but thanks to the strong intervention of General Anders, who literally snatched these children away, yet in the local press there has not been a single word of recognition for the general. The Government cannot smuggle these children across borders. The [Jewish] Agency must arrange this with the British. We have had difficulties because we took a certain number of non-military personnel with the troops, and in Cairo General Anders had to promise that this would not happen again. For this reason I was astonished when this was raised in our talks. Still, you need not be so worried about the fate of these children. Even if they cannot be brought to Palestine, nothing bad will happen to them, God forbid. They will travel with Polish children and be treated equally with them.

As to the Government and the National Council, General Sikorski has accomplished a great thing – he has split *Endecja* in two. One part sits in the Government and in the Council and has accepted [the Government's] declaration of principles.[4] However, instead of expressing satisfaction the Jews are up in arms. This is beyond my comprehension. We shall have to discuss all these matters at some length, in order to put what has been behind us and to work together for the future. I regret that this conversation is taking place in Tel Aviv, where my time is limited. I think that we should meet in Jerusalem where we shall be able to talk more freely.

The delegates of the Representation had to interrupt the Minister frequently, insisting that some of his arguments stem from ignorance of many facts. All reserved the right to reply to a number of accusations against the Jewish people and to refute them.

It was agreed that Dr. Rosmarin would inform us about the time of the next meeting after consulting with the Minister.

NOTES TO DOCUMENT NO. 3

1 Sanacja – the name given to the political movement led by Józef Piłsudski following his seizure of power in Poland in May 1926. On Polish Jewry's relations with Sanacja, see Pawel Korzec, *Juifs en Pologne: La question juive pendant l'entre-deux-guerres* (Paris, 1980), pp. 165–87 and passim; Moshe Landa, *Miut Lèumi Lohem; Màavak Yehudei Polin ba-Shanim 1918–1928* (Jerusalem, 1986), pp. 276–337.
2 On Polish-Jewish relations under Soviet occupation, see Engel, *Shadow of Auschwitz*, pp. 59–62.
3 Official statistics released by the Polish Embassy in the USSR held that over half of the employees of Polish-sponsored relief institutions in the Soviet Union were Jews; see 'Deportations of Polish Citizens from Soviet-Occupied Poland to the Interior of the USSR, 1940–1941', Hoover Institution Archives, Poland (Ambasada US), Box 30, File 8. These figures have been challanged by Kalman Nussbaum, *Ve-Hafach lahem le-Ròets: Ha-Yehudim ba-Tsava ha-Amami ha-Polani be-Vrit ha-Mòatsot*, Tel Aviv 1984, p. 64. Nussbaum maintains, on the basis, *inter alia*, of a comprehensive list of delegates and agents employed by the Embassy, that only a small minority were Jews.
4 The term *'Endecja'* refers here to the National Party (*Stronnictwo Narodowe*), the ideological heir of the former National Democratic Party (*Narodowa Demokracja*), to which the name 'Endecja' was first applied. The National Party, known for an ideological orientation strongly hostile to Jewish interests, was initially one of the four major parties that supported the Government-in-Exile. It objected, however, to the Polish-Soviet Agreement concluded in July 1941 and in consequence withdrew its support. Shortly thereafter the party divided, with one faction, led by former Minister Marian Seyda, favouring reconciliation with the Government and another, led by Tadeusz Bielecki, preferring to remain in opposition.

Document No. 4
[Unofficial Polish protocol of Kot's second meeting with the Representation of Polish Jewry. Hoover Institution Archives, Polish Government, Box 700, File 'Mniejszości Żydzi'][1]

THE REPRESENTATION OF POLISH JEWS, 5 December 1942 (Anshel Reiss, Dr. Moshe Kleinbaum, Dr. Abraham Stupp), declare;

The Representation of Polish Jews comprises representatives of the Jewish parties from Poland (except for the Bund and the Revisionists). Included in it are: the General Zionists, the Religious Zionists (Mizrahi), the left-wing socialist Zionist parties, and Agudas Yisroel. The tasks of the Representation include duties towards the Polish State and the creation of [decent] living conditions for the Jews in Poland. Our work began in April 1940, and contact with the Polish authorities was established. [Yet] as a representative body we have not found understanding on the part of the

Polish Government, nor have we found understanding or support on the part of Polish diplomatic offices here in Palestine. At present we cannot think calmly, for the events in the Homeland weigh heavily upon our thoughts. Several months ago we asked about facilitating contact for us inside Poland through the medium of the Polish Government. This matter is even more burning now. We have in Poland a group of active people with whom we wish to establish contact, and we request that you assist us in this task.

We should like to work together as much as possible in building the new foundations for a new Poland. The existing Jewish representation in the National Council is not entirely adequate.[2] Perhaps it would be possible to have our representative on the Planning Commission for the future order in Poland.

We believe that more could be done among the Polish population in this country to establish good relations between Poles and Jews. We have been making efforts aimed at achieving such relations and at removing antisemitism from Polish circles.

Unfortunately, the facts speak otherwise. [Consider] the Russian issue. There are many unpleasant facts. We do not know if there will be [any further] evacuation. People come to us and tell us that the Russian authorities will not exercise any control over evacuation lists prepared by the Polish military authorities. The question of the several hundred Jewish children in Teheran is important to us.

There has been talk about Jewish world power. How painful it is that we cannot get the children out of Teheran. We ask you for help.

We have succeeded in organizing a protest campaign throughout the Jewish world against the persecution of Jews in Poland. The Polish Government ought to take an appropriate stand as well.

[These are] the general outlines of Polish-Jewish problems. We expected this war to bring about a great turnabout [in the relations] between our two peoples, a turnabout of the spirit. We are disappointed. The impression is current throughout the world that the Polish Government has broken with the former regime in the areas of domestic and foreign policy. We do not have the same conviction with regard to the Jewish question. A turnabout in Polish opinion has not taken place. The Polish Government faces a difficult task here, for it does not have the courage to take a stand on the Jewish question that is not popular among the Poles.

We know that instructions issued by the army were attenuated when they reached the lower echelons. We know that more than one representative of the Polish Government explains the instructions on the Jewish question as a temporary expedient, an adaptation to Western European style.[3] This is not [meant as] a reproach on our part, but we pose it as a problem which has not even been taken up yet. We do not know how many Jews we represent; but the historic tie between Poles and Jews will not be broken with the end of the war, and it will be necessary to bring order into these relations. The Jewish problem will remain on a global scale as well. The attitude of Polish Jews towards the Polish question will influence world Jewry's attitude towards Poland. This is a historic moment for the Jewish people, which has stood together with the Allied nations, including the Poles. After this war the Jewish people must no longer be persecuted. The Jews must become free and self-dependent in Palestine, yet at the same time there must be equality for all Jews in other countries. There will be a great struggle over this. Our interests clash with the interests of the Allies, especially with British interests. We should like the British to recognize our position as their own. We are also concerned about Polish opinion in this matter and about conducting suitable propaganda and action. We are convinced that you have noticed that active Jewish life has been concentrated here in Palestine.

The Polish authorities have not taken up the offer we made two years ago.[4] We have not seen any desire to make use of our help. We have received only fragmentary replies. This must change, because we have been pushed into a blind alley. Perhaps we have not been active enough, but we have felt ourselves hampered by a lack of information as well as by the absence of any clear inclination on the part of the Polish Government to work together.

We know that protests have been sent to London from the Homeland as a result of Schwarzbart's talks on the radio. Has the Government undertaken any educational campaign? Why does Minister Stroński not mention Jewish issues in his talks to the Homeland?[5] We feel that the Polish Government is not inclined to use the opportunity to work together with the Representation.

The Minister's reply: I can speak [only] with telegraphic conciseness. It is possible to straighten out Polish-Jewish relations if nothing is left unclarified. Let us put aside the pluses and minuses of the Polish-Jewish question. Anti-semitism in Poland has been a sporadic phenomenon. Painful events have taken place, but these have never been mass phenomena. On the Jewish side some regrettable things have happened; [the Jews] weakened democracy [and] acted in solidarity with Piłsudski, both at home and abroad. In the course of the present war a large percentage of the Jews behaved abominably. Jews welcomed the Bolsheviks with flowers; they denounced the Poles. This has weighed heavily upon Polish-Jewish relations. No wonder that officers who experienced these wrongs were embittered. (The Jewish bourgeoisie behaved well and regretted this.)

During my stay in Russia on behalf of the Government I endeavoured to eradicate anti-semitism and hatred. The Embassy apparatus had the strictest instructions to improve the atmosphere and to establish harmony, brotherhood, and a sense of community. There was not a [single] case in which these instructions were broken. There was not a [single] Jew with whom we would not speak or whose matter would not be taken care of. There were several briefing sessions and orders issued by General Anders and General Bohusz firmly stressing that Jews must be well treated.[6] There were no physical attacks, although there were some grounds for them. I endeavoured to have several high-ranking anti-semitic officers dismissed. I employed Jews in the Embassy and in the relief missions. Jews from Bukhara wrote in praise of two former Endecja militants.

Please do not say that the Government is not carrying out educational work. Among the Jews there have been speculators and smugglers who have spoiled our opinion. I have a number of letters from Jews about this matter. You must keep in mind that Jews need to stop complaining and start working.

Where is the Jews' public declaration that Lwów and Wilno ought to be returned to Poland? Why have the Jews done nothing in this matter? Either the Jews express solidarity with Polish actions, or they refuse, in which case they have no right to complain about the Polish Government.

The Polish Government appointed Lieberman[7] minister and that led Poles to protest. When he died he was decorated with the Order of the White Eagle, and [this time] there were [no] protests from Poland.[8]

The Government expects warmth and support, not criticism.

The Government has been carrying out educational work. It split *Endecja* in two. Seyda[9] is head of one of the factions, and he condemns anti-semitism. This division is breaking apart the anti-semitic movement inside Poland. [But] instead of accepting this gratefully, the Jews express alarm. In looking over our mutual relations we have to consider what the Jews themselves can do to put an end to anti semitism in Poland. Zygielbojm[10] has stimulated unfavourable sentiments towards the Jews by his tactlessness.

In this country there are those who once belonged to Sanacja. The Jews, as citizens of Poland, must demonstrate an attitude befitting citizens. Here every trifle is magnified, and this creates a climate unfavourable to the Polish Government. The Soviets treat the Jews badly, but [at the same time] they spread gossip about Polish anti-semitism. Individual Jews express affection for Poland, but the [Jewish] organizations do not. Our contact with the Homeland is [maintained via] the radio and the parachute. We can help. I suppose that in Britain Jews are members of the Planning Commission for Europe. The attitude of the Jewish Agency in Teheran is strange. They refuse to hand us any documents. Mr. Grünbaum, instead of trying to come to terms with the Polish Government, sends appeals to America. This is unacceptable. This evacuation of Jewish children from Russia is the achievement of General Anders. [There has not been] even a single mention of this in the press. We have no way to influence Iraq to let these children pass through [its territory]. I am convinced of the necessity for an independent Palestine. The Jews must approach us in this matter.

The Representation: We have listened with patience to this lecture. We have the impression that you have overlooked certain points. We know that there were some unpleasant incidents in Eastern Poland. [However,] one should not forget what had been happening in Poland for several years before the outbreak of the war. We must seek a bridge. We have appealed to America on behalf of the Polish cause; we have not done everything because we could not. We need facts.

NOTES TO DOCUMENT NO. 4

1 Handwritten annotation at top of page – 'Nieautoryzowany [Unauthorized'].
2 In the first National Council (December 1939–July 1941) one Jew, Ignacy Schwarzbart, had represented Jewish interests in the name of the Representation of Polish Jewry; in the second Council (summoned in February 1942) he was joined by the representative of the Bund, Szmuel Zygielbojm. During the period preceding the summoning of the second Council the Representation had argued that Jews ought to be represented on it in proportion to their percentage of the total population in prewar Poland; since the Council included 31 delegates, the Representation felt that another Jew should be appointed. The Polish Government, on the other hand, explicitly rejected the notion of proportional representation for Jews; see Engel, *Shadow of Auschwitz*, p. 267.
3 This may be a reference to the infamous order issued by General Anders on 30 November 1941, which stated that although 'our policy – since it is at present completely and entirely connected with English policy – must be to relate positively to the Jewish question, whose influence in the Anglo-Saxon world is considerable ..., when we are masters in our own home ... we shall dispose of the Jewish question as the greatness and sovereignty of our homeland and ordinary human justice require'. Quoted in Engel, *Shadow of Auschwitz*, p. 136. However, since this order was published in Palestine only in 1943, it cannot be known for certain whether the leaders of the Representation were already familiar with its contents in December 1942.
4 The reference is evidently to the message sent to the Government-in-Exile by the Representation on 23 September 1940, at the time of the Representation's creation. This message included a statement that 'the Representation has expressed its complete solidarity with the struggle for the rebirth of an independent democratic Poland. . . .' See Reprezentacja, *Sprawozdanie*, p. 7.
5 In the event, only a week earlier Stroński had explicitly rejected the notion of exhorting the people of occupied Poland to assist their threatened Jewish fellow-citizens. See Engel, *Shadow of Auschwitz*, p. 201.
6 Anders issued such an order on 14 November 1941; see ibid., p. 135. Earlier, on 24 October 1941, a meeting had been held at the Polish Embassy in Kuibyshev between Anders and three Jewish leaders (Henryk Ehrlich and Wiktor Alter from the Bund and the General Zionist Ludwik Seidenman), during which Anders promised that Jews would be treated equally with all other soldiers in the Polish army. A facsimile of the minutes of this meeting is reproduced in Slowes, *Yàar Katyn*, pp. 227–30.

7 Herman Lieberman – leading Jewish member of Polish Socialist Party (PPS); served as minister of justice in the Government-in-Exile until his death in 1941.
8 Handwritten correction to text: 'były protesty [there were protests]' changed to 'nie było już protestów [this time there were no protests]'.
9 See Document No. 3, n. 4.
10 See above, n. 2.

Document No. 5
[Summary of a press conference. Hoover Institution Archives, Polish Government, Box 700, File 'Mniejszości Żydzi']

Minutes of the interview given on 5 December 1942 in Tel Aviv by Minister Professor Kot to the representatives of the Palestinian Press.[1]

[...][2]
To begin with, Mr Heftman, the president of the Union of Hebrew Journalists, greets the minister, stressing the community of fate between the Polish and Jewish peoples, the first to be attacked by the Germans; he expresses his confidence that the Polish Government will do everything possible to persuade the democracies to save Polish Jewry. Addressing his colleagues, the speaker declares that in the person of the minister he greets a spokesman of progressive Poland; at the same time he expects a declaration about the events in Poland and also about the situation of the Jews in Russia. In the press reports on the extermination of Jews in Europe Poland occupies the central place. The speaker asks [the minister] not to be surprised at the unusual questions that will be put to him; they are the consequence of an exceptional situation.

Minister Kot expresses thanks for the greetings and states that the assembled guests are the representatives of public opinion not only in Palestine but also of world Jewry. I have not come here for purposes of propaganda, but for the purpose of exchanging information. I have the impression that living in your beautiful and peaceful country you remain as if on the periphery of the colossal events taking place throughout the world, where the fate of the Poles and the Jews is being decided.

I shall disappoint you when I say that I intend to speak the candid truth, but only on condition that it will not be published, since I am speaking with you as representatives of [public] opinion and not of the press. Looking with enchantment upon Palestine as a paradise, I compare her with the places where the fate of the Poles and the Jews is being decided. In order to be able to talk calmly about these things one must be far removed from the events. I share the view of your president that the war is being waged against the Jews and the Poles. Suffice it to say that the war began in

Poland and that Hitler aims equally at the extermination of the Jews and the Poles. The Poles and the Jews are bound together as no other peoples. German rule in Poland began with the liquidation of the Poles in Polish Silesia, where people were herded together into enclosures and murdered. This was the first attempt. In Auschwitz experiments in the mass destruction of Poles were carried out. At first German fury expressed itself in robbery, destruction, and violence. We estimate the number of Poles murdered in cold blood at 120,000. Following this first period there began the biological extermination of the Jews. This action, unprecedented in world history, has been going on now for several months. The facts that have been published in the press reached the Polish Government in stages and were communicated to the Allies and to Jewish organizations. The Polish Government, horrified by the news, called conferences of the heads of the governments of interested countries, and Minister Mikołajczyk organized appropriate meetings.[3] With the deepest sorrow I must confirm that the facts reported in the press are true. I am not quite so certain about the numbers. The Polish Government's delegates in the Homeland are sending proposals aimed at stopping the extermination of the Jews in Poland. There are no illusions in the Homeland that protests can achieve the desired effect. The Germans have to be made to feel the force of a reaction against German elements who are within the Allies' reach. Moreover, it is certain that if international courts do not punish the Germans now, nothing will stop them. The impossibility of getting the Allies to agree to the aforementioned Polish proposals prevents their being made known publicly, for in this way the Germans would be given encouragement for even greater atrocities. Opinion is stronger than governments. Reports about German bestiality meet with the answer that it is only *Greuelpropaganda* [atrocity propaganda] aimed at undermining [the spirits of] the peaceful Anglo-Saxon nations who shudder at the thought of reprisals against the Germans. Should we be unable to convince public opinion and to arouse it, we shall lose and leave millions of people for prey. The Germans began with the Poles, then went on to the Jews, and now they intend to resume the annihilation of the Poles.[4] I emphasize that there are no differences here and that we have common aims. In Poland the common dangers have brought the Poles and the Jews closer together. Any suggestion that Poles are capable of collaborating with Germans must be treated cautiously. The Germans brought in a mass of Ukrainian and Lithuanian police. It sometimes happens that the Germans highlight irresponsible Polish elements in order to spread propaganda hostile to us. I declare with sorrow something that does not need to be made explicit, that the intelligentsia in Lithuania hate the Jews and the Poles. The details surpass anything imaginable. The Lithuanians use the arguments that it is necessary to liquidate the Polish element in Lithuania, and against the Jews [they speak of] revenge for what happened during the Soviet occupation. The Ukrainians behave in a similar fashion, although perhaps less blatantly. The Polish Government remains in contact with Jewish representatives in London and America about this matter. General Sikorski went to America to speak on behalf of all the governments in order to bring about a more rapid prosecution of the war, so that it will not be too late.

The editor-in-chief of *Davar*, Rubashov,[5] apologizes for asking an unusual question. You have arrived here at a time of mourning. Our information is even worse. Does the Polish state know that those being murdered are Polish citizens? What does the Polish Government intend to do about the murder of Jewish Polish citizens? We have heard that General Sikorski is in America, but is he organizing reprisals against the Germans? Might Poles and Jews act together in presenting this question and demand? The massive crimes of the Germans can happen only if the world watches them with indifference. We have heard that Poles in the Homeland have not taken part in any of this. We should like to believe this; we should like to know what the Polish Government and the Polish underground have done to counteract these atrocities. There is the radio. Has Minister Stroński spoken to the Homeland on this subject? The Polish Government has ties with the Vatican. Has the Vatican been approached by the Polish Government on this matter? If not, perhaps we could make an approach together? The evacuation from Russia has a dual significance. Distinctions are being made between Poles and Jews. We cannot understand how such distinctions can be made. History does not know such deportations as having recently taken place. We wish you success in your present work; we call for protection for the Jews and ask that the Polish Government not be silent in this matter.

Mr. Minc[6], the representative and editor of the newspaper *Ha-Tsofeh*: Why has the Polish Government taken so long to publicize the news in its possession? We have heard the protest of the National Council,[7] but we did not know of this earlier. I do not mean to complain. What steps has the Polish Government taken internationally, and first of all in the United States, to make it possible for Jews to leave Russia and to supply them with medicine and food? We know that distinctions have been made between Jews and Poles by lower-ranking officials in the Embassy and army in Russia. What does the Government intend to do about this matter?

Mr. Remba, representative of the daily *Ha-Mashkif*,[8] asks the fundamental question: how to save the millions of Jews people who have not yet been annihilated. We demand the creation of an independent Jewish army, appointment of a commission to bring the Germans to justice, and the constitution of a Jewish state.

Mr. Finkelstein, representing the daily *Ha-Arets*:[9] We have listened with interest to the information you have presented. We should like to know which of the Polish Government's proposals did not meet with the favour of the governments of the English-speaking countries. Perhaps a change is in the offing now. Could you not approach General Sikorski and ask him to raise this question in America once again?

Mr. Lipson, representing *Ha-Tsofeh*: German sources report about improper behaviour by Poles towards Jews. We know that in Lwów the Poles behaved badly. An investigation should be conducted.

Mr. Berger, representing *Heggeh*:[10] Perhaps there will be a miracle, and Jewish children from Poland will be saved. Perhaps now is the time to think where to place them.

Mr. Swislocki, representing *Ha-Zeman*:[11] Collections were taken up here for parcels to Poland, while at the same time the murders in Poland were already going on. We were not told anything about these murders.

Minister Kot expresses his thanks for the questions. I shall answer briefly. I have materials that one can pore over for several days and nights. In general my impression is that you are on the periphery of great power politics, and you do not know what is happening or what the prevailing climate is. There have been innumerable protests by our Government, first of all by Minister Mikołajczyk, who is in charge of matters concerning the Homeland. He has publicized statistical data that were communicated simultaneously to the Allied governments and to Jewish representatives. Apparently there is no communication between London and Palestine. This is an unpleasant surprise for me. With regard to the behaviour of the Poles in the Homeland, we have articles from the underground press of both the right and the left. Polish opinion is aroused but helpless. It is possible that some elements of the riffraff took part [in anti-Jewish actions]. If anything happened in Lwów, please send me a witness and the relevant documents. The former anti-semitic attitudes in Poland have changed. In a right-wing newspaper published in underground Poland, there is a description of an event in Oszmiana [. . .].[12] As to the question whether General Sikorski will demand reprisals, my answer is that we have been demanding it categorically for several months together with the Yugoslavs, who are working closely with us. Others are taking a less decisive stand. It is essential that circles that you can influence should exert pressure. History will note how the Polish Government is pressing its demands energetically and forcefully. There is no need to influence the Polish Government. There should not be any unresolved questions between Poles and Jews. The Polish side has suffered from statements made by some Jews against Poland. You must use your influence wherever you have access. I propose that you send a message to General Sikorski asking him to continue his efforts and declaring your support and desire to work together. This will make a better impression than would any message of mine. It is difficult for me to say what terms were put to the Allies. As for the Vatican, the Government has abandoned any intervention on behalf of the Poles. Except for the Poles and the Belgians, the Catholics are on

Hitler's side. The Pope's position is difficult. The Jesuits are against Hitler. The great statesman Archbishop Jałbrzykowski[13] was removed from his post, and his place was taken by a Lithuanian. The Jewish world could turn to the Vatican, and this may have greater impact than Polish intervention. With regard to relations in Poland, what is happening there is being carried out exclusively with the support of the German forces. There is no role to be played in rendering help to Jews by the Polish civilian population, which is isolated from what is going on. I would recommend not to have any illusions about the possibility of sending parcels, evacuating children, etc. This proves that people here are unaware about the conditions that prevail there. Our emissaries are sent to Poland, but they do not return.

I believe that the problem of persecutions in Poland has been exhausted. I move on to Russia. I shall clear up the complaints about the inequalities in Russia, but may I ask you not to make notes, even for your own recollection. We are speaking confidentially. After my arrival in Russia I realized that the Polish-Jewish situation was difficult. Some Jews had welcomed Soviet troops marching into Poland with flowers and had derided the Poles. The Jews in Russia were apprehensive about how the Polish Government would relate to them, for they knew that the number of incidents painful to the Poles was great. The Polish population was bitterly inclined against the Jews. I started out from the premise that the catastrophe that has befallen us must erase the memory of past events. I never asked how particular Jews behaved. Each one was eligible to receive the same assistance. I never discriminated between Jews and Poles. Matters of welfare were managed by people appointed by the Embassy but nominated from below. There were many Jews. There were cases in which Jews themselves demanded the removal of several [other] Jews. The colossal distances made it impossible for the Embassy to react immediately to complaints. I have lists of charges against Jews and Poles. That the Embassy did not make any distinctions has been thoroughly checked. You can be certain that I suffered a great deal of unpleasantness because I appointed a large number of Jewish agents [in the welfare apparatus]. In the South of Russia, where there is a large Jewish settlement, 30 of the 37 agents are Jews. 14 per cent of the Polish population, that has received 21 per cent of the total amount of aid distributed, lives there. 35 per cent of all medical stations and hospitals are located there.[14] I have impressed upon the entire Polish community in Russia that the Jews are entitled to occupy any of the various posts. Ambassador Romer continues in this fashion [. . .].[15]

There have been many complaints about the evacuation. It was an evacuation of the military, and it included the families of soldiers only in part. A portion of the families remained, as did a portion of Embassy officials. I demanded that the army punish officers who were guilty of improper behaviour towards Jews. I have also asked Jews for material, but no one has provided me with any. Against this background, it seems strange that the transportation of one thousand children from Russia to Teheran that General Anders arranged has not been mentioned in the press. I was opposed to the evacuation of the army and the civilian population. We have registers of Jews who have received certificates for Palestine whom the Soviet authorities do not wish to release now, as in their Polish passports their nationality is listed as Jewish [. . .].[16]

I have given proof of my highest confidence in talking to you about all these questions. Should anyone repeat what has been said here, it would harm the Jewish population in Russia greatly. There will not be another opportunity like the present one for proclaiming a Jewish state. This must not be overlooked. Finally, in the matter of a Jewish army, the Jews themselves must raise their voice.

At the conclusion of the meeting, President Heftman explained that nothing said at this conference may be published in the press.

I thank you for your work in Kuibyshev, and I bid you fond farewell. The Jewish community looks forward to Poland's [renewed] independence.

Minutes taken by the Vice-Consul of Poland, Andrzej Jenicz.

NOTES TO DOCUMENT NO. 5

1 Handwritten annotation at the top of the page: 'Nieautoryzowany [unauthorized]'.
2 List of those present ellipsised.
3 Stanisław Mikołajczyk – leader of Polish Peasant Party (*Stronnictwo Ludowe*); deputy prime minister of Government-in-Exile to July 1943; prime minister July 1943–November 1944. The reference here is probably to the press conference organized by Mikołajczyk on 9 July 1942 together with British Information Minister Brendan Bracken, at which news was presented of the 'wholesale extermination of the Jews' in Poland.
4 Although Polish spokesmen consistently maintained this position in public, there is evidence that this view may not have been accepted as axiomatic in Polish Government circles. See Jan Karski to Tadeusz Romer, 4 October 1943, Hoover Institution Archives, Jan Karski, Box 2, File 8.
5 In addition to serving as editor-in-chief of *Davar*, the influential daily of the Palestinian Jewish labour movement, Zalman Rubashov was also a member of the Jewish National Council (Våad Lèumi), a representative body of Palestinian Jewry charged with the governance of the Jewish community in non-political matters. On behalf of this body he drafted the manifesto responding to the news of the Holocaust received in November 1942. He later served as the third president of the State of Israel (after having Hebraized his surname to Shazar).
6 Binyamin Minc – leader of the non-Zionist, religiously orthodox, labour-oriented Po-alei Agudat Yisrael party. He was also a member of the Rescue Committee (Våad ha-Hatsalah) operated by the Jewish Agency Executive.
7 The reference is to the resolution adopted by the Polish National Council on

27 November 1942 protesting 'the German crimes directed against the Polish nation, and with particular bestiality against the Jewish population of Poland'.
8 *Ha-Mashkif* – daily newspaper of the Revisionist movement in Palestine.
9 *Ha-Arets* – non-party daily newspaper with middle-class liberal orientation.
10 *Heggeh* – daughter publication of *Davar* in simplified Hebrew for new immigrants.
11 *Ha-Zeman* – short-lived Tel Aviv morning daily with General Zionist tendencies.
12 Description of events paralleling that of same incident in Document No. 1.
13 Romuald Jałbrzykowski – archbishop of Wilno who endeavoured to mobilize the clergy in his area for the rescue of Jews.
14 For a description of the aid apparatus established by the Embassy, as well as for statistics on allocations to Jews, see 'Udzielona Pomoc i Opieka nad Ludnością Żydowską w ZSRR', Hoover Institution Archives, Poland (Ambasada USSR), Box 16.
15 Passages in which Kot read letters attesting to his previous statements ellipsised.
16 Three sentences giving examples of Soviet treatment of Jews omitted.

Document No. 6
[Summary of Kot's meeting with Polish Jewish religious leaders. Hoover Institution Archives, Polish Government, Box 700, File 'Mniejszości Żydzi']

Minutes of the interview given by Minister Kot on 5 December 1942 to representatives of Agudas Yisroel: E. Mazur, chairman of the Jewish community in Warsaw; Aizenstadt, a rabbi from Kraków; Minc, editor of HaTsofeh; *Loewenstein, from Zurich.*[1]

The guests say that they have sinned, for they have not cared sufficiently for the fate of their brethren. Now they are concerned for saving the life of even a single person in Poland. They do not know, however, where to direct the prospective refugees. It is a matter of concern to the delegation that the Polish Government guarantee that after the war the evacuees will not be a burden upon the countries in which they will be staying. There is little time left to save the Jews of Poland. What is your advice as to how to proceed? We ask for guidance.

After the war of 1914–18 the League of Nations appointed a commission to care for refugees. Is it not possible now to use the same channels to attempt to bring about the evacuation of Jews from Poland to neutral countries? The question of providing for these people is an important one. We are with Poland with all our hearts; we have families there, and we are all in despair. We say openly that we have various means; [however] to the Vatican, for example, we have no possibility of sending our delegates. We stand isolated. Please make it possible for us to send our people to Teheran and Istanbul. We have no contact with Poland; we ask you to make it possible for us. We ask for information from Russia, because there, too, we have relatives; perhaps there it will be possible to do something. We ask you to make it possible for Rabbi Prato, the chief rabbi of Rome, to go to Istanbul. We want to bring the Jewish children who are now in Teheran (those evacuated from Russia) to this country, so that they may be taken under the care of Aguda and educated in a religious spirit.

Minister Kot explained: These are all difficult matters. We have to look reality straight in the face. I do not believe that Jews will be let out of Poland. For a year and a half not a single Pole has left Poland. The reverberations from the Jews who have been let out of Poland recently will prevent the possibility that others will eventually be freed. Today there is not a power in the world which could force anything from Hitler through negotiations. I do not believe in intervening with the Vatican, but nothing ought to be neglected. We could act as confidential mediators in sending the Jews' message to the Pope. Sending people from here, especially sending Jews to Turkey, is a most difficult matter. You need British assistance here. From the Polish side it is almost impossible. I suggest that the Jews send a message to the King of Sweden. The Polish Government maintains links with the Homeland through the radio and through parachutists. It may be possible to talk about sending a very vigorous Jewish person to Poland via England by this route. The radio stations in Poland fall constantly into German hands. The personnel of these exposed radio stations commit suicide in order to avoid the possibility of compromising others. These are all long-term concerns. If all Jewish groups would send a clever message to General Sikorski, who is at present in Washington, this might achieve the desired effect. Such a message would have to reach America public opinion. Perhaps particular Jewish organizations could appeal to their respective American counterparts and keep them informed about the activities of the Polish Government in Jewish matters.

The example of the war of 1914–18 seems unrealistic if you are thinking of achieving the same thing now. The Swiss Legation in Berlin is honest, and it could be influenced through the Swiss Government. As for Russia, the Soviet Government must be pressured. I have a list of people who have certificates and whom the Russian authorities do not wish to let out. The Russian Government can be influenced only by the United States. It is better not to send packages to Russia. The question of Jewish children must be settled by Jewish organizations themselves.

Minutes taken by Andrzej Jenicz, Vice-Consul of the Polish Republic.

NOTE TO DOCUMENT NO. 6

1 Handwritten annotation at top of page: 'Nieautoryzowany [unauthorized]'.

Document No. 7.
[Minutes of Kot's meeting with leaders of Palestinian Jewry.
Hoover Institution Archives, Polish Government,
Box 700, File 'Mniejszości Żydzi']

Minutes of a Conference held on 6 December 1942 in Jerusalem

Minister Kot: welcomes the assembled guests. As a member of the Polish Government, he wishes to discuss Polish-Jewish relations in the present war together with the chairman of the [Jewish Agency] Executive, the chief Rabbi, representatives of world Jewry, [and] Jewish religious and labour [leaders].

I am sorry that this conversation is taking place at such a tragic moment for both Poles and Jews. Evil is raging in occupied Poland, and we are helpless against it. The present war is first and foremost a war against the Jews and against Poland. It has been in the making for years. The question of Poland's existence and her access to the sea provided the occasion for Hitlerite aggression as well as for checking German expansion eastward. The fact that the war is being waged against Jews and Poles demands a mutual alliance to win the war and above all to achieve [our] war aims. Hitler, or rather all Germany, began the work of destruction in Poland by annihilating the Poles, wiping out whole Polish villages, as if for experimental purposes. The first period [consisted of] mass shootings of Poles in the Western territories. The Jewish question was at that time peripheral; the Jews suffered merely humiliation of their human dignity, degradations, thefts, and insults. After the murder of some 120,000 Poles, the extermination of the Jews in the biological sense began, on a scale beyond the comprehension of civilized nations, without historical precedent, carried out entirely according to a preset plan. This has aroused the indignation of the Polish Government, which the Government has communicated to the Allies and to the Jews.

A message from the Government delegate in Warsaw, who represents all elements in Poland, contains demands addressed to the Allied powers. It contains information about the persecution and despair of the powerless population. Words or methods used before the war to counteract such barbarity are of no avail. Only by meting out an equal measure to German citizens in the Allied countries will it be possible to stop the Hitlerite barbarity. We must demand to bring the perpetrators to court. [We must demand their] punishment. [We must demand] a declaration by the Allies that more than one German will answer for the murder of each Pole or Jew. The Polish Government is adamant that the governments of the Allied countries fulfil these demands. In this it is supported by the Yugoslavs and by others, but it is most difficult to make the English-speaking countries grasp the scale of the Hitlerite atrocities. They believe that it is all exaggerated. Public opinion, which has never been prepared to grasp such atrocities, resists believing in them. There is fear of the term 'retaliation' and the notion 'revenge'. Especially in the United States, citizens of German, Italian, and Irish origin direct public opinion against Japan but soften it in relation to the Axis countries. This has caused Premier Sikorski to fly to Washington three times in order to explain the situation to Roosevelt, to make him aware that victory may come at a moment when no one will be left in Poland to celebrate the victory. I should hope that these activities of Polish citizens would find a parallel in the activities of Jewish citizens, so that our demands could be presented with the greatest possible force. Poland grieves at the tragedy of the slaughtered Jewish people not because Poles are threatened with the same fate, but for religious and humanitarian reasons. The protest meetings of the Polish people, such as those called at the initiative of the Polish bishop, are an expression of this. When I was in Russia I spoke with the chairman of the Soviet Republics and told him that at the moment Hitler is the greatest teacher of humanity, for he has taught nations to draw closer and act together, to forget mutual animosities. I have no doubt that neither Jews nor Poles need such a terrible teacher.

Please ask your questions; I am ready to explain anything regarding the Polish-Jewish problem, a matter that is of utmost concern to us all.

Ben Gurion: We appreciate the feelings that stand behind your words about the Jews' and Poles' community of tragic fate. When Hitler came to power and declared war against the Jews, it was clear to us that we were only the first victims and that after us would come all weak nations. It is regrettable that nobody shared that perception with us. We are disheartened that we are not in a position to do anything for our brethren anywhere in Europe, but perhaps there are things that the Polish Government can do. You are right when you say how difficult it is to convince the English and the Americans that the news about the Hitlerite atrocities is true, but there is someone whom the world would believe – the Vatican. Poland could help by exerting influence on the Vatican. The English-speaking countries are not Catholic, but they will believe the Vatican. Our second request is that the Polish Government facilitate sending our people to occupied Poland. Our people are ready, and we request that the Government help them. The third matter [is one] of which I speak with a certain reserve, as I am not familiar with these matters in detail: I ask the Polish Government, which gives aid to people in the Homeland, to tell the people in Poland to render aid to the Jews and to give them support. The fourth matter goes beyond purely Polish affairs. We are interested in obtaining the help of the Polish Government in creating a Jewish army, made up of Jews who are under no obligation to serve in armies of other countries.[1] Our situation is worse than that of other nations. The Jews are not in their own country; they have no government of their own. We ask the Polish Government to support us in the matter of the army as well as in obtaining representation among the Allied nations, so that after victory we might come to the peace conference with our own accounts and demands. Finally I add that I do not know how Jews might help Poland, but no people in the world is so ready to support the struggle of the Polish people as is the Jewish people.

Mr. Elmaleh,[2] in the name of the Palestine National Council[3] and of all Palestinian Jews thanks the minister for his expressions of feelings towards the Jewish people. In their meetings with Minister Kot the representatives of the Jewish people have heard words of consolation flowing from heart to heart. When Hitler launched his struggle against the Jews, Europe did not understand that this was only the beginning and that all Europe's turn would soon follow. Now we see the consequences of Europe's indifference towards the Jewish persecutions. Please convey our best wishes to Premier Sikorski and to all who are concerned with our problems; we shall not forget what anyone does for us.

Mr. Schmorak[4] [speaks] on behalf of the Jewish Agency and also as a Polish citizen. We do not know how the Polish underground organizations relate to the persecution of Jews and what instructions they have received from the Polish Government. We know that Belgian and Dutch citizens are demonstrating sympathy for the Jewish people; [we know] how they are helping them by providing shelters for them in Antwerp, Brussels, and in the villages. The situation of Poland is worse than that of Belgium or Holland, although I suppose that a great deal could be done for the Jews in Poland. Later on the Jews might be able to aid the Polish population. Would it not be advisable to let the mass of the Polish people know by radio what is at stake, for the people do not know how their leaders wish them to behave. For example, would it not be proper for the Church to bring to the consciousness of the people that helping Jews is a civic and Christian duty? Moreover, if the urban intelligentsia helped Jewish people, the suffering of many could be relieved. In this way solidarity in tragedy and misfortune would be expressed.

The Chief Rabbi of Palestine:[5] Thank you for your heartfelt words. I hope that Poland will exert pressure on the Vatican. I have already talked with representatives of the Vatican, but pressure is still needed; further steps are necessary. I am certain that Poland could have great influence upon the Vatican. We never despair; the language of Jews knows no such word. We have lived through everything and we shall begin anew. We bear with the Polish nation the same suffering and persecution. We have much in common with Poland. As a professor of history you know this best of all. Jewish history and culture are most closely connected with Poland. The greatest concentration of Jews was in Poland; they reached the greatest cultural and economic heights. The most famous Jewish schools were in Poland. The Zionist movement had its origins in Poland. From Poland came the most famous Jewish writers and poets. Because we are so strongly connected with Poland, we believe that Poland will help the dying Jewish people. I ask the Government to do all in its power to exert influence on the Allied powers to open their doors and accept those who are persecuted by the German murderers. Please exert pressure on Britain to open Palestine for the Jews. I do not say 'I hope'; I say 'I believe' that Poland will rise again; and I hope that Poland will help the Jewish nation, which seeks its full reconstitution. God bless the Allies.

Minister Kot: I thank you all for saying what is on your minds. I cannot give you a reassuring answer about everything. Let me indicate that I am speaking here in a small circle to statesmen, in complete confidence. The Vatican is divided. It should be borne in mind that with the exception of Poland all the great Catholic nations are on the side of the Axis. The Vatican must take this into account. The Poles complain not only that the Vatican does not defend the Polish population, but that it does not defend even the Polish clergy and church, which are being persecuted by the Germans. Nevertheless, I think that representatives of the Jews ought to appeal to the Vatican. The Polish Government cannot do this, because for a long time it has not received any sympathetic response from the Vatican; but an appeal by Jews to the Pope might have some effect. The Government's instructions to the population in the Homeland and to the underground organizations have clearly said not to be drawn into any anti-semitic acts; they were decisive and forceful, and they have achieved their full effect. Information on these matters reached me before my departure from Kuibyshev.[6] Some bandit groups that might resort to violence operate among the dregs of society, but the population of the Homeland knows that the Germans hide their crimes by highlighting people of Polish origin. There was a case in Warsaw in which Volksdeutsche demolished a Jewish shop, after which they brought together some street urchins, photographed them and distributed the photographs throughout the world in order to show how Poles demolish Jewish shops. It was then that all of the parties together, meeting secretly, issued a proclamation to the nation explaining the essence of German duplicity. Almost all of the organs of the underground press have unmasked these devilish German tactics. News has reached me from Poland in Kraków, Warsaw, and other Polish towns and villages Jewish people, children in particular, have been finding shelters. I know that there has arisen a brotherhood of misfortune between the two peoples. Eighteen months ago a leader of ONR[8] sent a letter to the premier in which he stressed that his organization would never enter into collaboration with the Germans over the Jewish question. In many reports from Poland we have been informed that the Germans, unable to find agents for the extermination of Jews among the Poles, have imported Lithuanian and Ukrainians. The Lithuanians who aim to achieve unity in their country, have become specialists in exterminating Poles and Jews. The Ukrainians, in annihilating both Poles and Jews, express their hatred of them. We receive photographs of Polish underground papers from Poland, representing both the right and the left. They are full of protest and indignation over the murder of the Jews. You have read the proclamation issued by the league of Catholic associations in Poland; we cannot help, but we cannot observe the persecution of Jews in Poland [in silence]. One of the underground papers from the Homeland describes that happened during the executions in Oszmiana in fall 1941 [. . .].[9]

Lately the German crimes are being perpetrated by Germans in uniforms, out of the sight of the civilian population. Jews are being annihilated by contingents, according to a plan, outside the ghetto walls. The Poles do not see what is happening. A testimony to the awful conditions in the ghettos is the suicide of the chairman of the Jewish community in Warsaw.[10] What Poles do see is that from trains in which Jews are being deported hundreds of corpses are thrown out even during the course of the journey. Jews are being transported in their thousands from Warsaw to Bełżec, and it is evident that they are being put to death, as the food rations are always the same. As to the endeavour to secure the opening of frontiers for the persecuted Jews, I must tell you that I do not believe that Hitler will agree to let these people go. For a year and a half not a single Pole has left the country legally. Hitler is not interested in exchange deals or in money; fearing defeat, he intends to chain the people of Germany to himself by claiming that he has freed them from the Jews, their greatest enemy. Of course, efforts should be made, even if their success is not plausible. For this reason I also think that every practical proposal ought to be carried out. Sending a number of Jews to Poland is feasible, but not at this moment. It could be done, but naturally we shall not discuss this in this rather broad forum.

You ask how the weak Jews might help Poland. It is not Poland that you need to help, but the Jews. We must conduct a single uniform policy of maintaining a sense of attachment to the Polish Homeland and culture. How much the Jews themselves desire that was demonstrated when Polish citizenship was withdrawn from the Jews in Russia and Soviet citizenship forced [upon them]. They turned to us with a cry for help: 'Do not permit this; we want to return to Poland as Polish citizens.' [. . .][11] Had you borne this in mind, some incidents would never have happened, such as the one that happened here in Palestine, when an appeal to aid Polish citizens in Russia was opposed by some circles on the grounds that distinctions had allegedly been made between Poles and Jews, evidently without taking into consideration that this is one of the greatest lies of foreign propaganda. A sense of solidarity joins all Polish citizens in Russia; I have seen former Jew-baiters who cooperated sincerely with Jews because they had all been dealt the same load. It may have happened that somewhere somebody did not receive something; Russia is a big place, and in the lower echelons of the welfare organization somebody might have annoyed somebody else. But there have also been complaints about Jewish welfare officials distributing aid to Jews but not to Poles. I possess reports – perhaps someone would like to look at them – [from which] it appears that wherever Jews were in the majority I appointed Jewish officials. We did not feel any differences there. Russia wants to separate the Jews from Polish citizens. In order to prevent this, I gave instructions in the first instance to assist Jews financially and materially. Only in the future will it be possible to prove to what extent we have given preference to Jews so as to deprive the Russians of their perfidious arguments. I asked Ambassador Romer for information regarding the concentrations of Jewish citizens in the south, and here is the communication I received: (text of Ambassador Romer's telegram).[12]

As to the evacuation, we need to recall that this was an evacuation of the army, not of civilians, and it was strictly circumscribed by Soviet regulations. Both my own family and the families of the great majority of my officials remained in Russia. You ought to be very careful before expressing your complaints. I heard among others an accusation that matzos were not distributed to Jews in Russia but were eaten by the army in Pahlevi after the evacuation. These matzos were not delivered because they had been stored in the north, in Mamlutka; one case of matzos reached the army, and the soldiers ate them because they had no bread. We have no control over the fate of each case in the transports because we do not have sufficient personnel. [. . .][13]

We have notified leading Jewish circles of this, and you cannot pretend that you did not know. We have been eager to seek the intervention of America, with whom the Kremlin reckons, but not through the press, for this could have harmed the Jews. We were refused intervention in this matter from Palestine. This is to the detriment of the Jewish people, just as is stopping the aid campaign from Palestine because fools and agents spread [rumours] that the distribution of aid is unjust. I am bitter; one day it will come to light who did this and for what purpose. You ask what you can do. I say [conduct] a uniform policy, stop sideswiping at us [in a way] that hurts Jews and Poles. The Poles, too, feel hurt by the Jews; they remember denunciations by Jews that caused many people to find themselves in jail. We must forget all this; we must put an end to misunderstandings which please others alone. Poles and Jews have lived well together. It is necessary to remember that among Jews in Russia too there were ruffians and criminals released from Polish jails; they are the ones who smuggled themselves out and spread the false rumours. We have a higher goal; we must take a critical attitude towards these complaints.

As to a Jewish army and government, inform the Government in concrete terms what you want.

Mr. Schmorak: I ask that we should not raise the Jewish Agency's complaints in this forum. Next to the essential questions, these are matters of secondary or even tertiary importance. I should like to raise these items at a separate meeting. However, let me indicate that I did approach the Polish Government, asking whether we ought to intervene. Then Grünbaum made another approach, stressing that we cannot remain inactive, for the sake of the Jews and of Poland alike, for this may turn out to be a [matter of] bilateral interest. We received no answer for six weeks. I despatched an urgent message. Finally, three weeks later came a reply that was so unclear that I did not understand it. I did not know whether intervention was advisable or not. I have reservations about the documents that you claim would demolish [our] accusations. I have done everything so that these [accusations] would not become public. Not everything in them was untrue. The Government cannot be held responsible for everything that [its] delegates do. I do not agree that all of the information comes from people of ill will; some of the accusations are undoubtedly authentic. This is a matter of secondary importance, but it could become important in a further evacuation. I ask to deal with the matter of complaints separately and to discuss it on another occasion. Those gathered here are not familiar with this material. When we intervened with the Soviet ambassador in the United States, we did what we had to. We did not inform the Polish Government because we had not received an answer to our question whether we ought to intervene. The intervention brought no results, and we are upset about this. As to stopping the aid campaign in Palestine, I think that before you put forth accusations you ought to give the other side a chance to present its case.

Minister Kot: I am sorry that your intervention was fruitless. I am glad that you did intervene, but this should have been done not with Litvinov[14] but through the Americans. You seek inefficient ways, while we have been looking forward to your intervention as a means of salvation, so that something could be done for these unfortunate Jews. I regret that you have not shown the same degree of scrupulousness as to whether something is good or necessary when you stopped the aid campaign for Polish citizens in Russia, when you gathered together petty complaints about trivial matters, or even downright falsehoods. You stopped the aid campaign for Polish citizens in Russia purportedly because the distribution of allocations was unequal. This is a charge against the Embassy, and it hurts me.

Mr. Schmorak: This problem requires clarification. You have been informed about it in a one-sided manner.

Minister Kot: The Polish Government is interested in the question of a [Jewish] army and the Jews' role in the peace conference and could interest other governments in this matter, since the Polish state contains the largest percentage of Jews. We do not know what we shall find after the war, what the numerical relations well be; but I think that this subject can be discussed in detail between the Polish Government and Jewish citizens. It is possible to participate in the peace conference if you have an army. The Jews must have an army, but you must indicate under what designation, in what size and numbers, so that you do not say later on that we want to throw the Jews out of Poland. The Government can help, but these issues must be presented in practical and concrete terms. [. . .]¹⁵

NOTES TO DOCUMENT NO. 7

1 On proposals to create a Jewish army, see, *inter alia*, Monty Noam Penkower, *The Jews Were Expendable: Free World Diplomacy and the Holocaust* (Urbana, 1983), pp. 3–29.
2 Avraham Rafael Elmaleh (Almaliah) – noted lexicographer, one of the leaders of the Sefardic Jewish community in Palestine.
3 See Document No. 5, n. 5.
4 Emil Schmorak – Zionist leader from Lwów, former chairman of Zionist Federation of East Galicia. In 1938 he took charge of the Department of Trade and Industry of the Jewish Agency Executive. He was a member of the Agency's Committee on Polish Jewry organized in 1940, which eventually evolved into the Rescue Committee.
5 The reference is to Rabbi Yitshak HaLevi Herzog, former chief rabbi of Ireland, who in 1936 was named Ashkenazic chief rabbi of Palestine. He was the father of the current president of Israel, Hayim Herzog.
6 Kuibyshev – city on Volga River, about 900 kilometres southeast of Moscow, which served as the temporary capital of the Soviet Union during the period of the German invasion (1941–43).
7 Volksdeutsche – ethnic Germans of foreign (in this case Polish) citizenship.
8 ONR – abbreviation for Obóz Narodowo-Radykalny (National Radical Camp), a right-wing Polish political organization established in 1934, which demonstrated strong anti-Jewish tendencies.
9 Description of events parallel to that in Document No. 1 omitted.
10 The reference is to the suicide of Adam Czerniakow, chairman of the Warsaw *Judenrat*, on 23 July 1942, at the outset of the mass deportation of Jews from the Warsaw ghetto to Treblinka. Czerniakow did not take his own life, as Kot implied, because of 'the awful conditions in the ghettos', but because he would not cooperate with the Germans in facilitating the deportation.
11 Passage referring to letters received from Jews attesting to this desire ellipsised.
12 The reference is evidently to telegram no. 218, despatched from Kuibyshev to London on 24 November 1942 by Tadeusz Romer, who had replaced Kot as Polish ambassador to the Soviet Union. This cable contained the information quoted by Kot in Document No. 5 (reference n. 14). Hoover Institution Archives, Lt. Colonel Borkowski, Box 1.
13 References to various reports on the situation of Jews in Russia ellipsised.
14 Maksim Litvinov – Soviet ambassador to the United States; former commissar for foreign affairs.
15 List of those present omitted.

THE POLISH GOVERNMENT-IN-EXILE AND THE HOLOCAUST 303

Document No. 8
[Description of Kot's first meeting with Grünbaum. Hoover Institution Archives, Władysław Anders, Box 70, Document 156]

Extract from the Minutes of the Meeting of the Executive of the Jewish Agency for Palestine, 17 December 1942

Mr. Grünbaum: He and Dr. Schmorak visited Professor Kot. During the visit Professor Kot read to them various horrifying documents about the situation of the Jews in Poland. At the conclusion of the talk Professor Kot asked Grünbaum to meet him again, and in the event he was invited to visit Professor Kot the next morning. The discussion was quite long and lasted, with a break for lunch, from 11:30 am to 6:30 pm; and it was not completed. Yesterday a second meeting with Professor Kot took place (at Mr. Grünbaum's apartment). This discussion, too, lasted from 11:30 to 4:30, with a break for lunch. These talks will continue. The members (of the Executive – translator's remark) will receive the minutes of these talks. (Here Mr. Grünbaum inserted in his own handwriting; 'not written due to lack of time').[1] He will endeavour on this occasion to give only a brief summary of the fundamental contents of the issues discussed with Professor Kot.

Regarding the question of acceptance of Jews into the Polish Army and the evacuation of Jewish refugees from Russia, Kot explained that at the beginning of the evacuation there was no interference on the part of the Russian authorities, while among the leaders of the Polish army there were those who had aimed to lower the number of Jews within the army. At the outset of the mobilization the number of Jews in the Polish army reached 30 per cent.

In the course of the talks, he hinted that some army officers exploited the Revisionist initiative to create a Jewish Legion within the Polish Army against the Jews.[2]

In the meantime the Russian Government interfered and issued detailed instructions to the effect that the Polish army should not accept candidates belonging to the national minorities who on 29 November 1939 were located in the territory occupied by Russia. At the same time the Russians tried to prove to the Jews that in fact it was the Poles who opposed accepting them into the army. He explained further that certain Polish officers took advantage of the Russian orders and expelled many Jews, but such officers were in a decided minority. He knows also that Russian officers sent groups of Jews and forced the Poles to induct them and transfer them from Russia with the Polish army. The Poles feared that this was a provocation on the Russian part. In general Professor Kot contended that the Russian Government changed its explanations and instructions in relation to the Polish army time after time; it made commitments but did not keep them. He holds the Russian Government responsible for the small number of Jews in the ranks of the Polish army and in the evacuation.

It is true that there are strong anti-Jewish tendencies in the Polish army; there have even been cases of anti-semitism. But he is ready to combat such incidents with all his might and to bring all those responsible before a court. He regrets that the Jews, and in particular the Jewish delegates in Teheran, have not supplied him with the relevant documents in these matters.

He repeated the same regarding the evacuation: what the right hand gives the left takes away. Once again he tried to prove that the main culprits are the Russians.

At this point Professor Kot argued that we have been mistaken in our assessment of General Anders's activities. It was he who brought the Jewish children to Teheran, and the Russians put obstacles even in their way.

With regard to aid, the charge that Jews were discriminated against in the distribution of aid is unfair. [. . .]³ He is aware that there are complaints and that there are those who make accusations, but each one of them has his own motives for this. He demands cooperation from us, especially that we do not hinder the action on behalf of Polish Jews in Russia that must be organized in Palestine. If we do not help now, our responsibility will be great indeed.

He asserted also that Jews have responded that while we have been receiving information about what is happening to the Jewish refugees in Russia, we do not take note of statements favourable to the Poles. As a result the documents in our possession are detrimental to the Polish authorities. Mr. Grünbaum firmly denied this and assured [Professor Kot] that he would present him all of the protocols and other materials, without names, of course, because many of the witnesses are in the army of the Polish [civil] service, and he would not wish anyone to come to any harm as a result. Professor Kot promised that no harm would be done to anybody, but Mr. Grünbaum stuck to his position.

Mr. Grünbaum asked Professor Kot to issue a recommendation to bring the Jewish children from Teheran to Palestine, where we would receive them. Professor Kot has not given an answer. At the same time he expressed surprise that we had not yet been able to secure a ship to transport these refugee children.

The discussion passed to the situation inside Poland. Mr. Grünbaum said that it was astonishing that the Germans were transporting Jews from all countries to Poland and killing them there alone. Professor Kot was shocked; he said: Is Mr. Grünbaum trying to say that this is because there is a more congenial climate in Poland for the killing of Jews?

Mr. Grünbaum's reply was that while there were indeed many Poles who helped Jews, on the other hand there was no general reaction on the part of the Poles against acts of extermination, such as there was in other countries. The Polish people should be stirred to help the Jewish people. Mr. Grünbaum received no answer to this suggestion.

Mr. Grünbaum also spoke with him about the need for the Polish Government to issue a declaration addressed to the neutral countries to the effect that Jewish refugees who found themselves in those countries would be allowed to return to Poland. This would greatly facilitate obtaining shelter for Jews in the neutral countries. Professor Kot did not reply to this either.

[. . .]4

Professor Kot told Mr. Grünbaum also that at a meeting of the National Council in London, Vice-Premier Mikołajczyk expressed his astonishment that some Jewish newspapers appear to be under the influence of the enemy in the conduct of their propaganda, since they consider it proper to agitate against Polish anti-semitism in these days of butchery. He added that the Government does not reveal anything about the activities of the Jewish police against the Jews themselves. It seems that there is much truth in these reports. The Government is concerned that if this information is published it would make a most unpleasant impression on the world.

NOTES TO DOCUMENT NO. 8

1 The passages in parentheses are the remarks of the person who translated the original Hebrew version of the minutes into Polish for the Document Bureau of the Polish army in Palestine. Many Jews were connected with the Document Bureau; prominent among them were members of the breakaway Revisionist wing of the Zionist movement. On this see David Engel, 'The Frustrated Alliance: The Revisionist Movement and the Polish Government-in-Exile, 1939–1945', *Studies in Zionism*, VII:1 (1986), pp. 27–8. The second parenthetic comment seems to suggest that the original Hebrew copy from which the Polish translation was made had at one time been in Grünbaum's possession; perhaps it was Grünbaum himself who supplied the copy.
2 The reference is to a proposal formally submitted to Anders in October 1941 by Marek Kahan and Miron Szeszkin, two activists in the Polish Revisionist Zionist movement, calling for the creation of separate Jewish units among the Polish forces then being mustered in the Soviet Union. On the genesis and ultimate fate of this proposal see Kalman Nussbaum, '"Legyon Yehudi" o Ahizat Einayim?' *Shvut*, X (1984), pp. 47–54. A facsimile of the original proposal by Kahan and Szeszkin has recently been reproduced in Shalom Slowes, *Yàar Katyn, 1940*, Tel Aviv 1986, pp. 225–26.
3 Arguments repeated from previous documents omitted.
4 Miscellaneous inconsequential matters omitted.

Document No. 9
[Description of Kot's second meeting with Grünbaum.
Hoover Institution Archives, Władysław Anders,
Box 70, Document 156]

Extract from the Minutes of the Meeting of the Executive of the Jewish Agency for Palestine, 24 January 1943

Mr. Grünbaum: He visited various places in Palestine together with Professor Kot. The weather was bad, and we could not carry out our complete plan. After their return to Jerusalem he had a conversation with him that lasted about five hours. Professor Kot told him that he would very much like to find a person or Jewish group with whom he could reach a general understanding and who would represent the Jewish people as the ally of the Polish Government. He did not find such a personality, and it is difficult to find a group; but it seems to him that the Zionist Organization is indeed a group with which it is possible to enter negotiations and to reach an agreement. They demand our assistance with regard to the Polish Government's call to the Allies in the matter of reprisals against the German Government. From Poland itself come calls to bomb German targets. They also demand that this be carried out by Polish airmen. The British Government is not prepared to provide planes for such a purpose, and they [the Polish Government] insist that we aid them in acquiring planes in [other] allied countries.

Mr. Grünbaum replied that in this matter there is no difference between us, and if there is any possibility we shall help the Polish Government. Professor Kot observed in passing that the military and civil authorities in Palestine regard the Jews and the Agency Executive with hostility.

Professor Kot also informed him that he did not enter into any talks with the Arabs. Poland has no interest in discussions with the Arabs. For him Palestine is the country of the Jews. Members (of the Jewish Agency Executive – translator's insertion)[1] certainly recall that the former Polish Government (before the war) had looked for a way to make a connection with the Arabs, and the Polish consulates in Palestine received instructions in this regard.

Continuing, Professor Kot said that it is necessary to prepare the peace now, and in this field the Jews possess the ability to help the Poles. Mr. Grünbaum explained to him that with regard to western Poland there will not be any differences of opinion at all; the heart of the matter is the territories of eastern Poland. This matter involves Russia in particular, and that complicates matters greatly. Mr. Kot said that with regard to western Poland the conviction prevails at present that it is indispensible to free East Prussia from the Germans, as well as Gdańsk and Silesia; but here one runs into Czechoslovakia, and the Czechs have recently retreated somewhat from their projected federation with Poland.

It is true that the question of the East concerns Russia in particular. The Russian Government left regular troops in the Ukraine to act as partisans. On their side the Germans mobilized some 150,000 Ukrainians who also act as partisans against the other ones. These groups live off the Ukrainian peasants, and for this reason the peasants have formed their own fighting units to fight against these other groups simultaneously. Thus there is complete chaos in the Ukraine. On the whole the Ukrainians joined with the Germans, and in Moscow there is open hatred of the Ukrainians. There is no doubt that at the conclusion of the war the Ukrainians will be liquidated by deporting millions of them to Siberia.

Mr. Grünbaum said that in relation to Bolshevism the Jewish attitude will depend on the régime. Should it appear the same as before the war, they [the Jews] would oppose any annexations to Russia, and their motives are understandable. It is, however, possible that a change of régime will take place, and then their attitude would also change.

Mr. Grünbaum expressed the conviction that the idea of the Polish Government's creating a Ministry of Jewish Affairs has been broached in Jewish circles because Jews in general do not give weight to declarations but demand action.

Mr. Kot expressed his surprise at our attitude towards declarations and expressed as well the fear that the matter of the ministry will encounter many difficulties that it will not be possible to overcome. In the course of discussion the issue was also raised of creating a separate department in the prime minister's office. Of course, these were more [in the nature of] ideas rather than conclusions. Regarding the latter idea, Kot said that it could be taken into consideration.

According to Professor Kot there is no hope at all that the evacuation of Polish citizens from Russia will still be possible. Our documents concerning the attitude of the Poles towards Jews in connection with the evacuation seem to him doubtful. In response to them Professor Kot claimed that he puts all the documents in his possession at our disposal, while we present him with extracts only. He is also certain that he will be able to defend the Government's position on this issue. In his reply Mr. Grünbaum explained that even without entering into a discussion of who is guilty or where the fault lies, it is a fact that only 6 per cent of those who arrived from Russia were Jews, while all estimates show that there are large masses of Jews there. No one will believe that there was no possibility of saving a greater number of Jews. Mr. Kot added that if the possibility of evacuation arises he will inform us immediately, so that we can present our claims for the consideration of the Polish Government.

Mr. Grünbaum raised issues concerning the Polish army. Mr. Kot read an extract from a report of a Polish general about Jews who came to

Palestine on the basis of our certificates. In spite of this they were brought to Polish army camps and inducted there. When they heard that they would have to submit once again to a medical examination, they disappeared and were consequently registered as deserters. The Jewish Agency demanded that these charges be withdrawn, and Professor Kot turned to the army command on this matter. A General replied that if these Jews would not return to Poland he would be prepared to cross their names off the list of deserters. Mr. Grünbaum explained that all who arrive in Palestine on the basis of immigrant certificates are potential citizens of Palestine, but it cannot be guaranteed that not a single one of them will wish to return to Poland. There is no justification for the conduct of the Polish command in registering them as deserters when they were brought to Palestine in Polish military vehicles holding immigrant certificates and discharge papers given them in Teheran in their hands. He firmly demanded that these accusations be withdrawn.

Professor Kot indicated that the Polish Government intends to call up all Polish citizens in Palestine to the ranks of the Polish army. Mr. Grünbaum reminded Mr. Kot of the agreement between us and the Polish Government about allowing Polish citizens to join Jewish units. Mr. Kot observed that this was not a negotiated agreement but that another order had been promulgated modifying the previous one. If the Agency Executive intends to bring about a change in this latest order, he suggests cabling Schwarzbart to make efforts in this direction. Should Schwarzbart not succeed, then we should approach him (i.e. Kot), and he would be ready to render assistance.

Also discussed was the question of aid for Jewish refugees in Russia. Professor Kot agreed to Mr. Grünbaum's proposal that we send special consignments and lists of persons to whom these consignments should be despatched. The lists would be given to Mr. Seide[n]man,[2] who will be appointed coordinator of all the matters pertaining to aid for Jews. If appropriate negotiations end successfully, this would free us from paying high duties to the Russian Government.

In the matter of the children and the demands made by the rabbis,[3] Mr. Grünbaum expects a visit from the representative of the Polish Government for refugee affairs. He asks Professor Kot that the Polish Government not interfere in this internal Jewish affair. It seems to him that Professor Kot accepted our point of view, but he has no definite answer. This morning we were notified that Rabbi Herzog wishes to consider this problem together with us. We informed him that our negotiations with the Polish Government have not yet been concluded, and only after their conclusion shall we approach him.

NOTES TO DOCUMENT NO. 9

1 See Document No. 8, n. 1.
2 Ludwik Seidenman (b. 1906) – Warsaw attorney active in the General Zionist movement. From 1941–43 he served as legal counsellor to the Polish Embassy in the USSR.
3 See Document No. 6.

THE STANISŁAW KOT COLLECTION, WARSAW

Bernadeta Tendyra

During a study trip to Poland in 1984 to collect material for my thesis on internal relations in General Sikorski's Polish Government in Exile 1939–43, I was given access to the Stanisław Kot Collection in the Peasant Movement History Institute Archives (AZHRL) which are kept at the United Peasant Party headquarters in Warsaw.

Professor Kot spent the last years of his life in exile, living in Paris and then London. Even before his death in 1975, his large archival collection was broken up. Part of it was transferred to Poland and deposited in the Peasant Party archives in 1969. Another part remained in the possession of the second wife of Kot's close friend, Professor Jan Hulewicz, in Kraków. Unfortunately, there is no access to these documents. The rest is deposited in the archives of the General Sikorski Historical Institute (GSHI) in London. Kot's academic works were transferred to the Jagiellonian Library in Kraków in 1964.

The Kot Collection in Warsaw is an invaluable source for research into the activities of the Polish wartime émigré government. Although it contains documents spanning a period from 1919 to 1949, eighty per cent of the material concerns the Second World War. It includes, amongst other things: Kot's personal files; reports from German-occupied Poland; the situation of Poles in former Eastern Poland (restricted access); Poles in Rumania, Hungary, France, Britain and the Middle East; the reconstruction of the Polish Armed Forces; the organization and activity of the Polish Government in Exile; the functioning of ministries and diplomatic bases; political parties in Poland; studies concerning post-war Poland; the emigre opposition to General Sikorski; press and propaganda; the situation of Polish prisoners and forced labourers in Germany; the plight of Jews in Poland, the USSR and in exile; finally, the activities of Polish émigrés in the USA. The remainder of the archive concerns inter-war Poland.

Two of the three following published documents are taken from Professor Kot's Warsaw Collection. The first is an extract from a report prepared by Mieczysław Harusewicz for the Polish Government authorities on the National Radical Camp (*ONR*), its work in Poland and attitude to activities in exile (AZHRL Stanisław Kot Collection File 82). The second is General Sikorski's reply to Harusewicz's request for admission to the National Council as *ONR* representative in exile (AZHRL Stanisław Kot Collection File 195). They form part of a rich and varied archive which should be more extensively researched by scholars of modern Polish history.

THE NATIONAL RADICAL CAMP (*ONR*)

The National Radical Camp came into being on 14 April 1934, when a group of young Warsaw activists broke with the National Party to form a new, extreme radical movement. Led by Henryk Rossman, Jan Mosdorf, Tadeusz Gluziński and Bolesław Piasecki, they had become disillusioned with the leadership's perceived inertia, lack of solutions to Piłsudski's coup and reluctance to implement the radical nationalist programme advocated by the *endecja* youth.

In December 1926, Roman Dmowski founded the Great Poland Camp (*OWP*), a new political structure aimed at unifying nationalist elements against the *sanacja* and at ending the dissipation which had contributed to the coup. Its long-term aim was an all-embracing national organization to take power from Piłsudski, deal with the Jews and the Left and begin constructing a great and powerful Poland. The *OWP*, based on hierarchy, discipline and personal responsibility, emulated but did not wholly approve the fascist dictatorships emerging in Germany and Italy. In search of its own solution to the Parliamentary crisis, it turned increasingly to extra-Parliamentary methods, working uncomfortably alongside first the Popular National Union (*ZLN*), then the National Party (*SN*), both of which advocated a more conventional, Parliamentary route to power.

The *OWP's* Youth Section, the *Młodzi*, who enjoyed considerable autonomy within the organization, came to dominate the whole national camp. Spurred on by Dmowski, their ideas grew increasingly radical. The main tenets included: supremacy of the nation, based on Roman Catholicism, civilization and statehood; strict union between Church and state, in the interests of God and the Polish nation; tradition, hierarchy and discipline in state affairs; rejection of defunct Parliamentarianism in favour of strong, dynamic leadership and resort to force to achieve it; a socio-economic system based on conservatism and the status quo; elimination of Jews from national life with a view to eventual forced migration; an equally energetic struggle against the Left; unlimited expansion east, with incorporation of populations spiritually or ethnically linked to Poland; finally, an acute awareness of the permanent and most dangerous German threat. The *Młodzi* strove to fuse traditional postulates of the nationalist movement with new ones characteristic of the emerging fascism. Set against the backdrop of economic collapse, their ideas proved particularly potent amongst the frustrated young middle class intelligentsia, which joined the party in large numbers.

The activity of the *Młodzi* became increasingly violent as Piłsudski consolidated his dictatorship. This, together with their growing membership and formal incorporation into the *OWP* Executive Committee, led the authorities to delegalize the *OWP* in March 1933. The disbanded organization now merged with the *SN*, which immediately created conflict between the *Młodzi*, used to having their way in the *OWP* and the so-called *Starzy*, who favoured a greater degree of democracy and cooperation with the legal opposition to Piłsudski. Ultimately the *Starzy*, whilst allowing the *Młodzi* a measure of autonomy, insisted upon their formal subordination to the *SN* leadership. This proved the sticking point which split the party.

The situation came to a head when a section of the Warsaw *Młodzi*, frustrated by the constraints and ideological conformity imposed by the *Starzy*, appealed to Dmowski to radicalize the *SN*. Dmowski, however, whilst inspiring their radical views, would not accept the creation of a new, fascist organization. When this failed, they left the *SN* to form the *ONR*. Another split occurred in Poznan with the formation of the Union of Nationalist Youth (*ZMN*), which eventually cooperated with the *sanacja*. At first, attempts were made to universalize the split amongst the *endecja Młodzi*, but opposition from the established party proved tougher than expected. The *ONR* ultimately remained a Warsaw organization and its membership never exceeded the 5000 mark. Links with the *SN Młodzi* remained strong.

The *ONR*'s structure and programme reflected the Dmowski young *endecja* school, whence it derived with a more extreme interpretation and its implementation outside the traditional national camp. It retained the *OWP*'s hierarchical structure with its various levels of initiation, the top level remaining hidden even from the formal highest party authorities. Its programme, launched on 14 April 1934, drew logical conclusions from the fascist trend sweeping the *Młodzi*, with selected exaggerations of accepted ideology. Unusually, it adopted a very different approach to socio-economic issues, emphasizing the need for greater social equality and justice; protection of the working man and family; agricultural reform; appropriation of large estates without compensation and nationalization of public assets. But in other areas, it was the degree rather than the ideology which differed. Extreme solutions to the Jewish question were adopted, with the *ONR* becoming notorious for its fighting squads and street attacks on Jews, socialists and other 'proscribed' elements. Nor did it hide its fascination for the dynamic totalitarian movements taking power abroad, seeing in their methods the means of building a great, strong, Catholic, all-Polish Poland. The immediate priority, however, was to remove the *Sanacja*, by force if necessary.

Not surprisingly, the *ONR*'s legal existence lasted just three months. On 16 June 1934, using Pieracki's assassination as a pretext, the authorities banned the organization and locked up its leaders in the Bereza Kartuska. Thereafter, the *ONR* continued its activities on a semi-legal basis, working through established national organizations, infiltrating the *SN* and *sanacja* youth movements and printing its weekly paper, the *ONR-ABC*. Its inability to operate openly, however, made the expansion of its cadres increasingly difficult. The *ONR* itself split in April 1935 when Bolesław Piasecki and his followers, wanting a single leader for the organization and dissatisfied with the *ONR*'s close links with the *SN*, its secret hierarchy from which Piasecki himself was excluded and some of its economic postulates, broke away to form the *ONR-Falanga* (named after the group's publication). This organization proved even more extreme and violent than its predecessor.

After Piasecki's departure, the *ONR-ABC* gradually changed its position from confrontation to that of negotiation with the *sanacja* (as also did Piasecki) but with limited success. The growing German threat made consolidation imperative; the negotiations aimed, therefore, to create a broad-ranging camp including the government, the Peasant Party 'Piast', the *SN* and the *ONR*. Ideological differences proved too great to bridge the divide. In the last years of the Second Republic, the Radical Movement's influence dwindled as the external threat grew, and it was to remain in this critical period on the more extreme fringes of Polish political life.

With the outbreak of the Second World War the *ONR*, wanting to fight the invader but also believing that a strong military organization would secure political power in post-war Poland, formed the *Związek Jaszczurczy* (*ZJ*) and the *Szaniec* Group to lead it (whilst Piasecki's group created the National Confederation). With its secret structure and semi-legal existence from before the War, it was better prepared for underground activity than most other parties. Almost immediately after the collapse of Warsaw, it began to produce a duplicated information bulletin from radio monitoring, which soon evolved into the Szaniec publication produced by Henryk Minich and Mieczysław Harusewicz. At the same time, the party's leadership and aims were formed, the first fighting units began training and contacts were established with other underground organizations.

A pressing problem was to ensure the *ONR*'s proper representation in the newly-formed Polish government in Paris. In October 1939, a former *ONR* leader, Jerzy Kurcjusz, announced his intention of going to France as the party's representative. This did not accord with the wishes of the party hierarchy, which decided to send one of its founding members,

Dr Tadeusz Gluziński, as delegate instead. Kurcjusz and Gluziński left Warsaw in December 1939 but the latter died whilst crossing the mountains to Hungary. To bridge this unexpected gap, Mieczysław Harusewicz was nominated to take Gluziński's place. Arriving in Paris around Easter 1940, he found the *ONR* formally represented in the National Council by Stanisław Jóźwiak who, while supporting the *ONR*'s programme before the War, had not been active in the party. Jóźwiak himself stated at the beginning of a speech in the National Council on 9 March 1940 that he represented the Polish gentry, not a particular party programme, even though he had been an *ONR* member in inter-war Poland.[1]

At the same time, Jerzy Kurcjusz, who had arrived in Paris before Harusewicz, began talks with Professor Kot for admission to the National Council as *ONR* representative. Harusewicz, meanwhile, had been instructed not to enter the government but to settle military matters and to join the Council, which he attempted to do immediately on arrival. The attached document, concerning the *ONR*'s attitude to working with the government, was prepared at this time as clarification of the organization's position. Harusewicz managed to persuade Kurcjusz to resign from his plans but he was less successful with Sikorski. After the government's evacuation to London, Sikorski sent a negative reply to Harusewicz's request (see attached document dated 23 August 1940). The Committee of the *ONR* in Exile retorted in a statement published in the *Jestem Polakiem* (I am a Pole) journal on 1 September 1940 (see attached document).

Sikorski clearly felt constrained by the opposition of the four parties forming the Government of National Unity. The Nationalist S(*SN*) probably backed Harusewicz's inclusion in the National Council but it is doubtful whether the Peasant Party (*SL*), the Party of Labour (*SP*) and the Polish Socialist Party (*PPS*) would welcome it. Sikorski was also under pressure from the British authorities over alleged anti-semitism in the Polish army and political circles. The Foreign and War Offices spent several months investigating these allegations, concluding that while the official Polish attitude was beyond reproach (most recently manifested by Sikorski's Order of the Day to the Army of 5 August 1940 denouncing divisions of creed or religion) the situation was different at the grass roots level.[2]

Grievances over alleged Polish anti-semitism focused on the *Jestem Polakiem* journal, with which the *ONR* was closely associated. The *Evening Standard* attacked the publication on 20 August 1940[3] and on 22 August, following complaints from constituents, W. Gallacher put a question in the House of Commons to Minister of Information Nicholson about *Jestem Polakiem*, in which a 'violently anti-Jewish' article by Marian Seyda had appeared.[4] Seyda subsequently denied that he had any connections with *Jestem Polakiem* but the damage had been done.[5] Sikorski had to be seen to act. Already on 21 August, he wrote to Mikołajczyk about British complaints and urged the latter to call a meeting of party leaders, demanding the suspension of all émigré political journals other than official government ones.[6] Moreover, in a report to the Central Department of 20 September, the British Ambassador to Poland, Sir Howard Kennard, related that Sikorski had personally condemned the anti-semitic activities of the *ONR* and *Jestem Polakiem* and had promised energetic measures to suppress them.[7] On 22 November, a Polish government communique appeared in the *Polish Daily*, stating that only one émigré political paper was to be published urging individuals to cease publication and denouncing the editors of *Jestem Polakiem*, who had refused to comply with the request.[8] *Jestem Polakiem* was finally suppressed by the British censors in April 1941.

After Harusewicz's understandable failure to secure a place in the National Council, the *ONR*'s Committee in Exile ceased to function effectively. Individual members involved themselves in the publication of *Jestem Polakiem* and later *Walka* (Battle) and Harusewicz maintained close contacts with Tadeusz Bielecki and Adam Demidowicz-Demidecki of the *SN* and Adam Doboszyński, Zygmunt Przetakiewicz and Father Edward Bełch, who edited the two publications. Members of both the *ONR-ABC* and *Falanga* joined Bielecki's National Camp Committee in Exile (*KZON*), which was formed in January 1942 in opposition to Sikorski's Russian policy. This committee remained in existence until the autumn of 1943, but its achievements never equalled its ambitions. The same could be said of the *ONR* in exile. (For the *ONR*'s activities in war-time and post-war Poland, in the *ZJ*, the *Szaniec* Group, later in the National Armed Forces [*NSZ*] and the Świętokrzyska Brigade and for Piasecki's post-war leadership of *PAX*, see Zbigniew Siemaszko's *Narodowe Siły Zbrojne*, London, 1982.)

NOTES

1 GSHI A. 5. 1/5 Fourth meeting of the National Council, 9 March 1940.
2 The issue of anti-semitism in the Polish Army and its investigation in 1940 are discussed in the following: C5143/5143/55; C6231/5143/55; C8802/5143/55; C8923/5143/55 FO 371/24481 PRO.
3 C8923/5143/55 FO 371/24481 PRO.
4 Parliamentary Debates (Commons) CCCLXIV col. 1493. See also: CCCLXIV col. 769; CCCLXV col. 145–6.
5 C9020/9020/55 FO 371/24483 PRO.
6 GSHI Dz.Cz.N.W. August 1940 Part I Sikorski to Mikołajczyk 21 August 1940.
7 C10125/5143/55 FO 371/24481 PRO.
8 C9020/9020/55 FO 371/24483 PRO.

DOCUMENTS

The Position of the *ONR* Regarding Activities in Exile

As early as last December the Leadership of the National Radical Camp [*ONR*] sent its delegate, the late Dr. Tadeusz Gluziński,[1] who was to declare to the Polish Government in Paris our readiness to cooperate in the cause of rebuilding the Polish State and its Army. As we know, our first delegate gave his life for his mission before reaching his goal. Counsellor Jerzy Kurcjusz,[2] who accompanied him, arrived in mid-February in Paris, where he found that the Government had received Gluziński's letter, which he wrote in the middle of January this year, announcing the arrival of our delegate.

Aware of our Organization's belief that any cooperation should officially commence with the admittance of our delegate to the National Council of the Polish Republic, immediately on his arrival, Counsellor Jerzy Kurcjusz raised this matter in talks with Government Leaders.

Regarding its participation in the National Council, the *ONR* is guided by the following premises: the unanimous view of the whole Country is that the National Council is its representative body, that is a kind of *Sejm* by proxy. The Polish Government, which was formed in exile in special circumstances and without the Nation's participation, by creating the Council has expressed its fundamental view that every government should be established and upheld by the public. This is entirely in agreement with the democratic principles which the present Government regards as the foundation of the future edifice of the Polish State.

The National Council includes not only representatives from all Polish political groups, but even an official Jewish representative, despite the fact that the name of the Council does not mirror the body of its members composed in that manner.

The *ONR*, which does not have a representative on the Council, trusts that the only reason for this state of affairs has been the absence in France so far of its delegate specifically authorized to represent the *ONR* on the National Council. That is why I have been sent in the capacity of this special delegate.

In every political organization stemming from a far-reaching ideological current which pervades society, the influence of the movement's leadership on its wider masses and tendencies and the emotional attitude of those masses to the leading elements conflict with and complement each other. The Leaders of the *ONR* see a quite considerable danger in continuing to leave our Movement outside regular participation in the life of the state in the perception of the broad masses of our supporters. What must be considered is that for six years now our movement has existed in these abnormal conditions and this was bound to have had some influence on the evolution of the 'desperado' and 'anti-state activist' mentality. Since there has been a tendency to attribute all administrative persecution which befell us to the influence of the Jews, the present situation – when there is a Jewish representative on the Council yet none from the *ONR*, cannot but have undesirable significance. At the same time it must be remembered that, in the light of the tremendous outrage felt against the Jews as a result of reports from the Eastern occupation zone, perhaps only the anti-semitic parties will be able to explain at the suitable time why the Jewish question should be solved by way of evolution and not revolution which would then be imminent.

Angers, 31st March 1940 (Signed) Ing. Harusewicz[3]

NOTES

1 Tadeusz Gluziński – one of the *ONR*'s founding members. In 1939, *ONR* delegate to the Polish Government in Exile.
2 Jerzy Kurcjusz – former member of *ONR*'s highest authorities. In 1939 self-appointed *ONR* emissary to the Polish Government-in-Exile, later Head of Continental Operations in Turkey.
3 Mieczysław Harusewicz – *ONR* delegate to the Polish Government-in-Exile 1940, later Head of Committee of *ONR* in Exile.

FROM THE CHAIRMAN OF THE COUNCIL OF MINISTERS

Reference: 2011/XIX/40

London, 23 August, 1940

Further to our conversation last week, I would like to inform you that during a meeting of party representatives yesterday the view was expressed (three against one) that in the present circumstances, in consideration of State interests, an increase in the number of *ONR* representatives on the National Council was not recommended. At the same time it was established (ascertained) that Mr Jóźwiak[4] represented that faction on the National Council.

There was also expressed the view that the recent, immature political manoeuvering, which led to the significant debate in the House of Commons yesterday, has made any nomination whatsoever of *ONR* representatives to the National Council impossible at present. This is because, rightly or wrongly, it would be interpreted by English public opinion as reinforcement of anti-democratic and racialist tendencies in the Polish camp. The representatives of the political parties also demanded that the attitude of the *ONR* group which you represent to other factions of that camp, which back at home are endeavouring to spread pro-nazi ideology and striving towards political collaboration with the Germans be clarified.

With reference to the information with which you supplied me, I regret having to state that it is wholly unfounded and based on your informers' ill-will. Should you, therefore, wish to acquaint yourself with the true state of affairs, please apply to the Secretary who will provide you with any information you may require in this matter.

In replying to your proposals and clarifying the matters raised by you, I appeal to you to abandon here, on English soil, the pursuit of the racialist and anti-democratic slogans which harm Poland. Appreciation of the political situation is a duty not only of the Government but also of all citizens, in particular those who, bearing in mind Poland's interest, want to engage in active work for her.

For my part, should I find your understanding for the only just position at the present time, you may count on my assistance in doing positive work for the Country.

(Signed) Sikorski[5]
Chairman of the Council of Ministers

To Mr. M. Harusewicz, Ing.
By Hand

NOTES

4 Stanisław Jóźwiak – *ONR* representative in the National Council, as recognized by the Polish Government authorities.
5 Władysław Sikorski - Premier of the Polish Government in Exile, Commander in Chief of the Polish Armed Forces.

PUBLISHED IN: *JESTEM POLAKIEM* 1 SEPTEMBER 1940

Exposé
Sir,

We, the Committee of the National Radical Camp [*ONR*] in Exile, would be grateful if you could publish the following statement in your popular publication: –

The National Radical Camp, which was born in the struggle against the evils that have reigned in Poland's public life in the last several years, did, as the vanguard of that struggle by the young generation, suffer the greatest persecution at the hands of the ruling régime since, on instruction of the administrative authorities, it was disbanded, thereby being deprived, through these totalitarian ruling methods, of the ability to participate officially in the political life of the country. In view of the establishment of the Government of National Unity as a result of Poland's defeat, the *ONR* regards it as its duty to express its approval of the actions of this government and its willingness to participate in these.

A specific expression of the *ONR* position was the successive dispatch from Poland of two special envoys to the Polish Government. The first of these, the late Dr Tadeusz Gluziński, gave his life for his mission on the way there. The next delegate, who successfully reached the seat of the Polish Government late this March, informed the Government of his mandate, which first and foremost carried with it the duty and the right to represent the *ONR* on the National Council, where, out of all the Polish parties, the *ONR* was the only one not represented.

Although the Head of the Government had declared that the Government's fundamental position, it being the Government of National Unity, was that of cooperation with every Polish party, and in spite of repeated promises of positive resolution in the matter of *ONR* representation, for five months the *ONR* delegate and Committee in Exile have loyally and hopefully waited in vain for the Government's official response to their application. Finally, a letter from the Chairman of the Council of Ministers, dated 23rd of this month, brought us a negative reply regarding the appointment of an *ONR* delegate to the National Council. The letter contained the following reasons:

(1) that Mr Stanisław Jóźwiak was the *ONR* representative on the National Council.
(2) That politically [sic] immature manoeuvres were making the nomination of an *ONR* representative impossible at present.
(3) that doubts existed as to the *ONR*'s attitude towards elements at home, advocating pro-Nazi ideology and striving for political cooperation with the Germans.

In view of the above, we feel it is our duty to make the following public statement:

(1) Mr Stanisław Jóźwiak neither has been nor is a representative of the *ONR*, as he himself clearly stated, prior to our delegate's arrival, in a speech at a National Council meeting on 8 March this year, declaring

that he did not represent the programme of any party. This speech was carried by the Polish press in Paris, including Issue 63 of *Narodowiec*, and the Government is obviously familiar with it.

(2) We see no causal connections between some unidentified, allegedly immature political manoeuvres and the matter of our representation on the National Council. For various reasons, our political activity in exile has so far been limited to contacts with top Polish state institutions, several members of the National Council and political figures.

(3) Our organization derives from the pan-Polish movement which, of all the Polish political movements, was the only one that, for dozens of years, consistently and without deviation, has been uncompromisingly fighting Germanism in all its forms. In this respect, no one is or will be able to level against us any accusation based on fact, particularly as regards our attitude to the most dangerous form of Germanism which is represented by Nazism. There is, however, a long list of facts, signified by the crosses that mark our graves and the crosses that mark our chests, which present an irrefutable record of our selfless participation in the Nation's struggle against our ancient foe.

In making the above public, we note that the *ONR*'s readiness to take on the burden of cooperation in and joint responsibility for working for Poland in exile has been undermined by the Government, that we are the only Polish political party deprived of the ability to participate officially in activities in exile and that the great masses of our devoted Polish youth, who have been working devotedly and sacrificing their lives from the first day of the war, are deprived of their representative on the National Council.

At the same time the *ONR* Committee in Exile declares that, in spite of the known state of affairs, the *ONR* will continue to work persistently for Poland and to fight her foes wherever it can. No promises or offers, nor attempts at intimidation or threats will prevent us or lead us astray from this, just as the six years of persecution and Bereza[6] and its fatalities in their time did not have the designed effect.

The Committee of the National Radical Camp in Exile London, 28 August 1940.

Names supplied for the Editor's information only, owing to links with Poland evident from the contents.

NOTES

6 Bereza Kartuska – isolation camp for political prisoners 1934–39, created by the *Sanacja* authorities.

COMMENTARY

THE POOR POLES LOOK AT THE GHETTO
Jan Błoński[1]

On more than one occasion Czesław Miłosz has spoken in a perplexing way of the duty of Polish poetry to purge the burden of guilt from our native soil which is – in his words – 'defiled, blood-stained, desecrated'.[2] His words are perplexing, because one can only be held accountable for the shedding of blood which is not one's own. The blood of one's own kind, when shed by victims of violence, stirs memories, arouses regret and sorrow, demands repect. It also calls for remembrance, prayer, justice. It can also allow for forgiveness, however difficult this may be. The blood of the other, however, even if spilt in a legitimate conflict, is quite another matter but it also does not involve desecration. Killing when in self-defence is legally condoned, though it is already a departure from Christian moral law: Christ ordered Peter to put away his sword. Whenever blood is spilt it calls for reflection and penance. Not always, however, can it be said to desecrate the soil.

What Miłosz means here is neither the blood of his compatriots nor that of the Germans. He clearly means Jewish blood, the genocide which – although not perpetrated by the Polish nation – took place on Polish soil and which has tainted that soil for all time. That collective memory which finds its purest voice in poetry and literature cannot forget this bloody and hideous stigma. It cannot behave as if it never happened. Occasionally one hears voices, especially among the young, who were not emotionally involved in the tragedy, saying: 'We reject the notion of collective responsibility. We do not have to return to the irrevocable past. It is enough if we condemn this crime *in toto* as we do with any injustice, any act of violence.' What I say to them is this: 'Our country is not a hotel in which one launders the linen after the guests have departed. It is a home which is built primarily on memory; memory is at the core of our identity. We cannot dispose of it at will, even though as individuals we are not directly responsible for it. We must carry it within us even though it is unpleasant or painful. We must also strive to expiate it.'

How should this be done? To purify after Cain means, above all, to remember Abel. This particular Abel was not alone, he shared our home, lived on our soil. His blood has remained in the walls, seeped into the soil. It has also entered into ourselves, into our memory. So we must cleanse ourselves, and this means we must see ourselves in the light of truth. Without such an insight, our home, our soil, we ourselves will remain tainted. This is, if I understand correctly, the message of our poet. Or, at any rate, this is how Miłosz sees his duty, while calling upon us at the same time to also assume this obligation.

How difficult this task is can be seen from Miłosz's celebrated poem *Campo di Fiori*. At the heart of it there is the image of the merry-go-round which was – by chance, but what a coincidence! – built in Krasiński Square in Warsaw just before the outbreak of the ghetto rising. When the fighting broke out, the merry-go-round did not stop; children, youngsters and passers-by crowded around it as before:

> ... Sometimes the wind from burning houses
> Would bring the kites along
> And people on the merry-go-round
> Caught the flying charred bits.
> This wind from the burning houses
> Blew open the girls' skirts
> And the happy throngs laughed
> On a beautiful Warsaw Sunday ...
>
> [translated by A. Gillon]

Miłosz compares 'the happy throng' to the crowd of Roman vendors who – only a moment after the burning at the stake of Giordano Bruno – went merrily about their business as before, enjoying their 'pink fruits of the sea' and 'baskets of olives and lemons' as if nothing had happened. He ends the poem with reflections of 'the loneliness of the dying', who have 'the word of the poet' for their only consolation. It is only the word, the poet seems to be saying, which can preserve what can still be saved. It purges the memory by voicing a protest against the passing away and 'the forgetting which is beginning to grow/Even before the flame dies down'.

The act of remembering and mourning fixes in the memory the image of the stake in the middle of the market place or that of a merry-go-round on the grave. The success of the poem itself – which is often quoted and has been translated into many languages – is a clear proof of that. In its Hebrew version, the poem may appear as evidence of the hostile indifference of the Poles in the face of the Holocaust. Years later Miłosz wonders 'whether there really was such a street in Warsaw. It existed and, in another sense, it did not. It did exist because there were indeed merry-go-rounds in the vicinity of the ghetto. It didn't because in other parts of town, at other moments Warsaw was quite different. It was not my intention to make accusations.'[3] The poem, he concedes, is too 'journalistic', allowing one too easily to draw conclusions. It simplifies truth and by so doing, soothes the conscience. Worse, the poet discovers that he has written 'a very dishonest poem'. Why? Because – I quote – 'it is written about the act of dying from the standpoint of an observer.' So it is; the piece is so composed that the narrator, whom we presume to be the poet, himself, comes off unscathed. Some are dying, others are enjoying themselves, all that he does is to 'register a protest' and walk away, satisfied by thus having composed a beautiful poem. And so, years later, he feels he got off too lightly. Matched against the horrors of what was occurring at the time, he says, the act of writing is 'immoral'. *Campo di Fiori* does not succeed in resolving the conflict between life and art. Miłosz adds in his defence that the poem was composed as 'an ordinary human gesture in the spring of 1943' and, of course, we must immediately concede that it was a magnanimous human gesture. During that tragic Easter, it saved – as someone put it somewhat grandiloquently – 'the honour of Polish poetry'. We agree with the poet, though, that the last word on the subject has yet to be spoken.

This agonizing over a poem may perhaps help us understand why we are still unable to come to terms with the whole of the Polish-Jewish past. Here then I shall abandon literature and draw directly on my personal experience. Perhaps, on reflection, not even very personal, as almost everybody who has travelled abroad, especially in the West, must have had this question put to him at one time or other: 'Are Poles anti-semites?' Or, more bluntly: 'Why are Poles anti-semites?' I myself have heard it so many times, and so many times I have tried to explain, that I could attempt a thumbnail sketch of some twenty or so of such conversations:

– Are Poles anti-semites?

– Why do you put your question in this way? There are Poles who are anti-semites, some others who are philo-semites, and a growing number who do not care either way.

– Well, yes, of course, but I am asking about the majority. Poles have always had a reputation for being anti-semites. Could this be an accident?

– What do you mean by 'always'? Wasn't it true that at a time when Jews were expelled from England, France and Spain, it was in Poland and not elsewhere, that they found refuge?

– Yes, maybe, but that was a long time ago, in the Middle Ages. At that time Jews were the objects of universal contempt. But at least since the mid-eighteenth century in Europe, there has always been a problem of Polish intolerance.

– But it is exactly at that time that Poland disappeared from the map of Europe!

– Polish society, however, continued to exist and the Jews could not find their place within it. Why?

– We were under foreign rule; we had to think of ourselves first.

– This is precisely what I mean. Why could you not think of yourselves together with the Jews?

– They were too numerous. We did not have sufficient resources. We could not provide for their education, judiciary, administration. Jews didn't even speak Polish: they preferred to learn Russian or German. But there were enlightened people among us who advocated the course of assimilation and strove to bring the two communities together.

– But why? Why couldn't Jews simply remain Jews? You were also responsible for pogroms, why?

– It is not true, the first pogroms took place in the Ukraine and they were provoked by the Tsarist police...

And so such discussions continue:

– When you regained independence, the fate of Jews did not improve. On the contrary, anti-semitism became even more vicious.

– You can't change society in only twenty years, and besides that, was it not much the same elsewhere in Europe at the time? In the aftermath of the First World War we received many Jews from Russia and after 1934, from Germany.

– That may be true, but you still treated them as second class citizens. During the war you saved too few.

– There is in Israel a place commemorating people who saved Jews during the war. Thirty per cent of the names on that list are Polish names.

– But the percentage of Jews who survived the war in Poland is low, the lowest in Europe in relation to a total number of the population.

– In 1942 there were four Jews for every eight Poles in Warsaw. Now, how is it possible for the eight to hide the four?

– It was indeed the Poles who used to identify Jews and passed them on to the Germans and to the police which was, let us not forget, Polish.

– In every society there is a handful of people without conscience. You have no idea what the German occupation in Poland was like. To hide one Jew, meant risking the life of one's whole family, children included.

– Yes, that's true, but there were equally brutal repressions for the

underground activities and a great number of people were involved in them. Following the war Jews did not wish to remain in Poland.
— Indeed. It was difficult for them to live surrounded by memories.
— It was difficult for them to live among Poles who did not wish to give them back their houses and shops and threatened and even killed some of them. Have you not heard of the pogroms in Kraków and Kielce?
— The pogrom in Kielce was a political provocation.
— Even if it was, so what? It did find a response. Ten thousand people besieged the Jewish house in Kielce. Ten thousand people can't be provocateurs.
— Jews were sometimes a target not for being Jews but for sympathizing with communists.
— In 1968, is it because they were communists that they had to leave Poland?

And so on, indeed, endlessly. The debates of historians resemble this discussion. The same arguments and events — only more carefully documented — appear time and again. There is a vast body of literature, both of a personal and documentary nature, of which we have very little idea in Poland. We should, however, know it better, because it also refers to us. It contains a wide range of viewpoints and opinions. There are books whose authors do not hide that they are motivated by hate. We cannot afford to ignore them; they are born of personal experiences the authenticity of which cannot be doubted. And, besides, haven't we ourselves produced works which are equally full of hatred, sometimes hysterical hatred, toward Jews?

There are also many books which are cautious and, as far as is possible, devoid of partisanship. These books carefully remind us of the intellectual as well as the material conditions of Polish-Jewish co-existence. They take into account the terror, unimaginable today, of life under the German occupation and a certain moral degradation of the society which was a direct result of life under this enormous pressure. This, in fact, was not a uniquely Polish experience; it happened also elsewhere.[4] They make a tacit assumption that tragedies of Eastern Europe cannot be measured by the yardstick of, say, the English experience. When the skies are literally falling in, even a kick can be an expression of sympathy and compassion. The truth, however, remains difficult to determine and difficult to accept. Two years ago I attended a discussion in Oxford between some foreign and some Polish specialists, and I must confess that it was a distressing experience. For us as well as for the Jewish participants, I suppose. We were a long way from agreeing with each other, but that is not the aim of such conferences. I was continuously aware of what was not being said there and what is the main reason why these discussions – friendly, for the most part – were painful for all concerned. It was later that I came to the conclusion that this was due to the sense of a kind of contamination, a feeling of being somehow soiled and defiled, which is what Miłosz had in mind in the passage noted above.

And that is why I would like to go back once more to the poet. In 1943 Miłosz wrote another poem about the destruction of the ghetto, a poem entitled 'A poor Christian looks at the ghetto'. It is more ambiguous, perhaps more difficult to understand. It opens with the image of destruction:

> It has begun: the tearing, the trampling on silks,
> It has begun: the breaking of glass, wood, copper, nickel,
>   silver, foam
> Of gypsum, iron sheets, violin strings, trumpets, leaves,
>   Balls, crystals,

And later:

> The roof and the wall collapse in flame and heat seizes
>   the foundations,
> Now there is only the earth, sandy, trodden down,
> With one leafless tree.

The city was destroyed, what remained is the earth, full of broken shells and débris. It is also full of human bodies. In this earth, or rather under it:

> Slowly, boring a tunnel, a guardian mole makes his way,
> With a small red lamp fastened to his forehead.
> He touches burned bodies, counts them, pushes on.
> He distinguishes human ashes by their luminous vapour,
> The ashes of each man by a different part of the spectrum.

Who this mole is, it is difficult to say. Is he a guardian, perhaps a guardian of the buried? He has got a torch, so he can see; better, at any rate than the dead can see. And the poet himself, he is as if among the buried. He lies there with them. He fears something. He fears the mole. It is a striking, startling image:

> I am afraid, so afraid of the guardian mole,
> He has swollen eyelids, like a Patriarch
> Who has sat much in the light of the candles
> Reading the great book of the species.

And so this mole has the features of a Jew, poring over the Talmud or the Bible. It seems more likely that it is the Bible, as this alone deserves the name of 'the great book of the species', meaning, of course, the human species.

> What will I tell him, I, a Jew of the New Testament,
> Waiting two thousand years for the second coming of Jesus?
> My broken body will deliver me to his sight
> And he will count me among the helpers of death:
> The uncircumcised.
> [translated by Cz. Miłosz]

It is a terrifying poem; it is full of fear. It is as if two fears co-exist here. The first is the fear of death; more precisely, the fear of being buried alive, which is what happened to many people who were trapped in the cellars and underground passages of the ghetto. But there is also a second fear: the fear of the guardian mole. This mole burrows underground but also underneath our consciousness. This is the feeling of guilt which we do not want to admit. Buried under the rubble, among the bodies of the Jews, the 'uncircumcised' fears that he may be counted among the murderers. So it is the fear of damnation, the fear of Hell. The fear of a non-Jew who looks at the ghetto burning down. He imagines that he might accidentally die then and there, and in the eyes of the mole who can read the ashes, he may appear 'a helper of death'. And so, indeed, the poem is entitled: 'A poor Christian looks at the ghetto'. This Christian feels fearful of the fate of the Jews but also – muffled, hidden even from himself – he feels the fear that he will be condemned. Condemned by whom? By people? No, people have disappeared. It is the mole who condemns him, or rather *may* condemn him, this mole who sees well and reads 'the book of the species'. It is his own moral conscience which condemns (may condemn) the poor Christian. And he would like to hide from this mole-consciousness, as he does not know what to say to him.

Miłosz, when asked what or who is represented by this mole, declined to answer. He said that he had written the poem spontaneously, not to promote any particular thesis. If this is so, the poem would be a direct expression of the terror which speaks through images, as is often the case in dreams and also in art. It makes tangible something which is not fully comprehended, something that was and perhaps still is, in other people's as much as in the poet's own psyche, but in an obscure, blurred, muffled shape. When we read such a poem, we understand ourselves better, since that which had been evading us until now is made palpable. As for myself, I have – as probably every reader does – filled in the gaps in my own reading of 'A poor Christian . . .'. I hope, however, that I have not strayed too far from the intentions of the poet.

Here I return to the hypothetical conversation. It is a simplified summary of dozens of arguments and discussions. What is immediately striking here? In the replies of my fictitious Pole one detects the very same fear which makes itself felt in 'A poor Christian ...'. The fear that one might be counted among the helpers of death. It is so strong that we do everything possible not to let it out or to dismiss it. We read or listen to discussions on the subject of the Polish-Jewish past and if some event, some fact which puts us in a less-than-advantageous light, emerges, we try our hardest to minimize it, to explain it away and make it seem insignificant. It is not as if we want to hide what happened or deny that it took place. We feel, though, that not everything is as it should be. How could it have been otherwise? Relations between communities, like the relations of two people, are never perfect. How much more relations as stormy and unhappy as these. We are unable to speak of them calmly. The reason is that, whether consciously or unconsciously, we fear accusations. We fear that the guardian mole might call to us, after having referred to his book: 'Oh, yes, and you too, have you been assisting at the death? And you, too, have you helped to kill?' Or, at the very least: 'Have you looked with acquiescence at the death of the Jews?'

Let us think calmly: the question will have to be asked. Everybody who is concerned with the Polish-Jewish past must ask these questions, regardless of what the answer might be. But we – consciously or unconsciously – do not want to confront these questions. We tend to dismiss them as impossible and unacceptable. After all, we did not stand by the side of the murderers. After all, *we* were next in line for the gas chambers. After all, even if not in the best way possible, we did live together with the Jews; if our relations were less than perfect, they themselves were also not entirely without blame. So do we have to remind ourselves of this all the time? What will others think of us? What about our self-respect? What about the 'good name' of our society? This concern about the 'good name' is ever present in private, and even more so, in public discussion. To put it differently, when we consider the past, we want to derive moral advantages from it. Even when we condemn, we ourselves would like to be above – or beyond – condemnation. We want to be absolutely beyond any accusation, we want to be *completely* clean. We want to be also – and only – victims. This concern is, however, underpinned by fear – just as in Miłosz's poem – and this fear warps and disfigures our thoughts about the past. This is immediately communicated to those we speak to. We do not want to have anything to do with the horror. We feel, nevertheless, that it defiles us in some way. This is why we prefer not to speak of it all. Alternatively, we speak of it only in order to deny an accusation. The accusation is seldom articulated but is felt to hang in the air.[5]

Can we rid ourselves of this fear? Can we forestall it? I think not, as it lies, in all truth, in ourselves. It is we ourselves who fear the mole who burrows in our subconscious. I think that we shall not get rid of him. Or, at least we shall not get rid of him by forgetting about the past or taking a defensive attitude towards it. We must face the question of responsibility in a totally sincere and honest way. Let us have no illusions: it is one of the most painful questions which we are likely to be faced with. I am convinced, however, that we cannot shirk it.

We Poles are not alone in grappling with this question. It may be helpful to realize this. Not because it is easier to beat one's breast in company. Not because in this way the blame may appear less weighty. Rather because in this way we shall be able to understand it better. To understand both our responsibility and the reason why we try to evade it.

We read not so long ago about John Paul II's visit to the Synagogue in Rome. We are also familiar with the Church documents in which – already at the time of Pope John XXIII – the relationship between Christians and Jews, or rather, between Christianity and Judaism, was redefined, hopefully for all time. In the Pope's speech as well as in these documents one aspect is immediately clear. They do not concern themselves with attributing blame nor with the consideration of reasons (social, economic, intellectual or whatever) which made Christians look upon Jews as enemies and intruders. One thing is stated loud and clear: the Christians of the past and Church itself were wrong. They had no reason to consider Jews as a 'damned' nation, the nation responsible for the death of Jesus Christ, and therefore as a nation which should be excluded from the community of nations.

If this did happen, it was because Christians were not Christian enough. The church documents do not state: we 'had to' defend ourselves, we 'could not' save Jews or treat them as brothers. They do not attempt to look for mitigating circumstances (and these can be found). Jews, being monotheists, were 'beyond the pale' already in antiquity. In the Middle Ages what cemented Europe together was religious unity. Let us bear in mind that the Church was, on the whole, more tolerant than the secular rulers. Nonetheless, all this does not change the basic situation and must be put aside. Instead, what has to be stressed is that the Church sustained hostility toward Jews, thereby driving them into isolation and humiliation. To put it briefly, the new Church documents do not attempt to exonerate the past, do not argue over extenuating circumstances. They speak clearly about the failure to fulfil the duty of brotherhood and compassion. The rest is left to historians. It is precisely in this that the Christian magnanimity of such pronouncements lies.

I think we must imitate this in our attitude to the Polish-Jewish past. We must stop haggling, trying to defend and justify ourselves. To stop arguing about the things which were beyond our power to do, during the occupation and beforehand. Nor to place blame on political, social and economic conditions. But to say first of all – Yes, we are guilty. We did take Jews into our home, but we made them live in the basement. When they wanted to come into the drawing-room, our response was – Yes, but only after you cease to be Jews, when you become 'civilized'. This was the thinking of our most enlightened minds, such as Orzeszkowa and Prus. There were those among Jews who were ready to adhere to this advice. No sooner did they do this, when we started in turn talking of an invasion of Jews, of the danger of their infiltration of Polish society. Then we started to put down conditions like that stated *expressis verbis* by Dmowski, that we shall accept as Poles only those Jews who are willing to cooperate in the attempts to stem Jewish influences in our society. To put it bluntly, those who are willing to turn against their own kith and kin.

Eventually, when we lost our home, and when, in its premises, the invaders set to murdering Jews, did we show solidarity towards them? How many of us decided that it was none of our business? There were also those (and I leave out of account common criminals) who were secretly pleased that Hitler had solved for us 'the Jewish problem'. We could not even welcome and honour the survivors, even if they were embittered, disorientated and perhaps sometimes tiresome. I repeat: instead of haggling and justifying ourselves, we should first consider our own faults and weaknesses. This is the moral revolution which is imperative when considering the Polish-Jewish past. It is only this that can gradually cleanse our desecrated soil.

What is easy in the case of words is, however, more difficult in practice. Its precondition is a change in the social awareness of the problem. For our part, we often demand of Jews (or their friends) an impartial and fair assessment of our common history. We should, however, first acknowledge our own guilt and ask for forgiveness. In fact, this something that they are waiting for – if, indeed, they are still waiting. I recall one moving speech at the Oxford conference, in which the speaker started by comparing the Jewish attitude to Poland to an unrequited love. Despite the suffering and all the problems which beset our mutual relations, he continued, the Jewish community had a genuine attachment to their adopted country. Here they found a home and a sense of security. There was, conscious or unconscious, an expectation that their fate would improve, the burden of humiliation would lighten, that the future would gradually become brighter. What actually happened was exactly the opposite. 'Nothing can ever change now,' he concluded. 'Jews do not have and cannot have any future in Poland. Do tell us, though,' he finally demanded 'that what has happened to us was not our fault. We do not ask for anything else. But we do hope for such an acknowledgement.'

This means for the Polish side the acceptance of responsibility. Here enters for the last time the guardian mole and asks: 'Full responsibility? Also a shared responsibility for the genocide?' I can already hear loud protests. 'How can that be? In God's name, we didn't take part in the genocide.' 'Yes, that is true' I shall reply. Nobody can reasonably claim that Poles as a nation took part in the genocide of Jews. From time to time one hears voices claiming just that. We must consider them calmly, without getting angry which might be taken as a mark of panic. To me, as for the overwhelming majority of people, these claims are unfounded. So why talk of genocide? And of shared responsibility? My answer is this: participation and shared responsibility are not the same thing. One can share the responsibility for the crime without taking part in it. Our responsibility is for holding back, for insufficient effort to resist. Who of us could claim that there was sufficient resistance in Poland? It is precisely because resistance was so weak, that we now honour those who did have the courage to take up this heroic risk. It may sound rather strange, but I may believe that this shared responsibility through failure to act, is the less crucial part of the problem we are considering. More significant is the fact that if only in the past we had behaved more humanely, had been wiser, more magnanimous, genocide would perhaps have been 'less imaginable', would probably have been considerably more difficult to carry out, and almost certainly would have met with much greater resistance than it did. To put it differently, it would not have met with the indifference and moral turpitude of the society in whose full view it took place.

A question arises immediately whether this could be said not only of the Poles, but equally well of the French, the English, the Russians, of the whole of the Christian world. Yes, indeed, it can. This responsibility is, indeed, our common responsibility. But it cannot be denied that it was in Poland where the greatest number of Jews lived (more than two thirds of the world's Jewry are Polish Jews, in the sense that their forefathers lived in the territories belonging to the Polish republic in the period before the Partitions). Consequently, we had the greatest moral obligation towards the Jewish people. Whether what was demanded of us was or was not beyond our ability to render, God alone must judge and historians will continue to debate. But, for us, more than for any other nation, Jews were more of a problem, a challenge which we had to face.

To refer once more the realm of literature: nobody understood this better than Mickiewicz. The thoughts and the vision of our romantic poet were more farsighted than that of any of his contemporaries. Unlike the majority of those who were well disposed to the Jews, Mickiewicz held a deep conviction that Israel, 'the older brother', should not only enjoy the same privileges in Poland as everybody else, but also at the same time retain the right to remain distinct in religion and custom. This was also Norwid's attitude; as far as we can judge, Słowacki was of the same opinion. So, at the very least, our literary greats stood on the side of truth and justice. The thinking of Mickiewicz was indeed visionary: he seems to have been aware that only such a path could save the Jews (if only partially) from extinction, and us from the moral turpitude. It would have been a truly extraordinary path to take and one which would have merited the epithet 'messianic' in the proper sense of the word. Reality, unfortunately, took exactly the opposite form to that dreamt of by the poets. It was nowhere else but in Poland, and especially in the twentieth century, that anti-semitism became particularly virulent. Did it lead us to participate in genocide? No. Yet, when one reads what was written about Jews before the war, when one discovers how much hatred there was in Polish society, one can only be surprised that words were not followed by deeds. But they were not (or very rarely). God held back our hand. Yes, I do mean God, because if we did not take part in that crime, it was because we were still Christians, and in the last moment we came to realize what a satanic enterprise it was. This still does not free us from sharing responsibility. The desecration of the Polish soil has taken place and we have not yet discharged our duty of seeking expiation. In this graveyard, the only way to achieve this is to face up to our duty of viewing our past truthfully.

NOTES

1 This article was first published in *Tygodnik Powszechny*, 11 January 1987.
2 E. Czarnecka, *Podróżny świata. Rozmowy z Cz. Miłoszem. Komentarze*, (New York, 1983), p. 119.
3 Ibid., pp. 63–4.
4 The victim cannot accept that he was not only wronged, but also humiliated and demeaned by his persecutor; that he was unable to stand up to the inhumanity of it all. In the years 1944–8, Polish opinion was not able to acknowledge the disintegration of all norms and moral debasement of the large part of our society in the aftermath of the war. The drastic treatment of these themes by writers such as Borowski and Różewicz aroused indignation. The readers of this journal (*Tygodnik Powszechny*) took exception to J. J. Szczepański's short story, *Buty* (Shoes). It was hard to accept the truth of the 'infection with death' (the term coined by K. Wyka). A rather similar attitude was, of course, also to be found among Jews.
5 That is the reason why there are so few literary words that treat the theme of Polish society's attitude to the Jewish Holocaust. It is not only because literature is rendered speechless in the face of genocide. The theme is too hot to handle; writers felt that they came into conflict with their readers' sensibility.

APPENDIX

CAMPO DI FIORI

In Rome, on the Campo di Fiori
baskets with olives and lemons
the pavement splattered with wine
and broken fragments of flowers.
The hawkers pour on the counters

the pink fruits of the sea,
and heavy armfuls of grapes
fall on the down of peaches.

Here, on this very square
Giordano Bruno was burned;
the hangman kindled the flame of the pyre
in the ring of the gaping crowd,
and hardly the flame extinguished
the taverns were full again
and hawkers carried on heads
baskets with olives and lemons.

I recalled Campo di Fiori
in Warsaw, on a merry-go-round,
on a fair night in the spring
by the sound of vivacious music.
The salvoes behind the ghetto walls
were drowned in lively tunes,
and vapors freely rose
into the tranquil sky.

Sometimes the wind from burning houses
would bring the kites along,
and people on the merry-go-round
caught the flying charred bits.
This wind from the burning houses
blew open the girls' skirts,
and the happy throngs laughed
on a beautiful Warsaw Sunday.

Perhaps one will guess the moral,
that the people of Warsaw and Rome
trade and play and love
passing by the martyr's pyre.
Another perhaps, will read
of the passing of human things,
of the oblivion growing
before the flame expired.

But I that day reflected
on the loneliness of dying men,
on the fate of lone Giordano;
that when he climbed the scaffold

he found no word in human tongue
with which to bid farewell
to those of mankind who remain.

Already they were on the run,
to peddle starfish, gulp their wine;
they carried olives and lemons
in the gay hum of the city.
And he was already remote
As though ages have passed,
and they waited a while
for his flight in the fire.

And those dying alone,
forgotten by the world,
their tongue grew strange to us,
like the tongue of an ancient planet.
And all will become a legend –
and then after many years
the poet's word shall stir revolt
on the new Campo di Fiori.

Warsaw, 1943 [trans. Adam Gillon]

A POOR CHRISTIAN LOOKS AT THE GHETTO

Bees build around red liver,
Ants build around black bone.
It has begun: the tearing, the trampling on silks,
It has begun: the breaking of glass, wood, copper, nickel, silver, foam
Of gypsum, iron sheets, violin strings, trumpets, leaves, balls, crystals.
Poof! Phosphorescent fire from yellow walls
Engulfs animal and human hair.

Bees build around the honeycomb of lungs,
Ants build around white bone.
Torn is paper, rubber, linen, leather, flax,
Fiber, fabrics, cellulose, snakeskin, wire.
The roof and the wall collapse in flame and heat seizes the foundations.

THE POOR POLES LOOK AT THE GHETTO

Now there is only the earth, sandy, trodden down,
With one leafless tree.

Slowly, boring a tunnel, a guardian mole makes his way,
With a small red lamp fastened to his forehead.
He touches buried bodies, counts them, pushes on.
He distinguishes human ashes by their luminous vapor,
The ashes of each man by a different part of the spectrum.
Bees build around a red trace.
Ants build around the place left by my body.

I am afraid, so afraid of the guardian mole.
He has swollen eyelids, like a Patriarch
Who has sat much in the light of candles
Reading the great book of the species.

What will I tell him, I, a Jew of the New Testament,
Waiting two thousand years for the second coming of Jesus?
My broken body will deliver me to his sight
And he will count me among the helpers of death:
The uncircumcised.

Warsaw, 1943.
(Translation C. Miłosz)

DEDICATION

You whom I could not save
Listen to me.
Try to understand this simple speech as I would be
   ashamed of another.
I swear, there is in me no wizardry of words.
I speak to you with silence like a cloud or a tree.

What strengthened me, for you was lethal.
You mixed up farewell to an epoch with the beginning
   of a new one,
Inspiration of hatred with lyrical beauty,
Blind force with accomplished shape.

Here is the valley of shallow Polish rivers. And an
   immense bridge

Going into white fog. Here is a broken city,
And the wind throws screams of gulls on your grave
When I am talking with you.

What is poetry which does not save
Nations or people?
A connivance with official lies,
A song of drunkards whose throats will be cut in a moment,
Readings for sophomore girls.
That I wanted good poetry without knowing it,
That I discovered, late, its salutary aim,
In this and only this I find salvation.

They used to pour on graves millet or poppy seeds
To feed the dead who would come disguised as birds.
I put this book here for you, who once lived
So that you should visit us no more.

1945

(Translation C. Miłosz)

POLISH-JEWISH RELATIONS DURING THE SECOND WORLD WAR: A DISCUSSION[1]

Professor Gutman[2]

I should like to begin making a methodological point. I am very concerned that not only we will speak in mutually incomprehensible terms and that the content of our statements will not enable us to discuss the essence of the problem with which we have to deal. We are representatives not only of nations which have suffered greatly over the last centuries, but we also represent a certain generation and we are not only historians, but actual witnesses and activists of a hard epoch. In English they talk of a 'unique period'. We bear upon our shoulders the weight of an uncommon responsibility, for this generation which has produced so many contradictory testimonies – there are Jewish testimonies and there are Polish testimonies – risks making the world believe that it has nothing clear and believable to say. Perhaps this will all lead to revisionism, to a flight from the truth. This is perfectly possible, for the substance of this period is so terrible and so strange that our human consciousness is inadequate to grasp that such a thing could happen.

The way in which I was taught history enjoined me to tell the truth, as far as the sources indicate that truth and even when it is very painful. I do not know if people learn from history. A small child who burns its fingers only once will not do it again, and yet everyone knows that humanity continues to wage wars, continues to murder, that the same or similar mistakes are committed again and again. So I do not know if people learn from history, but I regard it as our duty as historians to do everything we can to help people to do so. We must therefore always strive to learn, to teach and to speak the truth. It seems to me that we began to air the difficult problems today in the wrong way for there are certain guidelines which we must follow if our discussion is to be fruitful. The country in which I live has achieved many things. It is a very interesting country to be in, but it is not an easy place in which to live. It seems to me that speaking the historical truth is one of the achievements that Israel can be proud of. Even if the truth is very painful where the Jews are concerned, we feel we must admit it concerning our relations with others or the mistakes we have committed. We speak openly and today it seems natural that this truth is recorded in writing. When a responsible historian in Israel writes in an apologetic way, his work receives a very critical reception. This is what I teach my students and it is an elementary truth they must learn. It is my impression that, as far as Polish-Jewish relations are concerned, there is a certain weakness in our discussions for which both sides are, in a sense, responsible. There is a tendency not to state the truth plainly, but to 'colour' the truth, or to censor it, to use only those documents which are convenient, to forget those documents which raise difficulties. I respect Professor Bartoszewski greatly, and I know that this feeling is mutual, we have known each other for many years. Professor Bartoszewski writes in the wise introduction to his important book on Poles who saved Jews during the war that there were changes for the better as far as relations with the Jews were concerned after 1939 and that anti-semitism weakened during this period.[3] He gives the following reason: suffering unites people. There is no way of studying these things objectively, we have no materials, no studies of public opinion, we cannot say for certain how these things were. We express what are personal thoughts and conclusions or, in the case of Professor Władysław Bartoszewski, his own good will. That was how he wanted things to be, I think. I understand this perfectly. He also states that there were cases when people belonging to various political parties, behaved in their daily life, in their actions and in their attitude to Jews, in a way that contradicted their ideas and their socio-political views. I cannot agree with this central thesis, a thesis that reveals much good will, but also much naïvety. It is not true that suffering unites people, that terrorized people who suffer at the hands of a destructive power are inclined to unite or cooperate with each other. The truth is – and we know this from Oświęcim and from the work of such people as Hannah Arendt or Anna Pawełczyńska[4] in Poland – that it is in just such conditions that differences between people acquire enormous significance and create huge disparities between those who enjoy certain privileges and those who do not. Sometimes the privilege appears to be a trivial one, but it has great significance in such a situation. Dr Garliński[5] said rightly today that to speak with a Jew in Oświęcim was unheard of and dangerous. The Jews were prisoners and the Poles were prisoners but the difference between them was enormous. Just to give one example; as late as 1943 and 1944 the Poles, the French, the Belgians and the Czechs could receive parcels. The Jews did not receive parcels. Can anyone understand what this difference meant?

In 1943 the selection of Aryans was abandoned in Oświęcim, but not that of the Jews. Can anyone conceive the enormous difference this created between people and what it meant? It may seem strange but there is someone who wrote, I think it was Bettelheim, of how in the camps one can talk of different social classes. When we speak of classes we have in mind a kind of sociological construct, but the differences in the camps were perhaps even greater than in normal social conditions. So there is a great deal to discuss here.

It is also true that an historian cannot study historical processes in isolation, but must see the connections between them and the way they occur as part of a long term historical process. It would be wrong to take the period 1939–45 out of its historical context. One has to take into account that strong anti-semitism did exist in Poland between the wars. It would be equally incorrect to state simply that the Poles were anti-semites between the wars and to end the argument there. Every generalisation is mistaken. There were many noble and intelligent people in Poland, who were brave and daring during the interwar period; we have many records to this effect. Even from the political point of view the picture shows important variations. I sat once in London and studied the Polish newspaper *Gazeta Polska* – a very interesting record – and I looked for material concerning the Jews. I covered 1935 within 3 hours. Almost nothing. The only Jews who appear are Florian Sokolow and perhaps a few poems by Leśmian or Tuwim from time to time, that was all. 1936 – nothing. I spent two days reading that year, but for 1937 it took me two days to read only two months, there was a great difference. The truth is that these last few years, 1936–9, were a period when anti-semitism grew stronger in Poland and this anti-semitism influenced what came later. What occurred then is clear. The National Camp and a large part of Piłsudski's camp (even if not the whole) adopted the slogans of political anti-semitism.

The whole phenomenon is complex. One of the members of the National Radical Camp (*ONR*) at this time argued that Piłsudski had clearly legitimized anti-semitism. It may not be true but this was what he said and it was understandable given the influence of nationalism and fascism which were so strong in Europe at that time. Another right-wing leader, polemicizing with the Jews argued, 'How can you claim that Piłsudski had connections with the Jews? He was, after all, the first to defend the pact with Hitler'. I do not share his point of view but this argument was used in order to create a certain atmosphere and to strengthen the anti-semitic tendency in Poland.

This trend had a number of characteristics, a central one being the claim that there were too many Jews in Poland, and that their percentage was higher here than in any other nation in the world with the exception of Palestine. A second argument took the following form: Poland is an economically underdeveloped country, it is in the process of development. The Jews work above all in economic spheres such as local trade and in the markets, they are small tradesmen and there is no longer room for them in Poland. They can no longer support themselves by means of their customary occupations. This view was expressed not only by Dmowski, but also by Bogusław Miedziński. Yet in 1937 Bogusław Miedziński had nothing to say about what should actually happen to these Jews. At the time, when the problem of peasants was discussed, people also said: there are too many peasants in the villages, we must find a solution. Good solutions were proposed as well as bad ones. Yet when it came to the Jews there were no suggestions. There is no room. That was the view of the majority. I will not say it was a unanimous view, that would be unfair, but it was firmly held by a majority of Polish political parties. Bogusław Miedziński also stated in February 1937 in his capacity of deputy speaker of the *Sejm*: 'I like the Danes very much, but if there were three and a half million Danes in Poland then that would be quite unacceptable.' If Miedziński had been confronted with an American claim that millions of Poles in America were harming the economy because there was a serious unemployment problem would he not have declared this was an appalling assertion, and would he not have been right? Yet when it came to the Jews the idea that they were after hundreds of years, no longer strangers did not appeal and there was only one answer and it was the order of the day. The Jews should emigrate.

There were a number of approaches to this question. There was the *ONR* approach, shared to some extent by the *endecja*, who held that one should treat the Jews in such a way that would make them leave. There was also the approach of the pro-government Camp of National Unity (*OZON*) which said, No, such methods are abhorrent to us. We do not employ physical violence, we will not cause disturbances, we will not hear of such a thing, for if it begins it will not end with the Jews. Let us have an economic boycott if necessary. We will look for a way out for the Jews, they ought to emigrate.' But may I ask, where were these Jews to go?

I have great difficulty in explaining to my students that the world of the 1930s was not today's world. It was not an open world. Minds were not open and the gates of countries were not open. It is not like this now but it was then. The Jews were prepared to go, but where could they go to? Who was prepared to take them in? As for the ridiculous murmuring about Madagascar, that was a complete farce. It just goes to show how unfeasible these things were.

As far as Polish-Jewish relations are concerned, I immediately concede that Professor Bartoszewski, Irena Adamowicz, Jadwiga Dudziec, Alexander Kamiński and others like them were people who helped the Jews. I will go further – they were people who could not sleep peacefully at night because they knew that nearby other people were suffering simply because they were born who they were. This gave them no rest and they were compelled to do something. They can, in a certain sense, be regarded as honorary Jews. But they were few, taking the country as a whole, they were very few. What is more important, and what we must take responsibility for deciding, is what was the response of the political parties and above all of the organized Polish underground? For this was, after all, a remarkable Polish phenomenon, this solidarity of the Polish underground. It was an exceptional achievement, for Poland had existed for only 20 years following 130 years of partition. This feeling of identification of Poles from all social spheres and their anti-German solidarity is a previously unheard of historical achievement and one of Europe's greatest under Nazi occupation. I should like to make two things clear here. First, all accusations against the Poles that they were responsible for what is referred to as the 'Final Solution' are not even worth mentioning. Secondly, there is no validity at all in the contention that Polish anti-semitism or other Polish attitudes were the reason for the siting of the death camps in Poland.

Poland was a completely occupied country. There was a difference in the kind of 'occupation' countries underwent in Europe. Each country experienced a different occupation and almost all had a certain amount of autonomy, limited and defined in various ways. This autonomy did not exist in Poland. No one asked the Poles how one should treat the Jews. Yet Poland did have one source of strength which other countries did not possess. This lay in her internal organisation, the organised union of Polish patriots and the specifically Polish attitude to the enemy. This solidarity and the impulse to fight against the politics of the occupier was shared by almost all Poles but it did not exist in full with regard to the Jews. I believe that it did not really include the Jews. Professor Davies has written that when the *Judenrat* and a local council (*Zarząd Miejski*) were set up in Warsaw a barrier was created, and it was no longer possible to help them or to speak with anyone – there was simply no one to speak with.[6] Why? The *Judenrat* had, after all, existed in Warsaw before the establishment of the Ghetto in October and November 1940. When everything was still open and accessible and the Jews had full contact with the Poles, there were no barriers. For a time the *Judenrat* was a continuation of the Jewish *kahal*. Why, then, was there no contact? Iranek Osmecki writes in his book that the first contacts were established towards the end of 1942.[7] Witold Bieńkowski, Professor Bartoszewski's close friend, wrote the same in his report of 1944 addressed to the Polish Government in London.[8] He writes that from neither the objective or the subjective point of view was there any reason to become involved in the Jewish question or with the Jews before the end of 1941. Why? Perhaps Professor Bartoszewski can answer this question. For by the end of 1942, 100,000 Jews had died of starvation and disease in the Warsaw ghetto. How can it be that the organized forces of the underground did not provide either material or spiritual aid? I make no accusations here this is a straightforward historic fact which cannot be overlooked. Why did this happen, given that Poland was organized, that solidarity existed, that authorities existed. Stefan Korboński has written of an underground 'state'.[9] Why was that underground state not responsible from the civil and human point of view for the Jews? There is no answer, the question stands. I think that we as Jews, and the Poles as Poles should ask ourselves this question. I believe there are many points of contact between us and similarities in the fate we each suffered. I believe that nations cannot be described as 'good' or 'bad', but that the lessons of history have their own significance and cannot be ignored. I wish to mention briefly two more subjects – the Home Army (*AK*) and the question of Jews fighting and the issue of *Żegota* and aid to the Jews. The fact is that it was very difficult for Jews to gain entry to the *AK*, even if they were willing to fight. This enormously complicated the position of those Jews who wanted to resist. As for the Committee for Aid to the Jews (*Żegota*), one can only applaud unreservedly its efforts. But its members were a small and under-financed group who had to contend with the indifference of most of Polish society and the active hostility of a significant section.

Professor Bartoszewski[10]

As Professor Gutman began his talk from a personal and subjective point of view, I feel that I can be permitted to do the same. He made a number of points based on the personal experiences of a person of our generation, some dating from a period spent in a German camp and in active participation in the underground. Professor Gutman's experiences are thus very similar to my own. I have to say that I would not accept without question his statement that it is not true that suffering unites people, despite his reference to Pawełczynska's book which I also value greatly; sometimes suffering unites and sometimes it divides. It depends on what kind of people are involved and where and on how great the suffering is.

I do not consider myself to be an expert on the subject of suffering, but for the sake of accuracy I would like to mention that I have spent almost 8 years of my life in camps and prisons. The company was varied, Gestapo officers, petty and professional criminals, extortionists, not to speak of political prisoners. I therefore have some right to speak of my observations of people's behaviour and attitudes in very different conditions. A certain hypothesis is to be found in the writings of my fellow speaker which is also repeated during his address. He argues that since anti-semitism existed as an important element in the formation of Polish public opinion from 1918 to 1968, then there must be certain implications relevant to the period 1939–45. Incidentally, I am curious to know why anti-semitism should be considered an important element in Polish public opinion only up to 1968 and not to 1984?

I agree completely that anti-semitism in Poland was one of the prominent tendencies in public life, as it was in many other European countries, particularly in East-Central Europe. Poland was not an exception, which does not, of course, justify anything, but such was the situation. What was the nature of this anti-semitism? A library of books has been written on the subject, there is no single formula. I think it was significantly stimulated by customs – both religious and historic, by the economic situation and to some extent by the general level of civilization of the majority of Polish society which was characterized on the whole by hostility to all 'strangers'. Not only the Jews were looked down on in Poland, but the Czechs and the Lithuanians also. In fact, apart from the Hungarians (who were not really our neighbours), all our neighbours were looked down on, with the difference that our other neighbours, for example the Germans, were a force with a state behind them, while the Jews had no state to back them. Also, there were Jews living throughout the country and not just in one particular place.

There was, particularly in the last few years before the war, a noticeable antipathy towards the Jews on the part of the Poles. I will not say the majority felt this, for what exactly does the term mean? Only a few thousand people took part in the political life of the country. Perhaps a million. There were perhaps twenty two and a half million Poles in Poland when the second World War broke out. There are no statistics or questionnaires available which can tell us what the majority of them thought, insofar as they thought of these problems at all. We can rely only on the newspapers published by the political parties of the time which represent 0.5 per cent of public opinion, and we can rely on parliamentary elections. However, as the elections were boycotted in 1935 by the whole Polish opposition and by part of the Jewish opposition, they cannot be taken as a normal expression of the opinion of Polish society *as a whole*. In these conditions, as in many others, the use of such concepts as 'majority' or 'minority' is rather hazardous. But let us assume that for reasons of civilization, culture, religion, superstition or economic conflict, during a time of European crisis, the hostility of a large percentage of Poles was easily aroused towards those in whom they saw a rival, especially if they were incited to believe that this was a rival group. This does not mean to say that feelings of dislike or separateness necessarily lead to hostility and criminal acts. I know many honest Americans, who not only dislike Negroes, but Mexicans and Puerto-Ricans as well, and I also know many Englishmen who do not like Indians, but if we were to ask on this basis if they would be prepared to kill them what would be their answer? (Professor Gutman: I did not say that.) No, but a certain train of thought emerges here and I am simply making the deduction that we are left with if dislike and estrangement are put in a class with what can be held to be their logical consequences.

Of course, one basic consequence of estrangement is isolation and passivity and the thesis of my paper today was that the most characteristic phenomenon of Polish-Jewish relations before 1939 was mutual isolation or separateness.[11] The Poles saw no reason to approach the Jews, to get to know or to understand them. A notable proportion of Jews felt the same (of course we are not speaking here of Słonimski, or of the hundreds of professors, lawyers or doctors). They saw no clear reason why, in dealing with people of a different religion and different customs who treated them with suspicion, they should make any particular effort to win the hearts, the minds or the good will of the Poles. Both sides, whether for reasons of culture or upbringing – for one reason in Kraków and for others in Wilno, Nowogródek or Pińsk – isolated themselves from each other. Since Jewish autonomy in Poland was quite considerable, the Jews enjoyed the freedom to develop their life in all its aspects: internal, cultural, social, religious, sporting and so on. This meant that even if people did not thrive in a specifically Zionist or Communist tradition, they were at least brought up within the Jewish social tradition and contributed towards making Polish Jewry something special on a world scale. Nevertheless, all this went on outside and parallel to Polish society, and it is this fact which fills me with dismay and which I see as characteristic in the development of nationalism in Europe at that time. It was not that it would occur daily to the Poles to think, 'I don't like Jews', but rather that the Poles never thought at all about the Jews who were living alongside them. It was simply of no significance or interest to them. I was brought up on Bielańska Street in Warsaw, 200 metres from Nalewki Street, so I know this from experience not from books. I was one of the very few (if not the only) pupil in my class who had Jewish friends. In very small towns the situation was a little different. In bigger towns this segregation was almost automatic and dictated by class. The élite, professors, lawyers, doctors, was acceptable, anything lower was not so much worse as completely alien. That for me represents what was a characteristic state of affairs. It does not, in my opinion, lead inevitably to hostility at the time of and in the conditions of German occupation.

Professor Gutman has expressed the view, both in his paper[12] and to some extent in his address, that I, out of goodness and naïvety believe that Poles were better disposed towards the Jews than they actually were, because the true situation grieves me. Many things do grieve me, but as far as this is concerned I cannot yet accept that there is any proof indicating what percentage of Poles was of a particular disposition, just as there is nothing to indicate what percentage of the Jews was interested in Polish affairs or problems. Such evidence appeared when Poland was threatened by Hitler, and there were many moving instances of Jewish solidarity on the part of poor and middle-class Jews who supported the army and took part in defending the country. For many Poles this was a first, striking proof of patriotism which they had never previously suspected; it had been of no interest to them.

The war came. I see a very definite moral division arising during the war. Regardless of background, the better, moral, decent people believed that if someone was being murdered then things were very serious indeed. Liking or disliking someone was entirely another matter, but when someone was being murdered the situation was quite different. This is surely natural and is not so very difficult to understand. At a meeting connected with the Council for Aid to the Jews (*Żegota*) I met an old schoolmaster of mine, an *Endek* and a National Party activist who put forward the view that since the Germans had deprived the Jewish teachers of everything and were persecuting them, then he had certain responsibilities towards them. I had thought that since he was an *Endek* before the war, then during the war he would turn his back and have nothing to do with the Jews. I was young and principled but I was mistaken; these things were very complicated. For example, before the war there were careerists in the left-wing parties who during the war kept their distance and avoided any involvement in Jewish affairs.

I would like to draw your attention to the fact that in 1939 Poland was divided in half and that, according to the statistics of my colleague Ludwik Landau, who worked in the Information Bureau of the *AK* High Command, 62 per cent of Jews found themselves on the German side, and 38 per cent found themselves under Soviet occupation. In fact there were more in the latter category, as people were fleeing to the east. As a result the statistics relating to 1 September 1939 are inaccurate. There were Poles fleeing to the east and Jews also, for obvious reasons. Let us look at this situation more closely. Professor Gutman in his paper on the subject states that various accusations were levelled, but for Jews there was only one enemy, the Germans, and this simplified the question. In actual fact, the Germans became our sole common, Jewish and Polish enemy from the end of June 1941 which was when they occupied the whole of Poland. In a normal country every citizen regards any occupier as the enemy, but one must remember that between 1939 and 1941 there was a fundamental difference in the way the problem of occupation was perceived in Poland's eastern territories. For a considerable proportion of the Jewish population Soviet occupation meant salvation from the Germans and this fact overshadowed the problem of the loss and collapse of the state and the loss of independence. This was natural and understandable. Secondly, there were Jews living in this area who, until twenty years previously, had been brought up in two cultural traditions, their own and the Russian. Why should they feel any categoric hostility towards Russian culture in which they or their parents and grandparents had been brought up? Furthermore, groups which isolated themselves from the everyday life of the state, (even in Israel today certain extreme religious groups isolate themselves), were indifferent as to what state existed. Please note, however, that for the Poles living in the eastern territories this was the collapse of their beloved state for which they had waited 123 years. In the absence of any objective studies or research, I reject the slander that the Jews played an especially inauspicious role as collaborators with the occupier in the Eastern Territories. Such a role was also played partly by Poles, including people with a university education, partly by Ukrainians and partly by Byelorussians. In many circumstances the Jews also played such a role, like all other nationalities. Certain people conditioned by various ideological doctrines, played a harmful role. One set of statistics can probably be confronted with others representing the testimony of former Polish prisoners in Siberia, in which we find the same stories repeated hundreds of times about how a Jew had taken them in to the *NKVD* or had brought the *NKVD* to their homes. On other occasions, however, it was someone else who betrayed them – a Ukrainian, Byelorussian or Pole. I do not approach the subject from this aspect, but there are others who do, and there is evidence in reports from these areas, dating from 1941 when these terrains were united under German occupation, of Polish xenophobia, hostility and resentment.

The real passion of my life has been searching for what unites people, but one has to dig deep and it can sometimes be very hard. It seems to me now that something which could unite people in the future and which also played a part in uniting people during the war would be to make people aware of the Jews' role in fighting for Polish independence during the second World War, of Jews who fought at Monte Cassino and died during other Polish battles in substantial numbers. In theory, this information is acknowledged, but in practice it has not been absorbed into the nation's cultural and intellectual bloodstream. On every possible occasion I remind people that the Chief Rabbi of the Polish army was also murdered at Katyń.

There have been a number of misunderstandings here concerning the Home Army (*AK*). Like any other army, it was not the Home Army's task to provide social welfare or to save people. If it had been, the *AK* would have tried to rescue Poles from Oświęcim, from Pawiak, from Montelupich prison and from Lublin Castle. It would have helped displaced people and fugitives. Even before the ghettos had been established or the extermination of Jews had begun, the Tannenberg operation had occurred: 50,000 members of the Polish intelligentsia were murdered in the west, gallows were erected in marketplaces, executions were carried out. Jews were still being publicly humiliated then; they had to wear armbands and their property was confiscated, but they were not being killed *en masse*. So it was not the *AK*'s task to provide the Poles with social welfare. The task of providing such help was a substantial burden for the civilian sector, as in every state, although, of course, there was no 'state' in the normal sense, in spite of the manner in which the Polish underground is grandiloquently described. The *AK* was not the force Professor Gutman seems to think it was. It did not organize itself effectively until 1942. 1940–41 was a period when after the fall of France many people abandoned conspiracy, it was a year of collapse, when there was a lot of informing and thousands of arrests took place. *AK* members were deported to Oświęcim. It was a crucial period. This does not mean that people lacked commitment, but please take into account the fact that the greatest wave of serious and consecutive arrests of Polish activists swept through Poland in 1940–1.

How was it for the Jews in the *AK*? I was in the *AK* and the head of my detachment was a Jew, according to the criteria of the Nuremburg Laws. In my detachment, there were Landau, Stanisław Borenstein and others. I never encountered the problem of 'origin' among circles which published journals or appeals or who generally circulated information. The archives from which Professor Gutman gleaned so much information probably derived from these sources who also provided London with information about the Jewish situation and which was used by the Government-in-Exile. I cannot go into this because it would form the subject of a separate paper and there is not time. The *AK* was an army of 350,000 – 380,000 people. Is there an army anywhere in the world which, having 350,000 people, does not have 0.5 per cent of criminals or thugs? Volunteers working in conspiratorial circumstances cannot be controlled in the way that a normal army in barracks can. I know, of course, that there were a variey of people in the *AK*, because it was a volunteer army. There were élites. No one here has mentioned, not even Dr Dobroszycki who is an outstanding specialist on the subject, how harmful the activity of a section of the underground press was in forming opinions concerning Jewish affairs. I say this clearly and with complete openness, nothing should be hidden here. Yet one has to say that the press of the *AK* and of *Delegatura* (Representative Organ) was blameless in this respect. Many articles, appeals, information, opinions, and evaluations awakening solidarity and sympathy for the plight of the Jews can be cited. In contrast, the press of some political parties behaved as if the question did not exist, including Piasecki's group which acquired real status only after the war when, co-operating with the Polish People's Republic, it entered a position of authority for the first time. This group published journals in which it expressed the view, for example, that 'the Germans and the Jews had set the world on fire and they should perish together'.

If such things are written or expressed, then a certain percentage of people will believe them. But the influence of the *AK* press was incomparably greater than the influence of these groups and it is the task of the sociologist or historian to clarify how strong these groups were, how many members they had and how far their influence extended.

Professor Gutman said that we bear responsibility for the future and to conclude I would like to say the following. Was enough done in Poland to help the Jews during the occupation? No, Jews were not given enough help in Poland; they were given far too little. Was enough done for such victims anywhere in Europe? Nowhere. Anyone studying the problem of the Jews in Poland during the holocaust and particularly those who know this period from experience, knows how difficult it was; and knows what an enormous amount of energy went into the actions to rescue people, many of which were unsuccessful, for the number of attempts made to save people outnumbered by far the number of people actually saved. Any scholar will tell you that. What emerges from all this? People failed in their humanity, not for the first time, hopefully for the last time. People failed, and we are left with a moral question. We must ask ourselves now what would have been enough? Occasionally, someone Jewish tells me that I did *enough* in trying to help the Jews – my answer is, no, I did no such thing. Only those who died in the course of providing such help did *enough*. Only of them can we not say that from the moral point of view they did not do enough. Of everyone else who lived through this time, who confronted this question, whose eyes were open and who tried to do something, succeeding in one action but failing to perform another, one can say he did much, he did a little, he did something or he did a great deal. But only of those who died can we say – they did enough. That is how Christian philosophy views it (laying down one's life for one's neighbour) and this is how other philosophies and ethical systems view it, but of course it cannot be demanded every day of whole nations. I would be interested to see how other nations behaved in a similar situation – some better perhaps, or some maybe even worse. Finally, since Professor Gutman has appealed for educative action for the future, I would like to say that everyone draws conclusions from the past; I am no exception. I draw conclusions above all from the fact that all systems of hatred, of humiliating man or of limiting his rights are a potential threat for all who are weak. In some places the Jews may be at risk, in others it could be someone else. As a socialist Professor Gutman must undoubtedly agree. The conclusion I have come to is that the next generation should be brought up in that which unites, not that which divides. In my own sphere, in my own home I have tried to do this. Let others try to do the same instead of reproaching or accusing each other.

Dr Garliński[5]

There is a story of two partners who owned a cinema. On one night, one said, 'we are doing very badly, the cinema is half empty'. His friend contradicted him, 'the cinema is half full, we are doing good business'. This is the best example of two points of view. Both the speakers we have heard have quoted documents. Both know the subject well, I know them quite well, both are honest men. But they are so adamant in their different points of view that it is very difficult to have the same opinion. What is most difficult in this problem is that the majority of people never spent a day under German occupation. The majority of people in the world don't understand how difficult it is to do something proper under mental and physical pressure. They discuss theoretically what they would do if they were in this situation, but if their lunch is 30 minutes late, they are already uneasy because they are hungry. They don't understand what can happen if you are under pressure, if you know that when you do something against the Occupation Authorities you will be killed or your wife will be killed. This is the problem and when we are talking about this difficult problem we must all always remember what we would do if we were in this kind of situation.

The difference between the opinion of Poles and Jews under German occupation is that Jews were on the bottom and we were not. The same happened in Auschwitz. Jews were on the bottom. The life expectancy of a Jew in Auschwitz, once he had been accepted into the camp and not sent directly to the gas chamber, was three months. Some, like Professor Gutman, survived, but not many. The Poles had a better chance; as I said and I am honest, to speak to a Jew in Auschwitz or to be on friendly terms was dangerous. If the *SS* or a trustee who was a German criminal saw you, you could be in difficulty, that is the difference. Therefore the Jewish point of view is different to the Polish in the same situation and, of course, when somebody betrayed a Jew, when somebody Polish betrayed a Jew under the German occupation, we remember it. I will be frank with you, I was betrayed to the Gestapo by my friend, a Jew from my secondary school. I will not mention his name, even my wife does not know his name. I am sorry for him, he was under pressure, he was blackmailed to do it, I know. But I have no bad feeling towards him, I understand his situation, but this is a fact. Therefore when we finally finish this conference, this Polish-Jewish conference, let us try to finish with the feeling that we have exhausted these problems. They existed and they are history, but we have to think positively about what we can do in the future so that these things never happen again. It is not only in Polish-Jewish relations that Auschwitz must never happen again, that the holocaust must never happen again. We are settled in many countries of the world, especially in the United States, the greatest power in the world. That is our mission, we survived and we must bear witness. Don't quarrel, don't attack each other here in the future, remember we have a mission and we have to do it, otherwise we will have another holocaust, another Auschwitz, that is my message. When we lecture at universities and at schools, talking to young people – don't be neutral, don't say I couldn't care less, don't accept that other people will decide on behalf of you, because then we *will* have another Auschwitz, another holocaust. That is our message, that is our obligation.

Dr Polonsky[13]

Just before this conference, I had another look again at one of the classics of this period, Emanuel Ringelblum's *Polish-Jewish Relations during the Second World War*, a book written in clandestine conditions on the aryan side. In the introduction to this book Ringelblum writes that as he takes up his pen, he feels like a *sofer*, a Jewish scribe, who before he writes a word has to take a ritual bath, has to purify himself, has to prepare his mind because if he writes one letter wrong, everything he writes is worthless. And hearing the two speakers today, I felt very strongly how true were his observations. This is such a difficult subject to deal with because the moral pressures which were imposed on people under these conditions were such that normal human behaviour was effectively impossible. When we look at this subject it is extremely important constantly to bear this in mind. I am not saying we should have a moratorium on discussions on the holocaust. It is very important to discuss these subjects and to discuss them openly and to say what one feels. Yet at the same time I think we have to remember that this is a very weighty subject and a subject which does not lend itself to easy discussion or to easy understanding. In this context it seems to me that one can reproach Poles with many things, with anti-semitism before and after the war, but looking at the experience of the Second World War, it does not seem to me really that the behaviour of the Poles as a whole was significantly different from that in other European countries. We should not be too Polonocentric in looking at what happened. Everybody has a desire for secondary explanations. The primary explanation for the mass murder of the Jews during the Second World War is obvious – but this somehow seems unsatisfactory as a full explanation and for understandable reasons – it can't be so simple. Thus there is always the search for somebody who is responsible in addition to those primarily responsible – perhaps the Jews themselves were partly to blame, perhaps the Jews cooperated, perhaps the Allies could have done more. All of these things are in a sense true, but I think it should be remembered in all discussions of this subject where the primary reponsibility lay. Without Hitler and the people around him these things would not have happened.

Professor Gutman

As far as the *AK* is concerned, and this is an important point, I think that I agree with everything, or almost everything that you, Professor Bartoszewski, have said, especially about the Jews from the eastern territories. I am in perfect agreement – I think that you have presented the issue very objectively. I could not do it better myself, and agree with every word. However, the question of the *AK* as a whole is much more complicated. Its rescue operations are not the major question, although they too are important, of course. But in discussing the *AK* we should look first at the involvement of Jews in the Polish underground authorities. Ignacy Schwartzbart, for example, was one of the first members of the National Council in Paris and in London Shmul Zygelbojm was co-opted onto the Council and then Scherer. This indicates that some care was taken to ensure that Jews were represented within the Polish National Council (the exile parliament) for after all, Jews were also Polish citizens by descent and this was already accepted in exile in Rumania, an unprecedented event in Polish history.

However, there were no Jewish representatives in Poland itself. Where were they? They do not seem to have existed. There were no Jews in the *AK*, they do not appear in the authorities of any underground bodies. Professor Bartoszewski knows very well that from a certain time, that is from the end of 1941, groups of Jews who had organised themselves in Wilno, Warsaw, Białystok, Częstochowa or Zagłębie turned to the *AK* and begged for help in the armed struggle. This is a strange phenomenon. Someone was speaking today of Oświęcim, of how one fights when there is no sense in it, when it can achieve nothing. When there is no way out, when nothing can be done, then one does not fight. But the opposite is characteristic of the Jewish struggle and this kind of struggle occured, too, during the second World War. A rare phenomenon – the one form of struggle that could not lead to victory or gain any political advantage for the future or even simply save them. Such was the ghetto uprising, to fight in the ghetto was symbolic, it was a final cry of protest.

Most people here will be familiar with the despatches sent by a man whom everyone admires, Grot-Rowecki. He writes in February 1943: I gave them a few pistols. The Jews turn to me, there are communists among them too. I will not give them any more as we do not have enough ourselves.

'We do not have enough ourselves' – in these words we again see that huge difference which can be compared with the difference between the material conditions of the Poles and that of the Jews in the ghetto. This leads us to a second grave question that weighs us down, heavy as ballast, and gives us no peace, for what exactly is under discussion here? How many were fighting who needed to be armed? There is not enough time to discuss this now, but is something I have studied for many years. I could tell you what documents there are, what happened, what the response was in Wilno, in Białystok or Kraków. So we are not talking about rescue operations here, or even indifference, for it was a handful of people who wanted to undertake that last battle, which was a final human and national cry of protest, and who turned to the *AK* authorities. Something was also evidently amiss, for how could Bór-Komorowski, for example, give an account of this episode that does not correspond with reality at all?

So in this context Professor Bartoszewski has mentioned a very important point, namely that there were Jews in the *AK*, but there is another issue which should be raised. There are memoirs of people like Ludwik Hirszfeld, who can be regarded as a Jew or non-Jew depending on how you look at it. To the Germans he was a Jew, to the Poles he was one of many Polish scholars. Similarly Adolf Szyfman who was for many years the Director of the Polish Theatre and one of the most important figures in Polish culture between the wars. What do Szyfman and Hirszfeld write? That they could not walk the streets of Warsaw (Professor Bartoszewski: 'They were too well known') because they were recognised as Jews according to the Nuremberg laws and did not feel secure in Warsaw among the Poles. (Interruption: 'Rowecki also did not like wandering around Warsaw, Poles denounced him) Pardon me, but there is a great difference between Rowecki and the others I mentioned. Just look at what Hirszfeld says, it is very interesting when one comes to read it. He concludes his book *Historia jednego życia* by recounting how he was staying on a small estate not as a Jew but as a Pole with his daughter. He says she could not bear the way Jews were spoken of at table there. The reason why she did not survive this period is linked with the fact that she was forced to listen to these conversations. So it is a very complicated question. (Professor Bartoszewski: 'I can give you examples illustrating the opposite.')

I am convinced that many examples can be found to illustrate this. I wish to say this because Professor Bartoszewski has written a very important book and Mrs Prekerowa has also raised a very important subject here today, as far as *Żegota* is concerned which was an unprecedented phenomenon on a European level.[14] Much has been said about comparisons here today, there are very interesting comparisons to be made. If I had time I would go into this further. However, it appears that there were two main ways of thinking which determined what relationship people had with the Jews in the whole of occupied Europe and in the countries allied with the Axis. The first was subjective and the second political. The Italians provide an interesting example of a society which, from its lowest levels up, did not accept the adoption by their government of an anti-Jewish policy. In Italy a Jew could be calm and sure of himself among the rest of society and certain that they would not betray him precisely because he was a Jew. He found help in Italy. Unfortunately, I cannot say the same for Poland. (Professor Bartoszewski: 'Because unfortunately Poland was in a different situation – Italy was not an occupied country and did not lose 20 per cent of its population during the war.') The situation was the same when Italy was an occupied country. (Professor Bartoszewski: 'During the last few months Jews were also being murdered there'.) These differences are an indication of the development of a certain historical situation. There is also the political aspect. The truth is that the political parties in Poland during the Second World War, as Professor Bartoszewski has admitted, did not change their position and the occupier's press and the underground press spoke more or less the same language. In 1944 the idea of finding a place to which the Jews could emigrate was still being considered as an answer to the Jewish question. There were also factors which fed the seeds of anti-semitism and which must be seen as a result of the war situation. One is the situation which developed in Eastern Poland which Professor Bartoszewski has mentioned. The other concerns how Jews' fortunes were confiscated, how Jews lost their place in the economy, everything should be done to investigate the facts as they were. People did not want the Jews to return to reclaim their property.

Michał Borwicz

I would like to avoid all polemic and am concerned with setting out a few facts. It is very good that Professor Bartoszewski spoke about Lwów and that applies to a greater or lesser degree to all the Eastern lands. Much has been spoken and written on the subject of Jewish pro-Soviet sympathies. I have not, on the other hand, found any mention of facts indicating the opposite. As a refugee in Lwów at that time I had to visit various houses, which had been identified by individual Poles or groups involved in conspiracy, to make anti-Soviet contacts. The addresses were passed on to me and it just so happens that all the houses concerned belonged to Jews. It is interesting that no one writing about Lwów has bothered to make a note of these facts. Perhaps it is not possible in Poland but I have seen no mention of it in the émigré press either.

The Katyń murder has been mentioned here. It is a well-known fact that the Germans took advantage of the revelations regarding these crimes to strengthen their vicious anti-Jewish propaganda during the very weeks that the Warsaw ghetto insurrection took place. The outstanding chronicler Ludwik Landau, follows his description of the German hecatombs and hunting down of Jews in the heart of Warsaw by noting on 8 May 1943 that in the German 'rag' (as the newspaper produced by the occupier was called) they write of the soviet atrocities as the work of the Jews, which was supposedly proved by the lack of Jewish names among the victims. Landau comments that this statement contradicts the new list printed alongside in which names of undoubtedly Jewish origin appear. We now know that there were a considerable number of Jewish officers among the Katyń victims. Many years after the war when I turned to fellow-writers who had been studying the Katyń massacre, for a simple commentary, enquiring whether anyone had ever tried to calculate even the approximate number of Jewish victims, I received roughly the following answer: since Polish officers are involved and murdered ones at that, it would be *unfair* to inquire into their Jewish origin. In other words suppression of the fact of these officers' Jewish origin served first to strengthen anti-Jewish propaganda (during the most tragic moments of Jewish martyrdom!) and then after the war this same suppression of the facts was being legitimized by appealing to anti-racism. As if it were a question not of establishing the facts but of intending to reproach them.

In 1971 none other than Professor Adam Pragier, the outstanding émigré publicist and activist applied this theory to history also. When I mentioned in an article the Jews in Berek Joselewicz's regiments during the Kościuszko uprising and the Jews in the 1830 November uprising and the 1863 January uprising, Professor Pragier accused me of racism and of 'pinning a yellow star onto the uniforms of Polish soldiers' and a few lines later literally: 'like Hitler [!!!], Borwicz has attempted to revive [yellow stars] with regard to Polish soldiers of Jewish origin.' A few years earlier in Poland during the time of Moczar all Jews killed in Hitler's gas chambers were declared model Polish patriots and any mention of their Jewish origin was labelled as racism. They ceased to figure as Jews even in annual memorial speeches. At the same time living Jews, regardless of their patriotism or outlook, were regarded as an alien element and forced to leave Poland. It should be emphasized that the whole of the Polish émigré press objected to this policy very strongly.

Another point should be clarified concerning the officers. Certain detachments whose commanding officer was an extreme anti-semite could cause a lot of harm. Many had been appointed just before the war, especially during the last few years of independence. Naturally, one cannot generalize here, as during the occupation membership of the military did not necessarily presume that one also belonged to a political party. Furthermore, many right-wing people behaved correctly in this respect and sometimes very honourably.

Nevertheless, there were sporadic incidents which were all the worse for acquiring a certain official character. In the journal *Ziemie Wschodnie* ('The Eastern Lands'), a supplement to the official *Rzeczpospolita*, there was a column headed 'The activities of the *AK*'. One day I read in this column that in such a such a region and town Jewish forest bands had been molesting the peasants and the *AK* had liquidated these Jewish bandits. In reality, in order to live some groups of Jews had apparently stolen food. If the ordinary Polish partisans did the same it was called military requisitioning, but Jews were murdered for it. I remember notifying the Jewish underground in Warsaw who knew of such cases from other sources (or maybe even from the same paper). The Council for Aid to the Jews to whom I later sent a communiqué, informed us that they had managed to secure an interview with a Government Delegate and it was established that the *Delegatura* would provide such groups with food so that they would not be forced to steal. How far this programme was realized should be looked into.

Professor Juliusz Strojnowski[16]

Ladies and gentlemen, let us not hide our heads in the sand with regard to either of these issues. I have been studying the problem of fascism for many years and I have been able to collect a great deal of original material from the archive of the National Confederation (*Konfederacja Narodowa*). What is more, I have managed to bring this material to the West. Over 600 pages of reports and notes with precise figures showing how many people were killed and their names also often appear. Almost 40 per cent were Jews, 12 per cent (though this figure is unverified) were 'bolsheviks', the rest were 'lackeys of the Jews' or Poles who hid Jews. If a single Jew was found in a village then the whole peasant family who had sheltered him was also executed. We should not forget these things, but we should also take care not to forget another side of this issue. Did the Poles do too little or did they do enough? They undoubtedly did too little. But at the same time let us not forget the difficulty with which even that little was achieved. What percentage of Polish Jews could not speak Polish? How could they be placed with complete strangers who would know immediately who was involved? I remember how Professor Żera, Professor of Cardiology after the war at the hospital of the Sisters of St Elizabeth in Warsaw, got two important activists out of the ghetto in an ambulance completely bandaged up and plastered from head to toe because there was no other way of saving them. I remember how in 1941 I went to Lwów at the request of a colleague in order to bring back the Jewish wife of an important dignitary. Her appearance was such that she had to be bandaged up also in this way and I brought her back to Warsaw by train. There were difficulties which arose on a mass scale. How can more have been done in such conditions? No doubt there were opportunities but let us not overestimate either the good will of all the Poles or the material and moral conditions that existed.

Dr Józef Lichten[17]

I look at the clock and I see it is 3 minutes to 7 and, despite myself, at the end of this long hard day I think of one of the Jewish holy days, the Day of Atonement, when, often tired at the end of the day, we look at the clock, looking forward to the end of a day during which we have remembered many difficult things and revived personal memories. Professor Gutman spoke about boxing and I am very happy that I have the opportunity to speak before Professor Bartoszewski replies so that this day should not end with the discussion of minor and unimportant details which lead nowhere. Personally, I feel that too little has been said about the real perpetrators of all this grief. The 'occupier' has been mentioned here and there, but with a kind of timidity, without actually stating, 'The Germans did this.' It was not the Poles, it was not the Jews, it was the result of a treacherous attack by a foreign invader who bears complete responsibility for what happened. This should be remembered for there are people who, perhaps for personal reasons or experiences, would like to shift the blame onto other people or nations, even onto Poles, for example, or onto all Poles, thus commiting a grave error. I will not go into details, that is not why I asked to speak.

It seems to me that suffering does unite people and this is because in the end I rely simply on my own memories. I remember 1939 and the beginning of the war when the Poles and Jews dug trenches together, even Ringelblum in his chronicle mentions the strange atmosphere that fell over the country after war was declared. So there was some unifying element which brought out something closer that was shared, and not just the complete estrangement that I unfortunately had occasion to mention yesterday. It does not seem to me either that the weaker or stronger antisemitism that existed before the war influenced everything that happened during the war. It is possible that some newspaper influenced certain people here and there, but again we should bear in mind the main fact of the invasion.

Professor Bartoszewski has mentioned the underground. Personally, I was on the other end as I worked with the Government in London. I remember the dispatches we sent to the underground and I am perfectly aware and can confirm that for a very long time the so-called Polish underground was not at all organized, that it was a collection of representatives of political parties who quarrelled with each other and it was a long time before they were able to unite in some kind of common struggle.

This whole subject is not what it used to be, that is a subject with immediate contemporary relevance. For there are no Jews in Poland now, we cannot talk of economic or political affairs, we cannot discuss the press, we cannot speak of what unites or divides us. At this stage the question has moved to another level, that of culture and research. I feel that after forty five years not all of us should take an active part in public discussions of the subject. These sad, tragic and, I hope, unrepeatable events should be left to the researchers who will look calmly at the documents and slowly draw their conclusions. Personal animosities and memories lead nowhere and as the last speaker before Professor Bartoszewski I would like to say that I hope the next discussions will be led by researchers basing their work on the documentation that exists and that we should not conduct boxing matches here that lead nowhere.

Professor Bartoszewski

Ladies and gentlemen, I really had no intention of boxing with anyone, and anyone who reads my paper in English will surely not find a single sentence which would hurt or offend anyone. I hope the translation is accurate, but in discussion one sometimes has to adapt to the contingencies of argument and focus more sharply on certain things. I share the views of my colleague Professor Gutman completely in the case of such people as Hirszfeld and Szyfman. I should add, however, that attempts to rescue Hirszfeld from the ghetto were made systematically and he was rescued by Father M. Godlewski, who before the war was the founder of economic organisations which favoured boycotting the Jews. A priest of this type saved him, there were others deprived of culture who behaved badly. As to why Hirszfeld or Szyfman could not walk the streets of Warsaw, I can only say that the university lecturer Piotr Słonimski wandered around Warsaw without problems until 1944 and lived in his pre-war apartment on Puławska Street together with his son who was in the *AK* and who was imprisoned for that activity after the war in Poland. Piotr Słonimski, a doctor in the *AK*, was killed during the Warsaw uprising by a German bomb. But until the uprising he lived in the same house and walked about Warsaw and was as much a grandson of Chaim Zelig Słonimski as was his brother Antoni Słonimski who spent the war in London.

So far as the capabilities of the *AK* are concerned, I agree with Dr Borwicz, let us not overestimate them. On 19 February 1943, the Gestapo arrested a Delegate of the Government in Warsaw and the *AK* did not try to rescue him nor did it have an opportunity to do so. On 26 March 1943, three weeks before the ghetto uprising, the first armed action took place in Warsaw outside the Arsenal which is remembered to this day as the apogee of the *AK*'s armed achievements in Warsaw. The *AK* was not that strong at all as the following document illustrates – on 19 February 1943 the head of the *AK* telegraphed the Command of the Polish Armed Forces in London as follows: 'We have had 7 parachute drops and have received only 17 incomplete instead of the 100 promised. If this continues then not only will there be no question of equipping us for an uprising but I will not even be in a position to equip current diversive actions in the most urgent areas.' Of course, there is a difference between the meaning of 'much' and 'little', but this is not the point. The leadership of the *AK*, like that of any other army, worked according to the principle that the army would act on command. The *AK* leadership did not consider that premature action in the heart of Poland could be justified regardless of the suffering of people, Poles or Jews who wanted to fight in 1942 or 1943, for the front was then at the Volga.

Professor Strojnowski has said rightly that there are certain limits to human capabilities and I would like end by saying the following. I think Jan Józef Lipski's position is valid – let the Poles speak plainly to Poles about Polish anti-semitism and attempt to educate them, let the Jews warn the Jews of the dangers of xenophobia, prejudice and antagonism. Then we will get somewhere. It is very easy to speak to Poles about Jewish anti-polonism, to the Jews about Polish anti-semitism and to all of them about the soullessness of the world who looked on as the tragedy took place and for which we must all to some extent take responsibility.

NOTES

1 This discussion took place at the International Conference on Polish-Jewish Studies held in Oxford in September 1984.
2 Professor Yisrael Gutman, Max and Rita Haber Professor at the Institute of Contemporary Jewry and at the Hebrew University and Director of the Center of Holocaust Studies at Yad Vashem.
3 Ed. Władysław Bartoszewski, Zofia Lewin, *Righteous among Nations. How Poles Helped the Jews 1939–1945*, (English translation, London, 1969).
4 Anna Pawełczyńska, *Wartości a przemoc*, (Warsaw, 1973).
5 Dr Józef Garliński, a former Home Army officer and a former inmate of Auschwitz; a historian of the Second World War with several books to his credit.
6 N. Davies, *God's Playground: A History of Poland*, (Oxford, 1982), p.441.
7 K. Iranek-Osmecki, *Kto ratuje jedno życie*, (London, 1968).
8 The report is in the Studium Polski Podziemnej in London.
9 Stefan Korboński, *Polskie Państwo Podziemne*, (Paris, 1975).
10 Professor Władysław Bartoszewski, writer, historian, currently visiting Professor at Munich University.
11 For this paper see ed. C. Abramsky, M. Jachimczyk, A. Polonsky, *The Jews in Poland*, (Oxford, 1985), pp. 146–60.
12 For this paper, see *The Jews in Poland*, pp. 177–89.
13 Dr Antony Polonsky, Reader in International History, London School of Economics.
14 For this paper, see *The Jews in Poland*, pp. 161–76.
15. Michał Borwicz, writer and historian, from 1945 to 1947 Director of the Jewish Historical Commission in Kraków and deputy Director of the Central Jewish Historical Commission in Poland.
16 Professor Juliusz Strojnowski, Professor of history at the University of Cologne.
17 Dr. Józef Lichten, Professor of the Polish University Abroad, London and representative of the Anti-Defamation League of B'nai B'rith in Rome and at the Vatican.

REVIEW ESSAYS

IMAGES OF JEWISH POLAND IN THE POST-WAR POLISH CINEMA
Edward Rogerson

There is in the Polish literary tradition an identifiable 'Polish-Jewish' element, even though it is difficult to formulate an effective framework for critical analysis. The presence of a sizeable Jewish minority in the Polish lands is reflected in the vernacular literature – particularly in the century following the failure of the 1831 uprising – either through the writings of Polish-speaking Jews such as Bruno Schulz, or in the works of Polish writers such as Adam Mickiewicz or Władysław Reymont. Whether there is in mainstream literature any real attempt to come to terms with the Jewish experience is highly debateable; those same writers whose works comprise the classic texts of Polish Romantic literature also helped to formulate the Messianic sub-text which enables Poles to project a self-image of an exclusively Catholic Martyr Nation. Nevertheless, even if the growing polarisation of Polish society during the nineteenth and early twentieth centuries tended to exclude the national minorities from the cultural debate, the existence of a culturally significant Jewish minority could not be ignored by Polish writers. Literature is both an imperative force and a mirror for the society which engenders it.

In the problematic cultural atmosphere of People's Poland, cinema's adherents would claim that it has become the most significant imperative intellectual force in Polish culture and society. For Andrzej Wajda, the contemporary cinema has appropriated the leading cultural role which Polish literature developed during the nineteenth century.[1]

Perhaps. But this is special pleading, overstating the artistic autonomy of the contemporary Polish cinema. Wajda, of course, is teasing the geese; literary adaptations of classic texts form a significant part of his prolific output. He is keenly aware of the cultural supremacy of the Romantic tradition and of the continuing importance of the Polish classics – even if they remain largely unread by the bulk of the population. And if contemporary Polish literature has become conflated with cinematic output, it is in part because the Polish cinema reflects a self-consciously literary approach to artistic expression. Which is why, in the end, echoes of the Jewish past have survived – despite the virtual destruction of Jewish Poland in the Holocaust. Those Polish literary works which explore Jewish life and culture are not so close to the heart of the Romantic tradition as to allow film-makers to use them in the arcane Polish cultural games of political allusion and allegory, but the most important are readily available to directors such as Wajda for whom the cinema is a means of exploring and evaluating the Polish historical experience.[2]

The terrible finality of the Nazi Final Solution has both reduced and distorted the Jewish component of that experience. In effect, the continuity of Jewish Poland has been irrevocably broken, and the history of a millennium of Polish-Jewish life is thereby divorced from the Polish present. With the community either destroyed or dispersed, the strongest surviving manifestation of the Jewish influence on Polish culture is to be found in the literature of Jewish Poland's last, most troubled century.

Wajda's 1974 adaptation of *Ziemia obiecana* (Promised Land) is a case in point. Władysław Reymont's 1897 novel presents the process of industrialization in nineteenth century Łódź as a dehumanizing experience, in which normal human values become submerged under the pressures of the new urban society. In Reymont's novel, as in the film, the most powerful impression is of the emergent class and racial tensions. The 'good' characters prove ineffectual in this new world of greed and ruthlessness, while the leading protagonists – German, Jew and Pole – are morally flawed, bound together only by a simple community of interest and a determination to exploit the new tensions to their own advantage.

Wajda's literary aesthetic is highly idiosyncratic; in many of his cinematic adaptations of literary works, he has often consciously challenged established critical interpretations of the original texts. In *Ziemia obiecana*, he has attempted to modify the cumulative effect of Reymont's schematic approach to characterization. Wajda's leading characters are more rounded; the ties which bind together the three industrialists have a degree of genuine affection which is scarcely present in the novel.

But the schematic nature of Reymont's original characterization is too well established for Wajda to be able to dispel with any conviction the strangely passionless atmosphere which this inspires. With the exception of the three industrialists, Reymont's Łódź is an environment populated almost completely with passive fictional stereotypes, whose only function is to form a barely differentiated human background to the main narrative. This vast human canvas of dispossessed peasants turned wretched urban *lumpenproletariat* and unfeeling petty Jewish merchants and financiers, at first visually insistent and threatening, becomes increasingly unsatisfactory. There is none of the deftness of touch by which Zola or, in an earlier age, Dickens could invest even a minor character with genuine humanity.

As a result, Reymont's novel is curiously lacking in vitality, for all the fascination of the main narrative drive.

These are, of course, criticisms of the text with which the director has had to work. This fundamental sterility could be neutralized only at the risk of compromising the novel's underlying narrative structure. But even as it stands, the film challenges the unthinking prejudices which dominate Reymont's vision of industrial society. Wojciech Pszoniak's performance as the Jew, Moryc Welt, adds humanity to a character in which Reymont encapsulated his negative vision of Polish Jewry. There is in Pszoniak's performance a paradoxical sense of almost joyful urgency, as if being there at the heart of things was all that mattered. This is not the exercise of financial power for the sake of it, or for the sake of oppressing the Polish population. In Pszoniak's hands, Welt becomes a character of great complexity whose humanity defuses an important element in the anti-semitism which so disfigures the novel.

By contrast, Daniel Olbrychski's Polish *szlachcic*, Borowiecki, only partially overcomes Reymont's schematic characterization. Reymont's Borowiecki, unable finally to reject the values of his class, is emotionally destroyed by the consequence of his ambition. Wajda strengthens Borowiecki by emphasizing his single-mindedness in the face of the anti-commercial traditions of his class, and the hostility of his non-Polish commercial rivals. Even so, Reymont's characterization is occasionally difficult to counter. This is particularly noticeable in the soft-focus epilogue, a significant departure from Reymont's original narrative. When Borowiecki orders the Tsarist police to shoot Polish strikers, his initial reluctance to countenance the act is strangely at variance with the earlier vehemence with which he rejected his Polish background.

Wajda has engineered a remarkable transformation of Reymont's most difficult novel. In a sense, he has made a film *about* Reymont's *Ziemia obiecana*, a contribution to a critical debate about a writer whose work is so dominated by his own prejudices and obsessions as to weaken the unique quality of his artistic vision. There is always a sense of an authorial Wajda, standing apart from a work with which he has found it difficult to come to terms and providing instead a detached critical gloss on Reymont's flawed vision of the processes of urban industrialization. The effect is emotionally draining and dramatically exciting. Twelve years after its controversial first appearance, *Ziemia obiecana* still has the power to raise emotions – even though those emotional responses owe more to ideological fixed positions than to Wajda's artistic intent. Wajda's Łódź is no longer Reymont's violent urban environment, and in its sense of detachment the film is at times strangely un-Polish. But it still deserves its place among the finest of Wajda's works.

Ziemia obiecana is the work of an outsider hostile both to the new economic order of the industrial towns, and to the urban Jews who had left behind their traditional communities to move to the industrial centres. Reymont showed no interest in the environment which the urban Jews had abandoned, and even those Poles sympathetic to the Jewish population were remarkably ill-informed on their lives and traditions. The virtual destruction of Jewish Poland must now have ended any real hopes of a cultural *aggiornamento*. Those fragments of Jewish life to have survived the Holocaust are too few to be self-sustaining.

Polish cinema is effectively the product of a post-war society where Jewish Poland has ceased to play any positive role. In consequence, cinematic analysis of the Jewish experience must be seen as something of an exercise in literary and historical exegesis; a formerly vibrant Polish-Jewish culture now survives only where it has been committed to paper. Even where writers or directors have Jewish antecedents – such as Andrzej Munk – they too will effectively experience the richness of their cultural heritage only at second hand. Contemporary Poland's tiny Jewish population is living among the ruins of its past.

In a sense, literary archaeology is the real subject matter of *Sanatorium pod klepsydrą* (The Sanatorium under the sign of the Hourglass), an adaptation by Wojciech Jerzy Has from the short stories of the Polish-Jewish fantasist Bruno Schulz (1892–1942). Schulz, the antithesis of the urbanized Jews of Reymont's Łódź, lived and worked all his life in the small Carpathian town of Drohobycz (now in the Soviet Ukraine), rarely leaving his home and always returning as quickly as he could. He was shot dead in the street in November 1942, only a few yards from his birth-place – the victim of an internal Gestapo feud.[3]

Schulz wrote only twenty six short stories – more properly descriptive works with a narrative content – in the ten years preceding his death. He recreates a traditional Jewish world which had already passed into folk memory long before Eastern European Jewry was destroyed in the Nazi extermination camps and the ghettoes – the *Hasidim* in their long overcoats haggling over lengths of cloth, ambiguous religious and social rites, darkened streets of shabby façades and dust-filled interiors. The rhythms and patterns of traditional Jewish life, its habits and associations, exist for Schulz only in his dreams. He is celebrating – and it is a celebration – a lost world of mystery and terror, of time-honoured traditions filtered through the imagination of a sickly child born to parents already middle-aged. Everything about this imaginary Drohobycz is old and dust-ridden. Every cobwebbed cranny or shadowy perspective suggests a brooding menace which the lonely child can evade only by crawling under his bed, or by muttering mysterious incantations, garbled imitations of the Judaic liturgy whose meaning is known only to the child-magician.

The almost tangible opulence of this imagined dream-world creates an aura of exoticism which is far removed from the principal concerns of the Polish literary imagination. Nevertheless, Schulz attained some degree of popularity in Poland towards the end of his life. There is in Schulz's vision a sense of mysticism and decadence which appealed in the morbid cultural atmosphere of Poland in the late 1930s. Even though his following was strong only among those *avant-garde* Poles who had fallen under the influence of Surrealism, there is a perennial Polish fascination with the exotic. Schulz's images of a remote and fading Jewish culture transcended the narrow geographic limits of his provincial life.

But a community has life even in decline. Any controversy over the progressive impoverishment of Jewish Poland during the inter-war period is now overshadowed by the cruel destruction of the Jewish community in the Nazi Holocaust. When the Wojciech Has adaptation was released in 1973, the Schulz stories had acquired a new level of signification. In effect, it has become impossible to make or to watch such a film without being aware of the intervening tragedy.

To be fair to Has, he largely avoids the dangers of this strange metonymic historicism. His adaptation is faithful, both to the spirit of Schulz's works, and in many places to the original text. The claustrophobic sets exactly recreate the dusty cobwebbed atmosphere of the books, and the peculiar, almost monochromatic colour film stock used by the Polish film industry during the early 1970s helps to reinforce the impression of a world which exists only in dreams or fading photographs in dusty picture frames.

Sanatorium pod klepsydrą is no lost domain of childhood innocence; the terrors which afflict the narrator Józef, although nameless, are frighteningly real. But these nameless terrors of childhood become blunted, perhaps even lost, in the changed perspectives of the adult world. Schulz is alive to the real impossibility of returning to this past, of ever being able to understand one's own childhood.

Józef (Jan Nowicki) is at once participant and disinterested observer of the scenes from his childhood. This is perhaps the most innovative feature of the Wojciech Has screenplay; by placing Jan Nowicki directly into this recreation of Drohobycz, Has avoids the potential ambiguities of Schulz's narrative structure. The adult Józef relives his past, but his adult persona is forced to relearn the forgotten rules of his childish imagination. Only by being re-educated as a child can he understand how to escape the terrors and penetrate the secrets of the arcane rituals with which he filled his childhood. Józef's painful process of reintegration into this lost Jewish world is possible only by abandoning his adult sensitivities and preconceptions.

It is perhaps inevitable that Wojciech Has cannot avoid the problems of Polish chronology – that we should see glimpses of the future tragedy of Jewish Poland in the images of decadence and occasional violence which come to dominate the film. Nevertheless, when Schulz wrote obliquely about Cossack raids, he did not have in mind the German Nazis. It would require an absurdly recondite reading of the original stories to interpret Schulz as a contributor, *a posteriori*, to post-war Holocaust Studies; he was a victim, not a chronicler. But the perverse Polish sense of metaphor will always reassert itself; Schulz's celebration of Jewish traditions has become the epitaph of a culture destroyed.

As a result of the overwhelming tragedies of the Nazi Occupation, the complex life of Jewish Poland is effectively redefined in terms of its own destruction. The celebratory element in *Sanatorium pod klepsydrą* is compromised by these problems of historical perspective which have latterly come to dominate contemporary Polish explorations of the Jewish experience. This problem is implicit even where those reflections focus on wider aspects of Jewish life and culture in Poland. It is as though the whole Jewish experience in Poland in some sense prefigures the evident horrors of the Nazi Final Solution.

Austeria (The Inn), a 1983 adaptation by Jerzy Kawalerowicz of Julian Stryjkowski's 1966 novel, makes explicit this strong sense of metonymic historicity. The author draws his readers into complicity in a world which consciously prefigures the Nazi Holocaust. Put simply: a group of Jews shelter at a Galician inn remote from the Russian advance into Austrian Poland during the First World War. Their oasis of humanity is by degrees transformed into a death-trap; none of the refugees escapes from a fate which seems somehow pre-ordained. As the historical tragedy intrudes on the refugees, human values are gradually undermined. The patience and tolerance of the innkeeper prove in the end to be frail in the face of wartime destruction and violence. As a counter to the inhuman passions of the Russian forces, his tolerant philosophy is as futile as the blind panic which caused the Jews to seek refuge in the first place.

Austeria is perhaps the best post-war analysis of the Polish-Jewish experience, since the work is certainly not unsympathetic to the problems and dilemmas facing the Polish majority. Stryjkowski explores the central crisis of Jewish life in the Polish lands: that tolerance and anti-semitism often inhabited the same intellectual and emotional space. The uneasy cohabitation between Pole and Jew was fraught with hidden tensions, although it took outside intervention for these tensions to take on a deeper, tragic form.

Jerzy Kawalerowicz is careful to preserve much of Stryjkowski's original narrative and philosophical intentions. But the screen adaptation, as with much of Kawalerowicz's work, is curiously lacking in passion; he fails on the whole to engage the emotions. In part at least, this could stem from the relative unfamiliarity of a Polish audience with a remote episode from the periphery of the Polish experience. But the central dilemma stems from Kawalerowicz's long-standing avoidance of contention in his film output; he is a director who has survived by not giving offence, by avoiding the intellectual tangles with censorship which characterize the work of the more outspoken Polish film directors. His over-faithful, tentative approach to Stryjkowski's novel has the paradoxical effect of undermining its deeper intentions.

In truth, *Austeria* appeared fifteen years too late to have any real impact, except as a historical curiosity. The intellectual climate, still favourable when Stryjkowski's novel was published in 1966, deteriorated markedly after March 1968. As Poland's Communist regime, responding to its growing insecurity in the late 1960s, consciously appropriated more of the symbols and prejudices of the Polish national tradition, official discussion of Polish-Jewish relations became couched in increasingly circumspect terms. When the film finally appeared, in 1983, popular responses were muted; the issues had ceased to be important in a country where the centre of political debate had shifted towards the aspirations of a generation which had never known Jewish Poland.

Despite the frequent uneasiness of Polish-Jewish relations, there was almost nothing to prepare either community for the intensity of the tragedy which destroyed Jewish Poland. Guilt and horror, characteristic of Jewish responses to the Nazi Holocaust, can be identified in Polish images of the same events. But such reactions make up only part of the Polish response. Official Poland's reluctance to come to terms with its present has the effect of compromising its relation to the past. The Nazi Occupation still colours official attitudes.

For official Poland, the difference between the Nazi treatment of Pole and Jew is simply a matter of degree. The uniqueness of the Jewish experience is undermined: subtly, as in newsreel reflections on the sufferings of the two martyr nations; or more directly, as in 1968, when the political climate became openly anti-semitic and the 'Zionists' were accused of manipulating Polish compassion for their own political ends.

The more outspoken examples of official attitudes are to be found in newsreel and television treatments of the war-time experience. Nevertheless, official Poland retains the means of influencing the broad pattern of feature film output – at the very least, through the manipulation of the censorship mechanism. It is therefore to be expected that cinematic treatment of the Nazi Occupation should follow patterns of analysis dictated by official attitudes – perhaps even that shifts in official policy will be mirrored in cinematic output.

Official attitudes are certainly not too far from the surface in war-related film output from the first decade of People's Poland. *Ostatni etap* (The Last Stage, 1947), Wanda Jakubowska's semi-documentary study of Auschwitz, would probably fit more easily into a study of Socialist Realism. There is little of historical value to be extracted from Jakubowska's analysis; she creates a world of stereotypical banality – brutal Nazis, their *Kapo* helpers, the dignified prisoners dreaming of freedom and Joseph Stalin. With her use of Soviet technicians and her desire to uphold Poland's new social order, she entirely negates the value of her personal testimony as a former Auschwitz internee.

Or consider Aleksander Ford, the first head of Film Polski on its creation in 1945. He is a problematic figure in the Polish cinema: a Jewish radical with a strongly Polish cultural aesthetic. The film critic Jacek Fuksiewicz[4] identified a strange blend of romanticism and impressionism which was somewhat at variance to his political commitment to cinematic realism. But Ford was too astute a political survivor to challenge too directly the prevailing orthodoxy. It was the rebirth of official anti-semitism, not any need for freedom of artistic expression, which encouraged Ford to emigrate in 1968.

Ulica Graniczna (Border Street, 1948), Ford's semi-documentary study of the life and death of the Warsaw Ghetto, is therefore compromised by the director's apparent need to conform to the prevailing political climate. But the film escapes from these artistic restrictions to a considerable degree. There is a basic equivocation in the characterization, and Ford shows a willingness to discuss the recent past – Polish anti-semitism included – in a manner which has become more unusual since 1956, as the Communist authorities began to appropriate the symbols and concerns of the Polish national tradition. It could be argued that the attack on traditional anti-semitism was made easier by firmly identifying the phenomenon with the reactionary social structure of inter-war Poland. But Ford's use of children as the central element in the narrative, and his picture of a world governed by terror, comes closer than many Polish films to a fair cinematic analysis of the Nazi bureaucratization of anti-semitism – and of its tragic consequences.

Socialist Realism was something of a constricting factor for Polish feature film output; only with the restoration of a degree of artistic freedom after 1953 was it possible for a new generation of film directors to develop those familiar Polish themes of historical reflection and an exploration of the national mythology. Andrzej Wajda, the most potent cinematic investigator of Polish historical obsessions, has explored in several films the absorption of the war-time experience into the national tradition; the war remains, for his generation, the most significant formative experience and a source of reflection for the post-war Poland which emerged from the ruins.[5]

Because of Wajda's obsessions with the symbols and mythologies of Poland's recent past, his reflections on the Second World War offer a well-rounded analysis of the relationship between the destruction of Jewish Poland and the wider Polish experience. Echoes of the Holocaust can be found in several of his major works, although only in *Samson* (1961) does he approach the war from a Jewish perspective.

The Warsaw Ghetto Rising, and the initial reluctance of the Home Army to offer effective support to the Jewish fighters, is an important external dynamic in the action of *Pokolenie* (A Generation, 1954), Wajda's first feature. The death of a Jewish friend in the Ghetto fighting prompts the leading protagonists – though too late – to try to help the Jewish insurgents. The film is a powerful debut work, although it is an unsatisfactory example of the director's historical and cultural outlook; necessary compromises with Socialist Realist doctrines and artistic clashes with Aleksander Ford ensured that Wajda's film closely reflected official attitudes towards the issues and controversies of Polish resistance. Reflections on Polish history, Wajda's most important intellectual contribution to the Polish cinema, are subordinated in *Pokolenie* to the political dictates of an ideology whose legitimacy he has challenged in almost every subsequent film.

Krajobraz po bitwie (Landscape after a battle, 1970) offers a more balanced reflection on the impact of Nazi Occupation. Set in a refugee camp during the winter of 1945, the film depicts a Poland displaced emotionally and physically. The film has a loose structure; the product of a series of short stories. The unifying feature is the bitter emptiness of the refugees, survivors uprooted from their past. The social structure of the camp replicates the indifference and despair of Occupied Poland. A love affair between a Polish writer and a Jewish survivor ends in her death – needlessly shot by a nervous American sentry; the tragedy is met with indifference by the refugees. The experience of Occupation, the destruction of one nation and the demoralization of another, has broken the emotional spirit of Nazism's survivors.

Samson is Wajda's most complete attempt to explore this emotionally broken environment from the perspective of Nazism's principal victims. He is unable to escape fully from the schematic ideological determinism of Kazimierz Brandys' novella, which has a formulaic clumsiness typical of Socialist Realist fiction; despite this, the film is an interesting attempt to explore the strange pathology of one man's reaction to the destruction of the Jewish nation. Jakub Gold is a latter-day Samson, unaware of his strength and forced to confront impersonal historical forces from a position of isolated weakness. Imprisoned before the War for killing an anti-semitic thug in a street brawl, Jakub is released in 1939 only to be interned in the Warsaw Ghetto. He fights against his externally-imposed destiny, first by escaping from the Ghetto, and then by becoming involved in the armed resistance to Nazism. His death is inevitable, but it represents a personal reaction to the verdict of historical destiny. Wajda's reaction to the Jewish fate is highly personal; faced with the totality of the Holocaust, the director-historian can express his feelings of revulsion only by exploring 'the predicament of a hounded man'.[6]

During the first half of the 1960s, Polish creative artists were able to explore the complex dilemmas arising from the Nazi Occupation with some degree of openness. In several books and films, there is a basic honesty of approach which was later to be abandoned, in the anti-semitic disturbances of 1968. *Świadectwo urodzenia* (Birth certificate, 1961, Stanisław and Tadeusz Różewicz) is a further example of this exploration of the past. As with Wajda's more considered reflections on the War, *Świadectwo urodzenia* is concerned with the effects of the conflict; in three unconnected short stories, the film traces the lives of Polish children as they try to cope with the physical and emotional pressures of Nazi terror. The Jewish fate hovers on the periphery of all the stories, but it is in the third story, *A Drop of Blood*, that the Jewish experience is directly approached. A Jewish girl is sheltered from the Germans by a number of Polish families, and is placed in an orphanage under a false identity. A German spot-check – a scene of unashamed sentimentality – leads to her identification by a *Gestapo* racial expert as a child with 'pure Aryan characteristics'. As she tearfully protests her (false) identity, the Germans begin to make plans for her to be brought back into the Master Race.

Świadectwo urodzenia raises all the principal issues of the Jewish experience but in its even-handedness and its occasional lapses into sentimentalism, it cannot be said to engage the emotions beyond a relatively superficial level. It is as though the Różewicz brothers want to raise dilemmas without exploring the consequences too closely. Polish anti-semitism is directly countered at one point by a subsequent scene showing the Poles reluctantly though sincerely helping a victim of Nazism. This is a long-standing Polish intellectual game, and one is left to wonder at this apparent belief in an essentially over-riding goodness. It really is evading the issue to juxtapose conflicting images of characteristic Polish attitudes without making some attempt to differentiate between them.

There is now little scope for the further exploration of wartime dilemmas. Poland is a predominantly young country, and the remoteness of the Jewish dimension has transformed formerly controversial themes into a matter of recondite academic enquiry. *Kartka z podróży* (Postcard from a Journey, 1983, Waldemar Dziki) shows the extent to which this trend has affected the cinema.[7] The screenplay, from a Czech short story, follows the last actions of a middle-aged, cultured Jew who has received his expected deportation order from the German administration. This cultivated man, the antithesis of Nazi caricatures of Jewish sub-humanity, tries to retain his dignity as he confronts the first stage of his fatal journey to Treblinka.

Emotional distance compromises *Kartka z podróży*. There is little enough to engage the audience, and it fails to challenge received opinions of the Nazi deportations. As a result, the film's shortcomings and contradictions stand out more clearly; the portrait of the Ghetto is frankly unbelievable, and it is inconceivable that any Polish Jew would continue to entertain such beliefs in the basic civility of the German Occupiers. To that extent, the story is only too clearly not of Polish origin.

The Nazi Final Solution failed in its ultimate objective to destroy every last trace of Jewish life in Eastern Europe. Certainly, Poland has ceased to be the pre-eminent Jewish centre which it had been in the centuries before 1939, but echoes of the Jewish heritage have continued to be felt in Polish life and culture during the post-war period. This was not something which the Communist authorities could accept with equanimity. Several leading Communists – most notably Jakub Berman, Hilary Minc – were of Jewish origin, which created tensions within the Polish Party. As Poland's Communists began after Stalin's death to absorb the more disreputable elements of Polish nationalism, the perceived threat of the *Żydokomuna* was often called into service in the fractional in-fighting.

Although Jewish Poland has become a peripheral element in Polish life, the controversies generated by party fractionalism occasionally spilled out into Polish life – the 'anti-Zionist' campaign of March 1968 is the most pressing example. Two films made during the Solidarity period, *Przypadek* (Accident, Krzysztof Kieślowski) and *Matka Królów* (Mother of Kings, Janusz Zaorski), both allude to the effects of anti-semitism within the Party apparatus. In *Przypadek*, a multi-layered and disturbing account of a man who lives three consecutive lives – *partyjny, opozycyjny* and non-political – each ending with the same plane-crash, a friend from the hero's childhood suddenly leaves Poland in 1968. Only later does he discover that she was of Jewish origin. In *Matka Królów*, a semi-documentary epic spanning the period of the War and Polish Stalinism (1939–1956), the former lover of the heroine holds an important government post in the first decade of People's Poland. When he is dismissed in October 1956, it is because of his Jewish ancestry.

Both *Przypadek* and *Matka Królów* were abruptly shelved on completion, remaining unseen for some years before finally obtaining their Polish general release. The reasons for the delay are difficult to determine, but it is unlikely that the somewhat tangential Jewish dimension accounts for their apparent unacceptability to the Polish authorities. Perhaps, simply, the predominant images of a society in barely disguised conflict are a continuing source of official embarrassment in post-Solidarity Poland. It is post-war history itself, and not the fading memories of Jewish Poland, which most concerns Poland's rulers.

In truth, Jewish Poland is losing its power to provoke controversy. Polish sensitivity towards the Jewish heritage has been steadily eroded throughout the post-war period, an erosion mirrored in the almost incidental nature of recent cinematic references to lingering Polish anti-semitism. If a Polish director feels he must look to an original Czech story for his inspiration in a study of the Nazi Final Solution, then the tragedy of Jewish Poland and the Warsaw Ghetto is evidently losing its immediacy for the Poles – a strange eventuality for a nation with such a strong sense of history. It is as though the world which vanished in the Holocaust has finally been transformed into just another area of academic enquiry and historical research.

Which is not to say that the history of Jewish Poland is becoming devoid of emotional value for the Poles, nor to suggest that the present Polish government is somehow averse to using the Jewish experience for propaganda purposes. Claude Lanzmann's controversial and somewhat self-righteous epic *Shoah* was shown in Poland in 1985 in part because it was seen in official circles as a means of showing the Poles that the Catholic Church was morally flawed in its response to Jewish suffering.[8] Equally, the current official willingness to talk about Polish-Jewish reconciliation might well be motivated by something other than a spirit of altruism. . . .

Whatever the reasons for these political equivocations, the fact remains that the Jewish experience has been of limited apparent value as a source of inspiration for Polish feature film directors. Wajda's literary and historical aesthetic apart, it has been left for a few directors, mainly Jewish in origin, to record in their cinematic output a fragment of the diversity of Jewish life in Poland. The result is an incomplete record of an important historical experience. Countless newsreels and short documentaries have hinted at the richness of the Jewish heritage, but this past remains for most Poles a largely unexplored, perhaps even exotic, environment. Only in feature films concerned with the Second World War – in any case, a Polish obsession – does any of the diversity of the Jewish experience translate into the mainstream of feature film production. But, since the Polish film industry is essentially a post-war creation, it could perhaps hardly be otherwise.

NOTES

1 'The best literature in Poland today is found in screenplays. Most of the best films in recent years have been original stories for the screen.' From an interview with Andrzej Wajda in the French critical journal Cinéaste, February 1980.
2 I discuss these Polish cinematic 'games' of political allusion and allegorical expression in more detail in: 'Cultural Games in a Cold Climate' (Encounter, January 1987).
3 The Schulz short stories are available in English translation as follows: *The Street of Crocodiles* (McGibbon and Kee, 1963). *Sanatorium under the Sign of the Hourglass* (Hamish Hamilton, 1979). The Schulz stories have inspired *Street of Crocodiles*, a short feature from the Quay Brothers, which was released in 1986. The film is a remarkable puppet animation which recreates in miniature form the dusty claustrophobia of Schulz's imagination. The Quay Brothers' work is discussed by the British film director Peter Greenaway in: 'Street of Crocodiles' (Sight and Sound, Summer 1986).
4 Jacek Fuksiewicz, *Polish cinema*, (Interpress, 1973).
5 The essential paradox is that Wajda often feels himself to be constricted by the historical and literary tradition which is his major source of inspiration. 'I would gladly trade in this clutch of national symbols [. . .] for a handful of sexual symbols

from the Freudian textbooks.' 'Quoted in Bolesław Michałek: *Andrzej Wajda*, (London 1973).
6 Barbara Mruklik: *Andrzej Wajda*, (WAiF, Warsaw, 1969), quoted in Michałek.
7 *Kartka z podróży* won the 1983 Andrzej Munk Award for a début feature. It is ironic that such an unsatisfying film should receive an award given in honour of a man whose – sadly unfinished – film *Pasażerka* (1962) is probably the finest psychological study in the Polish cinema of the Nazi Concentration Camp system.
8 Neal Ascherson: 'The frontiers of art and history' (*The Observer*, 9.XI.1986).

THE HOLOCAUST – JEWS AND GENTILES IN MEMORY OF THE JEWS OF PACANÓW

Andrzej Bryk

Martin Gilbert. *The Holocaust: the Jewish Tragedy*. London: Collins. 1986. Pp. 959.

Richard Lukas. *Forgotten Holocaust: the Poles under German Occupation, 1939–1944*. Lexington: The University Press of Kentucky. 1986. Pp. 300.

Nechama Tec. *When Light pierced the Darkness: Christian Rescue of Jews in Nazi-Occupied Poland*. New York: Oxford University Press. 1986. Pp. 262.

Randolph Braham, editor. *Jewish Leadership during the Nazi Era: Patterns of Behaviour in the Free World*. New York: Social Science Monographs and Institute for Holocaust Studies of CUNY, distributed by Columbia University Press, New York. 1985. Pp. 154.

Deborah Lipstadt.*Beyond Belief: the American Press and the Coming of the Holocaust, 1933–1945*. New York: The Free Press. 1986. Pp. 370.

The Holocaust of European Jews, and especially the Holocaust of Jewish civilization between the Vistula and the Dnieper – with its language, culture, economic system – has become the subject of continuing academic research. Recently a series of works has appeared which examine the question afresh.

Gilbert's is by no means the classic history of the Holocaust. He has attempted to create a portrait based on the pain and despair of individuals. He has carried out interviews with hundreds of survivors, and managed to obtain diaries. He gives us 'an insight into the many different ways in which individuals met their death' (p. 419). Gilbert also writes about the witnesses: sympathetic and indifferent, rescuing and denouncing. But the question of the relationship between Jews and non-Jews does not interest him.

The author is not always consistent in his method. On occasions his attempts to make generalisations leave misleading impressions. He writes very little about the German Army. Yet the Holocaust did not only involve the SS. On several occasions he cites Churchill as chief spokesman on Jewish affairs in the West, although it is questionable whether Churchill should be used as a symbol of the free world's interest.

Gilbert writes a good deal about the lack of resistance from Jews themselves. He shows how the German policy of deception and trickery reinforced typical Jewish behavioural patterns which had developed over centuries: 'the traditional dependence upon the utmost restraint, and the reliance for survival upon every type of ingenuity' (p. 386). The Germans tried to convince them that the chance of survival still existed, if only they were prepared to exert their maximum efforts. So every means was attempted and each failed. And although (and in spite of the paralysing passivity) the book records every semblance of resistance, one can see clearly how Jewish culture did not prepare them for the Holocaust.

Jews were forced to choose between current, unprecedented experience and their whole cultural inheritance, which had taught them that what they were experiencing 'could not be real'.[1] Their abandonment of hope and initiation of a desperate struggle meant that their existence became reduced almost to the biological minimum.[2] None of the other peoples who were subjugated by the Nazis and chose to fight, even those subjected to mass murder, were forced to reject their cultural legacy in this way.

Gilbert's book is a monument in which the tragedy of six million people is not a matter of indifference. It is a major accomplishment. The Jews, alongside the Gypsies, were condemned to complete annihilation. But in Eastern Europe millions of others were murdered too. Richard C. Lukas writes of the fate of Poles under German occupation, and he asks historians of the Holocaust many questions hitherto ignored. He shows that Hitler's policy towards the Poles was one of destroying a whole people. The Nazis refused to acknowledge the Poles as fellow human beings and reduced them to the level of slaves.

The Germans started by liquidating the élite. During the war Poland lost 47 per cent of its doctors, 57 per cent of its lawyers, 40 per cent of its professors, 30 per cent of its technical workers and engineers, and over 18 per cent of its priests. Polish culture was irreparably damaged. Confiscations, starvation-level food rations, countryside seizures and requisitioning amounting to theft, caused a drastic impoverishment of the community. But worse of all were the executions. 'Poles were shot not only for resisting ... but also for simply being out after curfew or for selling on the black market, or for merely being Polish ... Frenchmen and Belgians were not rounded up and shot in street round-ups as Poles ... for no reason. People lived in constant fear of arrest, torture and death ....The principle of collective responsibility was applied' (p. 35–37). The Germans pacified over 300 villages, killing off their inhabitants. They built over 2,000 extermination camps, concentration camps and labour camps in Poland.

They were constructed here in an isolated country, cut off from the outside world, where terror reigned unchecked and where the greatest number of Jews were located.

The Germans did not find political collaborators in Poland, although one has to say that they did not look for them. Consequently, the Poles' only alternative was resistance. Lukas explains the complicated structure of the Polish underground. Independent groups gradually merged into one organization, the *AK* (Home Army), which remained politically subordinate to the Polish émigré government. The *AK* represented various shades of political opinion (apart from a handful of extreme right-wing and communist elements) and its commanders frequently had only nominal control over individual units. Until 1943 the *AK* organised for self-defence (executions of *SS*, Gestapo and collaborators), limiting its military operations owing to the bloody reprisals exacted by the Nazis. It also prepared plans for a rising against the Germans.

Against this background, Lukas analyses the controversial issue of the Home Army's attitude towards the Jews. He maintains that accusations from the Jewish side, that the *AK* as a whole was guilty of anti-semitism, are exaggerated. Such sentiments were alien to the *AK* command. Indeed signs of anti-semitism in the lower ranks of the *AK* reflected only the views of a group of right-wingers, who were in a minority overall. Under the auspices of the *AK*, furthermore, the organization *Żegota* was created in 1942 – an organization unique in the occupied countries which afforded help to Jews.

In Lukas' opinion the reason why so few Jews joined the ranks of the *AK* was not so much anti-semitism, as the fact that the majority of Jews were unassimilated. 'The vast majority of the members of the *AK* were civilians ... who went about their jobs and daily routines unnoticed. Most Jews could not function in that way. If they managed to escape from the ghettoes, they had to hide. The logical place to go was the forest in the East ... where ... they usually ... joined partisans organised by the Soviets and (Polish communists) ... because for a long time the *AK* did not place priority on partisan warfare' (p.79). The first *AK* units did not begin to appear in the forests until 1943. A group which was hostile towards the Jews, however, was the extreme right-wing *NSZ* (National Armed Forces), which did not recognise the authority of the *AK*. A minority of the *NSZ* did subordinate itself to the *AK* in 1944, but by then the majority of Jewish partisans were being murdered by the Germans. Sporadic attacks by the *AK* on Jewish partisans were motivated – claims Lukas – by political considerations. Since the Jews were for the most part involved with the communist movement 'it would seem implausible that in the struggle between the *AK* and the communists that went on in Eastern Poland, the *AK* units would have the time or inclination to differentiate between Jewish and non-Jewish Communist partisans before they fired on them'(p. 80). Lukas does not ignore the role that the stereotype of the Jew-Communist may have played in the ranks of the *AK*, but emphasizes that the situation was more complex.

Lukas explains the *AK*'s attitude of suspicion to the Jews' passivity during the early years of the occupation, adding that the majority of Jewish groups which were mobilized for action were of communist leanings. He also disputes the view that the *AK* did not provide arms in sufficient quantities for the 1943 ghetto rising in Warsaw. Without attempting to pass a moral judgment on the fears that the doomed rising might spread, he shows that the *AK* did not possess heavy arms, nor did it entirely control the arms distributed among the members of its organization, and a large proportion of the weaponry attributed to the *AK* was unsuitable for actual use. Only when air drops from England began in 1943 did the situation begin to improve, but even during the failed Warsaw Rising in August 1944, only 10 per cent of the 16,000 combatants were fully armed.

Lukas devotes a part of his study to the problem of anti-semitism in the Polish Army in the USSR (1941–2) and in the West. He claims that during the period when the greatest extermination of Jews was taking place, between 1942–4 the Western press devoted a disproportionate amount of attention to anti-semitic incidents in the Polish Army, which were exploited politically by Zionists. The Russians forbade the recruitment of Polish Jews to the army, granting this right only to ethnic Poles. The Polish Government protested and fought to obtain exit visas. Despite this the Jewish press maintained that Poles were responsible for removing Jews from the army. In the Middle East some of the Jews deserted, not so much because of anti-semitism – claims Lukas – but rather because of Zionist propaganda (which had the tacit approval of the Polish Command). In Great Britain the question of anti-semitism in the Polish Army was taken up in 1944 in connection with the recruitment of Jews – Polish citizens – and the arrest of some for desertion. A number of the Jews, insists Lukas, did not want to serve because of anti-semitism, but others simply did not want to fight. These desertions and the anti-Polish campaign continued owing to the activities of pro-Soviet members of parliament. On the other hand the Zionists were also actively involved, wanting to organise independent Jewish units and playing the card of Polish anti-semitism. The Polish Government, sensitive to such charges, issued an amnesty for the Jewish deserters. Of course, a considerable number of Jews served loyally throughout in the Polish Army.

Furthermore, the exiled Polish Government never let Polish Jews down. As early as 1940 this government, in which there were Polish Jewish representatives, informed Western public opinion of the persecution of the Jews and was the first to publish evidence that they were being exterminated. From 1942, it pressed for retaliatory bombing of, among other targets, the railway line to Auschwitz. It is true that at the beginning of the war, the government considered, and there was evidence for this, claims Lukas, that the situation of the Polish population was worse than that of the Jews. From 1941 however, after reports delivered by courier began to arrive, a change in attitude occurred. Nevertheless, claims Lukas, – 'a relationship of confidence never really developed between the Jewish community in England and the United States and the Polish Government'(p. 153). The main stumbling block was 'the anti-semitic orientation of prewar Polish governments . . . Sikorski was astonished at Jewish circles in the U.S. who emphasized Polish anti-semitism during the war – to the point that . . . they seemed oblivious to German murders of Jews' (p. 168). Lukas adds, however, that the Polish Government was ineffective in countering charges of anti-semitism and failed to set up a Ministry for Jewish Affairs.

Lukas devotes a great deal of space to relations between the Polish and Jewish communities under the occupation. Aid extended to the Jews was restricted not so much by anti-semitism – argues Lukas – but rather due to the Nazi terror. This apart, 'in Poland, where contacts between Poles and Jews were so limited before the war, it would be unrealistic to assume that their relationship during the war would be much different'(p. 126). In occupied Poland, uniquely in Europe, offering help of any kind to a Jew resulted in the death sentence both for oneself and for one's family. Alongside the quiescent mass of the population, whom Lukas regards as 'passively humanitarian', there were those who were active helpers. Estimates of the number of Poles who lost their lives for helping Jews varies from a few thousand to 50,000. Between 50,000 and 100,000 Jews survived as a result. The number of those concealed, but who did not survive, is also considerable. In total around a million people were engaged in rescue work. He considers the efforts made to rescue Jews were disproportionately high when compared with other countries in Europe.

Lukas describes many aspects of the German occupation in Poland and of Polish-Jewish relations – aspects as a rule insufficiently known – but he does leave out certain issues. He claims, that because Poles were victims of the terror, just as Jews were, the issue of Polish anti-semitism as a social fact becomes of less importance. The question of Polish nationalism during the war remains, however. A characteristic of the victim of nationalism is the 'reluctance to acknowledge in just measure that . . . the victim can also victimize.'[3] Without an answer to the question of whether there exists any link whatsoever between the prewar anti-semitism of a large section of the Polish community and the Germans' murdering of Polish Jews, this is not a reasonable way of examining Polish-Jewish relations. The anti-semitism of a large proportion of Poles during the war does not make them collaborators. There is a huge gulf between anti-semitism and a crime of this kind, but, on the other hand, it is not true that anti-semitism disappeared during the war and that its poisoned spring did not corrupt.

In September 1941 the commander of the *AK* reported to Sikorski: 'Please accept it as a fact that the overwhelming majority of the country is anti-semitic. . . . Anti-semitism is widespread now. Even secret organizations remaining under the influence of . . . the Democratic Club or the Socialist Party adopt the postulate of emigration as a solution of the Jewish problem.'[4] Indeed the courier, Jan Karski reported:

> The solution of the Jewish question . . . is . . . a dangerous tool in the hands of the Germans, leading to a "moral disarmament" of wide sectors of the Polish community . . . However true it may be that the country has a fundamental hatred (of the Germans), this issue creates almost a link by means of which the Germans are reaching a common understanding with a significant section of the Polish population . . . This situation threatens to demoralise large sections of the community . . . trying to establish some kind of . . . common front, one encounters immense difficulties from these groups within the Polish community, since anti-semitism has by no means diminished amongst them.[5]

Lukas does not include these documents, although he refers to Karski's report. And yet they are of central importance.

Lukas's book provides evidence of how difficult it is – in spite of objectivism – to grasp the whole truth about the Polish nation during those years. Poland 'rescuing' or 'passively humanitarian' was not inconsiderable and was greater than, for example, 'rescuing' France or Slovakia, but its importance should not be overestimated. Poles rescued Jews often despite the opposition of other Poles. The Germans murdered the Polish Jewish community, but nothing can excuse indifference hidden from conscience behind the screen of helplessness. In looking for the source of this indifference one must look into the legacy of Polish anti-semitism. This is, however, now a matter for Polish consciences, of which Lukas – recording facts – has no obligation to take account.

As for the Home Army, up until 1943 its chief aim was to prevent the community from becoming demoralised by establishing norms of community life, organising illegal education and the elimination of collaborators. Lukas nearly loses sight of the fact that this activity was directed not only against Germans, but that in the main it was for the benefit of Poles. The *AK* and its political annexe acted as a substitute for public life in Poland under the terror. It must be emphasized that neither the Polish Government in London, nor the *AK*, were a continuation of the pre-1939 political system. Sikorski's government was composed of representatives from the centre-left parties and of liberal elements from the National

Democratic party, and it was a democratic government.⁶ Apart from opposing the Germans, the task of the *AK* élite was to prepare and lead the community towards democracy. Poland's political culture before 1939 was nationalist in character and a large section of the Polish elite exacerbated the Jewish problem in an irresponsible way.⁷ However, Poland had a strong democratic opposition even then, and so it cannot be argued that the outbreak of war prevented the introduction of anti-Jewish legislation. The municipal elections of 1938 had already signalled a turning point, and indeed the 1940 elections could, according to some predictions, have led to victory for the opposition parties.⁸ These were the parties who provided the *AK* with the élites which, amongst other things, combatted anti-semitism. Only with the Holocaust of the Polish Jews and the decimation of ethnic Poles themselves, did the slow and hesitant process begin, set in motion by the *AK* élite, of forming a community of feeling, which – in the words of Vincenz – 'never awakened, never matured into full awareness'.⁹ From this perspective, it becomes easier to understand the role played by the *AK* élite with regard to the anti-semitism within the community. We can, and should, say, as Henryk Grynberg has done, that 'accusing the Poles of cooperating in crucifying the Jews is as inconsistent with the truth . . . as accusing the Jews of crucifying the Messiah.'¹⁰ But one should also take in the whole tragedy, when a Polish community raised to a significant degree in an anti-semitic culture and subconciously accepting the alien nature of Jews suddenly found itself in a situation where that culture did not offer any moral barrier to an easy acceptance of the fact of their annihilation.¹¹ The central *AK* press is witness to the fact that its élite perceived this danger. A few remarks about the Polish Army. After 1939 it was indeed a volunteer army, and the motivation leading to enlistment was true patriotism and not administrative pressure as we usually understand it. Under these conditions feelings of exclusivity rose to the surface. In the minds of many Poles the behaviour of Jews, when faced with the entry into Poland of Soviet forces in 1939, was pro-Soviet. This fact is cited as the reason for anti-semitism in the Polish Army. It is true that some Jews joined the Soviet administration, but large numbers shared the fate of the Poles.¹² Polish Jews were deported together with ethnic Poles in 1940 and many thousands died (amongst others, the Chief Rabbi of Warsaw, Moses Shorr and the Chief Rabbi of the Polish Army, Major Baruch Steinberg in Katyń). It is worth asking to what extent the attitude of some Poles towards the Jews, in the army that was later formed, was determined by social perception, the tendency to see what we want to see, something that is part of our conditioning. The conduct of some Jews in 1939 strengthened anti-semitic convictions, but did not cause them.

The question of whether Jews were refused enlistment to the Polish Army deserves further study. Statements by a number of Polish Jews indicate that they were ruled out not only by Soviet prohibitions, but also by Polish recruiting teams, although this was never the official policy of General Anders. In Lukas the line between the high command and a section of the officer corps and men, is blurred over. The role of Zionists was not inconsiderable here, but that problem in turn was settled politically in Palestine. Anti-semitism, however, did not disappear. It was provoked by National Democrat activists as early as 1940. They gained control of Polish offices in Palestine and started anti-Jewish activities. This had the result that Polish Jews, who after 1940 were well-disposed towards Polish refugees, later began to regard them as enemies.[14] This kind of policy had later consequences with the unjust Jewish accusations, fanned by the Russians, of discrimination during the evacuation from the USSR. Similarly, in spite of what Lukas assumes, Menachem Begin did not desert. Summoned by Irgun to take over its command, he refused because he did not want to desert. Successful intervention to have him released came from both the Polish and Jewish sides.[15]

The Polish Government in exile did not abandon Polish Jews, but it failed to carry out a number of important political gestures. It is true that as early as 1939 the government declared that its goal was the rebuilding of a just Poland in which all its citizens could live, but in 1942 the *Endecja* placed a resolution before the émigré parliament that Jews be encouraged to emigrate from Poland.[16] Sikorski, who was the first Polish leader since Dmowski to visit the United States, did not come out with a clear declaration aimed at American Jews. The provocative behaviour of Dmowski towards the Jews in 1918, described by the leader of the American Jewish Committee, L. Marshall as 'simply monstrous', caused, as Paderewski reported, 'immense harm to the Polish cause'.[17] Dmowski's arrogance resulted in Jewish community leaders deciding on an anti-Polish line. Faced with this situation, Sikorski did not take any decisive steps which would have changed the political orientation of American Jews towards Poland. However much American Jews may be accused of getting their priorities wrong, it was Polish policy which was, in this difficult area, unfortunate, and resulted from the entanglement in internal struggles with the *Endecja*. An assessment of the Polish position is also complicated by the fact that to date no-one has researched the question of the degree to which the conduct of the Polish Government towards American Jews might have been a bargaining counter prompted by the search for support over the Polish eastern border question.

In citing Polish losses suffered, Lukas states: 'Poland lost 6,028,000 of its citizens, or 22 per cent of its population, the highest ratio of losses to population of any country in Europe. About 50 per cent of these victims were Polish Christians and 50 per cent were Polish Jews. It's time to speak about the forgotten holocausts of WWII . . . .Because of lack of understanding of the Holocaust in its broadest terms writers have perpetuated . . . unrealistic and unhistorical judgements about the possibilities . . .

available to the Poles to render greater aid than they did to the Jews' (pp. 22 and 39).

Here two reservations must be expressed. Of the three million Poles, several hundred thousand died in the USSR.[18] Around 650,000 died fighting. A table of the statistics of murdered Jews and Poles, in itself of unsure value, since they were the citizens of the same state, can only be drawn up on the understanding that parity of losses is absolutely no indication of similar fates. It is true that the tragedy of the Poles is often dishonestly ignored, but using the concept of the Holocaust as a symbol of Nazi barbarism is a misuse of the term. The fate of Poles was not the same as that of the Jews.

During the occupation being a Pole – although equated with slavery – did not necessarily mean death; being a Jew did. Because of this some 90 per cent of Polish Jews perished, as compared with 10 per cent of Poles. The Holocaust cannot, therefore, be just a metaphor for bestiality. It is a part of Jewish history. Where then should one place the tragedy of non-Jews? The most reasonable solution seems to me to be that suggested by Yehuda Bauer – a '"continuum of evil" that would lead from mass murder ... through genocide to holocaust. Such a continuum does not imply a value judgement as to the degree of moral condemnation, so that one cannot argue that "mass murder" is in some way less reprehensible than genocide or holocaust.'[19] Of course, the failure of researchers to be sensitive to this 'continuum of evil', as practised by the Nazis, prevents a full understanding of the Holocaust as well, and in this respect the methodological points made by Lukas are entirely correct.

Previous studies of the Holocaust have never tried to find an empirically documented answer to the question: Who were the righteous among nations? This gap in the literature has recently been addressed. Nechama Tec studies Poland, which 'provides the key to an understanding of the Holocaust ... and the rescuing of Jews' (p. 11). She bases her study on published sources and interviews, which furnish information on 565 'just' Poles. Her general conclusions are based on an analysis of this group of subjects.

The first part of the study provides a description of the circumstances surrounding escape from the ghetto to non-Jewish areas and subsequent concealment. The second part details atypical cases: rescues carried out for financial gain, or else examples of people with anti-semitic views who hid Jews. The third part contains a psychological outline of the rescuing group and clarifies what motivated them. Tec questions the principle of entering into comparisons between the treatment of Jews by people in Western Europe (e.g. Denmark, Holland) and in Poland, emphasizing that here there were the greatest dangers in helping Jews, and yet despite this the same number of people proportionately (with the exception of Denmark) were rescued.

In 1941, the Germans issued a decree forbidding the Jews under pain of death to leave the ghetto, and issued death sentences on Poles helping Jews. One third of those Poles who nonetheless aided Jews initiated such help themselves. In two thirds of the cases it was not planned and no-one was waiting on the other side of the wall. Eighty per cent of those Jews saved were unassimilated and unable to live by using 'aryan' papers. She stresses the fact that Poles never entered into any political collaboration with the Germans, and defines the attitude of the majority as 'one of purposeful uninvolvement. Poles, struggling to survive, neither aided the Germans nor hindered them' (p. 40). The rescuing of Jews required Poles to overcome several hurdles. The most important – states Tec – were the Nazi terror and a non-aggressive, 'cultural' anti-semitism. For this reason the environment in which the 'righteous' Poles operated was far from a favourable one in which to try to rescue Jews. She adds, however, that 'the ultimate responsibility for the creation and implementation of the Final Solution lies with the Nazis' (p. 63).

Yad Vashem has accorded the title of 'righteous Christian' to 5742 people, of whom 1505 were of Polish origin. Tec estimates that this figure should be multiplied by a factor of ten. Moreover, we do not know how many Poles perished together with those to whom they had offered shelter. Here, by contrast with Lukas, Tec refrains from estimating a figure.

Some offered to help from motives of personal gain. In such cases the psychological links between shelterer and sheltered were weaker, resistance to the threat of danger lower, and desire to have the Jew off one's hands greater. There were also a number of rescuers, although only a small percentage, who were unambiguously anti-semitic. Their action was a form of defiance against the Germans. It demanded serious consideration of the consequences of one's deeds, and a moral and intellectual independence. It is no coincidence therefore that the anti-semites who came to the rescue of Jews were deeply devout Catholics or intellectuals who played a prominent role in society.

Tec attempts to determine to what extent social class, political leanings or religion throw light on the motives behind the actions of the 'righteous'. Those who tended to help mostly came from from the intelligentsia and the workers, but these did not exceed their proportional representation. As for political views, the Left did not have a monopoly on helping Jews. Tec is more interested however in the role of the AK. She manages here to make an extremely useful contribution, believing that the suggestions that help was offered only by communists or the left-wing of the AK are mistaken. She points out that the postwar persecution of the AK led to a belittling of its contribution in this area. This in turn led to a large part of the evidence being lost. It is necessary to add to this that the AK formally disbanded in January 1945 and it was regarded by the communists as a hostile organization, which led to its being outlawed and to thousands of

AK soldiers fleeing to the woods where they carried out anti-communist activities.[20] Also operating in the woods were the extreme right-wing *NSZ* groups and Ukrainian nationalists. The communists started to identify the former *AK* men with the right-wing extremists, accusing them also of murdering Jews. There were members of the *AK* at the time who, fearing retribution, did not admit to being members and to having helped Jews. Members of *Zegota* were also persecuted. Facts were falsified in publications dealing with relations between the *AK* and the Jews, shaping the opinions which were accepted later by historians and journalists in the West, which resulted in much misunderstanding.[21]

Tec devotes considerable space to the position of the Catholic Church in Poland, and to the influence of religious values on the decisions of those people who helped Jews. Traditionally, the teaching of the pre-war Church was anti-semitic, but this in turn required an altering of values based on the Decalogue. Generally speaking, neither the Vatican, nor the Polish Church mounted an official attack on the crimes against the Jews. With a lack of clear directions from the Vatican, the Polish clergy were in an ambiguous position. Tec leads us to understand that there existed some links between the Vatican and the Polish Church during the war and that the Polish Church did not make a public condemnation of crimes against Jews, only because it received no such instructions. But Pius XII was equally silent about the crimes committed against Poles and priests. During the war 3000 Polish priests died – 18 per cent of the clergy. Pius XII's silence, inexplicable to the Polish population, had widespread moral implications.[22] But the view that a directive from Rome might have been obliged the Church to resist betrays a lack of comprehension about the true nature of the Nazi occupation. The position of the Polish Church was incomparably better than that of the Jews, and yet during the occupation the Church was isolated and persecuted as never before in its history.[23] One should not, therefore, investigate the official position of the Polish Church – itself under the terror – but rather, and this is what Tec does, look at the activities of particular priests, religious orders and lay Catholics. She cites numerous examples of priests rescuing Jews. Nevertheless the behaviour of the Polish clergy was not uniform. The accounts are mixed. In the rescuing of children alone the contribution of the clergy was considerable. One of the basic means used was to teach Jewish children religion and baptize them. This was later to provoke fierce controversy. But – argues Tec – in purely objective terms, this course meant rescue. It was carried out without compulsion, and even when their guardians refused to agree to the children's christening, this had no effect on the decision to conceal them. For most of the rescuers, however, purely religious motivations were less relevant than compassion. Only in the case of the very devout did faith play a significant role.

In asking who were the people who rescued Jews, Tec introduces the concept of normative and autonomic altruism. Normative altruism is displayed when conduct directed to the benefit of others is expected, even rewarded by society. Autonomic altruism, by contrast, refers to disinterested help which may not receive society's approval. In Poland people who rescued Jews had to appeal to autonomic altruism, since their activity placed them in conflict with the cultural anti-semitism of the community.

This is a risky assumption. Where people extending help to Jews were concerned, overlaying everything was the fear of whether such action would jeopardize the lives of all those living under the same roof. No doctrine could prepare people for how they were to behave in the face of crime on a mass scale against a neighbouring group, when any attempt to help was threatened with death. There also remains the problem of the relation between anti-semitism and the general demoralization of the community under the terror (in which large numbers of Polish underground conspirators also became victims of betrayal). The criterion of how widespread is a conviction (in this case anti-semitism) and of the willingness to act in the light of it, is relative, something which is confirmed by Tec who in her study indicates that tens of thousands were saved. One should steer clear of generalizations, the more so since the Tec book shows (as does Lukas') that there was more than one Poland: rescuing, fear-struck, and indifferent.

One of the most dramatic questions linked with the Holocaust, concerns the attitude of the free world and the Jewish leaders in it. The subject is controversial owing to the accusations levelled after the war by Jewish spokesmen from occupied Europe, that Jews elsewhere took part in a 'conspiracy of silence'.

A collection of works edited by Rudolph L. Braham discusses this question with regard to the United States, Great Britain, Palestine, Switzerland, and Latin America. In it David Wyman shows that American Jewish organizations were unable to exert pressure on their government to undertake rescue activities, or to influence public opinion. They were divided and at odds with one another; nor could loose, ad hoc committees manage to develop a common strategy. After the Bermuda conference, the Zionists, until then the most active group, concentrated on gaining the support of the Jewish community for the idea of a Jewish state. They treated the rescuing of Jews as a marginal affair, and this ruled out any chance of cooperation with other groups. From 1943, when the Zionists became the largest Jewish organization in America, rescue activities assumed a secondary role. In the face of the slight hope that existed of saving Jews, it was felt essential to direct limited financial resources toward realistic and attainable goals. Equally, according to the Zionist philosophy of history, which treated the Holocaust not as an aberration, but as the culmination of centuries-long persecution of Jews, it was concluded that only the creation of a Jewish state could safeguard against the possibility of a further Holocaust. Wyman considers that the Zionists' assessment of the situation was faulty. Very much more could have been achieved, and this is confirmed by the activities of independent groups, sabotaged by the Jewish organizations.

The position of British Jews was different. They did not operate politically as an ethnic group – claims Bernard Wasserstein – because the idea of political activity of this kind was alien to British democracy. The Jewish leaders did not have the same opportunities to mobilize their community as in the United States. In spite of this British Jews did a great deal. From 1933 onwards they themselves covered the cost of maintaining Jewish refugees and only in 1939, when this action became too expensive, was it taken over by the government. After 1939, growing anti-semitism and the barring of further immigration to Palestine meant that the activities of the Jewish community were restricted and had – in the light of total war – particular implications. Only in 1942 did these efforts produce a positive reaction from British public opinion, although in practical terms, little was achieved. Nevertheless, insists Wasserstein, we should look favourably on the efforts of the British Jews who were united and knew how to reach public opinion. The fact that these efforts brought modest results was not their fault.

The attitude of the leaders of the *yishuv* is equally controversial. Bela Vago only discusses the position of the leaders of the Executive Committee of the Jewish Agency, this being the organization which considered itself as a government acting in the name of Jews worldwide. The policies of these leaders were not consistent. At the end of the thirties the leaders of the *yishuv* found themselves trapped in a vicious circle. Since they looked on themselves as the representatives of world Jewry they should have been in a position to initiate rescue work. But they were also representatives of a would-be state. The reconciliation of these two tasks was impracticable and the *yishuv* inclined toward the latter.

Even the outbreak of war did not bring about a change in these priorities. The initiatives taken to increase illegal immigration were the result of a grassroots movement and emanated from outside the circles of the leadership, which concentrated chiefly on forming Jewish units within the British Army. Only in 1943 was a Rescue Committee formed, but even here the chasm between the idea of strengthening *Eretz Israel*, and that of rescue operations, was evident. In 1944 the leaders of the *yishuv* began activities in support of Balkan and East-European Jews, but they were half-hearted. In summing up Vago argues that, 'the participation of the *yishuv* leadership in the help and rescue activities did not match its capacities and competence and it failed to fully exploit the given circumstances' (p. 65).

The essay by Riegner deals with Jewish organizations in Switzerland, although it does not discuss the activities of Jewish international organizations in that country. Switzerland, traditionally a haven for the oppressed, in the case of the Jews evinced considerable resistance. This coincided with a growth in anti-semitic feelings which led during the war to the notorious differentiation between 'political refugees' and 'racial refugees'. The latter were refused the right of asylum. From 1942, the government virtually closed its borders, but due to pressure of public opinion, influenced by the news of mass murders, some of the refugees were admitted. What is striking – states Riegner – is that although public opinion and Swiss organizations campaigned to have the law changed, Jews remained silent. This culminated in a crisis within the Jewish élite and the Jewish community's new leadership worked from 1943 in tandem with public opinion. Altogether around 30,000 Jews were admitted, but Switzerland could have accepted several hundreds of thousands more. Riegner concludes that the Jewish community did not exploit all the avenues open to it and irrespective of what motivations guided its actions, cannot be judged in a positive light.

The last of the essays in this volume deals with the Jews of Latin America. In the 1930s this community began to grow, its numbers increased by the addition of Jewish refugees from Europe. They found themselves in countries that were far distant from the theatres of battle. This meant that their significance increased dramatically. An assessment of the activities of this community requires even more detailed research. The one thing we do already know is that here too Jews did not profit from several opportunities to influence the immigration policies of the countries of the region.

Two observations: There emerges from these studies the picture of Jewish communities who were not up to the mark. It fell to them to take action in conditions where governments were unwilling to acknowledge the exceptional nature of the tragedy which had befallen the Jews, and these communities did not believe in cooperating with public opinion. Only by working through public opinion (as in England, Switzerland, to a certain extent in the United States) could success be achieved.

The second observation concerns the increase in anti-semitism in nearly all of the countries discussed, which occurred at the same time as the first waves of persecution. This was especially noticeable in England, where the growth in anti-semitism marked the end of a long period of playing the Jewish card. Certainly Britain joined the struggle against Hitler, but at the same time backing was given to the Arabs which was sound politically, but reactions to the Jews were increasingly cool, despite their persecution by Hitler. It was at this point – I believe – that the mystique surrounding Zionism in British circles began to disappear (a mystique which had not yet begun to surface in America and in other countries as a positive result of the Holocaust). The Jews were now the losers and no-one was willing to help them. This situation, where hope in the possibility of any normal development was shattered, provoked in some sections of the Jewish community a crisis of confidence in the value or purpose of their own activities and the possibility of devising fresh tactics.

The attitude of the American Government with regard to the Holocaust has already been extensively researched. There has remained, however, the lack of an analysis of the American press and its influence on public opinion. It is an important matter, since it is possible that the attitude of the American Government might have been different if public opinion had made clear its strong demand for action to rescue Jews.

Deborah E. Lipstadt argues that from 1933 the American press treatment of Nazi anti-semitism questioned the reliability of the information and the wisdom of retaliatory action. There were various reasons for this. In the course of the twentieth century the style of press operation in democratic societies underwent change when Governments discovered that it was possible to manipulate the press. This led to a change in attitude both amongst journalists and within public opinion; one was almost compelled to doubt everything. Linked with this were memories of the false reporting from the First World War in which it was claimed that the German Army committed atrocities.

However a basic reason for the doubts harboured by the press was the lack of understanding of the true nature of Nazi anti-semitic ideology. The first reports describing the persecution of Jews were received with scepticism although they were the product of firsthand witnesses. There was no understanding either of the way in which news was falsified by totalitarian regimes; reference was typically made to the information contained in Nazi newspapers, that contradicted American journalists. Naive attempts were made to explain persecutions: that Hitler wanted to turn the attention of the German people away from internal issues, that the Jews were being persecuted not for racial reasons but political ones, that the violence was the result of conflict within the party.

These explanations had their origin in the theory that Lipstadt calls 'nothing but ... a means of accomplishing something else' (p. 56). It was not understood that anti-semitism was one of the cornerstones of Nazi ideology. Only after Kristallnacht did the view begin to make itself heard, that this was the result of too compliant a policy at Munich, and that the way in which the world treated the Germans might affect their conduct of internal politics. Confronting Hitler would have signified a course of action that transgressed two main articles of American faith: neutrality, and the ban on a higher level of immigration. Added to this was American anti-semitism. They were indeed hostile toward Nazism, but 'a survey taken from 1940 ... shows that Jews were almost consistently seen as a greater menace to the welfare of the United States than were any other national, religious or social group' (p. 127).

The most astonishing point, however, was the attitude of the American press towards the 'Final Solution'. From the end of 1942 the mass murders in the East were already common knowledge. Because of this the manner in which the news of these crimes was reported was of fundamental importance. Hiding behind the formula that 'it is difficult to verify', these were published on the inside pages of the newspapers, and the annihilation of the Jews was treated on the same level as murders carried out against other nationalities. 'On occasion', says Lipstadt, 'the Allied press did a better job of suppressing, or casting doubt upon the news of the Final Solution than did the Nazis' (p. 142). The press accepted the official line of the government – which wanted to avoid any kind of rescue action – that rescue could come only through victory. In 1944 the press reacted cynically to the slogan 'open ports', being well aware that a demand of this kind would not be accepted either by public opinion or by the government. As a result scarcely 1,000 Jews entered in a situation where the immigration quota was 91 per cent unfulfilled. In the summer of 1944 evidence of the existence of gas chambers was buried deep in the inside pages of newspapers. Discussion concerning the rescue of Hungarian Jews was abandoned. When the camps were liberated, a section of the press still failed to understand the distinction between a concentration camp and an extermination camp. Consequently the press can be accused of a monstrous 'failure of imagination'.

Lipstadt does not provide much for this phenomenon. The Holocaust revealed a fundamental truth: Democratic, liberal societies have great difficulties in understanding the true nature of totalitarian systems since they think in pragmatic and not in ideological terms. So the slave labour of the Jews was comprehended as a pragmatic order of activity. Murder on ideological grounds fell outside this categorisation. Ideology has an automotive character. 'Totalitarianism is disclosed,' writes Kateb, 'as the disposition to live a fiction ... Totalitarianism is a systematic way of refusing the given reality and remaking it with an absolute lack of resistance ... An absolute absence of restraint sustained the leaders in the initiation ... .of the fiction ... It was a self-realizing fiction because no restraint stood in the way of realization.'[24] In a situation such as this ideology retreats only when faced by the brute force of reality. A decision of the liberal democracies not to capitulate to Hitler could have constituted brute force of this kind. Instead they chose appeasement.

The reticence of the American press and that of the whole civilized world had yet one more measure – a cultural one. In the 1930s America entered an era of euphemisms: 'to die' became 'to pass away', 'crippled' became 'handicapped'. Hitler too used euphemisms – he spoke of the 'Final Solution' instead of 'murder'. This phenomenon occurred at the same time as a reevaluation of the ethnic element in American culture. Hitler's policies forced America to confront anti-semitism seriously. During this period there had been a desire to forget about this problem, and especially to efface the figure of the Jewish hero from mass culture. While it was just at this point that American Jews were achieving great success in the cultural field, they were equally well aware that their popularity resulted from the non-Jewish character of their creations. It was because of this that the *New York Times* was fearful of exposing the Holocaust, and Hollywood directors did not show Jews on the cinema screen. For the same reason American Jewish élites were inactive and the answer throughout America to Hitler's anti-semitism was silence or else description of the problem in categories of 'nothing but . . .'. De facto – nobody wanted to fight a war over the Jews.

During the war the Germans were well aware of this phenomenon and at times purposely released news of the Holocaust, in order to provoke the Allies into stronger efforts to save the Jews. Some Nazi elements believed that using the Jewish card would weaken the Allied soldiers will to fight. And here the Allies accepted the Nazi rules of the game and were careful not to create the appearance of waging war over the Jews.

There was no knowledge of how to deal on an intellectual level with the free world's Christian tradition of anti-semitism. The Nazi tradition of anti-semitism, which had come to light as early as 1933, was treated as something known and familiar (hence the 'Nothing but . . .' syndrome). So it was condemned, but not combatted in such a way as to force departure from the established rules of international dealings, since it was in a way traditional. There was no comprehension that the Nazi form of anti-semitism was anti-Christian. Confusion reigned in the press. An open admission that they were fighting in the Jewish cause would have required revising their own anti-semitic tradition, opposing Nazi anti-Christian anti-semitism with it, and acknowledging in addition, that they were fighting for a culture in which Jews were equal. Hitler sensed perfectly this ambiguity of Christian anti-semitism and played on it to the end. In reality Jews had never been acknowledged as equal in the culture of the free world and so – paradoxically – they were made equal in the process of persecution. Thus the Holocaust and the political reactions to it, pose an equally basic question about Christian anti-semitism, which is frequently unconscious.

Was the Final Solution avoidable? Even if ideological theory (L. Dawidowicz) is rejected in favour of functional theory (R. Hilberg) the question raised above remains unanswered. Initially, this ideological acceleration took the form of honing ideology.'Totalitarian leaders show latent murderousness inherent in aestheticism: a readiness to sacrifice anything to the "consonance of their own system".'[25] This was made manifest in the 'aesthetic cleansing' of Germany, carried out in order to improve the system. And for as long as Jews were still leaving the country, this was only persecution fanned by the policy of 'appeasement'. This effective 'cleansing' of Germany lost its rationale in 1939 and 1941 when the Reich again found itself in possession of millions of Jews. Until the 23 October 1941 (when the frontiers of the Reich were closed) the Jewish problem was a problem of persecution, of emigration and of murders, but it did not constitute a Holocaust.[26] If refugees had then been accepted by the free world, perhaps the logic of ideology would not have turned in the direction of the Holocaust; even if the number of those accepted had not been in proportion to the number of Jews in the East, a permanent system of informal links with Hitler would then have been established.[27] The silence on the part of the free world led to the 'institutionalization' of ideology, to the *Endlösung*.

NOTES

1 See R. Zimand, *Dziennik Adama Czerniakowa – próba lektury*, (Paris 1979), p. 36.
2 In its most drastic form this can be seen in the memoirs of Marek Edelmann. See Hanna Krall, *Zdążyć przed Panem Bogiem*, (Kraków, 1977).
3 T. Garton Ash, 'The Life of Death', *New York Review of Books*, 19 December 1985, p. 32.
4 J. Gross, *Polish Society under German Occupation*, (Princeton, 1979), pp. 184–5).
5 Quotation taken from R. F. Scharf: 'Cum Ira et Studio', *Puls*, no. 24 (1985), p. 75.
6 A. Polonsky, *The Little Dictators – the History of Eastern Europe since 1918*, (London–Boston, 1975), p. 43.
7 C. Milosz, *Native Realm*, (New York, 1968), p. 106.
8 J. Rothschild, *East Central Europe Between Two World Wars*, (Seattle-London, 1983), p. 72.
9 S. Vincenz, *Tematy żydowskie*, (London, 1977), p. 88.
10 H. Grynberg, *Prawda nieartystyczna*, (West Berlin, 1984), p. 48.
11 Władysław Bartoszewski, a member of *Żegota*, writes: 'I must state honestly; if I had assimilated everything I heard at school and at Church on the subject of Jews, I would have become an anti-semite. Only an inner resistance to stupidity and compulsion of thought led to my being able to defend Jews during the war', in *Warto być Przyzwoitym*, (Paris, 1986), p. 79.
12 See the key work by J. T. Gross, *Polish Society under Soviet Occupation, 1939–1941*, (Princeton University Press, forthcoming).
13 According to calculations carried out by the Polish Embassy in Kujbyshev, 30 per cent of all those transported from the Polish eastern territories during the Stalinist mass deportations were Polish Jews. See S. Swianiewicz, *W cieniu Katynia*, (Paris, 1983), p. 181.
14 W. Pobóg-Malinowski, *Najnowsza Historia Polityczna Polski*, vol. 3, (London, 1983), pp. 289–90.
15 Ibid., p. 280.
16 B. K. Johnpoll, *The Politics of Futility: The General Jewish Workers' Bund of Poland, 1917–1943*, (Ithaca, New York, 1967), pp. 247–8. The proposal was supported by a Zionist close to the Polish Government – Ignacy Schwarzbart – who suggested Palestine as the only goal for those wishing to emigrate.
17 W. Sukiennicki, *East Central Europe During World War I. From Foreign Domination to National Independence*, vol. 2, (Boulder, Colorado, 1984), p. 895.
18 The figures provided by Polish sources are at this point fairly imprecise, but the number of victims seems to be the overall figure, both under the German and under the Soviet occupations.

19 Y. Bauer, 'The Place of the Holocaust in Contemporary History', in Jonathan Frankel, ed., *Studies in Contemporary Jewry*, vol. 1, (Indiana, 1984), p. 214.
20 R. F. Leslie, ed., *The History of Poland since 1863*, (Cambridge, 1983), p. 282.
21 See Adam Ciolkosz, 'Broń dla Getta Warszawy' *Kultura* vol. 170, (Paris 1969), pp. 15–45.
22 J. Garlinski, *Polska w Drugiej Wojnie Swiatowej*, (London, 1982), pp. 70–87.
23 For example, many religious orders imposed on their members throughout the country the duty of helping Jews.
24 G. Kateb, *Hannah Arendt – Politics, Conscience, Evil*, (Ottawa, 1983), pp. 79–80.
25 Ibid.
26 See M. Marrus, *The Unwanted: European Refugees in the XX Century*, (New York, Oxford, 1985), pp. 227–33.
27 Paradoxically, the one chance of escape in this prevention of Nazi ideology from crystalizing into the 'Final Solution' was perceived subconsciously by Avraham Stern. See Conor Cruise O' Brien, *The Siege – the Saga of Israel and Zionism*, (New York, 1986), p. 246.

JEWS AS A POLISH PROBLEM
Władysław T. Bartoszewski

ANEKS* is a Polish political quarterly published in London. In 1986 a double issue appeared, devoted largely to Polish – Jewish relations. Seven articles, 130 pages in total, were published in a section entitled 'Jews as a Polish Problem'. This followed in the footsteps of two Catholic monthlies from Poland, which published special issues on Jewish history and Jews in Poland (*WIĘŹ*, April 1983 and *ZNAK*, February – March 1983). The latter (407 pages long) was reviewed in the first volume of *POLIN*.

Articles in this issue of *ANEKS* deal mainly with the Holocaust, although the period after the war is also discussed and the questions raised are not only historical, but also moral and philosophical. In almost all Claude Lanzman's film *Shoah* is discussed or at least mentioned. The character of the papers varies. Jakub Karpiński's 'Asymmetry' and Włodzimierz Goldkorn's 'The Sense of History and the Destruction of Jews' are historico-philosophical. Jacek Kuroń presents his personal memoirs in 'Zośka'; Timothy Garton Ash and Israel Shahak put forward two different approaches to the film *Shoah*. Jan Tomasz Gross reconstructs Polish-Jewish relations during the war, which are also among the issues discussed in Aleksander Smolar's historical and political essay.

Smolar in his 'Taboo and Innocence' offers in many ways the boldest and most interesting analysis of Polish-Jewish relations during and after the war. He stresses that the core of the issue is a moral problem – the attitudes of Poles towards the Jews – which, given Polish powerlessness, could have had little practical consequence for the fate of the Jews. Smolar disagrees with both typical Jewish and Polish historical treatments of this issue. He rejects the view that Polish attitudes during the war constituted a continuum with pre-war anti-semitism. Equally, he questions the claims that the tragic experiences of the war changed completely Polish attitudes. Polish-Jewish relations during and after the war were immensely complex and often peculiar and absurd. It is an irony of history that in Poland there were anti-semites who helped the Jews during the war, but did not like them either before or after. Polish anti-semites have not disappeared, because unlike the situation in other European countries there was no crisis of right-wing ideology. As Smolar says: the Polish right was nationalistic, anti-German, anti-Soviet, and anti-semitic. It was not, however, compromised by the links with fascism, collaboration, and hostility towards democracy (p. 109). Conversely, the stereotypes of the Catholic Pole and the communist Jew became reinforced. This was a result of perceiving Jews as collaborators with the Soviets in 1939–1941 and later, when many Jews occupied important positions in the post-war Polish government, especially in the security apparatus. I agree with Jakub Karpiński when he argues in *ANEKS* ('Asymmetry') that the Poles have no right to blame the Jews for the murders and abuses of power perpetrated by the secret police, the prosecutors and the judiciary, because although often staffed with Jews they were not Jewish, but communist institutions (p. 9). Unfortunately, such was the perception of many Poles just after the war. Jews, as Smolar points out, ceased to be 'an economic problem' and became 'a political one'. This influenced the way the Church looked at the Jews after the war. Not only was the Polish government in their eyes 'Jewish', but it was also accusing the patriotic opposition, that is the majority of Polish society, of anti-semitism, hoping that this would diminish Western support for the anti-communists. It has since been claimed, with some versimilitude, that the government even organized pogroms for this purpose. Thus, concludes Smolar, any pro-Jewish pronouncement coming from the Church could have been interpreted as an act of support or endorsement for the alien communist ruler (p. 114). He takes a very critical view of the official Church's attitude in this and later periods, although he praises the numerous efforts of priests, nuns and whole Orders in saving Jews during the war. One of the main factors in the preservation of anti-semitism in Poland after the majority of Jews had been killed was the terrible fate of non-Jewish Poles. Poland suffered proportionally bigger losses than any other country. Three million Polish Jews and three million Gentile Poles died as a result of the war. Many people were unwilling to grant the Jews a special status, arguing that death itself was more important than its probability, circumstances, criteria of selection and the process of destruction. In 1945–7 Poland, already devastated by the war, was entering a period of foreign domination and was not ready for reflection on the crisis of European civilisation (p. 128).

Shoah provoked an exchange between Timothy Garton Ash, whose 'The Life of Death' is a translation of the relevant part of his article from *The New York Review of Books* (19.12.1985), and Israel Shahak ('Normality in an Inhuman World'). Garton Ash wrote his paper after the British première of *Shoah* organized by the Institute for Polish-Jewish Studies in Oxford, which was followed by a discussion and a meeting with Claude Lanzman. This enabled Lanzman to clarify many points which puzzled the audience of the film, but certain issues still remained unresolved. Garton Ash's review was the first detailed account of the film and its relation to history. It was long, complex and written under the strong impression *Shoah* makes on nearly all viewers. The review itself has been widely considered one of the most important commentaries on Lanzman's work. Garton Ash writes very well and tries to be as objective as possible. He does not, however, escape various traps set for the unwary by *Shoah*. The impact of the film is such that one can analyse it effectively only after a long reflection. I do not propose to engage in a thorough critique of it, but certain aspects, at least those discussed by Garton Ash, must be examined.

I too consider *Shoah* to be a cinematographic masterpiece of great moral importance, but I want rather to concentrate on Lanzman's (and Garton Ash's) treatment of history, since the film has now become a source of historical knowledge for the general public.

One of the major problems facing a critic of an historical film is what criteria to apply for judging this kind of work. Is it a documentary or is it a work of fiction? And if it is an historical fiction, to what extent is it based on historical truth? Garton Ash seems to be confused about this at times, which is not surprising if one takes into consideration the somewhat incoherent and incompatible statements of Lanzman himself. The director stresses emphatically that *Shoah* is not a documentary; it is a work of art (incidentally, do these two have to be in opposition?). Lanzman claims, however, that this is a work of art which is historically accurate in every respect and detail. Garton Ash devotes space to both aspects of this claim.

Lanzman claimed boldly in Oxford that he was the leading specialist on the Holocaust and Garton Ash supports this view when he states:

> Accuracy is the second extraordinary feature of this work ... In Oxford, faced with some of the world's leading experts on Jewish and Polish affairs, he answered every criticism on points of factual detail with what seemed to me overwhelming knowledge, conviction and something more: the justified sense that he had done what none of these historians had done (p. 38).

Such ill-judged comments force Garton Ash (and still more Lanzman) into historical quicksand. *Shoah* consists of interviews with the survivors and witnesses of the Holocaust. American publishers of the text of *Shoah* even claim that this is 'an oral history of the Holocaust'. What in this context is the meaning of the claim that the film is accurate in all factual details? Only one thing, namely that when Lanzman heard historically inaccurate statements, he corrected them during his filmed conversations or edited them afterwards (out of 350 hours of material *Shoah* uses nine and a half – providing ample scope for editing). This was not the case. It is not at all surprising that in a work of this kind and magnitude there should be some factual mistakes. Anybody who specialises in oral history or anthropology knows that people talking about the past make various and numerous mistakes about dates, places, names and other facts. This may not be of crucial importance, but one has to acknowledge the phenomenon and a special methodology is required to deal with it. One does not look for total accuracy in the accounts of events which took place 45 years ago given by witnesses. In *Shoah* there are a number of small mistakes, something which in itself I do not consider important. I mention this only because Lanzman denies it vehemently and Garton Ash does not seem to notice it. There are as well a few serious mistakes, at least one of which is critically examined by Garliński in the last issue of *POLIN*.[1]

There is, however, another omission of far greater consequence. This is something which Garton Ash calls 'the Polish backdrop', in other words the history of Polish-Jewish relations during the war. I do not agree with Garton Ash when he says that this backdrop receives 'more prominence in the film than its strict historical relevance to his [C.L.] main theme might dictate' (p. 41). I think Garton Ash here misses the point. *Shoah* is a film *à thèse* and shows only those things which support its thesis. The Polish backdrop is set out in a way which fits Lanzman's preconceptions and plays a large role in the film. Other aspects of conditions in Poland which could contradict the *thèse* are consistently and conspicuously absent. When Lanzman said in Oxford that 'nothing essential' about the Poles was left out, it is not too strong to claim that he was falsifying history. Garton Ash admits this. He thinks that, although incomplete, 'the Polish past is historically secondary'. But it is not. The *thèse* of Lanzman is that firstly, the Holocaust is the logical conclusion of the centuries of anti-semitism (this is verbalised in the film by Raul Hilberg) and secondly, that the Jews were abandoned to their fate and that the bystanders to their tragedy (mainly Poles, as the destruction of European Jewry took place amongst them) looked on passively, 'they mastered the routine of extermination. No one was troubled by it.'[2] Moreover, in Oxford, Lanzman stated that what happened in Poland could not have happened in France, where extermination camps would have been impossible. This arrogant and morally dubious statement clearly brings the Polish backdrop to the fore.[3]

Garton Ash appeals to us not to trust the artist, but rather his tale. This particular tale cannot just be taken on trust since it conveys both a strong moral and an historical message. It has to be examined, especially as Lanzman insists on being both an artist and an historian. As the former he succeeds; as the latter he fails.

On this point Garton Ash is not consistent. At first he praises the historical accuracy of Lanzman. Later he acknowledges that some essential elements are left out, but considers this to be of little importance (p.40). Eventually he ends his article by saying that 'only the historians give us the standards by which we can judge and "place" . . . *Shoah*.' Historians protect us from the great dictators – film directors (p.51).

Let me then try to offer some protection. The most obvious flaw in *Shoah* is, as I have already mentioned, the lack of any material which does not support Lanzman's point of view. Since the film is constructed around people and their recollections, the key problem is that of selection. Who is to be shown and interviewed, and who may be left out? What are the criteria of selection? Is the final result fair, representative and complete – to borrow Garton Ash's adjectives? It is characteristic that Lanzman obstinately refused to answer this question in Oxford. After a long and heated exchange with academics he eventually admitted that the criteria were his 'obsessions'. This is of course perfectly acceptable on the condition that the work does not pretend to be history. As Garton Ash aptly remarks, *Shoah* 're-creates the life of death'. It does not, however, re-create history; it *creates* it. This may seem to be a harsh judgment, especially as the film is very moving and largely true, but it follows the rules suggested by Garton Ash for examining historical works.

Lanzman decided not to interview or show people who would tell stories he did not like, irrespective of their importance.[4] His explanations for various noticeable omissions are quoted by Garton Ash. Some people were 'weak' on the screen, could not 'relive' the past; others wanted to lecture him; some were busy or ill. All these excuses are legitimate for an artist, but not for an historian. Worse still, people who were not included fell within certain categories, which were not represented as a result. There was not a single Pole who helped Jews during the war, and yet those who survived had to rely almost exclusively on Polish help. Members of the Jewish resistance were virtually ignored as well. The problem is not, as Garton Ash would have it, that these groups were of secondary importance to the main theme, but that this theme would have been seriously weakened by their evidence. The idea that Jews went to their death because the Poles were totally indifferent could not have been sustained.

The point I would like to make is this. All Poles must bear responsibility for what took place on our soil during the war. One must not be complacent about this. Jan Błoński discusses this moral issue admirably elsewhere in this volume of POLIN. Historically, the terrible truth remains that the overwhelming majority of Polish Jews were doomed regardless of the degree of Polish help and Jewish resistance. I believe that both could have been safely mentioned in *Shoah* without fear that the message would have somehow become blurred. The problem is that by ignoring them Lanzman forfeited his claim to present historical truth accurately. The excuses he offered in Oxford were intellectually dishonest.

There are other troubling factors related to what has just been said. One is the manipulation of the material. This has been pointed out by one of the interviewees, Jan Karski. Karski was the courier for the Polish underground who in 1942 succeeded in bringing to the West information about the extermination of Jews and the appeals for help. He was the first person who talked with Anthony Eden, Roosevelt and others about the desperate position of Polish Jews – all in vain. And yet Lanzman, out of eight hours of interview with Karski, decided to show his description of the suffering in the ghetto and to ignore the only part of the testimony which makes it absolutely unique![5] Karski himself has commented on this:

> The inclusion of this material in the film, as well as even general information about those who tried to help Jews, would have presented the destruction of Jews in a proper historical perspective. Leaders of nations, powerful governments decided about this destruction or participated in this destruction, or kept indifferent towards it. People, normal people, thousands of people sympathised with the Jews or helped them.[6]

Another problem is Lanzman's *modus operandi*. Many interviews in the film come from peasants. The way Lanzman conducts his field work among them may be fascinating to watch, but the evidence thus collected would be considered inadmissible by anthropologists. One is not allowed to bully informers and to try forcing answers one wants to hear, because such responses are of dubious value. Again, I would stress that this procedure may be artistically justifiable and indeed brings results in *Shoah*. Still, it is not acceptable for a person researching in oral history.

Here I should clarify one misunderstanding shared by Garton Ash and many others, including Poles. There is a famous scene in the film in front of the church in Chełmno. Peasants tell a story about a rabbi persuading the Jews on their way to extermination to accept this as a punishment for sentencing Christ to death. 'His blood is on us.' The scene is powerful, but ought to be put in a proper context. Peasants in Poland accepted until the war that Jews were part of their world and their cosmology. As Alina Cała rightly points out, if a peasant had been asked: should Jews assimilate or emigrate (two favourite ways of solving 'the Jewish problem'), he would not understand this alternative.

> The Jews ... were part of life as created by God, testimony to the Passion of Christ, something threatening and strange, but necessary and unalterable. Their destruction could only be determined by Him alone and it would constitute a sign that the end of the world had arrived.[7]

For peasants this invocation is the way to rationalize something which even intellectuals find difficult to explain adequately – the Holocaust. It is pointless to accuse the peasants of being simple and primitive. They still largely accept the traditional, 'closed' concept of the world in which all elements have their own appropriate place.

Garton Ash claims that there are two 'intolerable facts' for nationalists, whether Polish or Jewish (in the broadest sense) to accept. For Poles 'There was virulent and widespread anti-semitism in Poland during the Second World War.' For Jews 'The conditions of German occupation were worse for the Poles than for any other nation except the Jews' (p. 43). Garton Ash thinks that these statements are obvious, but I question both 'facts'. Firstly, there was anti-semitism in Poland during the war, but it is impossible to conclude how widespread it was, and its virulence is also open to question (it is also difficult for an historian to measure). To quote one document without its proper context is not enough.[8] General Grot-Rowecki, the commander of the Home Army (*AK*) sent a message to the Polish Government-in-Exile which commented that 'the overwhelming majority of the country is anti-semitically disposed.'[9] This was written in September 1941, three months after the Germans attacked the Soviet Union, their rapid advance uniting Poland under one occupying authority. For the first time since September 1939 news from eastern Poland reached Warsaw. Amongst other information there were details about the behaviour of Jews towards the Soviets during these twenty-one months. There were widespread rumours that the overwhelming majority of Jews participated in the Soviet oppression of Poles. There are no detailed studies about this phenomenon and one should therefore examine this information with caution.[10] Another article in the same issue of *ANEKS*, Aleksander Smolar's 'Taboo and Innocence' takes a very critical view of the Jewish attitudes towards the Soviets and the Poles in this period. He quotes the same document as Garton Ash and then concludes:

> In no other European country during the war was there such a dramatic collision of interests and attitudes between the Jews and the nation among which they lived, as during the Soviet occupation 1939–41. Elsewhere Jews had discordant interests with a part of the society around them (for example with collaborators), but in solidarity, in a relationship with the rest of society. In eastern Poland, however, it was the Jews who were perceived as collaborators (p. 98).

That Jews were perceived as collaborators should not prejudge the issue, which ought to be examined. It does, however, put the message of Grot-Rowecki into context.

Similar reservations apply to the second 'fact' about conditions under German occupation. These were worse for the Poles than for any other nation except the Jews only from the western perspective. The situation of other nations behind the eastern front was no better than that of the Poles. The position of Gypsies was comparable only with that of the Jews. This is a point made also by Israel Shahak in his reply to Garton Ash's paper. Shahak, a survivor of the Warsaw ghetto, is well known for his pro-Palestinian views. This leads some people reject all his arguments *a priori*. I cannot accept such a position. After scrutiny some of Shahak's arguments are still valid and some not. Shahak questions the very idea of the uniqueness of the Holocaust. He considers other acts of genocide (Tasmania, Armenia, China) and also the African slave trade, to be comparable with the Holocaust in their effect and the sufferings they involved. He is concerned mainly with the human condition and human behaviour irrespective of nationality. His message is: it is pointless to accuse this or that nation, because people of all nations can be good or bad, and always behave with a varying degree of decency. People occasionally fail as human beings and horrors follow. One can agree with the universal aspect of this viewpoint. As Shahak argues, all people have a need for normalcy and this included even the Jews in the ghettos and people in concentration camps. In order to live, people had to return to the state of normality (however illusory) and conduct their 'normal' life. Here the Jews behaved liked the Poles, because both were motivated by human nature. Shahak's particular, historical arguments are more open to dispute. True, the destruction of Jews cannot be considered in total separation from the Nazi crimes perpetrated on other nations. At the same time it does not seem to be appropriate to equate the Holocaust with the other mass-exterminations. Historically speaking, one can find horrors, both before and after, which are quantitatively comparable, or even worse. Qualitatively the Jewish experience was different. The creation of a special, dispassionate, bureaucratic structure to carry out the task of extermination is only one aspect of this problem. The crucial distinction was analysed recently by George Steiner. It lies in the symbolic and metaphysical – theological realm[11] and I do not propose to discuss it here. Włodzimierz Goldkorn's article in *ANEKS*, 'The Sense of History and the Destruction of Jews' embodies a similar approach. Jews look at their history through the prism of the Holocaust; all events are examined with the destruction in mind. All the Jews are survivors. Goldkorn argues, after Yerushalmi, that for the Jews history not only has a meaning, but is also a ground where God's will is realized with human help. God made a pact with the Jewish nation and every Jew has to participate in bringing God's projects to fruition.[12] How can the Holocaust be interpreted within these terms of reference? Traditional ideologies and programmes of political parties, economic and social theories did not prevent the extermination of Jews and cannot offer the explanation now. Steiner presents deep and troubling thoughts on this problem.[13]

Goldkorn disagrees with Raul Hilberg that the Holocaust is the logical conclusion of the centuries of anti-semitism. Anti-semitism may have led to pogroms, often to the killing of Jews, but from this there is no logical step to total destruction. Goldkorn points out that Polish anti-semitism has nothing to do with Holocaust and that many Polish antisemites helped the Jews during the war *while remaining anti-semitic*. This is a peculiar phenomenon mentioned also by Nechama Tec.[14] As both Goldkorn and Smolar point out, it is because Polish anti-semitism did not contemplate the Nazi solution to 'the Jewish problem', and because even the right-wing parties were anti-Nazi, that the Poles have not reflected enough on the Holocaust and have not considered themselves morally or historically responsible.

The question of the moral responsibility of the Poles is also raised in a very suggestive introductory essay by Jakub Karpiński ('Asymmetry'). He discusses Polish-Jewish relations in general terms, but concentrates at controversial episodes (like the Kielce pogrom). His essay is lucid and reserved in tone. The same cannot be said about another paper on what is probably the most disputed issue in Polish-Jewish history: relations during the Second World War. Jan Tomasz Gross, the author of a book on Polish society under the German occupation presents a socio-historical analysis of these relations. It was originally delivered as a lecture in Oxford. *ANEKS* published a version of it under a different title: 'He Is From My Homeland ... But I Do Not Like Him.'[15] The article, like its title, is provocative. The author clearly feels very passionately about the subject and engages in a forceful polemic with Polish historians and literary figures. The problem is that this has an adverse effect on his historical judgment. Individual documents are quoted out of context. For example a reference to a report of Jan Karski from the spring of 1940, which Gross claims was falsified because it contained information about antisemitic attitudes in Poland is followed by two others (from the Delegate of the Government-in-Exile and from the commander of the Home Army – *AK*, Grot-Rowecki), both from the autumn 1941. Both supposedly reinforce the image conveyed by that of Karski. After quoting Grot-Rowecki's message mentioned above, Gross states: ' And this attitude was not to change with the passage of time, that is with the increasing mass destruction of Jews.' He then quotes the fourth and last of his documents, coming from July 1944, a report of Andrzej Chciuk ('Celt'), saying that the Polish Government-in-Exile 'goes too far in its philo-semitism, especially as Jews are not liked in the country' (p. 29). Gross concludes that from these four fragments we can make definite conclusions about the attitude of Poles towards Jews, since the reports presented a summary of the current knowledge of the subject. He also suggests that there was a continuity of anti-semitism and anti-Jewish feelings in occupied Poland (at least from early 1940 until July 1944). The question arises: why does Gross not quote any reports from 1942 and 1943 when the extermination of Jews took place? A large amount of space in these was devoted to the description of horrors and to the appeals for help, and also to the revulsion of the Polish population witnessing these criminal deeds. Karski's report was written in the spring of 1940 when nobody expected 'the Final Solution'. From the first months of the occupation Jews were discriminated against and oppressed by the Germans. At the same time Jews were not considered, and did not consider themselves, to be in mortal danger.[16] This was the time when Germans conducted a thorough campaign of extermination of the Polish élites. The first large ghettos in the *Generalgouvernement* were created and enclosed later – in November 1940 in Warsaw, in March 1941 in Kraków. Despite very harsh conditions and brutal treatment some Jews and Poles thought that it was safer in the ghettos than outside. There were mass arrests and execution of Poles in various parts of the country, which lent support to the suspicion that the Polish nation was in immediate danger.[17] This is the backround to the first reports. I have already mentioned the situation in the autumn of 1941, when the news from eastern Poland reached Warsaw. This should not be overlooked by Gross when he talks about attitudes, even if he disapproves of them. After all he wrote in 1979: '... when the Russians occupied the eastern half of the country in 1939, it was primarily from among the Jews that they managed to enlist collaborators to set up the new administration'.[18] Finally, after the curious omission of 1942–3 we have a report of 'Celt'.[19] This can be interpreted in a variety of ways. The report continued: 'The Delegate wished to state that according to him the Government exaggerates in its love for Jews' (p. 29). One could argue that he personally thought the Government should make more balanced pronouncements, or that he was conveying the views of right-wing parties, which as a Delegate he was also representing, and which objected to the pro-Jewish policy of the Government-in-Exile. Does Gross read too much in the phrase: 'Jews are not liked in the country' (p. 29)? I think he might. The continuity of anti-semitic attitudes of 'the overwhelming majority' that Gross claims to describe is not proven. From the crucial period of 1942–3 Gross quotes only the underground press: *Słowa Prawdy*, *Polska*, and a pamphlet published by *Stronnictwo Pracy*. All these are anti-Jewish, some virulently so. They are not, however, representative of the entire political spectrum in occupied Poland, or of the underground press. If Gross had claimed that the extreme right-wing parties had not changed their anti-semitic views, one could agree with him. It is a misrepresentation to claim that these were the views of the majority. The large majority of underground publications took a very different line. *Biuletyn Informacyjny*, the official organ of ZWZ and later the Home Army, was filled with stories about Jewish suffering, appeals for help and warnings that taking advantage of the Jewish fate would be severely punished. The latter was not an empty threat as blackmailers, if discovered, were sentenced to death and shot.[20] When talking about the underground press it is relevant to examine the relative influence and importance of different newspapers. It is misleading to quote a small right-wing publication (with a circulation of around a thousand copies) without mentioning *Biuletyn Informacyjny* the most important clandestine journal representing the views of the High Command of the Home Army which was published throughout the period of occupation as a weekly reaching at times 50,000 copies.

Gross argues that had the Polish population helped the Jews with equal zeal as it engaged itself in armed conspiracy against the Germans, many more Jews could have been saved. He claims that the Poles were much more willing to take the risk of taking part in conspiracy than in saving Jews, and that there was a social stigma attached to those who helped, but not to the conspirators. This, according to Gross, enabled the Germans to persecute both the Jews and the Poles who helped them with greater effectiveness, because they were isolated in their own society. Conspiracy was punishable by death, and yet people participated in it; helping the Jews met with the same punishment, but only a small number of people did it.

Gross makes here some wrong assumptions. Firstly, to be caught conspiring against Germans was not equivalent to death. Such activities were not automatically punishable by death. People were sent to prison, often tortured, sent to concentration camps. Some were killed but many survived. To be caught helping a Jew was met with a death penalty for the entire family, sometimes an entire village.[21] Helping the Jews was much more difficult often for very banal reasons: their appearance, occasionally their speech, logistical problems with flats, false papers and money. Conspirators led a double life – one 'normal', the other secret. The majority of Jews could not have any 'normal' life, because they had what Germans considered to be Semitic features, or could not speak the language fluently, or were well-known figures. They had to be protected at all times. The underground was not massively engaged in this help. It was created long before anybody had any idea about Hitler's plans. The underground's role was primarily a military one. The rules of conspiracy precluded combining help to Jews with underground activities. The more help, the greater the risk for the underground. *Volksdeutsche*, Polish profiteers, blackmailers and denouncers were present in large numbers, as Gross describes elsewhere. One person could ruin the long efforts of many. Jews were the easiest victims, but not the only ones. Despite the high esteem in which the overwhelming majority of society surrounded the leaders of the underground state and Home Army, they were not immune to denouncers. General Grot-Rowecki himself was a victim of such a Pole, who with two others successfully betrayed 200 people.[22]

There are no accurate figures as to how many Jews survived the war in German-occupied Poland. The estimates vary from fifty to over one hundred thousand.[23] Almost all of them were helped – it was not possible to survive otherwise. Many did not survive despite that help. The number of people involved in helping was far greater than the number of people rescued. On many occasions one person had to be helped by ten or fifteen others (this is testified by the survivors and their memoirs and by those who organized help). The number of people involved, often only very briefly, will remain unknown. The estimates are that they were around a few hundred thousand. This was not enough, but should it be called 'a relatively small group of people' (p. 32)? In terms of Christian morality yes. Would an historical judgment be the same? Gross ends his article with a comment about the emptiness of the Holocaust, the loss, from which nothing can be saved, and the wasted sacrifice, which did not bear fruit (p. 34). As he refers to the Warsaw ghetto uprising, let us remember the words of the Jewish Fighting Organization (ζOB) in its leaflet issued on 23 April 1943, the fifth day of the fight which was undertaken: 'For your and our human, social and national honour and dignity.' The values of this appeal, shared by those who helped, were saved.

NOTES

* ANEKS, 41/42 (London, 1986), pp.236.
1 See J. Garliński, 'The Underground Movement in Auschwitz Concentration Camp', in *POLIN. A Journal of Polish Jewish Studies*, vol. 1 (1986), pp. 212–26.
2 Claude Lanzman in his interview with *L'Express* (Paris), 17 May 1985.
3 Lanzman displays here a particular lack of knowledge about war-time France. He does not seem to be familiar with two books showing the substantial degree of help received by the Germans in their extermination of Jews from the French: S. Klarsfeld, *Le Memorial de la Déportation des Juifs de France* (Paris, 1978), and M. R. Marrus and R. O. Paxton, *Vichy et les Juifs* (Paris, 1981).
4 For instance: the head of the first separate Jewish Section of the Bureau of Information and Propaganda of the Chief Command of the Home Army (*AK*), Henryk Woliński, or Marek Edelman, one of the commanders of ζOB (Jewish Fighting Organization) during the Warsaw ghetto uprising, and many others.
5 Karski's mission is described in detail in J. Karski *Story of a Secret State* (Boston, 1944) and W. Laqueur, *The Terrible Secret. Supression of the Truth about Hitler's "Final Solution"* (London, 1980). In 1985 I saw an hour-long interview with Karski, which will be a part of a documentary film on Polish history. His recollections of the Western response to Jewish and Polish pleas for help were vivid and very dramatic.
6 Jan Karski, 'Shoah (Zagłada)', *Kultura* (1985), no. 11, p. 124.
7 Alina Cała, 'The Question of the Assimilation of Jews in the Polish Kingdom (1864–1897): An Interpretative Essay', in *POLIN. A Journal of Polish-Jewish Studies*, vol. 1 (1986), p. 148. Cała makes it clear that although the article deals with the 19th century, the opinion has remained valid (see note 19, op. cit. p. 150).
8 As I understand this was probably done for the reasons of space.
9 In *The New York Review of Books* Garton Ash quotes a bad translation from Jan T. Gross *Polish Society under German Occupation. The Generalgouvernement 1939–1944* (Princeton, 1979), p. 184. Since then other people have used Gross's translation. The correct version is mentioned by Norman Davies in 'Poles and Jews: An Exchange', *The New York Review of Books*, 9 April 1987, p. 43. In *ANEKS* the disputed phrase appears in Polish, as in the original report.

10 This is noted in W. Bartoszewski 'Some Thoughts on Polish-Jewish Relations' *POLIN. A Journal of Polish-Jewish Studies*, vol. 1 (1986), pp. 282-3.
11 George Steiner, 'The Long Life of Metaphor. An Approach to "the Shoah", *Encounter* (February 1987), p. 57.
12 Y. H. Yerushalmi, *Zakhor: Jewish History and Jewish Memory* (Seattle, 1982).
13 G. Steiner, op. cit., pp. 55-61.
14 Nechama Tec, *When Light Pierced the Darkness: Righteous Christians and the Polish Jews* (Oxford, 1986).
15 This title strikes me as a very unfortunate one. 'He Is From My Homeland' is a title of a poem by Antoni Słonimski devoted to all people who share and sympathise with the suffering of others. The poem ends: 'He is from my homeland . . . he is a Man'. This poem was used as the motto of a book describing help offered to Jews by Poles: *Ten jest z ojczyzny mojej . . . Polacy z pomocą Żydom 1939–1945* (2nd ed., Kraków, 1969), edited by W. Bartoszewski and Z. Lewinówna. Gross's parody of it distorts both the message of the poem and in a sense denigrates those who helped.
16 A message sent to the Government-in-Exile in July 1941 says after describing the poor and deteriorating situation of Jews in the ghettos:

> The attitudes amongst Jews are despite all optimistic, though they suppose that the poorer and weaker will not last till the end of the war.

'Uwagi ogólne za czas od marca do 15 kwietnia', General Sikorski Historical Institute (London), PRM-K-85.
17 See Bartoszewski, 'Some Thoughts . . .', op. cit., pp. 283-4.
18 Gross, *Polish Society* . . . , op. cit., p. 20.
19 There is no reference to where Gross found this report in either *ANEKS* or in his book, where the report is quoted and discussed on pp. 185-6. In another place he mentions 'Celt's Report' from 'Kot Collection, 25/9', Gen. Sikorski Historical Institute, London.
20 Such executions, carried out explicitly for denouncing Jews, were published afterwards for instance in '*Biuletyn Informacyjny*' no. 37, 16 September 1943; no. 49, 9 December 1943; 9 March 1944; no. 13, 30 March 1944, and many others. See W. Bartoszewski, *Los Żydów Warszawy 1939–1943* (London, 1983), pp. 66-8.
21 See Szymon Dattner, *Las sprawiedliwych. Karta z dziejów ratownictwa Żydów w okupowanej Polsce* (Warsaw, 1968).
22 See Tadeusz Żenczykowski, *General Grot. U kresu walki* (London, 1983), p. 170.
23 There are serious difficulties in establishing the exact number of survivors, which results in such divergent estimates. One approach is to count the number of Jews living in Poland in 1946 and deduct those who came back after the war from the Soviet Union. According to Józef Garliński, there were 240 thousand Jews in Poland in 1946, out of which 157 thousand returned from the Soviet Union. On this basis he calculates that around 83 thousand Jews survived the war on the German occupied territory of Poland (J. Garliński, *Polska w Drugiej Wojnie Światowej*, London 1982, p. 252).

BOOK REVIEWS

Nahum Gross, ed. *Yehudim ba-Kalkalah*. Jerusalem:
the Zalman Shazar Center. 1985. Pp. 437.

Though entitled 'Jews in Economic Life', this volume is not a systematic and structurally cohesive history of the economic activities of Jews (like the *Economic History of the Jews* by S. W. Baron, A. Kahan et. al. or M. Arkin's *Aspects of Jewish Economic History*) but a collection of individual studies that cannot be viewed as a whole, its common subject matter notwithstanding. It comprises papers presented at the seventh annual conference of the Historical Society of Israel, which took place in Jerusalem in 1982 thanks to the Zalman Shazar Center, and presents a variety of studies relating to different historical periods and geographic areas, loosely connected, divergent in methodology and uneven in the manner of exposition. Moreover, certain lacunae in the table of contents initially envisaged could not be avoided because all conference participants did not submit their papers for publication.

Many of the twenty-five essays deal with Jewish occupations and Jewish entrepreneurs, or entrepreneurship, in the traditional descriptive way, based on primary or secondary documentation for inductive conclusions, emphasizing the measure of the 'Jewish contribution', with little or no reference to relevant or underlying socio-economic and political factors. The redeeming merit of this category of studies is that most are devoted to specific topics and/or less well-known, marginal and 'extraneous' geographic areas. One contribution, of essential value, deals with the economic activities of Jews in the Caribbean in colonial times, which played such a vital role in the link between Sephardic refugees-marranos and the colonization of the New World (a subject discussed extensively by Peter Wiernik in his *History of the Jews in America* published in 1912). The other papers in this category include such questions as Herod's sources of revenue to fund his enormous building projects, agricultural variations in different areas of the Golan in the Talmudic period, cosmetics as the main commodity of the Jewish itinerant peddler in Roman Palestine, Jewish guilds in Turkey, and other specific economic functions of Jews in such places as Izmir, the Ottoman Empire in general, Sherifian Morocco and Moldavia. This widening of the geographic horizon as it relates to different periods provides new perspectives for a wider understanding.

In that respect, one should single out the opening paper of the volume – Shmuel Ettinger's comprehensive survey of Jewish economic activities through the ages, in Christian Europe as well as Islamic countries. It presents the salient developments in the economic involvement of Jews in a way that is admirably succinct and dialectical, including a sound treatment of the restrictions imposed and the negative stereotyping of Jews that so often put them at an economic disadvantage.

In terms of a broader methodological approach which takes into account the pertinent and interrelated sociological and political elements as well as comparative factors, there are at least five papers to note. Most significant in that respect is the very title of M. Toch's paper, 'The German economy in the 13th–14th centuries: the framework and conditions for the economic activity of the Jews'. It demonstrates a sophisticated and desirable approach in its historical treatment of Jewish occupations and other aspects of Jewish life. Similarly, A. Barkai's essay about the 'Changes in economic life of German Jewry in the age of industrialization' emphasizes, besides general economic developments, the process of emancipation, greater mobility, better education, and the changing demographic profile as crucial factors in the generally improved economic situation of the Jews in Germany. W. D. Rubinstein's treatment of the 'Jewish economic élite in Britain in 1815–1939' stands out through his comparative approach to the subject and his integrating his theme with specific British socio-political changes. Moreover, this treatment also includes the changing influences, both positive and negative, of the rich Jewish élite on British policies during that period.

A paper which adopts an approach that is as much sociological as economic, within the wider framework of historical circumstances, is that by A.Y. Bornstein concerning 'The Jewish poor in the era of the "Great Entrepreneurs"'. Different and novel in the sense of dealing with the economically passive, rather than the well-to-do, of the Jewish community in Germany in 1850–1914, the study examines not only the underlying reasons for poverty among segments of the Jewish population but also goes into the character of Jewish organized welfare in relation to the general welfare structure in Germany at the time.

The scholarly piece by Arcadius Kahan, to whose memory the conference proceedings and the book are dedicated, must be particularly cited. Although essentially a study demonstrating the importance of the economic contribution made by Jewish entrepreneurs to the industrialization of

Tsarist Russia, this essay is noteworthy for its exposition of the inner dialectical evolution of that contribution in accordance with categories of economic theory, forming a concise and lucid synthesis of all the pertinent evidence and its economic interpretation.

Of the remaining papers, three may be categorized, without minimizing their academic quality, as fascinating stories about particular individuals. S. D. Chapman's 'dramatic' account of the inner workings in the rise of Nathan Mayer Rothschild as the dominant figure in the international banking family; M. Zimmerman's essay about Ludolf Holst (1756–1825), a German writer in Hamburg, demonstrated to be the prototype of Werner Sombart (1863–1941) and the precursor in formulating a pattern of distorted and biased theories about the role of Jews in the economic sphere; and Hagit Lavsky's interesting personal drama of Salman Schocken, reflecting the ideological tensions in the Zionist Organization on the economic development of the *yishuv* in the 1920s and the possibility of a professional, non-political approach, free from interference of political parties.

Two other papers describe economic topics and activities in Palestine, in terms of Zionist history – one, essentially descriptive, deals with the *kollelim* and *haluka* system of providing financial support and social services to Ashkenazic communities in Palestine in the late nineteenth century; the other is about the economic achievements and merits of the five leading industrialists in Palestine in the 1920s.

With respect to methodological questions, the only paper on this subject in the volume, by H. Wasserman, provides a critical discussion of the tendency of most historians, Jews and non-Jews, to utilize a 'reference group' for their conclusions while neglecting to seek a 'control group' in order to arrive at more objective judgements, as illustrated by the author's study of the economic mobility of German Jews during their period of emancipation.

Finally, the essays pertaining to Poland. Here again the reader is given, in three essays, the conventional utilization of evidence – some primary but mostly secondary sources published in Poland after World War II – to reach conclusions which had been presented by Yitzhak Schipper a long time ago, whether to do with the contribution made by Polish Jews to the progressive evolution of the organization of producing and marketing salt in the sixteenth century (Sh. A. Cygielman); or the factual character and extent of Jewish commercial activities in Poland in the sixteenth and seventeenth centuries (G. D. Hundert); or 'the other side' in the relationship between Jewish *arendar* and the Polish noblemen to 'discover' that the position of the former was not as disadvantageous and contemptible as Dubnow would have us believe (M. J. Rosman). Indeed, it was not always, depending on any number of factors and circumstances. Disregarding the archival material in the Czartoryski Library in Kraków utilized by the author, the 'other side' in the business of leasing is well known to those historians who do not proceed from the mistaken notion that the literature on the subject is limited.

The subject of the worsening situation of the Jewish labourer in Poland between the two World Wars is well documented and convincingly presented by B. Grantzarska-Kadari, who stresses correctly that despite conditions of economic deprivation, this generation of Jewish labourers exemplified a life style in which pride in one's labour as well as one's cultural activities was truly paramount.

In all, the wide variety of topics, vertical and horizontal, under the general heading of Jewish economic participation, together with the numerous details and substantiating materials will undoubtedly be instructive and enlightening to students of Jewish history as well as interested readers. Moreover, the volume as a collection of researched monographs provides another beneficial tool in the hands of the Jewish historian. A list of the contributing scholars showing their professional positions and addresses would have been useful as, indeed, are the twenty-four pages of English summary.

Jacob Litman
New York University

Jonathan I. Israel. *European Jewry in the Age of Mercantilism: 1550–1750*. Oxford: Clarendon Press. 1985. Pp. xxi, 293.

When did modern Jewish history begin? The early architects of Jewish historiography, and their successors, suggested the second half of the eighteenth century as the turning point which ended the 'Jewish Middle Ages'. That period, marked by the French Revolution on the one hand, and by the work of Moses Mendelssohn on the other, is pictured as ushering in a new era involving fundamental changes in Jewish culture and political status. On this convention rests the common claim that, 'the period known as "early modern" in Western Europe was, for most Jews, a continuation of the Middle Ages'.[1] In the book under review, Professor Jonathan Israel of the University of London attempts to show that the early modern period was an essentially new phase in Jewish history, and to draw a firm dividing-line between the medieval and early modern epochs. The beginning of the early modern era is to be dated in 1570 and the period came to an end in the second quarter of the eighteenth century.

The author's central claim is based on a clearly expressed criterion for the evaluation of the Jewish historical experience, namely, the 'significance' or the 'impact' of the Jews on the economy and culture of Europe.

On this basis he identifies a profound change beginning around 1570 and reaching a 'high point' in the period between 1650 and 1713. It was in the second half of the seventeenth century that Jews had the most profound and pervasive significance ever in European history. This heyday of Jewish influence came to an end during the eighteenth century which the author depicts as a period of decline.

In the first chapter, entitled 'Exodus from the West', it is stressed that the Iberian expulsions of the late fifteenth century (Spain 1492, Portugal 1497, Navarre 1498) were part of a broader European trend which saw the banishment of numerous Central European Jewish communities during the same decade (Geneva 1490, Mecklenburg and Pomerania 1492, Halle and Magdeburg 1493, etc.; the 1495 expulsion from Lithuania is not mentioned). A further wave of expulsions, during the mid-sixteenth century, was more 'ideological' and systematic because of the tensions generated by the Reformation and the Counter-Reformation. This second phase came to an end in 1570. By that time Jewish life and culture had been virtually eliminated from Central and Western Europe. New centres were established in the Ottoman Empire and in Poland-Lithuania. This was more than a simple movement of population, 'the great trek to the east was a form of economic emancipation.' Not only were the new communities characterized by much greater occupational diversity and vastly increased significance in the economies of their new states, but concomitantly the Jews' position in society was much stronger and more secure than it had been in Western Europe.

The great turning-point, the sign of which was the initially tentative re-admission of Jews to West European states, reversed previous trends which prevailed, 'everywhere west of Poland'. This change was made possible by the combined influence of two related developments. Out of the competing, deadlocked claims of the Catholic and the various reformed Churches arose a kind of radical scepticism. Important thinkers of the period like Bodin, Lipsius and Bacon, sought the truth in all sources including the Scriptures and the post-Biblical literature of the Jews. There emerged a school of philosemitic scholarship and at the same time a 'philosemitic mercantilism'. The pursuit of the economic interests of the state irrespective of religion and tradition was a political expression of the rejection of received truths by the radical sceptics: 'it is no mere chance that Bodin stood at the centre of both initiatives'. Thus, Jews began to re-appear in Western and Central Europe, and particularly Iberian Jews. The changes in policy which made this possible were chiefly the work of absolutist princes determined to foster the prosperity of their states. After describing some examples of these developments, Israel goes on to propose that in the period between 1550 and 1650, there were profound changes in Jewish culture as well.

While the Jewish cultural atmosphere in that period was more autonomous and coherent than ever before, and while there was much in it that was resistant to non-Jewish intellectual and anti-rationalist trends, 'there can be no mistaking its novel and . . . rather modern character'. The novel elements identified by Israel include, first of all, the most potent current of mysticism in Jewish history. Emanating from Safed, it served to reinforce the links between Sephardic and Ashkenazic Jews. He also points to a new involvement in poetry, music and dance, citing Sephardic and Italian examples. The intensified political and historical awareness of Jews, exemplified in the work of David Gans, Ibn Yahya, Samuel Usque and Ibn Verga is cited. Here, the author might have debated Yosef Haim Yerushalmi's rather adamant contention that, 'the attitude toward historiography among sixteenth-century readers was no different . . . from what it had been in prior ages'.[2] Even more seriously, Professor Israel's West European orientation becomes most problematic in this discussion of Jewish culture. Isserles and Luria are mentioned in two sentences as examples of the trend toward reconciling traditional Jewish learning, mysticism, and some elements of philosophy and science! Major works on East European Jewish culture such as those of Ben Sasson, Shmeruk and Zinberg are not even listed in the bibliography. As will be seen, one of the merits of this book is the author's success in showing the economic links between Sephardic and Ashkenazic Jews, but in the realm of culture, it is not at all clear that the diverse works of Moses Cordovero, Judah Loew and the polemics of Elijah Montalto can be linked together successfully. And there are serious questions about the relative weight assigned here to the various dimensions of Jewish culture in the sixteenth and seventeenth centuries.

The Thirty Years War accelerated the trends begun after 1570 and particularly the re-settlement of Jews and their growing demographic and economic significance. Jewish army provisioners laid the groundwork for the later appearance of the *Hofjuden*. In making these claims, Israel entirely rejects the historiographical convention that the German Jewish population declined during the period of the war. He finds that the contending forces tended to protect Jews precisely because of their increasing economic importance. Similarly, the Jewish population of Poland-Lithuania expanded in this period with the Chmielnicki massacres seen as 'less a turning-point in the history of Polish Jewry than a brutal but relatively short interruption in its steady growth and expansion'. All of these developments formed the prelude for the 'high point' reached by European Jewish society in the period between 1650 and 1713.

The 'high point' period marked the culmination of the political and cultural trends which led to the prominence of the Jews in Western Europe. The role of the Court Jews, a phenomenon which Israel asserts was not limited to Central Europe but embraced Jews playing similar roles in Holland, in Italian territories and in Poland as well, was most important at this time. He also includes in this group New Christian financiers in Spain. Similarly, the participation of Jews in the importing of colonial goods and in the transit trade between Germany and Poland and between Italy and the Balkans was most significant in this period. The strong vertical ties within Jewish society, and the economic interdependence of European Jewish communities, east and west, Sephardic and Ashkenazic, are stressed. Indeed, Israel shows how important these links were for the rapid mobilization of capital by Court Jews, and he attempts to prove also that the Sephardic importers of Amsterdam, Hamburg and southwestern France made possible 'the grip of Ashkenazic Jewry over the jewel, precious metal, tobacco and spice trades in Central and Eastern Europe'.

Complementing this unprecedented prominence of Jews in the European economy was a dramatic expansion of the Jewish population at a time when the population of Europe as a whole was stagnant or declining. Consequently, the Jewish proportion of the European population grew significantly, and particularly in Poland-Lithuania. It is in this period, after 1650, that Jewish society in Europe can be characterized most accurately as 'A Republic Apart'. Everywhere in Europe, Jewish autonomous institutions reached their fullest and most ramified stage of development before waning from the early decades of the eighteenth century. These developments, however, were accompanied by a 'Spiritual Crisis' which took diverse forms.

If I understand him correctly, Professor Israel maintains that the general European crisis of faith which led to the splintering of the Church and the rise of scepticism, enabled the integration of Jews in Western Europe, but those same 'corrosive forces at work generally now also entered the body politic and spiritual of Jewry.' He accepts Scholem's thesis that the Sabbatian movement engulfed all of Jewry, rich and poor, Sephardic and Ashkenazic, and that its influence persisted long after the messiah's apostasy. He claims as well that a second dimension of this spiritual crisis, 'the Spinozist Revolt', not only contributed to the anti-Jewish animus which eventually characterized the European Enlightenment, but also significantly affected western Sephardic society. The anti-Christian writings created by (Sephardic) Jews in the new atmosphere of freedom and in an attempt to recover from the Sabbatian debacle found their analogue in the splendid new synagogues built in Amsterdam in the 1670s. At the same time, Jewish influence on European culture as a whole reached unprecedented proportions – clearly reflected in the work of Grotius, Rembrandt, Milton, Newton, Racine, Pascal and others. Nevertheless, there also appeared in this period some new elements of Jew-hatred, particularly in the writings of the Deist precursors of the Enlightenment, and most notoriously in Eisenmenger's *Entdecktes Juden-*

thum. The latter work was primarily a reaction against the currency and influence of Jewish anti-Christian writings.

Signs of decline became evident in the second decade of the eighteenth century. Jewish population growth faltered and began to lag behind the general expansion of the European population. Although this was not the case in certain German territories, and certainly not in Poland-Lithuania, Israel stresses that in those areas the Jewish population did become widely dispersed with no large concentrations in the great cities. At the same time there was a loosening of communal allegiance detectable not only among Sephardic Jews and *Hofjuden* but expressed also in a general crisis of authority leading to the progressive collapse of Jewish autonomous institutions. Reference to the work of Azriel Shohet and Jacob Katz would have deepened this discussion and other parts of Israel's book as well. The demographic and institutional decline was accompanied by the waning of Jewish significance within the European economy, and by the spread of the anti-Jewish animus of the European Enlightenment.

Professor Israel has made a significant contribution to scholarship with this new book. Not only is there new information, based on research in West European archives, on Sephardic economic and political activities, but he has posed a number of significant broader questions about the European Jewish experience which, one suspects, will be debated for some time to come. By way of conclusion, I should like to take up, very briefly, one of these central issues.

By what criteria shall we periodize Jewish history? Clearly, the position taken in the present work is that the criterion ought to be the change in the role of the Jews in European society. I do not believe, however, that one must resort to the teleological fallacies of the Zionist school of Jewish historiography to question this position.[3] One ought to be able to evaluate developments within Jewish society and culture on a basis other than one that depends on whether these developments impinged in some way on the societies within which Jews lived. And surely, within the realm of Jewish history, if one wishes to describe the early centuries of the modern era, one should attend to the largest and most creative concentrations of Jews. Yet in this work, Ottoman Jewry is barely mentioned and the Jews of Poland-Lithuania, though they receive more attention, lie tellingly outside the central hypotheses of the work. This is not to gainsay Professor Israel's achievement; his is an important book worthy of the attention of all European and Jewish historians.

Gershon David Hundert
McGill University

NOTES

1 Robert Seltzer. *Jewish People, Jewish Thought: The Jewish Experience in History* (New York and London, 1980), p. 454.
2 *Zakhor: Jewish History and Jewish Memory* (Seattle and London, 1982), p. 69.
3 G. D. Hundert, 'Reflections on the "Whig" interpretation of Jewish history: *ma'assei banim siman le'avot*' in *Truth and Compassion: Essays in Memory of Rabbi Solomon Frank*, ed. H. Joseph et. al. (Waterloo, Ontario, 1983), pp. 113-14.

Lucy S. Dawidowicz. *The Golden Tradition.*
Jewish Life and Thought in Eastern Europe.
New York: Schocken Books. 1984. Pp. 10, 502.

Lucy Dawidowicz writes in the introduction to this recently republished book: 'This is a book about East European Jews in crisis, challenge and creativity from the end of the eighteenth century until their cataclysmic destruction in the Second World War.' She has prepared a collection of extracts from the autobiographies of eminent Jews or memoirs which show the deep changes which have occurred in the last two centuries in Jewish life in East Europe. She argues that '. . . the most direct form of history, the autobiography, is history's most intimate disclosure, a man's assessment of his life, his acts and ideas, successes and failures . . .'. I feel that there is some exaggeration in these words. Autobiographical documents and memoirs differ greatly in their value and even the best of them should not be considered uncritically as historical sources. Some are indeed really of great importance. Others, however, have served as self-justification for authors trying to hide some dark side of their past and who therefore present only what they consider noble. Sometimes the authors omit important facts. One of the representatives of the *Haskala*, Moses Leib Lilienblum, quoted in this book, has written: 'Luzzato's autobiography is as hollow as the parched ears of corn in Pharoah's dream.' Every historian should bear this statement in mind in using documents of this kind. Dawidowicz is, however, aware of this problem and has chosen truly important memoirs, works that reveal many different sides of Jewish life and thought.

The book does not present Jewish life in all its real variety. The life of Jewish shopkeepers, artisans, farmers, workers and *luftmenshen* is far less represented than that of scholars, rabbis, rebbes, teachers and artists. The autobiographies and memoirs contained in this book concern mainly the Jewish intellectual élite and the life of common people appears only on the margin. Even in this sphere there are *lacunae*. The most important gap is the paucity of material on the twentieth century. Most of the memoirs are connected with the evolution of the Jewish intellectual and political life before the First World War. Only in a few cases do we find anything about the period 1918–1939 (and almost exclusively about Polish Jewry), nothing about the First World War. The importance of these years in Jewish life does not need to be stressed.

Of course, every selection of documents, especially when a vast amount of material is to be included in a single volume, can be criticized because of the lack of this or that important text. The merit of the book is that Lucy Dawidowicz has chosen documents presenting very different and often contradictory ways of life and attitudes which, as a whole, give a vivid and complete picture of the Jewish élite from the second half of the eighteenth century to the beginning of the twentieth century. We find here the hasidic *rebbes*, *mitnagdim*, orthodox rabbis, *maskilim*, philanthropists in the traditional style, scholars, writers, journalists, assimilationists, *apikorsim*, Zionists, socialists, teachers. In general, the lives of these men – which often develop dramatically – illustrate the changing world of Jews in East Europe from the end of the feudal order, with the special legal status it assigned to Jews, to capitalism which brought the legal emancipation of groups of people previously classed as inferior.

The book is thus an excellent manual for every student who wants to understand how the Jews in this part of Europe, previously a religious community, were transformed into the contemporary nation. Perhaps its division into eleven chapters (composed of a total of 57 fragments of autobiographies and memoirs) may be questioned. It is sometimes difficult to ascertain the principles on which the chapters have been divided up. Yet, it is also true that every possible structure has its good and weak sides, and the book in its present form does help the student to understand the complicated problems involved. It would have been useful to have inserted a separate chapter concerning *mitnagdim*, seeing that early *hasidim* and *haskala* have their own chapters.

The book has its origins as a textbook for university students which has influenced its shape and the scope of commentaries. Yet some important inconsistencies have crept into the notes concerning the persons presented in the book. Sometimes, elementary biographical information is provided, while in other cases the role a given person played in Jewish intellectual life is discussed, omitting even the basic biographical details. For the professional historian, who can also profit greatly from this volume, an indication of what has been omitted from the extracts would be valuable.

The book opens with an outline (almost ninety pages) on the intellectual and political development of East Central European Jewry from the eighteenth century to 1939. This is a brilliant introduction to the problems which are encountered in the memoirs down to the First World War. There are, however, some minor misunderstandings. It is incorrect to write of the Jews in Lemberg that they were 'surrounded by a Greek

Catholic population . . .' (p. 34); the Jews of this city lived among a mainly Polish population, while the Ukrainians lived, for the most part, mainly in the villages. The story of Jewish emancipation in Congress Poland (p. 35) is also more complicated than is suggested by Dawidowicz's account.

More important misunderstandings are to be found on pages concerning the inter-war period but a short review is not the right place to discuss them. There is, however, one question worth studying in the future. Dawidowicz writes: 'No Jewish strategy succeeded in Poland; none could have in accelerating dictatorship' (p. 79). This opinion is shared by some other historians studying the past of the Polish Jews. I think, however, that this question should be discussed in the context of the history of Poland in that time. Taking into consideration the dramatic developments of this short period of twenty-one years and its tragic end in September 1939, a similar opinion could be formulated not only concerning Jewish strategies but also about Polish ones. In the very difficult economic situation without any possibility of fundamental changes in the economic and social policy, in the dramatic international situation of the whole of Central Europe which depended ultimately on the policy of the Big Powers, no strategy seems capable of solving the most important problems of the Polish Republic and its inhabitants, and the end in 1939 under external blows was certainly tragic. Yet, however critical one's opinion about the inter-war period (and I am not inclined to be over-optimistic) nobody can say anything with certainty. It was – and is still today – difficult, if not impossible, to predict how international market conditions would have developed if peace had been preserved; this was one of the most important factors influencing the internal situation in Poland. I would therefore rather be more cautious in expressing any opinion concerning the Jewish – and not only Jewish – strategies in the inter-war period in Poland.

Jerzy Tomaszewski
University of Warsaw

Joseph Weiss. *Studies in Eastern European Jewish Mysticism*. Edited by David Goldstein. Oxford: The Littman Library of Jewish Civilization, Oxford University Press. 1986. Pp. 272.

Seventeen years have passed since the tragic death of Professor Joseph Weiss, when the appearance of the volume of his collected studies in English proves once again how central and dominant his work is in the study of Hasidism. The lapse of time has not diminished the impact of his new ideas and approaches, and it seems that in many cases recent scholarship still operates within the parameters set down a generation or more ago by him. I have no doubt that this new volume will re-emphasize the importance of reading and re-reading Joseph Weiss's works if a scholarly, historically accurate and philologically sound approach to Hasidism is to be sought.

Two subjects were central to Weiss's study of Hasidism. One was the understanding of the unique figure of Rabbi Nahman of Braslav, the grandson of Rabbi Eliezer Besht, the founder of Hasidism; the second was the emergence of Hasidism in its early stages, from the groups which preceded and surrounded the Besht until the organization and teachings of the young movement were streamlined by the work of the Great Maggid, Rabbi Dov Baer of Mezhirech, in the third quarter of the eighteenth century. As to the first subject, Weiss's studies were collected and edited by M. Piekarz and published in Hebrew (The Bialik Institute, Jerusalem, 1971), whereas his studies of early Hasidism were until now scattered in various journals (especially the *Journal of Jewish Studies*, which he edited for many years), and many have remained unpublished. David Goldstein presents us with a collection of these papers, some published for the first time. Of special importance are the additions to several of Weiss's studies which Goldstein found in his papers, and printed together with the previously published studies. Reading this book together with the Piekarz volume, the scholar can finally have a clear picture of the results of Professor Weiss's diligent and intuitive concept of the history and development of the Hasidic movement.

One of the most brilliant contributions of Professor Weiss to the study of Hasidic origins is his thesis concerning the social stratum from which this movement emerged, and the impact of its spiritual problems on the later development of Hasidism. This thesis was presented by him in an extensive article published in Hebrew in 1951 (*Zion*, vol. 16, pp. 46–105). and is now summarized in the article that opens the collection, 'Some Notes on the Social Background of Early Hasidism'. Weiss presents in this essay a description of the group of itinerant preachers, many of them influenced by ideas originating in the various schools of Sabbatian heretics, who laid the ideological foundations of some of the most prominent ideas found in the traditions attributed to the Besht. The nature of Hasidic leadership and the theory of the powers of the *tsaddik* originated, according to Weiss, in the social and theological problems faced by this group. This is followed by one of Weiss's classical studies of Hasidic origins – the description of the circle of 'pre-Hasidic Hasidim' around Rabbi Nahman of Kosov.

The main body of this collection is devoted to Weiss's study of the central ideas of the early *Hasidim*, mainly using the texts of the sermons of Rabbi Dov Baer of Mezhirech. Weiss analysed in great detail the obscure and scattered references which together comprise the elements of the Hasidic mystical approach to religious life: the elements of contemplation, the novel way of Torah study, the 'via passiva' attitude in religious practice, the mystical conception of the intentions during prayers (*kavanot*), the meaning of Hasidic faith and trust in God, and other themes which helped Hasidic masters turn Hasidism into one of the most meaningful spiritual phenomena of modern Jewish history. Most of these subjects were never studied in detail before Professor Weiss published these articles, and they have served as the basis for later studies of Hasidic mysticism.

The last part of this collection of studies includes a selection of Weiss's studies of later Hasidic teachers, and especially of the two most profound phenomena of third-generation Hasidism – the mass movement of Habad Hasidism and the small, esoteric sect of Braslav Hasidism. The differences between these two sects, both emerging from the same source but creating radically divergent historical movements, interested Weiss greatly. No study of Rabbi Nahman himself is included in the collection, but a brief description can be found in 'Sense and Nonsense in Defining Judaism – The Strange Case of Nahman of Braslav'. In this article Weiss used the uniqueness of Rabbi Nahman's teachings and personality to demonstrate the wide variety of religious phenomena produced by Judaism, and he shows how feeble are all attempts to define Judaism when compared with the richness and profundity of its spiritual movements. Another indication of such diversity can be found in Weiss's study of the unique theology of Rabbi Mordecai Joseph Leiner, the founder of Izbica Hasidism.

It seems appropriate to me that the editor entitled the volume 'Eastern European Jewish Mysticism'. While Weiss dedicated a significant part of his efforts to elucidating social and historical problems connected with Hasidic history, his main aim was always to understand and explain the nature of Hasidic mysticism per se. He always viewed Hasidism as the modern manifestation of Jewish mysticism, and therefore an expression not only of a mass movement but also of great mystics such as the Maggid of Mezhirech and Rabbi Nahman. His brilliant description of this phenomenon is now readily available and will undoubtedly serve to enrich the study of Jewish spirituality.

Joseph Dan
The Hebrew University, Jerusalem

Mathias Bersohn.
Kilka słów o dawniejszych bóżnicach drewnianych w Polsce. Part I,
Kraków 1895; part II, Kraków 1900: the Committee for Research
of the Kraków Academy of Science. Part I, Warsaw, 1903.
Pp. 66. Reprint by the National Library, Warsaw 1985.

Scholars and art experts, both Jewish and non-Jewish, have shown an interest in the wooden synagogues of Poland, Lithuania, and the Ukraine that is unparalleled with regard to any other branch of the artistic-religious creative tradition of the Jews of Eastern Europe, rich and varied though it is.

The researchers and art experts who drew attention to these small synagogues around the turn of the century and highlighted their originality and Jewishness as well as their beauty and charm are most certainly worthy of recognition. The value of their contribution has, tragically, been further enhanced since the Holocaust and the German war of annihilation against the Jews, and every expression of their cultural and material creativity, completely destroyed the surviving examples of such religious art in Eastern Europe and particularly Poland.

Some three years ago, the National Library in Warsaw made a splendid gesture of tribute to the memory of one of the pioneers of research into the art of Polish synagogues, Mathias Bersohn, by publishing a new, illustrated edition of one of his most important works on Polish-Jewish art, *Kilka słów* .... Warsaw-born Bersohn, historian of Polish Jewry and founder of the Jewish Antiquities Museum of the Warsaw community, was one of the first to appreciate the beauty of these synagogues and to realize their importance in the history of Jewish folk architecture.

Bersohn's prodigious activity in researching the history of Polish Jewry resulted in a succession of studies written between 1861 and 1906, of which the best known is a collection of historical documents on Polish Jewry between 1388 and 1782 drawn from the state archives and a biographical dictionary of Jewish scholars in Poland in the sixteenth, seventeenth and eighteenth centuries.

Bersohn's most important publication, however, in some ways, the seminal work in the field of the religious art of Polish Jewry, was his *Kilka słów* ..., published between 1895 and 1903 as a special publication of the Committee for Research into the History of Art of the Kraków Academy of Sciences. He wrote in the Introduction:

> In several Polish towns inhabited mostly by Jews there are old, wooden synagogues frequently of unusual shape and of a style that seems to defy description. The inherent conservatism – and perhaps even more the poverty of the Jewish community of these towns –

means that only a few of these highly original structures have survived in their original form to the present time.

Bersohn describes many such monuments, including several he saw with his own eyes on the travels he took throughout Congress Poland, Lithuania, Volyhnia and Podolia. Even though Bersohn writes more as an amateur enthusiast of Jewish folk art than as an art historian, his writings do not lack scholarly merit. He preceded his descriptions of the synagogues with interesting historical material, and complemented his own drawings of the synagogues with architects' plans and drawings of their *objets d'art* and religious appurtenances.

In this period in and around the late nineteenth century, the study of Jewish religious art was undertaken mostly by amateur art enthusiasts and folklore experts who were not Jewish; very few Jews actually took an interest in this field of research. Accordingly, little attention was paid to the Jewish builders and craftsmen who constructed them. The anonymity surrounding these skilled artisans denies us the opportunity not only of knowing their identities but also of knowing something about their ways of living and working while engaged in the holy task of religious building and decoration in the various plastic arts. Only occasionally does Bersohn mention the names of Jewish craftsmen. But none of this was sufficient proof, in Bersohn's opinion, of the existence of Jewish synagogue builders. 'Despite rigorous searches in these directions,' he wrote, 'and many written requests to the committees of the longer-established communities, we do not yet know of any Jewish builder from the seventeenth and eighteenth centuries.'

Bersohn's research was instrumental in opening the way to the study of the wooden synagogues of Poland and elsewhere; and moreover, thanks to his links with the Polish world of learning as a member of the Committee for the History of Art of the Kraków Academy of Science and the Viennese Scientific Society, he succeeded in arousing enthusiasm among the scholars of Poland and other countries with regard to this long-established and original form of Jewish building.

David Dawidowicz
Tel Aviv

Magdalena Opalski. *The Jewish Tavern-Keeper and his Tavern in Nineteenth Century Polish Literature*. Jerusalem: Centre for Research on the History and Culture of Polish Jews and the Zalman Shazar Center. 1986. Pp. 109.

Under the system of *propinacja* in Poland, dating from the Middle Ages, the landlord had the sole right to distil and sell alcohol and continued to have this right even after the Partitions of the eighteenth century. It was abolished in Prussia in 1845, in Galicia in 1889 and in Russian Poland only in 1898. Normally the agent of the *szlachcic* in the sale of alcohol was a Jew. Under this system the landlord could dispose of part of the grain harvest in the form of alcohol and thus cream off from the peasantry such money as they might earn on their own account. The implication was that he and the Jewish innkeeper had an interest in encouraging the consumption of alcohol and thus of acting in the worst interests of the peasants. In addition, the innkeeper could give credit for those periods when the peasants did not possess money and thus obtain an additional income from the interest he charged on the debts incurred. This was a situation which the reformers of the eighteenth century deplored as a social evil. In his *Przestrogi dla Polski*, published in 1790, Stanisław Staszic had written that 'aside from lawless serfdom, Jews are the second great cause of laziness, stupidity, drunkenness and poverty among the peasants.' This was an attitude which a political thinker could adopt in search for measures to reform the Polish Commonwealth. In the nineteenth century, writers tended to look at society as it was. Opalski's book, the fourth in a series of works from the Center for Research on the History and Culture of Polish Jews, does not examine the problem from an economic point of view, but, as the title states, analyzes the attitudes of Polish authors to the role of Jewish innkeepers in the Polish countryside. Her view is that nineteenth-century fiction tended to be silent about the role of the noble in using the tavern as a means of exploiting the peasantry. They accepted the fact that the Jewish innkeeper in fact was part of the community. Often it is difficult to draw a distinction between myth and reality. The innkeeper is sometimes represented as being on the fringe of society, having connections with crime and smuggling. The Jew is certainly a source of information about the wider world. The 'Jewish Post' (*poczta żydowska*), which might almost be translated as 'the bush telegraph', provided news of what was happening beyond the immediate area of the village. It even emerges that the Jew is often trusted by the peasant, who prefers his advice to that which he might receive from the noble landlord. Yet as the nineteenth century progressed, the Jewish innkeepers began to drift away from the countryside, leaving Christians to take over the taverns. Evidently they did not fill the social vacuum created by the disappearance of the traditional system. More and more the taverner, especially after the insurrection of 1863, begins to emerge as the entrepreneur. Bolesław Prus's *Anielka* (1879) presents the innkeeper as seeking to maintain a neutral position between the peasants and the impoverished landowner, who now appears in fiction as the person suffering from the crisis of bankruptcy. In short, the Jew begins to emerge as a moderately successful capitalist. Junosza's novel on the career of Symcha Boruch Kaltkugel goes to extremes. Symcha Boruch is represented as an innkeeper with a wide range of activities, which yield him a fortune large enough to enable him to set up in the city as a moneylender, respected by the community and with younger daughters who converse with one another in French. On the whole, however, the Jewish innkeeper retains his traditional role in Polish fiction. As Opalski says, the taverner is an 'isolated island locked in the confines of the noble's estate and lives well beyond the dimension of history'. Symcha Boruch is an exception. We can hardly disagree with her when she writes that 'in Polish literature as a whole, the tavernkeeper remained a negative figure'. Her work is in fact a warning against assessing the role of the Jewish innkeeper from the point of view of Polish writers, who in the period of the Partitions were assessing their society with the outlook of the *szlachta*, however much they might be critical of the noble class. The innkeeper was presented as a feature of Polish society from a point of view external to Jewish society itself. This work gives food for thought and excites the wish that it might be possible to obtain a picture of Polish society from a Jewish taverner's point of view. Conditions may have varied from estate to estate and from region to region, but the suspicion remains that the evil practices which some Polish writers detect in Jewish taverners may have been the result of the pressures placed upon them by the landowners anxious to exploit to the full the advantages given to them by the right of *propinacja*. It was the landlord who established the rent for the taverner and kept it as high as he could. Evils which arose were laid at the door of the taverner.

R. F. Leslie
Charlbury

Steven J. Zipperstein. *The Jews of Odessa: A Cultural History, 1794–1881*. Stanford: Stanford University Press. 1985. Pp. 212.

Steven Zipperstein's book on Odessa should be seen as an example of a new and valuable trend in which Jewish history is viewed from the vantage point of the local community. This historiographical departure has altered the focus of Jewish history writing, from the macrocosmic to the microcosmic, or, more precisely, from a concentration on general factors presumably relevant to Jewry as a whole to the local Jewish sphere. Increasingly this is the dominant tendency of Jewish historical work, though several recent exceptions easily come to mind. In the past, books were produced, of course, on specific urban Jewish communities but these were generally undertaken to commemorate centres of Jewish life destroyed in the Holocaust. Rarely were they written by professional historians.

This rather recent emphasis on urban historiography originated in the United States, which perhaps helps explain the early initiative of the

Jewish Publication Society of America in publishing a series of books on major urban Jewish communities such as Vienna, Frankfurt, Cologne, and Vilna among others. These were followed by monographs on key communities in the United States, such as New York (Grinstein, Goren), Detroit (Gartner) and elsewhere. Outside the United States this trend made little headway. With regard to Eastern Europe, very few historical works on particular communities were produced: Fin, Maggid and Klausner on Vilna, Shatzsky on Warsaw and a handful of others. The bulk of the studies written on Jewish communities in Russia and Poland belong to the post-Holocaust 'commemorative' school and are of uncertain value as scholarly investigations.

No doubt, if one were to choose only one East European Jewish community for study Odessa would be the first and ideal choice. This was a community that came into existence only at the end of the eighteenth century, and it developed in the region of New Russia that was new to Jewish settlement and whose substantial distance from the older and more established centres of Jewish life in Eastern Europe permitted it to develop with relative independence. Alexander Orbach made an attempt to study Odessa Jewry in *New Voices of Russian Jewry* (Leiden, 1980), but he focused exclusively on the Jewish press of the 1860s and showed little interest in the community's social history.

The fact that the Jewish community of Odessa originated and developed along with the city of Odessa itself provides the researcher with an unusual opportunity to study Jewish history within a larger context. And the articles of Patricia Herlihy on Odessa history offer the Jewish historian an appropriate and convenient basis for research.

This relatively liberal and cosmopolitan seaport gave Jews a rare opportunity for extensive involvement in the social, economic and political life of a Russian city, as well as unique freedom in the building of their own communal life. In this respect Odessa led the way for other New Russian cities such as Nikolaev, Ekaterinoslav, Kherson, and Elizavetgrad (see Zipperstein's discussion of this factor on pp. 134–9).

This book focuses on the period from the end of the eighteenth century until the pogroms of the 1880s. It follows the rather paradoxical process whereby Odessa came to serve as a paradigm for Jewish acculturation in Eastern Europe in contrast to the assimilation model characterized by Warsaw. But at the same time that these developments were engendering high hopes among Jews for the improvement of their legal status, came the pogrom of 1871 – a model antithetical to the one anticipated by local Jewry. The prosperity, social acculturation, and political influence of Odessa's Jewish minority (pp. 55, 132–3) engendered an antagonism from segments of the surrounding community for which the Jews were ill-prepared. The Odessa pogrom was the precursor not only of the pogroms that were to spread from the cities of southern Russia to those elsewhere in

Poland and Russia in the 1890s, but also of the rise of modern antisemitism in Western Europe beginning a decade earlier. Most disturbed by this turn of events in Odessa were those who had given enthusiastic support to the process of acculturation – that is, the intelligentsia and it was they who were now responsible for a reassessment (pp. 114–34, 139–50). The Jewish community as a whole, however, continued as before, with the traditional being continually pushed aside by the forces of secularization; the time for more widespread reassessment was yet to come.

The change in the attitude of society and the authorities in Odessa to the Jews paralleled a blow to the city's prosperity as the unchallenged major centre of commercial activity in the Black Sea region. The extensive railway building of the 1860s and 70s opened up other centres, as the author describes (p. 134–9). This process also led to the migration of the maskilic centre of Russian Jewry, which now moved from Odessa to St. Petersburg, elsewhere in Russia and abroad. Zipperstein, who mentions this last point, might have devoted somewhat more attention to it.

Zipperstein's research spans a period of some eighty years, from the end of the eighteenth century to the 1880s, and he focuses primarily (because of the sources available to him) on the last thirty years. Writing the history of an urban community generally means that the research uses municipal archives and community records. In this case such records were unattainable and, accordingly, Zipperstein relies mainly on the Jewish and non-Jewish press along with memoirs relating to the period with the best coverage beginning in the late 1850s.

The study endeavours to present a comprehensive social history of the Jews of Odessa, with attention given to the development of community institutions, education, culture and economic development. How best to balance all these various factors is quite naturally problematic and the transition in this book between socioeconomic-demographic history to cultural and educational history is not always smooth. Perhaps separate chapters on each of these areas would have been better, although to some extent the various themes are dealt with by Zipperstein in separate sections. The author provides extraordinarily interesting data on the demography and economy of the Odessa community along with comparable information on other communities in New Russia. The fact that he combines this data with an analysis of the community's social and cultural history gives the reader an absorbing and dynamic picture of the development of Odessa Jewry.

This book is full of new insights. For instance, Zipperstein shows how education in Odessa, rather than promoting new cultural and ideological programmes, served to further Jews' social and economic integration in the city. A great deal of attention is devoted by the author to the relationship between the Galician and native Russian Jewish communities of the city, to the interaction between them and the dynamics of local communal power.

In the course of the study Zipperstein alters the standard viewpoint that education and acculturation were first brought to Odessa by the immigrants from Galicia: he shows that it was the conditions of life in Odessa that attracted the Galician immigration, and it was these conditions that helped fashion Odessa's unusual openness to education and modernity (see esp. p. 40). At the same time he demonstrates that the German education introduced by the Galician immigrants held sway, at least until the sixties. The growth of these 'modern' Jewish community institutions was encouraged by the authorities (p. 43) who favoured the Galicians at the expense of the local elements. This is illustrated in Zipperstein's book by the struggle for hegemony within the community that surrounded the choice of Rabbi Schwabacher (pp. 74, 86–92), by the establishment of modern synagogues and the widespread availability of local modern Jewish education (pp. 56–67). The great success of general education for Jews in Odessa, both in Russian schools and in Jewish governmental schools (pp. 55, 108, 130) remained unrivalled in Russia and Poland until the end of the nineteenth century. The impact of Jewish enlightenment is described by Zipperstein in a vivid fashion which highlights how external conditions and *Haskalah* as a way of life for the individual paralleled and even anticipated the elaboration of a maskilic programme. Zipperstein shows how the maskilic revolution in Jewish life in its full sense can be said to have occurred only after the local social institutions had absorbed new developments and this took place only in the 1860s.

The study also successfully portrays the central characters in Odessa cultural life, including Bezalel Stern and Osip Rabinovich, alongside sympathetic Russian figures such as Governor-General Vorontsov and Pirogov (curator of the Odessa educational district), figures who had counterparts nowhere in Russia.

The book demonstrates, I believe, how Odessa's religious pluralism, its openness to Jewish economic initiative and its political congeniality had no positive consequences for the ultimate destiny of its Jews. In the end – despite periods of relative success in economic, social and cultural spheres – Jewish acculturation in the cities of New Russia did not prevent and may have even contributed to the disturbances of the 1880s which hit these communities first. This blow led to the politicization and even the radicalization of much of Odessa Jewry in particular and the Jews of the New Russia region in general, where large numbers of Jews now embraced Jewish nationalism, socialism, and emigration. Zipperstein has so well succeeded in clarifying the historical background to Russian Jewry's political transformation in the last years of the nineteenth century that his contribution can neither be overrated nor exaggerated.

Joseph Salmon
Ben Gurion University of the Negev

Stephen M. Berk. *Year of Crisis, Year of Hope. Russian Jewry and the Pogroms of 1881–1882*. Westport, Connecticut: Greenwood Press. 1985. Pp. 288.

The pogrom movement of 1881–82 had both an immediate and a long-range impact on the subsequent development of modern Jewish history. Firstly, the pogroms gave rise to a massive Jewish emigration from tsarist lands that served to redistribute dramatically the world Jewish population. Secondly, the existing Jewish communities of central and western Europe, confronted by the plight of their Russian co-religionists, were forced to evaluate their own identities as Jews and their relationships to both foreign Jews and to fellow non-Jewish citizens in the lands they were living in. Finally, the assessment of the pogroms, and especially the subsequent hostile response to the Jewish community by the Russian government, led numbers of Jews to question whether the liberal, integrationist path remained the most effective means by which to attain true equality for the Jews of Russia. For such writers, the picture of a genuinely harmonious co-existence of Jews and non-Jews in a context of mutual respect and acceptance did not appear to be credible in the aftermath of the riots. Hence, the post-1881 development of those Jewish movements and ideologies which focused attention primarily on Jewish needs and interests rather than on the general perfection of society can be traced to a Jewish reading of the pogroms as they focused attention on the modern forms of anti-semitism in Russia and in other European locations. In retrospect then, Jewish responses to and evaluations of the events of 1881–82 have been especially significant as they have contributed to the subsequent Jewish effort to deal with the new realities of life, be they in new geographical locations, or in new understandings of identity, or in the forging of new relationships with the non-Jewish world.

In assessing the character of modern Jewish history in recent years, scholars have been paying more and more attention to the 1881–82 period as they have analyzed the impact that Jewish responses to the pogroms played in the shaping of the last one-hundred years of Jewish history. While Stephen Berk's book belongs to this general body of literature, it is not one of the stronger representatives of such scholarship. In the main, this is because Berk is more interested in describing the events of 1881 rather than in examining, in a critical manner, the reactions to or internalizations of those events by either the Jews or the Russians. Thus, this emerges as that kind of book that is intended to set the stage for that later, in-depth, examination of the repercussions to that explosion herein described. As such, this book really should have been published years ago, that is, before the current scholarly interest in the impact of pogroms on world Jewry began to make its appearance.

Berk's narrative begins with a background review of Jewish life in the Empire since the era of Nicholas I (1825–55). In seeking to explain the pogrom movement, Berk makes a sustained effort at uncovering the general causes that served to ignite the pogroms in the first place. However, here, too, he is content with a summary rather than with a close analysis which would have led to conclusive findings. Even after this exposition, the reader is still left with a number of specific questions on both the Russian disturbances and their general relationship to contemporary anti-Jewish activities and attitudes both in Russia and in Europe as a whole.

Berk's strength is in his organizational and literary abilities. He presents his narrative in a clear and well-written exposition. In his survey, he does touch on all of the pertinent developments in Russia including the ambivalent stance of the Russian radical movement to the pogroms and the emergence of the Jewish nationalist camp in the wake of those riots. Berk concludes his story by tracing the movement of the fleeing Russian emigrants to North America as he highlights the host of difficulties they encountered as they tried to integrate themselves into a very new and quite alien society. While the author's focus on the difficulties confronting the immigrant in the United States is of interest to his American readers and does stay within the parameters of the work as established by the title, the topic is, as presented, extraneous to the central issues raised by the theme of the pogroms, that is, the manner in which Jews understood what had just transpired and how they were to deal with it.

Stephen Berk's book is much more valuable to the reader interested in the general flow of those events associated with 1881. The author does cover nearly all of the topics associated with those developments and does so in a clear and straightforward manner. However, this book will prove to be a disappointment for the student searching either for new insights into the pogrom movement itself and its general relationship to the issue of Russian relations with the local Jewish communities, or for that student eager to see a fresh appraisal of some aspect of the Jewish understanding of those events, understandings that proved to be crucial for the development of Jewish history in the twentieth century.

Alexander Orbach
University of Pittsburgh

Hans Rogger. *Jewish Policies and Right-Wing Politics in Imperial Russia.* London: Macmillan. 1985. Pp. 289.

Hans Rogger's book is largely devoted to a study of Russian government policy towards the Jews from the mid-nineteenth century until the fall of the monarchy. The book's last two chapters, on the other hand, look at the non-official groups and parties, all of them to a greater or lesser extent antisemitic, which sprang up in the early twentieth century. Lucid in style, balanced in judgement and packed with valuable information, Rogger's book will be an invaluable source for students of late imperial Russia for a long time to come. Almost all the book's chapters are reprinted articles written by Rogger over many years of a distinguished academic career and it is a mark of the author's stature that they fully retain their freshness and their value.

Rogger's first chapter, newly written for this book, looks at Russian antisemitism in the European mirror. It shows that, while Russian policies towards Jews and their emancipation shared much in common with other Euorpean states up to the mid-nineteenth century, subsequently they diverged. Much of Rogger's work is devoted to explaining why this was the case, and why the Russian government became a byword in Europe for its illiberal and brutal treatment of the Jews. Subsequent chapters contain both general surveys of ministerial attitudes and policies towards the Jews, and more detailed studies of the Beilis affair, the issues of land and the peasantry, and the question of emigration.

As already stated, the last chapters on the formulation of Russian right-wing parties and the existence or otherwise of a Russian fascism differ somewhat in subject from the book's core. Rogger concludes that the radical right parties which sprang up around 1905, and in particular the quite powerful Union of the Russian People, were not created by the government, never came fully under its control and, at least initially, favoured not only a very new populist and mobilizational style in politics but also quite radical policies on social and economic questions. By 1908, however, the radical right was in disarray and decline, partly because the government and the traditional élites, now firmly re-established in the saddle, needed it less and could better afford to give vent to their dislike of the new right's crudity and demagogy. Rogger concludes that Russian fascism could never really get off the ground in pre-revolutionary Russia because liberalism, capitalism and the emancipation of the Jews had not advanced sufficiently nor displaced the traditional conservative élites from power. There was not enough modern civilization in Russia against which mass resentment could be mobilized, nor could one rant about the bankruptcy of liberalism in a society governed by an increasingly unpopular traditional conservative regime. Moreover, an obvious but important point; so long as the Russian right glorified the tsar as the centre-piece of its political world, it was tied both to the actual personality of Nicholas II and, to some extent, to the governmental system he represented. This put real constraints on its mass appeal and its radicalism, not to mention its ability to recruit the politically ambitious.

As regards the core of his book, namely the attitudes and policies of the

Russian central government towards the Jews, Rogger comes to a number of key conclusions. He does not of course deny that deep and irrational prejudices informed many ministers' attitudes towards the Jews. On the whole, however, he stresses that these top officials were rational and pragmatic men for whom the existence of a large and 'alien' Jewish minority in a poor but modernizing peasant country caused real difficulties. Rogger argues that top officials were far too scared of mass disorder themselves to encourage it by deliberately loosing pogroms. He also concludes that no evidence exists to indict them on this score. Rogger stresses the anxiously defensive nature of Russian bureaucratic conservatism, combined with the government's deep conviction that peasants were defenseless and potentially dangerous children whom the state must protect against the full effects of rapid capitalist modernization. Such attitudes, which lay behind the decades of support for the peasant commune, also explained in part the government's policies towards the Jews. The latter were for the most part seen as much more enterprising and financially stronger then the peasantry, which had to be guarded by the state against the effects of its own improvidence and naivety. Hence the Jews must be locked away in the Pale, deprived of the chance of buying land, and constrained in their efforts to compete even with non-peasant Christians for professional educations and careers. Failure to check Jewish aspirations in this manner led, in the opinion of Russian ministers, to the mass disorders they so deeply feared.

This traditional bureaucratic attitude, never of course universally held, continued to dominate ministerial thinking down to the revolution, but, as the upper bureaucracy became more politicized after 1905 and more aware of the need to mobilize mass support, other attitudes began to surface. Thus, as regards the Beilis affair, Rogger concludes that I. G. Shcheglovitov was seeking to cultivate myths around which Russian authoritarian conservatism could rally. Faced with the advance of constitutionalism, which in Shcheglovitov's view would never be an effective means of governing Russia, the minister of justice was seeking to found a counter-movement grounded in popular anti-liberal sentiment. Whether, had imperial Russia survived, Shcheglovitov's activities would have represented the 'wave of the future', cannot be stated with any certainty, but one has only to read the minister of justice's speeches to sense that a new and sometimes sinister vocabulary was just beginning to make its mark in high official circles.

Dominic Lieven
London School of Economics and Political Science

Hans Rogger. *Jewish Policies and Right-Wing Politics in Imperial Russia.* London: Macmillan. 1985. Pp. 289.

The latest book of Professor Rogger, whose previous publications on Russia in the eighteenth and nineteenth centuries enjoy high reputation, consists of eight rather loosely connected articles that appeared originally between 1964–1976. Only one, the introductory essay, which is devoted to the question of Jewish emancipation as seen from the perspective of modern European history, appears for the first time. The remaining articles are but slightly modified versions of the original texts. Most examine various aspects of the 'Jewish question' in late imperial Russia under Alexander III and Nicholas II. Among the topics covered are attitudes towards Jews after 1881 (chapter 2), the infamous Beilis case and its relation to the internal politics of pre-war Russia (chapter 3), solutions to the Jewish question proposed by such leading statesment as Ignatiev and Goremykin (chapter 4), Jewish policies in context of the liberation of the serfs (chapter 5), official restrictions on emigration (chapter 6). Somewhat different problems are explored in the final chapters which discuss the formation of right-wing Russian organizations at the beginning of the twentieth century. Yet, here too, the author retains the same basic approach and the book can be treated as a coherent whole. Twenty years separate the writing of some of these essays, yet Rogger's views on the subject have not changed.

The central question that links all the essays concerns the reasons why Russia's policy towards the Jews was both so inconsistent and so radically different from the policies of other European countries. In trying to explain why, for instance, the Pale of Settlement remained largely intact until the First World War, Rogger rejects most standard explanations. Nothing that occurred is treated as either obvious or inevitable: he rejects Richard Pipes's theory that attributes the especially virulent Russian form of anti-semitism to the impact of Orthodox Christianity and also questions 'scapegoat theories' since these do not sufficiently take into account the social and economic reality. In Rogger's opinion, the treatment of Jews here was the direct consequence of a peculiarity of their position in imperial society. This does not mean that he denies the existence of anti-semitic feelings. Quite to the contrary, the analysis presented in chapter 4 in the period between 1881–1917 leads him to conclude that 'Russian policy makers in the period under discussion were anti-Semites of varying degrees of intensity, that they had little sympathy and less understanding for the Jews and that they were imbued with deep anti-Jewish prejudices' (p. 106). Yet he also stresses that anti-semitism is not a sufficient explanation for Russian policy. It was not Judeophobia but a harsh reality without parallel in other parts of Europe that dictated the decisions of the

Russian ministers. Those who determined Russia's policies, writes Rogger, were convinced that the problem of the Jews could not be solved by lifting their legal disabilities. However much that view was shaped by fear and prejudice, it had correlates and objective grounds – in Jewish numbers, in an underdeveloped economy, in the structure and values of Russian society and government – that were absent or weaker in the West (p. 14). Russia never developed the social and economic conditions that facilitated the emancipation of Western Jews. Anti-semitism is not seen here as either endemic or the major factor in shaping policy but as a consequence of economic backwardness that would have altered had the situation changed. The general scheme seems plausible, but Rogger's opinions on Jewish policies are somewhat separated from the social reality, since, with the exception of some rather general demographic data and information on legal restrictions, the condition of Jews is not examined in detail. The author relies heavily on the classic works of Dubnow, Gessen or Baron. What primarily interests him is the Jewish Question as reflected in the consciousness of Russia's political élite – the fears, prejudices, and hopes of the various ministers coping with the problem. His attempt to reproduce their motives and to understand them is indeed so successful that the careless reader might surmise that he shares their point of view. But he is far from identifying with them and constantly stresses their shortsightedness, inability to make decisions and their biased approach. At the same time, he sees Russian Jews responsible for indisputable and taxing problems and while he reproaches Russian ministers for their unwillingness to take a more liberal stance he shows sympathy, or, at least, understanding, for their lack of courage. It is only natural that radical reforms were viewed by bureaucrats as being a leap into the darkness; it does not necessarily follow that the impact of such reforms would have confirmed earlier anxieties. Had the author placed greater stress on a comparative approach he would, I think, be less certain that the problems confronting late nineteenth-century Russia were unique. Even the 1862 emancipation of the Jews in Congress Poland is ignored by him as a point of reference. His purview is limited strictly to the fifteen western provinces of the Pale.

There is much in the book that is new and convincing. Rogger shows how, instead of one line of conduct in governmental policy toward Jews, he detects several, often contradictory, ones that testify neither to a concerted effort toward russification nor efforts to a commitment to push Jews out of the Empire by way of mass emigration. Just the opposite; the state tried to limit emigration and its activity in this area is reminiscent of the policy of the Soviet Union. Moreover, the author asserts that neither tsars nor their ministers were responsible for periodic waves of pogroms even though some of them treated such incidents as a proof of the nation's patriotic feelings. However, he does not exclude the possibility that some pogroms may have been organized by the local or central police. Very well documented is his analysis of the Beilis case which leads to the conclusion that this macabre, almost ludicrous, affair, far from being part of a 'grand design' prearranged by the ruling group, was in reality 'an experiment, conducted by a small band of unsuccessful politicians and honest maniacs ...' (p. 55). In comparing ethnic conflict in the rural and urban areas, Rogger convincingly proves that all incidents in fact started in the cities. The last two chapters, which concentrate on the attitudes of men representing the extreme right of the Russian political spectrum, supplement earlier assertions to a smaller degree, but Rogger's skilful examination of the Union of Russian People as 'a kind of Tory democracy in Slavophile dress' (p. 200) is worth reading. His general conclusion, that in view of their limited political goals and lack of dynamism, such organizations had little in common with modern European fascist movements, is fully substantiated.

In sum, the articles in *Jewish Policies and Right-Wing Politics in Imperial Russia* are characterized by a desire to look at late tsarism and its Jewish question without prejudice and to scrutinize assumptions unsupported by solid facts. Although some of this revisionism goes too far, this book, dedicated to the memory of the author's grandparents who were victims of the Holocaust, is worthy of the highest esteem.

Daniel Grinberg
Warsaw

Heide W. Whelan, *Alexander III and the State Council: Bureaucracy and Counter-Reform in Late Imperial Russia*. New Brunswick, New Jersey: Rutgers University Press. 1982. Pp. 244.

The initial article of the first code of fundamental laws of the Russian Empire stated that 'the emperor of Russia is an autocratic and unlimited monarch'. It may cause some astonishment, therefore, to learn that one of the most determined tsars of the nineteenth century, Alexander III (1881–1894), continually found his desires blocked by the very institutions of government which were supposed to serve the autocratic principle. This discovery was certainly an unpleasant surprise for Alexander, who railed against the 'windbag lawyers' who thwarted his will. The more so, because Alexander found to his chagrin that he could not do without their expertise. Heide W. Whelan explores the strange relationship between Alexander and his own bureaucracy, exemplified by the highest legislative organ of the realm, the State Council.

Alexander's dilemma was tied to the political evolution of the Russian Empire. To function effectively amidst a flood of day-to-day problems, the Empire required a framework of law and legality. This need, in turn, spawned a bureaucracy possessed of a dual loyalty: to the person of the emperor and his autocratic power, and to the abstract ideal of the 'state' or the 'people'. Professor Whelan suggests that there thus arose a fatal schism in the bureaucratic mind between autocracy (or 'patriarchal power', as she calls it), and 'modern principles'. The combination of autocracy and legality, she argues, required a good deal of wishful thinking from tsars and servitors.

Yet was the average *chinovnik* – to say nothing of the average tsar – really such a schizophrenic as to be unable to see this obvious contradiction? Or did it really exist in such stark terms? No tsar, from the first, Ivan IV, to the last, Nicholas II, was ever as free as the autocratic ideal suggested. The 'patriarchal' Russian state placed a number of constraints upon the tsar, in the form of religious norms, traditions and disdain for *proizvol*, or arbitrariness. While every tsar strayed from the ideals of proper conduct, they were all compelled to pay obeisance to them. This phenomenon in itself was part of the evolution of Russia into a modern state with a modern bureaucratic élite, committed to the rule of law. The clash of real and ideal was a normal occurrence, and nowhere near as unique as Whelan implies.

Whelan examines the functions, organisation and composition of the State Council and offers a number of test cases of it in action. This activity took place within the context of the 'counter-reforms', the assault on the liberalizing reforms of Alexander II. The test cases are the three most important legal initiatives of Alexander III's reign: the reorganisation of the judiciary with a view to weakening its independence, the institution of a conservative functionary in the countryside, the land captain, and the restructuring of the institutions of local self-government. In each case, she finds, the State Council proposed to mutilate or destroy the essence of the proposed counter-reform. In the case of the land captain, the tsar's direct intervention was necessary to secure acceptance of a version which he preferred. In the two other cases the will of the sovereign was effectively circumvented.

The State Council proved so recalcitrant, Whelan contends, because it was dominated by individuals who had begun their service careers under the tsar-reformer, Alexander II, and who were committed to the ideal of legality which the great reforms exemplified. They were sufficiently loyal to the sovereign to respond at once to a direct command, as in the case of the land captain project, but when left to their own devices they resisted the emasculation of the great reforms, in the name of the preservation of legality.

Alexander could not simply 'pack' the State Council with more pliable members. Appointment to the prestigious body followed strict traditions of seniority, rank and expertise which could not be easily flouted by a sovereign, especially one devoted to the preservation of conservative values. State Council work required juridical skills, and the training and ethos of the legal profession emphasised legality. Lawyers who despise the rule of law do not long remain in the profession. For these reasons, Alexander found it difficult even to appoint chairmen of the State Council who were entirely acceptable to him.

The struggles which Professor Whelan chronicles make fascinating reading. She goes too far when she suggests that they would have prevented Alexander from attaining his counter-reform goals. To be sure, Alexander could not abolish the State Council, since he would have had to replace it with a similar agency. But other expedients were available. Since all legal projects were supposed to be reviewed and passed by the State Council, he would have had to replace it with a similar agency. But other expedients were available. All legal projects were supposed to be reviewed and passed by the State Council, with the tsar giving final approval. Alexander and his ministers simply began to ignore this route and rely on ministerial decrees, as a form of short-term legislation.

The legal treatment of the Jews provides a good example, though the issue is not examined by Whelan. The position of Russian Jewry continually declined under Alexander III. Restrictions were tightened on Jewish residence in and out of the Pale of Settlement, and on occupational rights, especially in the liquor trade. Jews were driven from the free professions and from secondary and advanced education. These measures were attained through ministerial circulars and through strict enforcement of statutes, which had been allowed to lapse in practice. As far as possible, unsympathetic bodies were by-passed. The Minister of Internal Affairs, N. P. Ignat'ev, did not trust the Council of Ministers – and still less the State Council – to pass his draft project of the notoriously restrictive 'May Laws' in 1882. His attempt to gain imperial confirmation of the project outside of legal channels failed, however, and it was indeed gutted by the Council of Ministers. Such infighting discouraged a comprehensive resolution of the Jewish Question. The efforts of the Pahlen Commission to draft a comprehensive code failed amidst the squabbles of rival factions. Alexander's bureaucrats even failed to secure a straightforward and long-sought objective, a uniform code of laws for the Jews in the Empire and in the Kingdom of Poland. In short, while the reign of Alexander II was a 'time of troubles' for Russian Jewry, Professor Whelan's study reveals indirectly why it was not incomparably worse.

John D. Klier
Fort Hays State University

Mary Antin. *The Promised Land*.
With a Foreword by Oscar Handlin. Princeton:
Princeton University Press. 1985. Pp. xxii, 373.

If ever there was a prose hymnal inscribed to America by an immigrant to appear at just the right moment and to strike just the right note, surely it was *The Promised Land*. Published in 1912, Mary Antin's loveletter became a household word. In her lifetime, it was to go into thirty-four printings and sell 85,000 copies. At a time when immigration was averaging a million a year and there was increasing fear that the country was being polluted by degraded hordes from eastern and southern Europe, *The Promised Land* turned its thirty-one year old author into an instant celebrity. Amid mounting pressures for restriction, notes Oscar Handlin in a characteristically penetrating and succinct foreword to the Princeton imprint, the book 'cast a beam of reassuring light', reminding Americans that theirs was a great nation still.

Like Booker T. Washington's *Up From Slavery*, to which it was compared, *The Promised Land* is the testament of a pilgrim. While Masha merely became Mary, unlike the great black leader who in an inspired moment named himself after the nation's founder, both Jewish Mary and black Washington had discovered a predestined new world from which there was no returning. Thirteen years earlier, Mary's gifts had been unveiled in her first book, *From Plotzk to Boston*, more correctly Polotzk (Russia), rather than Plock (Poland), a typographical error, for which the precocious author forgave the printer. Originally composed in Yiddish by a thirteen year old, at the request of her uncle, as a series of letters detailing the epic journey, she then translated it into English. 'Like most modern Jewesses who have written,' wrote Israel Zangwill in the preface, 'she is . . . destined to spiritual suffering.' The noted English man of letters would be proved right, for Mary, the poet, was never to find her full voice. 'All the processes of uprooting, transportation, replanting, acclimatization, and development took place in my own soul,' wrote Mary in *The Promised Land* (xxii) but she was unequipped to probe further. For her, the move from Russia was so gigantic a step out of a medieval old world into the modern new Canaan, from Tsarist despotism to the land of the free, that it left no place for an ongoing complexity. For a young woman with Mary's mind and sensibilities the opportunity to develop her individuality in ways barely foreshadowed in Polotzk was a sacred service. Every manifestation of that process was to her a virtual revelation of divine selfhood, an experience that many others, without her rare gifts of expression, would share.

Mary Antin's opening lines strike a note of exaltation and rebirth, if not reincarnation, that becomes the refrain of an earthbound pilgrim for whom America-Boston had become the celestial city.

I was born, I have lived, and I have been made over. Is it not time to write my life's story? I am just as much out of the way as if I were dead, for I am absolutely other than the person whose story I have to tell. . . . (xix)

For the daughter of the East European ghetto, release from her mother's kitchen into an American classroom was a revolutionary act. 'At a formative stage in American Jewish life, Jewish women were given the chance, virtually for the first time, to occupy themselves seriously with study, not Talmudical study, of course,' Alvin Rosenfeld reminds us (*The American Autobiography*. ed. Albert E. Stone. 1981. p. 138), but the study, 'forbidden up until not so long ago, of magnetic new realms of mind and spirit'. In discarding an unenfranchised Jewish woman's past and blithely embracing an unfettered American future, Mary was becoming a new woman, an unconscious and reluctant pioneer of her sex. 'The type of the Intellectual as Hero', a genre of American literature proverbially associated with Jewish writers, was 'prominently established in our literature by a woman,' (ibid.), argues Rosenfeld.

Curiously, despite the rich harvest of women's history, little has been written of the Jewish woman's revolution in its transatlantic aspects. Manifest already in the 1870s in Russia, it would invade household and classroom, insinuate its way into public life, and lead to revolutionary organization and a quest for martyrdom by young Jewish women extending from Emma Goldman to Golda Meir to Betty Friedan. Quite undesignedly, Mary Antin's immigrant girl story may well be the inadvertent world manifesto of the Jewish woman's revolution that courses through our own time.

Moses Rischin
San Francisco State University

John Bodnar. The Transplanted:
A History of Immigrants in Urban America.
Bloomington: Indiana University Press. 1985. Pp. xxi, 294.

As his title implies, John Bodnar's treatment of the European immigrant experience in America's cities focuses on the social and economic matrices in which the immigrants' lives became embedded once they passed through the portals into their new country. Indeed, the chief value of the work rests on Bodnar's perception that the immigrants were not simply 'uprooted' — the term used by Oscar Handlin in his now classic study of the Great Immigration — and pitted against the social machinery of a new society, but that in 'confront[ing] the imperatives of this new economic and social order ... they helped to divide society into divergent classes, cultures and ideologies'. Collectively, then, if not individually, the immigrants transformed urban American society and in fact did much to determine its tone.

In *The Transplanted* Bodnar attempts to demonstrate this by collating and pointing to the interrelating implications of many specialized studies of villages and regions of immigrant origin in Europe, specific immigrant groups, the immigrant family, fraternal orders, immigrant labour and the industrial economy, immigrant entrepreneurs and social mobility, and churches, schools and politics as both integrative and fragmenting factors in the ethnic American context. It is an experiment at achieving a synoptic view of a great diversity of social phenomena, at 'transcending older categories of "old" and "new" immigration ... [and] moving beyond the restricted field of vision' of earlier immigration scholarship. The key word in this book, therefore, is not comparison, but synthesis.

Bodnar, who has written in the past on immigrants and industrial relations, understands the process of transplantation chiefly in terms of a response to the development of capitalism. This central explanatory mechanism provides the mortar, the unifying conceptualization, so necessary in this type of work. He asserts the absolute interdependence between capitalism – its dislocating impact on rural society and small manufacture in Europe and its determining influence on the nineteenth-century American economy – and push-pull phenomena of mass immigration. Yet, where this type of analysis has in the past led to what Bodnar sees as a too-restrictive focus on class factors in the immigrant experience to the detriment of an appreciation for cultural and other social factors, his own goal is to integrate 'political history and private history'. To this end, he is constantly harking back to the realm of the individual and the family as the plane on which the 'relationship between immigration and capitalism' primarily took shape; hence, the subtitle of the book refers to 'a history of immigrants' rather than 'immigration'.

Citing over 350 previous studies, this book is chock-full of illuminating data on the origins of immigrant streams, the spatial mobility of immigrant industrial workers, the rates of return-migration among various ethnic groups, education strategies, family networks, cultural associations and voting patterns. Bodnar's summarizing of major and innovative findings performs an essential service for the non-specialist who will not himself master this vast and ever-growing literature. The specialist will find here a critical review of the opposing points of view among contemporary scholars, as well as a social-historical argument that deserves further discussion in its own right.

If the book suffers from anything in particular, it is an inbuilt disproportion between the theoretical superstructure and the extremely telescoped and capsule-summarized bits of data which are piled up (sometimes no more than listed) to support it. Although this does work occasionally – the material on pinpointing emigration from specific regions and countries is particularly well argued – elsewhere the result is less satisfactory. One disturbing tendency is the verbal magnification of extremely prosaic facts to fit the book's 'big screen' approach: seeking a larger family income becomes 'a decision to deal with capitalism'; family and ethnic community were 'a preoccupation ultimately not because they were familiar but because they represented somewhat manageable and understandable systems'; the all-encompassing need to support oneself and one's family becomes the basis for a 'culture of everyday life'.

The other manifestation which becomes irksome is the repetitiveness of the examples cited to illustrate a given point, alongside a lack of opportunity to examine any case studies in greater detail. The one-line summaries of sociological and historical findings have a negative consequence for precision and accuracy, at least in some instances. Scanning Bodnar's references to Jewish immigrant life, for example, we find such over-generalized assertions as that 'young Jews were attracted to cities such as Vilna, where they studied religion less and the gospel of socialism more' (p. 49). The non-initiated will certainly find the stark and solitary sentence, 'Some Jewish leaders called for adaptation through a modernization of Jewish customs' less than illuminating (p. 49). There would seem to be no justification for viewing the establishment of the First Hebrew Ladies Benevolent Society as an instance of loosened ties to the home among Jewish women (p. 80). Jacob Schiff, it is true, was part of the German-Jewish élite in New York; but his involvement in lobbying for diplomatic pressure against official Russian anti-semitism could hardly be called an instance of 'initial efforts at public education and mobilization of support emanat[ing] from élites' (p. 201). The Jewish élite did not have to rouse or educate their middle-class and working-class constituencies on this issue; quite the reverse was the perceived case in downtown New York.

Such misunderstandings and overgeneralizations may be unavoidable in a work of this scope, and one wonders whether the overall purpose would not be better served by a collective work by area specialists. But this, of course, would destroy the chance for a seamless argument. Bodnar is to be admired for the attempt and credited for the grand design. Caveats as to his execution merely point to the possibilities for an ongoing discussion of the vital historical issues that he raises.

Eli Lederhendler
Tel Aviv University

Michael R. Weisser. *A Brotherhood of Memory:
Jewish Landsmanshaftn in the New World*.
New York: Basic Books. 1985. Pp. xiii, 283.

The rise and fall of Jewish *landsmanshaftn* in New York during the first five decades or so of this century constitutes a topic of major importance for the understanding of Jewish folk memory and the cultural construction of ethnic identity. During the period of the great migration to the United States there surfaced the names of literally thousands of Eastern European towns and villages that became labels for newcomers anxious to form themselves into smaller or larger groups, according to their respective places of origin, for the ostensible purpose of ensuring their social welfare. The consolidation and institutionalization of the community memories that lay behind the formation of these benevolent societies give us today the opportunity to glimpse a good sociological refraction of life in the shtetl, as well as of the so-called 'shtetl mentality', while the eventual disintegration of the *landsmanshaftn* in more recent years attests to the fading of these memories and the rise of newer preoccupations in determining the nature of modern Jewish identities. Not that this book charts such things as the romantic rags-to-riches stories or a mythologized, sentimental view of the shtetl; on the contrary, Michael Weisser's explicit aim is to convey the depth and the trauma of the migration experience as mirrored in the history of these societies, formed by those immigrants who chose to remain fundamentally unassimilated. It is a subject which has for far too long been overlooked in the ordinary understanding of Jewish readjustment in the modern world. He is to be warmly commended for this conscientious, sympathetic and highly readable study, which firmly establishes the 'organizations of fellow countrymen' as an essential element in the structural evolution of modern Jewish society.

While his brief, five-page Appendix on 'The Ethnicity Debate' reveals a certain familiarity with the current social science literature, bolstered elsewhere in the footnotes by the occasional comparative reference to peasant studies, Weisser's methodological techniques are, however, a little too diffuse for comfort. He himself admits in the Preface that his exposition rests on what he calls '*bubbe mayse* history', viz. '... a mixture of facts, anecdotes, fairy tales, fables, innuendos, truths, half-truths, memories, experiences, and even some outright lies'. Doubtless an excellent definition of the genre, but in this particular case it could unfortunately be taken as too close a parody of his subject-matter itself – which is a pity – even though it does succeed quite well in reproducing the hopes, fears and insecurities of those first-generation immigrants whose world-view it is that he is out to document. But apart from the statistical tables and the bibliographic references (chiefly to certain *landsmanshaft* archives held at YIVO and the

Joint Distribution Committee), he does not make a habit of distinguishing between the various components of *bubbe mayse* history: between 1880 and 1920 in Eastern Europe, for example, were there 'more than one million' Jewish deaths from hunger, famine and disease (p. 112), or were there 'two million' (p. 25)? How could there have been 'more than 200,000' Jewish dead as a result of pogroms in Eastern Europe between 1919 and 1922 (p. 113) if there were 'more than 250,000' deaths from this cause in the Ukraine alone between December 1918 and April 1919 (p. 67)?

Where the oral history method more seriously lets him down, however, is in his failure properly to explore the assumption, maintained throughout the book, that the *landsmanshaftn* in turning their backs on assimilation thus recreated the world and values of the shtetl – that they were in effect replacement Old World communities within a New World context. This is certainly how they were perceived by the American-born children and grandchildren of the immigrants, and hence was one of the factors that led to their demise – but apart from constant reference to fear, xenophobia and the minimizing of risk, there is too little elaboration of the evidence in support of this view. How much of a shared identity did residents of a particular shtetl actually possess prior to migration? What kind of fission within the shtetl reproduced itself in New York? How common was it for migrants from a particular set of adjoining shtetlach to set up a single *landsmanshaft* on arrival in America? How, in short, was a *landsman* actually defined? Kin ties would have been significant, one supposes, but what about (for example) liturgical and other shared ritual behaviour? Weisser indicates that traditional Jewish law was always followed at *landsmanshaft* funeral arrangements and in the provision of kosher food at society meetings, but has little further to say about religion, surely an important shtetl value (let alone the existence of *yeshivas* or Hasidic groups predicated on presumed common places of origin); and apart from a solitary reference to herrings and potatoes at p. 259, he never gets round to dealing with food. Dress, or rites of passage such as circumcisions or weddings, are similarly omitted from the account. But attention is given to the recruitment of women into the societies – doubtless quite a significant development. If, then, the case for the simple reaffirmation of shtetl values is to be seriously maintained, more details regarding cultural continuities and discontinuities in matters of this sort need to be provided – a more inclusive scheme, in other words, for comprehending the process of cultural reconstruction in the new setting.

But in other respects Weisser skilfully leads the reader through a number of themes raised by the history of the *landsmanshaftn*. Minutes of society meetings reveal how crucial they were in oganizing relief to European Jews during the upheavals after the First World War (1200 missions were undertaken by 1923), and after the Holocaust they were uniquely well-placed to provide survivors with the incalculably important psychological support needed to deal with the trauma of readjustment. Within the world of immigrant Jews in New York one of their prime *raisons d'être* was to cope with sickness and death: they were the principal purchasers of cemetery space and in fact acted as the primary vehicle for dealing with death among immigrant Jews until at least the end of the 1930s. It is truly remarkable, therefore, that these societies have been so totally passed by: although, for example, there were approximately three thousand of them at the beginning of the 1920s, when probably one in every two Jewish immigrants joined a *landsmanshaft*, an otherwise comprehensive 1500-page Communal Register drawn up by the New York kehillah in 1918 almost entirely neglected their existence, devoting only eleven pages to them and mentioning not one of them by name. *Landsmanshaft* identities, with their emphasis on shtetl communalism, were seen right from the outset as intrinsically contradictory to the presumed character of modern Jewish life in America. Weisser carefully traces the reasons for their decline – the geographical dispersion of members and their reluctance or inability to cope with social change, the rise of larger and much more powerful Jewish charities, the assimilation and general *embourgeoisement* of Jewish society, the divorce between home and workplace in modern industrial society, the decline of neighbourhood-based face-to-face daily interaction, and so on – but as he points out they were always perceived as socially and economically marginal, dominant in important areas of Jewish life though they evidently were. In that sense one suspects that their decline belongs to a different area of reality – after all, what do we know about the one thousand *landsmanshaftn* still believed to be in existence as recently as 1980?

Cultural memory in the Jewish folk tradition is thus not easily measurable, although if some prestige is involved the remembrance of origins seems especially tenacious. Or should the *landsmanshaftn* be seen as an adaptation based on an economic strategy for survival? Now that the shtetlach themselves have vanished from the real-world map after the Holocaust, one might be forgiven for thinking that these erstwhile identities are now truly irrecoverable, and that they will finally pass into oblivion from the minds and hearts of the descendants of those poverty-stricken immigrants fleeing persecution. But perhaps it is only after this interval of a century since the beginning of the great migration that we can begin to develop a sense of the existence of more than one set of assimilation trajectories among the migrants. Who knows, for instance, where the contemporary interest in 'roots' will lead? The publication of Michael Weisser's book is itself an important event in this more recent sequence in the restoration of the details of the memory of Eastern Europe; further refinements of his subject seem bound to follow.

Jonathan Webber
Oxford Centre for Postgraduate Hebrew Studies

Henryk Piasecki. *Sekcja Żydowska PPSD i Żydowska Partia Socjalno-Demokratyczna 1892–1919/20*. Żydowski Instytut Historyczny. Wrocław: Zakład Narodowy im. Ossolinskich. 1983. Pp. 380.

The relations of the Jewish community and the Polish Social Democratic Party in Galicia at the end of the nineteenth and the beginning of the twentieth century may seem a matter of minor importance, but this work places the problem in a broad perspective and reveals the tensions which occurred everywhere in Eastern Europe. It may be deduced from the census of 31 December 1900 that there were 811,183 Jews in Galicia, the majority being employed in the crafts and light industry, though a substantial section was occupied in agriculture and mining, which was unusual for Jewish communities in Eastern Europe. Their conditions were exceptionally hard. Wages were low and hours long. Comparisons of the population figures for 1890 and 1900 suggest that over 100,000 Jews emigrated during that period. For those who remained there arose the problem of organizing the defence of their interests. The Po'alei Zion movement, which emerged as a formal organization in 1903, though it took its stand on an eight-hour day and a rest period of thirty-six hours to cover the sabbath, tended at first to attract only white-collar workers. Labourers on the other hand were drawn into cooperation with the Polish Social-Democratic Party. Here, however, a complication arose. The Polish Social Democrats thought in terms of a united working class movement with the common language of Polish, whereas Jewish leaders thought they would be more effective if they used the 'jargon', a term for Yiddish certainly not used generally in that sense in English-speaking countries. Thus the Social-Democratic desire for solidarity conflicted with the Jewish desire to obtain the widest possible currency for their views. The result was that the Jewish Section of the Polish Social Democratic Party came under criticism and there arose in 1907 the Jewish Social Democratic Party.

It should be noted, however, that at election times Jews voted tactically according to which candidate seemed most likely to be returned, irrespective of his party label. As time passed the language problem uncovered the problem of Jewish nationality. A similar problem had arisen in Russia, where the Bund, founded in 1897 in Wilno, worked side by side with the Social Democrats. In Galicia the older generation among the Jewish intelligentsia accepted the possibility of assimilation with the Poles and adhered to the Social Democrats, but the younger sections and the mass of Jewish workers looked to the Jewish Social Democratic Party. The official attitude was one of non-recognition on the grounds that the Jews were not a nation and that Yiddish was 'the dialect of local Jews in Galicia and Bukovina', not a recognized language within the boundaries of

Austria-Hungary. Curiously enough this view struck a chord with the Zionists, whose view was that Hebrew was the national language of the Jews. The Poalei Zion group thought that there were two languages, Yiddish in the lands of the Diaspora and Hebrew in the future in Palestine. Some Social Democrats took a neutral point of view, while other socialists spoke of Polish as a 'comrade' language. The Jewish Social Democratic Party, however, declared that Yiddish was the only national language of the Jewish workers. The Fourth Congress of the party took place on 25–26 October 1910, at which the language question was seen as part of the struggle for national cultural autonomy. In the census of 1910 language was to be defined not as the mother tongue, but the language of general social intercourse. Yiddish was not recognized by the state. According to a Jewish Social Democratic leaflet in 1900 there were, in the light of religious statistics 1,224,711 Jews, of whom 419,210 were assigned by the criterion of language to the German nationality and 622,235 to the Polish, with the rest parcelled out among the Italians, Hungarians and South Slavs. In spite of fierce protests the same system was applied in 1910. In Galicia in 1910 it is estimated that there were 871,084 Jews out of a total population of 8,025,675 or 10.6 per cent of the whole. Although there was a rise in the total number of Jews by comparison with 1900, their percentage of the population had fallen by 0.5 per cent, which seems to indicate the operation of the factor of emigration. There was a slight fall in the numbers employed in industry, the crafts and trade. It would appear that there was a constant stream of emigration to the United States among professionally qualified persons.

There was a reconciliation of the Jewish Social Democratic Party with the Polish Social Democratic Party in 1911, but the underlying problems remained. The Poles claimed the hegemony of the working class movement. The First World War and the collapse of the Austro-Hungarian Empire threw this problem and all the other problems of the Jews of Galicia into the melting pot. The old system of religious communities ceased to have any influence. Jewish National Councils arose in 1918 to protect Jewish interests. In the new conditions of the revived Polish state the Jewish Social Democratic Party united with the Bund in 1920. Possibly the most interesting of the author's observations are contained in his epilogue. He interprets Jewish politics in the light of social changes in a society emerging from its medieval structure into the modern capitalist economy. Jews who obtained a secondary education or who went to universities and polytechnics tended to adopt Polish as their first language and were thus assimilated into Polish society. For this reason the Jewish Section of the Polish Social Democratic Party lost its significance, whereas the Jewish Social Democratic Party maintained its connections with the Jewish workers. It must be remembered that Jewish workers concentrated in small-scale industry or cottage industry were relatively stronger with regard to their employers than they would have been in large-scale industry which could offer stiffer resistance to strikes. Curiously enough it was the Jewish miners who were all Zionists, seeing no future in the existing system and desiring to sever contact with it by creating a new life elsewhere. There was also the factor of the generation gap. Adolescents were attracted to political and cultural activities which coincided with the Sabbath. This brought them into conflict with their parents who adhered to the old religious way of life. Trade union premises were treated not only as political centres, but also as places of education and entertainment. The activities of the Jewish Social Democrats thus had a far wider importance for Jews than corresponding political movements had for Christians. The author's work is thought-provoking and invites us to wish to know more about Jewish problems elsewhere in Eastern Europe.

R. F. Leslie
Charlbury

Ber Borochov, *Class Struggle and the Jewish Nation. Selected Essays in Marxist Zionism*. Edited by Mitchell Cohen. New Brunswick/London: Transaction Books. 1984. Pp. 218.

Ber Borochov, the founding father of Marxist Zionism, is largely a forgotten figure today. For the international labour movement and in particular, for the Marxist Left, his effort to synthesize socialist internationalism with Jewish nationalism must appear today even more bizarre, not to say illegitimate, than it did to Lenin shortly before World War I. Even in Israel, where the labour movement owed much to his theoretical inspiration, his legacy seems increasingly irrelevant to a society preoccupied with altogether different issues. The contemporary Israeli or Jewish reader will find nothing in this or any other of Borochov's writings to illuminate his understanding of the conflicts between Israelis and Arabs, Sephardis and Ashkenazis, religious or secular Jews; let alone to guide him in grasping the larger issues confronting the Zionist movement today in its relations with the international community or the Jewish diaspora.

This is not of course surprising. Borochov died in 1917, at the early age of 38, barely a month after the Bolshevik Revolution and the Balfour Declaration, two events which were to profoundly transform Jewish history in the twentieth century. His commitment to a theory of revolutionary class struggle, so characteristic of the Russian milieu from which he came, never had much relevance to the sociological realities in *Eretz Israel*, even in Borochov's own time. Moreover, the social base of Borochov's theorizing, the existence of a world-wide Jewish proletariat which was not only landless but increasingly displaced from its traditional sources of livelihood, subject to discrimination at home and to alien laws in the lands of emigration abroad, has long since ceased to exist. What then is left of the edifice of Borochovism, that almost mathematical mode of Marxist determinism with its insistence on the iron laws of historical necessity and at the same time its burning faith in the charismatic idea of socialism? What remains of this 'pioneering social scientist of the Jews', who in 1906 believed that Palestine would be the future land of spontaneous waves of Jewish immigration or who thought that the Inquisition and mass expulsions could never recur? (Borochov, like other Zionist theorists, was deeply pessimistic about the diaspora, but never remotely imagined the possibility of a genocidal anti-semitism.)

Mitchell Cohen, in an introduction of exemplary clarity, argues that Borochov's importance resides in his analysis of nationalism. Unlike other Marxist theoreticians of his time, Borochov did not regard the national question as being of secondary, temporary or merely tactical significance. He sought to find an original, materialist explanation for its continuing acuity and relevance, as much to the proletariat as to the other classes in modern capitalist society. His political struggle to establish *Poalei Zionism* in Russia (against the intense rivalry of the Bund and the various territorialist splinter-groups in the Jewish labour movement) further sharpened his perception of the centrality of the national question for the proletariat, especially for extra-territorial minorities like the Jews.

Borochov was convinced that the Jews suffered from a chronic, almost pathological sickness in their socio-economic structure that could only be cured by territorial concentration in Palestine. Socialist Zionism was for him the most radical therapy imaginable, the one solution which would go to the root of the Jewish problem – i.e. the landlessness, the exile and the consequent divorce of the Jewish people from nature and from the primary processes of production. Borochov tried to explain the necessity for Zionism in rigorous Marxist terms, but by 1917 he seemed to have renounced many of his earlier theories, though not the need for class struggle. Thus the last text of Borochov in this anthology, 'Eretz Israel in Our Program and Tactics' (1917) speaks a far more emotional language than the somewhat dry, geometrical propositions of early Borochovism. Here, we find a clear demand for *Eretz Israel* as a *National Home*, a rejection of mechanical conceptions about immigration (including his own theory of the 'stychic' process), support for co-operatives in Palestine, for participation in a world Jewish congress and for independent socialist initiatives in building up the country. (Almost by way of an aside, Borochov also remarked: 'Normal relations between the Jews and Arabs will and must prevail.')

In other texts such as his analysis of the 'Jubilee of the Jewish labour movement' (1912) or 'The Aims of Yiddish Philology' (1913) the reader encounters a Borochov who was much more than a Marxist propagandist or ideologue. The breadth of his scholarly interests, the intellectual curiosity, the passionate commitment to the Jewish people come through strongly in these pieces, as well as the crystal-clear precision of his formulations. Borochov was in many ways a brilliant observer and analyst of the social realities of his epoch, in spite of the fact that so much of what he had to say will seem dated to the contemporary reader. For this reason alone one can welcome the re-edition of these texts in English, making Borochov's creative applications of Marxist methodology to the sociology of the Jewish people accessible to a wider public.

Robert S. Wistrich
Hebrew University of Jerusalem
Oxford Centre for Postgraduate Hebrew Studies

Ehud Luz. *Makbilim Nifgashim* Tel Aviv: Am Oved. 1985.

The relationship between the Jewish religion and modern nationalism was, since the 1880s, the subject of great interest and this shows no sign of abating. Central to this discussion are a number of questions: should Jewish nationalists conduct themselves according to the standards of religious values, as established in exile or according to new European ones? Do modern values contradict the religious ones, or is there a prospect for synthesis? What will be the relationship between the religious and the secular members of the Movement? Who will lead it and according to what cultural and religious criteria? Should the movement include in its agenda cultural and educational activity? If so, what sort of 'traditional' or 'modern' Jewish activities should it promote? Ironically, such questions are no less relevant in present-day Israel than they were during the lifetime of the *Hibbat Zion*. The wide-ranging changes that have affected Jews – wholesale emigration from Eastern Europe and the establishment of a new and dominant diaspora community in the United States, rapid secularization and a far-reaching economic transition, even the Holocaust and the establishment of the State of Israel – none of these have either answered these questions or served to blunt their importance.

The *Hibbat Zion* Movement and the subsequent Zionist Movement relied on a tenuous balance, largely East European, between *maskilim* and the religious, the *haredim*. Both realized the impossibility of forcing its value on the other and were thus resigned to working together.

However, every now and then the disagreements intensified and an immediate solution was imperative. How was agricultural settlement to proceed during the biblically ordained *Shemita* year (the seventh fallow year)? What values and teaching methods should be introduced into the school curriculum in Palestine? Should the institutions of the Zionist Organization operate on the Sabbath? Solutions to these and similar problems were urgently required from the movement's leadership but were not always forthcoming. On the contrary, inside as well as outside the movement, some leaders, public figures, writers and rabbis tried to utilize these issues to challenge Zionism's position on religion. Some set about doing this by invoking monolithic theories to prove that a new sort of agreement and regulations be introduced based on new, less vague, less elastic assumptions.

In his book *Makbilim Nifgashim*, Ehud Luz traces relations between the orthodox and *maskilim* in *Hibbat Zion* and later in the Zionist movement. He shows how members tried to solve these problems and to bridge the rift created between religion and nationalism. He also describes the factors that caused the differences between these groups, the means employed to bridge and occasionally also to blur them, and also the attempts to widen them on the part of various groups outside the movement. A discussion of these issues has in recent years occupied a central position in Zionist historiography. Particularly over the course of the last decade, many studies have examined these struggles which divided the movement, precipitated splits in Zionist Congresses and brought into existence new factions, and even federations.

Yet Luz's book is unique in its ambitions. It attempts to show that the Zionist movement constituted a solution to the cultural conflict that existed in Eastern Europe in the second half of the nineteenth century between the *maskilim* and traditionalists. In contrast to others who view clashes between the two as part of larger social, political or cultural processes, Luz tries to prove that Zionism was created out of the urgent need for rapprochement between camps who had before the establishment of the movement been distant from and even hostile to each other. In other words, the Jewish national movement was a product of cultural-social processes that took place within the Jewish people. Cooperation between the camps of the religious and the *maskilim* was 'the result of the experience of the re-discovery of ethnic solidarity which had remained alive in Eastern Europe despite the social schism. . . . It was this experience which pushed the two camps towards making an effort at mutual rapprochement which was to strengthen national unity.'

Luz's thesis raises many difficulties. The book hardly deals at all with the search for 'national unity' sought by the various sides in the dispute and instead treats only those attempts to achieve a monolithic ideology for one camp or the other. Luz provides a profound, even brilliant, analysis of the views held by the main personalities he deals with in his book – on the secular side: Ahad Ha'am, Berdychewski, Bernstein-Cohen and Mandelstamm, and on the other: Pines, Rabinowitz (from Poltava) and Reines. He tells us that they did not want co-existence but generally tried to fit the Zionist movement into their own respective world views. The book describes various stages in the development of the controversy between the religious and the *maskilim*, beginning with the struggle over the image of *Hibbat Zion* and the Zionist movement, until the Uganda crisis.

In the face of his masterly portrait of profound social and cultural differences within the Zionist movement one wonders how its various components managed to remain together without breaking into numerous splinters? Furthermore, how can one explain the cooperation between the different factions which made up the movement on the political level, so lucidly portrayed by the author, against the background of increasing ideological polarization? How could those who saw Zionism as 'The Jewish people's answer to the Torah in its traditional meaning' march together with those who viewed the Jewish religion as one whose 'historical function had been fulfilled and which ought to vacate its place to secular nationalism, the future mainstream of Jewish existence?' The book provides no answer. It cannot, because the attempt to portray the development of such historical processes through the prism of ideological debates is doomed to failure. Some historical reality is doubtlessly reflected in ideological controversies, but in most instances attempts are made to conceal a different reality behind such conflicts. Serious disagreements on a political, personal or social level, or the desire to control positions of power, appeared more honourable when presented against the background of ideological conflict. What was simpler on the part of Rabbi Mohilever or members of the *Mizrahi*, for instance, than to present their conflict against a background of ideological disagreements rather than admit that what they wanted was political control? What is more honourable than to present the struggle of *B'nei Moshe* or the 'Democratic Faction' as a struggle of one ideology against another rather than as a struggle for domination and power?

Except for his treatment of cultural-social conflict, Luz's explanations are consistently unsatisfactory. Brilliant as are the author's analyses of the ideologies held by the various parties, his explanations of historical processes are not always relevant, and one discovers errors and much haziness. This is not the place to enumerate all of these. I shall merely point out that his analysis of the establishment of *Hibbat Zion* and the Odessa Committee, the development of *B'nei Moshe*, the description of the Zionist movement's origins in Russia or his description of the factions that existed in Russian society, are full of almost amazing over-simplifications. The reason why an author who shows such profundity in his textual analyses makes so many errors in his analyses of historical processes is due to the documentary material that he uses. On examination it can be seen that more or less all of them represent the theories of the book's heroes. On the other hand, sources dealing with the development of Zionism are almost non-existent, or are taken from secondary sources such as Klausner, Grünbaum and Böhm. The shallowness of their conclusions is well known by specialists. Luz is a scholar with a brilliant analytical ability, whose overall explanation regarding the influence of the religious debate on the Zionist movement is unsatisfactory.

Joseph Goldstein
Haifa University
Everyman's University, Tel Aviv

Shmuel Nitzan, editor. *Tnu'at Dror be'Galicia*.
Tel Aviv: Beit Lohamei ha-Gettaot and ha-Kibbutz ha-Meuhad.
1984.

The collection under review is the seventh in a series on the subject of the training farms (*kibbutzei ha-hakhshara*) in those parts of Poland formerly under Russian rule. Like them, it consists of a wide range of contributions, such as recently written reminiscences, authentic source material, excerpts from the press, minutes from meetings of organizations, letters from party activists, and so on. The volume also has a lengthy introduction which successfully places *Dror* and the movements which established it, namely *Freiheit* and *he-Halutz ha-Tsa'ir*, in the wider context of Jewish Galicia.

The contributions are not of uniform quality. The memoirs, written decades after the events, must be treated with circumspection, in part due to their sometimes nostalgic and sentimental tone. On the other hand, the older sources published here are of considerable importance. They are certain to help constitute a basis for future work on the history of the Jews in the region.

The volume offers further evidence, if more was really needed, of the importance of the regional traditions in the life of Polish Jewry, even when all parts of the country were united within the framework of the new Polish state. This was the result of the specific development of the various parts of Poland under the rule of the occupying power, which established the distinctive character of the Jewish settlements in the different regions. This tradition proved too strong to be overcome even within the new political framework, and, as a result, all attempts at unification on the part of the Zionist or other Jewish organizations failed. Such regional differences had their impact on the political disagreements of the Jewish representatives in the *Sejms* (which did much to weaken their impact), on the character of the pioneer movement and on the Zionist youth movements, where tensions between western and eastern Galician Jewry were abiding and significant.

Dror was established in 1929 as a *kibbutz* training farm shared by two movements, *Freiheit* and *he-Halutz ha-Tsa'ir*. The former was the youth movement of that part of the *Po'alei Zion* that refused to embrace rapprochement with the Comintern and which established an independent movement in 1920. *Freiheit* was intended to train the movement's young recruits. It was devoted to social radicalism, the need to address local needs, and also to the cultural importance of Yiddish. Self-fulfilment in the Land of Israel and zeal for the Hebrew language were far removed from its ideology. It was only in the course of time that it began to adopt these values without abandoning older commitments.

He-Halutz ha-Tsa'ir, on the other hand, derived its ideology from entirely different sources. Right from the beginning it educated its members to reject the diaspora, to embrace the Hebrew language and to self-fulfilment within the exclusive framework of *he-Halutz*. It aspired to become an independent movement with its own ideology, whose training was open to both sexes and to the graduates of other youth movements, as well as to young people without a prior youth movement background and with an overall affiliation with the *Kibbutz Meuchad* movement in the *Yishuv*. Though both movements embodied populist tendencies and appealed largely to the young Jewish workers, their outlook differed to such an extent that even after they founded *Dror*, which was their common *kibbutz hakhshara*, (in 1929) it took another nine years before they were organizationally united.

Moreover, in contrast to *he-Halutz* in Russian Poland, the Galician counterpart lacked a history of its own; in fact, it served as a kind of loose organization, federal framework for the distribution of Palestinian certificates, formerly the prerogative of *Ha-Shomer ha-Tsa'ir*. *He-Halutz* merely served in this respect as an organizational meeting-place with the real educational work taking place in *ha-Shomer* and *Gordonia*. *Ha-Shomer ha-tsa'ir* educated its members for life inside the movement's *kibbutzim*; *Gordonia* trained members to live in its *kvutsot*. The joint attempt by *Freiheit* and *he-Halutz ha-Tsa'ir* to turn *he-Halutz* into a movement with ideological and educational characteristics of its own failed as a result of the strong opposition from *Ha-Shomer ha-Tsa'ir* and *Gordonia*.

One of the central features of the volume is the awareness on the part of *he-Halutz's* membership of discrimination, of the feeling that the young movement was forced to struggle for its right to exist against forces stronger than itself. It may be said that while in those parts of Poland which had formerly been under Russian rule, the majority in *he-Halutz* considered themselves to represent the mainstream of the Palestinian worker's movement, in Galicia *Dror* represented a rather small minority.

The volume covers mainly the decade before the Second World War. Success began to come its way way in the late 1920s with the establishment of *Kibbutz Dror* which united graduates of *Freiheit* and *he-Halutz ha-Tsa'ir*. This resulted from influences outside Galicia with the ideological crystalization of *he-Halutz* and with the establishment of a permanent training programme whereby members were required to pursue a pioneering life style before immigration to Palestine even if this was a long way off. Of great influence in this respect was the end of the Fourth *Aliya* and the new restrictive stance of many countries previously open to immigration. The situation of Jewish youth was adversely affected also by the world-wide economic recession whose consequences were especially severe in Poland and particularly so in economically backward Galicia. The increasingly anti-semitic policy only made a bad situation still worse. As a result of these factors, large numbers of young people joined the ranks of *he-Halutz* and *Kibbutz Dror*. This included youth not motivated by ideology, but mainly by the desire to emigrate. Between the years 1932–6 *Kibbutz Dror* grew from two units, numbering thirty-eight members, to fifteen numbering a total of 450 with a reserve of some 2,500 people who had completed the obligatory training period and were waiting to immigrate to Palestine or were preparing themselves for a future move. This wave did not last very long. With the outbreak of riots and the cessation of immigration, all the pioneer movements, including *Dror*, began to decline, and in 1939 *Dror* had only two training *kibbutzim*. Not all new members, especially those without a youth movement education, were prepared to remain on *hakhshara* for as long as six years. Those parts of the book that examine this period note the serious problems that plagued the *hakhshara* in this period. The situation improved somewhat only in 1939 with the beginnings of the illegal *aliya*.

As we said, the two movements that came to establish *Dror* appealed to the lower classes rather than to students and this helped determine the movement's basic character. It was also a movement based in the small towns. Unlike *ha-Shomer ha-Tsa'ir*, *Dror* did not succeed in taking root in the larger settings. Thus, the *Freiheit* branch in Kraków consisted mostly of members from small towns who had moved there in search of work. The situation was much the same elsewhere. The growth of *he-Halutz* was indicative of the uneven processes of modernization and radicalization in Jewish society which led to the disintegration or weakening of the traditional East European social framework. This process was far more profound in the cities than in the small towns. In small towns, the Jewish national framework retained its importance once youth from these settings joined in *hakhshara*.

The *hakhshara's* professed aim was mainly productivization, meaning the promotion of agricultural work and orienting members for life on a *kibbutz*. However, in the harsh reality of Poland, the members of *Kibbutz Dror*, like their colleagues in other *hakhasharot*, were compelled to take on any work that came their way.

Another problem discussed in the volume is the problems faced by female members. If a son's decision to leave home in order to join the *hakhshara* frequently meant a serious crisis, the fate of a girl was typically much worse. Traditionally girls were allotted well-defined roles within the family and the communal hierarchy; hence many Zionist girls literally escaped from their homes without their parents' knowledge. Hasidic fathers in particular did not easily consent to their daughters' pioneering activities and not infrequently such conflict resulted in a complete break with the family. This situation tended to weigh heavily upon the girls and this is still evident in memoirs written half a century later. Even when females entered *kibbutzim* they did not find it easy to achieve equality, despite the institution's declared commitment to sexual equality. Their struggle for an equal position in this new society represents one of the most interesting chapters in the history of the pioneering movement.

The political texture of Jewish life in Poland (including Galicia) was complex, a reflection of both resilient influences of the past and the daunting challenge of the new reality. The volume under review illuminates these problems very well. It makes no pretensions to scientific objectivity, but it will certainly have a decisive impact on the writing of Zionist history in Eastern and East Central Europe.

Israel Oppenheim
Ben-Gurion University of the Negev
Beer Sheva

Ritchie Robertson. *Kafka: Judaism, Politics, and Literature*. Oxford: Oxford University Press. 1985. Pp. 330.

Anyone who follows the oscillations of literary criticism over the past twenty years cannot escape the impression that we are moving away from the tendency to treat literary works in isolation of their context characteristic of structuralism and post-structuralism and back towards the notion that the literary text refers to some sort of reality which really exists beyond the limits of the linguistic artifact. History and historicism are back. David Lodge, shrewdly utilizing Roman Jacobson's now famous binary schema built on the metaphoric/metonymic polarity, describes this movement from the autotelic to the referential as one from the metaphoric to the metonymic poles. This schema is particularly apt for a description of Kafka criticism since Kafka's own writing is a dazzling mélange of metaphoric and metonymic utterances. In addition to the metaphoric/metonymic aspects of the fiction, the reader is always confronted by the fact that Kafka, while working on his fiction, which was usually patently free of references to specific objects or events in the external world, wrote reams of letters and diary entries, much of it heavily referential.

Kafka's interest in Jewish affairs and his obsession with his Jewish identity is a case in point: while the diaries and letters are full of references to these matters, his fiction is singularly free of them. It is not surprising that this disparity has intrigued readers and inspired scholars to search for the latent Jewish subtext in his fiction. The materials that enable one to pursue this avenue of research have been considerably expanded in the past decade by such biographical works as Ronald Hayman's *K: A Biography of Kafka* (1981) and Ernst Pawel's *The Nightmare of Reason: A Life of Franz Kafka* (1984), both leaning heavily on Helmut Binder's and Klaus Wagenbach's biographical studies which have updated and corrected Max Brod's early – indispensable though not always reliable – biography.

Ritchie Robertson's book admittedly builds on the efforts of his predecessors, but attempts to utilize the historical information to interpret Kafka's works. The subtitle of his book: 'Judaism, Politics and Literature' is supposed to give a rough idea of its scope, but is both inadequate and misleading. This erudite volume is not merely a study of the thematics of Kafka's fiction; it purports to use both the historical background (including Kafka's reading) and the narrative techniques, to arrive at fresh interpretations of many of his works. As such, this is an ambitious exercise written for specialists (all the quotes are in German) and makes heavy use of a wide range of books Kafka definitely read or might have read, primarily in German; the author's familiarity with the scholarly literature on Kafka is truly impressive.

The two categories, Judaism and Politics, are curiously separated, since 'Judaism' is defined as anything pertaining to Jewish identity while 'Politics' is restricted to Zionism which, as Robertson correctly argues, was primarily a question of identify for Kafka and his Jewish contemporaries, particularly after 1916–17. In general, the specific historical background which the author adduces to enrich his interpretation of the works is primarily Jewish, beginning with the oft-cited encounter with the Yiddish actors who performed in Prague in 1911–12, and radically intensified by the massive influx into Prague in the winter of 1915 of 15,000 Galician Jewish refugees, many of them *Hasidim*. Though this information is not new, Robertson shapes it adroitly to recreate the cultural milieu of Prague Jewry, and Kafka's colleagues in particular, at that period. In this respect, the theoretical dichotomy posited by Central European intellectuals between 'gemeinschaft' and 'gesellschaft' was given concrete, existential meaning: the Ostjuden, often called 'Die Polnischen Juden', especially the *Hasidim*, were often looked upon by the westernized, deracinated Jews of Prague as the authentic Jews. Allied to this pervasive sense of restlessness, one finds in Kafka, in particular, a heightened self-consciousness which induces an agonized estrangement from any sense of reality. Robertson employs to good effect the dichotomy between consciousness and being in

Chapters 3, 5 and 6, which deal with *The Trial*, 'The Zurau Aphorisms', and *The Castle*.

Robertson objects in his preface to the 'academic interpreters of Kafka, who contend that his writings have nothing substantive to say, however indirectly, about the world, but are designed to frustrate the reader's desire for meaning and force him to reflect on the unreliability of his own mental operations' (p. ix). Robertson obviously refers to a variety of 'post-structuralist' critics who point to Kafka as a proof-text for 'indeterminacy', one of the features of what is currently called 'post-modernist' narrative technique. In general, Robertson's efforts provide a welcome antidote to many of the excesses of this criticism, but in doing so, raise equally problematic questions regarding the validity of interpretation. Frequently, as one reads through this book, one questions the validity of an interpretation built on fragments of intertextual references and extrinsic historical data. Three brief examples will demonstrate our argument.

'The Judgment' has long been hailed as Kafka's 'breakthrough' story since it is the first work of such sustained narrative intensity and effectiveness that it, in retrospect, catapulted Kafka from a frustrated writer of fragments to a world-class prose writer. Robertson attributes the artistic success of this story to Kafka's renewed interest in Jewish culture in 1911–12. Robertson traces the influence on the story which Kafka, himself, admits to in his Diaries, specifically the synthesis of two genres: the German novella and the Yiddish family drama. And yet this thorough exercise in intertextuality all but obscures the moving referentiality of the story to a very real situation in Kafka's private life which was rendered in the story as an excruciatingly exacerbated version of the prevalent conflicts between the generations at a specific moment and place in history, a rendition so vivid that it endows the story both with its unity and its power to move us even after successive readings.

'A Report to an Academy', on the other hand, is not explained through an extensive investigation of sources, but rather through the testimony of Brod that this story was understood by its contemporaries as a satire of the deracinated westernized Jew, here represented as a mimicking ape. Robertson adduces as further evidence the statement by Nordau – and other Zionist leaders – that westernized Jews merely mimic the cultures in which they live, but never really assimilate them fully. This interpretation raises an interesting theoretical issue. While one can, in fact, read this story as a satire on westernized Jews, one can also read it as a satire on modern civilization and its pretences. There is nothing at all in the story which necessitates the first reading. If the story is so free of specific references to Jews or any other national or religious groups, what is there to determine the particularistic reading? If, furthermore, one espouses the particularistic reading, that the story really refers to Jews, shouldn't one call attention to the massive repression of any detail which would allow the average competent reader to associate this story with Jews? This question has far-reaching implications for the interpretation of Kafka's entire corpus and one would expect more extensive treatment of it by an author who has the above-mentioned hermeneutic goals in mind.

Robertson's interpretation of *The Castle* is his boldest and least satisfying chapter. Building on the scantiest data base, he posits that K, the protagonist of the novel, is a messianic pretender whom Kafka condemns:

> *Das Schloss* is deeply indebted to Kafka's knowledge of the Messianic tradition. Through the figure of K. Kafka expressed the Messianic impulse, examines it critically, and finally condemns it. K. resembles the would-be Messiahs of history, not only in the pun implicit in his profession, but in four of his salient characteristics (p. 232).

The pun referred to is embedded in two Hebrew words: *mashoah* (land-surveyor) and *mashiah* (messiah). While *mashiah* is a common word in Hebrew, *mashoah* is extremely rare and one doubts the viability of such a pun: puns to be effective have to be recognized. Here, as elsewhere in this chapter, Robertson draws sweeping conclusions from rather flimsy evidence. For instance, one reads about Zionism and Hasidism, learns of Kafka's interest in both, but finds it difficult to accept the leap to a statement like 'What saved Kafka's writings from becoming totally hermetic is Zionism' (p. 225).

These three examples, each in its own way, demonstrate the problematics of Robertson's hermeneutics. One would be on safer ground in assigning to the historical background – including Kafka's reading – a primarily heuristic value; by considering the extrinsic historical material as the grounds for a definitive interpretation one returns, however unwittingly, to the intentional fallacy. Historicism, finally, does not relieve the critic of his responsibility for explaining the relentless repression of historical – particularly Jewish – references in Kafka's fictions.

Arnold J. Band
University of California, Los Angeles

Sander L. Gilman. *Jewish Self-Hatred:*
Anti-Semitism and the Hidden Language of the Jews.
Baltimore and London: The Johns Hopkins University Press.
1986. Pp. 461.

Sander Gilman, an authority on both German literature and medical history, has already published several important studies of stereotyping, most recently *Difference and Pathology* (1985). Stereotypes are not based on objective perceptions of social groups: 'the very concept of color is a quality of Otherness, not of reality' (p. 6). Instead, they belong to systems of representations which are distorted by the power-group's desire to withhold cultural authority and political power from the encroaching Other. In this book Gilman moves into new territory by discussing the reactions of a minority group, the German Jews, to the stereotyping applied to it by the majority. The first substantial study of Jewish self-hatred, this supersedes everything previously written on the topic.

The introduction explains with remarkable clarity the complex generation of self-hatred. The power-group is always divided, since it claims that whoever satisfies its criteria may join its ranks, yet preserves its identity by defining those criteria so elusively that outsiders can never fully satisfy them. Unable to admit that the power-group they long to join is flawed by contradiction, the outsiders introject this division, and thus place themselves in a double bind. To join the power-group, outsiders must accept its values. But this means admitting that their own distinctive qualities must always exclude them from the power-group.

The immutable qualities of German Jews were thought to include linguistic distinctiveness. Since Jews in the Diaspora were normally bilingual, their peculiar languages, Hebrew and Yiddish, always aroused suspicion. 'Jewish books' were publicly burnt in 1244 as well as in 1933. After the eighteenth century's elevation of language as the most intimate expression of national identity, Jews were thought incapable of mastering German without somehow contaminating it by their 'hidden language'. Gilman's ample documentation justifies him in making this concept central to his analysis of self-hatred, though his concentration on written texts prevents him from considering other aspects of language, such as intonation, gesture, and facial expression, which were supposed to distinguish the Jew.

Gilman also shows perceptively how the Jews' marginality was confirmed by their association with other stereotypes. They were variously perceived as unmanly, hence like women; as swarthy, hence like blacks; as excitable, hence like the insane. I. J. Singer's *The Family Carnovsky* helps to illustrate the latter two associations.

Most of the book examines successive discourses within which different sorts of double bind were imposed on the German Jews. Gilman begins with the discourse of religion as the setting for the controversy between the humanist Reuchlin and the convert Pfefferkorn. Then, in the universalist discourse of the Enlightenment, we see Mendelssohn helping to create the images of the 'good' Jew who can be Europeanized and the 'bad' Yiddish-speaking, often Polish Jew. An especially valuable chapter studies three Polish Jews, Ephraim Kuh, Salomon Maimon and Issachar Behr, who mastered German literary forms but were painfully excluded from cultured German society. Next Gilman examines the early nineteenth-century discourse of liberal and francophile journalism practised by Borne, Heine and Marx. Its stylistic variety and wit caused this discourse to be classified as 'Jewish' by contrast with the more homogeneous, ponderous and Latinate 'German' style.

Later in the nineteenth century, science lent its authority to the new discourse of race, which represented the Jews' 'hidden language' as an ineradicable biological feature. Jews like Fritz Mauthner composed philosophies of language which dismissed 'Jewish' languages as inferior. This context enables Gilman to shed more light than any previous writer on the exaggerated linguistic purism of Karl Kraus. The same period saw 'the invention of the Eastern Jew', and Gilman's account of this extraordinary episode forms a useful supplement to Steven Aschheim's *Brothers and Strangers* (1982). Hostility to Polish Jews was transferred to semi-assimilated Jews in Germany, while the Yiddish-speaking Jews of Poland and Galicia were travestied as unspoilt primitives by neo-Romantics like Buber, who had no notion that Yiddish literature was already entering European modernism.

Gilman also shows the concept of Jewish self-hatred developing within medical discourse from Charcot to Bettelheim. He argues that its simple antithetical structure, derived from the German experience, has been misapplied to the more complex situation of American Jews, who can contrast themselves with blacks as well as with WASPs. Finally, he examines the reconstruction of Jewish identity in the writings of four Holocaust survivors: Canetti and Koestler, who fled to Britain, and Jerzy Kosinski and Jurek Becker, who were both born in Łódź and now live in America and East Germany respectively. His last chapter investigates the self-hatred attributed to Philip Roth's Zuckerman tetralogy.

One of Gilman's strengths is his ability to interpret autobiographical, journalistic and scientific texts, showing that they are not transparent windows on the world but forms of representation which reward a literary and psychological analysis. Outstanding successes include his discussion of Maimon's autobiography and his account of Marx's Jewish identity. Though his elucidation of Heine's *Hebräische Melodien* breaks new ground, he does not always seem happy with fictional texts. The closing discussion of Bellow, Richler and Roth is schematic, while his treatment of Kafka is notably uncertain. And he seems reluctant to concede that gifted writers, constrained to use stereotypes, can qualify and question them. Thus he does not discuss the explicit sympathy which qualifies Heine's revulsion from the Jews of Poland, nor the richly ambivalent figure of Hirsch-Hyacinth in *Die Bäder von Lucca*.

All German quotations and titles are translated, though it seems odd to refer to the periodicals *Der Kunstwart* and *Der Stürmer* only as *The Artguard* and *The Attacker*. Translations of German passages are sometimes clumsy and faulty, and some potentially bewildering misprints have been overlooked: 'context' and 'content' p. 139, 'work-formulation' for 'word-formation' (p. 196), 'dialectally' for 'dialectically' (p. 217), and perimeters' for parameters' (p. 371). On p. 322 'the Polish poet Marina Zwetajewa' should be the 'Russian poet Marina Tsvetayeva'.

Despite these trivial irritations, this is a rich, dense, endlessly stimulating and rewarding book, a brilliant interdisciplinary crossing of social psychology with textual analysis. It is equal in importance, and much superior in conceptual clarity, to Edward Said's well-known study of stereotyping, *Orientalism* (1978). Historians of German Jewry will learn from it how interpretative techniques can disclose new meanings in familiar texts; literary scholars will learn how social psychology can enlarge their interpretative equipment.

Ritchie Robertson
Downing College, Cambridge

Edward D. Wynot. *Warsaw Between the World Wars: Profile of the Capital City in a Developing Land, 1918–1939.* New York: Columbia University Press. 1983. Pp. vii + 375

The idea for this book, which forms part of the Columbia University Press series of Eastern European Monographs, arose from a symposium held in Warsaw on the role of the city in the development of interwar Poland. The approach to the subject is specific, as Wynot treats Warsaw as the capital of a 'developing' and 'emerging' nation, following the colonial rule of Russia, Prussia and Austria. He uses models of post-colonial capitals in the Third World as his comparative framework. He tries to discover within this scheme how Warsaw coped with its new role as capital of an independent nation. He asks to what extent the city was an integrating factor in interwar Poland in relation to its influence on the social, political, economic and cultural development of the country; he is also concerned to discover whether it was past pre-independence forces or future trends which had the most impact on the city's evolution.

After an introductory chapter, providing a brief summary of the city's history from the Middle Ages, Wynot deals with the economy, society, politics and urbanization of inter-war Warsaw, the city's operational and human (as he describes them) municipal services, and its cultural and intellectual life. There were many good and also many bad features to life in Warsaw between the wars. In his survey, Wynot stresses the way in which the capital matured and developed in these years, though it remained strongly under the control of the central government which intervened continually in its affairs. As a result, as he demonstrates, Warsaw did not nessarily reflect national political trends and voting patterns. It was a town with many civil servants and people linked with the government, and, as a consequence, the pro-government *BBWR* (non-party bloc for cooperation with the government) did better here than in other Polish cities, while both the right and the left were weaker. Wynot describes the interesting beginnings of urban planning in the city, and the evolution of the capital as the Polish centre of national culture.

Of particular interest is the attention paid to the Jewish aspect of the city and the details provided. This emphasis is more than justified due to the numerical preponderance and economic role of the Jews in the city: in 1921 the Jews constituted 33.1 per cent of the total population, falling to 29.1 per cent in 1939. The other minorities represented about one per cent of the population. Wynot elaborates on Jewish voting patterns at national and municipal elections, on the Jews' commercial and occupational activities, on the Jewish *heder* system in Warsaw, and on the Jewish literary and theatrical scene. He regards Warsaw as the centre of both Polish national culture and Polish Jewish culture, 'essentially the triumph of private efforts on both the individual and group levels'. The Polish theatre was not handicapped by lack of Jewish support. The Jewish theatrical ventures were thwarted by financial problems due to the difficulty of winning patronage from the Jewish community; according to Wynot, the Orthodox and Conservative Jews shunned the theatre, the wealthy and professional scorned it as a diversion for the 'rabble', Assimilationists disliked the use of Yiddish instead of Polish and the Zionists wanted the introduction of Hebrew. Even though these factors contributed to lowering standards, Wynot regards the Jewish theatre as a remarkably dynamic subculture.

Wynot deals with Warsaw as a municipal city relative mainly to the powers and activities of the government and the Town Hall. Though the work is informative, the approach tends to be somewhat dry and statistical. He does not attempt to portray the city as a community; we learn little of the residents themselves, little of the substance, colour and drama of their lives. This would necessitate a different approach and the use of other sources. However, the work is supported by detailed footnotes and a good bibliography, and is based on a comprehensive selection of Polish sources. This makes it not only an important study on the history of interwar Warsaw but also a useful addition to the works on this period already available.

Joanna K. M. Hanson
London

Aleksander Biberstein. *Zagłada Żydów w Krakowie*.
Kraków: Wydawnictwo Literackie. 1985. Pp. 275.

This is a document of singular importance. It is a comprehensive and faithful record by an eye-witness of the systematic process of destruction — material, moral and physical — of one of the most important Jewish communities in Europe, as carried out by the German administration, from its chief organ the Gestapo and its many instruments, down to the ill-famed Jewish 'Ordnungsdienst'. The process of destruction was based on a central plan and, as observed and described here, was applied throughout Poland, with local refinements according the degree of depravity of the officials on the spot.

The strangulation of the Jewish community was designed to be carried out in stages: by setting them apart from the Polish population, restricting their movement, causing their economic ruin, locking them up in ghettoes, decimating them by forced labour and finally by sending them to their death in gas chambers.

Dr Aleksander Biberstein was an eye-witness to all these stages bar the last. From the moment the Germans marched into Kraków, he kept a notebook of events wherein he recorded what he saw and heard. He knew this was an important task and he guarded his notes as his most valued possession. When the ghetto was liquidated and he was moved to the camp in Płaszów, he kept the notebooks on him and continued making entries. From Płaszów he was transported to the concentration camp in Gross-Rosen and the notebooks were lost. Through a sequence of improbable coincidences — as is the case with virtually every survivor — Biberstein ended up in Brunnlitz, as one specimen in the famous 'Schindler's Ark'. After the liberation he stayed on in Poland until 1958, when he emigrated to Israel.

The text in our possession is his own reconstruction of the original notebooks, his remarkable memory refreshed and amplified by probing conversations with other survivors and examination of documents in the archives. The manuscript of over one thousand pages has been ably edited and the 'Wydawnictwo Literackie' in Kraków, a publishing house of good repute, is to be congratulated on the production of this book. (A small cavil: the dustjacket has a photograph of two bearded Jews in gaberdines and ghetto armbands sweeping the road. The caption relating to the picture says: 'Jewish lawyers in the ghetto.' This, of course, is a mistake. No Jewish lawyer ever looked like this.)

Biberstein draws a detailed picture of Jewish life in Kraków and its environs, with precise topographical details, the activities of the various institutions, and the demographic statistics. He concentrates on the health-sector since he himself was the founder and director of the hospital for infectious diseases.

The first chapter ends in March 1941, with the creation of the ghetto, in the district of Podgórze, where in an area inhabited before the war by 3,000 people, 20,000 were squeezed to live in unimaginable squalor. In the first week of June 1942 there began the daily deportations from the ghetto to the 'East' – as it turned out the destination was the death-camp in Bełżec. Further 'resettlement' took place in October 1942. In March 1943 the ghetto was liquidated and the remaining population was transferred to a labour camp – later 'upgraded' to a fully-fledged concentration camp in Płaszow.

In that move from the ghetto to the camp, children up to fourteen years of age were not allowed to go with their parents but were supposed to be sent to a 'kinderheim'. The scenes of the enforced separation, even in Biberstein's dry description, are enough to turn day into night.

Biberstein throws light on the vexatious problem of the *Judenrat*. He describes how the members of the Council (of which his brother, Marke Biberstein, was the first appointed chairman) were men of good standing in the community and strove incessantly and at grave personal risk to soften the relentless repression, mainly through bribes to the German officials. It becomes clear how, sooner rather than later, these individuals could no longer, in conscience, do the Germans' bidding and they were imprisoned, deported or shot – giving room to the pliable self-seekers who obediently, if sometimes with excess of zeal, did as they were told until they, too, were slaughtered. This was the pattern, in Kraków as elsewhere.

One step further down the slope is the 'Ordnungsdienst' – the Jewish policemen, agents and informers – there was no shortage of those, and Biblerstein has forgotten none of them. The Germans quite deliberately chose for their servants those of weak character, potential and actual criminals who, given a semblance of power over their fellow-men, were quickly corrupted and reduced to the bestial level of their paymasters. One must remember that the lowliest German had the life of any Jew at his mercy. The threat of torture and death not to the individual alone but also to his family posed moral choices so cruel and insoluble that often the only escape from them was suicide. One should, perhaps, be slow in passing retrospective judgment on behaviour in situations which, in saner times, are beyond imagining.

Biberstein also gives an account (not quite accurate, in the light of other sources) of the heroic and pathetic efforts of a group of young men and women to organize themselves into an underground movement to fight the Germans, whatever that could mean in the context – not a single member of that group lived for long.

To a Krakovian, like this reviewer, these pages are inexpressibly poignant. Whilst they relate to events of more than forty years ago – the wound feels fresh. Since Kraków was a closely-knit community, most of the names mentioned, doctors, lawyers, merchants, teachers, religious leaders, fighters and, also, some of the canaille of the 'Ordnungsdienst', were quite familiar, and bring back to my mind the faces of those people – a ghostly multitude flooding the memory. Survivors, indelibly marked by their experience, are people apart. Their voices have a resonance which will not fade.

In the archives of Yad Vashem in Jerusalem there are many thousands of diaries and testimonies of eye-witnesses of the destruction of European Jewry, written in the ghettoes, in the camps, in the forests, and on the 'Aryan' side – in Polish, Yiddish, Hebrew, Hungarian, French. It is, of course, only a fraction of all that was written and that, largely accidentally, survived and found its way to the archives. These records vary greatly as to their documentary and literary value, but they all deserve to be studied, evaluated and published as irrefutable evidence of events which beggar belief. These diaries were often written at the risk of their author's lives; the writers were haunted by the thought that the world would not know how they lived and died – leaving a trace in writing made dying easier.

It is a melancholy thought that these documents, but for an occasional researcher, lie fallow to this day – the human and financial resources of Yad Vashem are, seemingly, too scarce to be devoted to this task. It must be left to some Foundation, an Institute, an Endowment or a private benefactor to fund this project: to research, edit, translate and publish, wholly or in part, the diaries and testimonies contained in these archives. Anybody listening?

Rafael F. Scharf
London

Shmuel Krakowski. *The War of the Doomed: Jewish armed resistance in Poland, 1942–1944*. Translated by Orah Blaustein. New York: Holmes and Meier. 1984. Pp. xii, 340, maps.

Shmuel Krakowski, chief archivist of Yad Vashem, lectures on the Holocaust at the University of Tel Aviv, and is exceptionally well placed to treat this subject: what happened to those Jews in German-occupied Poland who determined to try and fight, instead of going as ordered to the death camps. He deals only with the rump of Poland, the original *General Gouvernement*, in its four districts of Warsaw, Lublin, Kraków and Radom. He omits the fifth district, of East Galicia, centred on Lwów, which was thrown in with the rest in August 1941 by German administrators, because its primarily Ukrainian population posed different problems from those in the other four, primarily Polish, districts.

To have any reasonable chance of success a resistance movement against an occupier needs hope, arms, leadership, intelligence, security, and propaganda to induce popular support; help from an outside power is often indispensable as well. The Jews in occupied Poland had few resources of this kind: no outside support, no propaganda vehicle beyond gossip and the occasional poster, feeble intelligence, weak security (because of the proliferation of Gestapo agents), hardly any arms, and no hope. There were a few leaders of distinction; most of them found early deaths. Even the one tactical advantage usually open to guerillas – the initiative in seizing the moment for an ambush – was unavailable to those of the Jews inside the Warsaw ghetto who were determined to resist: they were surprised by a German incursion on 18 January 1943, before they were ready to riposte. The four days' impromptu scuffling that followed gave useful lessons to the survivors, so that the Germans' final incursion on 19 April led to several weeks' bitter fighting, house to house, cellar to cellar, sewer to sewer. Most of it was over by late May; a few tiny groups hung on, without friends, without light, almost without food, until October. A few more handfuls of men managed to tunnel their way out of the ghetto and go on with the war; several dozen fought in the Warsaw rising of August-September 1944, a very few survived it.

Besides the partisan groups in the forests, and the ghettoes – Kraków and Częstochowa fought, as well as Warsaw, and he lists fourteen other combatant towns – Krakowski deals also with the camps: in which Jewish resisters, like the rest, persevered in their struggle against all the odds. From Treblinka and Sobibor there were even mass break-outs. One man at least got all the way from Sobibor to Berlin, with the Red Army; another survived the world war, to be killed in action in the Israeli War of Independence.

After these mass break-outs, scores of successful escapers who entrusted themselves to the local peasantry were handed back by them to the Germans because they were Jews. Nothing can bring out more forcefully the hopelessness of the Jewish struggle in Poland, in a war that was polygonal rather than two-sided. Among the partisans, there were several cases of Jews being killed – for their arms – by *AK* units, or by Russians; one case at least of a killing by the *AL*. The *AL* did at least try, sometimes, to cooperate with Jewish partisan bands or to recruit from them when they were broken up; the *AK* did not, and Krakowski observes the lack of any statement by the *AK*'s commanders that recognized the fact of Jewish resistance. In towns, those Jews who tried to survive, passing for Aryans with forged papers, had to depend on their neighbours' charity not to be denounced; and by no means always received it.

Krakowski has worked primarily among the archives in Jerusalem and in Warsaw; he has been able to use the papers of the Polish Ministry of Internal Affairs and of the Polish Communist Party. Soviet archives have no more been opened to him than to any other foreigner working in this or related topics. He has not attempted the London archives, and does not even mention SOE, which arranged arms drops for the *AK*. He has also read widely in English, German and Polish. Mastery of his materials and a strong sense of historical order have enabled him to write a remarkable book, which pays due and dignified tribute to men and women who came to horrible ends, because they were Jews in Hitler's Poland and had the will to resist.

M. R. D. Foot
London

Nechama Tec. *When Light Pierced the Darkness. Christian Rescue of Jews in Nazi-Occupied Poland.*
New York, Oxford: Oxford University Press. 1986. Pp. 226.

The subject of Christian attitudes towards Europe's Jews is an important one at all times, above all for the years 1933 to 1945 when the Nazi regime with its racist and anti-Jewish ideology and policies ruled first in Germany and then over virtually the whole of continental Europe. Some argue that it was the history and background of Christian anti-Jewishness and anti-semitism (the two are different and should always be differentiated) which brought about the eventual Nazi Holocaust of European Jewry during the Second World War. This is a mistaken view since both, by themselves, would never have resulted in such a policy of the wholesale murder of European Jewry just like that. It took the emergence of the historical figure of Adolf Hitler and the special conditions and nature of his Nazi régime to put into effect what, admittedly, many thousands of non-Jews – and most of them could hardly be described as 'Christian' in either belief or practice – had been thinking and proposing for many years. Any analysis of the context of Nazi Germany's persecution and then extermination of Russian and European Jewry must first of all contend with the specific nature of the Nazi regime and its use of terror in various forms to control German and European society before any wholesale condemnation of 'Christian Europe' is allowed to pass. But having said this, it is a fact nevertheless that the Nazi extermination of European Jewry during the Second World War took place in what was supposedly a 'Christian' environment. This raises any number of questions about the political and religious beliefs of those 'willing hands' who actually put the Nazi 'Final Solution' into operation, and even about those others, the majority of Europe's citizens under Nazi occupation, who were aware of or who witnessed what was going on. In turn, these questions relate also to the vexed issue of the so-called 'rescue' of Europe's Jews during the Holocaust.

Nechama Tec's book is an attempt to deal with some of these issues by examining aspects of the Christian response in Nazi-occupied Poland to the Nazi campaign against the Jews. This has always been a controversial subject because of the often vicious anti-Jewish atmosphere and policies of the pre-1939 Polish republic and society, and because following the Nazi invasion in September 1939, nothing much seemed to change in Polish attitudes towards the Polish Jews. This was even remarked upon by the SS, one officer commenting upon one Polish denunciation of the Jews thus: 'You Poles are a strange people. Nowhere in the world is there another nation which has so many heroes and so many denouncers' (p. 51). Not surprisingly, a number of Polish writers and historians, chief among them Władysław Bartoszewski, have produced works showing how Jews were in fact helped or resuced by Christian Poles during the dark days of the Nazi occupation. Tec, a Jewish survivor herself and a sociologist, believes however that the bulk of Holocaust literature about these 'righteous Christians' contains 'no overall systematic and comprehensive explanations' (p. 12). Her book then, as the title of Chapter 10 shows, is intended to arrive at 'A New Theory of Rescue and Rescuers' (p. 150 ff.). But how successful is she in this enterprise?

In principle her basic approach is a valid analytical one as shown by the problems examined in individual chapters: how Jews were or were not able to 'pass over' to the Christian side, how they were hidden and supported by Christian Poles, what factors contributed to individual Poles aiding or even rescuing Jews, what rôle money played in this whole process, how even some acknowledged anti-semites helped or even rescued Jews, and how class, politics, friendship, and religion affected the attitudes of Poles towards the oppressed Jews. While there is much that is of interest in the book, there is also a great deal which is not so good. Partly the problem lies within the subject itself and the methods of analysis adopted. As soon as one investigates the reasons for any kind of human behaviour in particular forms of society, and however much the investigator attempts to separate these into clearly identifiable patterns, the basic problem remains that there will always be as many explanations or reasons for human behaviour as there are human beings. Time and again Tec finds herself having to acknowledge this basic fact. But at the same time her own approach to the work, rather than overcoming this problem, tends to accentuate the diffuse effect one is left with. This is because the amount of space devoted to actual analysis tends to be overwhelmed by the space given to the quoted testimony of survivors and rescuers so that in parts and increasingly the book takes on the feel of a 'popular oral history' instead of a more serious piece of historical analysis.

This criticism is really underlined by the author's failure to set her own analysis and the recorded testimony against any recognizable contextual or chronological background. There were many important phases in the development of Nazi Germany's anti-Jewish policies in Poland towards the Polish Jews, even before Jews from western Europe began to be transported to the ghettos and camps of the east and even before the onset of the Final Solution in the extermination camps of Poland. Likewise, there were different phases in the German treatment of the Poles, from outright oppression and extermination of intellectuals and political leaders early on to the change of emphasis in 1943 after Stalingrad and Katyń, when a more positive German policy towards the Poles could be seen, for a number of reasons. These different phases of Nazi Germany's anti-Jewish and anti-Polish policies affected not only the situation and circumstances of Jews and Poles, but it most certainly affected – at different times – the attitudes of Poles towards the notion and action of aiding, hiding, or even rescuing Jews. The great pity about this book is that this important aspect of the subject is largely absent. Had it been present, greater point would have been given to the author's initial purpose and to the analytical points she does make at times. Nevertheless, the book should be read for a number of reasons, not least of which is to remind us all how frail the human spirit is and how charity (or rather selfishness) really does begin and end with the individual and not with other human beings who might be in greater need of help and protection.

John P. Fox
London

W Czterdziestą Rocznicę: Agonia, walka i śmierć warszawskiego getta. London: Polska Fundacja Kulturalna. 1983. Pp. 91.

Janina Jaworska. *Henryka Becka 'Bunkier 1944 roku'*. Wrocław. Ossolineum. 1982.

These two small books deal in totally different ways with the plight of Jews on both sides of the ghetto walls in Poland during the Second World War. The two main characters Marek Edelman and Henryk Beck had little in common with each other apart from their Jewish background and medical profession.

W Czterdziestą Rocznicę is primarily a collection of recollections by Marek Edelman, a Bundist and one of the ŻOB commanders during the Ghetto Uprising. *Henryka Becka 'Bunkier 1944 roku'* is a collection of artistic recollections of a 110-day-long stay in the ruins of deserted Warsaw following the collapse of the Warsaw Uprising in 1944.

W Czterdziestą Rocznicę, edited by Józef Garliński, was published on the fortieth anniversary of the Ghetto Uprising. It contains an introduction by Garliński following by the complete text of Edelman's *Getto walczy (Udział Bundu w obronie getta warszawskiego)*, originally published in Poland in 1945. This is followed by two interviews with Edelman, one which the Polish journalist Hanna Krall originally included in her book *Zdążyć przed Panem Bogiem* (Kraków, 1977) and the second appeared in the Solidarity weekly, *Tygodnik Mazowsze*. There is also an open letter of Edelman explaining why he refused the invitation to participate in the Honorary Committee for the Celebrations of the 40th Anniversary of the Uprising in the Warsaw Ghetto, which were officially organized in Warsaw in 1983 and were the cause of considerable controversy. Also included in the book are a selection of documents from the archives of the Polish Underground Study Trust in London and those of W. Bartoszewski. They relate to certain problems raised in the texts e.g. German regulations, Polish reaction to the plight of the Jews, help for the Jews, death sentences carried out by the Polish underground on Poles for betraying Jews. Finally there is the entire text of Pope John Paul II's homily given during the mass he took on the site of the Auschwitz-Birkenau Concentration Camp in June 1979.

Edelman's main text having been written so soon after the event is a very authentic and vivid one. It deals not only with the fighting but the whole question of attitudes in the Ghetto, especially those of the Bund, and thus it has a specific political and historical value. He describes in detail Ghetto conditions, the transportations, he tries to convey the essence of the problems of fear and disbelief that existed, the varying opinions on the question of armed resistance and he discusses the role of the Jewish police. The other two texts do not concern themselves so much with details as the whole question of Ghetto values, the significance of and motivation for the Uprising, its symbolism and why merely for a Jewish uprising to take place against the Nazis can be considered a victory.

The second book, *Henryka Becka, 'Bunkier 1944, roku'*, although specifically about Beck's paintings when catacombed in devastated Warsaw is also biographical. Beck, a Catholic, was born in Lwów of Jewish parents. He was to become a highly respected gynaecologist, but also had a passion for drawing. The first years of the war, having fought in the September campaign, he spent in Lwów. The German attack on the Soviet Union in June 1941 forced him into hiding, frequently changing his shelters. During the Warsaw Uprising he was director of one of the insurgent hospitals. Following the fall of the capital he remained in the city with his Polish wife hiding with a group of thirty-three others in the ruins, living in indescribable conditions and fear. There were quite a number of people and groups hiding in parts of the post-insurgent city, including a considerable percentage of Jews. Edelman also hid for a while with such a group.

This book is really concerned with the drawings Beck made during that period of 110 days. They portray and convey the life and fears of that underground existence. The paintings, varied in style, present a haunting and rare document. His complete collection which he himself titled *Bunkier 1944 roku* is reprinted in the book, forty-six in black and white and eight in colour. Janina Jaworska has written an extremely well researched biography to accompany them and also a comprehensive description of the paintings. There are summaries in English, French, German and Yiddish.

Both these books provide a moving documentation of human suffering and endurance and are an important contribution to the understanding of Jewish-Polish relations during the Second World War.

Joanna K. M. Hanson
London

Hanna Krall. *Sublokatorka* Paris:
Librairie Libella S. A. R. L. 1985. Pp. 156.

The current movement of Poles and Jews towards some sort of dialogue inevitably confronts an obstacle of nearly insurmountable dimensions: the incommensurability of Polish and Jewish memories of the Nazi occupation and its aftermath. Poles and Polish Jews both inhabited the geographical centre of the Nazi hell, but their experiences were profoundly and irreducibly different. Yet too often, the attempt to understand founders before the assault of 'facts': comparing numbers of Polish and Jewish dead, the relative prevalence of *szmalcownicy* (who blackmailed Jews) versus 'righteous gentiles' (who sheltered Jews), the proportion of Jews in the security apparatus of post-war Polish governments, and so on. Efforts are further thwarted because in the intervening forty years, Poles and Jews, for the most part geographically separated, have developed vastly different world-views rooted to a large extent in their disparate memories of the war and its aftermath.

Hanna Krall, born Jewish, survived the war as a child concealed in a succession of Polish homes, then remained in Poland through all the difficult years since, an active participant in Polish cultural and intellectual life. She is therefore a Jewish survivor in a double sense: of the war and in contemporary Poland. She is 'Jewish', however, if her books are any indication, purely by virtue of her war-time experience, that is, by virtue of having survived; Jewish history or culture are *terra incognita* to her. There are some others like her in contemporary Poland, but none, to my knowledge, who have chosen to write about it. Her previous book, about Marek Edelman, Łódź cardiologist and last survivor of the leadership of the Warsaw Ghetto Uprising, assaulted our conventional notions of heroism;[1] Krall here reaches not for the 'facts', but for the deeper truth of her own life, and in so doing touches some of the darkness at the root of contemporary Polish-Jewish relations.

This is a difficult book to read; from all indications it was certainly a difficult one to write. The narrative spans a period beginning with the author's concealment during the Nazi occupation (hence the title), and ends on 13 December 1981, the day on which martial law was declared in Poland. It is far, however, from being a chronological account, nor is it an autobiography in any conventional sense. For most of the book, the voice which addresses us is that of Marysia, the daughter of the patriotic Polish family with whom Marta, the 'sub-tenant', hides. Marysia remains in contact with her friend through all the vicissitudes of the post-war years, and recounts her own story as well as Marta's. But 'Marysia', as the narrator frequently confesses, is a pretence, a device for approaching memories which cannot otherwise be approached, and for keeping 'her', the sub-tenant, in the more manageable third person. And the narrative as a whole, jumping backwards and forwards in time, returning to phrases and images, experimenting with various versions of 'Marysia', momentarily breaking into the 'author's' first person voice only to withdraw again behind 'Marysia', is a kind of exorcism, an attempt to speak out, and perhaps be rid of, a child's most private agony at the heart of contemporary evil.

Marysia and Marta embody two mutually-exclusive ways of living, rooted in two ways of dying. The seed of this distinction is already present in the book about Edelman, where the author contrasts the fate of Krystyna Krahelska, a heroine of the Polish underground who, having 'pinned behind her long bright hair', written a patriotic song, and nursed a wounded fighter, met her death running through a field of sunflowers, and the 'unimpressive' fate of starving Ryfka Urman, sitting in her Warsaw Ghetto courtyard surrounded by a silent crowd, next to the half-eaten remains of her child.[2] The split between 'brightness' (*jasność*, which resonates with particular intensity in Polish as an attribute, for example, of the Virgin) and 'blackness' (*czerń*) becomes, for the narrator of *Sublokatorka*, an obsession: the fundamental human distinction. It is, first of all, an aesthetic distinction: the 'bright' are beautiful, tall and immaculate in body and spirit; the 'black', ugly, crooked and dirty. It is also a psychological distinction: the 'black' are the eternal isolated victims, carrying within them a sense of their own worthlessness; the 'bright' are filled with their own value and that of their comrades – heroism and self-sacrifice is their instinctive response to oppression, as self-preservation is for the 'black'. These categories, applied with a vengeance to divide the world in two, verge on pretension, and what is worse on ideology, as the narrator herself realizes and mocks her conception, as when Marysia considers returning to school to study the new discipline of 'victimology', recently developed by two Israeli jurists seeking a therapy for making the 'black' become 'bright'. In one realm, however, the categories acquire particular force: that of morality. Marysia, for example, recalls her home: 'Mama, sad but brave, takes up various work, deals in cigarettes or bakes cookies, but never losing any of her dignified self-respect, also greatly looks after her external appearance, so every evening she washes out her one blue blouse and irons it at dawn, but as for me, she doesn't let me laugh loudly, "Maria", she repeats – in important matters she always addresses me by my given name – "one may not laugh, daddy and the Fatherland are enslaved"' (p. 14). This 'bright' and solid world is that of moral privilege, wherein one is born into right and wrong as into one's own heroic national history and noble family lineage. It is, of course, archetypically Polish, and parodies the ethos which has nurtured Polish national survival for the past two hundred years. It is a world closed to five-year-old Marta, who spends her days locked alone in Marysia's family's apartment, ever so careful to avoid the window, and on the rare occasions when she is taken for a walk with her 'family', must constantly remember to keep her Jewish eyes fixed on the sidewalk. When, as the narrator confides only toward the end of the book, Marta's real mother arrives one day, weeping with remorse over the meaningless 'mistake' of having handed Marta's father money instead of food as the Nazis took him, 'you [i.e., Marta] stand next to her in calm silence. "Too bad", you say at last. "For that I am alive." You pull your hand out of hers and quickly leave the room, terrified that you won't make it, that somewhere yet her grief may overtake you'(p. 135). This moral world, shaped by helpless isolation, is a trackless waste wherein all choices are equally horrendous. Perhaps one can choose to survive, but with a terrible price: a hidden childhood memory forever haunts one with a horror comparable to Ryfka Urman's act. This is the world of 'blackness', and, for a narrator who counts it among her earlier memories, it is archetypically Jewish.

What links these childhood memories to subsequent moments in Polish history is not just a function of autobiography, but the emphasis, characteristically Polish, on the moral dimension of one's response to history. This becomes most clear in another pair of 'doubles' whose stories counterpoint those of Marysia and Marta. Marysia's father, Major Jan Ludwik Krall, is a pre-war Polish officer and the grandson of a 'January insurrectionist'. Slapped in the face before his wife's eyes by a German officer (an event which, Marysia relates, 'forever remained our family's most powerful experience of the occupation' [p. 15]), he then fights with an AK^3 group which is subsequently incorporated into the Red Army, arrested by Soviet military police, and after a post-war trial in a Polish court, sentenced to a prison from which none return. Major Krall's 'black' double is Bernard Rajnicz, the Polish Jewish political officer of Krall's Soviet regiment. If Major Krall is the archetype of the martyred Polish freedom fighter, then Bernard seems to incarnate the post-war Polish stereotype of the Jewish communist preying on Polish patriots at Moscow's command. Yet this stereotype is soon betrayed. Like Marta, Bernard's earliest memories are of humiliation, but in his case, in a comical, lower-middle-class Jewish family; his real life begins when aged sixteen shortly before the war, converted by a pamphlet on 'profit and surplus value and class struggle', he goes among 'Jewish hovels' to announce 'to his friends, a hunch-backed seamstress and an unemployed baker, [. . .] that they have a splendid affinity with a certain idea which will shortly triumph universally' (p. 36). Like Marta, in the post-war years Bernard desperately seeks to shed his 'blackness' for 'brightness', yet repeatedly confronts his isolation. When, for example, he realizes that if not for communism and his comrades, he would never have escaped the Nazi invasion of Lwów, he sadly and ironically concludes that 'he couldn't even be a revisionist like others, couldn't even hate Stalin like others, but had to love him a little after all' (p. 64). Bernard, who, also like Marta, is 'from nowhere', must repeatedly confront with no resources but his own conscience the deadly choices which post-war Polish history hurls at him. 'Interviewing' Bernard, the narrator asks: '"What is that moment before a decision [. . .] That spasm. Is it already brightness, because one has chosen. Or still blackness, terror before the choice?" "It is terror before blackness", answered Bernard R. [. . .] without reflection' (p. 69). Yet Bernard, out of his private 'blackness', repeatedly manages somehow to choose on the side of human dignity. Called as a prosecution witness in Major Krall's trial, he rejects the pre-arranged testimony, and tells the 'ordinary, objective' truth, a choice which, duly noted, returns to haunt him in the 'anti-Zionist' purges of 1968. And on December 13, 1981, Bernard finds himself explaining to his bored young police interrogator, who is interested only in names and addresses, that the reason he 'hooked up to all this' was 'to rehabilitate an idea for which he had gained, long ago, several bakers from the suburbs of Lwów', (p. 143) while to himself he reflects that at last he has joined the 'bright': 'He is one of them, finally one of them . . .' (p. 145).

On the same day, Marysia, riveted in the snow amidst a huge crowd, paralyzed by the dream-like nature of the events around her, encounters Marta busily writing down the names of internees. In Poland, the term *stan wojenny* (martial law, literally state of war) was quickly abridged to *Wojna* (the War), and the events assimilated by collective memory to the model of the heroic Polish Uprising of 1944. Marta's reaction to 13 December is therefore profoundly ironic: for her too it recalls the Uprising, but with a characteristically 'black' twist. Her memory of the start of the Uprising is that of the first day on which she could raise her eyes on the street. 'It's terrible', Marysia had then said, to which Marta had responded: 'It's terrible for everyone, isn't it?' (p. 74). These same words are now exchanged between Marysia and Marta on 13 December. Marta, like Bernard R., can now become fully 'bright', should she choose to. The invitation is made by Marysia on the last page of *Sublokatorka*, attempting to convince Marta that the sight of a magnificent landscape belongs to her as well. When Marta, who feels that only a gas chamber is truly hers, protests that such an appropriation is a grievous sin, Marysia answers: 'But we bright ones take it upon ourselves. Together with the punishment, naturally. It's true that the punishment for the sin of our pride touches everyone, you people too, but as it is, you get quite a bit. You can be with us. Only then, in our abasement and terror, when they are shooting at everyone. So you have quite a bit. AT LAST YOU CAN BE WITH US' (pp. 155–56). To which one is tempted to retort with Marta's words earlier in the book: 'One can free oneself from blackness, but brightness is incurable' (p. 139).

Strong words these, and not, on the face of it, tending to encourage 'Polish-Jewish dialogue'. Yet what, after all, are the uses of 'blackness'? 'The only thing one can sensibly do with blackness', concludes the narrator of *Sublokatorka* at one point, 'is to transform it into art, as Chaplin, Woody Allen and [Bruno] Schultz did' (p. 106). This Krall accomplishes, in a subtle and endlessly ironic play of character and incident which constantly eludes, I should stress, the effort to schematize it. For Marysia and Marta are the parts of single maimed Polish-Jewish, Jewish-Polish identity, as are Major Krall, Bernard R., and the other compromised and compromising personages who populate these pages. They are the cast of a comic nightmare summoned by a 'sub-tenant' in a two-fold sense: a being who inhabits the catacombs of both individual consciousness and recent Polish history. This art does not heal our wounds, but exposes them. Healing is something else again, but can only be conceived when we truly perceive the hurt.

Michael C. Steinlauf
Brandeis University

NOTES

1 *Zdążyć przed Panem Bogiem* [*Getting There Before God Does*], Kraków: Wydawnictwo Literackie, 1977; translated by Joanna Stasinska and Lawrence Weschler as *Shielding the Flame: an Interview with Marek Edelman, One of the Last Surviving Leaders of the Warsaw Ghetto Uprising*, New York: Henry Holt & Company, 1986.
2 *Zdążyć przed Panem Bogiem*, pp. 16–17; *Sublokatorka*, p. 18.
3 Armia Krajowa (Home Army): the anti-communist forces commanded by the Polish government-in-exile in London.

Randolph L. Braham and Bélo Vágó, editors.
The Holocaust in Hungary: Forty Years Later.
New York: Columbia University Press. 1985. Pp. 256.

This book of essays is the result of various lectures and conferences. The forty years noted in the title serves as a commemoration for 1944 and the events of the Holocaust in Hungary. The facts are, of course, well known. During the last stages of the Second World War the killing of most of the 800,000 Hungarian Jews who perished during the Holocuast was done with almost uncanny expertise and frightening speed by the *SS* 'specialists' and the Hungarian bodies attached to them, especially the Hungarian gendarmie which took part in the deportations. Between 15 May and 10 July 1944, 437,402 persons alleged to be Jews were taken to certain death to Auschwitz. Apart from Budapest's 200,000 Jews, all were deported. The forced marches and the brutality of the Hungarian fascists decimated even the relatively protected ones. But the ghetto in Pest and most of the Jews in the capital survived the War.

The book includes short and some longer essays by the finest specialists in the field. The work is not exclusively academic and included are personal confessions and literary essays as well as more standard historical studies. Some of the authors themselves were victims. The different viewpoints aired and the contrasts of opposing opinions make this collection especially valuable. The most striking difference between the essays written in Hungary and those produced by foreigners is that while the Hungarian writers aim to describe and understand the facts, some of the other researchers, from Israel and the United States, seek to identify criminals. They condemn both the representatives of the Hungarian cultural and political life and the elected leaders of the Jews. The essays in the first part of the volume study the roots of the German-Hungarian anti-semitic traditions, the network of the Hungarian-Jewish, Jewish-Hungarian bonds, the features of the political and ideological life between the World Wars. Nathaniel Katzburg, Gyorgy Száraz, Ivan T. Berend and Istavan Deak describe the route to the Holocaust through the institutionalization of anti-semitism. Gula Juhász lists the various authors and intellectual trends that sustained racism.

Raphael Patai examines the Hungarian Jewish intelligentsia. Elsewhere authors focus on the tragic year of 1944. Gyorgy Ranki and Béla Vágó analyse the respective role and responsibility of Germans and Hungarians. Elek Karsaw – who died not long ago – tells about the response of the local administrating bodies. Raphael Vágó writes about the hostile attitudes of the Palestine *Yishuv*. The fate of Raul Wallenberg is also evaluated.

Randolph Braham, a co-editor of the book and a well-known expert, condemns Jewish leaders for failing to enlighten their people about impending disaster. Ivan Sanders analyses the image of the Holocaust as reflected in contemporary Jewish literature. Andras Kovacs undertakes a particularly difficult task when, in his speculative essay, he studies the conflicts within Hungarian Jews after 1945 and their efforts toward integration.

The book raises a wide range of questions: was the devastation of the Hungarian Jews inevitable? Is it valid or illuminating to examine the responsibility of the political leaders and Jewish leaders? Perhaps most important, what would I do in such circumstances?

Maria Schmidt
Budapest

Les Livres du Souvenir: Mémoriaux juifs de Pologne.
Présenté par Annette Wieviorka et Yitzhok Niborski.
Paris: Editions Gallimard/Julliard.
1983. Pp. 185, 16 pp. photographs.

This modest volume presents a sampling drawn from perhaps fifteen out of the many hundred memorial books written by Polish Jews after World War II. The format of the 'Archives' collection in which this volume appears dictates that the editors frame the excerpts with commentary and background information. The background information provides little that is surprising or objectionable to scholars. The critical comments, on the other hand, constitute an implicit sociology of the *yizker-bukh* genre itself. The criteria suggested to distinguish the genre seem appropriate enough: 'The existence of a typical structure, the mélange of documents, the presence of several first-hand accounts which we find in the immense majority of these books authorize us to speak of a literary genre' (p. 25). The editors take this 'authorization' seriously. In most cases the commentary treats the relevant excerpts not merely as characteristic of what may be found in the original books, but as an illustration of an important aspect of the entire genre. The strategy is stimulating but is risky.

Neither the sources of the theory underlying the commentary, nor the theory itself, are made explicit. The editors' references to 'collective memory', however, suggest the French concept of the sociology of memory set out in Maurice Halbwachs' *La Mémoire Collective* (Presses Universitaires de France, [1950] 1968), where he writes:

> When we return to a city where we have been before, what we perceive helps us reconstitute a tableau, many of whose parts had been forgotten. If what we see today takes its place in the framework

of our memories, inversely these memories adapt to the ensemble of our current perceptions (ibid. p. 1).

But this prosaic example poses an obvious difficulty if we want to apply it to the memorial books: for those who committed their memory to *yizker-bikher*, there was no possibility of return. The point may be made relevant to the *yizker-bikher* in the following way: all memory exists within sets of relations (the 'tableau') and is inherently social. We retain memories because they provide evidence of our social identity at the time when the memories are set. We bring them to a conscious level and share them because of the significance they hold for our social identity in the present.

The memories contained in the memorial books accordingly serve a dual purpose. They reconstitute a past social world, which the survivor needs in order to give substance to life history; and they provide a portrait of that world which can serve the survivors as a basis for a unified group identity of which they can be proud in their lives after the destruction of the world from which they come.

Several examples will illustrate the strengths and dangers of this approach. The editors note the frequency of articles about the secular Jewish schools founded between the wars. They provide a suggestive explanation:

> We see something fundamental here. Secularism, of which the authors of these articles were both products and advocates can only justify itself if it is not treason against Jewish affirmation, if it can rebut the accusation that it is a first step toward the assimilation and disappearance of the Jews as such. This accusation is particularly grave at a moment when genocide has annihilated a major portion of our people. It is therefore vital to show that secular Judaism has the same educative capacity as traditional Judaism, that it could take over the reins of the educational system which had assured the continuity of Judaism for two millenia (p. 108).

In a chapter entitled 'The Romance of the Shtetl', the editors discuss the prevalence of character portraits in the books. They note that traditional communal figures tend to be identified, in additional to their given names, either by their functions or by patronymics: Moyshele Shoykhet, Mendl Reb Khayim's:

> Surnames are reserved for the hoi polloi. If this habit can be explained by the fact that before the 19th century the Jews lived in tiny communities and that the use of family names was imposed on them late ... we may see here also, in these texts [written] after the

genocide, a desire to regain the familiarity of the epoch and to make these personnages picturesque (p. 162).

This – where historical ethnography is synthesized with a critical analysis of the memorial books – represents the best possibilities of the editors' approach.

Unfortunately, at a number of points the editors base gross generalizations on isolated excerpts. Since their analysis rests on the insertion of the individual into the collective, it is not surprising that they choose a description of one town's fraternal societies in which harmony reigns supreme: 'No conflict ... no rivalry, neither for power nor for money' (p. 78). The problem is not that these societies were, in fact, riddled with disputes over power and money; Wieviorka and Niborski know that. Yet while they are correct in asserting that social strife *does* tend to be glossed over in the memorial book, a more thorough review of them would reveal many accounts of such disputes.

At one or two points the analysis is so forced as to appear patronizing. Referring to one author who asserts that even the local gentiles were deeply impressed by Theodor Herzl when he visited their town, the editors wonder whether this is 'the return of the old fantasy of the Jews to give themselves a king, so that they may be equal to the nations and assure themselves of recognition?' (p. 130). Such unfettered 'psychohistory' leaves a bad taste.

Certain excerpts contained here read like excellent first-hand social history and leave one to doubt whether a firm distinction can by drawn between collective memory and history. Others are of an unusual literary quality and embody the ironic genius of the *yizker-bikher*, such as the piece which explains that Chelm's reputation as a city of fools was deliberately fostered to gain publicity for the town and make Jews stop and spend money there (p. 155).

The book ends with a discussion of the contradiction between these books' stated goals of transmitting the past to future generations, and the fact that the survivors' children and grandchildren hardly know of their existence. By presenting revealing selections from this vast literature to a new audience, Wieviorka and Niborski hope to overcome this lack. More generally, they offer a sensitive attempt at understanding the convoluted paths of memory which link the survivors' (and émigrés') youth with the post-war world they share with each other and with their descendants.

Jonathan Boyarin
YIVO Institute for Jewish Research

LETTER TO THE EDITORS

Professor Maurycy Horn's review

The review of *Jewish Privileges in the Polish Commonwealth* by Professor Maurycy Horn, published in volume 1 of POLIN (pp. 351–54) contains a series of errors, misunderstandings and inaccuracies which require clarification.

1. The privilege granted to the Jews in the town of Wilkowiszka (pp. 359–66) has, indeed been preserved in the Polish language, but was entered in the minute-book (*pinkas*) of this *kahal* written with Hebrew characters. I published it both in this form and in a transliteration to the Latin alphabet

2. The privilege which has been preserved in German and which was published by me in this form was that granted to Lwówek in Wielkopolska (pp. 184–91) and not Lwów as was incorrectly stated in the review.

3. Professor Horn asserts that 'The most important weakness of the work is the failure to take into account the privileges of a dozen odd Jewish communities which are mentioned in the Księgi Spraw Publicznych used by Goldberg (the so-called Kanclerski catalogue no. KK) (p. 354). Yet at the beginning of my volume, I wrote that the privileges I was publishing '... were collected ... until 1967 during the time I was able to work there.' When in 1981 I had the opportunity of working again in Polish archives, the present volume was already in the press and I was unable to add the new unpublished privileges which I had found! (pp. vii–viii). I believed that the matter had been set out clearly, but evidently Professor Horn did not share this view and came to the conclusion I have quoted. I should add that the list he provides of privileges which I did not publish is incomplete. I have in my possession many more unpublished documents of this type which are intended for my next volume. In addition two of the privileges mentioned by Professor Horn (those for Kraków and Oswięcim) are

merely re-statements of general privileges and therefore in accordance with the stated principles of my edition could not have been included.

Thus, 'the most important weakness' of Professor Horn's review is his failure to take into account the statements and editorial pre-suppositions of this author and publisher.

Yours sincerely

Jacob Goldberg

CONTRIBUTORS

Władysław Teofil Bartoszewski is a Research Fellow at St Antony's College, Oxford University, where he also teaches modern history. His book *The Jew in the Mind of the Polish Peasant* will appear shortly in Jerusalem. He is Associate Editor of Polin.

Eugene C. Black is Ottilie Springer Professor of History at Brandeis University. He is author of *The Association: British Extra-parliamentary Organization, 1769–1793* (Cambridge, Mass., 1963) and editor of *European Political History* 1815–70 (New York, 1967) and *Victorian Culture and Society* (London, 1973). At present he is working on a study of the political activity of Lucien Wolf.

Andrzej Bryk is a lecturer at the Institute for Constitutional History of the Jagiellonian University Krakow. He has written articles in various journals on the history of political ideas and Polish-Jewish relations.

Jan Błoński is Professor of the History of Polish Literature at the Jagiellonian University in Kraków. His many publications include *Poeci i inn* (Poets and others, 1956), *Zmiana Warty* (The Changing of the Guard, 1961) and *Odmarsz* (Departure).

Shmuel A. Cygielman, Senior Lecturer in Jewish History at the Ben-Gurion University of the Negev in Bersheva, is mainly engaged in research on the social, economic and legal history of Polish Jewry down to the nineteenth century. Among his works are *Sources to the History of Polish Jewry until 1948* (forthcoming) and numerous articles.

David Engel teaches the history of Polish Jewry at Tel-Aviv University and is editor of *Gal-Ed*, a Hebrew-language journal devoted to Polish-Jewish history. The first part of his comprehensive study on the Polish government-in-exile and the Jews will appear in autumn 1987.

Mieczysław Inglot is Professor of Polish Literature at the University of Wrocław. His publications include *Polskie czasopisma literackie ziem litewsko-ruskich w latach 1832–1851* (Polish literary periodicals of the Lithuanian-Ukrainian lands in the years 1832–1851, 1966), *Norwid. Z dziejów recepcji twórczości* (Norwid. The history of his critical reception, 1983) and *Świat komedii fredrowskich* (The world of Fredro's comedies, 1986).

Paul Latawski is Assistant Professor of International Relations at New England College, Arundel, Sussex. He has published articles concerning East Euroean history and is a contributor to the official history series of the United States Army.

Eli Lederhendler, a graduate of the Jewish Theological Seminary of America, lectures in Jewish history at Tel-Aviv University. He is also Managing Editor of *Studies in Contemporary Jewry*, the annual publication of the Institute of Contemporary Jewry of the Hebrew University. He is the author of several essays on Russian-Jewish and Jewish immigration history, and of a forthcoming book, *The Road to Modern Jewish Politics: Political Tradition and Political Reconstruction in the Jewish Community of Tsarist Russia*.

George J. Lerski is emeritus professor of Modern European History at the University of Chicago and Vice-President of the Polish-American Congress. Among his publications are *A Polish Chapter in Jacksonian America* (Wisconsin, 1958), *Herbert Hoover and Poland* (Stanford, 1977), *Emisariusz JUR* (The emissary Jur, London, 1984) and, together with his wife Halina, *Polish-Jewish Co-existence, 1772–1939: A Topical Bibliography* (Greenwood Press, 1986).

Józef Lewandowski is a historian specializing in the area of Central and Eastern Europe. His most important books are *Federalizm. Litwa i Białoruś w polityce obozu belwederskiego* (Federalism. Lithuania and Byelorussia in the politics of the Piłsudski-ite camp, Warsaw, 1962), *Imperializm słabości* (The imperialism of weakness, Warsaw, 1967) and *The Swedish contribution to the Polish Resistance Movement* (Uppsala, 1979). From 1969, he has been a political refugee in Sweden, where he is Professor of History at Uppsala University. He has written articles for *Kultura* and *Aneks*.

Maria and Kazimierz Piechotka are architects and architectural historians. They have practised as architects in post-war Poland and together have written over 130 books and articles on the history of architecture, housing developments and the mechanization of construction. Among their works are *Bóznice dzewniane* (Wooden synagogues, Warsaw, 1955), which was translated into English (Warsaw, 1959) and *Zalozenia techniczne zintegrowanego przemysłu budowlanego* (The technical bases of an integrated building industry, Warsaw, 1978).

CONTRIBUTORS

Edward Rogerson writes on various aspects of East European culture and history. His articles on contemporary Polish cinema have appeared in *Sight and Sound* and *Encounter*. He is currently preparing a study of the social reconstruction of post-war Poland.

Szyman Rudnicki is a Docent and deputy Director of the Historical Institute of the University of Warsaw. His principal interest is twentieth-century political and social groups in Poland. His works include *Dzialalność polityczna polskich konserwatystów 1918–1926* (The political activity of Polish conservatives 1918–1926, Wrocław, 1981) and *Oboz Narodowo-Radykalny. Geneza i działalność* (The National Radical Camp. Its evolution and development, Warsaw 1985).

Michael Steinlauf is completing a doctoral dissertation at Brandeis University on Polish-Jewish contacts in the theatre. He was a Fulbright fellow in Poland in 1983–4 where he undertook research for his doctorate as well as on the role of Yitzhak Leibl Perełz as a political and cultural activist in fin-de-siècle Warsaw.

Daniel Stone is Professor of History at the University of Winnipeg. His books include *The Polish Memoirs of William John Rose* (Toronto, 1975), *Polish Politics and National Reform 1775–1778* (Boulder, Colorado, 1976) and many articles.

Bernadeta Tendyra is a research student at the London School of Economics, completing a doctoral thesis on the internal politics of General Sikorski's Polish Government in Exile 1939–43. She was recently Assistant Editor of the LSE's *Millenium: A Journal of International Studies*.

Anna Żuk is a lecturer in the Institute of Philosophy and Sociology at the Marie Curie Sklodkowska University in Lublin. Her main interest is in the interpretive reconstruction of the philosophical context of Judaism, on which she has published a number of articles.

OBITUARY

Eric Sosnow

Eric Sosnow, who died on 20 February 1987, was one of the most outstanding representatives of that generation of young Jews who left behind the insecurity of their native Eastern Europe to come to this country on the eve of World War Two. Born in Kolno, Poland, in 1910 he studied at Wilno University and moved to London in 1935 as correspondent for a number of Polish newspapers including *Kurjer Wileński*, *Nasz Prezgląd* and *Der Tag*. He also found time to study for the M.Sc. (Econ.) at the London School of Economics and Political Science and to act as secretary to Nahum Sokolow, one of the leaders of the world Zionist movement. A man of considerable linguistic skills he pursued a successful career as a journalist, writing extensively on Eastern Europe, not only in Polish and Yiddish, but also for a number of English papers, above all the *Sunday Times* and the *Economist*. His journalism was sharp and perceptive. In a long article in the *Economist* in January 1939 he spotlighted the growing German economic penetration of Poland and the dangers this posed for Polish independence. He retained throughout his life the love of the written word, remaining a member of the London Foreign Press Association and co-editing the commemorative two volume history of his home town, published in Israel in 1971. To this, he also contributed two chapters on the town's economic development.

His forte was however commerce, to which he turned at the beginning of the war, establishing an international trading company, United City Merchants, which he built up with great skill and enterprise. His commercial contracts were worldwide and the regions with which he dealt included South Asia, the Middle East, Africa, Eastern Europe and the Soviet Union. He was energetic in the pursuit of his business interests, but his real love lay elsewhere. Particularly after the tragic accident of the death of his son Norman at the age of 23 in 1967, he dedicated himself more and

OBITUARY

Eric Sosnow, 1910–1987

more to charitable and educational concerns, a reflection of the interest in the young and their welfare. In 1968 he established the Norman Sosnow travelling scholarships to enable undergraduates in history and economics at Christ's to travel the world, a scheme which benefited a large number of young people and which was extended in 1982 to the L.S.E. He set up the Norman Sosnow distinguished visiting scholarship for senior academics at Christ's, sat on the College Investment Committee and was a fellow commoner of the College. One of the rooms in the College new building is named after his son.

He was a member of the Board of Governors of the L.S.E. and an honorary fellow and his generosity helped to establish the Norman Sosnow Chair in Banking and Finance at the School in 1985. He was interested in the link between theoretical and practical knowledge and this was reflected in his endowment of a careers room at Rugby School. He was always deeply concerned with developments in Eastern Europe and particularly in Poland, where he contributed to a fund for the welfare of children and arranged for medical journals to be sent to Polish Universities. He was also closely associated with the Institute for Polish–Jewish Studies in Oxford from its inception and his advice and guidance was crucial in its development, and in the establishment of *POLIN*. Among his decorations were the Commendador of the Republic of Portugal and the Polish Order of Merit.

As a man, Eric was unfailingly kind and generous. He had known both suffering and gladness and his love of life and his desire to aid others was undiminished by the passage of time. Eric was always a joy to be with – his optimism was unfailing and his sense of humour infectious. He was a man at home in many worlds, a natural survivor from a world now largely gone. The widespread affection he aroused was reflected in the many tributes which followed his death. Mervyn King, Professor of Economics at the L.S.E. wrote, 'His enthusiasm for and belief in education and research were those of a man fifty years his junior and an example to us all.' Sir Claus Moser remarked on his 'wonderful warmth, kindness, gentleness and humour' and observed that he 'was such a totally good man, someone who invariably thought of others before himself, whose generosity was quiet but total.' Sir John Plumb formerly Master of Christ's College, Cambridge, wrote of his 'gusto, love of family and friends, endless generosity and passion for the good things in life – of art, scholarship, all in fact that adorns the life of man.' He conluded, 'Eric was a good man, generous to a fault, but his greatest gift was to transmit his happiness to others.' His loss will be deeply felt by his many friends, but above all by his devoted wife, Sylvia, his daughter Fiona and her husband Ronnie Fattal, his brother Morris and his sister Henia.

Antony Polonsky

Arthur M. Sackler

Dr Arthur M. Sackler, the great scientist and philanthropist, died of a heart attack in New York on 26 May 1987 at the age of 73. A brilliant researcher he was a pioneer in biological psychiatry, neuro-endocrinology, experimental medicine and the author of more than 140 scientific papers. A great entrepreneur in advertising and publishing in his own field, his *Medical Tribune* and other similar publications in 10 languages now have offices in 11 countries. He was also a member of numerous specialized learned societies, often acting as their president. Dr Sackler will, however, be best remembered for his widely distributed benefactions in the fields of the arts and humanities as well as in medical studies, and for his remarkable art collections, which were always destined for the enjoyment of the widest public.

His medical and scientific benefactions include: the Sackler School of Medicine of Tel-Aviv University in Israel, The Sackler Institute of Gradute Biomedical Science at New York University (his alma mater), the Arthur M. Sackler Sciences Center at Clark University in Worcester, Massachusetts, the Arthur M. Sackler Center for Health Communications at Tufts University, Boston and a therapeutic research centre at Brooklyn College of Pharmacy.

In the arts, an area in which he collected widely and eclectically, the Metropolitan Museum in New York owes to his munificence the Arthur M. Sackler Gallery of early Chinese Stone Sculpture (of which many were gifts from him), the Sackler wing housing the Egyptian Temple of Dendur and the Japanese collections of the Museum, Harvard University the splendid Arthur M. Sackler Museum (conceived by James Stirling and inaugurated in the Fall of 1985); an Arthur M. Sackler Museum on the Mall in the Smithsonian Institution in Washington, which opened in mid-September of this year, endowed with an initial gift of over 1,000 prime items from Dr Sackler's extensive collection of Chinese, Near Eastern and Islamic Art. There is also an Arthur M. Sackler Gallery at Princeton University. Last year an Arthur M. Sackler Museum was set up in the University of Peking in China. It will be devoted to Chinese archaeology and become a centre for training Chinese students in museology.

His unexpected and premature death occurred at a moment when he was planning an archaeological Museum in Jerusalem, whilst extending his holdings in European Art of Old Testament subjects, which he also intended to give to that city, which was always very close to his heart.

His collecting, which started in the 1940s, was avid and wide-ranging, although probably the most significant part is in the field of Chinese art, particularly early jades, bronzes, stone sculpture, ceramics and paintings, his infallible taste and curiosity led him to assemble masterpieces of New Eastern and Islamic art, early Renaissance, Impressionist and School of Paris paintings, master-drawings ranging from a spectacular collection of Piranesi to drawings by sculptors, Italian majolica, European sculptures in terracotta (a medium he particularly appreciated) and Renaissance and Baroque bronzes. He was also deeply involved as a collector in Graeco-Roman sculpture and pre-Columbian art. Altogether his holdings go into tens of thousands of items, of an unequalled quality. He also supported many young contemporary artists.

Always underlining that 'Great Art doesn't belong to anybody. Never did. Never will,' Dr Sackler's collections (or selections from them) were shown in most of the great museums in the United States, Great Britain, China and in Jerusalem. As befitted a man of his taste and knowledge, these exhibitions were usually accompanied by remarkable and beautifully produced catalogues, which alone would be a monument to him.

In the last years he took a strong and acquisitive interest in paintings by Polish Avant-garde painters. 'the painters of protest' as he called them and was also a keen follower of the activities of the Polish-Jewish Institute at Oxford and the planned international conference on the history and culture of Polish Jews to be held in Jerusalem in early 1988.

He will be missed by many for his intellectual brilliance, friendship, inspiration and unequalled generosity.

Andrew S. Ciechanowiecki

www.ingramcontent.com/pod-product-compliance
Ingram Content Group UK Ltd.
Pitfield, Milton Keynes, MK11 3LW, UK
UKHW021315180426
11947UKWH00015B/1251